ECONOMICS TODAY

THE MICRO VIEW

THE ADDISON-WESLEY SERIES IN ECONOMICS

Ninth
Edition

ECONOMICS TODAY

THE MICRO VIEW

ROGER LeROY MILLER

INSTITUTE FOR UNIVERSITY STUDIES, ARLINGTON, TEXAS

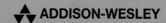 **ADDISON-WESLEY**

An imprint of Addison Wesley Longman, Inc.

Reading, Massachusetts • Menlo Park, California • New York • Harlow, England
Dan Mills, Ontario • Sydney • Mexico City • Madrid • Amsterdam

Photo Credits
Page 3, Frank Siteman/Stock, Boston; page 17, Hans Halberstadt/Photo Researchers; page 45, Jeff Greenberg, PhotoEdit; page 73, Jean-Marc Giboux/Gamma-Liaison; page 94, AP/Wide World; page 116, © Martin Rogers/Stock, Boston; page 413, Frederik Bodin/Stock, Boston; page 439, © D & I MacDonald/The Picture Cube; page 461, © Savino/The Image Works; page 481, Monkmeyer/Goodwin; page 508, Steve Starr/Stock, Boston; page 533, Peter Menzel/Stock, Boston; page 557, © David Young-Wolff/PhotoEdit; page 583, AP/Wide World; page 605, © Joe Sohm/Chromosome/Stock, Boston; page 628, AP/Wide World; page 631, © Skjold/The Image Works; page 649, UPI/Bettmann; page 666, © Ramey/Stock, Boston; page 679, © Bob Kramer/The Picture Cube; page 694, © David Witbeck/The Picture Cube; page 711, © Christopher Brown/Stock, Boston; page 733, © Jon Burbank/The Image Works; page 753, © Jeff Greenberg/The Picture Cube; page 761, © Brookins/Richmond Times-Dispatch; page 775, Sanguinetti/Monkmeyer.

Executive Editor: John Greenman
Developmental Editor: Vicki Cohen
Project Editor: Ellen MacElree
Supplements Editor: Julie Zasloff
Design Manager: John Callahan
Cover Designer: Kay Petronio
Text Designer: A Good Thing, Inc.
Cover Photos:
Front cover: Brazil slum: K. McGlynn/The Image Works; seedling: © 1986, George Turner/ Photo Researches; newspapers: PhotoDisk, Inc.; Earth: PhotoDisk, Inc.; satellite dish: Joe Sohm/ The Image Works; heads of State: Reuters/Archive; vote sign: Crandall/The Image Works; soldiers: Photoreporters.
Back cover: Train wreck: Reuters/Bettmann; takeout food window: Spunbarg/Picture Cube; smokestacks: Digital Stock Corp.; ATM machine: PhotoDisk, Inc.; military: Reuters/Bettmann; shopping mall: Nettis/Photo Researchers.
Art Studio: ElectraGraphics, Inc.
Photo Researcher: Mira Schachne
Electronic Production Manager: Su Levine
Desktop Administrator: Laura Leever
Electronic Page Makeup: Laura Leever
Printer and Binder: R. R. Donnelley & Sons Company
Cover Printer: Phoenix Color

Library of Congress Cataloging-in-Publication Data
Miller, Roger LeRoy.
  Economics today: the micro view / Roger LeRoy Miller. — 9th ed.
    p.   cm. — (The Addison-Wesley series in economics)
  Includes index.
  ISBN 0-673-98055-3 perm. paper)
    1. Microeconomics. 2. Economics. I. Title.
HB171.5.M6426   1996
338.5—dc20   96-2363
                                                                CIP

Copyright © 1997 by Addison-Wesley Educational Publishers Inc.

ISBN 0-673-98055-3
 2345678910—DOW— 979899

To Sabine T. Miller
Courage to the max.
R.L.M.

CONTENTS IN BRIEF

In this volume, Chapter 6 is followed by Chapter 19.

CONTENTS IN DETAIL

In this volume, Chapter 6 is followed by Chapter 19.

PART 7   MARKET STRUCTURE, RESOURCE ALLOCATION, AND REGULATION   479

Chapter 22: The Firm: Cost and Output Determination   481

Chapter 23: Perfect Competition   508

PART 8   PRODUCTIVE FACTORS, POVERTY, THE ENVIRONMENT, AND INTEREST GROUPS   603

EXAMPLES

INTERNATIONAL EXAMPLES

Why Are There So Many Brush Fires in Corsica?

The True Cost of the Military Draft in France

Consumption Versus Capital Goods in the United States and Japan

Why Foreign Graduate Students Specialize When Studying in the United States

Cross-Border Shopping in Europe

The Slump in Worldwide Sales of Cigars

Changing Technology and the Supply of Salmon

Mexico's Price Freeze and the Shopping Cops

Rent Controls in Bombay

Are Lighthouses a Public Good?

Chile's Privatized Social Security System

A Booming Business in Facelifts by Russian Plastic Surgeons

A Tale of Two Countries

China Eliminates Saturday Work

The Price Elasticity of Demand for Newspapers

A Pricing Decision at Disneyland Paris

Europeans Use More Capital

The Global Coal Market

"We're Just Trying to Keep the Market Stable"

Fuji Film Price Discrimination

Collapsing Oil Prices

European Post Offices: Natural Monopolies and How to Evade Them

European Merchant Guilds, the Original Craft Unions

Europe's Management-Labor Councils

One Consequence of Privatizing Italian Banks: Loan Sharking

Viager, or Betting on an Early Death (Someone Else's)

Relative Income Inequality Throughout the Richest Countries

Poverty Worldwide and How to Cure It: Suggestions from the UN Summit

Deterioration in the United Kingdom's National Health Care System

The Black Sea Becomes the Dead Sea: The Results of Externalities

Agriculture and an Effective Interest Group

The Importance of International Trade in Various Countries

International Trade and the Alphabet

The Importation of Priests into Spain

Industrialized Poverty

The World Bank and the Development of Poor Nations (or Lack Thereof)

International Policy Examples

Who Should Pay the High Cost of a Legal System?

Should Ivory Imports Be Banned Worldwide?

Can Citizens Recycle Too Much? The Case of Germany

Should School Tuition Vouchers Be Used in Developing Countries?

DOMESTIC EXAMPLES

The Increasing Native American Population

When It Is Rational *Not* to Learn New Technology

The Perceived Value of Gifts

Getting Directions

Garth Brooks, Used CDs, and the Law of Demand

The Future of College Teaching

Dinosaurs and the Price of Amber

Technology and the Death of Middlemen

Ph.D.s Need Not Apply

The Most Progressive Tax System of All: College Financial Aid

Newspaper Vending Machines Versus Candy Vending Machines

What Do Real-World Price Elasticities of Demand Look Like?

Traffic Fatalities, Rising Incomes, and Alcohol Consumption

The Long-Run Effectiveness of "Sin" Taxes

How to Read the Financial Press: Stock Prices

Explaining the Success of at Least One Multibillionaire

Making Executives Own a Share of the Company

Goods Versus Ideas

Whittling Away at Apple's Profit Margins

"Intel Inside"

Patents as Intellectual Property

Domestic Policy Examples

THINKING CRITICALLY ABOUT THE MEDIA

ISSUES AND APPLICATIONS

T O THE INSTRUCTOR

In a sense, part of our work as educators is being done for us by politicians whose every economic pronouncement, regardless of its accuracy, is duly reported by the media. Our students are constantly bombarded by differing economic views of the world. One of our jobs is to teach these very same students to distinguish truth from fiction and fact from opinion. As professional economists, most of us are quite convinced that an understanding of the economic way of thinking provides a powerful engine of analysis for today's students so that they can in fact separate the "chaff" from the "wheat." One of the key new features in this ninth edition of *Economics Today: The Micro View* explicitly addresses the media.

THINKING CRITICALLY ABOUT THE MEDIA

At least once, and sometimes two or three times, in a chapter there is a set-off feature titled "Thinking Critically About the Media" with an appropriate subheading. Each topic has been selected so as to highlight a newsworthy event and to go beyond the media's coverage of it, often with surprising results. The topics are listed on page xxi.

DID YOU KNOW THAT . . . ?

To entice your students further, each chapter begins with a provocative and often significant set of facts, introduced in the form of a question: "Did You Know That . . .?" Your students cannot fail to be intrigued.

THE CUTTING EDGE—TODAY'S TECHNOLOGY

What's new in telecommunications, computers, digital sound and imaging, and other marvels of the world of electronics is perhaps more familiar to students than to many professors. So it is not by chance that I use cutting-edge high-tech examples throughout the text to illustrate the basic principles of economics. Your students demand a modern look and feel in their study materials—and that is what they get in the ninth edition of *Economics Today: The Micro View.*

A WORLD OF GLOBAL EXAMPLES

High-speed telecommunications coupled with the opening up of the former Soviet Union and Eastern Europe, as well as increased trade with Latin America, Asia, and a booming mainland China, dictate a globalization of the principles of economics text. The ninth edition is truly global in scope. In every chapter, your students are exposed to economic principles demonstrated in set-off features, preceded by a globe, called simply "International Example." There are 36 international examples in this edition. You can see the full list on page xix.

Examples Closer to Home

Of course, the United States has its share of relevant and exciting examples that can be used to demonstrate economic principles. In this edition, there are 42 new domestic examples. A full list is presented on pages xix–xx.

Policy Matters

Many of the economic discussions presented by the media involve important policy issues. In the ninth edition, your students are explicitly exposed to important policy questions both on the domestic and international fronts. There are 4 international and 17 domestic policy examples. A full list appears on pages xix–xx.

ISSUES AND APPLICATIONS

It has been a tradition in all editions of *Economics Today: The Micro View* to present at the end of each chapter a section titled "Issues and Applications." The 23 "Issues and Applications" are *all new*. Their format is designed to encourage your students to apply economic concepts and to think critically about how they have applied those concepts. To this end, each "Issues and Applications" section has a list of *concepts applied* at the beginning and is followed by two or three critical-thinking questions titled "For Critical Analysis." You will find suggested answers to these critical-thinking questions in the *Instructor's Resource Binder.* The titles of the new "Issues and Applications" features for the ninth edition are found on page xxii.

Critical Thinking Throughout

In addition to the set-off features concerning the media, your students are exposed to further critical-thinking exercises at the end of each example. The questions following each example are headed "For Critical Analysis." They attempt to get your students to take the analysis one step further to develop their critical-thinking skills. Essentially, the students are asked to "think like economists." The answers to all "For Critical Analysis" questions are found in the *Instructor's Manual.*

As stated earlier, two or three additional critical-thinking questions appear at the end of each "Issues and Applications" section.

PEDAGOGY WITH A PURPOSE

You and your students will notice how carefully the pedagogy in each chapter fits together as a whole. My purpose continues to be to guide your students in their study of our science with a positive approach. The result is what I believe to be state-of-the-art motivational, conceptual, and review pedagogy:

- A *chapter-opening issue* that relates directly to the "Issues and Applications" section at the end of that chapter
- A list of *preview points* and completely self-contained answers
- A *chapter outline*

- *Marginal definitions,* with important terms boldfaced when first introduced in the text
- *Concepts in brief* summarized at the end of major sections
- A *point-by-point end-of-chapter summary*
- *Problems,* with answers for every odd-numbered problem provided at the back of the book
- A session in *computer-aided instruction* for each chapter, available on a free diskette

Interacting with the Internet

The number of Internet users, as well as the number of World Wide Web sites, is growing daily. To help your students use this increasingly valuable resource, I have put together a chapter-ending feature called "Interacting with the Internet." In Chapter 1, your students will get a brief introduction to using the Internet. In appropriate chapters throughout the rest of the text, Internet addresses are provided so that your students can obtain additional information about material covered in the chapter.

The Core of Economics: Theory, Theory, and More Theory

While your students will have their interest piqued by the myriad new examples in this ninth edition, all of those examples serve one basic purpose—to drive home the application of the theory just presented. You will find the latest theoretical concepts in this ninth edition, presented in a logical manner for ease of understanding.

For more specific details on the presentation of theory, see the listing at the end of this preface under the heading "What's New in the Ninth Edition."

Complete Teaching Flexibility

One of the keys to the success of *Economics Today: The Micro View* is that it is suitable for many teaching styles. Instructors who wish to stress theory can do so. Those who wish to stress applications and examples can do that. Furthermore, chapters that are often skipped in shorter courses are placed at the ends of units. The numerous supplements for both instructors and students allow for even further flexibility.

THE REMAINDER OF THE TEACHING AND LEARNING PACKAGE

As you will discover, the ninth edition of *Economics Today: The Micro View* has the most comprehensive, usable, and effective teaching and learning package ever developed for a principles of economics text.

Printed Materials for Students
- *Extended-Coverage Topics*—free booklet
- Reproducible homework assignments—two separate versions
- *Your Economics Life: The Practical Applications of Economics*—free with every new copy
- *Student Learning Guide*

Computer Software for Students
- ET9 Computer-Assisted Instruction
- Graphing Tutorial
- *Economics Tutor*—"games" that teach theory
- Micro Tutorial

Multimedia for Your Students

Not only are the examples in *Economics Today: The Micro View* on the cutting edge, but so are the supplementary materials for classroom presentation and individual study. They include the following:

Videos

To go with this edition, HarperCollins offers *Economics at Work,* a package of 11 short videos of five to seven minutes each, free to adopters, including such titles as *Cigarettes, Addiction, and Elasticity; A Talk with Investment Bankers;* and *Stock Answer: A Guide to the Market.*

Printed Materials for Instructors
- *Test Banks 1, 2,* and *3*—almost 8,000 multiple-choice questions and 500 short-essay questions available on three separate test banks, fully classroom-tested
- *Instructor's Resource Binder*—complete with reproducible supplementary information
- *Instructor's Manual*
- *Instructor's Course Planning Guide and Media Handbook*
- *Economics Today* newsletter

Software for Instructors
- *TestMaster*—in a flexible format
- *QuizMaster-TM*
- Computerized *Instructor's Manual*

Transparencies and Acetates
- LOTS: Lecture Outline and Transparency System
- Full-color acetates and acetate overlays
- Transparency masters

WHAT'S NEW IN THE NINTH EDITION

- *Chapter outline* at the beginning of each chapter
- Chapter opening "Did You Know That . . .?"
- "Thinking Critically About the Media" feature
- "Interacting with the Internet" feature
- 23 new "Issues and Applications" sections
- 42 new domestic examples
- 36 new international examples
- 21 new international and domestic policy examples
- New videos
- A new videodisc
- *Economics Today* CD-ROM

Changes Throughout the Body of the Text

- Marginal definitions all coincide with in-text definitions.
- The link between the preceding theory text and all examples is consistently made clear.

Part 1: Introduction

Chapter 1
- The role of incentives is stressed.

Chapter 2
- Human capital is explicitly mentioned as a separate factor of production.
- Comparative advantage in trade is introduced early.

Chapter 3
- More examples of shifts in supply and demand curves are presented.

Chapter 4
- A discussion of transactions costs and intermediaries is now included.
- An expanded discussion of alternative rationing systems is presented.
- Price supports and minimum wages are now used as examples.

Chapter 5
- There is a complete discussion of correcting for externalities as well as an explicit discussion of property rights.

Chapter 6
- The chapter has been renamed "Economies in Transition" to reflect the worldwide movement toward market systems.
- The role of incentives is further expanded in this chapter, which now includes the four faces of capitalism and a discussion of the transitional phase, called *frontier capitalism,* including the development of the legal system and privatization as well as political opposition to it.
- There is the latest information on Russia and China, as well as where future economic power shifts will lie.

Part 6: Dimensions of Microeconomics

Chapter 19
- The origins of utility theory are explained.
- The explanation of marginal utility has been made clearer.
- The principle of substitution and the real-income effect have been added.

Chapter 20
- The explanation of how to calculate elasticity has been made easier.

Chapter 21
- A new table presents the difference between stocks and bonds.
- Primary and secondary markets are discussed.
- How to read the financial press is fully explained.
- Problems in corporate governance are reviewed, including asymmetric information, adverse selection, and moral hazard.

Part 7: Market Structure, Resource Allocation, and Regulation

Chapter 22
- A simpler explanation of average and marginal physical product is provided, as well as a better example of diminishing returns.

Chapter 23
- Constant reminders are provided that the average and total cost curves include a normal rate of return on investment.

Chapter 24
- The rise of natural monopolies is explained more fully.
- There is more material on cartels.

Chapter 25
- The topic of advertising as signaling behavior is discussed.
- A new discussion is provided of efficiency and resource allocation with oligopoly.
- Game theory is applied to pricing strategies.
- Opportunistic behavior is discussed.

Chapter 26
- The feedback effects of regulation are explored.
- There is more on the costs of regulation.
- The market-share test and the enforcement of antitrust laws are now covered.

Part 8: Productive Factors, Poverty, the Environment, and Interest Groups
- Discussion of public choice and the economics of interest groups has been moved to the end of the unit (Chapter 32).

Chapter 27
- Explanation of the determinants of demand elasticity for inputs has been simplified.
- The topics of efficiency wages and insiders versus outsiders are now discussed in relation to wage determination.

Chapter 28
- There is more on the current status of labor unions.
- Discussion of the upward-sloping supply curve for a monopsonist has been expanded.

Chapter 29
- A clearer explanation of economic rents is provided.
- Specific examples are given of economic rents to labor and why they are not useless.
- The long-run effects of taxing away economic rents are discussed.

Chapter 30

- There is more on the distribution of total wealth in the United States.
- Equality and its trade-off with efficiency are discussed.
- Household incomes and household spending are compared.
- The earned income tax credit program (EITC) is now covered.
- A more economic-theoretic explanation is provided of the rise in health care spending.
- Moral hazard and deductibles analysis are used to explain the quantity of medical care demanded.
- Moral hazard as it affects physicians and hospitals is discussed.
- The topic of medical savings accounts (MSAs) is introduced.

Chapter 31

- Wild species, common property, and trade-offs are analyzed.

Chapter 32

- Agricultural subsidies are examined as an example of the economics of interest groups.
- A detailed analysis of the difference between market and collective decision making is provided.
- The iron triangle is discussed.
- Political rent seeking is explained more fully.

Part 9: Global Economics

Chapter 33

- Exhausting mutual gains from exchange is explained.
- The transmission of ideas is presented as an additional benefit from international trade.
- There is more on the cost of protecting American jobs.
- Graphical explanation of the effects of quotas and of tariffs has been simplified.
- Voluntary quotas, including voluntary restraint agreements (VRAs) and voluntary import expansion (VIEs), are discussed.
- The World Trade Organization is covered.

Chapter 34

- A more complete explanation of the mirror image relationship between the capital account and the current account is provided.

Chapter 35

- The importance to economic development of an open economy and an educated population is emphasized.
- The commission of Type II errors because of protectionism is explained.
- The topic of creative destruction is introduced.
- The relationship between population growth and economic development is explored.
- The consequences of foreign aid are analyzed.

ACKNOWLEDGMENTS

For many years now, I have had the good fortune of receiving numerous comments and criticisms from users of *Economics Today: The Micro View.* All of you who have continued to support my work will see the results of your comments in the ninth edition. Specifically, I would like to thank the following reviewers who went beyond the call of duty to help me improve the manuscript of the ninth edition:

John Adams, Northeastern University

Kari Battaglia, University of North Texas

Michael Bull, DeAnza College

Kevin Carey, University of Miami

Richard J. Cebula, Georgia Institute of Technology

Young Back Choi, St. John's University

Carol Cies, Rose State College

Joy L. Clark, Auburn University at Montgomery

Marsha Clayton, University of Arkansas at Monticello

Eleanor D. Craig, University of Delaware

Andrew J. Dane, Angelo State University

James A. Dyal, Indiana University of Pennsylvania

Ishita Edwards, Oxnard College

Frank Falero, California State University, Bakersfield

Alexander Garvin, Indiana University of Pennsylvania

J. P. Gilbert, Mira Costa College

Richard J. Gosselin, Houston Community College

Gary Greene, Manatee Community College

Mehdi Haririan, Bloomsburg University of Pennsylvania

John M. Hill, Delgado Community College

R. Bradley Hoppes, Southwest Missouri State University

Grover Howard, Rio Hondo College

R. Jack Inch, Oakland Community College

Randall G. Kesselring, Arkansas State University

Philip G. King, San Francisco State University

Janet Koscianski, Shippensburg University

Peter Kressler, Rowan College of New Jersey

Margaret Landman, Bridgewater State College

George Lieu, Tuskegee University

Stephen E. Lile, Western Kentucky University

James J. McLain, University of New Orleans

Mary Lou Madden, Sheldon Jackson College

Dan C. Messerschmidt, Lynchburg College

Margaret D. Moore, Franklin University

George L. Nagy, Hudson Valley Community College

Randall E. Parker, East Carolina University

Raymond A. Pepin, Stonehill College

Reneé Prim, Central Piedmont Community College

Robert W. Pulsinelli, Western Kentucky University

Rod D. Raehsler, Clarion University of Pennsylvania

Sandra Rahman, Newbury College

Gautam Raychaudhuri, Northern Illinois University

Barbara Ross-Pfeiffer, Kapiolani Community College

Phil Smith, DeKalb College

Richard L. Sprinkle, University of Texas at El Paso

Rebecca Summary, Southeast Missouri State University

Gary Theige, City College of San Francisco

Deborah Thorsen, Palm Beach Community College

Lee J. Van Scyoc, University of Wisconsin, Oshkosh

Mark A. Wilkening, Blinn College

Peter R. Wyman, Spokane Falls Community College

Whitney Yamamura, American River College

Alex A. Yguado, Mission College, Los Angeles

Those who reviewed previous editions:

Esmond Adams
John R. Aidem
M. C. Alderfer
Leslie J. Anderson
Fatima W. Antar
Aliakbar Ataiifar
Leonard Atencio
Glen W. Atkinson
Thomas R. Atkinson
James Q. Aylesworth
Charlie Ballard
Maurice B. Ballabon
G. Jeffrey Barbour
Daniel Barszcz
Robin L. Bartlett
Robert Becker

Charles Beem
Glen Beeson
Charles Berry
Scott Bloom
M. L. Bodnar
Mary Bone
Karl Bonnhi
Thomas W. Bonsor
John M. Booth
Wesley F. Booth
Thomas Borcherding
Tom Boston
Barry Boyer
Maryanna Boynton
Ronald Brandolini
Fenton L. Broadhead

Elba Brown
William Brown
Maureen Burton
Ralph T. Byrns
Conrad P. Caligaris
Dancy R. Carr
Doris Cash
Thomas H. Cate
Richard Chapman
Carol Cies
Gary Clayton
Warren L. Coats
Ed Coen
Pat Conroy
James Cox
Stephen R. Cox

Eleanor D. Craig
Joanna Cruse
John P. Cullity
Thomas Curtis
Andrew J. Dane
Mahmoud Davoudi
Edward Dennis
Carol Dimamro
William Dougherty
Barry Duman
Diane Dumont
Floyd Durham
G. B. Duwaji
Robert P. Edwards
Alan E. Ellis
Mike Ellis

Frank Emerson
Zaki Eusufzai
John L. Ewing-Smith
Frank Fato
Grant Ferguson
David Fletcher
James Foley
John Foreman
Ralph G. Fowler
Arthur Friedberg
Peter Frost
E. Gabriel
Steve Gardner
Peter C. Garlick
Joe Garwood
Otis Gilley

Frank Glesber
Jack Goddard
Allen C. Goodman
Nicholas Grunt
William Gunther
Demos Hadjiyanis
Martin D. Haney
Ray Harvey
E. L. Hazlett
Sanford B. Helman
John Hensel
Robert Herman
Gus W. Herring
Charles Hill
Morton Hirsch
Benjamin Hitchner

James Horner
Nancy Howe-Ford
R. Jack Inch
Christopher Inya
Tomotaka Ishimine
E. E. Jarvis
Parvis Jenab
S. D. Jevremovic
J. Paul Jewell
Frederick Johnson
David Jones
Lamar B. Jones
Paul A. Joray
Daniel A. Joseph
Craig Justice
Septimus Kai Kai
Devajyoti Kataky
Timothy R. Keely
Ziad Keilany
Norman F. Keiser
E. D. Key
M. Barbara Killen
Bruce Kimzey
Philip G. King
Terrence Kinal
E. R. Kittrell
David Klingman

Charles Knapp
Jerry Knarr
Michael Kupilik
Larry Landrum
Margaret Landman
Keith Langford
Anthony T. Lee
George Lieu
Stephen E. Lile
Lawrence W. Lovick
Warren T. Matthews
Robert McAuliffe
Howard J. McBride
Bruce McClung
John McDowell
E. S. McKuskey
John L. Madden
Glen Marston
John M. Martin
Paul J. Mascotti
James D. Mason
Paul M. Mason
Tom Mathew
Warren Matthews
G. Hartley Mellish
Mike Melvin
Herbert C. Milikien

Joel C. Millonzi
Glenn Milner
Thomas Molloy
Margaret Moore
William E. Morgan
Stephen Morrell
Irving Morrissett
James W. Moser
Martin F. Murray
Jerome Neadly
James E. Needham
Claron Nelson
Douglas Nettleton
Gerald T. O'Boyle
Lucian T. Orlowski
Diane S. Osborne
Jan Palmer
Gerald Parker
Martin M. Perline
Timothy Perri
Jerry Petr
Maurice Pfannesteil
James Phillips
Raymond J. Phillips
I. James Pickl
Dennis Placone
William L. Polvent

Reneé Prim
Robert W. Pulsinelli
Kambriz Raffiee
John Rapp
Ron Reddall
Mitchell Redlo
Charles Reichhelu
Robert S. Rippey
Ray C. Roberts
Richard Romano
Duane Rosa
Richard Rosenberg
Larry Ross
Philip Rothman
John Roufagalas
Patricia Sanderson
Thomas N. Schaap
William A. Schaeffer
William Schaniel
David Schauer
A. C. Schlenker
Scott J. Schroeder
William Scott
Dan Segebarth
Robert Sexton
Augustus Shackelford

Richard Sherman Jr.
Liang-rong Shiau
David Shorow
Vishwa Shukla
R. J. Sidwell
David E. Sisk
Alden Smith
Howard F. Smith
Lynn A. Smith
Steve Smith
William Doyle Smith
Lee Spector
George Spiva
Herbert F. Steeper
William Stine
Allen D. Stone
Osman Suliman
J. M. Sullivan
Rebecca Summary
Joseph L. Swaffar
Frank D. Taylor
Daniel Teferra
Robert P. Thomas
Richard Trieff
George Troxler
William T. Trulove

William N. Trumbull
Arianne K. Turner
John Vahaly
Jim VanBeek
Lee J. Van Scyoc
Roy Van Til
Robert F. Wallace
Henry C. Wallich
Milledge Weathers
Robert G. Welch
Terence West
Wylie Whalthall
Everett E. White
Michael D. White
Raburn M. Williams
James Willis
George Wilson
Travis Wilson
Ken Woodward
Donald Yankovic
Alex Yguado
Paul Young
Shik Young
Mohammed Zaheer
Ed Zajicek
William J. Zimmer Jr.

As always, a major revision cannot be done by the author alone. The entire staff at Addison-Wesley proved tireless in helping me finish this project. My longtime editor, John Greenman, continued to come up with new ideas and made sure that they were carried out correctly. My developmental editor, Vicki Cohen, made sure that the manuscript was complete and accurate. My project editor, Ellen MacElree, was a hard taskmaster, but I appreciate her getting the book out on time. My copyeditor, Bruce Emmer, smoothed out the manuscript. Dr. Willard W. Radell carefully checked every single graph. Masterful proofing was done by Judy Kiviat, Marie-Christine Loiseau, and Daniel K. Benjamin. Julie Zasloff in wizardly fashion produced all of the printed supplements and made sure they all corresponded to the text and came out on time. Finally, Sue Jasin of K&M Consulting probably retyped more than she thought was possible for a revision. To all of these people I wish to extend my sincere thanks and esteem.

If you or your students have comments, be sure to write to me. I am always eager to find ways to improve this text.

R. L. M.

ECONOMICS
TODAY
THE MICRO VIEW

PART 1

INTRODUCTION

CHAPTER 1

THE NATURE OF ECONOMICS

For most people, choosing a spouse has never been an inexpensive or easy activity. Not long ago, some people were arguing that the institution of marriage was dying. Yet recent statistics show that the opposite is true: The percentage of Americans getting married has increased. Spouse selection is clearly an activity that most people eventually choose to engage in. A variety of considerations are involved. For example, the ease or difficulty of obtaining a divorce may have an effect on how spouses are chosen; so may the factor called love. Is there a rational, economic reason why individuals prefer a marriage in which there is mutual love? To answer this question, you need to know about the nature of economics.

PREVIEW QUESTIONS

1. What is the difference between microeconomics and macroeconomics?

2. What role does rational self-interest play in economic analysis?

3. Why is the study of economics a science?

4. What is the difference between positive and normative economics?

3

Did You Know That . . . since 1987, the number of fax machines in U.S. offices and homes has increased by over 10,000 percent? During the same time period, the number of bike messengers in downtown New York City *decreased* by over 65 percent. The world around us is definitely changing. Much of that change is due to the dramatically falling cost of communications and information technology. By the late 1990s the computers inside video games will cost only a few hundred dollars yet have 50 times the processing power that a $10 million IBM mainframe had in 1975. Not surprisingly, since the start of the 1990s, American firms have been spending more on communications equipment and computers than on new construction and heavy machinery.

Cyberspace, the information superhighway—call it what you want, but your next home (if not your current one) will almost certainly have an address on it. The percentage of U.S. households that have at least one telephone is close to 100 percent, and those that have video game players is approaching 50 percent. Over 35 percent of homes have personal computers, and more than half of those machines are set up to receive and access information via phone lines. Your decisions about such things as when and what type of computer to buy, whether to accept a collect call from a friend traveling in Europe, and how much time you should invest in learning to use a new multimedia system involve an untold number of variables: where you live, the work your parents do, what your friends think, and so on. But, as you will see, there are economic underpinnings for nearly all the decisions you make.

THE POWER OF ECONOMIC ANALYSIS

Knowing that an economic problem exists every time you make a decision is not enough. You also have to develop a framework that will allow you to analyze solutions to each economic problem—whether you are trying to decide how much to study, which courses to take, whether to finish school, or whether America should send troops abroad or raise tariffs. The framework that you will learn in this text is based on the *economic way of thinking*.

This framework gives you power—the power to reach informed conclusions about what is happening in the world. You can, of course, live your life without the power of economic analysis as part of your analytical framework. Indeed, most people do. But economists believe that economic analysis can help you make better decisions concerning your career, your education, financing your home, and other important areas. In the business world, the power of economic analysis can help you increase your competitive edge as an employee or as the owner of a business. As a voter, for the rest of your life you will be asked to make judgments about policies that are advocated by a particular political party. Many of these policies will deal with questions related to international economics, such as whether the U.S. government should encourage or discourage immigration, prevent foreigners from investing in domestic TV stations and newspapers, or restrict other countries from selling their goods here. Finally, just as taking an art, music, or literature appreciation class increases the pleasure you receive when you view paintings, listen to concerts, or read novels, taking an economics course will increase your understanding when watching the news on TV or reading the newspaper.

DEFINING ECONOMICS

What is economics exactly? Some cynics have defined *economics* as "common sense made difficult." But common sense, by definition, should be within everyone's grasp. You will encounter in the following pages numerous examples that show that economics is, in fact, pure and simple common sense.

Economics
The study of how people allocate their limited resources to satisfy their unlimited wants.

Economics is part of the social sciences and as such seeks explanations of real events. All social sciences analyze human behavior, as opposed to the physical sciences, which generally analyze the behavior of electrons, atoms, and other nonhuman phenomena.

> **Economics is the study of how people allocate their limited resources in an attempt to satisfy their unlimited wants. As such, economics is the study of how people make choices.**

To understand this definition fully, two other words need explaining: *resources* and *wants*. **Resources** are things that have value and, more specifically, are used to produce things that satisfy people's wants. **Wants** are all of the things that people would consume if they had unlimited income.

Resources
Things used to produce other things to satisfy people's wants.

Wants
What people would buy if their incomes were unlimited.

Whenever an individual, a business, or a nation faces alternatives, a choice must be made, and economics helps us study how those choices are made. For example, you have to choose how to spend your limited income. You also have to choose how to spend your limited time. You may have to choose how much of your company's limited funds to spend on advertising and how much to spend on new-product research. In economics, we examine situations in which individuals choose how to do things, when to do things, and with whom to do them. Ultimately, the purpose of economics is to explain choices.

MICROECONOMICS VERSUS MACROECONOMICS

Economics is typically divided into two types of analysis: **microeconomics** and **macroeconomics.**

Microeconomics
The study of decision making undertaken by individuals (or households) and by firms.

Macroeconomics
The study of the behavior of the economy as a whole, including such economywide phenomena as changes in unemployment, the general price level, and national income.

> **Microeconomics is the part of economic analysis that studies decision making undertaken by individuals (or households) and by firms. It is like looking through a microscope to focus on the small parts of our economy.**

> **Macroeconomics is the part of economic analysis that studies the behavior of the economy as a whole. It deals with economywide phenomena such as changes in unemployment, the general price level, and national income.**

Microeconomic analysis, for example, is concerned with the effects of changes in the price of gasoline relative to that of other energy sources. It examines the effects of new taxes on a specific product or industry. If price controls were reinstituted in the United States, how individual firms and consumers would react to them would be in the realm of microeconomics. The raising of wages by an effective union strike would also be analyzed using the tools of microeconomics.

By contrast, issues such as the rate of inflation, the amount of economywide unemployment, and the yearly growth in the output of goods and services in the nation all fall into the realm of macroeconomic analysis. In other words, macroeconomics deals with **aggregates,** or totals—such as total output in an economy.

Aggregates
Total amounts or quantities; aggregate demand, for example, is total planned expenditures throughout a nation.

Be aware, however, of the blending of microeconomics and macroeconomics in modern economic theory. Modern economists are increasingly using microeconomic analysis—the study of decision making by individuals and by firms—as the basis of macroeconomic analysis. They do this because even though in macroeconomic analysis aggregates are being examined, those aggregates are made up of individuals and firms.

THE ECONOMIC PERSON: RATIONAL SELF-INTEREST

Economists assume that individuals act *as if* motivated by self-interest and respond predictably to opportunities for gain. This central insight of economics was first clearly articulated by Adam Smith in 1776. Smith wrote in his most famous book, *An Inquiry into the*

Nature and Causes of the Wealth of Nations, that "it is not from the benevolence of the butcher, the brewer, or the baker that we expect our dinner, but from their regard to their own interest." Otherwise stated, the typical person about whom economists make behavioral predictions is assumed to look out for his or her own self-interest in a rational manner. Because monetary benefits and costs of actions are often the most easily measured, economists most often make behavioral predictions about individuals' responses to ways to increase their wealth, measured in money terms. Let's see if we can apply the theory of rational self-interest to explain an anomaly concerning the makeup of the U.S. population.

EXAMPLE
The Increasing Native American Population

Look at Figure 1-1. You see that the proportion of Native Americans increased quite dramatically from 1970 to 1990. Can we use Adam Smith's ideas to understand why so many Native Americans have decided to rejoin their tribes? Perhaps. Consider the benefits of being a member of the Mdewakanton *(bday-WAH-kan-toon),* a tribe of about 100 that runs a casino in which in a recent year gamblers wagered over $500 million. Each member of the tribe received over $400,000. There is now a clear economic reason for Native Americans to return home. Over 200 of the nation's 544 tribes have introduced gambling of some sort, and almost half of those have big-time casinos. Reservations are grossing almost $6 billion a year from gaming. Tribe members sometimes get direct payments and others get the benefits of better health care, subsidized mortgages, and jobs. Self-identified Native Americans increased in number by 137 percent between 1970 and 1990.

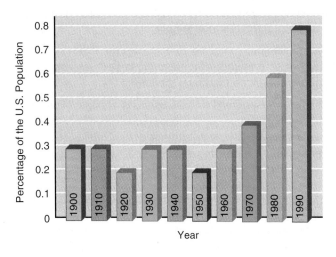

FIGURE 1-1

Native American Population of the United States, 1900–1990
The percentage of the U.S. population identifying itself as Native American has increased substantially in recent decades. Is there an economic explanation for this demographic trend?

FOR CRITICAL ANALYSIS: What nonmonetary reasons are there for Native Americans to rejoin their tribes? ●

The Rationality Assumption

The **rationality assumption** of economics, simply stated, is as follows:

We assume that individuals do not intentionally make decisions that would leave them worse off.

Rationality assumption
The assumption that people do not intentionally make decisions that would leave them worse off.

The distinction here is between what people may think—the realm of psychology and psychiatry and perhaps sociology—and what they do. Economics does *not* involve itself in analyzing individual or group thought processes. Economics looks at what people actually do in life with their limited resources. It does little good to criticize the rationality assumption by stating, "Nobody thinks that way" or "I never think that way" or "How unrealistic! That's as irrational as anyone can get!"

Take the example of driving. When you consider passing another car on a two-lane highway with oncoming traffic, you have to make very quick decisions: You must estimate the speed of the car that you are going to pass, the speed of the oncoming cars, the distance between your car and the oncoming cars, and your car's potential rate of acceleration. If we were to apply a model to your behavior, we would use the laws of calculus. In actual fact, you and most other drivers in such a situation do not actually think of using the laws of calculus, but to predict your behavior, we could make the prediction *as if* you understood the laws of calculus.

In any event, when you observe behavior around you, what may seem irrational often has its basis in the rationality assumption, as you can see by the following example.

EXAMPLE
When It Is Rational *Not* to Learn New Technology

The standard young person's view of older people (particularly one's parents) is that they're reluctant to learn new things. The saying "You can't teach an old dog new tricks" seems to apply. Young people, in contrast, seem eager to learn about new technology—mastering computers and multimedia, playing interactive games, cruising the information superhighway. But there is a rational reason for older people's reduced willingness to learn new technologies. If you are 20 years old and learn a new skill, you will be able to gain returns from your investment in learning over the course of many decades. If you are 60, however, and invest the same amount of time and effort learning the same skill, you will almost certainly not be able to reap those returns for as long a time period. Hence it is perfectly rational for "old dogs" not to want to learn new tricks.

FOR CRITICAL ANALYSIS: Some older people do learn to use new technologies as they emerge. What might explain this behavior? •

Responding to Incentives

If it can be assumed that individuals never intentionally make decisions that would leave them worse off, then almost by definition they will respond to different incentives. We define **incentives** as the potential rewards available if a particular activity is undertaken. Indeed, much of human behavior can be explained in terms of how individuals respond to changing incentives over time.

Schoolchildren are motivated to do better by a variety of incentive systems, ranging from gold stars and certificates of achievement when they are young to better grades with accompanying promises of a "better life" as they get older. There are, of course, negative incentives that affect our behavior, too. Children who disrupt the class are given after-school detention or sent to the vice principal for other punishment.

Implicitly, people react to changing incentives after they have done some sort of rough comparison of the costs and benefits of various courses of action. In fact, making rational choices invariably involves balancing costs and benefits.

Incentives
Rewards for engaging in a particular activity.

The linked concepts of incentive and costs and benefits can be used to explain seeming anomalies in the world around us.

INTERNATIONAL EXAMPLE
Why Are There So Many Brush Fires in Corsica?

Every summer on Corsica, a French island in the Mediterranean less than half the size of the state of New Jersey, 10,000 to 40,000 acres of brush go up in flames. As many as 37 brush fires have been reported on a single day. One might attribute the prevalence of brush fires to the island's physical differences from other European locations, but that is not the explanation. Rather, the European Union (EU) has provided an incentive for some Corsicans to set brush fires deliberately. When brush is burned, more grazing land becomes available, and most Corsican cattle are left to roam freely on common land. Corsicans who claim that they tend at least 100 head of cattle receive a "suckling cow premium" from the EU, equal to more than $2,000 a month. The large number of brush fires on the island of Corsica is no accident.

FOR CRITICAL ANALYSIS: *The average cow in Europe is three years old before she gives birth, whereas in Corsica the average age is a year and a half. Why do you think Corsicans breed their cows faster than other Europeans?* •

Defining Self-Interest

Self-interest does not always mean increasing one's wealth measured in dollars and cents. We assume that individuals seek many goals, not just increased wealth measured in monetary terms. Thus the self-interest part of our economic-person assumption includes goals relating to prestige, friendship, love, power, helping others, creating works of art, and many other matters. We can also think in terms of enlightened self-interest whereby individuals, in the pursuit of what makes them better off, also achieve the betterment of others around them. In brief, individuals are assumed to want the right to further their goals by making decisions about how things around them are used. The head of a charitable organization usually will not turn down an additional contribution, because accepting it lets that person control how that money is used, even if it is always for other people's benefit.

Otherwise stated, charitable acts are not ruled out by self-interest. Giving gifts to relatives can be considered a form of charity that is nonetheless in the self-interest of the giver. But how efficient is such gift giving?

EXAMPLE
The Perceived Value of Gifts

Every holiday season, aunts, uncles, grandparents, mothers, and fathers give gifts to their college-aged loved ones. Joel Waldfogel, an economist at Yale University, surveyed several thousand college students after Christmas to find out the value of holiday gifts. He found that compact discs and outerwear (coats and jackets) had a perceived intrinsic value about equal to their actual cash equivalent. By the time he got down the list to socks, underwear, and cosmetics, the students' valuation was only about 85 percent of the cash value of the gift. He found out that aunts, uncles, and grandparents gave the "worst" gifts and friends, siblings, and parents gave the "best."

FOR CRITICAL ANALYSIS: *What argument could you use against the idea of substituting cash or gift certificates for physical gifts?* •

CONCEPTS IN BRIEF

- Economics is a social science that involves the study of how individuals choose among alternatives to satisfy their wants, which are what people would buy if their incomes were unlimited.

- Microeconomics, the study of the decision-making processes of individuals (or households) and firms, and macroeconomics, the study of the performance of the economy as a whole, are the two main branches into which the study of economics is divided.

- In economics, we assume that people do not intentionally make decisions that will leave them worse off. This is known as the rationality assumption.

- Self-interest is not confined to material well-being but also involves any action that makes a person feel better off, such as having more friends, love, power, affection, or providing more help to others.

ECONOMICS AS A SCIENCE

Economics is a social science that makes use of the same kinds of methods used in other sciences, such as biology, physics, and chemistry. Similar to these other sciences, economics uses models, or theories. Economic **models,** or **theories,** are simplified representations of the real world that we use to help us understand, explain, and predict economic phenomena in the real world. There are, of course, differences between sciences. The social sciences—especially economics—make little use of laboratory methods in which changes in variables can be explained under controlled conditions. Rather, social scientists, and especially economists, usually have to examine what has already happened in the real world in order to test their models, or theories.

Models, or **theories**
Simplified representations of the real world used as the basis for predictions or explanations.

Models and Realism

At the outset it must be emphasized that no model in *any* science, and therefore no economic model, is complete in the sense that it captures *every* detail or interrelationship that exists. Indeed, a model, by definition, is an abstraction from reality. It is conceptually impossible to construct a perfectly complete realistic model. For example, in physics we cannot account for every molecule and its position and certainly not for every atom and subparticle. Not only is such a model impossibly expensive to build, but working with it would be impossibly complex.

The nature of scientific model building is such that the model should capture only the *essential* relationships that are sufficient to analyze the particular problem or answer the particular question with which we are concerned. *An economic model cannot be faulted as unrealistic simply because it does not represent every detail of the real world.* A map of a city that shows only major streets is not necessarily unrealistic if, in fact, all you need to know is how to pass through the city using major streets. As long as a model is realistic in terms of shedding light on the *central* issue at hand or forces at work, it may be useful.

A map is the quintessential model. It is always a simplified representation. It is always unrealistic. But it is also useful in making (refutable) predictions about the world. If the model—the map—predicts that when you take Campus Avenue to the north, you always run into the campus, that is a (refutable) prediction. If our goal is to explain observed behavior, the simplicity or complexity of the model we use is irrelevant. If a simple model can explain observed behavior in repeated settings just as well as a complex one, the simple model has some value and is probably easier to use.

Assumptions

Every model, or theory, must be based on a set of assumptions. Assumptions define the set of circumstances in which our model is most likely to be applicable. When scientists predicted that sailing ships would fall off the edge of the earth, they used the *assumption* that the earth was flat. Columbus did not accept the implications of such a model. He assumed that the world was round. The real-world test of his own model refuted the flat-earth model. Indirectly, then, it was a test of the assumption of the flat-earth model.

EXAMPLE
Getting Directions

Assumptions are a shorthand for reality. Imagine that you have decided to drive from your home in San Diego to downtown San Francisco. Because you have never driven this route, you decide to get directions from the local office of the Automobile Association of America (AAA).

When you ask for directions, the travel planner could give you a set of detailed maps that shows each city through which you will travel—Oceanside, San Clemente, Irvine, Anaheim, Los Angeles, Bakersfield, Modesto, and so on—and then, opening each map, show you exactly how the freeway threads through each of these cities. You would get a nearly complete description of reality because the AAA travel planner will not have used many simplifying assumptions. It is more likely, however, that the travel planner will simply say, "Get on Interstate 5 going north. Stay on it for about 500 miles. Follow the signs for San Francisco. After crossing the toll bridge, take any exit marked 'Downtown.'" By omitting all of the trivial details, the travel planner has told you all that you really need and want to know. The models you will be using in this text are similar to the simplified directions on how to drive from San Diego to San Francisco—they focus on what is relevant to the problem at hand and omit what is not.

FOR CRITICAL ANALYSIS: In what way do small talk and gossip represent the use of simplifying assumptions? ●

The *Ceteris Paribus* Assumption: All Other Things Being Equal. Everything in the world seems to relate in some way to everything else in the world. It would be impossible to isolate the effects of changes in one variable on another variable if we always had to worry about the many other variables that might also enter the analysis. As in other sciences, economics uses the **ceteris paribus assumption.** *Ceteris paribus* means "other things constant" or "other things equal."

Consider an example taken from economics. One of the most important determinants of how much of a particular product a family buys is how expensive that product is relative to other products. We know that in addition to relative prices, other factors influence decisions about making purchases. Some of them have to do with income, others with tastes, and yet others with custom and religious beliefs. Whatever these other factors are, we hold them constant when we look at the relationship between changes in prices and changes in how much of a given product people will purchase.

Ceteris paribus [KAY-ter-us PEAR-uh-bus] assumption
The assumption that nothing changes except the factor or factors being studied.

Deciding on the Usefulness of a Model

We generally do not attempt to determine the usefulness, or "goodness," of a model merely by evaluating how realistic its assumptions are. Rather, we consider a model good if it yields usable predictions and implications for the real world. In other words, can we use the model to predict what will happen in the world around us? Does the model provide useful implications of how things happen in our world?

Once we have determined that the model does predict real-world phenomena, the scientific approach to the analysis of the world around us requires that we consider evidence. Evidence is used to test the usefulness of a model. This is why we call economics an **empirical** science, *empirical* meaning that evidence (data) is looked at to see whether we are right. Economists are often engaged in empirically testing their models.

Consider two competing models for the way students act when doing complicated probability problems to choose the best gambles. One model predicts that, based on the assumption of rational self-interest, students who are paid more for better performance will in fact perform better on average during the experiment. A competing model might be that students whose last names start with the letters *A* through *L* will do better than students with last names starting with *M* through *Z,* irrespective of how much they are paid. The model that consistently predicts more accurately is the model that we would normally choose. In this example, the "alphabet" model did not work well: The first letter of the last name of the students who actually did the experiment at UCLA was irrelevant in predicting how well they would perform the mathematical calculations necessary to choose the correct gambles. The model based on rational self-interest predicted well, in contrast.

Models of Behavior, Not Thought Processes

Take special note of the fact that economists' models do not relate to the way people *think;* they relate to the way people *act,* to what they do in life with their limited resources. Models tend to generalize human behavior. Normally, the economist does not attempt to predict how people will think about a particular topic, such as a higher price of oil products, accelerated inflation, or higher taxes. Rather, the task at hand is to predict how people will act, which may be quite different from what they say they will do (much to the consternation of poll takers and market researchers). The people involved in examining thought processes are psychologists and psychiatrists, not typically economists.

POSITIVE VERSUS NORMATIVE ECONOMICS

Economics uses *positive analysis,* a value-free approach to inquiry. No subjective or moral judgments enter into the analysis. Positive analysis relates to statements such as "If A, then B." For example, "If the price of gasoline goes up relative to all other prices, then the amount of it that people will buy will fall." That is a positive economic statement. It is a statement of *what is.* It is not a statement of anyone's value judgment or subjective feelings. For many problems analyzed in the hard sciences such as physics and chemistry, the analyses are considered to be virtually value-free. After all, how can someone's values enter into a theory of molecular behavior? But economists face a different problem. They deal with the behavior of individuals, not molecules. That makes it more difficult to stick to what we consider to be value-free or **positive economics** without reference to our feelings.

When our values are interjected into the analysis, we enter the realm of **normative economics,** involving *normative analysis.* A positive economic statement is "If the price of

---

Empirical
Relying on real-world data in evaluating the usefulness of a model.

Positive economics
Analysis that is strictly limited to making either purely descriptive statements or scientific predictions; for example, "If A, then B." A statement of *what is.*

Normative economics
Analysis involving value judgments about economic policies; relates to whether things are good or bad. A statement of *what ought to be.*

gas rises, people will buy less." If we add to that analysis the statement "so we should not allow the price to go up," we have entered the realm of normative economics—we have expressed a value judgment. In fact, any time you see the word *should,* you will know that values are entering into the discussion. Just remember that positive statements are concerned with *what is,* whereas normative statements are concerned with *what ought to be.*

Each of us has a desire for different things. That means that we have different values. When we express a value judgment, we are simply saying what we prefer, like, or desire. Because individual values are diverse, we expect—and indeed observe—people expressing widely varying value judgments about how the world ought to be.

A Warning: Recognize Normative Analysis

It is easy to define positive economics. It is quite another matter to catch all unlabeled normative statements in a textbook such as this one (or any other), even though an author goes over the manuscript many times before it is printed. Therefore, do not get the impression that a textbook author will be able to keep all personal values out of the book. They will slip through. In fact, the very choice of which topics to include in an introductory textbook involves normative economics. There is no value-free, or objective, way to decide which topics to use in a textbook. The author's values ultimately make a difference when choices have to be made. But from your own standpoint, you might want to be able to recognize when you are engaging in normative as opposed to positive economic analysis. Reading this text will help equip you for that task.

CONCEPTS IN BRIEF

- A model, or theory, uses assumptions and is by nature a simplification of the real world. The usefulness of a model can be evaluated by bringing empirical evidence to bear on its predictions.

- Models are not necessarily deficient simply because they are unrealistic and use simplifying assumptions, for every model in every science requires simplification compared to the real world.

- Most models use the *ceteris paribus* assumption, that all other things are held constant, or equal.

- Positive economics is value-free and relates to statements that can be refuted, such as "If A, then B." Normative economics involves people's values, and normative statements typically contain the word *should.*

How Relevant Is Love in a Marriage Contract?

Concepts Applied: *Rationality assumption, costs, benefits*

Economist Gary Becker argues that dating can be understood in terms of the rationality assumption. For instance, the better off an individual thinks he or she may be in a marriage, the more that individual is willing to invest in finding the right mate.

Looking for a mate can be analyzed from a sociological, psychological, or anthropological point of view. Here we want to examine this activity in terms of the rationality assumption developed in this chapter. We present an economic analysis based in part on the work of Nobel Prize–winning economist Gary Becker.

Minimizing Costs

According to the rationality assumption, individuals will not knowingly engage in activities that will make them worse off. Consequently, we predict that in choosing a spouse, individuals will naturally want to marry someone with whom they get along. So we predict that likes will attract more often than not: Individuals will tend to marry others with similar values. Dating and "courting" can be viewed as resource-using activities designed to determine with more certainty the values that each potential marriage partner has.

The more benefits one believes can be derived from the marriage contract, the more costs one will incur in searching for a spouse. The longer one searches, the more costs are incurred due to dating and courtship activities. The more durable the marriage contract, the greater the investment people will be willing to make in trying to find the "right" spouse.

Divorce and Wrong Partner Choices

The most durable marriage contract occurs in a legal setting in which divorce is impossible. One benefit is that a spouse cannot later leave because he or she prefers someone else. In many societies, the tendency has been toward fewer restrictions on divorce.

As divorces have become easier (that is to say, less costly), the durability of the marriage contract has seemed to decline. This result follows, at least in part, from economic analysis: As the expected durability of marriage declines, individuals implicitly have less incentive to incur longer searches for the "right" partner. The result: more wrong choices about a partner and hence more frequent divorces.

Why Love Matters

One aspect of love is that the level of happiness of the person loved affects the well-being of the other person. The more one loves another person, the more one is motivated to help that other person. Within a marriage, each spouse is dependent on the other.

When one spouse fails to uphold his or her end of the bargain, this tends to reduce the well-being of the other. Within a marriage, there is no actual iron-clad agreement about who provides what, how, and when. Therefore, it is relatively easy for one spouse not to do what he or she is supposed to do or at least not do it very well. The more love is involved, however, the more each spouse wants to make the other spouse better off. So we predict that marriages work out better the more spouses love each other. Hence individuals generally want to be in a marriage environment in which there is mutual love.

FOR CRITICAL ANALYSIS

1. Is there any difference between what economics predicts about a "good" marriage and what most people believe anyway?
2. If divorce is impossible, how does this affect spouse selection?

CHAPTER SUMMARY

1. Economics as a social science is the study of how individuals make choices to satisfy wants. Wants are defined as what people would buy if their incomes were unlimited.

2. Economics is usually divided into microeconomic analysis, which is the study of individual decision making by households and firms, and macroeconomics, which is the study of nationwide phenomena, such as inflation and unemployment.

3. The rationality assumption is that individuals never intentionally make decisions that would leave them worse off.

4. We use models, or theories, to explain and predict behavior. Models, or theories, are never completely realistic because by definition they are simplifications using assumptions that are not directly testable. The usefulness of a theory, or model, is determined not by the realism of its assumptions but by how well it predicts real-world phenomena.

5. An important simplifying assumption is that all other things are held equal, or constant. This is sometimes known as the *ceteris paribus* assumption.

6. No model in economics relates to individuals' thought processes; all models relate to what people do, not to what they think or say they will do.

7. Much economic analysis involves positive economics; that is, it is value-free. Whenever statements embodying values are made, we enter the realm of normative economics, or how individuals and groups think things ought to be.

DISCUSSION OF PREVIEW QUESTIONS

1. What is the difference between microeconomics and macroeconomics?

Microeconomics is concerned with the choice-making processes of individuals, households, and firms, whereas macroeconomics focuses on the performance of the economy as a whole.

2. What role does rational self-interest play in economic analysis?

Rational self-interest is the assumption that individuals behave in a reasonable (rational) way in making choices to further their interests. In other words, we assume that individuals' actions are motivated primarily by their self-interest, keeping in mind that self-interest can relate to monetary and nonmonetary objectives, such as love, prestige, and helping others.

3. Why is the study of economics a science?

Economics is a science in that it uses models, or theories, that are simplified representations of the real world to analyze and make predictions about the real world. These predictions are then subjected to empirical tests in which real-world data are used to decide whether or not to reject the predictions.

4. What is the difference between positive and normative economics?

Positive economics deals with *what is,* whereas normative economics deals with *what ought to be.* Positive economic statements are of the "if . . . then" variety; they are descriptive and predictive and are not related to what "should" happen. Normative economics, by contrast, is concerned with what ought to be and is intimately tied to value judgments.

PROBLEMS

(Answers to the odd-numbered problems appear at the back of the book.)

1-1. Construct four separate models to predict the probability that a person will die within the next five years. Include only one determining factor in each of your models.

1-2. Does it matter whether all of a model's assumptions are "realistic"? Why or why not?

1-3. Give a refutable implication (one that can be disproved by evidence from the real world) for each of the following models:

    a. The accident rate of drivers is inversely related to their age.

    b. The rate of inflation is directly related to the rate of change in the nation's money supply.

    c. The wages of professional basketball players are directly related to their high school grade point averages.

    d. The rate at which bank employees are promoted is inversely related to their frequency of absenteeism.

1-4. Is gambling an example of rational or irrational behavior? What is the difference between gambling and insurance?

1-5. Over the past 20 years, first-class mail rates have more than tripled, while prices of long-distance phone calls, televisions, and sound systems have decreased. Over a similar period, it has been reported that there has been a steady decline in the ability of high school graduates to communicate effectively in writing. Do you feel that this increase in the relative price of written communication (first-class mail rates) is related to the alleged decline in writing ability? If so, what do you feel is the direction of causation? Which is causing which?

1-6. If there is no way to test a theory with real-world data, can we determine if it is a good theory? Why is empirical evidence used to validate a theory?

1-7. Identify which of the following statements use positive economic analysis and which use normative economic analysis.

    a. The government should not regulate the banking system because recent problems have demonstrated that it does not know what it is doing.

    b. The elimination of barriers to the free movement of individuals across European borders has caused wages to become more equal in many industries.

    c. Paying members of Congress more provides them with less incentive to commit wrongful acts.

    d. We need more restrictions on companies that pollute because air pollution is destroying our way of life.

COMPUTER-ASSISTED INSTRUCTION

Key elements of the scientific way of thinking are illustrated by applying them to everyday situations.

Complete problem and answer appear on disk.

INTERACTING WITH THE INTERNET

The Internet is a web of educational, corporate, and research computer networks around the world. Today, over 40 million people are using it, and more than 60,000 networks are connected to it. Perhaps the most interesting part of the Internet is the World Wide Web, commonly called the Web, which is a vast interlinked network of computer files all over the world. You can use the Internet to find discussion groups, news groups, and electronic publications. The most common use of the Internet is for electronic mail (e-mail).

At many colleges and universities, you can get an e-mail address and a password. Your address is like a mailbox at which you will receive electronic information. Many of the chapters in this ninth edition of *Economics Today* end with Internet addresses and activities that you will find helpful in your study of the principles of economics. In any event, you should get an Internet address now. Pick up a copy of the new user's handbook and start using e-mail.

You can also roam through the user-friendly **gopher** menus. You first open your connection the way you would to send or receive electronic mail. Then you type **gopher** and hit the return (enter) key. (On Windows-based systems, you begin a gopher session by double-clicking on the gopher icon.) You will then be presented with a first-level menu of choices. Choose one by moving the cursor (arrow) up or down to the item you want to open (at the blinking cursor, type in the number of your choice). When you are done playing around, type in **Q.** The largest gopher site is at the University of Minnesota. To reach it, type **gopher** and then type

tc.umn.edu

If you want to "surf" (browse) economics resources immediately, go directly to Resources for Economists on the Internet by typing in

http://econwpa.wustl.edu/EconFAQ/EconFAQ.html

This site is maintained by Professor William Goffe of the University of Southern Mississippi. This is his "home page," the table of contents for a particular Web site. On this page you will find a catalog of "hypertext" pointers, which are highlighted words or phrases that you can click on to connect to places around the Web.

To get in the last laugh, you might want to look up some economist jokes at

http://www.etla.fi/pkm/joke.html

Happy surfing!

CHAPTER 2

SCARCITY AND THE WORLD OF TRADE-OFFS

Is anything more precious than life itself? Most people would say no, though few of us actually act as if life was our most treasured gift. We routinely act in ways that decrease our expected life, include smoking, having an improper diet, not exercising, exceeding the speed limit, not buckling our seat belts, and passing carelessly on two-lane roads. Government policymakers pass laws to protect human life, but they cannot eliminate every risk that exists. They can, however, force society to spend resources to reduce risk to human life. When they do, a trade-off is involved because risk reduction involves the use of things that are scarce.

PREVIEW QUESTIONS

1. Do affluent people face the problem of scarcity?

2. Fresh air may be consumed at no charge, but is it free of cost to society?

3. Why does the scarcity problem force individuals to consider opportunity costs?

4. Can a "free" college education ever be truly free?

id You Know That . . . Chris Van Horn, president of CVK Group in Washington, D.C., grosses over $200,000 a year for having people wait in line? Adam Goldin loves working as a "line waiter" because he gets paid for "doing nothing." His job is to arrive early in the morning on Capitol Hill to hold places for lobbyists who must attend congressional hearings. Van Horn charges his more than 100 lobbyists and law firm clients $27 an hour and pays his part-time line waiters like Mr. Goldin $10 an hour. The lawyers and lobbyists who pay professional line waiters are able to use the time they save more productively and earn well above the $27 an hour they have to pay the line waiters. They do not miss the opportunity to be making more income this way. After all, such lobbyists and lawyers do not have an unlimited amount of time. Time is scarce to them.

SCARCITY

Whenever individuals or communities cannot obtain everything they desire simultaneously, choices occur. Choices occur because of *scarcity*. **Scarcity** is the most basic concept in all of economics. Scarcity means that we do not and cannot have enough income or wealth to satisfy our *every* desire. Scarcity exists because human wants always exceed what can be produced with the limited resources and time that nature makes available.

Scarcity
A situation in which the ingredients for producing the things that people desire are insufficient to satisfy all wants.

What Scarcity Is Not

Scarcity is not a shortage. After a hurricane hits and cuts off supplies to a community, TV newscasts often show people standing in line to get minimum amounts of cooking fuel and food. A news commentator might say that the line is caused by the "scarcity" of these products. But cooking fuel and food are always scarce—we cannot obtain all that we want at a zero price. Therefore, do not confuse the concept of scarcity, which is general and all-encompassing, with the concept of shortages as evidenced by people waiting in line to obtain a particular product.

Scarcity is not the same thing as poverty. Scarcity occurs among the poor and among the rich. Even the richest person on earth faces scarcity because available time is limited. Low income levels do not create more scarcity. High income levels do not create less scarcity.

Scarcity is a fact of life, like gravity. And just as physicists did not invent gravity, economists did not invent scarcity—it existed well before the first economist ever lived. It exists even when we are not using all of our resources.

Scarcity and Resources

The scarcity concept arises from the fact that resources are insufficient to satisfy our every desire. Resources are the inputs used in the production of the things that we want. **Production** can be defined as virtually any activity that results in the conversion of resources into products that can be used in consumption. Production includes delivering things from one part of the country to another. It includes taking ice from an ice tray to put it in your soft-drink glass. The resources used in production are called *factors of production,* and some economists use the terms *resources* and *factors of production* interchangeably. The total quantity of all resources that an economy has at any one time determines what that economy can produce.

Factors of production can be classified in many ways. Here is one such classification:

1. **Land. Land** encompasses all the nonhuman gifts of nature, including timber, water, fish, minerals, and the original fertility of land. It is often called the *natural resource.*

Production
Any activity that results in the conversion of resources into products that can be used in consumption.

Land
The natural resources that are available from nature. Land as a resource includes location, original fertility and mineral deposits, topography, climate, water, and vegetation.

Labor
Productive contributions of humans who work, involving both mental and physical activities.

Physical capital
All manufactured resources, including buildings, equipment, machines, and improvements to land that is used for production.

Human capital
The accumulated training and education of workers.

Entrepreneurship
The factor of production involving human resources that perform the functions of raising capital, organizing, managing, assembling other factors of production, and making basic business policy decisions. The entrepreneur is a risk taker.

2. **Labor. Labor** is the human resource, which includes all productive contributions made by individuals who work, such as steelworkers, ballet dancers, and professional baseball players.

3. **Physical capital. Physical capital** consists of the factories and equipment used in production. It also includes improvements to natural resources, such as irrigation ditches.

4. **Human capital. Human capital** is the economic characterization of the education and training of workers. How much the nation produces depends not only on how many hours people work but also on how productive they are, and that, in turn, depends in part on education and training. To become more educated, individuals have to devote time and resources, just as a business has to devote resources if it wants to increase its physical capital. Whenever a worker's skills increase, human capital has been improved.

5. **Entrepreneurship.** The factor of production known as **entrepreneurship** (actually a subdivision of labor) involves human resources that perform the functions of organizing, managing, and assembling the other factors of production to make business ventures. Entrepreneurship also encompasses taking risks that involve the possibility of losing large sums of wealth on new ventures. It includes new methods of doing common things and generally experimenting with any type of new thinking that could lead to making more money income. Without entrepreneurship, virtually no business organization could operate.

Goods Versus Economic Goods

Goods
All things from which individuals derive satisfaction or happiness.

Economic goods
Goods that are scarce.

Goods are defined as all things from which individuals derive satisfaction or happiness. Goods therefore include air to breathe and the beauty of a sunset as well as food, cars, and CD players.

Economic goods are a subset of all goods—they are goods derived from scarce resources about which we must constantly make decisions regarding their best use. By definition, the desired quantity of an economic good exceeds the amount that is directly available from nature at a zero price. Virtually every example we use in economics concerns economic goods—cars, CD players, computers, socks, baseball bats, and corn. Weeds are a good example of *bads*—goods for which the desired quantity is much *less* than what nature provides at a zero price.

Services
Mental or physical labor or help purchased by consumers. Examples are the assistance of doctors, lawyers, dentists, repair personnel, housecleaners, educators, retailers, and wholesalers; things purchased or used by consumers that do not have physical characteristics.

Sometimes you will see references to "goods and services." **Services** are tasks that are performed for someone else, such as laundry, cleaning, hospital care, restaurant meal preparation, car polishing, psychological counseling, and teaching. One way of looking at services is thinking of them as *intangible goods*.

WANTS AND NEEDS

Wants are not the same as needs. Indeed, from the economist's point of view, the term *needs* is objectively undefinable. When someone says, "I need some new clothes," there is no way to know whether that person is stating a vague wish, a want, or a life-saving necessity. If the individual making the statement were dying of exposure in a northern country during the winter, we might argue that indeed the person does need clothes—perhaps not new ones, but at least some articles of warm clothing. Typically, however, the term *need* is used very casually in most conversations. What people mean, usually, is that they want something that they do not currently have.

Humans have unlimited wants. Just imagine if every single material want that you might have were satisfied. You can have all of the clothes, cars, houses, CDs, tickets to concerts, and other things that you want. Does that mean that nothing else could add to your total level of happiness? Probably not, because you might think of new goods and services that you could obtain, particularly as they came to market. You would also still be lacking in fulfilling all of your wants for compassion, friendship, love, affection, prestige, musical abilities, sports abilities, and so on.

In reality, every individual has competing wants but cannot satisfy all of them, given limited resources. This is the reality of scarcity. Each person must therefore make choices. Whenever a choice is made to do or buy something, something else that is also desired is not done or not purchased. In other words, in a world of scarcity, every want that ends up being satisfied causes one or more other wants to remain unsatisfied or to be forfeited.

CONCEPTS IN BRIEF

- Scarcity exists because human wants always exceed what can be produced with the limited resources and time that nature makes available.

- We use scarce resources, such as land, labor, physical and human capital, and entrepreneurship, to produce economic goods—goods that are desired but are not directly obtainable from nature to the extent demanded or desired at a zero price.

- Wants are unlimited; they include all material desires and all nonmaterial desires, such as love, affection, power, and prestige.

- The concept of need is difficult to define objectively for every person; consequently, we simply consider that every person's wants are unlimited. In a world of scarcity, satisfaction of one want necessarily means nonsatisfaction of one or more other wants.

SCARCITY, CHOICE, AND OPPORTUNITY COST

The natural fact of scarcity implies that we must make choices. One of the most important results of this fact is that every choice made (or not made, for that matter) means that some opportunity had to be sacrificed. Every choice involves giving up another opportunity to do or use something else.

Consider a practical example. Every choice you make to study one more hour of economics requires that you give up the opportunity to do any of the following activities: study more of another subject, listen to music, sleep, browse at a local store, read a novel, or work out at the gym. Many more opportunities are forgone also if you choose to study economics an additional hour.

Because there were so many alternatives from which to choose, how could you determine the value of what you gave up to engage in that extra hour of studying economics? First of all, no one else can tell you the answer because only you can *subjectively* put a value on the alternatives forgone. Only you know what is the value of another hour of sleep or of an hour looking for the latest CDs. That means that only you can determine the highest-valued, next-best alternative that you had to sacrifice in order to study economics one more hour. It is you who come up with the *subjective* estimate of the expected value of the next-best alternative.

The value of the next-best alternative is called **opportunity cost.** The opportunity cost of any action is the value of what is given up—the next-highest-ranked alternative—

Opportunity cost
The highest-valued, next-best alternative that must be sacrificed to attain something or to satisfy a want.

because a choice was made. When you study one more hour, there may be many alternatives available for the use of that hour, but assume that you can do only one thing in that hour—your next-highest-ranked alternative. What is important is the choice that you would have made if you hadn't studied one more hour. Your opportunity cost is the *next-highest-ranked* alternative, not *all* alternatives.

In economics, cost is always a forgone opportunity.

One way to think about opportunity cost is to understand that when you choose to do something, you lose. What you lose is being able to engage in your next-highest-valued alternative. The cost of your choice is what you lose, which is by definition your next-highest-valued alternative. This is your opportunity cost.

Let's consider the opportunity cost of forcing young men to serve time in the military service.

INTERNATIONAL EXAMPLE
The True Cost of the Military Draft in France

In 1996, the president of France, Jacques Chirac, announced that the government would end the military draft over the following six years. Ultimately, France will end up with 150,000 fewer soldiers. Chirac warned that the change would not result in any budget savings because the smaller professional army would cost the same as the then-current draft system. Each year, a professional military person "costs" 15 times more than a conscript. The annual salary of a professional military person is about 185,000 francs (about $38,000), whereas a conscript is only paid 12,500 francs (about $2,575).

But what is the true cost of a conscript in France? Remember that cost is always a forgone opportunity. If a conscript was making 100,000 francs a year (about $20,000) before being drafted, that is his opportunity cost. In other words, that is the opportunity cost to the nation whether or not that individual is paid the 100,000 francs a year by the French army. Resources are not saved by a nation engaging in conscription. Rather, the true cost to the military is simply hidden from the people.

FOR CRITICAL ANALYSIS: What are some other costs to the nation associated with a military draft? •

THE WORLD OF TRADE-OFFS

Whenever you engage in any activity using any resource, even time, you are *trading off* the use of that resource for one or more alternative uses. The value of the trade-off is represented by the opportunity cost. The opportunity cost of studying economics has already been mentioned—it is the value of the next-best alternative. When you think of any alternative, you are thinking of trade-offs.

Let's consider a hypothetical example of a one-for-one trade-off between the results of spending time studying economics and accounting. For the sake of this argument, we will assume that additional time studying either economics or accounting will lead to a higher grade in the subject studied more. One of the best ways to examine this trade-off is with a graph. (If you would like a refresher on graphical techniques, study Appendix A at the end of this chapter before going on.)

Graphical Analysis

In Figure 2-1, the expected grade in accounting is measured on the vertical axis of the graph, and the expected grade in economics is measured on the horizontal axis. We simplify the world and assume that you have a maximum of 10 hours per week to spend studying these two subjects and that if you spend all 10 hours on economics, you will get an A in the course. You will, however, fail accounting. Conversely, if you spend all of your 10 hours studying accounting, you will get an A in that subject, but you will flunk economics. Here the trade-off is a special case: one-to-one. A one-to-one trade-off means that the opportunity cost of receiving one grade higher in economics (for example, improving from a C to a B) is one grade lower in accounting (falling from a C to a D).

The Production Possibilities Curve (PPC)

The graph in Figure 2-1 illustrates the relationship between the possible results that can be produced in each of two activities, depending on how much time you choose to devote to each activity. This graph shows a representation of a **production possibilities curve (PPC).**

Consider that you are producing a grade in economics when you study economics and a grade in accounting when you study accounting. Then the graph in Figure 2-1 can be related to the production possibilities you face. The line that goes from A on one axis to A on the other axis therefore becomes a production possibilities curve. It is defined as the maximum quantity of one good or service that can be produced, given that a specific quantity of another is produced. It is a curve that shows the possibilities available for increasing the output of one good or service by reducing the amount of another. In the example in Figure 2-1, your time for studying was limited to 10 hours per week. The two possible outputs were grades in accounting and grades in economics. The particular production possibilities curve presented in Figure 2-1 is a graphical representation of the opportunity cost of studying one more hour in one subject. It is a *straight-line production possibilities curve,* which is a special case. (The more general case will be discussed next.) If you decide to be at point *x* in Figure 2-1, 5 hours of study time will be spent on accounting and 5 hours will be spent on economics. The expected grade in each course will be a C. If you are more interested in getting a B in economics, you will go to point *y* on the production possibilities curve, spending only 2.5 hours on accounting but 7.5 hours on economics. Your expected grade in accounting will then drop from a C to a D.

Production possibilities curve (PPC)
A curve representing all possible combinations of total output that could be produced assuming (1) a fixed amount of productive resources of a given quality and (2) the efficient use of those resources.

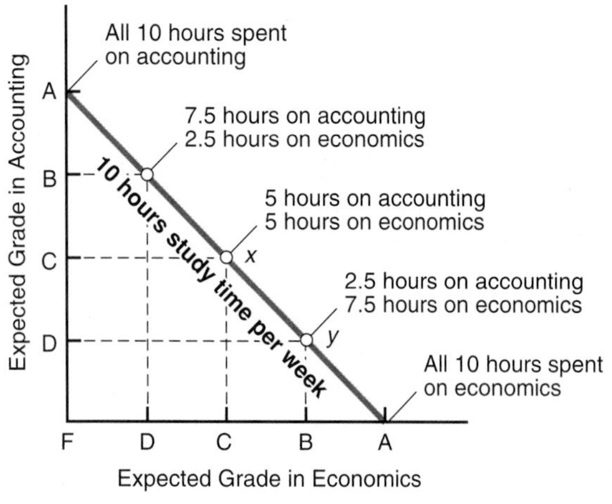

FIGURE 2-1

Production Possibilities Curve for Grades in Accounting and Economics (Trade-offs)
We assume that only 10 hours can be spent per week on studying. If the student is at point *x*, equal time (5 hours a week) is spent on both courses and equal grades of C will be received. If a higher grade in economics is desired, the student may go to point *y*, thereby receiving a B in economics but a D in accounting. At point *y*, 2.5 hours are spent on accounting and 7.5 hours on economics.

Note that these trade-offs between expected grades in accounting and economics are the result of *holding constant* total study time as well as all other factors that might influence a student's ability to learn, such as computerized study aids. Quite clearly, if you wished to spend more total time studying, it would be possible to have higher grades in both economics and accounting. In that case, however, we would no longer be on the specific production possibilities curve illustrated in Figure 2-1. We would have to draw a new curve, farther to the right, to show the greater total study time and a different set of possible trade-offs.

CONCEPTS IN BRIEF

- Scarcity requires us to choose. When we choose, we lose the next-highest-valued alternative.
- Cost is always a forgone opportunity.
- Another way to look at opportunity cost is the trade-off that occurs when one activity is undertaken rather than the next-best alternative activity.
- A production possibilities curve (PPC) graphically shows the trade-off that occurs when more of one output is obtained at the sacrifice of another. The PPC is a graphical representation of, among other things, opportunity cost.

THE CHOICES SOCIETY FACES

The straight-line production possibilities curve presented in Figure 2-1 can be generalized to demonstrate the related concepts of scarcity, choice, and trade-offs that our entire nation faces. As you will see, the production possibilities curve is a simple but powerful economic model because it can demonstrate these related concepts. The example we will use is the choice between the production of M-16 semiautomatic rifles and CD-ROM players. We assume for the moment that these are the only two goods that can be produced in the nation. Panel (a) of Figure 2-2 on page 24 gives the various combinations of M-16s and CD-ROM players that are possible. If all resources are devoted to M-16 production, 10 billion per year can be produced. If all resources are devoted to CD-ROM player production, 12 billion per year can be produced. In between are various possible combinations. These combinations are plotted as points *A, B, C, D, E, F,* and *G* in panel (b) of Figure 2-2. If these points are connected with a smooth curve, the nation's production possibilities curve is shown, demonstrating the trade-off between the production of M-16 semiautomatic rifles and CD-ROM players. These trade-offs occur *on* the production possibilities curve.

Notice the major difference in the shape of the production possibilities curves in Figures 2-1 and 2-2. In Figure 2-1, there is a one-to-one trade-off between grades in economics and in accounting. In Figure 2-2, the trade-off between CD-ROM production and M-16 production is not constant, and therefore the production possibilities curve is a *bowed* line. To understand why the production possibilities curve for a society is typically bowed outward, you must understand the assumptions underlying the PPC.

Assumptions Underlying the Production Possibilities Curve

When we draw the curve that is shown in Figure 2-2, we make the following assumptions:

1. That resources are fully employed
2. That we are looking at production over a specific time period—for example, one year

Panel (a)

Combination	M-16 Rifles (billions of units per year)	CD-ROM Players (billions of units per year)
A	10.0	0
B	9.6	2
C	9.0	4
D	8.0	6
E	6.6	8
F	4.5	10
G	0	12

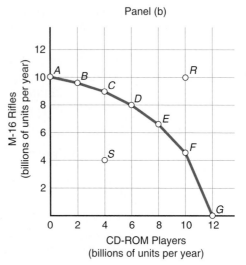

Panel (b)

FIGURE 2-2

Society's Trade-off Between M-16 Rifles and CD-ROM Players
Both the production of M-16 semiautomatic rifles and the production of CD-ROM players are measured in billions of units per year. The various combinations are given in panel (a) and plotted in panel (b). Connecting the points A–G with a relatively smooth line gives the society's production possibilities curve for M-16 rifles and CD-ROM players. Point R lies outside the production possibilities curve and is therefore unattainable at the point in time for which the graph is drawn. Point S lies inside the production possibilities curve and therefore represents an inefficient use of available resources.

3. That the resource inputs, in both quantity and quality, used to produce M-16 rifles or CD-ROM players are fixed over this time period
4. That technology does not change over this time period

Technology is defined as society's pool of applied knowledge concerning how goods and services can be produced by managers, workers, engineers, scientists, and craftspeople, using land and capital. You can think of technology as the formula (or recipe) used to combine factors of production. (When better formulas are developed, more production can be obtained from the same amount of resources.) The level of technology sets the limit on the amount and types of goods and services that we can derive from any given amount of resources. The production possibilities curve is drawn under the assumption that we use the best technology that we currently have available and that this technology doesn't change over the time period under study.

Technology
Society's pool of applied knowledge concerning how goods and services can be produced.

Being off the Production Possibilities Curve

Look again at panel (b) of Figure 2-2. Point R lies *outside* the production possibilities curve and is *impossible* to achieve during the time period assumed. By definition, the production possibilities curve indicates the *maximum* quantity of one good given some quantity of the other.

It is possible, however, to be at point S in Figure 2-2. That point lies beneath the production possibilities curve. If the nation is at point S, it means that its resources are not being fully utilized. This occurs, for example, during periods of unemployment. Point S and all such points within the production possibilities curve are always attainable but usually not desirable.

Efficiency

The production possibilities curve can be used to define the notion of efficiency. Whenever the economy is operating on the PPC, at points such as *A, B, C,* or *D,* we say that its production is efficient. Points such as *S* in Figure 2-2, which lie beneath the production possibilities curve, are said to represent production situations that are not efficient.

Efficiency
The case in which a given level of inputs is used to produce the maximum output possible. Alternatively, the situation in which a given output is produced at minimum cost.

Efficiency can mean many things to many people. Even within economics, there are different types of efficiency. Here we are discussing efficiency in production, or productive efficiency. An economy is productively efficient whenever it is producing the maximum output with given technology and resources.

A simple commonsense definition of efficiency is getting the most out of what we have as an economy. Clearly, we are not getting the most that we have if we are at point *S* in panel (b) of Figure 2-2. We can move from point *S* to, say, point *C,* thereby increasing the total quantity of M-16s produced without any decrease in the total quantity of CD-ROM players produced. We can move from point *S* to point *E,* for example, and have both more M-16s and more CD-ROM players. Point *S* is called an **inefficient point,** which is defined as any point below the production possibilities curve.

Inefficient point
Any point below the production possibilities curve at which resources are being used inefficiently.

The concept of economic efficiency relates to how goods are distributed among different individuals and entities. An efficient economy is one in which people who value specific goods relatively the most end up with those goods. If you own a vintage electric Fender guitar, but I value it more than you, I can buy it from you. Such trading benefits you and me mutually. In the process, the economy becomes more efficient. The maximum efficiency an economy can reach is when all such mutual benefits through trade have been exhausted.

The Law of Increasing Relative Cost

In the example in Figure 2-1, the trade-off between a grade in accounting and a grade in economics is one-to-one. The trade-off ratio was fixed. That is to say, the production possibilities curve was a straight line. The curve in Figure 2-2 is a more general case. We have re-created the curve in Figure 2-2 as Figure 2-3. Each combination, *A* through *G,* of M-16s and CD-ROM players is represented on the production possibilities curve. Starting with the production of zero CD-ROM players, the nation can produce 10 billion units of M-16s with its available resources and technology. When we increase production of CD-ROM players from zero to 2 billion units per year, the nation has to give up in M-16s that first vertical arrow, *Aa.* From panel (a) of Figure 2-2 you can see that this is .4 billion M-16s a

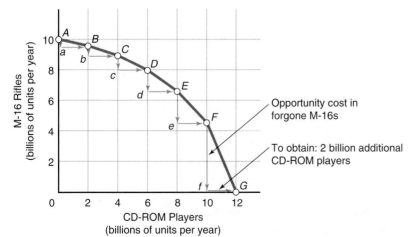

FIGURE 2-3

The Law of Increasing Relative Cost
Consider equal increments of CD-ROM player production, as measured on the horizontal axis. All of the horizontal arrows—*aB, bC,* and so on—are of equal length (2 billion units). The opportunity cost of going from 10 billion CD-ROM players per year to 12 billion *(Ff)* is much greater than going from zero units to 2 billion units *(Aa).* The opportunity cost of each additional equal increase in CD-ROM production rises.

year (10.0 billion − 9.6 billion). Again, if we increase production of CD-ROM players by 2 billion units per year, we go from *B* to *C*. In order to do so, the nation has to give up the vertical distance *Bb,* or .6 billion M-16s a year. By the time we go from 10 billion to 12 billion CD-ROM players, to obtain that 2 billion unit increase, we have to forgo the vertical distance *Ff,* or 4.5 billion M-16s. In other words, we see an increase in the opportunity cost of the last 2 billion units of CD-ROM players—4.5 billion M-16s—compared to an equivalent increase in CD-ROM players when we started with none being produced at all—.4 billion M-16s.

What we are observing is called the **law of increasing relative cost.** When society takes more resources and applies them to the production of any specific good, the opportunity cost increases for each additional unit produced. The reason that, as a nation, we face the law of increasing relative cost (which causes the production possibilities curve to bow outward) is that certain resources are better suited for producing some goods than they are for other goods. Resources are generally not *perfectly* adaptable for alternative uses. When increasing the output of a particular good, producers must use less efficient resources than those already used in order to produce the additional output. Hence the cost of producing the additional units increases. With respect to our hypothetical example here, at first the electronic technicians in the armed services would shift over to producing CD-ROM players. After a while, though, janitors and army cooks would be asked to help. Clearly, they would be less effective in making CD-ROM players.

As a rule of thumb, *the more specialized the resources, the more bowed the production possibilities curve.* At the other extreme, if all resources are equally suitable for CD-ROM player production or M-16 production, the curves in Figures 2-2 and 2-3 would approach the straight line shown in our first example in Figure 2-1.

Law of increasing relative cost
The observation that the opportunity cost of additional units of a good generally increases as society attempts to produce more of that good. This accounts for the bowed-out shape of the production possibilities curve.

CONCEPTS IN BRIEF

- Trade-offs are represented graphically by a production possibilities curve showing the maximum quantity of one good or service that can be produced, given a specific quantity of another, from a given set of resources over a specified period of time—for example, one year.

- A PPC is drawn holding the quantity and quality of all resources fixed over the time period under study.

- Points outside the production possibilities curve are unattainable; points inside are attainable but represent an inefficient use or underuse of available resources.

- Because many resources are better suited for certain productive tasks than for others, society's production possibilities curve is bowed outward, following the law of increasing relative cost.

ECONOMIC GROWTH AND THE PRODUCTION POSSIBILITIES CURVE

Over any particular time period, a society cannot be outside the production possibilities curve. Over time, however, it is possible to have more of everything. This occurs through economic growth (why economic growth occurs will be discussed in a later chapter). Figure 2-4 shows the production possibilities curve for M-16 rifles and CD-ROM players shifting outward. The two additional curves shown represent new choices open to an economy that has experienced economic growth. Such economic growth occurs because of

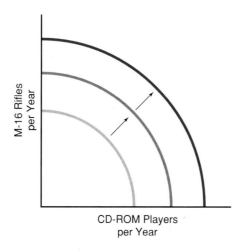

FIGURE 2-4

Economic Growth Allows for More of Everything

If the nation experiences economic growth, the production possibilities curve between M-16 rifles and CD-ROM players will move out, as is shown. This takes time, however, and it does not occur automatically. This means, therefore, that we can have more M-16s and more CD-ROM players only after a period of time during which we have experienced economic growth.

many things, including increases in the number of workers and productive investment in equipment.

Scarcity still exists, however, no matter how much economic growth there is. At any point in time, we will always be on some production possibilities curve; thus we will always face trade-offs. The more we want of one thing, the less we can have of others.

If a nation experiences economic growth, the production possibilities curve between M-16 rifles and CD-ROM players will move outward, as is shown in Figure 2-4. This takes time and does not occur automatically. One reason it will occur involves the choice about how much to consume today.

THE TRADE-OFF BETWEEN THE PRESENT AND THE FUTURE

Consumption
The use of goods and services for personal satisfaction.

The production possibilities curve and economic growth can be used to examine the trade-off between present **consumption** and future consumption. When we consume today, we are using up what we call consumption or consumer goods—food and clothes, for example. And we have already defined physical capital as the manufactured goods, such as machines and factories, used to make other goods and services.

Why We Make Capital Goods

Why would we be willing to use productive resources to make things—capital goods—that we cannot consume directly? For one thing, capital goods enable us to produce larger quantities of consumer goods or to produce them less expensively than we otherwise could. Before fish are "produced" for the market, equipment such as fishing boats, nets, and poles are produced first. Imagine how expensive it would be to obtain fish for market without using these capital goods. Catching fish with one's hands is not an easy task. The price per fish would be very high if capital goods weren't used.

Forgoing Current Consumption

Whenever we use productive resources to make capital goods, we are implicitly forgoing current consumption. We are waiting for some time in the future to consume the fruits that will be reaped from the use of capital goods. In effect, when we forgo current consumption to invest in capital goods, we are engaging in an economic activity that is forward-looking—we do not get instant utility or satisfaction from our activity. Indeed, if we were to produce only consumer goods now and no capital goods, our capacity to produce consumer goods in the future would suffer. Here we see a trade-off situation.

The Trade-off Between Consumption Goods and Capital Goods

To have more consumer goods in the future, we must accept fewer consumer goods today. In other words, an opportunity cost is involved here. Every time we make a choice for more goods today, we incur an opportunity cost of fewer goods tomorrow, and every time we make a choice of more goods in the future, we incur an opportunity cost of fewer goods today. With the resources that we don't use to produce consumer goods for today, we invest in capital goods that will produce more consumer goods for us later. The trade-off is shown in Figure 2-5. On the left in panel (a), you can see this trade-off depicted as a production possibilities curve between capital goods and consumption goods.

Assume that we are willing to give up $1 trillion worth of consumption today. We will be at point A in the left-hand diagram of panel (a). This will allow the economy to grow. We will have more future consumption because we invested in more capital goods today. In the right-hand diagram of panel (a), we see two goods represented, food and recreation. The production possibilities curve will move outward if we collectively decide to restrict consumption each year and invest in capital goods.

In panel (b), we show the results of our willingness to forgo more current consumption. We move to point C, where we have many fewer consumer goods today but produce a lot

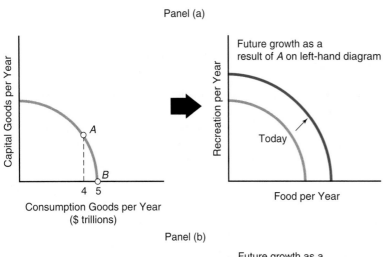

FIGURE 2-5

Capital Goods and Growth
In panel (a), the nation chooses not to consume $1 trillion, so it invests that amount in capital goods. In panel (b), it chooses even more capital goods. The PPC moves even more to the right on the right-hand diagram in panel (b) as a result.

more capital goods. This leads to more future growth in this simplified model, and thus the production possibilities curve in the right-hand side of panel (b) shifts outward more than it did in the right-hand side of panel (a).

In other words, the more we give up today, the more we can have tomorrow, provided, of course, that the capital goods are productive in future periods and that society desires the consumer goods produced by this additional capital.

INTERNATIONAL EXAMPLE
Consumption Versus Capital Goods in the United States and Japan

The trade-off represented in Figure 2-5 on the production possibilities curve of capital versus consumption goods can be observed in real life when we compare different countries. The Japanese, for example, have chosen to devote more than twice the amount of resources each year to the production of capital goods than we have in the United States. Not surprisingly, the Japanese have until recently experienced economic growth at a much higher rate than the United States has. In effect, then, Japan is represented by panel (b) in Figure 2-5—choosing more capital goods—and America by panel (a)—choosing fewer capital goods.

FOR CRITICAL ANALYSIS: Does this analysis apply to the trade-off between consumption and human capital for you as an individual? If so, how? ●

CONCEPTS IN BRIEF

- The use of capital requires using productive resources to produce capital goods that will later be used to produce consumer goods.

- A trade-off is involved between current consumption and capital goods or, alternatively, between current consumption and future consumption because the more we invest in capital goods today, the greater the amount of consumer goods we can produce in the future and the smaller the amount of consumer goods we can produce today.

SPECIALIZATION AND GREATER PRODUCTIVITY

Specialization
The division of productive activities among persons and regions so that no one individual or one area is totally self-sufficient. An individual may specialize, for example, in law or medicine. A nation may specialize in the production of coffee, computers, or cameras.

Specialization involves working at a relatively well-defined, limited endeavor, such as accounting or teaching. It involves a division of labor among different individuals and regions. Most individuals, in fact, do specialize. For example, you could change the oil in your car if you wanted to. Typically, though, you take your car to a garage and let the mechanic change the oil. You benefit by letting the garage mechanic specialize in changing the oil and in doing other repairs on your car. The specialist will get the job finished sooner than you could and has the proper equipment to make the job go more smoothly. Specialization usually leads to greater productivity, not only for each individual but also for the nation.

Absolute Advantage

Absolute advantage
The ability to produce a good or service at an "absolutely" lower cost, usually measured in units of labor or resource input required to produce one unit of the good or service.

Specialization occurs because different individuals and different nations have different skills. Sometimes it seems that some individuals are better at doing everything than anyone else. A president of a large company might be able to type better than any of the typists, file better than any of the file clerks, and wash windows better than any of the window washers. The president has an **absolute advantage** in all of these endeavors—he uses fewer labor hours for each task than anyone else in the company. The president does not, however, spend his time doing those other activities. Why not? Because he is being paid the most for undertaking the president's managerial duties. The president specializes in one particular task in spite of having an absolute advantage in all tasks. Indeed, absolute advantage is irrelevant in predicting how he uses his time; only *comparative advantage* matters.

Comparative Advantage

Comparative advantage is the ability to perform an activity at the lowest opportunity cost. You have a comparative advantage in one activity whenever you have the lowest opportunity cost of performing that activity. Comparative advantage is always a *relative* concept. You may be able to change the oil in your car; you might even be able to change it faster than the local mechanic. But if the opportunity cost you face by changing the oil exceeds the mechanic's opportunity cost, the mechanic has a comparative advantage in changing the oil. The mechanic faces a lower opportunity cost for that activity.

> **Comparative advantage**
> The ability to produce a good or service at a lower opportunity cost compared to other producers.

You may be convinced that everybody can do everything better than you. In this extreme situation, do you still have a comparative advantage? The answer is yes. What you need to do to discover your comparative advantage is to find a job in which your *disadvantage* relative to others is the smallest. You do not have to be a mathematical genius to figure this out. The market tells you very clearly by offering you the highest income for the job for which you have the smallest disadvantage compared to others. Stated differently, to find your comparative advantage no matter how much better everybody else can do the jobs that you want to do, you simply find which job maximizes your income.

The coaches of sports teams are constantly faced with determining each player's comparative advantage. Babe Ruth was originally one of the best pitchers in professional baseball when he played for the Boston Red Sox. After he was traded to the New York Yankees, the owner and the coach decided to make him an outfielder, even though he was a better pitcher than anyone else on the team roster. They wanted "The Babe" to concentrate on his hitting. Good pitchers do not bring in as many fans as home-run kings. Babe Ruth's comparative advantage was clearly in hitting homers rather than practicing and developing his pitching game.

Scarcity, Self-Interest, and Specialization

In Chapter 1, you learned about the assumption of rational self-interest. To repeat, for the purposes of our analyses we assume that individuals are rational in that they will do what is in their own self-interest. They will not consciously carry out actions that will make them worse off. In this chapter, you learned that scarcity requires people to make choices. We assume that they make choices based on their self-interest. When they make these choices, they attempt to maximize benefits net of opportunity cost. In so doing, individuals choose their comparative advantage and end up specializing. Ultimately, when people specialize, they increase the money income they make and therefore become richer. When all individuals and businesses specialize simultaneously, the gains are seen in greater material well-being. With any given set of resources, specialization will result in higher output.

INTERNATIONAL EXAMPLE
Why Foreign Graduate Students Specialize When Studying in the United States

Specialization is evident in the fields of endeavor that foreign students choose when they come to the United States for graduate studies. Consider the following statistics: More than

60 percent of U.S. doctorates in engineering and 55 percent of those in mathematics, computer science, and the physical sciences are earned by foreign-born students. Yet foreign nationals are awarded relatively few advanced degrees in business, law, or medicine. The reason has nothing to do with intelligence or giftedness; it is simply that many more of the best American students choose schools in these professional fields rather than ones offering science and engineering programs.

Why does this specialization occur? For American students, the greatest returns for about the same effort come from business, law, and medicine. In contrast, foreign-born graduate students face fewer language and cultural obstacles (and hence better job prospects) if they choose technical subjects.

When students from foreign countries come to American graduate schools to obtain their Ph.D. degrees, more than 70 percent of them remain in the United States after graduation, thereby augmenting America's supply of engineers and scientists. Such specialization has helped the United States maintain its leadership in both the technoscientific and sociocultural areas.

FOR CRITICAL ANALYSIS: What type of capital do foreign-born students bring with them to the United States? ●

THE DIVISION OF LABOR

Division of labor
The segregation of a resource into different specific tasks; for example, one automobile worker puts on bumpers, another doors, and so on.

In any firm that includes specialized human and nonhuman resources, there is a **division of labor** among those resources. The best-known example of all time comes from one of the earliest and perhaps most famous economists, Adam Smith, who in *The Wealth of Nations* (1776) illustrated the benefits of a division of labor in the making of pins, as depicted in the following example:

> One man draws out the wire, another straightens it, a third cuts it, a fourth points it, a fifth grinds it at the top for receiving the head; to make the head requires two or three distinct operations; to put it on is a peculiar business, to whiten the pins is another; it is even a trade by itself to put them into the paper.

Making pins this way allowed 10 workers without very much skill to make almost 48,000 pins "of a middling size" in a day. One worker, toiling alone, could have made perhaps 20 pins a day; therefore, 10 workers could have produced 200. Division of labor allowed for an increase in the daily output of the pin factory from 200 to 48,000! (Smith did not attribute all of the gain to the division of labor according to talent but credited also the use of machinery and the fact that less time was spent shifting from task to task.)

What we are discussing here involves a division of the resource called labor into different kinds of labor. The different kinds of labor are organized in such a way as to increase the amount of output possible from the fixed resources available. We can therefore talk about an organized division of labor within a firm leading to increased output.

COMPARATIVE ADVANTAGE AND TRADE AMONG NATIONS

Though most of our analysis of absolute advantage, comparative advantage, and specialization has dealt with individuals, it is equally applicable to nations. First consider the United States. The Plains states have a comparative advantage in the production of grains and other agricultural goods. The states to the north and east tend to specialize in industrialized production, such as automobiles. Not surprisingly, grains are shipped from the

Plains states to the northern states, and automobiles are shipped in the reverse direction. Such specialization and trade allow for higher incomes and standards of living. If both the Plains states and the northern states were politically defined as separate nations, the same analysis would still hold, but we would call it international trade. Indeed, Europe is comparable to the United States in area and population, but instead of one nation, Europe has 15. What in America we call *interstate* trade, in Europe they call *international* trade. There is no difference, however, in the economic results—both yield greater economic efficiency and higher average incomes.

Political problems that do not normally arise within a particular nation often do between nations. For example, if California avocado growers develop a cheaper method than growers in southern Florida to produce a tastier avocado, the Florida growers will lose out. They cannot do much about the situation except try to lower their own costs of production or improve their product. If avocado growers in Mexico, however, develop a cheaper method to produce better-tasting avocados, both California and Florida growers can (and likely will) try to raise political barriers that will prevent Mexican avocado growers from freely selling their product in America. U.S. avocado growers will use such arguments as "unfair" competition and loss of American jobs. In so doing, they are only partly right: Avocado-growing jobs may decline in America, but jobs will not necessarily decline overall. If the argument of U.S. avocado growers had any validity, every time a region in the United States developed a better way to produce a product manufactured somewhere else in the country, employment in America would decline. That has never happened and never will.

When nations specialize where they have a comparative advantage and then trade with the rest of the world, the average standard of living in the world rises. In effect, international trade allows the world to move from inside the global production possibilities curve toward the curve itself, thereby improving worldwide economic efficiency.

THINKING CRITICALLY ABOUT THE MEDIA

International Trade

If you watch enough news on TV or frequently read the popular press, you get a distinct impression that international trade is somehow different from trade within our borders. At any given time, the United States is either at economic war with Japan or other countries in Asia or we are fighting with the European Union over whether American films should be allowed to dominate cinema offerings there. International economics is just like any other type of economics; trade is just another economic activity. Indeed, one can think of international trade as a production process that transforms goods that we sell to other countries (exports) into what we buy from other countries (imports). International trade is a mutually beneficial exchange that occurs across political borders. If you imagine a world that was just one country, trade would still exist worldwide, but it would not be called international trade.

CONCEPTS IN BRIEF

- With a given set of resources, specialization results in higher output; in other words, there are gains to specialization in terms of greater material well-being.

- Individuals and nations specialize in their areas of comparative advantage in order to reap the gains of specialization.

- Comparative advantages are found by determining which activities have the lowest opportunity cost—that is, which activities yield the highest return for the time and resources used.

- A division of labor occurs when different workers are assigned different tasks. Together, the workers produce a desired product.

Risk Reduction and the Value of a Human Life

Concepts Applied: *Scarcity, opportunity costs, trade-offs*

Are some lives worth more than others? The U.S. Department of Transportation values a human life at $2.6 million. Researchers examine the wage premiums that must be paid to the workers in dangerous jobs, such as certain construction work, to determine the value of a life.

How much is a human life worth? That is the question that researchers both in and out of government have had to grapple with ever since government began setting safety standards. None of us act as if life is priceless, yet we could virtually eliminate death in automobile accidents by implementing and enforcing a 5-mile-an-hour speed limit. Most people are willing to trade off some probability of injury or death in an automobile accident against the opportunity to travel faster and hence use less time in transit (in other words, to lower the opportunity cost of travel). As in almost everything else, there is an opportunity cost to preventing accidental death.

How to Value a Life

To make decisions about the net benefits of accident-avoiding government regulation, we need to estimate the value of a human life. One way to do so is simply to look at the lost earnings potential of someone who might die. This method is often used in courtroom battles between the survivors of accident victims and insurance companies.

Most people would, in contrast, be ready (if not able) to pay more than their lost future earnings to avoid death or injury. This willingness-to-pay methodology has been used to estimate the value of human lives in different countries. Researchers examine, for example, how much

of a premium workers in dangerous jobs (construction workers on high steel beams, for example) have to be paid to compensate them for the increased probability of death or injury. The U.S. Department of Transportation examined 50 such studies and came up with a value of human life ranging from $1 million to $4 million. It settled on the figure of $2.6 million. Using similar research methods, other countries have come up with similar numbers, as you can see in Table 2-1.

Opportunity Cost

Looking at Table 2-1, it seems as though some lives are worth more than others. Philosophically, this is obviously absurd; but from an economic point of view, most of the differences are a function of the differences in average annual income per person. In richer countries, individuals can obviously pay more to improve safety because they earn more.

When Prevention Is Not Worth the Cost

Given that we live in a world of scarcity, the use of resources for the prevention of injury or death necessarily

TABLE 2-1

The Value of a Human Life

Country	Value (in U.S. dollars)
United States	2,600,000
Sweden	1,236,000
New Zealand	1,150,000
Britain	1,100,000
Germany	928,000
Belgium	400,000
France	350,000
Netherlands	130,000

Source: R. Willike and S. Beyhoff, "Economic Cost of Road Accidents," as derived from national transportation departments in various countries, cited in "The Price of Life," *The Economist*, December 4, 1993, p. 74.

involves an opportunity cost. The Harvard School of Public Health's Center for Risk Analysis undertook a "lifesaving study" that examined whether we are spending too much on certain types of death and injury prevention. The median cost of a year of life saved by various techniques is represented in Table 2-2. Be aware that the table does not show the cost per life saved but rather the cost *per year* of life saved. This means that radiation control does save lives, but at the cost of about $27 million *per year of life saved.*

The Actual Trade-offs Involved

So trade-offs are clearly involved here. According to the risk analysis study, if the $21.3 billion a year spent on 185 major lifesaving programs were reallocated so that more went to the most beneficial measures, 60,000 deaths a year could be averted.

Consider one possibility. The Environmental Protection Agency proposed rules in 1995 that would increase the cost of paper production but save the lives of some workers engaged in that industry. The estimated cost: $1.9 million per life saved. In contrast, cervical cancer screenings every four years would cost only $10,000 per life saved.

Real Risk Is Falling

Crime and automobile and airplane accidents are in the news daily, but does this mean that the United States is becoming a more dangerous place in which to live? Not according to the National Safety Council, which estimated that the accidental death rate per 100,000 people in the United States fell from about 95 in 1910 to around 30

TABLE 2-2

The Cost of Saving a Year of Life

Preventive Measure	Cost per Year of Life Saved (in U.S. dollars)
Childhood immunization	negligible
Flu shot	600
Water chlorination	4,000
Breast cancer screening	17,000
Home radon control	141,000
Asbestos control	1,900,000
Radiation control	27,400,000

Source: Harvard University, School of Public Health.

today. Though this does not mean that all is well in America, the nation is not as unsafe as people normally think. Although a larger percentage of the population is subject to death or injury due to crime today than in the past, a smaller percentage of the population dies in automobile and air transportation accidents. Moreover, a much smaller percentage of the population suffers fatal injuries on the job than ever before.

FOR CRITICAL ANALYSIS

1. Why is opportunity cost such an important concept in analyzing government programs to save lives?
2. What activities do you engage in to reduce the chances of your premature death? What activities do you engage in that increase such chances?

CHAPTER SUMMARY

1. All societies at all times face the universal problem of scarcity because we cannot obtain everything we want from nature without sacrifice. Thus scarcity and poverty are not synonymous. Even the richest persons face scarcity because they also have to make choices among alternatives.
2. The resources we use to produce desired goods and services can be classified into land, labor, physical and human capital, and entrepreneurship.

3. Goods are all things from which individuals derive satisfaction. Economic goods are those for which the desired quantity exceeds the amount that is directly available from nature at a zero price. The goods that we want are not necessarily those that we need. The term *need* is undefinable in economics, whereas humans have unlimited *wants,* which are defined as the goods and services on which we place a positive value.

4. We measure the cost of anything by what has to be given up in order to have it. This cost is called opportunity cost.
5. The trade-offs we face as individuals and those we face as a society can be represented graphically by a production possibilities curve (PPC). This curve shows the maximum quantity of one good or service that can be produced, given a specific quantity of another, from a given set of resources over a specified period of time, usually one year.
6. Because resources are specialized, production possibilities curves bow outward. This means that each additional increment of one good can be obtained only by giving up more and more of the other goods. This is called the law of increasing relative cost.
7. It is impossible to be outside the production possibilities curve, but we can be inside it. When we are, we

are in a situation of unemployment, inefficiently organized resources, or some combination of the two.
8. There is a trade-off between consumption goods and capital goods. The more resources we devote to capital goods, the more consumption goods we can normally have in the future (and less currently). This is because more capital goods allow the economy to grow, thereby moving the production possibilities curve outward.
9. One finds one's comparative advantage by looking at the activity that has the lowest opportunity cost. That is, one's comparative advantage lies in the activity that generates the highest income. By specializing in one's comparative advantage, one is assured of reaping the gains of specialization.
10. Division of labor occurs when workers are assigned different tasks.

DISCUSSION OF PREVIEW QUESTIONS

1. Do affluent people face the problem of scarcity?
Scarcity is a relative concept and exists because wants are great relative to the means of satisfying those wants (wealth or income). Even though affluent people have relatively and absolutely high levels of income or wealth, they nevertheless typically want more than they can have (in luxury goods, power, prestige, and so on).

2. Fresh air may be consumed at no charge, but is it free of cost to society?
Individuals are not charged a price for the use of air. Yet truly fresh air is not free to society. If a good were free to society, every person would be able to use all that he or she wanted to use; no one would have to sacrifice anything in order to use that good, and people would not have to compete for it. In the United States, different groups compete for air; for example, environmentalists and concerned citizens compete with automobile drivers and factories for clean air.

3. Why does the scarcity problem force people to consider opportunity costs?
Individuals have limited incomes; as a consequence, an expenditure on an automobile necessarily pre-

cludes expenditures on other goods and services. The same is true for society, which also faces the scarcity problem; if society allocates specific resources to the production of a steel mill, those same resources cannot be allocated elsewhere. Because resources are limited, society is forced to decide how to allocate its available resources; scarcity means that the cost of allocating resources to produce specific goods is ultimately assessed in terms of other goods that are necessarily sacrificed. Because there are millions of ways in which the resources allocated to a steel mill might otherwise be allocated, one is forced to consider the *highest-valued* alternative. We define the opportunity cost of a good as its highest-valued alternative; the opportunity cost of the steel mill to society is the highest-valued output that those same resources could otherwise have produced.

4. Can a "free" college education ever be truly free?
Suppose that you were given a college education without having to pay any fees whatsoever. You could say that you were receiving a free education. But someone is paying for your education because you are using scarce resources—buildings, professors' time, electricity for lighting, etc. The opportunity

cost of your education is certainly not zero, so in that sense it is not free. Furthermore, by going to college, you are giving up the ability to earn income during that time period. Therefore, there is an opportunity cost to your attending classes and studying. You can approximate that opportunity cost by estimating what your current after-tax income would be if you were working instead of going to school.

PROBLEMS

(Answers to the odd-numbered problems appear at the back of the book.)

2-1. The following sets of numbers represent hypothetical production possibilities for a nation in 1998. Plot these points on graph paper.

Butter	Guns
4	0
3	1.6
2	2.4
1	2.8
0	3.0

Does the law of increasing relative cost seem to hold? Why? On the same graph, plot and draw the production possibilities curve that will represent 10 percent economic growth.

2-2. There are 150,000 conscripts (draftees) in the French army, each paid $2,000 a year. The average salary of each conscript prior to military service was $18,500 per year. What does it cost for conscripts in France each year?

2-3. Answer the questions using the following information.

Employee	Daily Work Effort	Production
Ann Jones	4 hours	8 jackets
	4 hours	12 ties
Ned Lopez	4 hours	8 jackets
	4 hours	12 ties
Total daily output		16 jackets
		24 ties

a. Who has an absolute advantage in jacket production?
b. Who has a comparative advantage in tie production?
c. Will Jones and Lopez specialize?
d. If they specialize, what will total output equal?

2-4. Two countries, Workland and Playland, have similar populations and identical production possibilities curves but different preferences. The production possibilities combinations are as follows:

Point	Capital Goods	Consumption Goods
A	0	20
B	1	19
C	2	17
D	3	14
E	4	10
F	5	5

Playland is located at point *B* on the PPC, and Workland is located at point *E*. Assume that this situation continues into the future and that all other things remain the same.

a. What is Workland's opportunity cost of capital goods in terms of consumption goods?
b. What is Playland's opportunity cost of capital goods in terms of consumption goods?
c. How would the PPCs of Workland and Playland be expected to compare to each other 50 years in the future?

2-5. Which of the following are part of the opportunity cost of going to a football game in town instead of watching it on TV at home? Explain why.

a. The expense of lunch in a restaurant prior to the football game.

b. The value of one hour of sleep lost because of a traffic jam after the game.

c. The expense of a babysitter for your children if they are too young to go to a football game.

2-6. Assume that your economics and English exams are scheduled for the same day. How would you determine how much time you should spend study-ing for each exam? Does the grade you are cur-rently receiving in each course affect your deci-sion? Why or why not?

2-7. Some people argue that air is not an economic good. If you agree with this statement, explain why. If you disagree, explain why. (Hint: Is all air the same?)

COMPUTER-ASSISTED INSTRUCTION

If you are given a production possibilities table, can you calculate the opportunity cost of successive units of one good in terms of forgone units of the other? By requiring specific calculations, the concept of opportunity cost is revealed.

Complete problem and answer appear on disk.

READING AND WORKING WITH GRAPHS

A graph is a visual representation of the relationship between variables. In this appendix, we'll stick to just two variables: an **independent variable,** which can change in value freely, and a **dependent variable,** which changes only as a result of changes in the value of the independent variable. For example, if nothing else is changing in your life, your weight depends on the amount of food you eat. Food is the independent variable and weight the dependent variable.

A table is a list of numerical values showing the relationship between two (or more) variables. Any table can be converted into a graph, which is a visual representation of that list. Once you understand how a table can be converted to a graph, you will understand what graphs are and how to construct and use them.

Consider a practical example. A conservationist may try to convince you that driving at lower highway speeds will help you conserve gas. Table A-1 shows the relationship between speed—the independent variable—and the distance you can go on a gallon of gas at that speed—the dependent variable. This table does show a pattern of sorts. As the data in the first column get larger in value, the data in the second column get smaller.

Now let's take a look at the different ways in which variables can be related.

DIRECT AND INVERSE RELATIONSHIPS

Two variables can be related in different ways, some simple, others more complex. For example, a person's weight and height are often related. If we measured the height and weight of thousands of people, we would surely find that taller people tend to weigh more than shorter people. That is, we would discover that there is a **direct relationship** between height and weight. By this we simply mean that an *increase* in one variable is usually associated with an *increase* in the related variable. This can easily be seen in panel (a) of Figure A-1.

Let's look at another simple way in which two variables can be related. Much evidence indicates that as the price of a specific commodity rises, the amount purchased decreases—there is an **inverse relationship** between the variable's price per unit and quantity purchased. A table listing the data for this relationship would indicate that for higher and higher prices, smaller and smaller quantities would be purchased. We see this relationship in panel (b) of Figure A-1.

Independent variable
A variable whose value is determined independently of, or outside, the equation under study.

Dependent variable
A variable whose value changes according to changes in the value of one or more independent variables.

TABLE A-1
Gas Mileage as a Function of Driving Speed

Miles per Hour	Miles per Gallon
45	25
50	24
55	23
60	21
65	19
70	16
75	13

Direct relationship
A relationship between two variables that is positive, meaning that an increase in one variable is associated with an increase in the other and a decrease in one variable is associated with a decrease in the other.

Inverse relationship
A relationship between two variables that is negative, meaning that an increase in one variable is associated with a decrease in the other and a decrease in one variable is associated with an increase in the other.

FIGURE A-1
Relationships

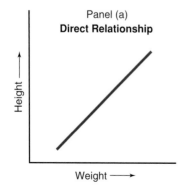

Panel (a)
Direct Relationship

Height →

Weight →

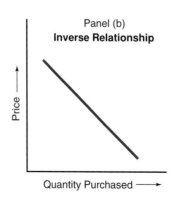

Panel (b)
Inverse Relationship

Price →

Quantity Purchased →

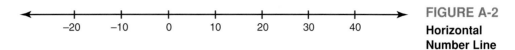

CONSTRUCTING A GRAPH

Let us now examine how to construct a graph to illustrate a relationship between two variables.

A Number Line

Number line
A line that can be divided into segments of equal length, each associated with a number.

The first step is to become familiar with what is called a **number line.** One is shown in Figure A-2. There are two things that you should know about it.

1. The points on the line divide the line into equal segments.
2. The numbers associated with the points on the line increase in value from left to right; saying it the other way around, the numbers decrease in value from right to left. However you say it, what we're describing is formally called an *ordered set of points*.

On the number line, we have shown the line segments—that is, the distance from 0 to 10 or the distance between 30 and 40. They all appear to be equal and, indeed, are equal to $\frac{1}{2}$ inch. When we use a distance to represent a quantity, such as barrels of oil, graphically, we are *scaling* the number line. In the example shown, the distance between 0 and 10 might represent 10 barrels of oil, or the distance from 0 to 40 might represent 40 barrels. Of course, the scale may differ on different number lines. For example, a distance of 1 inch could represent 10 units on one number line but 5,000 units on another. Notice that on our number line, points to the left of 0 correspond to negative numbers and points to the right of 0 correspond to positive numbers.

Of course, we can also construct a vertical number line. Consider the one in Figure A-3. As we move up this vertical number line, the numbers increase in value; conversely, as we descend, they decrease in value. Below 0 the numbers are negative, and above 0 the numbers are positive. And as on the horizontal number line, all the line segments are equal. This line is divided into segments such that the distance between −2 and −1 is the same as the distance between 0 and 1.

Combining Vertical and Horizontal Number Lines

By drawing the horizontal and vertical lines on the same sheet of paper, we are able to express the relationships between variables graphically. We do this in Figure A-4.

FIGURE A-3

Vertical Number Line

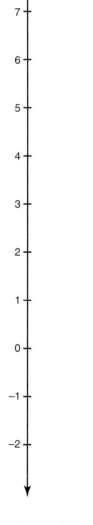

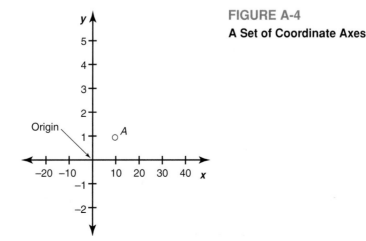

FIGURE A-4

A Set of Coordinate Axes

We draw them (1) so that they intersect at each other's 0 point and (2) so that they are perpendicular to each other. The result is a set of coordinate axes, where each line is called an *axis.* When we have two axes, they span a plane.

For one number line, you need only one number to specify any point on the line; equivalently, when you see a point on the line, you know that it represents one number or one value. With a coordinate value system, you need two numbers to specify a single point in the plane; when you see a single point on a graph, you know that it represents two numbers or two values.

The basic things that you should know about a coordinate number system are that the vertical number line is referred to as the **y axis,** the horizontal number line is referred to as the **x axis,** and the point of intersection of the two lines is referred to as the **origin.**

Any point such as A in Figure A-4 represents two numbers—a value of *x* and a value of *y*. But we know more than that; we also know that point A represents a positive value of *y* because it is above the *x* axis, and we know that it represents a positive value of *x* because it is to the right of the *y* axis.

Point A represents a "paired observation" of the variables *x* and *y;* in particular, in Figure A-4, A represents an observation of the pair of values *x* = 10 and *y* = 1. Every point in the coordinate system corresponds to a paired observation of *x* and *y,* which can be simply written (*x, y*)—the *x* value is always specified first, then the *y* value. When we give the values associated with the position of point A in the coordinate number system, we are in effect giving the coordinates of that point. A's coordinates are *x* = 10, *y* = 1, or (10, 1).

GRAPHING NUMBERS IN A TABLE

Consider Table A-2. Column 1 shows different prices for T-shirts, and column 2 gives the number of T-shirts purchased per week at these prices. Notice the pattern of these numbers. As the price of T-shirts falls, the number of T-shirts purchased per week increases. Therefore, an inverse relationship exists between these two variables, and as soon as we represent it on a graph, you will be able to see the relationship. We can graph this relationship using a coordinate number system—a vertical and horizontal number line for each of these two variables. Such a graph is shown in panel (b) of Figure A-5.

y axis
The vertical axis in a graph.

x axis
The horizontal axis in a graph.

Origin
The intersection of the *y* axis and the *x* axis in a graph.

TABLE A-2
T-Shirts Purchased

(1) Price of T-Shirts	(2) Number of T-Shirts Purchased per Week
$10	20
9	30
8	40
7	50
6	60
5	70

FIGURE A-5

Graphing the Relationship Between T-Shirts Purchased and Price

Panel (a)

Price per T-Shirt	T-Shirts Purchased per Week	Point on Graph
$10	20	I (20, 10)
9	30	J (30, 9)
8	40	K (40, 8)
7	50	L (50, 7)
6	60	M (60, 6)
5	70	N (70, 5)

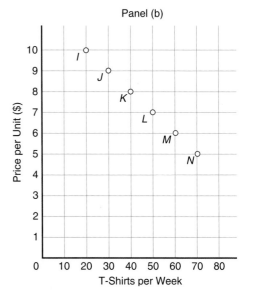

Panel (b)

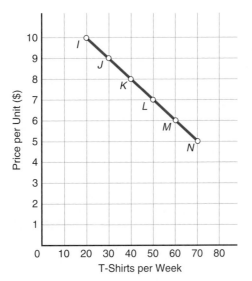

FIGURE A-6

Connecting the Observation Points

In economics, it is conventional to put dollar values on the *y* axis. We therefore construct a vertical number line for price and a horizontal number line, the *x* axis, for quantity of T-shirts purchased per week. The resulting coordinate system allows the plotting of each of the paired observation points; in panel (a), we repeat Table A-2, with a column added expressing these points in paired-data (*x*, *y*) form. For example, point *J* is the paired observation (30, 9). It indicates that when the price of a T-shirt is $9, 30 will be purchased per week.

If it were possible to sell parts of a T-shirt ($\frac{1}{2}$ or $\frac{1}{20}$ of a shirt), we would have observations at every possible price. That is, we would be able to connect our paired observations, represented as lettered points. Let's assume that we can make T-shirts perfectly divisible. We would then have a line that connects these points, as shown in the graph in Figure A-6.

In short, we have now represented the data from the table in the form of a graph. Note that an inverse relationship between two variables shows up on a graph as a line or curve that slopes *downward* from left to right. (You might as well get used to the idea that economists call a straight line a "curve" even though it may not curve at all. Much of economists' data turn out to be curves, so they refer to everything represented graphically, even straight lines, as curves.)

THE SLOPE OF A LINE (A LINEAR CURVE)

An important property of a curve represented on a graph is its *slope*. Consider Figure A-7 on page 42, which represents the quantities of shoes per week that a seller is willing to offer at different prices. Note that in panel (a) of Figure A-7, as in Figure A-5, we have expressed the coordinates of the points in parentheses in paired-data form.

Slope
The change in the *y* value divided by the corresponding change in the *x* value of a curve; the "incline" of the curve.

The **slope** of a line is defined as the change in the *y* values divided by the corresponding change in the *x* values as we move along the line. Let's move from point *E* to point *D* in panel (b) of Figure A-7. As we move, we note that the change in the *y* values, which is the change in price, is +$20, because we have moved from a price of $20 to a price of $40 per pair. As we move from *E* to *D*, the change in the *x* values is +80; the number of pairs of shoes willingly offered per week rises from 80 to 160 pairs. The slope calculated as a change in the *y* values divided by the change in the *x* values is therefore

$$\frac{20}{80} = \frac{1}{4}$$

FIGURE A-7

A Positively Sloped Curve

Panel (a)

Price per Pair	Pairs of Shoes Offered per Week	Point on Graph
$100	400	A (400,100)
80	320	B (320, 80)
60	240	C (240, 60)
40	160	D (160, 40)
20	80	E (80, 20)

Panel (b)

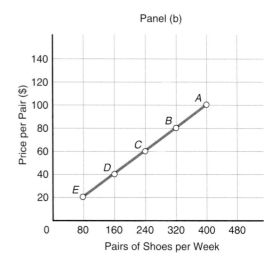

It may be helpful for you to think of slope as a "rise" (movement in the vertical direction) over a "run" (movement in the horizontal direction). We show this abstractly in Figure A-8. The slope is measured by the amount of rise divided by the amount of run. In the example in Figure A-8, and of course in Figure A-7, the amount of rise is positive and so is the amount of run. That's because it's a direct relationship. We show an inverse relationship in Figure A-9. The slope is still equal to the rise divided by the run, but in this case the rise and the run have opposite signs because the curve slopes downward. That means that the slope will have to be negative and that we are dealing with an inverse relationship.

Now let's calculate the slope for a different part of the curve in panel (b) of Figure A-7. We will find the slope as we move from point B to point A. Again, we note that the slope, or rise over run, from B to A equals

$$\frac{20}{80} = \frac{1}{4}$$

A specific property of a straight line is that its slope is the same between any two points; in other words, the slope is constant at all points on a straight line in a graph.

We conclude that for our example in Figure A-7, the relationship between the price of a pair of shoes and the number of pairs of shoes willingly offered per week is *linear,* which simply means "in a straight line," and our calculations indicate a constant slope. Moreover, we calculate a direct relationship between these two variables, which turns out to be an

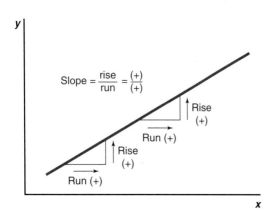

FIGURE A-8

Figuring Positive Slope

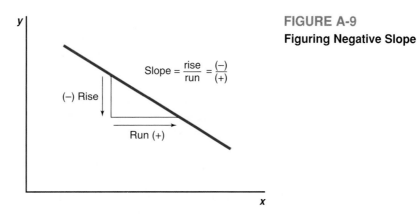

FIGURE A-9
Figuring Negative Slope

upward-sloping (from left to right) curve. Upward-sloping curves have positive slopes—in this case, it is $+\frac{1}{4}$.

We know that an inverse relationship between two variables shows up as a downward-sloping curve—rise over run will be a negative slope because the rise and run have opposite signs as shown in Figure A-9. When we see a negative slope, we know that increases in one variable are associated with decreases in the other. Therefore, we say that downward-sloping curves have negative slopes. Can you verify that the slope of the graph representing the relationship between T-shirt prices and the quantity of T-shirts purchased per week in Figure A-6 is $-\frac{1}{10}$?

Slopes of Nonlinear Curves

The graph presented in Figure A-10 indicates a *nonlinear* relationship between two variables, total profits and output per unit of time. Inspection of this graph indicates that at first, increases in output lead to increases in total profits; that is, total profits rise as output increases. But beyond some output level, further increases in output cause decreases in total profits.

Can you see how this curve rises at first, reaches a peak at point *C*, and then falls? This curve relating total profits to output levels appears mountain-shaped.

Considering that this curve is nonlinear (it is obviously not a straight line), should we expect a constant slope when we compute changes in *y* divided by corresponding changes in *x* in moving from one point to another? A quick inspection, even without specific numbers, should lead us to conclude that the slopes of lines joining different points in this curve, such as between *A* and *B*, *B* and *C*, or *C* and *D*, will *not* be the same. The curve slopes upward (in a positive direction) for some values and downward (in a negative direction) for

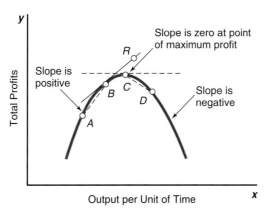

FIGURE A-10
The Slope of a Nonlinear Curve

other values. In fact, the slope of the line between any two points on this curve will be different from the slope of the line between any two other points. Each slope will be different as we move along the curve.

Instead of using a line between two points to discuss slope, mathematicians and economists prefer to discuss the slope *at a particular point*. The slope at a point on the curve, such as point B in the graph in Figure A-10, is the slope of a line *tangent* to that point. A tangent line is a straight line that touches a curve at only one point. For example, it might be helpful to think of the tangent at B as the straight line that just "kisses" the curve at point B.

To calculate the slope of a tangent line, you need to have some additional information besides the two values of the point of tangency. For example, in Figure A-10, if we knew that the point R also lay on the tangent line and we knew the two values of that point, we could calculate the slope of the tangent line. We could calculate rise over run between points B and R, and the result would be the slope of the line tangent to the one point B on the curve.

APPENDIX SUMMARY

1. Direct relationships involve a dependent variable changing in the same direction as the change in the independent variable.
2. Inverse relationships involve the dependent variable changing in the opposite direction of the change in the independent variable.
3. When we draw a graph showing the relationship between two economic variables, we are holding all other things constant (the Latin term for which is *ceteris paribus*).
4. We obtain a set of coordinates by putting vertical and horizontal number lines together. The vertical line is called the y axis; the horizontal line, the x axis.

5. The slope of any linear (straight-line) curve is the change in the y values divided by the corresponding change in the x values as we move along the line. Otherwise stated, the slope is calculated as the amount of rise over the amount of run, where rise is movement in the vertical direction and run is movement in the horizontal direction.
6. The slope of a nonlinear curve changes; it is positive when the curve is rising and negative when the curve is falling. At a maximum or minimum point, the slope of the nonlinear curve is zero.

PROBLEMS

(The answer to Problem A-1 appears at the back of the book.)

A-1. Complete the schedule and plot the following function:

$y = 3x$

y	x
	4
	3
	2
	1
	0
	-1
	-2
	-3
	-4

A-2. Complete the schedule and plot the following function:

$y = x^2$

y	x
	4
	3
	2
	1
	0
	-1
	-2
	-3
	-4

CHAPTER 3

DEMAND AND SUPPLY

During the 1974–1975 academic year, foreign students comprised 1.5 percent of all college students. Today, foreign students represent over 3 percent of all college students—an increase of more than 100 percent in their relative proportions. During the same time period, average grades have risen dramatically, particularly at our nation's best-known private universities. Finally, some private universities are actually starting to give discounts on tuition. To understand how these seemingly unrelated phenomena are actually closely related, you will need the tools of supply and demand analysis.

PREVIEW QUESTIONS

1. Why are relative prices important in understanding the law of demand?

2. How can we distinguish between a change in *demand* and a change in *quantity demanded*?

3. Why is there normally a direct relationship between price and quantity supplied (other things being equal)?

4. Why will the market clearing price occur at the intersection of the supply and demand curves rather than at a higher or lower price?

Did **You Know That . . .** more than 22 million people currently own portable cellular phones? This is a huge jump from the mere 200,000 who owned them in 1985. Since 1992, two out of every three new telephone numbers have been assigned to cellular phones. There are several reasons for the growth of cellular phones, not the least being the dramatic reduction in both price and size due to improved and cheaper computer chips that go into making them. There is something else at work, though. It has to do with crime. In a recent survey, 46 percent of new cellular phone users said that personal safety was the main reason they bought a portable phone. In Florida, for example, most cellular phone companies allow users simply to dial *FHP to reach the Florida Highway Patrol. The rush to cellular phones is worldwide. Over the past decade, sales have grown by nearly 50 percent every year outside the United States.

We could attempt to explain the phenomenon by saying that more people like to use portable phones. But that explanation is neither satisfying nor entirely accurate. If we use the economist's primary set of tools, *demand and supply,* we will have a better understanding of the cellular phone explosion, as well as many other phenomena in our world. Demand and supply are two ways of categorizing the influences on the price of goods that you buy and the quantities available. As such, demand and supply form the basis of virtually all economic analysis of the world around us.

As you will see throughout this text, the operation of the forces of demand and supply take place in *markets.* A **market** is an abstract concept referring to all the arrangements individuals have for exchanging with one another. Goods and services are sold in markets, such as the automobile market, the health market, and the compact disc market. Workers offer their services in the labor market. Companies, or firms, buy workers' labor services in the labor market. Firms also buy other inputs in order to produce the goods and services that you buy as a consumer. Firms purchase machines, buildings, and land. These markets are in operation at all times. One of the most important activities in these markets is the setting of the prices of all of the inputs and outputs that are bought and sold in our complicated economy. To understand the determination of prices, you first need to look at the law of demand.

THE LAW OF DEMAND

Demand has a special meaning in economics. It refers to the quantities of specific goods or services that individuals, taken singly or as a group, will purchase at various possible prices, other things being constant. We can therefore talk about the demand for microprocessor chips, French fries, compact disc players, children, and criminal activities.

Associated with the concept of demand is the **law of demand,** which can be stated as follows:

> **When the price of a good goes up, people buy less of it, other things being equal. When the price of a good goes down, people buy more of it, other things being equal.**

The law of demand tells us that the quantity demanded of any commodity is inversely related to its price, other things being equal. In an inverse relationship, one variable moves up in value when the other moves down. The law of demand states that a change in price causes a change in the quantity demanded in the *opposite* direction.

Notice that we tacked onto the end of the law of demand the statement "other things being equal." We referred to this in Chapter 1 as the *ceteris paribus* assumption. It means, for example, that when we predict that people will buy fewer CD-ROM players if their

Market
All of the arrangements that individuals have for exchanging with one another. Thus we can speak of the labor market, the automobile market, and the credit market.

Demand
A schedule of how much of a good or service people will purchase at any price during a specified time period, other things being constant.

Law of demand
The observation that there is a negative, or inverse, relationship between the price of any good or service and the quantity demanded, holding other factors constant.

price goes up, we are holding constant the price of all other goods in the economy as well as people's incomes. Implicitly, therefore, if we are assuming that no other prices change when we examine the price behavior of CD-ROM players, we are looking at the *relative* price of CD-ROM players.

The law of demand is supported by millions of observations of people's behavior in the marketplace. Theoretically, it can be derived from an economic model based on rational behavior, as was discussed in Chapter 1. Basically, if nothing else changes and the price of a good falls, the lower price induces us to buy more over a certain period of time because we can enjoy additional net gains that were unavailable at the higher price. For the most part, if you examine your own behavior, you will see that it generally follows the law of demand.

Relative Prices Versus Money Prices

Relative price
The price of a commodity expressed in terms of another commodity.

Money price
The price that we observe today, expressed in today's dollars. Also called the *absolute, nominal,* or *current price.*

The **relative price** of any commodity is its price in terms of another commodity. The price that you pay in dollars and cents for any good or service at any point in time is called its **money price.** Consider an example that you might hear quite often around parents and grandparents. "When I bought my first new car, it cost only fifteen hundred dollars." The implication, of course, is that the price of cars today is outrageously high because the average new car might cost $19,000. But that is not an accurate comparison. What was the price of the average house during that same year? Perhaps it was only $12,000. By comparison, then, given that houses today average about $140,000, the price of a new car today doesn't sound so far out of line, does it?

The point is that money prices during different time periods don't tell you much. You have to find out relative prices. Consider an example of the price of CDs versus cassettes from last year and this year. In Table 3-1, we show the money price of CDs and cassettes for two years during which they have both gone up. That means that we have to pay out in today's dollars and cents more for CDs and more for cassettes. If we look, though, at the relative prices of CDs and cassettes, we find that last year, CDs were twice as expensive as cassettes, whereas this year they are only $1\frac{3}{4}$ times as expensive. Conversely, if we compare cassettes to CDs, last year they cost only half as much as CDs, but today they cost about 57 percent as much. In the one-year period, while both prices have gone up in money terms, the relative price of CDs has fallen (and, equivalently, the relative price of cassettes has risen).

TABLE 3-1
Money Price Versus Relative Price
The money price of both compact discs (CDs) and cassettes has risen. But the relative price of CDs has fallen (or conversely, the relative price of cassettes has risen).

	Money Price		Relative Price	
	Price Last Year	Price This Year	Price Last Year	Price This Year
CDs	$12	$14	$\frac{\$12}{\$6}=2.0$	$\frac{\$14}{\$8}=1.75$
Cassettes	$6	$8	$\frac{\$6}{\$12}=0.5$	$\frac{\$8}{\$14}=0.57$

INTERNATIONAL EXAMPLE
Cross-Border Shopping in Europe

The increase in cross-border shopping is a good example of how individuals respond to relative prices rather than absolute, or money, prices. Several times a week, bargain-conscious Basques from Bilbao, Spain, cross the French border (which is without customs or immigration control because it is part of the European Union) to shop for food. At current exchange rates, similar-quality food costs about 40 percent less on the French side of the border. For cost-conscious consumers in Switzerland who live along the border with France, such trips are frequent. Professor Stephen Stearns, of Basel, Switzerland, claims that shopping in France saves a typical family more than 30 percent on its weekly food bill. At current exchange rates, pork and beef cost only half as much in France, and cheese is 40 percent less expensive. Germans and Belgians who live on the border with Luxembourg and the Netherlands often travel to those countries to buy food and consumer products, such as shampoo. The British frequently make a relatively long trip by ferry to France to buy alcoholic beverages, which cost 50 percent less than in Britain. All this border crossing bears out the fact that relative prices, not absolute (money) prices, determine people's shopping habits.

FOR CRITICAL ANALYSIS: How would we calculate the net benefit to cross-border shopping for the people who engage in it? (Hint: What are some of the costs of such shopping?) ●

THINKING CRITICALLY ABOUT THE MEDIA

The Real Price of Stamps

The press is fond of pointing out the rise in the price of a particular good, such as a stamp for first-class mail. In the 1940s, a first-class stamp cost only 3 cents, but by the mid-1990s, it had climbed to 32 cents. That is the absolute price of postage, however. What about the relative price, the price relative to the average of all other prices? The relative price of postage is actually lower today than when it reached its peak in 1975. Many other relative prices have fallen over the years, ranging from gasoline prices to the president's salary. Indeed, relatively speaking, the president's current $200,000-a-year salary is peanuts compared to what President Truman earned in 1947. In relative terms (dollars in 1947), the current president only earns about $30,000, even though in absolute terms, the current president makes more. Remember, everything is relative.

CONCEPTS IN BRIEF

- The law of demand posits an inverse relationship between the quantity demanded of a good and its price, other things being equal.
- The law of demand applies when other things, such as income and the prices of all other goods and services, are held constant.

THE DEMAND SCHEDULE

Let's take a hypothetical demand situation to see how the inverse relationship between the price and the quantity demanded looks (holding other things equal). We will consider the quantity of diskettes demanded *per year*. Without stating the *time dimension*, we could not make sense out of this demand relationship because the numbers would be different if we were talking about the quantity demanded per month or the quantity demanded per decade.

In addition to implicitly or explicitly stating a time dimension for a demand relationship, we are also implicitly referring to *constant-quality* units of the good or service in question. Prices are always expressed in constant-quality units in order to avoid the problem of comparing commodities that are in fact not truly comparable.

In panel (a) of Figure 3-1, we see that if the price were $1 per diskette, 50 of them would be bought each year by our representative individual, but if the price were $5 per diskette,

FIGURE 3-1

The Individual Demand Schedule and the Individual Demand Curve

In panel (a), we show combinations A through E of the quantities of diskettes demanded, measured in constant-quality units at prices ranging from $5 down to $1 per disk. In panel (b), we plot combinations A through E on a grid. The result is the individual demand curve for diskettes.

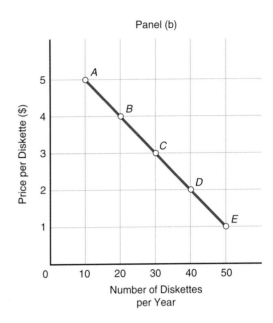

Panel (b)

Panel (a)

Combination	Price per Constant-Quality Diskette	Quantity of Constant-Quality Diskettes per Year
A	$5	10
B	4	20
C	3	30
D	2	40
E	1	50

only 10 diskettes would be bought each year. This reflects the law of demand. Panel (a) is also called simply demand, or a *demand schedule,* because it gives a schedule of alternative quantities demanded per year at different possible prices.

The Demand Curve

Tables expressing relationships between two variables can be represented in graphical terms. To do this, we need only construct a graph that has the price per constant-quality diskette on the vertical axis and the quantity measured in constant-quality diskettes per year on the horizontal axis. All we have to do is take combinations A through E from panel (a) of Figure 3-1 and plot those points in panel (b). Now we connect the points with a smooth line, and *voilà,* we have a **demand curve.**[1] It is downward-sloping (from left to right) to indicate the inverse relationship between the price of diskettes and the quantity demanded per year. Our presentation of demand schedules and curves applies equally well to all commodities, including toothpicks, hamburgers, textbooks, credit, and labor services. Remember, the demand curve is simply a graphical representation of the law of demand.

Demand curve
A graphical representation of the demand schedule; a negatively sloped line showing the inverse relationship between the price and the quantity demanded (other things being equal).

Individual Versus Market Demand Curves

The demand schedule shown in panel (a) of Figure 3-1 and the resulting demand curve shown in panel (b) are both given for an individual. As we shall see, the determination of price in the marketplace depends on, among other things, the **market demand** for a particular commodity. The way in which we measure a market demand schedule and derive a

Market demand
The demand of all consumers in the marketplace for a particular good or service. The summing at each price of the quantity demanded by each individual.

---

[1]Even though we call them "curves," for the purposes of exposition we often draw straight lines. In many real-world situations, demand and supply curves will in fact be lines that do curve. To connect the points in panel (b) with a line, we assume that for all prices in between the ones shown, the quantities demanded will be found along that line.

market demand curve for diskettes or any other commodity is by summing (at each price) the individual demand for all those in the market. Suppose that the market demand for diskettes consists of only two buyers: buyer 1, for whom we've already shown the demand schedule, and buyer 2, whose demand schedule is displayed in column 3 of panel (a) of Figure 3-2. Column 1 shows the price, and column 2 shows the quantity demanded by buyer 1 at each price. These data are taken directly from Figure 3-1. In column 3, we show the quantity demanded by buyer 2. Column 4 shows the total quantity demanded at each price, which is obtained by simply adding columns 2 and 3. Graphically, in panel (d) of Figure 3-2, we add the demand curves of buyer 1 [panel (b)] and buyer 2 [panel (c)] to derive the market demand curve.

There are, of course, literally tens of millions of potential consumers of diskettes. We'll simply assume that the summation of all of the consumers in the market results in a demand schedule, given in panel (a) of Figure 3-3, and a demand curve, given in panel (b). The quantity demanded is now measured in billions of units per year. Remember, panel (b) in Figure 3-3 shows the market demand curve for the millions of users of diskettes. The "market" demand curve that we derived in Figure 3-2 was undertaken assuming that there were only two buyers in the entire market. That's why the "market" demand curve for two

.FIGURE 3-2

The Horizontal Summation of Two Demand Schedules

Panel (a) shows how to sum the demand schedule for one buyer with that of another buyer. In column 2 is the quantity demanded by buyer 1, taken from panel (a) of Figure 3-1. Column 4 is the sum of columns 2 and 3. We plot the demand curve for buyer 1 in panel (b) and the demand curve for buyer 2 in panel (c). When we add those two demand curves horizontally, we get the market demand curve for two buyers, shown in panel (d).

Panel (a)

(1) Price per Diskette	(2) Buyer 1 Quantity Demanded	(3) Buyer 2 Quantity Demanded	(4) = (2) + (3) Combined Quantity Demanded per Year
$5	10	10	20
4	20	20	40
3	30	40	70
2	40	50	90
1	50	60	110

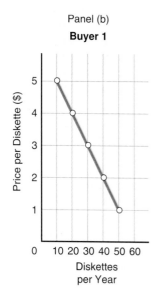

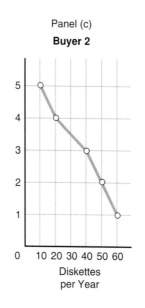

FIGURE 3-3

The Market Demand Schedule for Diskettes
In panel (a), we add up the millions of existing demand schedules for diskettes. In panel (b), we plot the quantities from panel (a) on a grid; connecting them produces the market demand curve for diskettes.

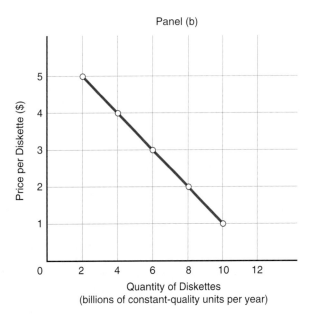

Panel (b)

Panel (a)

Price per Constant-Quality Diskette	Total Quantity Demanded of Constant-Quality Diskettes per Year (billions)
$5	2
4	4
3	6
2	8
1	10

buyers in panel (d) of Figure 3-2 is not a smooth line, whereas the true market demand curve in panel (b) of Figure 3-3 is a smooth line with no kinks.

Now consider some special aspects of the market demand curve for compact discs.

EXAMPLE
Garth Brooks, Used CDs, and the Law of Demand

A few years ago, country singer Garth Brooks tried to prevent his latest album from being sold to any chain or store that also sells used CDs. His argument was that the used-CD market deprived labels and artists of earnings. His announcement came after Wherehouse Entertainment, Inc., a 339-store retailer based in Torrance, California, started selling used CDs side by side with new releases, at half the price. Brooks, along with the distribution arms of Sony, Warner Music, Capitol-EMI, and MCA, was trying to quash the used-CD market. By so doing, it appears that none of these parties understands the law of demand.

Let's say the price of a new CD is $15. The existence of a secondary used-CD market means that to people who choose to resell their CDs for $5, the cost of a new CD is in fact only $10. Because we know that quantity demanded is inversely related to price, we know that more of a new CD will be sold at a price of $10 than of the same CD at a price of $15. Eliminating the used-CD market would in effect reduce the sales of new CDs.

One reason why CDs command a higher price than vinyl records or cassettes is that they are more durable. This increases their value in the secondary market. Eliminating the used-CD market would cause the real net price of new CDs to rise, leading to fewer purchases of new CDs, more taping off the radio or from friends, and an increase in radio listening.

FOR CRITICAL ANALYSIS: Can you apply this argument to the used-book market, in which both authors and publishers have long argued that used books are "killing them"? ●

CONCEPTS IN BRIEF

- We measure the demand schedule both in terms of a time dimension and in constant-quality units.

- The market demand curve is derived by summing the quantity demanded by individuals at each price. Graphically, we add the individual demand curves horizontally to derive the total, or market, demand curve.

SHIFTS IN DEMAND

Assume that the federal government gives every student registered in a college, university, or technical school in the United States a personal computer that uses diskettes. The demand curve presented in panel (b) of Figure 3-3 would no longer be an accurate representation of total market demand for diskettes. What we have to do is shift the curve outward, or to the right, to represent the rise in demand. There will now be an increase in the number of diskettes demanded *at each and every possible price*. The demand curve shown in Figure 3-4 will shift from D_1 to D_2. Take any price, say, $3 per diskette. Originally, before the federal government giveaway of personal computers, the amount demanded at $3 was 6 billion diskettes per year. After the government giveaway, however, the new amount demanded at $3 is 10 billion diskettes per year. What we have seen is a shift in the demand for diskettes.

The shift can also go in the opposite direction. What if colleges uniformly outlawed the use of personal computers by any of their students? Such a regulation would cause a shift inward—to the left—of the demand curve for diskettes. In Figure 3-4, the demand curve would shift to D_3; the amount demanded would now be less at each and every possible price.

The Other Determinants of Demand

The demand curve in panel (b) of Figure 3-3 is drawn with other things held constant, specifically all of the other factors that determine how much will be bought. There are many such determinants. The major other determinants are income; tastes and preferences; the prices of related goods; expectations regarding future prices, future incomes, and future product availability; and population (market size). Let's examine each determinant more closely.

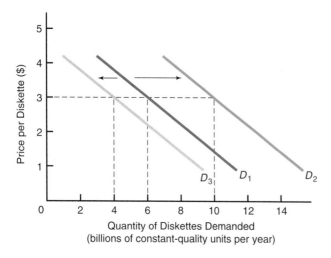

FIGURE 3-4

A Shift in the Demand Curve
If some factor other than price changes, the only way we can show its effect is by moving the entire demand curve, say, from D_1 to D_2. We have assumed in our example that the move was precipitated by the government's giving a free personal computer to every registered college student in America. That meant that at *all* prices, a larger number of diskettes would be demanded than before. Curve D_3 represents reduced demand compared to curve D_1, caused by a law prohibiting computers on campus.

Income. For most goods, an increase in income will lead to an increase in demand. The phrase *increase in demand* always refers to a comparison between two different demand curves. Thus for most goods, an increase in income will lead to a rightward shift in the position of the demand curve from, say, D_1 to D_2 in Figure 3-4. You can avoid confusion about shifts in curves by always relating a rise in demand to a rightward shift in the demand curve and a fall in demand to a leftward shift in the demand curve. Goods for which the demand rises when income rises are called **normal goods.** Most goods, such as shoes, computers, and CDs, are "normal goods." For some goods, however, demand *falls* as income rises. These are called **inferior goods.** Beans might be an example. As households get richer, they tend to spend less and less on beans and more and more on meat. (The terms *normal* and *inferior* are merely part of the economist's terminology; no value judgments are associated with them.)

Remember, a shift to the left in the demand curve represents a fall in demand, and a shift to the right represents a rise, or increase, in demand.

Normal goods
Goods for which demand rises as income rises. Most goods are considered normal.

Inferior goods
Goods for which demand falls as income rises.

Tastes and Preferences. A change in consumer tastes in favor of a good can shift its demand curve outward to the right. When Frisbees® became the rage, the demand curve for them shifted outward to the right; when the rage died out, the demand curve shifted inward to the left. Fashions depend to a large extent on people's tastes and preferences. Economists have little to say about the determination of tastes; that is, they don't have any "good" theories of taste determination or why people buy one brand of product rather than others. Advertisers, however, have various theories that they use to try to make consumers prefer their products over those of competitors.

INTERNATIONAL EXAMPLE
The Slump in Worldwide Sales of Cigars

Cigar manufacturers worldwide are finding out what happens to the demand for their product when there is a shift in tastes. Although the Belgians are the heaviest cigar smokers in the world, they are stubbing out more and more of their cigars. Health scares and increased public pressure in Europe not to pollute indoor spaces are the cause. Between 1988 and 1996, the sales of cigars dropped by over 15 percent worldwide. ERC Statistics International predicts that by the end of the twentieth century, annual cigar smoking will drop at least another 10 percent. Some European manufacturers are looking to Eastern Europe to fill the void in sales. Others are trying to encroach on the cigarette market by launching cigarillos that look like cigarettes.

FOR CRITICAL ANALYSIS: Many countries (including the United States) now ban the advertising of cigars and cigarettes. What do you think this has done to the demand curve for cigars? ●

Prices of Related Goods: Substitutes and Complements. Demand schedules are always drawn with the prices of all other commodities held constant. That is to say, when deriving a given demand curve, we assume that only the price of the good under study changes. For example, when we draw the demand curve for butter, we assume that the price of margarine is held constant. When we draw the demand curve for stereo speakers, we assume that the price of stereo amplifiers is held constant. When we refer to *related goods,* we are talking about goods for which demand is interdependent. If a change in the price of one good shifts the demand for another good, those two goods are related. There are two types of related goods: *substitutes* and *complements*. We can define and distinguish between substitutes and complements in terms of how the change in price of one commodity affects the demand for its related commodity.

Butter and margarine are **substitutes.** Let's assume that each originally cost $2 per pound. If the price of butter remains the same and the price of margarine falls from $2 per pound to $1 per pound, people will buy more margarine and less butter. The demand curve for butter will shift inward to the left. If, conversely, the price of margarine rises from $2 per pound to $3 per pound, people will buy more butter and less margarine. The demand curve for butter will shift outward to the right. In other words, an increase in the price of margarine will lead to an increase in the demand for butter, and an increase in the price of butter will lead to an increase in the demand for margarine. For substitutes, a price change in the substitute will cause a change in demand *in the same direction.*

For **complements,** the situation is reversed. Consider stereo speakers and stereo amplifiers. We draw the demand curve for speakers with the price of amplifiers held constant. If the price per constant-quality unit of stereo amplifiers decreases from, say, $500 to $200, that will encourage more people to purchase component stereo systems. They will now buy more speakers, at any given speaker price, than before. The demand curve for speakers will shift outward to the right. If, by contrast, the price of amplifiers increases from $200 to $500, fewer people will purchase component stereo systems. The demand curve for speakers will shift inward to the left. To summarize, a decrease in the price of amplifiers leads to an increase in the demand for speakers. An increase in the price of amplifiers leads to a decrease in the demand for speakers. Thus for complements, a price change in a product will cause a change in demand *in the opposite direction.*

Are new learning technologies complements or substitutes for college instructors? Read on.

Substitutes

Two goods are substitutes when either one can be used for consumption to satisfy a similar want—for example, coffee and tea. The more you buy of one, the less you buy of the other. For substitutes, the change in the price of one causes a shift in demand for the other in the same direction as the price change.

Complements

Two goods are complements if both are used together for consumption or enjoyment—for example, coffee and cream. The more you buy of one, the more you buy of the other. For complements, a change in the price of one causes an opposite shift in the demand for the other.

EXAMPLE
The Future of College Teaching

In this class and in others, you have probably been exposed to some of the new (and old) instructional technologies, some of which include films and videos, interactive computer software, and interactive CD-ROM learning systems. Your professors have used these new technologies as a complement to their teaching, but in the future they may in fact become a substitute for what your professors do in the classroom.

The University of North Dakota, North Dakota State University, and North Dakota State College of Science together offer enough TV courses that a student can earn a college degree in business administration, nursing, or education without ever attending a class. Televised lectures allow a given number of professors to teach a greater number of students. Now consider interactive CD-ROM learning systems. In principle, virtually every college course could be put on CD-ROM, thereby eliminating the need for instructors entirely. Going one step further, institutions of higher learning are now using the Internet to provide instruction. "Distance learning" is already being used by the University of Michigan in conjunction with companies in Hong Kong, South Korea, and Europe. Michigan offers a global M.B.A. through a combination of interactive video classroom instruction, high-speed Internet connections, e-mail, and shared application computing. A professor teaches a course "live" via video and uses the software program Lotus Notes, which allows course information to be sent via the Internet. Students submit their homework assignments the same way.

FOR CRITICAL ANALYSIS: *What do you predict will happen to the demand curve for college professors in the future?* ●

Expectations. Consumers' expectations regarding future prices, future incomes, and future availability may prompt them to buy more or less of a particular good without a change in its current money price. For example, consumers getting wind of a scheduled 100 percent price increase in diskettes next month may buy more of them today at today's prices. Today's demand curve for diskettes will shift from D_1 to D_2 in Figure 3-4 on page 52. The opposite would occur if a decrease in the price of diskettes were scheduled for next month.

Expectations of a rise in income may cause consumers to want to purchase more of everything today at today's prices. Again, such a change in expectations of higher future income will cause a shift in the demand curve from D_1 to D_2 in Figure 3-4.

Finally, expectations that goods will not be available at any price will induce consumers to stock up now, increasing current demand.

Population. An increase in the population in an economy (holding per capita income constant) often shifts the market demand outward for most products. This is because an increase in population leads to an increase in the number of buyers in the market. Conversely, a reduction in the population will shift most market demand curves inward because of the reduction in the number of buyers in the market.

Changes in Demand Versus Changes in Quantity Demanded

We have made repeated references to demand and to quantity demanded. It is important to realize that there is a difference between a *change in demand* and a *change in quantity demanded.*

Demand refers to a schedule of planned rates of purchase and depends on a great many nonprice determinants. Whenever there is a change in a nonprice determinant, there will be a change in demand—a shift in the entire demand curve to the right or to the left.

A quantity demanded is a specific quantity at a specific price, represented by a single point on a demand curve. When price changes, quantity demanded changes according to the law of demand, and there will be a movement from one point to another along the same demand curve. Look at Figure 3-5 on page 56. At a price of $3 per diskette, 6 billion diskettes per year are demanded. If the price falls to $1, quantity demanded increases to 10 billion per year. This movement occurs because the current market price for the product changes. In Figure 3-5, you can see the arrow pointing down the given demand curve D.

When you think of demand, think of the entire curve itself. Quantity demanded, in contrast, is represented by a single point on the demand curve.

A change or shift in demand causes the *entire* **curve to move. The** *only* **thing that can cause the entire curve to move is a change in a determinant** *other than its own price.*

In economic analysis, we cannot emphasize too much the following distinction that must constantly be made:

A change in a good's own price leads to a change in quantity demanded, for any given demand curve, other things held constant. This is a movement *on* **the curve.**

A change in any other determinant of demand leads to a change in demand. This causes a movement *of* **the curve.**

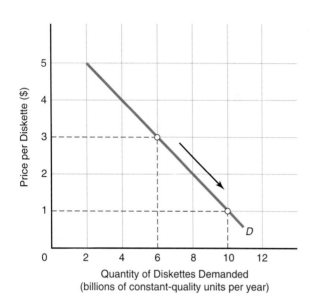

FIGURE 3-5

Movement Along a Given Demand Curve
A change in price changes the quantity of a good demanded. This can be represented as movement along a given demand schedule. If, in our example, the price of diskettes falls from $3 to $1 apiece, the quantity demanded will increase from 6 billion to 10 billion units per year.

CONCEPTS IN BRIEF

- Demand curves are drawn with determinants other than the price of the good held constant. These other determinants are (1) income; (2) tastes and preferences; (3) prices of related goods; (4) expectations about future prices, future incomes, and future availability of goods; and (5) population (number of buyers in the market). If any one of these determinants changes, the demand schedule will shift to the right or to the left.

- A change in demand comes about only because of a change in the other determinants of demand. This change in demand shifts the demand curve to the left or to the right.

- A change in the quantity demanded comes about when there is a change in the price of the good (other things held constant). Such a change in quantity demanded involves a movement along a given demand curve.

THE LAW OF SUPPLY

The other side of the basic model in economics involves the quantities of goods and services that firms are prepared to *supply* to the market. The **supply** of any good or service is the amount that firms are prepared to sell under certain conditions during a specified time period. The relationship between price and quantity supplied, called the **law of supply,** can be summarized as follows:

> **At higher prices, a larger quantity will generally be supplied than at lower prices, all other things held constant. At lower prices, a smaller quantity will generally be supplied than at higher prices, all other things held constant.**

There is generally a direct relationship between quantity supplied and price. For supply, as the price rises, the quantity supplied rises; as price falls, the quantity supplied also falls. Producers are normally willing to produce and sell more of their product at a higher price than at a lower price, other things being constant. At $5 per diskette, 3M, Sony, Maxell, Fuji, and other manufacturers would almost certainly be willing to supply a larger quantity than at $1 per unit, assuming, of course, that no other prices in the economy had changed.

Supply
A schedule showing the relationship between price and quantity supplied for a specified period of time, other things being equal.

Law of supply
The observation that the higher the price of a good, the more of that good sellers will make available over a specified time period, other things being equal.

As with the law of demand, millions of instances in the real world have given us confidence in the law of supply. On a theoretical level, the law of supply is based on a model in which producers and sellers seek to make the most gain possible from their activities. For example, as a diskette manufacturer attempts to produce more and more diskettes over the same time period, it will eventually have to hire more workers, pay overtime wages (which are higher), and overutilize its machines. Only if offered a higher price per diskette will the diskette manufacturer be willing to incur these higher costs. That is why the law of supply implies a direct relationship between price and quantity supplied.

THE SUPPLY SCHEDULE

Just as we were able to construct a demand schedule, we can construct a *supply schedule*, which is a table relating prices to the quantity supplied at each price. A supply schedule can also be referred to simply as *supply*. It is a set of planned production rates that depends on the price of the product. We show the individual supply schedule for a hypothetical producer in panel (a) of Figure 3-6. At $1 per diskette, for example, this producer will supply 20 million diskettes per year; at $5, this producer will supply 55 million diskettes per year.

The Supply Curve

Supply curve
The graphical representation of the supply schedule; a line (curve) showing the supply schedule, which generally slopes upward (has a positive slope), other things being equal.

We can convert the supply schedule in panel (a) of Figure 3-6 into a **supply curve,** just as we earlier created a demand curve in Figure 3-1. All we do is take the price-quantity combinations from panel (a) of Figure 3-6 and plot them in panel (b). We have labeled these combinations *F* through *J*. Connecting these points, we obtain an upward-sloping curve that shows the typically direct relationship between price and quantity supplied. Again, we have to remember that we are talking about quantity supplied *per year,* measured in constant-quality units.

FIGURE 3-6

The Individual Producer's Supply Schedule and Supply Curve for Diskettes
Panel (a) shows that at higher prices, a hypothetical supplier will be willing to provide a greater quantity of diskettes. We plot the various price-quantity combinations in panel (a) on the grid in panel (b). When we connect these points, we find the individual supply curve for diskettes. It is positively sloped.

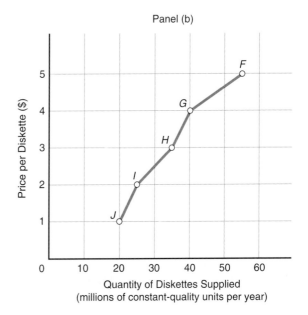

Panel (b)

Panel (a)

Combination	Price per Constant-Quality Diskette	Quantity of Diskettes Supplied (millions of constant-quality units per year)
F	$5	55
G	4	40
H	3	35
I	2	25
J	1	20

The Market Supply Curve

Just as we had to sum the individual demand curves to get the market demand curve, we need to sum the individual producers' supply curves to get the market supply curve. Look at Figure 3-7, in which we horizontally sum two typical diskette manufacturers' supply curves. Supplier 1's data are taken from Figure 3-6; supplier 2 is added. The numbers are presented in panel (a). The graphical representation of supplier 1 is in panel (b), of supplier 2 in panel (c), and of the summation in panel (d). The result, then, is the supply curve for diskettes for suppliers 1 and 2. There are many more suppliers of diskettes, however. The total market supply schedule and total market demand curve for diskettes are represented in Figure 3-8, with the curve in panel (b) obtained by adding all of the supply curves such as those shown in panels (b) and (c) of Figure 3-7. Notice the difference between the

Panel (a)

(1) Price per Diskette	(2) Supplier 1 Quantity Supplied (millions)	(3) Supplier 2 Quantity Supplied (millions)	(4) = (2) + (3) Combined Quantity Supplied per Year (millions)
$5	55	35	90
4	40	30	70
3	35	20	55
2	25	15	40
1	20	10	30

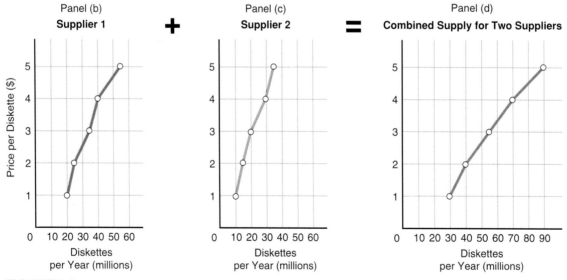

FIGURE 3-7

Horizontal Summation of Supply Curves
In panel (a), we show the data for two individual suppliers of diskettes. Adding how much each is willing to supply at different prices, we come up with the combined quantities supplied in column 4. When we plot the values in columns 2 and 3 on grids in panels (b) and (c) and add them horizontally, we obtain the combined supply curve for the two suppliers in question, shown in panel (d).

FIGURE 3-8

The Market Supply Schedule and the Market Supply Curve for Diskettes

In panel (a), we show the summation of all the individual producers' supply schedules; in panel (b), we graph the resulting supply curve. It represents the market supply curve for diskettes and is upward-sloping.

Panel (a)

Price per Constant-Quality Diskette	Quantity of Diskettes Supplied (billions of constant-quality units per year)
$5	10
4	8
3	6
2	4
1	2

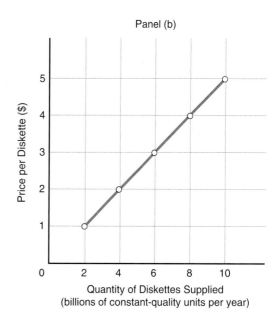

Panel (b)

market supply curve with only two suppliers in Figure 3-7 and the one with a large number of suppliers—the entire true market—in panel (b) of Figure 3-8. There are no kinks in the true total market supply curve because there are so many suppliers.

Notice what happens at the market level when price changes. If the price is $3, the quantity supplied is 6 billion diskettes. If the price goes up to $4, the quantity supplied increases to 8 billion per year. If the price falls to $2, the quantity supplied decreases to 4 billion diskettes per year. Changes in quantity supplied are represented by movements along the supply curve in panel (b) of Figure 3-8.

CONCEPTS IN BRIEF

- There is normally a direct, or positive, relationship between price and quantity of a good supplied, other things held constant.

- The supply curve normally shows a direct relationship between price and quantity supplied. The market supply curve is obtained by horizontally adding individual supply curves in the market.

SHIFTS IN SUPPLY

When we looked at demand, we found out that any change in anything relevant besides the price of the good or service caused the demand curve to shift inward or outward. The same is true for the supply curve. If something relevant changes besides the price of the product or service being supplied, we will see the entire supply curve shift.

Consider an example. A new method of putting magnetic material on diskettes has been invented. It reduces the cost of producing a diskette by 50 percent. In this situation, diskette producers will supply more product at *all* prices because their cost of so doing has fallen dramatically. Competition among diskette manufacturers to produce more at each and

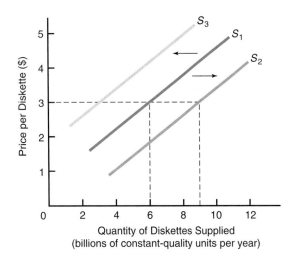

FIGURE 3-9

A Shift in the Supply Schedule
If the cost of producing diskettes were to fall dramatically, the supply schedule would shift rightward from S_1 to S_2 such that at all prices, a larger quantity would be forthcoming from suppliers. Conversely, if the cost of production rose, the supply curve would shift leftward to S_3.

every price will shift the supply schedule of diskettes outward to the right from S_1 to S_2 in Figure 3-9. At a price of $3, the quantity supplied was originally 6 billion diskettes per year, but now the quantity supplied (after the reduction in the costs of production) at $3 a diskette will be 9 billion diskettes a year. (This is similar to what has happened to the supply curve of personal computers and fax machines in recent years as computer memory chip prices have fallen.)

Consider the opposite case. If the cost of the magnetic material needed for making diskettes doubles, the supply curve in Figure 3-9 will shift from S_1 to S_3. At each and every price, the number of diskettes supplied will fall due to the increase in the price of raw materials.

The Other Determinants of Supply

When supply curves are drawn, only the price of the good in question changes, and it is assumed that other things remain constant. The other things assumed constant are the costs of resources (inputs) used to produce the product, technology and productivity, taxes and subsidies, producers' price expectations, and the number of firms in the industry. These are the major nonprice determinants of supply. If *any* of them changes, there will be a shift in the supply curve.

Cost of Inputs Used to Produce the Product. If one or more input prices fall, the supply curve will shift outward to the right; that is, more will be supplied at each and every price. The opposite will be true if one or more inputs become more expensive. For example, when we draw the supply curve of new cars, we are holding the cost of steel (and other inputs) constant. When we draw the supply curve of blue jeans, we are holding the cost of cotton fixed.

Technology and Productivity. Supply curves are drawn by assuming a given technology, or "state of the art." When the available production techniques change, the supply curve will shift. For example, when a better production technique for diskettes becomes available, the supply curve will shift to the right. A larger quantity will be forthcoming at each and every price because the cost of production is lower.

INTERNATIONAL EXAMPLE
Changing Technology and the Supply of Salmon

One example of how changes in technology can shift the supply curve out to the right involves salmon. In 1980, the total worldwide catch of salmon (wild and farmed) was just over 10,000 metric tons. Since 1980, new technology has been developed in what is called aquaculture, or the farm-raising of fish and related products. Aquaculture currently generates over $30 billion in worldwide revenues and is one of the world's fastest-growing industries. Farmed salmon from Chile, Scotland, Canada, Norway, and Iceland now exceeds 240,000 metric tons a year. Thus it is not surprising that despite a depletion of many wild salmon fishing grounds and a worldwide increase in the consumer demand for salmon, the retail price of salmon today (corrected for inflation) is about 50 percent of what it was in 1980.

FOR CRITICAL ANALYSIS: What might slow down the growth in salmon farming throughout the world? •

Taxes and Subsidies. Certain taxes, such as a per-unit tax, are effectively an addition to production costs and therefore reduce the supply. If the supply curve were S_1 in Figure 3-9, a per-unit tax increase would shift it to S_3. A **subsidy** would do the opposite; it would shift the curve to S_2. Every producer would get a "gift" from the government of a few cents for each unit produced.

Subsidy
A negative tax; a payment to a producer from the government, usually in the form of a cash grant.

Price Expectations. A change in the expectation of a future relative price of a product can affect a producer's current willingness to supply, just as price expectations affect a consumer's current willingness to purchase. For example, diskette suppliers may withhold from the market part of their current supply if they anticipate higher prices in the future. The current amount supplied at each and every price will decrease.

Number of Firms in the Industry. In the short run, when firms can only change the number of employees they use, we hold the number of firms in the industry constant. In the long run, the number of firms (or the size of some existing firms) may change. If the number of firms increases, the supply curve will shift outward to the right. If the number of firms decreases, it will shift inward to the left.

Changes in Supply Versus Changes in Quantity Supplied

We cannot overstress the importance of distinguishing between a movement along the supply curve—which occurs only when the price changes for a given supply curve—and a shift in the supply curve—which occurs only with changes in other nonprice factors. A change in price always brings about a change in quantity supplied along a given supply curve. We move to a different coordinate on the existing supply curve. This is specifically called a *change in quantity supplied.* When price changes, quantity supplied changes, and there will be a movement from one point to another along the same supply curve.

When you think of *supply,* think of the entire curve itself. Quantity supplied is represented by a single point on the supply curve.

A change or shift in supply causes the entire curve to move. The *only* thing that can cause the entire curve to move is a change in a determinant *other than price.*

Consequently,

> **A change in the price leads to a change in the quantity supplied, other things being constant. This is a movement *on* the curve.**

> **A change in any other determinant of supply leads to a change in supply. This causes a movement *of* the curve.**

CONCEPTS IN BRIEF

- If the price changes, we *move along* a curve—there is a change in quantity demanded or supplied. If some other determinant changes, we *shift* a curve—there is a change in demand or supply.

- The supply curve is drawn with other things held constant. If other determinants of supply change, the supply curve will shift. The other major determinants are (1) input costs, (2) technology and productivity, (3) taxes and subsidies, (4) expectations of future relative prices, and (5) the number of firms in the industry.

PUTTING DEMAND AND SUPPLY TOGETHER

In the sections on supply and demand, we tried to confine each discussion to supply or demand only. But you have probably already realized that we can't view the world just from the supply side or just from the demand side. There is an interaction between the two. In this section, we will discuss how they interact and how that interaction determines the prices that prevail in our economy. Understanding how demand and supply interact is essential to understanding how prices are determined in our economy and other economies in which the forces of supply and demand are allowed to work.

Let's first combine the demand and supply schedules and then combine the curves.

Demand and Supply Schedules Combined

Let's place panel (a) from Figure 3-3 (the market demand schedule) and panel (a) from Figure 3-8 (the market supply schedule) together in panel (a) of Figure 3-10. Column 1 shows the price; column 2, the quantity supplied per year at any given price; and column 3, the quantity demanded. Column 4 is merely the difference between columns 2 and 3, or the difference between the quantity supplied and the quantity demanded. In column 5, we label those differences as either excess quantity supplied (a surplus) or excess quantity demanded (a shortage). For example, at a price of $1, only 2 billion diskettes would be supplied, but the quantity demanded would be 10 billion. The difference would be −8 billion, which we label excess quantity demanded (a shortage). At the other end of the scale, a price of $5 per diskette would elicit 10 billion in quantity supplied, but quantity demanded would drop to 2 billion, leaving a difference of +8 billion units, which we call excess quantity supplied (a surplus).

Panel (a)

(1) Price per Constant-Quality Diskette	(2) Quantity Supplied (diskettes per year)	(3) Quantity Demanded (diskettes per year)	(4) Difference (2) – (3) (diskettes per year)	(5) Condition
$5	10 billion	2 billion	8 billion	Excess quantity supplied (surplus)
4	8 billion	4 billion	4 billion	Excess quantity supplied (surplus)
3	6 billion	6 billion	0	Market clearing price—equilibrium (no surplus, no shortage)
2	4 billion	8 billion	– 4 billion	Excess quantity demanded (shortage)
1	2 billion	10 billion	– 8 billion	Excess quantity demanded (shortage)

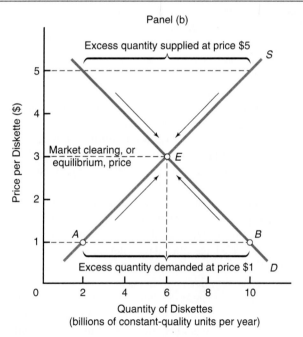

Panel (b)

FIGURE 3-10

Putting Demand and Supply Together

In panel (a), we see that at the price of $3, the quantity supplied and the quantity demanded are equal, resulting in neither an excess in the quantity demanded nor an excess in the quantity supplied. We call this price the equilibrium, or market clearing, price. In panel (b), the intersection of the supply and demand curves is at *E,* at a price of $3 per constant-quality diskette and a quantity of 6 billion per year. At point *E,* there is neither an excess in the quantity demanded nor an excess in the quantity supplied. At a price of $1, the quantity supplied will be only 2 billion disks per year, but the quantity demanded will be 10 billion. The difference is excess quantity demanded at a price of $1. The price will rise, so we will move from point *A* up the supply curve and point *B* up the demand curve to point *E.* At the other extreme, $5 elicits a quantity supplied of 10 billion but a quantity demanded of only 2 billion. The difference is excess quantity supplied at a price of $5. The price will fall, so we will move down the demand curve and the supply curve to the equilibrium price, $3 per diskette.

Now, do you notice something special about the price of $3? At that price, both the quantity supplied and the quantity demanded per year are 6 billion diskettes. The difference then is zero. There is neither excess quantity demanded (shortage) nor excess quantity supplied (surplus). Hence the price of $3 is very special. It is called the **market clearing price**—it clears the market of all excess supply or excess demand. There are no willing consumers who want to pay $3 per diskette but are turned away by sellers, and there are no willing suppliers who want to sell diskettes at $3 who cannot sell all they want at that price. Another term for the market clearing price is the **equilibrium price,** the price at which there is no tendency for change. Consumers are able to get all they want at that price, and suppliers are able to sell the amount that they want at that price.

Market clearing, or **equilibrium, price**
The price that clears the market, at which quantity demanded equals quantity supplied; the price where the demand curve intersects the supply curve.

Equilibrium

We can define **equilibrium** in general as a point from which there tends to be no movement unless demand or supply changes. Any movement away from this point will set into motion certain forces that will cause movement back to it. Therefore, equilibrium is a stable point. Any point that is not at equilibrium is unstable and cannot be maintained.

Equilibrium
The situation when quantity supplied equals quantity demanded at a particular price.

The equilibrium point occurs where the supply and demand curves intersect. The equilibrium price is given on the vertical axis directly to the left of where the supply and demand curves cross. The equilibrium quantity demanded and supplied is given on the horizontal axis directly underneath the intersection of the demand and supply curves. Equilibrium can change whenever there is a *shock*.

A shock to the supply-and-demand system can be represented by a shift in the supply curve, a shift in the demand curve, or a shift in both curves. Any shock to the system will result in a new set of supply-and-demand relationships and a new equilibrium; forces will come into play to move the system from the old price-quantity equilibrium (now a disequilibrium situation) to the new equilibrium, where the new demand and supply curves intersect.

Panel (b) in Figure 3-3 and panel (b) in Figure 3-8 are combined as panel (b) in Figure 3-10 on page 63. The only difference now is that the horizontal axis measures both the quantity supplied and the quantity demanded per year. Everything else is the same. The demand curve is labeled D, the supply curve S. We have labeled the intersection of the supply curve with the demand curve as point E, for equilibrium. That corresponds to a market clearing price of $3, at which both the quantity supplied and the quantity demanded are 6 billion units per year. There is neither excess quantity supplied nor excess quantity demanded. Point E, the equilibrium point, always occurs at the intersection of the supply and demand curves. This is the price toward which the market price will automatically tend to gravitate.

EXAMPLE
Dinosaurs and the Price of Amber

When there is a shift in either supply or demand, there is a movement toward equilibrium that usually involves a change in the equilibrium quantity and the equilibrium price. A good example is found in the market for amber, a semiprecious stone that often preserves fossil plants and animals from millions of years ago. In Figure 3-11, you see the original supply and demand curves for amber, labeled S and D_1. The equilibrium price is P_1, and the equilibrium quantity is Q_1. Then along came a book, and later a movie, called *Jurassic Park*, written by Michael Crichton. In the story, million-year-old mosquitoes that had feasted on dinosaurs were trapped in amber. Scientists were able to clone

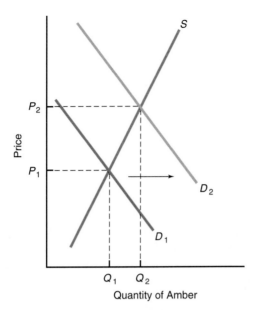

FIGURE 3-11

The Changing Price of Amber
With stable supply, a shift in the demand curve
for amber from D_1 to D_2 will cause the equilibrium price of amber to rise from P_1 to P_2 and
the equilibrium quantity to increase from Q_1
to Q_2.

various dinosaurs by removing the DNA from the dinosaur blood inside the mosquitoes.
(The technique remains in the realm of science fiction.) The success of the book and the
movie in the early 1990s made amber suddenly popular; in economic terms, the demand
curve for amber shifted outward to D_2. Very quickly, the price rose to P_2 and the equilibrium quantity increased to Q_2.

FOR CRITICAL ANALYSIS: *It has been a few years since the dinosaur craze peaked in
the United States. How would you represent what is now occurring in the market in amber
using supply and demand curves?* •

Shortages

The demand and supply curves depicted in Figure 3-10 represent a situation of equilibrium.
But a non-market-clearing, or disequilibrium, price will put into play forces that cause the
price to change toward the market clearing price at which equilibrium will again be sustained. Look again at panel (b) in Figure 3-10 on page 63. Suppose that instead of being at
the market clearing price of $3 per diskette, for some reason the market price is $1 per
diskette. At this price, the quantity demanded exceeds the quantity supplied, the former
being 10 billion diskettes per year and the latter, 2 billion per year. We have a situation of
excess quantity demanded at the price of $1. This is usually called a **shortage.** Consumers
of diskettes would find that they could not buy all that they wished at $1 apiece. But forces
will cause the price to rise: Competing consumers will bid up the price, and suppliers will
raise the price and increase output, whether explicitly or implicitly. (Remember, some buyers would pay $5 or more rather than do without diskettes. They do not want to be left out.)
We would move from points *A* and *B* toward point *E*. The process would stop when the
price again reached $3 per diskette.

    At this point, it is important to recall a distinction made in Chapter 2:

    Shortages and scarcity are not the same thing.

Shortage
A situation in which quantity
demanded is greater than quantity supplied at a price below
the market clearing price.

A shortage is a situation in which the quantity demanded exceeds the quantity supplied at a price *below* the market clearing price. Our definition of scarcity was much more general and all-encompassing: a situation in which the resources available for producing output are insufficient to satisfy all wants. Any choice necessarily costs an opportunity, and the opportunity is lost. Hence we will always live in a world of scarcity because we must constantly make choices, but we do not necessarily have to live in a world of shortages.

Surpluses

Now let's repeat the experiment with the market price at $5 per diskette rather than at the market clearing price of $3. Clearly, the quantity supplied will exceed the quantity demanded at that price. The result will be an excess quantity supplied at $5 per unit. This excess quantity supplied is often called a **surplus.** Given the curves in panel (b) in Figure 3-10, however, there will be forces pushing the price back down toward $3 per diskette: Competing suppliers will attempt to reduce their inventories by cutting prices and reducing output, and consumers will offer to purchase more at lower prices. Suppliers will want to reduce inventories, which will be above their optimal level; that is, there will be an excess over what each seller believes to be the most profitable stock of diskettes. After all, inventories are costly to hold. But consumers may find out about such excess inventories and see the possibility of obtaining increased quantities of diskettes at a decreased price. It behooves consumers to attempt to obtain a good at a lower price, and they will therefore try to do so. If the two forces of supply and demand are unrestricted, they will bring the price back to $3 per diskette.

> **Surplus**
> A situation in which quantity supplied is greater than quantity demanded at a price above the market clearing price.

Shortages and surpluses are resolved in unfettered markets—markets in which price changes are free to occur. The forces that resolve them are those of competition: In the case of shortages, consumers competing for a limited quantity supplied drive up the price; in the case of surpluses, sellers compete for the limited quantity demanded, thus driving prices down to equilibrium. The equilibrium price is the only stable price, and all (unrestricted) market prices tend to gravitate toward it.

What happens when the price is set below the equilibrium price? Here come the scalpers.

 POLICY EXAMPLE
Should Shortages in the Ticket Market
Be Solved by Scalpers?

If you have ever tried to get tickets to a playoff game in sports, a popular Broadway play, or a superstar's rock concert, you know about "shortages." The standard ticket situation for a Super Bowl is shown in Figure 3-12. At the face-value price of Super Bowl tickets (P_1), the quantity demanded (Q_2) greatly exceeds the quantity supplied (Q_1). Because shortages last only so long as prices and quantities do not change, markets tend to exhibit a movement out of this disequilibrium toward equilibrium. Obviously, the quantity of Super Bowl tickets cannot change, but the price can go as high as P_2.

Enter the scalper. This colorful term is used because when you purchase a ticket that is being resold at a price that is higher than face value, the seller is skimming an extra profit off the top. Every time an event sells out, ticket prices by definition have been lower than

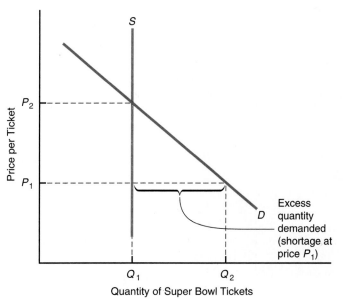

FIGURE 3-12

Shortages of Super Bowl Tickets

The quantity of tickets for any one Super Bowl is fixed at Q_1. At the price per ticket of P_1, the quantity demanded is Q_2, which is greater than Q_1. Consequently, there is an excess quantity demanded at the below–market clearing price. Prices can go as high as P_2 in the scalpers' market.

market clearing prices. Sellouts indicate that the event is very popular and that there may be people without tickets willing to buy high-priced tickets because they place a greater value on the entertainment event than the actual face value of the ticket. Without scalpers, those individuals would not be able to attend the event. In the case of the Super Bowl, various forms of scalping occur nationwide. Tickets for a seat on the 50-yard line have been sold for more than $2,000 a piece. In front of every Super Bowl arena, you can find ticket scalpers hawking their wares.

In most states, scalping is illegal. In Pennsylvania, convicted scalpers are either fined $5,000 or sentenced to two years behind bars. For an economist, such legislation seems strange. As one New York ticket broker said, "I look at scalping like working as a stockbroker, buying low and selling high. If people are willing to pay me the money, what kind of problem is that?"

FOR CRITICAL ANALYSIS: *What happens to ticket scalpers who are still holding tickets after an event has started?* •

CONCEPTS IN BRIEF

- The market clearing price occurs at the intersection of the market demand curve and the market supply curve. It is also called the equilibrium price, the price from which there is no tendency to change unless there is a change in demand or supply.

- Whenever the price is greater than the equilibrium price, there is an excess quantity supplied (a surplus).

- Whenever the price is less than the equilibrium price, there is an excess quantity demanded (a shortage).

How Higher Education Has Responded to Changes in Supply and Demand

Concepts Applied: *Demand and supply, shifts in demand and supply, relative prices*

Dwindling numbers of high school graduates forced colleges to aggressively recruit international students to make up for falling revenues in the past two decades. International students are even more desirable because there is a smaller percentage of them who qualify for financial aid, allowing schools to bring in more revenues.

During the decades after World War II, the pool of high school graduates rose virtually every year until the beginning of the 1980s. In other words, the potential supply of college students only stopped growing about a decade and a half ago. Not surprisingly, during this time period and until just recently, average tuitions at four-year colleges were rising faster than the rate of inflation. But today things are different. High schools now graduate 2.5 million students per year, down from 3.1 million a decade ago. In addition, the Bureau of Labor Statistics says that of the 18 million college graduates expected to enter the labor force between 1992 and 2005, only about 14 million will get jobs that require college training.

Figure 3-13 shows the demand curve for higher education shifting inward from D_1 to D_2. Clearly, at current prices, P_1, there is an excess quantity of higher education supplied. Something has to give.

Increasing Enrollment of Foreign College Students

Figure 3-14 shows the gradual increase in the number of foreign students enrolling in American colleges and universities. There are two reasons why American colleges have been "beating the global bushes" for new students.

The first, of course, is that they constitute an additional supply of potential students to make up for the dwindling supply of U.S. high school graduates. Second, and perhaps more important for many private universities, a much higher percentage of foreign students than American students pay full tuition. Now there are even firms that specialize in organizing foreign recruiting tours for American university admissions officials.

The Effect of Grade Inflation

The cost of attending college obviously includes tuition and textbooks. How much a student has to work to get a good grade is also a part of the cost of going to college. Not surprisingly, as the demand curve has shifted inward starting in the 1980s, colleges and universities throughout the nation have allowed grades to inflate. When Stanford University abolished Ds and Fs, it saw 93 percent of all grades awarded rise to As and Bs. At Harvard University, less than

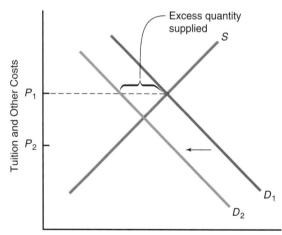

FIGURE 3-13

The "Soft" Market for College Applicants
For a variety of reasons, the demand for higher education has shifted from D_1 to D_2. With a stable supply curve, S, there exists an excess quantity of higher education supplied. Colleges and universities have therefore recruited more foreign students and started discounting tuition.

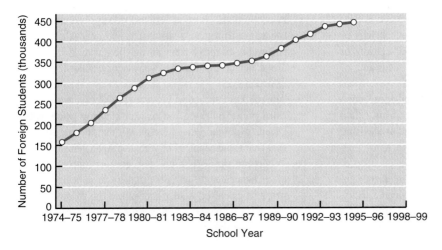

FIGURE 3-14
Foreign College Students in the United States
This graph shows the number of foreign students enrolled in all universities and colleges by school year in the United States.
Source: Institute of International Education.

20 percent of the student body has below a B average, and at Smith College, almost 90 percent of the students get As and Bs.

The Art of Discounting

Private universities are in competition with state universities. A New York resident who attends the University of Rochester and pays full tuition, including room and board, pays $2\frac{1}{2}$ times what the same student would pay to attend a campus of the State University of New York. In order to attract students, private universities have had to offer financial aid. At the University of Rochester, 70 percent of the students receive financial aid that averages $11,000 a year. So when private universities raise tuition, they have to offer even higher scholarships to attract qualified students. They consequently manage to keep only as little as 10 percent of the funds generated by a tuition increase.

What universities have started to do is give discounts on tuition. They may not call them that, but that is what they are. Continuing with the University of Rochester,

starting in the 1995–1996 school year, it cut fees for about half of its incoming freshman class by about 20 percent. George Washington University has been doing the same since 1988. Some colleges are going one step further by offering a type of money-back guarantee. For example, St. John Fisher College in Rochester, New York, offers students up to $5,000 cash if they do not find a job within six months after graduation.

Universities have discovered that the law of demand applies to them, too.

FOR CRITICAL ANALYSIS

1. Investigative reporters from the *Wall Street Journal* recently discovered that some colleges and universities have routinely falsified the SAT data of their incoming students in order to boost their reputations. Would you have expected as many U.S. colleges and universities to have acted this way prior to the 1980s? Why or why not?

2. Assume that a university gave only As to its students. How might this grading policy hurt its graduates?

CHAPTER SUMMARY

1. The law of demand says that at higher prices, individuals will purchase less of a commodity and at lower prices, they will purchase more, other things being equal.

2. Relative prices must be distinguished from absolute, or money, prices. During periods of rising prices, almost all prices go up, but some rise faster than others.

3. All references to the laws of supply and demand refer to constant-quality units of a commodity. A time period for the analysis must also be specified.

4. The demand schedule shows the relationship between various possible prices and their respective quantities purchased per unit time period. Graphically, the demand schedule is a demand curve and is downward-sloping.

5. The determinants of demand other than price are (a) income, (b) tastes and preferences, (c) the prices of related goods, (d) expectations, and (e) population, or market, size. Whenever any of these determinants of demand changes, the demand curve shifts.

6. The supply curve is generally upward-sloping such that at higher prices, more will be forthcoming than at lower prices. At higher prices, suppliers are willing to incur the increasing costs of higher rates of production.

7. The determinants of supply other than price are (a) input costs, (b) technology and productivity, (c) taxes and subsidies, (d) price expectations, and (e) entry and exit of firms.

8. A movement along a demand or supply curve is not the same thing as a shift in the curve. A change in price causes movement along the curve. A change in any other determinant of supply or demand shifts the entire curve.

9. The demand and supply curves intersect at the equilibrium point, marking the market clearing price, where quantity demanded just equals quantity supplied. At that point, the plans of buyers and sellers mesh exactly.

10. When the price of a good is greater than its market clearing price, an excess quantity is supplied at that price; it is called a surplus. When the price is below the market clearing price, an excess quantity is demanded at that price; it is called a shortage.

DISCUSSION OF PREVIEW QUESTIONS

1. Why are relative prices important in understanding the law of demand?

People respond to changes in relative prices rather than absolute prices. If the price of CDs rises by 50 percent next year, while at the same time the prices of everything else, including your wages, also increase by 50 percent, the relative price of CDs has not changed. If nothing else has changed in your life, your normal quantity demanded of CDs will remain about the same. In a world of generally rising prices (inflation), you have to compare the price of one good with the average of all other goods in order to decide whether the relative price of that one good has gone up, gone down, or stayed the same.

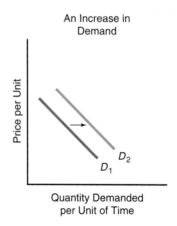

An Increase in Demand

2. How can we distinguish between a change in *demand* and a change in *quantity demanded*?

Use the accompanying graphs to aid you. Because demand is a curve, a change in demand is equivalent to a *shift* in the demand curve. Changes in demand result from changes in the other determinants of demand, such as income, tastes and preferences, expectations, prices of related goods, and population. A change in quantity demanded, given demand, is a movement along a demand curve and results only from a change in the price of the commodity in question.

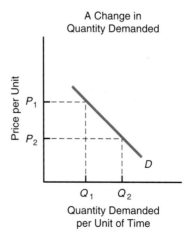

A Change in Quantity Demanded

3. Why is there generally a direct relationship between price and quantity supplied (other things being equal)?

In general, businesses experience increasing *extra* costs as they expand output in the short run. This means that additional units of output, which may be quite similar in physical attributes to initial units of output, actually cost the firm more to produce. Consequently, firms often require a higher and higher price (as an incentive) in order to produce more in the short run; this "incentive" effect implies that higher prices, other things being constant, lead to increases in quantity supplied.

4. Why will the market clearing price occur at the intersection of the supply and demand curves rather than at a higher or lower price?

Consider the accompanying graph. To demonstrate that the equilibrium price will be at P_e, we can eliminate all other prices as possibilities. Consider a price above P_e, $8 per unit. By inspection of the graph, we can see that at that price, the quantity supplied exceeds the quantity demanded for this product ($B > A$). Clearly, sellers cannot sell all they wish at $8, and they therefore find it profitable to lower price and decrease output. In fact, this surplus situation exists at *all* prices above P_e. Sellers, competing for sales, will reduce prices if a surplus exists.

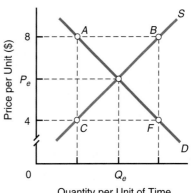

Consider a price of $4 per unit, where the quantity demanded exceeds the quantity supplied ($F > C$); a shortage of this commodity exists at a price of $4 per unit. Buyers will not be able to get all they want at that relatively low price. Because buyers are competing for this good, buyers who are willing to give up more of other goods in order to get this one will offer higher and higher prices. By doing so, they eliminate buyers who are not willing to give up more of other goods. An increase in price encourages sellers to produce and sell more. A shortage exists at *any* price below P_e, and therefore price will rise if it is below P_e.

At P_e, the quantity supplied equals the quantity demanded, Q_e, and both buyers and sellers are able to realize their intentions. Because neither group has an incentive to change its behavior, equilibrium exists at P_e.

PROBLEMS

(Answers to the odd-numbered problems appear at the back of the book.)

3-1. Construct a demand curve and a supply curve for skateboards, based on the data provided in the following tables.

Price per Skateboard	Quantity Demanded per Year
$75	3 million
50	6 million
35	9 million
25	12 million
15	15 million
10	18 million

Price per Skateboard	Quantity Supplied per Year
$75	18 million
50	15 million
35	12 million
25	9 million
15	6 million
10	3 million

What is the equilibrium price? What is the equilibrium quantity at that price?

3-2. "Drugs are obviously complementary to physicians' services." Is this statement always correct?

3-3. Five factors, other than price, that affect the demand for a good were discussed in this chapter. Place each of the following events in its proper category, and state how it would shift the demand curve in parentheses.

   a. New information is disclosed that large doses of vitamin C prevent common colds. (Demand for vitamin C)
   b. A drop in the price of educational interactive CD-ROMs occurs. (Demand for teachers)
   c. A fall in the price of pretzels occurs. (Demand for beer)

3-4. Examine the following table, and then answer the questions.

	Price per Unit Last Year	Price per Unit Today
Heating oil	$1.00	$2.00
Natural gas	.80	3.20

What has happened to the absolute price of heating oil? Of natural gas? What has happened to the price of heating oil relative to the price of natural gas? What has happened to the relative price of heating oil? Will consumers, through time, change their relative purchases? If so, how?

3-5. Suppose that the demand for oranges remains constant but a frost occurs in Florida that could potentially destroy one-third of the orange crop. What will happen to the equilibrium price and quantity for Florida oranges?

3-6. "The demand has increased so much in response to our offering of a $75 rebate that our inventory of portable laptop computers is now running very low." What is wrong with this assertion?

3-7. Analyze the following statement: "Federal farm price supports can never achieve their goals because the above-equilibrium price floors that are established by Congress and the Department of Agriculture invariably create surpluses (quantities supplied in excess of quantities demanded), which in turn drive the price right back down toward equilibrium."

3-8. Suppose that an island economy exists in which there is no money. Suppose further that every Sunday morning, at a certain location, hog farmers and cattle ranchers gather to exchange live pigs for cows. Is this a market, and if so, what do the supply and demand diagrams use as a price? Can you imagine any problems arising at the price at which cows and pigs are exchanged?

3-9. Here is a supply and demand schedule for rain in an Amazon jungle settlement where cloud seeding or other scientific techniques can be used to coax rainfall from the skies.

Price (cruzeiros per yearly centimeter of rain)	Quantity Supplied (centimeters of rain per year)	Quantity Demanded (centimeters of rain per year)
0	200	150
10	225	125
20	250	100
30	275	75
40	300	50
50	325	25
60	350	0
70	375	0
80	400	0

What are the equilibrium price and the equilibrium quantity? Explain.

COMPUTER-ASSISTED INSTRUCTION

By examining the consequence of a specific price change, we examine the roles of the substitution effect and the income effect in producing the law of demand.

Complete problem and answer appear on disk.

CHAPTER 4

EXTENSIONS OF DEMAND AND SUPPLY ANALYSIS

It was billed as the battle of grunge against greed. Eddie Vedder and the other members of Seattle grunge band Pearl Jam decided that the service charges required by Ticketmaster, the biggest distributor of tickets nationwide, were too high. Pearl Jam took the case to Congress, claiming that Ticketmaster was extracting its "pound of flesh" from poor fans nationwide by exploiting its unique position as a middleman in the live rock concert business. As soon as the word *middleman* was uttered, members of Congress started nodding their heads in agreement. To understand about middlemen is to understand about markets and exchange and how the forces of supply and demand can be altered by government actions, all topics discussed in this chapter.

PREVIEW QUESTIONS

1. Does an increase in demand always lead to a rise in price?

2. Can there ever be shortages in a market with no restrictions?

3. How are goods rationed?

4. When would you expect to encounter black markets?

id You Know That . . . millions of pounds of chemicals called chlorofluoro-carbons (such as Freon) are being illegally imported into the United States every year? Why does a thriving black market in these chemicals exist? Legislation intended to protect the earth's ozone layer has effectively eliminated or taxed heavily the sale of Freon in the United States. Yet because Americans own hundreds of millions of air-conditioned vehicles, home refrigerators, and air conditioners, all of which require Freon, demand for the chemical remains high. When an air conditioner needs fixing, it is often cheaper to pay for illegally imported Freon than to have the unit modified to use a replacement product. Illegal markets such as the one for Freon can be analyzed using the supply and demand analysis you learned in Chapter 3. Similarly, you can use this analysis to examine purport-ed shortages of apartments in Berkeley, Santa Monica, and New York City; the "surplus" of Ph.D.s in engineering and science; and many other similar phenomena. All of these exam-ples are part of our economy, which we can characterize as a price system.

THE PRICE SYSTEM

A **price system,** otherwise known as a *market system,* is one in which relative prices are constantly changing to reflect changes in supply and demand for different commodities. The prices of those commodities are the signals to everyone within the system as to what is relatively scarce and what is relatively abundant. Indeed, it is the *signaling* aspect of the price system that provides the information to buyers and sellers about what should be bought and what should be produced. In a price system, there is a clear-cut chain of events in which any changes in demand and supply cause changes in prices that in turn affect the opportunities that businesses and individuals have for profit and personal gain. Such changes influence our use of resources.

Price system
An economic system in which relative prices are constantly changing to reflect changes in supply and demand for different commodities. The prices of those commodities are signals to everyone within the system as to what is relatively scarce and what is relatively abundant.

EXCHANGE AND MARKETS

The price system features **voluntary exchange,** acts of trading between individuals that make both parties to the trade subjectively better off. The **terms of exchange**—the prices we pay for the desired items—are determined by the interaction of the forces underlying supply and demand. In our economy, the majority of exchanges take place voluntarily in markets. A market encompasses the exchange arrangements of both buyers and sellers that underlie the forces of supply and demand. Indeed, one definition of a market is a low-cost institution for facilitating exchange. A market in essence increases incomes by helping resources move to their highest-valued uses by means of prices. Prices are the providers of information.

Voluntary exchange
An act of trading, done on a voluntary basis, in which both parties to the trade are subjectively better off after the exchange.

Terms of exchange
The terms under which trading takes place. Usually the terms of exchange are equal to the price at which a good is traded.

Transaction Costs

Individuals turn to markets because markets reduce the cost of exchanges. These costs are sometimes referred to as **transaction costs,** which are broadly defined as the costs associated with finding out exactly what is being transacted as well as the cost of enforcing contracts. If you were Robinson Crusoe and lived alone on an island, you would never incur a transaction cost. For everyone else, transaction costs are just as real as the costs of produc-

Transaction costs
All of the costs associated with exchanging, including the informational costs of finding out price and quality, service record, and durability of a product, plus the cost of contracting and enforcing that contract.

tion. High-speed large-scale computers have allowed us to reduce transaction costs by increasing our ability to process information and keep records.

Consider some simple examples of transaction costs. The supermarket reduces transaction costs relative to your having to go to numerous specialty stores to obtain the items you desire. Organized stock exchanges, such as the New York Stock Exchange, have reduced transaction costs of buying and selling stocks and bonds. In general, the more organized the market, the lower the transaction costs. One group of individuals who constantly attempt to lower transaction costs are the much maligned middlemen.

The Role of Middlemen

As long as there are costs to bringing together buyers and sellers, there will be an incentive for intermediaries, normally called middlemen, to lower those costs. This means that middlemen specialize in lowering transaction costs. Whenever producers do not sell their products directly to the final consumer, there are, by definition, one or more middlemen involved. Farmers typically sell their output to distributors, who are usually called wholesalers, who then sell those products to supermarkets.

Recently, technology has reduced the need, and hence the job prospects, for middlemen.

EXAMPLE
Technology and the Death of Middlemen

For decades, most airline travelers did not buy tickets directly from the airlines. Instead, they relied on travel agents, who at one time numbered over 30,000. In 1995, the big airline carriers cut commissions paid to these middlemen, usually by capping them at $50 per ticket rather than the normal 10 percent of ticket purchase price. Basically, the airlines have realized that there are high-tech alternatives to travel agents for the distribution of their tickets. On-line computer services, such as CompuServe, allow subscribers to consult airline timetables and to reserve airline tickets from their home personal computers. As people become more and more familiar with how to use computers, modems, and on-line services, the trend toward cutting out the middlemen, at least in airline travel, will continue.

FOR CRITICAL ANALYSIS: How can travel agents more effectively compete with on-line computer services that offer airplane reservations? •

CHANGES IN DEMAND AND SUPPLY

It is in markets that we see the results of changes in demand and supply. In certain situations, it is possible to predict what will happen to equilibrium price and equilibrium quantity when a change occurs in demand or supply. Specifically, whenever one curve is stable while the other curve shifts, we can tell what will happen to price and quantity. Consider the four possibilities in Figure 4-1 on page 76. In panel (a), the supply curve remains stable but demand increases from D_1 to D_2. Note that the result is both an increase in the market clearing price from P_1 to P_2 and an increase in the equilibrium quantity from Q_1 to Q_2.

In panel (b), there is a decrease in demand from D_1 to D_3. This results in a decrease in both the relative price of the good and the equilibrium quantity. Panels (c) and (d) show the

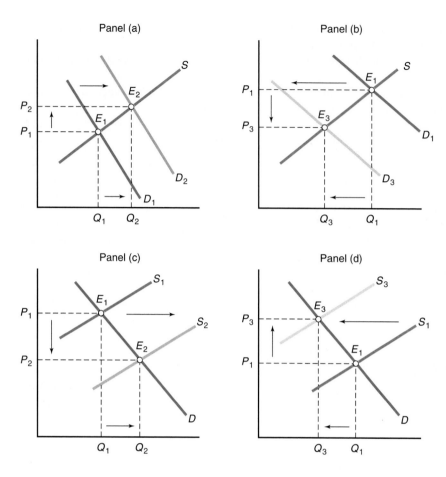

Panel (a)

Panel (b)

Panel (c)

Panel (d)

FIGURE 4-1

Shifts in Demand and in Supply: Determinate Results
In panel (a), the supply curve is stable at S. The demand curve shifts outward from D_1 to D_2. The equilibrium price and quantity rise from P_1, Q_1 to P_2, Q_2, respectively. In panel (b), again the supply curve remains stable at S. The demand curve, however, shifts inward to the left, showing a decrease in demand from D_1 to D_3. Both equilibrium price and equilibrium quantity fall. In panel (c), the demand curve now remains stable at D. The supply curve shifts from S_1 to S_2. The equilibrium price falls from P_1 to P_2. The equilibrium quantity increases, however, from Q_1 to Q_2. In panel (d), the demand curve is stable at D. Supply decreases as shown by a leftward shift of the supply curve from S_1 to S_3. The market clearing price increases from P_1 to P_3. The equilibrium quantity falls from Q_1 to Q_3.

effects of a shift in the supply curve while the demand curve is stable. In panel (c), the supply curve has shifted rightward. The relative price of the product falls; the equilibrium quantity increases. In panel (d), supply has shifted leftward—there has been a supply decrease. The product's relative price increases; the equilibrium quantity decreases.

When Both Demand and Supply Shift

The examples given in Figure 4-1 each showed a theoretically determinate outcome of a shift in either the demand curve holding the supply curve constant or the supply curve holding the demand curve constant. When both supply and demand curves change, the outcome is indeterminate for either equilibrium price or equilibrium quantity.

When both demand and supply increase, all we can be certain of is that equilibrium quantity will increase. We do not know what will happen to equilibrium price until we determine whether demand increased relative to supply (equilibrium price will rise) or supply increased relative to demand (equilibrium price will fall). The same analysis applies to decreases in both demand and supply, except that in this case equilibrium quantity falls.

We can be certain that when demand decreases and supply increases, the equilibrium price will fall, but we do not know what will happen to the equilibrium quantity unless we actually draw the new curves. If supply decreases and demand increases, we can be sure that equilibrium price will rise, but again we do not know what happens to equilibrium quantity without drawing the curves. In every situation in which both supply and demand change, you should always draw graphs to determine the resulting change in equilibrium price and quantity.

PRICE FLEXIBILITY AND ADJUSTMENT SPEED

We have used as an illustration for our analysis a market in which prices are quite flexible. Some markets are indeed like that. In others, however, price flexibility may take the form of indirect adjustments such as hidden payments or quality changes. For example, although the published price of bouquets of flowers may stay the same, the freshness of the flowers may change, meaning that the price per constant-quality unit changes. The published price of French bread might stay the same, but the quality could go up or down, thereby changing the price per constant-quality unit. There are many ways to change prices without actually changing the published price for a *nominal* unit of a product or service.

We must also consider the fact that markets do not return to equilibrium immediately. There must be an adjustment time. A shock to the economy in the form of an oil embargo, a drought, or a long strike will not be absorbed overnight. This means that even in unfettered market situations, in which there are no restrictions on changes in prices and quantities, temporary excess quantities supplied and excess quantities demanded may appear. Our analysis simply indicates what the market clearing price ultimately will be, given a demand curve and a supply curve. Nowhere in the analysis is there any indication of the speed with which a market will get to a new equilibrium if there has been a shock. The price may overshoot the equilibrium level. Remember this warning when we examine changes in demand and in supply due to changes in their nonprice determinants.

Now consider how long it takes the labor market to adjust to changes in supply and demand.

EXAMPLE
Ph.D.s Need Not Apply

During the late 1980s, news articles, TV shows, and radio commentaries proclaimed that the nation was facing a shortage of scientists. The growth in high-tech industries was going to create demands for scientists and engineers that would not be met. The government even suggested that this shortage would endanger national security. The result was an increase in the number of students seeking postgraduate education, especially doctoral degrees in engineering, the sciences, mathematics, and computer science. For example, in 1981–1982, a total of 2,621 Ph.D.s were granted in engineering; by 1991–1992, the number had more than doubled, to 5,488. Similar, though less dramatic, increases were seen in the number of doctorates awarded in the sciences and mathematics.

Yet halfway through the 1990s, joblessness among chemists was at a 20-year high. There were 3 percent fewer jobs for engineers than there had been a decade earlier, and more than 12 percent of 1995 recipients of doctorates in math could not find a job after graduation. What we were seeing was a classic case of adjustment taking time after market forces change. During the 1990s, defense industries downsized, forcing thousands of scientists and engineers out of work. When the particle accelerator being built in Texas was terminated, 1,000 physicists and engineers were "released." Pharmaceutical and biotech firms contracted and merged in the early 1990s. Academia experienced downsizing, too, drying up even more of the demand for Ph.D.s.

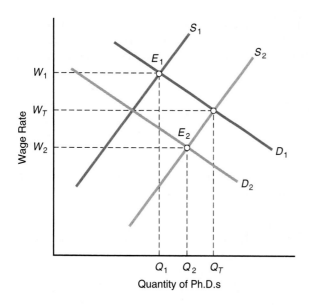

Wage Rate

Quantity of Ph.D.s

FIGURE 4-2

Falling Wages for Recent Ph.D.s

In the 1980s, the supply and demand for Ph.D.s yielded an equilibrium wage rate of W_1. Since then, the supply has shifted outward to S_2, while the demand has decreased to D_2. Wages have fallen somewhat, say, to W_T, but not yet to their equilibrium level of W_2. In the meantime, there is an "oversupply" of Ph.D.s at W_T.

You can see what happened using the supply and demand curves in Figure 4-2. The supply curve shifted from S_1 to S_2 during the period after 1987, reflecting the increase in the number of Ph.D.s being awarded. The demand curve shifted inward from D_1 to D_2, reflecting the decrease in the number of available positions. At the initial equilibrium E_1, the wage rate was W_1, and the equilibrium quantity of Ph.Ds in science, math, and engineering was Q_1. When the supply curve shifted to S_2 and the demand curve to D_2, there was an excess quantity supplied at wage rate W_1. While the wage rate has probably fallen somewhat below that, say, to W_T, it has not yet reached its new equilibrium at W_2. Until it gets to that point, there will be an excess quantity supplied of engineers, scientists, and computer specialists with Ph.D.s.

FOR CRITICAL ANALYSIS: *"The longer the time needed to learn a specialty, the more risk is involved." Analyze this quotation.* •

CONCEPTS IN BRIEF

• The terms of exchange in a voluntary exchange are determined by the interaction of the forces underlying demand and supply. These forces take place in markets, which tend to minimize transaction costs.

• When the demand curve shifts outward or inward with a stable supply curve, equilibrium price and quantity increase or decrease, respectively. When the supply curve shifts outward or inward given a stable demand curve, equilibrium price moves in the direction opposite of equilibrium quantity.

• When there is a shift in demand or supply, the new equilibrium price is not obtained instantaneously. Adjustment takes time.

THE RATIONING FUNCTION OF PRICES

A shortage creates a situation that forces price to rise toward a market clearing, or equilibrium, level. A surplus brings into play forces that cause price to fall toward its market

Water "Rationing"

More and more these days, we hear about the lack of water in some city, state, or country. For seven successive years in the 1980s and 1990s, California suffered droughts and was "forced" to "ration" water. Puerto Rico suffered a drought when rainfall dropped to 35 percent below normal; residents of San Juan were subjected to water cutoffs every other day. These stories about "running out of water" always focus on the supply of water, never on the demand. The demand curve for water slopes downward, just like that for any other good or service. When the supply of strawberries increases in the summer, their prices go down; when the supply decreases, their prices go up. When the supply of water falls because of a drought, one way to ration a smaller supply is to increase the price. For some reason, politicians and media announcers reject this possibility, implying that water is different. Beware when you see the word *rationing* in the media; it typically means that the price of a good or service has not been allowed to reach equilibrium.

clearing level. The synchronization of decisions by buyers and sellers that creates a situation of equilibrium is called the *rationing function of prices*. Prices are indicators of relative scarcity. An equilibrium price clears the market. The plans of buyers and sellers, given the price, are not frustrated.[1] It is the free interaction of buyers and sellers that sets the price that eventually clears the market. Price, in effect, rations a commodity to demanders who are willing and able to pay the highest price. Whenever the rationing function of prices is frustrated by government-enforced price ceilings that set prices below the market clearing level, a prolonged shortage situation is not allowed to be corrected by the upward adjustment of the price.

There are other ways to ration goods. *First come, first served* is one method. *Political power* is another. *Physical force* is yet another. Cultural, religious, and physical differences have been and are used as rationing devices throughout the world.

Consider first come, first served as a rationing device. In countries that do not allow prices to reflect true relative scarcity, first come, first served has become a way of life. We call this *rationing by queues*, where *queue* means "line," as in Britain. Whoever is willing to wait in line the longest obtains meat that is being sold at less than the market clearing price. All who wait in line are paying a higher *total* price than the money price paid for the meat. Personal time has an opportunity cost. To calculate the total price of the meat, we must add up the money price plus the opportunity cost of the time spent waiting.

Lotteries are another way to ration goods. You may have been involved in a rationing-by-lottery scheme during your first year in college when you were assigned a university-provided housing unit. Sometimes for popular classes, rationing by lottery is used to fill the available number of slots.

Rationing by *coupons* has also been used, particularly during wartime. In the United States during World War II, families were allotted coupons that allowed them to purchase specified quantities of rationed goods, such as meat and gasoline. To purchase such goods, you had to pay a specified price *and* give up a coupon.

Rationing by waiting may occur in situations in which entrepreneurs are free to change prices to equate quantity demanded with quantity supplied but choose not to do so. This results in queues of potential buyers. The most obvious conclusion seems to be that the price in the market is being held below equilibrium by some noncompetitive force. That is not true, however.

The reason is that queuing may also arise when the demand characteristics of a market are subject to large or unpredictable fluctuations, and the additional costs to firms (and ultimately to consumers) of constantly changing prices or of holding sufficient inventories or providing sufficient excess capacity to cover these peak demands are greater than the costs to consumers of waiting for the good. This is the usual case of waiting in line to purchase a fast-food lunch or to purchase a movie ticket a few minutes before the next show.

---

[1]There is a difference between frustration and unhappiness. You may be unhappy because you can't buy a Rolls Royce, but if you had sufficient income, you would not be frustrated in your attempt to purchase one at the current market price. By contrast, you would be frustrated if you went to your local supermarket and could get only two cans of your favorite soft drink when you had wanted to purchase a dozen and had the necessary income.

The Essential Role of Rationing

In a world of scarcity, there is, by definition, competition for what is scarce. After all, any resources that are not scarce can be had by everyone at a zero price in as large a quantity as everyone wants, such as air to burn in internal combustion engines. Once scarcity arises, there has to be some method to ration the available resources, goods, and services. The price system is one form of rationing; the others that we mentioned are alternatives. Economists cannot say which system of rationing is best. They can, however, say that rationing via the price system leads to the most efficient use of available resources. This means that generally in a price system, further trades could not occur without making somebody worse off. In other words, in a freely functioning price system, all of the gains from mutually beneficial trade will be exhausted.

CONCEPTS IN BRIEF

- Prices in a market economy perform a rationing function because they reflect relative scarcity, allowing the market to clear. Other ways to ration goods include first come, first served; political power; physical force; lotteries; and coupons.

- Even when businesspeople can change prices, some rationing by waiting will occur. Such queuing arises when there are large unexpected changes in demand coupled with high costs of satisfying those changes immediately.

THE POLICY OF GOVERNMENT-IMPOSED PRICE CONTROLS

The rationing function of prices is often not allowed to operate when governments impose price controls. **Price controls** typically involve setting a **price ceiling**—the maximum price that may be allowed in an exchange. The world has had a long history of price ceilings applied to some goods, wages, rents, and interest rates, among other things. Occasionally a government will set a **price floor**—a minimum price below which a good or service may not be sold. These have most often been applied to wages and agricultural products. Let's consider price controls in terms of price ceilings.

Price controls
Government-mandated minimum or maximum prices that may be charged for goods and services.

Price ceiling
A legal maximum price that may be charged for a particular good or service.

Price floor
A legal minimum price below which a good or service may not be sold. Legal minimum wages are an example.

Price Ceilings and Black Markets

As long as a price ceiling is below the market clearing price, imposing a price ceiling creates a shortage, as can be seen in Figure 4-3. At any price below the market clearing, or equilibrium, price of P_e, there will always be a larger quantity demanded than quantity supplied, that is, a shortage. This was discussed initially in Chapter 3. Normally, whenever a shortage exists, there is a tendency for price and output to rise to equilibrium levels. This is exactly what we pointed out when discussing shortages in the labor market. But with a price ceiling, this tendency cannot be fully realized because everyone is forbidden to trade at the equilibrium price.

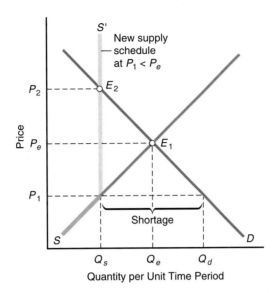

FIGURE 4-3

Black Markets

The demand curve is D. The supply curve is S. The equilibrium price is P_e. The government, however, steps in and imposes a maximum price of P_1. At that lower price, the quantity demanded will be Q_d, but the quantity supplied will only be Q_s. There is a shortage, and black markets develop. The implicit price (including nonprice costs) rises to P_2.

Nonprice rationing devices
All methods used to ration scarce goods that are price-controlled. Whenever the price system is not allowed to work, nonprice rationing devices will evolve to ration the affected goods and services.

Black market
A market in which goods are traded at prices above their legal maximum prices or in which illegal goods are sold.

The result is fewer exchanges and **nonprice rationing devices.** In Figure 4-3, at an equilibrium price of P_e, the equilibrium quantity demanded and supplied (or traded) is Q_e. But at the price ceiling of P_1, the equilibrium quantity offered is only Q_s. What happens if there is a shortage? The most obvious nonprice rationing device to help clear the market is queuing, or long lines, which we have already discussed.

Typically, an effective price ceiling leads to a **black market.** A black market is a market in which the price-controlled good is sold at an illegally high price through various methods. For example, if the price of gasoline is controlled at lower than the market clearing price, a gas station attendant may take a cash payment on the side in order to fill up a driver's car (as happened in the 1970s in the United States during price controls on gasoline). If the price of beef is controlled at below its market clearing price, the butcher may give special service to a customer who offers the butcher great seats at an upcoming football game. Indeed, the number of ways in which the true implicit price of a price-controlled good or service can be increased is infinite, limited only by the imagination. (Black markets also occur when goods are made illegal.)

Whenever a nation attempts to freeze all prices, a variety of problems arise. Many of them occurred a few years ago in Mexico.

INTERNATIONAL EXAMPLE
Mexico's Price Freeze and the Shopping Cops

The mid-1990s marked a low point for the Mexican economy when its currency, the peso, plunged in value relative to the dollar and other international currencies. In anticipation of rapidly rising domestic prices, the Mexican government imposed a temporary freeze on all prices. Almost immediately, shoppers began complaining about supermarkets, department stores, car dealerships, and mom and pop stores that were illegally raising their prices. In response, the Mexican Consumer Attorney General's Office sent out a small army of "shopping cops" to impose fines as necessary and temporarily closed hundreds of stores. During one national sample of commercial establishments, the Mexican Consumer Attorney General's Office reported that 70 percent were found to be cheating on the price freeze.

One way merchants got around government price controls was to place "sold" stickers on merchandise. Consumers then had to agree to pay a higher price in order to obtain the goods. Many automobile dealerships refused to deliver cars bought prior to the dramatic reduction in the value of the Mexican peso. Indeed, the number of ways to evade price controls were limited only by the imagination of buyers and sellers.

FOR CRITICAL ANALYSIS: How would you graphically illustrate the situation in Mexico using a supply and demand diagram? •

CONCEPTS IN BRIEF

- Government policy can impose price controls in the form of price ceilings and price floors.
- An effective price ceiling is one that sets the legal price below the market clearing price and is enforced. Effective price ceilings lead to nonprice rationing devices and black markets.

THE POLICY OF CONTROLLING RENTS

Over 200 American cities and towns, including Santa Monica, Berkeley, and New York City, operate under some kind of rent control. **Rent control** is a system under which the local government tells building owners how much they can charge their tenants in rent. In the United States, rent controls date back to at least World War II. The objective of rent control is to keep rents below levels that would be observed in a freely competitive market.

Rent control
The placement of price ceilings on rents in particular cities.

The Functions of Rental Prices

In any housing market, rental prices serve three functions: (1) to promote the efficient maintenance of existing housing and stimulate the construction of new housing, (2) to allocate existing scarce housing among competing claimants, and (3) to ration the use of existing housing by current demanders.

Rent Controls and Construction. Rent controls have discouraged the construction of new rental units. Rents are the most important long-term determinant of profitability, and rent controls have artificially depressed them. Consider some examples. In a recent year in Dallas, Texas, with a 16 percent rental vacancy rate but no rent control laws, 11,000 new rental housing units were built. In the same year in San Francisco, California, only 2,000 units were built. The major difference? San Francisco has only a 1.6 percent vacancy rate but stringent rent control laws. In New York City, except for government-subsidized construction, the only rental units being built are luxury units, which are exempt from controls. In Santa Monica, California, new apartments were not being constructed at all until 1996 when that city's rent control law was softened by the state legislature. New office rental space and commercial developments have always been exempt from rent controls.

Effects on the Existing Supply of Housing. When rental rates are held below equilibrium levels, property owners cannot recover the cost of maintenance, repairs, and capital improvements through higher rents. Hence they curtail these activities. In the extreme situation, taxes, utilities, and the expenses of basic repairs exceed rental receipts. The result is abandoned buildings. Numerous buildings have been abandoned in New York City. Some owners have resorted to arson, hoping to collect the insurance on their empty buildings before the city claims them for back taxes.

In Santa Monica, the result is bizarre contrasts: Run-down rental units sit next to homes costing more than $500,000, and abandoned apartment buildings share the block with luxury car dealerships. With the new law, such an anomaly should gradually disappear.

Rationing the Current Use of Housing. Rent controls also affect the current use of housing because they restrict tenant mobility. Consider the family whose children have gone off to college. That family might want to live in a smaller apartment. But in a rent-controlled environment, there can be a substantial cost to giving up a rent-controlled unit. In New York City, for example, rents can be adjusted only when a tenant leaves. That means that a move from a long-occupied rent-controlled apartment to a smaller apartment can involve a hefty rent hike. This artificial preservation of the status quo has become known in New York as "housing gridlock."

Attempts at Evading Rent Controls

The distortions produced by rent controls lead to efforts by both landlords and tenants to evade the rules. This leads to the growth of expensive government bureaucracies whose job it is to make sure that rent controls aren't evaded. In New York City, landlords have an incentive to make life unpleasant for tenants or to evict them on the slightest pretense. This may be the only way the landlord can raise the rent. The city has responded by making evictions extremely costly for landlords. Eviction requires a tedious and expensive judicial proceeding. Tenants, for their part, routinely try to sublet all or part of their rent-controlled apartments at fees substantially above the rent they pay to the owner. Both the city and the landlords try to prohibit subletting and typically end up in the city's housing courts—an entire judicial system developed to deal with disputes involving rent-controlled apartments. The overflow and appeals from the city's housing courts is now clogging the rest of New York's judicial system. Santa Monica has a similar rent control board. Its budget grew 500 percent in less than a decade. The landlords pay for it through a special annual assessment of more than $150 per rental unit per year.

Who Gains and Who Loses from Rent Controls?

The big losers from rent controls are clearly landlords. But there is another group of losers—low-income individuals, especially single mothers, trying to find their first apartment. Some observers now believe that rent controls have worsened the problem of homeless people in such cities as New York.

Typically, landlords of rent-controlled apartments often charge "key money" before a new tenant is allowed to move in. This is a large up-front cash payment, usually illegal but demanded nonetheless—just one aspect of the black market in rent-controlled apartments. Poor individuals cannot afford a hefty key money payment, nor can they assure the landlord that their rent will be on time or even paid each month. Because controlled rents are usually below market clearing levels, there is little incentive for apartment owners to take any risk on low-income-earning individuals as tenants. This is particularly true when a prospective tenant's chief source of income is a welfare check. Indeed, a large number of the litigants in the New York housing courts are welfare mothers who have missed their rent payments due to emergency expenses or delayed welfare checks. Often their appeals end in evictions and a new home in a temporary public shelter—or on the streets.

Who benefits from rent control? Ample evidence indicates that upper-income professionals benefit the most. These are the people who can use their mastery of the bureaucracy and their large network of friends and connections to exploit the rent control system. Consider that in New York, actresses Mia Farrow and Cicely Tyson live in rent-controlled apartments, paying well below market rates. So do State Senate Democratic leader Man-fred Ohrenstein, the director of the Metropolitan Museum of Art, the chairman of Pathmark Stores, and writer Alistair Cooke.

The average subsidy from rent regulation in New York City has been about $345 a month for tenant households with annual incomes above $75,000 but only $176 a month for households with incomes between $10,000 and $20,000. The results of a study by the Pacific Legal Foundation concerning rent controls in Santa Monica and Berkeley are instructive. Since the institution of rent controls in those two communities, they have become more exclusive in terms of median income and average education level compared to surrounding communities. In other words, both Santa Monica and Berkeley have experienced significant declines in the populations that the legislation was intended to protect.

INTERNATIONAL EXAMPLE
Rent Controls in Bombay

In the mid-1990s, the most expensive capital in the world with respect to rents was Bombay, India. The annual rent per square foot for *available* unleased space was estimated at about $177, compared to $45 in midtown Manhattan. In addition, most land-lords insist on receiving a year's rent in advance plus an additional security deposit equal to two years' rent. For major businesses, this can add up to millions of dollars, which are usually returned, but in three to five years and without payment of any interest.

One reason why Bombay rents are so high is the existence of rent controls and other laws intended to protect tenants. These controls and restrictions have kept out real estate developers and even scared owners of rentable property from renting that property, be it commercial or residential. One rent control law makes it almost impossible for a landlord to evict a tenant or to raise rents. Tenants can obtain what is called *statutory tenancy,* which allows them and their descendents to remain without a lease in any property they currently rent. There are situations in Bombay in which renters from 50 years ago still live in the same apartment, paying approximately the same rent as they originally did. Not surprisingly, unleased rental space is hard to find and hence quite expensive.

FOR CRITICAL ANALYSIS: What effect do you think Bombay's high rents might have on foreign firms' desire to operate in that city? •

CONCEPTS IN BRIEF

- Rental prices perform three functions: (1) allocating existing scarce housing among competing claimants, (2) promoting efficient maintenance of existing houses and stimulating new housing construction, and (3) rationing the use of existing houses by current demanders.

- Effective rent controls reduce or alter the three functions of rental prices. Construction of new rental units is discouraged. Rent controls decrease spending on maintenance of existing ones and also lead to "housing gridlock."

- There are numerous ways to evade rent controls; key money is one.

PRICE FLOORS IN AGRICULTURE

Another way that government can affect markets is by imposing price floors or price supports. In the United States, price supports are most often associated with agricultural products.

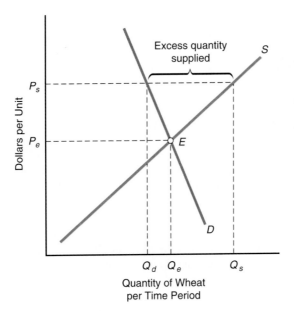

FIGURE 4-4

Agricultural Price Supports
Free market equilibrium occurs at E, with an equilibrium price of P_e and an equilibrium quantity of Q_e. When the government set a support price at P_s, the quantity demanded was Q_d, and the quantity supplied was Q_s. The difference was the surplus, which the government bought. Note that farmers' total income was from consumers ($P_s \times Q_d$) plus taxpayers [$(Q_s - Q_d) \times P_s$].

Price Supports

During the Great Depression, the federal government swung into action to help farmers. In 1933, it established a system of price supports for many agricultural products. Until recently there were price supports for wheat, feed grains, cotton, rice, soybeans, sorghum, and dairy products. The nature of the supports was quite simple: The government simply chose a *support price* for an agricultural product and then acted to ensure that the price of the product never fell below the support level. Figure 4-4 shows the market demand and supply of wheat. Without a price support program, competitive forces would yield an equilibrium price of P_e and an equilibrium quantity of Q_e. Clearly, if the government sets the support price at P_e or below, nothing will happen, because farmers can sell all they want at the market clearing price of P_e.

Until 1996, however, the government set the support price *above* P_e, at P_s. At a support price of P_s, the quantity demanded is only Q_d, but the quantity supplied is Q_s. The difference between them is called the *excess quantity supplied,* or *surplus.* As simple as this program seems, two questions arise: (1) How did the government decide on the level of the support price P_s? (2) How did it prevent market forces from pushing the actual price down to P_e?

If production exceeded the amount consumers wanted to buy at the support price, what happened to the surplus? Quite simply, the government had to buy the surplus—the difference between Q_s and Q_d—if the price support program was to work. As a practical matter, the government acquired the quantity $Q_s - Q_d$ indirectly through a government agency. The government either stored the surplus or sold it to foreign countries at a greatly reduced price (or gave it away free of charge) under the Food for Peace program.

Who Benefited from Agricultural Price Supports?

Traditionally advocated as a way to guarantee a decent wage for low-income farmers, most of the benefits of agricultural price supports were skewed toward owners of very large farms. Price supports were made on a per-bushel basis, not on a per-farm basis. Thus traditionally, the larger the farm, the bigger the benefit from agricultural price supports. In addition, *all* of the benefits from price supports ultimately accrued to *landowners* on whose land price-supported crops could grow. Except for peanuts, tobacco, and sugar, the price-support program was eliminated in 1996.

PRICE FLOORS IN THE LABOR MARKET

The **minimum wage** is the lowest hourly wage rate that firms may legally pay their workers. Proponents want higher minimum wages to ensure low-income workers a "decent" standard of living. Opponents claim that higher minimum wages cause increased unemployment, particularly among unskilled minority teenagers.

Minimum wage
A wage floor, legislated by government, setting the lowest hourly rate that firms may legally pay workers.

The federal minimum wage started in 1938 at 25 cents an hour, about 40 percent of the average manufacturing wage at the time. Typically, its level has stayed at about 40 to 50 percent of average manufacturing wages. It was increased to $4.25 in 1991 and may be higher by the time you read this. Many states and cities have their own minimum wage laws that sometimes exceed the federal minimum.

What happens when the government passes a floor on wages? The effects can be seen in Figure 4-5. We start off in equilibrium with the equilibrium wage rate of W_e and the equilibrium quantity of labor demanded and supplied equal to Q_e. A minimum wage, W_m, higher than W_e, is imposed. At W_m, the quantity demanded for labor is reduced to Q_d, and some workers now become unemployed. Note that the reduction in employment from Q_e to Q_d, or the distance from B to A, is less than the excess quantity of labor supplied at wage rate W_m. This excess quantity supplied is the distance between A and C, or the distance between Q_d and Q_s. The reason the reduction in employment is smaller than the excess supply of labor at the minimum wage is that the latter also includes a second component that consists of the additional workers who would like to work more hours at the new, higher minimum wage. Some workers may become unemployed as a result of the minimum wage, but others will move to sectors where minimum wage laws do not apply; wages will be pushed down in these uncovered sectors.

In the long run (a time period that is long enough to allow for adjustment by workers and firms), some of the reduction in labor demanded will result from a reduction in the number of firms, and some will result from changes in the number of workers employed by each firm. Economists estimate that a 10 percent increase in the real minimum wage decreases total employment of those affected by 1 to 2 percent.[2]

QUANTITY RESTRICTIONS

Governments can impose quantity restrictions on a market. The most obvious restriction is an outright ban on the ownership or trading of a good. It is presently illegal to buy and sell human organs. It is also currently illegal to buy and sell certain psychoactive drugs such as cocaine, heroin, and marijuana. In some states, it is illegal to start a new hospital without obtaining a license for a particular number of beds to be offered to patients. This licensing requirement effectively limits the quantity of hospital beds in some states. From 1933 to

---

[2]Because we are referring to a long-run analysis here, the reduction in labor demanded would be demonstrated by an eventual shift inward to the left of the short-run demand curve, *D*, in Figure 4-5.

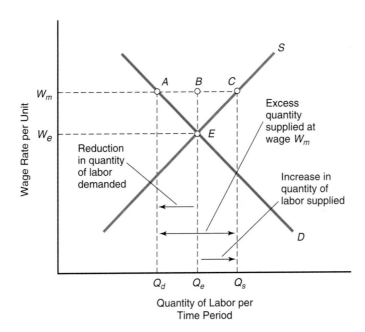

FIGURE 4-5

The Effect of Minimum Wages

The market clearing wage rate is W_e. The market clearing quantity of employment is Q_e, determined by the intersection of supply and demand at point E. A minimum wage equal to W_m is established. The quantity of labor demanded is reduced to Q_d; the reduction in employment from Q_e to Q_d is equal to the distance between B and A. That distance is smaller than the excess quantity of labor supplied at wage rate W_m. The distance between B and C is the increase in the quantity of labor supplied that results from the higher minimum wage rate.

1973, it was illegal for U.S. citizens to own gold except for manufacturing, medicinal, or jewelry purposes.

Some of the most common quantity restrictions exist in the area of international trade. The U.S. government, as well as many foreign governments, imposes import quotas on a variety of goods. An **import quota** is a supply restriction that prohibits the importation of more than a specified quantity of a particular good in a one-year period. The United States has had import quotas on tobacco, sugar, and immigrant labor. For many years, there were import quotas on oil coming into the United States. There are also "voluntary" import quotas on certain goods. Japanese automakers have agreed since 1981 "voluntarily" to restrict the amount of Japanese cars they send to the United States.

Import quota

A physical supply restriction on imports of a particular good, such as sugar. Foreign exporters are unable to sell in the United States more than the quantity specified in the import quota.

POLICY EXAMPLE

Should the Legal Quantity of Cigarettes Supplied Be Set at Zero?

Nicotine has been used as a psychoactive drug by the native people of the Americas for approximately 8,000 years. Five hundred years ago, Christopher Columbus introduced tobacco to the Europeans, who discovered that once they overcame the nausea and dizziness produced by chewing, snorting, or smoking the tobacco, they simply could not get along without it. Nicotine quickly joined alcohol and caffeine as one of the world's principal psychoactive drugs of choice.

In the century after Columbus returned from the Americas with tobacco, the use of and addiction to nicotine spread quickly around the world. There followed numerous efforts to quash what had become known as the "evil weed." In 1603, the Japanese prohibited the use of tobacco and repeatedly increased the penalties for violating the ban, which wasn't lifted until 1625. By the middle of the seventeenth century, similar bans on tobacco were in place in Bavaria, Saxony, Zurich, Turkey, and Russia, with punishments ranging from confiscation of property to execution. Even in the early twentieth century, several state governments in the United States attempted to ban the use of tobacco.

A proposed quantity restriction—outright prohibition—was in the news again a few years ago when the head of the Food and Drug Administration announced that his agency had finally determined that nicotine is addictive. He even argued that it should be classified with marijuana, heroin, and cocaine.

What can we predict if tobacco were ever completely prohibited today? Because tobacco is legal, the supply of illegal tobacco is zero. If the use of tobacco were restricted, the supply of illegal tobacco would not remain zero for long. Even if U.S. tobacco growers were forced out of business, the production of tobacco in other countries would increase to meet the demand. Consequently, the supply curve of illegal tobacco products would shift outward to the right as more foreign sources determined they wanted to enter the illegal U.S. tobacco market. The demand curve for illegal tobacco products would emerge almost immediately after the quantity restriction. The price people pay to satisfy their nicotine addiction would go up.

FOR CRITICAL ANALYSIS: What other goods or services follow the same analysis as the one presented here? •

CONCEPTS IN BRIEF

- With a price support system, the government sets a minimum price at which, say, qualifying farm products can be sold. Any farmers who cannot sell at that price can "sell" their surplus to the government. The only way a price support system can survive is for the government or some other entity to buy up the excess quantity supplied at the support price.

- When a floor is placed on wages at a rate that is above market equilibrium, the result is an excess quantity of labor supplied at that minimum wage.

- Quantity restrictions may take the form of import quotas, which are limits on the quantity of specific foreign goods that can be brought into the United States for resale purposes.

ISSUES AND APPLICATIONS

Grunge Meets Greed

Concepts Applied: Markets, exchange, price system, middlemen, rationing, supply and demand

Pearl Jam's Eddie Vedder refused to sell tickets for the '95–'96 tour through Ticketmaster because the distributor adds on a hefty fee to tickets. Are Ticketmaster's services of convenient ticket purchasing worth the price they charge? Pearl Jam didn't think so.

Arguably, the Seattle grunge band Pearl Jam is one of the most successful rock bands of our time. Not only is it one of the most popular bands in America, but it is also the most revolutionary. Pearl Jam refused to make videos for MTV and VH-1 for its second successful album, *Vs.*, and didn't release any singles from that album in the United States. When the band finally decided to tour after an intentionally long hiatus, it demanded a $20 ceiling on ticket prices, including a top service charge of 10 percent from the nation's leading ticket distributor, Ticketmaster.

Ticketmaster's Position as the Middleman

Ticketmaster distributes tickets nationwide for major entertainment events using a highly sophisticated computer system. When asked about Pearl Jam's claims that Ticketmaster was "gouging" fans, the head of the company, Fred Rosen, said that Ticketmaster's investment in that computer system makes it easier for performers to sell large numbers of tickets. Each year, Ticketmaster sells between 50 and 60 million tickets. Rosen believes that Ticketmaster has the right to be paid for such services and notes that "if Pearl Jam wants to play for free, we will be happy to distribute their tickets for free." Ticketmaster currently charges a fee of $4 to $18 per ticket.

Competition Among Middlemen

In most markets, there is competition among middlemen, and that competition lowers the price of their services. Prior to 1991, Ticketmaster's main competitor was Ticketron. In the 1980s, Ticketron began losing millions of dollars a year and eventually sold out to Ticketmaster in 1991. Apparently Ticketron was not operating as efficiently as Ticketmaster.

The Value That Ticketmaster Adds

Goods have little or no value if consumers cannot obtain them. The value of a good therefore depends on its availability. Middlemen add value to goods without physically changing them by simply making it easier for consumers to purchase them. As a middleman, this is what Ticketmaster does. Major entertainment events, such as a Pearl Jam concert, are most profitable and add value to more consumers when they are performed in large venues, such as football stadiums. It would be virtually impossible to service all of the fans desiring to attend a Pearl Jam concert if tickets were sold only at the box office of the venue where the concert was being held. A computerized nationwide system allows popular bands to sell tickets efficiently for concerts at large-capacity venues.

Pearl Jam's Failed Alternative Distribution System

Pearl Jam originally decided to give concerts without the use of Ticketmaster by distributing tickets through a lottery. Some 175,000 people sent in postcards for the two concerts that were to be held at Constitution Hall in Philadelphia, which seats 3,700 people. Of course, many people who saw those concerts paid extravagant prices by using the services of scalpers. One of the things that Pearl Jam cannot control is the value that fans place on seeing and hearing the band perform live. As long as different fans have different valuations of an activity, there will be some who will willingly give up their tickets at a high enough price, which others will gladly pay.

Neither the lottery nor any other alternatives that Pearl Jam tried to get around the intermediary services of Ticketmaster worked. The band canceled its 1995–1996 tour. Its spokespersons claimed that "touring without Ticketmaster was too complicated." About the same time, the congressional investigation into Ticketmaster for allegedly keeping ticket prices too high quietly closed without any action taken.

Competition for Ticketmaster may be on the horizon, with Massachusetts-based NEXT Ticketing selling tickets via a high-tech phone system and the Internet.

FOR CRITICAL ANALYSIS

1. Assume that Ticketmaster distributes 100 percent of all tickets to live entertainment events in the United States. Why wouldn't Ticketmaster charge an even higher service charge per ticket, say, $50?
2. If Congress passed a law restricting Ticketmaster to a $2 charge per ticket, what might happen as a result?

CHAPTER SUMMARY

1. A price system, otherwise called a market system, allows prices to respond to changes in supply and demand for different commodities. Consumers and business managers' decisions on resource use depend on what happens to prices.
2. Exchanges take place in markets. The terms of exchange—prices—are registered in markets that tend to minimize transaction costs.
3. With a stable supply curve, a rise in demand leads to an increase in equilibrium price and quantity; a decrease in demand leads to a reduction in equilibrium price and quantity. With a stable demand curve, a rise in supply leads to a decrease in equilibrium price and an increase in equilibrium quantity; a fall in supply leads to an increase in equilibrium price and a decrease in equilibrium quantity.
4. When both demand and supply shift at the same time, indeterminate results occur. We must know the direction and degree of each shift in order to predict the change in equilibrium price and quantity.
5. When there is a shift in demand or supply, it takes time for markets to adjust to the new equilibrium. During that time, there will be temporary shortages or surpluses.
6. In a market system, prices perform a rationing function—they ration scarce goods and services. Other ways of rationing include first come, first

served; political power; physical force; lotteries; and coupons.
7. Government-imposed price controls can take the form of price ceilings and price floors. Effective price ceilings—ones that are set below the market clearing price and enforced—lead to nonprice rationing devices and black markets.
8. Rent controls interfere with many of the functions of rental prices. For example, effective rent controls discourage the construction of new rental units. They also encourage "housing gridlock." Landlords lose during effective rent controls. Other losers are typically low-income individuals, especially single mothers, trying to find their first apartments.
9. A price floor can take the form of a government-imposed price support for agricultural products. This creates an excess quantity supplied at the supported price. To maintain that price, the government must buy up the surplus agricultural products. A price floor can apply to wages. When the government-imposed minimum wage exceeds the equilibrium wage rate, an excess quantity of labor is supplied. The result is higher unemployment for the affected group of workers.
10. Quantity restrictions can take the form of import quotas, under which there is a limit to the quantity of the affected good that can be brought into the United States and sold.

DISCUSSION OF PREVIEW QUESTIONS

1. Does an increase in demand always lead to a rise in price?

Yes, provided that the supply curve doesn't shift also. If the supply is stable, every rise in demand will cause a shift outward to the right in the demand curve. The new equilibrium price will be higher than the old equilibrium price. If, however, the supply curve shifts at the same time, you have to know in which direction and by how much. If the supply curve shifts outward, indicating a rise in supply, the equilibrium price can rise if the shift is not as great as in demand. If the increase in supply is greater than in demand, the price can actually fall. We can be sure, though, that if demand increases and supply decreases, the equilibrium price will rise. This can be seen in the accompanying graph.

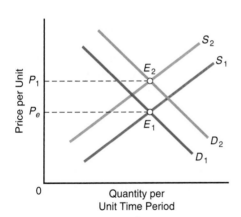

2. Can there ever be shortages in a market with no restrictions?

Yes, there can, because adjustment is never instantaneous. It takes time for the forces of supply and demand to work. In all our graphs, we draw new equilibrium points where a new supply curve meets a new demand curve. That doesn't mean that in the marketplace buyers and sellers will react immediately to a change in supply or demand. Information is not perfect. Moreover, people are often slow to adapt to higher or lower prices. Suppliers may require months or years to respond to an increase in the demand for their product. Consumers take time to respond to new information about changing relative prices.

3. How are goods rationed?

In a pure price system, prices ration goods. Prices are the indicators of relative scarcity. Prices change so that quantity demanded equals quantity supplied. In the absence of a price system, an alternative way to ration goods is first come, first served. In many systems, political power is another method. In certain cultures, physical force is a way to ration goods. Cultural, religious, and physical differences among individuals can be used as rationing devices. The fact is that given a world of scarcity, there has to be some method to ration goods. The price system is only one alternative.

4. When would you expect to encounter black markets?

Black markets occur in two situations. The first occurs whenever a good or service is made illegal by legislation. There are black markets in the United States for prostitution, gambling, and drugs. Second, there are black markets whenever a price ceiling (one type of price control) is imposed on any good or service. The price ceiling has to be below the market clearing price and enforced for a black market to exist, however. Price ceilings on rents in cities in the United States have created black markets for rental units.

PROBLEMS

(Answers to the odd-numbered problems appear at the back of the book.)

4-1. This is a graph of the supply and demand for oranges.

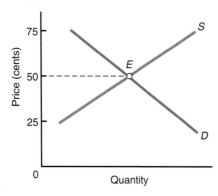

Explain the effect on this graph of each of the following events.

a. It is discovered that oranges can cure acne.
b. A new machine is developed that will automatically pick oranges.
c. The government declares a price floor of 25 cents.
d. The government declares a price floor of 75 cents.
e. The price of grapefruits increases.
f. Income decreases.

4-2. What might be the long-run results of price controls that maintained a good's money price below its equilibrium price? Above its equilibrium price?

4-3. Here is a demand schedule and a supply schedule for scientific hand calculators.

Price	Quantity Demanded	Quantity Supplied
$10	100,000	0
20	60,000	0
30	20,000	0
40	0	0
50	0	100,000
60	0	300,000
70	0	500,000

What are the equilibrium price and the equilibrium quantity? Explain.

4-4. This is a graph of the supply and demand for raisins.

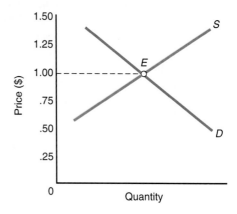

The following series of events occurs. Explain the result of the occurrence of each event.

a. An advertising campaign for California raisins is successful.
b. A fungus wipes out half the grape crop (used to make raisins) in California.
c. The price of bran flakes (a complement) increases.
d. The price of dried cranberries (a substitute) increases.
e. The government declares a price floor of 75 cents.
f. The government imposes and enforces a price ceiling of 75 cents.
g. Income increases (assume that raisins are an inferior good).

4-5. Below is a demand schedule and a supply schedule for lettuce.

Price per Crate	Quantity Demanded (crates per year)	Quantity Supplied (crates per year)
$1	100 million	0 million
2	90 million	10 million
3	70 million	30 million
4	50 million	50 million
5	20 million	80 million

What are the equilibrium price and the equilibrium quantity? At a price of $2 per crate, what is the quantity demanded? The quantity supplied? What is this disequilibrium situation called? What is the magnitude of the disequilibrium, expressed in terms of quantities? Now answer the same questions for a price of $5 per crate.

4-6. What is wrong with the following assertion? "The demand has increased so much in response to our offering of a $500 rebate that our inventory of cars is now running very low."

4-7. Rent control is a price ceiling. There are also legislated price floors. Assume that the equilibrium price for oranges is 10 cents each. Draw the supply and demand diagram to show the effect of a government-imposed price floor, or minimum price, of 15 cents per orange. Be sure to label any shortages or surpluses that result. Then show the effect of a price floor of 5 cents per orange.

COMPUTER-ASSISTED INSTRUCTION

A set of price ceiling and price floor situations is presented. You are asked to predict different outcomes for each situation in both the short and the long run.

Complete problem and answer appear on disk.

CHAPTER 5

THE PUBLIC SECTOR

In the United States over the course of a year, hundreds of thousands of tax attorneys and accountants labor alone or with clients to help those clients reduce their tax liabilities and fill out their tax returns. American taxpayers are each estimated to spend approximately 32 hours a year preparing their taxes. The opportunity cost exceeds $100 billion a year. And that is not the end of the story—many individuals spend a lot of valuable time figuring out ways to change their behavior so as to reduce the taxes they owe. Although there is never any way to avoid the cost of a tax system completely, there are ways to reduce compliance costs to society. One way is to switch to a more simplified tax system. To understand this issue, you need to know more about government and the public sector.

PREVIEW QUESTIONS

1. What problems will you encounter if you refuse to pay a portion of your income tax because you oppose national defense spending?

2. Will you benefit from many so-called tax loopholes when you first start working?

3. In what ways do regressive, proportional, and progressive tax structures differ?

4. Who pays the corporate income tax?

Did You Know That . . . the average American works from January 1 through May 7 each year to pay for all local, state, and federal taxes? The average New York resident works approximately three weeks longer to pay for all of the taxes owed each year. Looked at another way, the average American in a typical eight-hour day works about 2 hours and 42 minutes to pay for government at all levels. Every citizen, including children, averages about $8,000 a year in taxes of all kinds. The total amount paid exceeds $2 trillion. What is a trillion dollars? It is a million times a million. Thus it would take more than 2 million millionaires to have as much money as is spent each year by government. So we cannot ignore the presence of government in our society. Government exists, at a minimum, to take care of what the price system does not do well.

WHAT A PRICE SYSTEM CAN AND CANNOT DO

Throughout the book so far, we have alluded to the benefits of a price system. High on the list is economic efficiency. In its most ideal form, a price system allows resources to move from lower-valued uses to higher-valued uses through voluntary exchange. The supreme point of economic efficiency occurs when all mutually advantageous trades have taken place. In a price system, consumers are sovereign; that is to say, they have the individual freedom to decide what they wish to purchase. Politicians and even business managers do not ultimately decide what is produced; consumers decide. Some proponents of the price system argue that this is its most important characteristic. A market organization of economic activity generally prevents one person from interfering with another in respect to most of his or her activities. Competition among sellers protects consumers from coercion by one seller, and sellers are protected from coercion by one consumer because other consumers are available.

Sometimes the price system does not generate these results, with too few or too many resources going to specific economic activities. Such situations are called **market failures.** Market failures prevent the price system from attaining economic efficiency and individual freedom, as well as other social goals. Market failures offer one of the strongest arguments in favor of certain economic functions of government, which we now examine.

Market failure
A situation in which an unrestrained market economy leads to too few or too many resources going to a specific economic activity.

CORRECTING FOR EXTERNALITIES

In a pure market system, competition generates economic efficiency only when individuals know the true opportunity cost of their actions. In some circumstances, the price that someone actually pays for a resource, good, or service is higher or lower than the opportunity cost that all of society pays for that same resource, good, or service.

Consider a hypothetical world in which there is no government regulation against pollution. You are living in a town that until now has had clean air. A steel mill moves into town. It produces steel and has paid for the inputs—land, labor, capital, and entrepreneurship. The price it charges for the steel reflects, in this example, only the costs that the steel mill incurred. In the course of production, however, the mill gets one input—clean air—by simply taking it. This is indeed an input because in the making of steel, the furnaces emit smoke. The steel mill doesn't have to pay the cost of using the clean air; rather, it is the people in the community who pay that cost in the form of dirtier clothes, dirtier cars and houses, and more respiratory illnesses. The effect is similar to what would happen if the steel mill could take coal or oil or workers' services free. There has been an **externality,** an external cost. Some of the costs associated with the production of the steel have "spilled over" to affect **third parties,** parties other than the buyer and the seller of the steel.

Externality
A consequence of an economic activity that spills over to affect third parties. Pollution is an externality.

Third parties
Parties who are not directly involved in a given activity or transaction.

External Costs in Graphical Form

Look at panel (a) in Figure 5-1. Here we show the demand curve for steel to be D. The supply curve is S_1. The supply curve includes only the costs that the firms have to pay. The equilibrium, or market clearing, situation will occur at quantity Q_1. Let us take into account the fact that there are externalities—the external costs that you and your neighbors pay in the form of dirtier clothes, cars, and houses and increased respiratory disease due to the air pollution emitted from the steel mill; we also assume that all other suppliers of steel use clean air without having to pay for it. Let's include these external costs in our graph to find out what the full cost of steel production really is. This is equivalent to saying that the price of an input used in steel production increased. Recall from Chapter 3 that an increase in input prices shifts the supply curve inward to the left. Thus in panel (a) of the figure, the supply curve shifts from S_1 to S_2. If the external costs were somehow taken into account, the equilibrium quantity would fall to Q_2 and the price would rise to P_2. Otherwise, that price is implicitly being paid for, but by two different groups of people. The lower price, P_1, is being explicitly paid for by the purchasers of steel and steel products. The difference between P_2 and P_1 represents the cost that third parties are bearing in the form of dirtier clothes, houses, and cars and increased respiratory illnesses.

External Benefits in Graphical Form

Externalities can also be positive. To demonstrate external benefits in graphical form, we will use the example of inoculations against communicable disease. In panel (b) of Figure

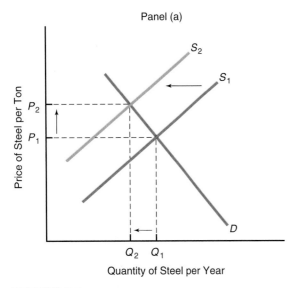

Panel (a)

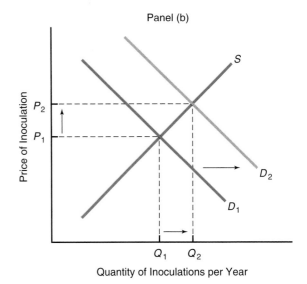

Panel (b)

FIGURE 5-1

External Costs and Benefits

In panel (a), we show a situation in which the production of steel generates external costs. If the steel mills ignore pollution, at equilibrium the quantity of steel will be Q_1. If the mills had to pay for the additional cost borne by nearby residents that is caused by the steel mill's production, the supply curve would shift inward to the left to S_2. If consumers were forced to pay a price that reflected the spillover costs, the quantity demanded would fall to Q_2. In panel (b), we show the situation in which inoculations against communicable diseases generate external benefits to those individuals who may not be inoculated but who will benefit because epidemics will not occur. If each individual ignores the external benefit of inoculations, the market clearing quantity will be Q_1. If external benefits are taken into account by purchasers of inoculations, however, the demand curve would shift rightward to D_2. The new equilibrium quantity would be Q_2 and the price would be higher, P_2.

5-1, we show the demand curve as D_1 (without taking account of any external benefits) and the supply curve as S. The equilibrium price is P_1, and the equilibrium quantity is Q_1. We assume, however, that inoculations against communicable diseases generate external benefits to individuals who may not be inoculated but will benefit nevertheless because epidemics will not break out. If such external benefits were taken into account, the demand curve would shift outward from D_1 to D_2. The new equilibrium quantity would be Q_2, and the new equilibrium price would be P_2. With no corrective action, this society is not devoting enough resources to inoculations against communicable diseases.

When there are external costs, the market will tend to *overallocate* resources to the production of the good or service in question, for those goods or services will be deceptively low-priced. With the example of steel, too much will be produced because the steel mill owners and managers are not required to take account of the external cost that steel production is imposing on the rest of society. In essence, the full cost of production is unknown to the owners and managers, so the price they charge the public for steel is lower than it would be otherwise. And of course, the lower price means that buyers are willing and able to buy more. More steel is produced and consumed than is socially optimal.

When there are external benefits, the market *underallocates* resources to the production of that good or service because the good or service is relatively too expensive (because the demand is relatively too low). In a market system, too many of the goods that generate external costs are produced and too few of the goods that generate external benefits are produced.

How the Government Corrects Negative Externalities

The government can in theory correct externality situations in a variety of ways in all cases that warrant such action. In the case of negative externalities, at least two avenues are open to the government: special taxes and legislative regulation or prohibition.

Special Taxes. In our example of the steel mill, the externality problem originates from the fact that the air as a waste disposal place is costless to the firm but not to society. The government could make the steel mill pay a tax for dumping its pollutants into the air. The government could attempt to tax the steel mill commensurate with the cost to third parties from smoke in the air. This, in effect, would be a pollution tax or an **effluent fee.** The ultimate effect would be to reduce the supply of steel and raise the price to consumers, ideally making the price equal to the full cost of production to society.

Regulation. To correct a negative externality arising from steel production, the government could specify a maximum allowable rate of pollution. This action would require that the steel mill install pollution abatement equipment within its facilities, that it reduce its rate of output, or some combination of the two. Note that the government's job would not be that simple, for it still would have to determine the level of pollution and then actually measure its output from steel production in order to enforce such regulation.

How the Government Corrects Positive Externalities

What can the government do when the production of one good spills *benefits* over to third parties? It has several policy options: financing the production of the good or producing the good itself, subsidies (negative taxes), and regulation.

Government Financing and Production. If the positive externalities seem extremely large, the government has the option of financing the desired additional production facilities so that the "right" amount of the good will be produced. Again consider inoculations

Effluent fee
A charge to a polluter that gives the right to discharge into the air or water a certain amount of pollution. Also called a *pollution tax.*

against communicable diseases. The government could—and often does—finance campaigns to inoculate the population. It could (and does) even produce and operate centers for inoculation in which such inoculations would be free.

Subsidies. A subsidy is a negative tax; it is a payment made either to a business or to a consumer when the business produces or the consumer buys a good or a service. In the case of inoculations against communicable diseases, the government could subsidize everyone who obtains an inoculation by directly reimbursing those inoculated or by making payments to private firms that provide inoculations. If you are attending a state university, taxpayers are helping to pay the cost of providing your education; you are being subsidized by as much as 80 percent of the total cost. Subsidies reduce the net price to consumers, thereby causing a larger quantity to be demanded.

Regulation. In some cases involving positive externalities, the government can require by law that a certain action be undertaken by individuals in the society. For example, regulations require that all school-age children be inoculated before entering public and private schools. Some people believe that a basic school education itself generates positive externalities. Perhaps as a result of this belief, we have regulations—laws—that require all school-age children to be enrolled in a public or private school.

CONCEPTS IN BRIEF

- External costs lead to an overallocation of resources to the specific economic activity. Two possible ways of correcting these spillovers are taxation and regulation.

- External benefits result in an underallocation of resources to the specific activity. Three possible government corrections are financing the production of the activity, subsidizing private firms or consumers to engage in the activity, and regulation.

THE OTHER ECONOMIC FUNCTIONS OF GOVERNMENT

Besides compensating for externalities, the government performs many other functions that affect the way in which exchange is carried out in the economy. In contrast, the political functions of government have to do with deciding how income should be redistributed among households and selecting which goods and services have special merits and should therefore be treated differently. The economic and political functions of government can and do overlap.

Let's look at four more economic functions of government.

Providing a Legal System

The courts and the police may not at first seem like economic functions of government (although judges and police personnel must be paid). Their activities nonetheless have important consequences on economic activities in any country. You and I enter into contracts constantly, whether they be oral or written, expressed or implied. When we believe that we have been wronged, we seek redress of our grievances within our legal institutions. Moreover, consider the legal system that is necessary for the smooth functioning of our system. Our system has defined quite explicitly the legal status of businesses, the rights of private ownership, and a method for the enforcement of contracts. All relationships among consumers and businesses are governed by the legal rules of the game. We might consider the government in its judicial function, then, as the referee when there are disputes in the economic arena.

Much of our legal system is involved with defining and protecting *property rights*. **Property rights** are the rights of an owner to use and to exchange his or her property. One might say that property rights are really the rules of our economic game. When property rights are well defined, owners of property have an incentive to use that property efficiently. Any mistakes in their decision about the use of property have negative consequences that the owners suffer. Furthermore, when property rights are well defined, owners of property have an incentive to maintain that property so that if those owners ever desire to sell it, it will fetch a better price.

Establishing and maintaining a well-functioning legal system is not a costless activity, as you can see in the following example.

Property rights
The rights of an owner to use and to exchange property.

INTERNATIONAL POLICY EXAMPLE
Who Should Pay the High Cost of a Legal System?

When a huge multinational gets into a lengthy and expensive "shouting match" with its detractors, the public ends up footing part of the legal bill. McDonald's operates worldwide with annual sales of about $40 billion. It has property rights in the goodwill associated with its name. When two unemployed British social activists published a pamphlet with such chapter headings as "McDollar, McGreedy, McCancer, McMurder, McRipoff, McTorture, and McGarbage," McDonald's was not pleased. The pamphlet accused the American company of torturing animals, corrupting children, and exploiting the Third World. So McDonald's went to court in London. When the case began, there were 26 preliminary hearings spread over a four-year time period, and when it went to trial, 180 witnesses were called. McDonald's itself will end up spending many millions of dollars, but British taxpayers will foot the entire bill for the use of the court system. According to the Lord Chancellor's Department, British taxpayers will pay at least £2.5 million (well over $4 million).

Should taxpayers continue to pay for all of the court system? No, according to policymakers in Britain. They have a plan to make litigants pay the full cost of court services, specifically judges' salaries. Once the plan was announced, Scotland increased its courtroom fees, in some cases by 1,000 percent. Such a system that forces litigants to pay for the full opportunity cost of the legal system has yet to be instituted in the United States or elsewhere.

FOR CRITICAL ANALYSIS: What other costs, besides judges' salaries, do citizens implicitly pay for in their legal system? ●

Promoting Competition

Many people believe that the only way to attain economic efficiency is through competition. One of the roles of government is to serve as the protector of a competitive economic system. Congress and the various state governments have passed **antitrust legislation.** Such legislation makes illegal certain (but not all) economic activities that might, in legal terms, restrain trade—that is, prevent free competition among actual and potential rival firms in the marketplace. The avowed aim of antitrust legislation is to reduce the power of **monopolies**—firms that have great control over the price of the goods they sell. A large number of antitrust laws have been passed that prohibit specific anticompetitive business behavior. Both the Antitrust Division of the Department of Justice and the Federal Trade Commission attempt to enforce these antitrust laws. Various state judicial agencies also expend efforts at maintaining competition.

Antitrust legislation
Laws that restrict the formation of monopolies and regulate certain anticompetitive business practices.

Monopoly
A firm that has great control over the price of a good. In the extreme case, a monopoly is the only seller of a good or service.

Providing Public Goods

The goods used in our examples up to this point have been **private goods.** When I eat a cheeseburger, you cannot eat the same one. So you and I are rivals for that cheeseburger, just as much as rivals for the title of world champion are. When I use a CD-ROM player, you cannot use the same player. When I use the services of an auto mechanic, that person cannot work at the same time for you. That is the distinguishing feature of private goods—their use is exclusive to the people who purchase or rent them. The **principle of rival consumption** applies to all private goods by definition. Rival consumption is easy to understand. With private goods, either you use them or I use them.

There is an entire class of goods that are not private goods. These are called **public goods.** The principle of rival consumption does not apply to them. That is, they can be consumed *jointly* by many individuals simultaneously. National defense, police protection, and the legal system, for example, are public goods. If you partake of them, you do not necessarily take away from anyone else's share of those goods.

Characteristics of Public Goods. Several distinguishing characteristics of public goods set them apart from all other goods.[1]

1. **Public goods are often indivisible.** You can't buy or sell $5 worth of our ability to annihilate the world with bombs. Public goods cannot usually be produced or sold very easily in small units.
2. **Public goods can be used by more and more people at no additional cost.** Once money has been spent on national defense, the defense protection you receive does not reduce the amount of protection bestowed on anyone else. The opportunity cost of your receiving national defense once it is in place is zero.
3. **Additional users of public goods do not deprive others of any of the services of the goods.** If you turn on your television set, your neighbors don't get weaker reception because of your action.
4. **It is difficult to design a collection system for a public good on the basis of how much individuals use it.** It is nearly impossible to determine how much any person uses or values national defense. No one can be denied the benefits of national defense for failing to pay for that public good. This is often called the **exclusion principle.**

One of the problems of public goods is that the private sector has a difficult, if not impossible, time in providing them. There is little or no incentive for individuals in the private sector to offer public goods because it is so difficult to make a profit in so doing. Consequently, a true public good must necessarily be provided by government.

INTERNATIONAL EXAMPLE
Are Lighthouses a Public Good?

One of the most common examples of a public good is a lighthouse. Arguably, it satisfies all the criteria listed in points 1 through 4. In one instance, however, a lighthouse was not a public good in that a collection system was devised and enforced on the basis of how much individuals used it. In the thirteenth century, the city of Aigues-Mortes, a French southern port, erected a tower, called the King's Tower, designed to assert

---

Private goods
Goods that can be consumed by only one individual at a time. Private goods are subject to the principle of rival consumption.

Principle of rival consumption
The recognition that individuals are rivals in consuming private goods because one person's consumption reduces the amount available for others to consume.

Public goods
Goods to which the principle of rival consumption does not apply; they can be jointly consumed by many individuals simultaneously at no additional cost and with no reduction in quality or quantity.

Exclusion principle
The principle that no one can be excluded from the benefits of a public good, even if that person hasn't paid for it.

---

[1]Sometimes the distinction is made between pure public goods, which have all the characteristics we have described here, and quasi- or near-public goods, which do not. The major feature of near-public goods is that they are jointly consumed, even though nonpaying customers can be, and often are, excluded—for example, movies, football games, and concerts.

the will and power of Louis IX (Saint Louis). The 105-foot tower served as a lighthouse for ships. More important, it served as a lookout so that ships sailing on the open sea, but in its view, did not escape paying for use of the lighthouse. Those payments were then used for the construction of the city walls.

FOR CRITICAL ANALYSIS: Explain how a lighthouse satisfies the characteristics of public goods described in points 1, 2, and 3. ●

Free-rider problem
A problem that arises when individuals presume that others will pay for public goods so that, individually, they can escape paying for their portion without causing a reduction in production.

Free Riders. The nature of public goods leads to the **free-rider problem,** a situation in which some individuals take advantage of the fact that others will take on the burden of paying for public goods such as national defense. Free riders will argue that they receive no value from such government services as national defense and therefore really should not pay for it. Suppose that citizens were taxed directly in proportion to how much they tell an interviewer that they value national defense. Some people will probably tell interviewers that they are unwilling to pay for national defense because they don't want any of it—it is of no value to them. Many of us may end up being free riders when we assume that others will pay for the desired public good. We may all want to be free riders if we believe that someone else will provide the commodity in question that we actually value.

The free-rider problem is a definite problem among nations with respect to the international burden of defense and how it should be shared. A country may choose to belong to a multilateral defense organization, such as the North American Treaty Organization (NATO), but then consistently attempt not to contribute funds to the organization. The nation knows it would be defended by others in NATO if it were attacked but would rather not pay for such defense. In short, it seeks a "free ride."

Ensuring Economywide Stability

The government attempts to stabilize the economy by smoothing out the ups and downs in overall business activity. Our economy sometimes faces the problems of unemployment and rising prices. The government, especially the federal government, has made an attempt to solve these problems by trying to stabilize the economy. The notion that the federal government should undertake actions to stabilize business activity is a relatively new idea in the United States, encouraged by high unemployment rates during the Great Depression of the 1930s and subsequent theories about possible ways by which government could reduce unemployment. In 1946, the government passed the Employment Act, a landmark law concerning government responsibility for economic performance. It established three goals for government accountability: full employment, price stability, and economic growth. These goals have provided the justification for many government economic programs during the post–World War II period.

CONCEPTS IN BRIEF

- The economic activities of government include (1) correcting for externalities, (2) providing a judicial system, (3) promoting competition, (4) producing public goods, and (5) ensuring economywide stability.

- Public goods can be consumed jointly. The principle of rival consumption does not apply as it does with private goods.

- Public goods have the following characteristics: (1) They are indivisible; (2) once they are produced, there is no opportunity cost when additional consumers use them; (3) your use of a public good does not deprive others of its simultaneous use; and (4) consumers cannot conveniently be charged on the basis of use.

THE POLITICAL FUNCTIONS OF GOVERNMENT

At least two areas of government are in the realm of political, or normative, functions rather than that of the economic ones discussed in the first part of this chapter. These two areas are (1) the regulation and/or provision of merit and demerit goods and (2) income redistribution.

Merit and Demerit Goods

Certain goods are considered to have special merit. A **merit good** is defined as any good that the political process has deemed socially desirable. (Note that nothing inherent in any particular good makes it a merit good. It is a matter of who chooses.) Some examples of merit goods in our society are museums, ballets, plays, and concerts. In these areas, the government's role is the provision of merit goods to the people in society who would not otherwise purchase them at market clearing prices or who would not purchase an amount of them judged to be sufficient. This provision may take the form of government production and distribution of merit goods. It can also take the form of reimbursement for payment on merit goods or subsidies to producers or consumers for part of the cost of merit goods. Governments do indeed subsidize such merit goods as concerts, ballets, museums, and plays. In most cases, such merit goods would rarely be so numerous without subsidization.

Demerit goods are the opposite of merit goods. They are goods that, through the political process, are deemed socially undesirable. Heroin, cigarettes, gambling, and cocaine are examples. The government exercises its role in the area of demerit goods by taxing, regulating, or prohibiting their manufacture, sale, and use. Governments justify the relatively high taxes on alcohol and tobacco by declaring them demerit goods. The best-known example of governmental exercise of power in this area is the stance against certain psychoactive drugs. Most psychoactives (except nicotine, caffeine, and alcohol) are either expressly prohibited, as is the case for heroin, cocaine, and opium, or heavily regulated, as in the case of prescription psychoactives.

Merit good
A good that has been deemed socially desirable through the political process. Museums are an example.

Demerit good
A good that has been deemed socially undesirable through the political process. Heroin is an example.

Income Redistribution

Another relatively recent political function of government has been the explicit redistribution of income. This redistribution uses two systems: the progressive income tax (described later in this chapter) and *transfer payments*. **Transfer payments** are payments made to individuals for which in return no services or goods are concurrently rendered. The three key money transfer payments in our system are welfare, Social Security, and unemployment insurance benefits. Income redistribution also includes a large amount of income **transfers in kind,** as opposed to money transfers. Some income transfers in kind are food stamps, Medicare and Medicaid, government health care services, and low-cost public housing.

The government has also engaged in other activities as a form of redistribution of income. For example, the provision of public education is at least in part an attempt to redistribute income by making sure that the very poor have access to education.

Transfer payments
Money payments made by governments to individuals for which in return no services or goods are concurrently rendered. Examples are welfare, Social Security, and unemployment insurance benefits.

Transfers in kind
Payments that are in the form of actual goods and services, such as food stamps, low-cost public housing, and medical care, and for which in return no goods or services are rendered concurrently.

CONCEPTS IN BRIEF

- Political, or normative, activities of the government include the provision and regulation of merit and demerit goods and income redistribution.

- Merit and demerit goods do not have any inherent characteristics that qualify them as such; rather, collectively, through the political process, we make judgments about which goods and services are "good" for society and which are "bad."

• Income redistribution can be carried out by a system of progressive taxation, coupled with transfer payments, which can be made in money or in kind, such as food stamps and Medicare.

PAYING FOR THE PUBLIC SECTOR

Jean-Baptiste Colbert, the seventeenth-century French finance minister, said the art of taxation was in "plucking the goose so as to obtain the largest amount of feathers with the least possible amount of hissing." In the United States, governments have designed a variety of methods of plucking the private-sector goose. To analyze any tax system, we must first understand the distinction between marginal tax rates and average tax rates.

Marginal and Average Tax Rates

If somebody says, "I pay 28 percent in taxes," you cannot really tell what that person means unless you know if he or she is referring to average taxes paid or the tax rate on the last dollars earned. The latter concept has to do with the **marginal tax rate.**[2]

The marginal tax rate is expressed as follows:

$$\text{Marginal tax rate} = \frac{\text{change in taxes due}}{\text{change in taxable income}}$$

It is important to understand that the marginal tax rate applies only to the income in the highest **tax bracket** reached, where a tax bracket is defined as a specified level of taxable income to which a specific and unique marginal tax rate is applied.

The marginal tax rate is not the same thing as the **average tax rate,** which is defined as follows:

$$\text{Average tax rate} = \frac{\text{total taxes due}}{\text{total taxable income}}$$

Taxation Systems

No matter how governments raise revenues—from income taxes, sales taxes, or other taxes—all of those taxes can fit into one of three types of taxation systems—proportional, progressive, and regressive, expressing a relationship between the percentage tax, or tax rate, paid and income. To determine whether a tax system is proportional, progressive, or regressive, we simply ask the question, What is the relationship between the average tax rate and the marginal tax rate?

Proportional Taxation. **Proportional taxation** means that regardless of an individual's income, his or her taxes comprise exactly the same proportion. In terms of marginal versus average tax rates, in a proportional taxation system, the marginal tax rate is always equal to the average tax rate. If every dollar is taxed at 20 percent, then the average tax rate is 20 percent, as is the marginal tax rate.

A proportional tax system is also called a *flat-rate tax.* Taxpayers at all income levels end up paying the same *percentage* of their income in taxes. If the proportional tax rate were 20 percent, an individual with an income of $10,000 would pay $2,000 in taxes, while an individual making $100,000 would pay $20,000, the identical 20 percent rate being levied on both.

---

[2]The word *marginal* means "incremental" (or "decremental") here.

Marginal tax rate
The change in the tax payment divided by the change in income, or the percentage of additional dollars that must be paid in taxes. The marginal tax rate is applied to the highest tax bracket of taxable income reached.

Tax bracket
A specified interval of income to which a specific and unique marginal tax rate is applied.

Average tax rate
The total tax payment divided by total income. It is the proportion of total income paid in taxes.

Proportional taxation
A tax system in which regardless of an individual's income, the tax bill comprises exactly the same proportion. Also called a *flat-rate tax.*

Progressive Taxation. Under **progressive taxation,** as a person's taxable income increases, the percentage of income paid in taxes increases. In terms of marginal versus average tax rates, in a progressive system, the marginal tax rate is above the average tax rate. If you are taxed 5 percent on the first $10,000 you make, 10 percent on the next $10,000 you make, and 30 percent on the last $10,000 you make, you face a progressive income tax system. Your marginal tax rate is always above your average tax rate.

Progressive taxation
A tax system in which as income increases, a higher percentage of the additional income is taxed. The marginal tax rate exceeds the average tax rate as income rises.

EXAMPLE
The Most Progressive Tax System of All: College Financial Aid

Strangely enough, it is not a government agency that imposes the most progressive tax system in the United States but rather colleges and universities. Through their financial aid programs, they severely punish parents who earn progressively more income during the years that their children are attending college and receiving financial aid. Starting at very low annual parents' income, most college financial aid departments begin reducing financial aid as parents' incomes rise. This constitutes an implicit additional marginal income tax. In Figure 5-2, you see that federal marginal tax rates start at zero, rise to 19 percent, and then rise again to 32 percent at about $60,000. When one adds the effective impact of the reduction in financial aid for parents in these different tax brackets, the actual marginal tax rate reaches as high as 79 percent. This is because the effective marginal tax rate of losing financial aid as income rises is between 22 and 47 percent, all added on top of local, state, and federal income taxes.

FOR CRITICAL ANALYSIS: What effect do you think this system of college financial aid has on parents' incentive to earn more income while their children are in college? •

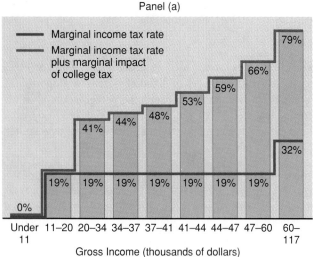

Panel (a)

- Marginal income tax rate
- Marginal income tax rate plus marginal impact of college tax

Gross Income (thousands of dollars)

Panel (b)

- Expected annual parental contribution ($)

Annual Family Income (thousands of dollars)

FIGURE 5-2

College Financial Aid and High Implicit Marginal Income Tax Rates for Parents
Because most college and university financial aid officers decrease aid to students whose families earn more, parents of college-enrolled children face relatively high implicit marginal income tax rates. At an income of $60,000 the actual rate faced is almost 80 percent.

Source: Data from *Forbes,* January 17, 1994, p. 74.

Regressive taxation
A tax system in which as more dollars are earned, the percentage of tax paid on them falls. The marginal tax rate is less than the average tax rate as income rises.

Regressive Taxation. With **regressive taxation,** a smaller percentage of taxable income is taken in taxes as taxable income increases. The marginal rate is *below* the average rate. As income increases, the marginal tax rate falls, and so does the average tax rate. The U.S. Social Security tax is regressive. Once the legislative maximum taxable wage base is reached, no further Social Security taxes are paid. Consider a simplified hypothetical example: Every dollar up to $50,000 is taxed at 10 percent. After $50,000 there is no Social Security tax. Someone making $100,000 still pays only $5,000 in Social Security taxes. That person's average Social Security tax is 5 percent. The person making $50,000, by contrast, effectively pays 10 percent. The person making $1 million faces an average Social Security tax rate of only .5 percent in our simplified example.

CONCEPTS IN BRIEF

- Marginal tax rates are applied to marginal tax brackets, defined as spreads of income over which the tax rate is constant.
- Tax systems can be proportional, progressive, or regressive, depending on whether the marginal tax rate is the same as, greater than, or less than the average tax rate as income rises.

THE MOST IMPORTANT FEDERAL TAXES

The federal government imposes income taxes on both individuals and corporations and collects Social Security taxes and a variety of other taxes.

The Federal Personal Income Tax

The most important tax in the U.S. economy is the federal personal income tax, which accounts for about 41 percent of all federal revenues. All American citizens, resident aliens, and most others who earn income in the United States are required to pay federal income taxes on all taxable income. The rates that are paid rise up to a specified amount, depending on marital status, and then fall, as can be seen in Table 5-1. Marginal income tax rates at the federal level have varied from as low as 1 percent after the passage of the Sixteenth Amendment to as high as 94 percent (reached in 1944). There were 14 separate tax brackets prior to the Tax Reform Act of 1986, which reduced the number to three. Advocates of a more progressive income tax system in the United States argue that such a system redistributes income from the rich to the poor, taxes people according to their ability to pay, and

TABLE 5-1

Federal Marginal Income Tax Rates
These rates became effective in 1996. The highest rate includes a 10 percent surcharge on taxable income above $263,750.

Single Persons		Married Couples	
Marginal Tax Bracket	Marginal Tax Rate	Marginal Tax Bracket	Marginal Tax Rate
$0–$24,000	15%	$0–$40,100	15%
$24,001–$58,150	28%	$40,101–$96,900	28%
$58,151–$121,300	31%	$96,901–$147,700	31%
$121,301–$263,750	36%	$147,701–$263,750	36%
$263,751 and up	39.6%	$263,751 and up	39.6%

Source: U.S. Department of the Treasury.

taxes people according to the benefits they receive from government. Although there is much controversy over the redistributional nature of our progressive tax system, there is no strong evidence that in fact the tax system has never done much income redistribution in this country. Currently, about 85 percent of all Americans, rich or poor, pay roughly the same proportion of their income in federal income taxes.

The Treatment of Capital Gains

The difference between the buying and selling price of an asset, such as a share of stock or a plot of land, is called a **capital gain** if it is a profit and a **capital loss** if it is not. As of the middle of 1996, short-term capital gains were taxed at ordinary income marginal tax rates.

Capital gains are not always real. If you pay $100,000 for a house in one year and sell it for 50 percent more 10 years later, your nominal capital gain is $50,000. But what if, during those 10 years, there had been inflation such that average prices had also gone up by 50 percent? Your *real* capital gain would be zero. But you still have to pay taxes on that $50,000. To counter this problem, many economists have argued that capital gains should be indexed to the rate of inflation. This is exactly what is done with the marginal tax brackets in the federal income tax code. Tax brackets for the purposes of calculating marginal tax rates each year are expanded at the rate of inflation, or the rate at which the average of all prices is rising. So if the rate of inflation is 10 percent, each tax bracket is moved up by 10 percent. The same concept could be applied to capital gains. Thus far, Congress has refused to enact such a measure.

Capital gain
The positive difference between the purchase price and the sale price of an asset. If a share of stock is bought for $5 and then sold for $15, the capital gain is $10.

Capital loss
The negative difference between the purchase price and the sale price of an asset.

The Corporate Income Tax

Corporate income taxes account for about 12 percent of all federal taxes collected and almost 8 percent of all state and local taxes collected. Corporations are generally taxed on the difference between their total revenues (or receipts) and their expenses. The federal corporate income tax structure is given in Table 5-2.

Double Taxation. Because individual stockholders must pay taxes on the dividends they receive, paid out of *after-tax* profits by the corporation, corporate profits are taxed twice. If you receive $1,000 in dividends, you have to declare them as income, and you must pay taxes at your marginal tax rate. Before the corporation was able to pay you those dividends, it had to pay taxes on all its profits, including any that it put back into the company or did not distribute in the form of dividends. Eventually the new investment made possible by those **retained earnings**—profits not given out to stockholders—along with borrowed funds will be reflected in the increased value of the stock in that company. When you sell your stock in that company, you will have to pay taxes on the difference between

Retained earnings
Earnings that a corporation saves, or retains, for investment in other productive activities; earnings that are not distributed to stockholders.

Corporate Taxable Income	Corporate Tax Rate
$0–$50,000	15%
$50,001–$75,000	25%
$75,001–$10,000,000	34%
$10,000,000 and up	35%

Source: Internal Revenue Service.

TABLE 5-2
Federal Corporate Income Tax Schedule
The rates were in effect through 1997.

what you paid for the stock and what you sold it for. In both cases, dividends and retained earnings (corporate profits) are taxed twice.

Who Really Pays the Corporate Income Tax? Corporations can exist only as long as consumers buy their products, employees make their goods, stockholders (owners) buy their shares, and bondholders buy their bonds. Corporations per se do not do anything. We must ask, then, who really pays the tax on corporate income. This is a question of **tax incidence.** (The question of tax incidence applies to all taxes, including sales taxes and Social Security taxes.) There remains considerable debate about the incidence of corporate taxation. Some economists say that corporations pass their tax burdens on to consumers by charging higher prices. Other economists believe that it is the stockholders who bear most of the tax. Still others believe that employees pay at least part of the tax by receiving lower wages than they would otherwise. Because the debate is not yet settled, we will not hazard a guess here as to what the correct conclusion should be. Suffice it to say that you should be cautious when you advocate increasing corporation income taxes. You may be the one who ultimately ends up paying the increase, at least in part, if you own shares in a corporation, buy its products, or work for it.

Tax incidence
The distribution of tax burdens among various groups in society.

CONCEPTS IN BRIEF

- Because corporations must first pay an income tax on most earnings, the personal income tax shareholders pay on dividends received (or realized capital gains) constitutes double taxation.

- The corporate income tax is paid by one or more of the following groups: stockholder-owners, consumers of corporate-produced products, and employees in corporations.

Social Security and Unemployment Taxes

An increasing percentage of federal tax receipts is accounted for each year by taxes (other than income taxes) levied on payrolls. These taxes are for Social Security, retirement, survivors' disability, and old-age medical benefits (Medicare). As of 1996, the Social Security tax was imposed on earnings up to $62,700 at a rate of 6.2 percent on employers and 6.2 percent on employees. That is, the employer matches your "contribution" to Social Security. (The employer's contribution is really paid, at least in part, in the form of a reduced wage rate paid to employees.) A Medicare tax is imposed on all wage earnings at a combined rate of 2.9 percent. These taxes and the base on which they are levied will rise in the next decade. Social Security taxes came into existence when the Federal Insurance Contributions Act (FICA) was passed in 1935.

There is also a federal unemployment tax, which obviously has something to do with unemployment insurance. This tax rate is 0.8 percent on the first $7,000 of annual wages of each employee who earns more than $1,500. Only the employer makes the tax payment. This tax covers the costs of the unemployment insurance system and the costs of employment services. In addition to this federal tax, some states with an unemployment system impose an additional tax of up to about 3 percent, depending on the past record of the particular employer. An employer who frequently lays off workers will have a slightly higher state unemployment tax rate than an employer who never lays off workers.

It has been argued that Social Security is a system in which current workers subsidize already retired workers. It is also argued that the system is not an insurance system because Social Security benefits are legislated by Congress; they are not part of the original Federal Insurance Contributions Act. Therefore, future generations may decide that they do not want to give large Social Security benefits to retired workers. Even if workers had paid large amounts into Social Security, they could conceivably be denied the benefits of a Social Security retirement income.

INTERNATIONAL EXAMPLE
Chile's Privatized Social Security System

Since 1981, Chile has gradually transformed its government-sponsored social security system into a private pension plan. Entrants into the labor force have been required to contribute 10 percent of their gross monthly earnings to private pension fund accounts that they own outright. During this time period, and even today, virtually anyone still in the public social security system can decide to leave it. Those who choose to leave the public system are given a type of bond that is deposited in their new private pension account to be redeemed at retirement. Fully 94 percent of Chile's labor force is enrolled in 20 competing private pension plans.

FOR CRITICAL ANALYSIS: Under what circumstances might American workers choose to "opt out" of the current federal Social Security system if they were offered the same options as Chilean workers? ●

SPENDING, GOVERNMENT SIZE, AND TAX RECEIPTS

The size of the public sector can be measured in many different ways. One way is to count the number of public employees. Another is to look at total government outlays. Government outlays include all of its expenditures on employees, rent, electricity, and the like. In addition, total government outlays include transfer payments, such as welfare and Social Security. In Figure 5-3, you see that government outlays prior to

THINKING CRITICALLY ABOUT THE MEDIA

Social Security

Countless articles have been written about the problem with the Social Security system in America. They all make reference to the employer and employee "contributions" to the Social Security trust fund. One gets the impression that Social Security payments by employees go into a special government account and that employees do not pay for their employers' "contribution" to this account. Both concepts are not merely flawed but grossly misleading. Though there may be an official Social Security trust fund in the accounts of the U.S. government, "contributing" employees simply have no legal claim on the assets of that trust fund. Indeed, they are just commingled with the rest of government taxes collected and spent every year. Social Security "contributions" are not contributions at all; they are merely taxes paid to the federal government. The so-called employer contribution, which matches the employee payments, is not in fact paid for by employers but rather by employees because of the lower wages that they are paid. Anybody who quits a job and becomes self-employed finds this out when the time comes to pay one's self-employment taxes (Social Security "contributions"), which effectively double the payments previously being made as an employee.

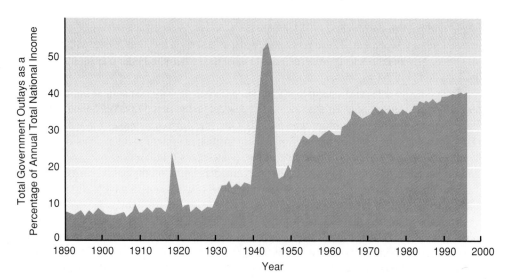

FIGURE 5-3

Total Government Outlays over Time
Here you see that total government outlays (federal, state, and local combined) remained small until the 1930s, except during World War I. Since World War II, government outlays have not fallen back to their historical average.

Sources: Facts and Figures on Government Finance and Economic Indicators, various issues.

Federal

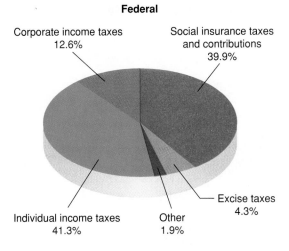

Corporate income taxes
12.6%

Social insurance taxes
and contributions
39.9%

Individual income taxes
41.3%

Other
1.9%

Excise taxes
4.3%

Fiscal Year 1996 Estimate

State and Local

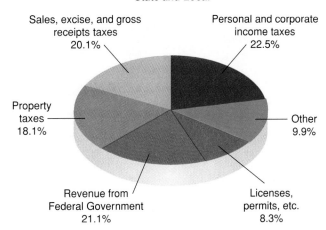

Sales, excise, and gross
receipts taxes
20.1%

Personal and corporate
income taxes
22.5%

Property
taxes
18.1%

Other
9.9%

Revenue from
Federal Government
21.1%

Licenses,
permits, etc.
8.3%

Fiscal Year 1995 Estimate

FIGURE 5-4

Sources of Government Tax Receipts

Over 80 percent of federal revenues come from income and Social Security taxes, whereas state government revenues are spread more evenly across sources, with less emphasis on taxes based on individual income.

Source: U.S. Department of Commerce, Bureau of Economic Analysis.

World War I did not exceed 10 percent of annual national income. There was a spike during World War I, a general increase during the Great Depression, and then a huge spike during World War II. Contrary to previous postwar periods, since World War II government outlays as a percentage of total national income have not gradually fallen but rather have risen fairly regularly.

Government Receipts

The main revenue raiser for all levels of government is taxes. We show in the two pie diagrams in Figure 5-4 the percentage of receipts from various taxes obtained by the federal government and by state and local governments.

The Federal Government.   The largest source of receipts for the federal government is the individual income tax. It accounts for 41.3 percent of all federal revenues. After that come social insurance taxes and contributions (Social Security), which account for 36.9 percent of total revenues. Next come corporate income taxes and then a number of other items, such as taxes on imported goods and excise taxes on such things as gasoline and alcoholic beverages.

State and Local Governments.   As can be seen in Figure 5-4, there is quite a bit of difference between the origin of receipts for state and local governments and for the federal government. Personal and corporate income taxes account for only 22.5 percent of total state and local revenues. There are even a number of states that collect no personal income tax. The largest source of state and local receipts is from property taxes (used by local government), sales taxes (used mainly by state governments), and corporate income taxes.

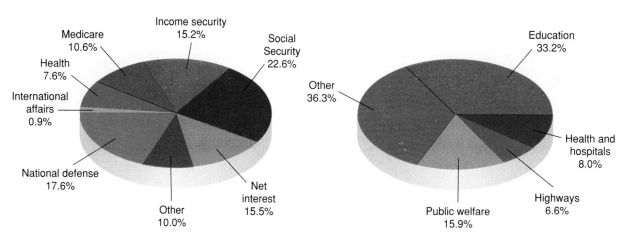

FIGURE 5-5

Federal Government Spending Compared to State and Local Spending

The federal government's spending habits are quite different from those of the states and cities. On the left you can see that the categories of most importance in the federal budget are defense, income security, and Social Security, which make up 55.4 percent. The most important category at the state and local level is education, which makes up 33.2 percent.

Sources: Budget of the United States Government; Government Finances.

Comparing Federal with State and Local Spending. A typical federal government budget is given in Figure 5-5. The largest three categories are defense, income security, and Social Security, which together constitute 55.4 percent of the total federal budget.

The makeup of state and local expenditures is quite different. Education is the biggest category, accounting for 33.2 percent of all expenditures.

CONCEPTS IN BRIEF

• Total government outlays including transfers have continued to grow since World War II and now account for about 40 percent of yearly total national output.

• Government spending at the federal level is different from that at the state and local levels. At the federal level, defense, income security, and Social Security account for about 55 percent of the federal budget. At the state and local levels, education comprises 33 percent of all expenditures.

Should We Switch to a Flat Tax?

Concepts Applied: *Average versus marginal tax rates, opportunity cost, progressive income tax system*

Each year, American taxpayers spend numerous hours preparing their taxes or hire accountants to do so for them. Switching to a national sales tax, one alternative to our current system, would eliminate the Internal Revenue Service and all of the expenses associated with that organization.

Since the enactment of the federal income tax, Americans have faced a progressive system. The top marginal tax rate soared to 94 percent in 1944, dropped to 92 percent in 1952, dropped again to 91 percent in 1954, and settled in at 50 percent starting in 1982. The Tax Reform Act of 1986 and other acts lowered it to 28 percent in 1988; today it stands at about 40 percent. The idea behind a progressive tax system is that the "rich" should pay more. In actuality, what happens is quite a different story. In Figure 5-6 on page 112, you see that regardless of what the top tax rate is, the federal government obtains around 20 percent of a nation's annual income as tax revenues.

Why? Because people respond to incentives. At high marginal tax rates, the following occurs: (1) Rich people hire more tax lawyers and accountants to help them figure out loopholes in the tax system to avoid high marginal tax rates; (2) some people change their investments to take advantage of loopholes that allow them to pay lower marginal tax rates; (3) some people drop out of the labor force, particularly secondary income earners, such as lower-paid working women; and (4) more people engage in off-the-books "underground" activities for cash on which no income taxes are paid.

An Alternative: The Flat Tax

For decades, many economists have argued in favor of scrapping our progressive income tax system and replacing

it with a so-called flat tax. Several members of Congress and presidential candidates praised the approach as well. The idea behind a flat tax is simple. To calculate what you owe, simply subtract the appropriate exemption from your income and multiply the rest by the flat tax, say, 20 percent. For example, a family of four might be able to earn as much as $25,000 or $35,000 a year before it paid any income tax. The major benefits of such a system, according to its advocates, would be the following: (1) fewer resources devoted to figuring out one's taxes, (2) fewer tax attorneys and accountants, who could then be engaged in more productive activities; (3) higher saving and investment; and (4) more economic growth. According to Professor Dale Jorgenson of Harvard University, switching from our current progressive tax system to a flat tax would add about $2.5 trillion to today's current annual national income. Opponents of a flat tax argue that (1) federal revenues will fall and the federal budget deficit will rise; (2) homeowners will no longer get the benefit of deducting their mortgage interest payments from income before taxes are calculated; and (3) the rich will pay few taxes.

Another Alternative: A National Sales Tax

Alternatively, we could apply some form of a national sales tax in place of the current income tax. Such a national sales tax could be in the form of a *value-added tax (VAT)*, which is common throughout Europe. A value-added tax is assessed on the value added by a firm at each stage of production. It is a tax on the value of products that firms sell minus the value of the materials that it bought and used to produce the products. Such a tax is collected by all businesses and remitted directly to the federal government. One of the major benefits of a national sales tax is that it would greatly reduce the Internal Revenue Service and the expenses associated with that organization. A national sales tax or a value-added tax of, say, 15 to 20 percent in lieu of a federal income tax would be quite similar to a consumption tax.

A Consumption Tax

With a *consumption tax,* taxpayers pay taxes only on what they consume (spend) out of income, not what they

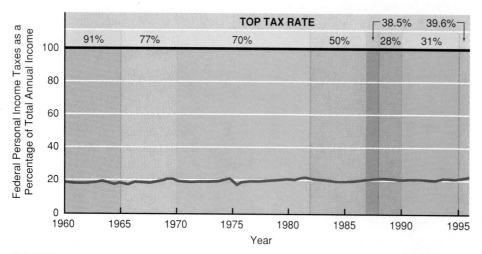

FIGURE 5-6

Changing Maximum Marginal Income Tax Rates and Revenues Collected
At the top of the diagram, you can see listed the top marginal tax rates from 1960 to the present. On the side is the percentage of total annual income collected by the federal government from the income tax system. No matter how high the marginal income tax rate has been, the government has collected about the same percentage of national income in taxes.

Source: Internal Revenue Service.

earn. One way to determine such consumption in any year is simply to subtract what is saved from what is earned. The difference is consumption, and that is the base to which a consumption tax would apply. (A consumption tax is actually equivalent to a national sales tax on all goods and services purchased.) In essence, a consumption tax provides an unlimited deduction for saving. As such, it encourages more saving. As you learned in Chapter 2, the less people choose to consume today, the faster the production possibilities curve will shift outward to the right, leading to more economic growth. Professor Lawrence J. Kitlikoff of Boston University estimated that a switch to a national sales tax or a consumption tax would generate a 27 percent greater capital stock over the 20 years following the introduction of such a system.

What About Fairness?

Every time a new tax system is discussed, the issue of fairness arises. Is it fair, as with a flat federal income tax, that everybody pay the same marginal tax rate, no matter how much he or she earns? Stephen Entin of the Institute for Research on the Economics of Taxation thinks it is:

"It is hard to find a definition of 'fairness' more compelling than the idea that every citizen is treated equally." What about a national sales tax, which might be regressive because the poor spend a larger portion of their income than the rich? Is that a "fair" system? For most economists, these are difficult questions, because they are in the realm of the normative, the value-laden. We can point out that an examination of the evidence shows what reality is. Simply stated, when marginal income tax rates are high, the rich do not, in fact, pay a higher average tax rate than when marginal tax rates are lower. It behooves the rich to find methods to reduce tax liabilities and to expend resources to influence members of Congress to insert an increasing number of loopholes in the Internal Revenue Code in order to reduce effective marginal tax rates on those who earn a lot.

FOR CRITICAL ANALYSIS
1. Do you think employees in the Internal Revenue Service would be for or against the flat-tax system? Explain your choice.
2. Why is a flat-tax system more efficient than a progressive income tax system?

CHAPTER SUMMARY

1. Government can correct external costs through taxation, legislation, and prohibition. It can correct external benefits through financing or production of a good or service, subsidies, and regulation.
2. Government provides a legal system in which the rights of private ownership, the enforcement of contracts, and the legal status of businesses are provided. In other words, government sets the legal rules of the game and enforces them.
3. Public goods, once produced, can be consumed jointly by additional individuals at zero opportunity cost.
4. If users of public goods know that they will be taxed on the basis of their expressed valuation of those public goods, their expressed valuation will be low. They expect to get a free ride.
5. Merit goods (chosen as such, collectively, through the political process) may not be purchased at all or not in sufficient quantities at market clearing prices. Therefore, government subsidizes or provides such

merit goods at a subsidized or zero price to specified classes of consumers.
6. When it is collectively decided that something is a demerit good, government taxes, regulates, or prohibits the manufacture, sale, and use of that good.
7. Marginal tax rates are those paid on the last dollars of income, whereas average taxes rates are determined by the proportion of income paid in income taxes.
8. With a proportional income tax system, marginal rates are constant. With a regressive system, they go down as income rises, and with a progressive system, they go up as income rises.
9. Total government outlays including transfers have continued to grow since World War II and now account for about 40 percent of yearly total national output.
10. Government spending at the federal level is different from that at the state and local levels. Defense, income security, and Social Security account for about 55 percent of the federal budget.

DISCUSSION OF PREVIEW QUESTIONS

1. **What problems will you encounter if you refuse to pay a portion of your income tax because you oppose national defense spending?**

   You must share in national defense collectively with the rest of the country. Unlike private goods, national defense is a public good and must be consumed collectively. You receive national defense benefits whether you choose to or not; the exclusion principle does not work for public goods, such as national defense. The government could make the exclusion principle work better by deporting you to foreign shores if you don't wish to pay for national defense. This is typically not done. If you were allowed to forgo taxes allocated to national defense, the IRS would be swamped with similar requests. Everyone would have an incentive to claim no benefits from national defense (whether true or not) because it must be consumed collectively. So, if you refuse, you may go to jail.

2. **Will you benefit from many so-called tax loopholes when you first start working?**

   Probably not, for you will not be making enough income to put you into the highest marginal income tax bracket. Tax loopholes are more beneficial the more they save you in taxes. At low incomes, your marginal tax rate is low, so each dollar in tax saved because of your use of a tax loophole yields you very little additional after-tax income. If you're in the 15 percent marginal tax bracket, you only benefit by 15 cents for every dollar in tax loopholes you find. Compare this to the benefit for someone in the 39.6 percent marginal tax bracket.

3. **In what ways do regressive, proportional, and progressive tax structures differ?**

   Under a regressive tax structure, the average tax rate (the percentage of income paid in taxes) falls as income rises. The marginal tax rate is below the average tax rate. Proportional tax structures are those in which the average tax rate remains constant as income rises; the marginal tax rate equals the average tax rate. Under a progressive tax structure, the average tax rate rises as income rises; the marginal tax rate is above the average tax rate. Our federal personal income tax system is an example of a progressive system.

4. Who pays the corporate income tax?

Ultimately, only people can be taxed. As a consequence, corporate taxes are ultimately paid by people: corporate owners (in the form of reduced dividends and less stock appreciation for stockholders), consumers of corporate products (in the form of higher prices for goods), and/or employees working for corporations (in the form of lower wages).

PROBLEMS

(Answers to the odd-numbered problems appear at the back of the book.)

5-1. Consider the following system of taxation, which has been labeled *degressive*. The first $5,000 of income is not taxed. After that, all income is assessed at 20 percent (a proportional system). What is the marginal tax rate on $3,000 of taxable income? $10,000? $100,000? What is the average tax rate on $3,000? $10,000? $100,000? What is the maximum average tax rate?

5-2. You are offered two possible bonds to buy as part of your investing program. One is a corporate bond yielding 9 percent. The other is a tax-exempt municipal bond yielding only 6 percent. Assuming that you are certain you will be paid your interest and principal on these two bonds, what marginal tax bracket must you be in to decide in favor of the tax-exempt bond?

5-3. Consider the following tax structure:

Income Bracket	Marginal Tax Rate
$0–$1,500	0%
$1,501–$2,000	14%
$2,001–$3,000	20%

Mr. Smith has an income of $2,500 per annum. Calculate his tax bill for the year. What is his average tax rate? His highest marginal tax rate?

5-4. Assume that Social Security tax payments on wages are 7.65 percent of wages, on wages up to $51,300. No *further* Social Security payments are made on earnings above this figure. Calculate the *average* Social Security tax rate for annual wages of (a) $4,000, (b) $51,300, (c) $56,000, (d) $100,000. Is this Social Security system a progressive, proportional, or regressive tax structure?

5-5. Briefly, what factors could be included as part of the requirements for a "good" tax structure?

5-6. What is meant by the expression "market failure"?

5-7. Is local police protection a public good? Explain.

5-8. TV signals have characteristics of public goods, yet TV stations and commercial networks are private businesses. Analyze this situation.

5-9. Assume that you live in a relatively small suburban neighborhood called Parkwood. The Parkwood Homeowners' Association collects money from homeowners to pay for upkeep of the surrounding stone wall, lighting at the entrances to Parkwood, and mowing the lawn around the perimeter of the area. Each year you are asked to donate $50. No one forces you to do it. There are 100 homeowners in Parkwood.

a. What percentage of the total yearly revenue of the homeowners' association will you account for?

b. At what level of participation will the absence of your $50 contribution make a difference?

c. If you do not contribute your $50, are you really receiving a totally free ride?

5-10. Assume that the only textile firm that exists has created a negative externality by polluting a nearby stream with the wastes associated with production. Assume further that the government can measure the external costs to the community with accuracy and charges the firm for its pollution, based on the social cost of pollution per unit of textile output. Show how such a charge will lead to a higher selling price for textiles and a reduction in the equilibrium quantity of textiles.

5-11. Label two columns on your paper "Private Goods" and "Public Goods." List each of the following under the heading that describes it better.

a. Sandwich
b. Public television
c. Cable television
d. National defense
e. Shirt
f. Elementary education
g. College education
h. Health clinic flu shots
i. Opera
j. Museum
k. Automobile

COMPUTER-ASSISTED INSTRUCTION

The decisions made by people in the government (bureaucrats) and people in the private sector often differ because of the different constraints they face. We show the impact of this on innovation in the ethical drug industry.

Complete problem and answer appear on disk.

INTERACTING WITH THE INTERNET

For both detailed and summary information on the U.S. federal budget, see
> **gopher://sunny.stat-usa.gov/11/BudgetFY96**

(Future budgets should have a similar name.) It also includes extensive historical and projected future information. Of particular interest is "A Citizen's Guide to the Federal Budget." At
> **http://www.ssa.gov/**

you can find material on the Social Security System; it is oriented toward both recipients and people interested in how the system works. The Justice Department can be accessed at
> **http://www.usdoj.gov/**

and the Federal Trade Commission (FTC) at
> **http://www.ftc.gov/**

CHAPTER **6**

ECONOMIES IN TRANSITION

If you visit one of the thousands upon thousands of hilly fields in Peru, you will likely meet a peasant family. That family probably has been tilling the soil in the same spot for decades. Most of these families eke out an existence. Very few of them could, if they wanted to, sell the land they have been tilling for so many years to pursue an alternative line of work. To understand why this is so in Peru requires a grasp of the changes that are occurring in the world's economies in transition.

PREVIEW QUESTIONS

1. Why does the scarcity problem force all societies to answer the questions *what, how,* and *for whom?*

2. How can economies be classified?

3. Why do we say that *all* economies are mixed economies?

4. What are the "three *Ps*" of pure capitalism?

You Know That . . . there used to be a country called the Soviet Union whose
f of state in 1960 took off his shoe at the United Nations and pounded it on the
shouting, "We will bury you"? That person was Nikita Khrushchev; he died in
k quite a few more years for his country to die, but die it did. The Soviet Union
he 74-year experiment in trying to run an economy without using the price, or
will go down in history as one of the greatest social and economic failures
because the Soviet Union dissolved itself at the end of 1991 does not mean
rld economy automatically became like that of the United States. In par-
iblics of the former Soviet Union, the Soviet "satellite" countries of East-
er nations, including China, are what we call *economies in transition.*
ne, every nation has its own **economic system,** which can be defined
eans through which resources are used to satisfy human wants. No
nal means—marketplace or government—a nation chooses to use,
questions must always be answered.

Economic system
The institutional means through
which resources are used to
satisfy human wants.

Resource allocation
The assignment of resources to
specific uses by determining
what will be produced, how it
will be produced, and for whom
it will be produced.

THE THREE BASIC ECONOMIC QUESTIONS

In every nation, no matter what the form of government, what the type of economic system,
who is running the government, or how poor or rich it is, three basic economic questions
must be answered. They concern the problem of **resource allocation,** which is simply how
resources are to be allocated. As such, resource allocation answers the three basic economic
questions of *what, how,* and *for whom* goods and services will be produced.

1. *What and how much will be produced?* Literally billions of different things could be
   produced with society's scarce resources. Some mechanism must exist that causes
   some things to be produced and others to remain as either inventors' pipe dreams or
   individuals' unfulfilled desires.
2. *How will it be produced?* There are many ways to produce a desired item. It is possible to use more labor and less capital or vice versa. It is possible to use more unskilled
   labor and fewer units of skilled labor. Somehow, in some way, a decision must be made
   as to the particular mix of inputs, the way they should be organized, and how they are
   brought together at a particular place.
3. *For whom will it be produced?* Once a commodity is produced, who should get it? In
   a market economy, individuals and businesses purchase commodities with money
   income. The question then is what mechanism there is to distribute income, which then
   determines how commodities are distributed throughout the economy.

THE PRICE SYSTEM AND HOW IT ANSWERS
THE THREE ECONOMIC QUESTIONS

As explained in Chapter 4, a price (or market) system is an economic system in which (relative) prices are constantly changing to reflect changes in supply and demand for different
commodities. In addition, the prices of those commodities are the signals to everyone within the system as to what is relatively scarce and what is relatively abundant. Indeed, it is the
signaling aspect of the price system that provides the information to buyers and sellers
about what should be bought and what should be produced. The price system, which is
characteristic of a market economy, is only one possible way to organize society.

What and How Much Will Be Produced?

In a price system, the interaction of demand and supply for each good determines what and how much to produce. Note, however, that if the highest price that consumers are willing to pay is less than the lowest cost at which a good can be produced, output will be zero. That doesn't mean that the price system has failed. Today consumers do not purchase their own private space shuttles. The demand is not high enough in relation to the supply to create a market. But it may be someday.

How Will It Be Produced?

The question of how output will be produced in a price system relates to the efficient use of scarce inputs. Consider the possibility of using only two types of resources, capital and labor. A firm may have the options given in Table 6-1. It can use various combinations of labor and capital to produce the same amount of output. Two hypothetical combinations are given in the table. How, then, is it decided which combination should be used? In the price system, the **least-cost combination** (technique B in our example) will in fact be chosen because it maximizes profits. We assume that the owners of business firms act as if they are maximizing profits. Recall from Chapter 1 that we assume that individuals act *as if* they are rational.

Least-cost combination
The level of input use that produces a given level of output at minimum cost.

In a price system, competition *forces* firms to use least-cost production techniques. Any firm that fails to employ the least costly technique will find that other firms can undercut its price. In other words, other firms that choose the least-cost production technique will be able to offer the product at a lower price and still make a profit. This lower price will induce consumers to shift purchases from the higher-priced firm to the lower-priced firm. Inefficient firms will be forced out of business.

For Whom Will It Be Produced?

This last question that every economic system must answer involves who gets what. In a market system, the choice about what is purchased is made by individuals, but that choice is determined by the ability to pay. Who gets what is determined by the distribution of money income.

Determination of Money Income. In a price system, a consumer's ability to pay for consumer products is based on the size of that consumer's money income. That in turn depends on the quantities, qualities, and types of the various human and nonhuman resources that the individual owns and supplies to the marketplace. It also depends on the prices, or payments, for those resources. When you are selling your human resources as labor

---

TABLE 6-1

Production Costs for 100 Units of Product X
Technique A or B can be used to produce the same output. Obviously, B will be used because its total cost is less than A's. Using production technique B will generate a $2 savings for every 100 units produced.

		A		B	
Inputs	Input Unit Price	Production Technique A (input units)	Cost	Production Technique B (input units)	Cost
Labor	$10	5	$50	4	$40
Capital	8	4	32	5	40
Total cost of 100 units			82		80

services, your money income is based on the wages you can earn in the labor market. If you own nonhuman resources—physical capital and land, for example—the level of interest and rents that you are paid for your physical capital and land will clearly influence the size of your money income and thus your ability to buy consumer products.

Which Consumers Get What? In a price system, the distribution of finished products to consumers is based on consumers' ability and willingness to pay the market price for the product. If the market price of compact discs is $9, consumers who are able and willing to pay that price will get those CDs. All others won't.

Here we are talking about the *rationing* function of market prices in a price system. Rather than have a central political figure or agency decide which consumers will get which goods, those consumers who are willing and able to pay the market price obtain the goods. That is to say, relative prices ration the available resources, goods, and services at any point in time among those who place the highest value on those items. If scarcity didn't exist, we would not need any system to ration available resources, goods, and services. All of us could have all of everything that we wanted without taking away from what anyone else obtained.

CONCEPTS IN BRIEF

- Any economic system must answer three questions: (1) *What* will be produced? (2) *How* will it be produced? (3) *For whom* will it be produced?

- In a price system, supply and demand determine the prices at which exchanges take place.

- In a price system, firms choose the least-cost combination use of inputs to produce any given output. Competition forces firms to do so.

- In a price system, who gets what is determined by consumers' money income and choices about how to use that money income.

TODAY'S INCREASINGLY ALL-CAPITALIST WORLD

Communism
In its purest form, an economic system in which the state has disappeared and individuals contribute to the economy according to their productivity and are given income according to their needs.

Socialism
An economic system in which the state owns the major share of productive resources except labor. Socialism also usually involves the redistribution of income.

Capitalism
An economic system in which individuals own productive resources; these individuals can use the resources in whatever manner they choose, subject to common protective legal restrictions.

Not long ago, textbooks presented a range of economic systems, usually capitalism, socialism, and communism. **Communism** was intended as a system in which the state disappeared and individuals contributed to the economy according to their productivity and received income according to their needs. Under **socialism,** the state owned a major share of productive resources except labor. **Capitalism** has been defined as a system under which individuals hold government-protected private property rights to all goods, including those used in production, and their own labor.

Pure Capitalism in Theory

In its purest theoretical form, market capitalism, or pure capitalism, has the following attributes:

1. Private property rights exist and are upheld by the judicial system.
2. Prices are allowed to seek their own level as determined by the forces of supply and demand. In this sense, pure capitalism is a price system.
3. Resources, including human labor, are free to move in and out of industries and geographic locations. The movement of resources follows the lure of profits—higher expected profits create an incentive for more resources to go where those profits might occur.

4. Risk takers are rewarded by higher profits, but those whose risks turn out to be bad business decisions suffer the consequences directly in terms of reduced wealth.

5. Decisions about what and how much should be produced, how it should be produced, and for whom it should be produced are left to the market. In a pure market capitalist system, all decisions are decentralized and made by individuals in a process of *spontaneous coordination* throughout the economy.

One way to remember the attributes of pure capitalism is by thinking of the three *P*s: prices, profits, and private property.

The role of government is limited to provision of certain public goods, such as defense, police protection, and a legal framework within which property rights and contracts are enforced.

Pure capitalism has also been called a **laissez-faire** system. The French term means "leave [it] alone" or "let [it] be." A pure capitalist system is one in which the government lets the economic actors in the economy make their own decisions without government constraints.

Laissez-faire
French for "leave [it] alone"; applied to an economic system in which the government minimizes its interference with the economy.

The Importance of Incentives

Though it is doubtful that full-blown communism ever really existed or could survive in a whole economy, various forms of socialism, in which the state owned important parts of the economy, have existed. Indeed, one can argue that the most important distinguishing feature between capitalist countries and everywhere else is the lack of private property rights. Economics predicts that, for example, when an apartment building is owned by no one (that is, owned by the "state"), there is less incentive for anyone to take care of it. This analysis has predicted well with respect to public housing in the United States. Just imagine an entire country for which all housing is public housing. That is what the former Soviet Union was like. (Note that we are not passing judgment on a system that has few private property rights. Rather, we are simply pointing out the predictions that economists can make with respect to how individuals treat such property.)

We pointed out in Chapter 4 that in a world of scarcity, resources must always be rationed. In economic systems in which prices were not allowed to be the rationing device, other methods had to be used. In the former Soviet Union, rationing by queuing (waiting) was one of the most prevalent. Some economists estimated that the average Russian spent as many hours a week waiting in lines as the average American spends watching television.

Today one might say that the collapse of communism has left the world with one system only, the **mixed economy,** in which decisions about how resources are used are made partly by the private sector and partly by the public sector—capitalism with government. Figure 6-1 represents the size of government relative to annual national output. You can see that even among the traditional capitalist countries of the world, there are great variations. These can be regarded as the different faces of capitalism.

Mixed economy
An economic system in which decisions about how resources should be used are made partly by the private sector and partly by the government, or the public sector.

CONCEPTS IN BRIEF

• Communism is an economic system in which, in theory, individuals would produce according to their abilities and consume according to their needs. Under socialism, the state owns most major capital goods and attempts to redistribute income.

• Pure capitalism allows for the spontaneous coordination of millions of individuals by allowing the free play of the three *P*s—prices, profits, and property rights. Often, pure capitalism is called a laissez-faire system.

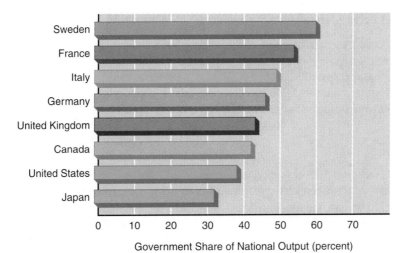

FIGURE 6-1

Percentage of National Yearly Output Accounted for by Government in Various Countries
Even among countries that have embraced capitalism for a long time, government plays an important, but widely different, role. It constitutes over 60 percent of the economy in Sweden, but less than 40 percent in the United States.

- Incentives matter in any economic system; therefore, in countries that have had few or unenforced property rights, individuals lacked the incentives to take care of most property that wasn't theirs.

- Most economies today can be viewed as mixed in that they combine private decisions and government controls.

THE DIFFERENT FACES OF CAPITALISM

The world is left with a single economic system that, thanks to the diversity of human cultures, has a variety of faces. Table 6-2 presents one way to categorize today's economic systems.

TABLE 6-2

Four Faces of Capitalism

Type of Capitalism	Examples	Characteristics	Problem Areas
Consumer	Canada, United States, New Zealand, Australia, United Kingdom	Borders are relatively open; focus is on profit maximization and laissez-faire.	Low saving and investment rates; income inequality
Producer	Japan, France, Germany	Production is emphasized over consumption; employment is a major policy issue; state controls a relatively large part of the economy.	Consumer dissatisfaction; potential slow future growth rates; inertia within the economy
Family	Indonesia, Malaysia, Thailand, Taiwan	Extended clans dominate business and capital flows.	Lack of modern corporate organizations; lack of money markets
Frontier	Russia, China, Ukraine, Romania, Albania	Many government enterprises pursue for-profit activities; new entrepreneurs emerge every day.	Difficulty of crossing borders; rising criminal activity

Source: Based on, in part, "21st Century Capitalism," *Business Week,* February 23, 1995, p. 19.

THE TRANSITIONAL PHASE: FRONTIER CAPITALISM

Frontier capitalism describes economies in transition from state ownership and control of most of the factors of production to a system of private property rights in which the price system is used to answer the basic economic questions. Table 6-3 presents theoretical stages in the development of frontier capitalism. Two aspects appear to be the most important: developing the legal system and selling off state-owned businesses.

Development of the Legal System

In the United States and many other countries, we take a well-established legal system as a given. That does not imply the total absence of a legal system in countries where we are now seeing frontier capitalism. To be sure, the former Soviet Union had a legal system, but virtually none of it had to do with economic transactions, which were carried out by state dictates. Individuals could not own the factors of production, and therefore, by definition, there were no legal disputes over property rights involving them. Consequently, the legal system in the former Soviet Union and its Eastern European satellites consisted of many volumes of criminal codes—laws against robbery, murder, rape, and theft as well as so-called economic crimes.

Enter the new world of private property rights and unfettered exchange of those rights among buyers and sellers. Now what happens when a buyer claims that a seller breached a particular agreement? In the United States, lawyers, courts, and the Uniform Commercial Code can be used to settle the dispute. Yet until recently in the frontier economies of the former Soviet Union, there was nothing even vaguely comparable. The rule of law in the United States and Great Britain has developed over hundreds of years; we cannot expect that in countries in transition toward full capitalism, an entire body of law and procedure can be developed overnight.

Privatization

The transition toward capitalism requires that the government lessen its role in the economy. This transition involves what has become known as *privatization*. **Privatization** is the transfer of ownership or responsibility for businesses run by the government, so-called *state enterprises,* to individuals and companies in the private sector. Even in capitalist countries, the government has owned and run various parts of the economy. During and after World War II, it became fashionable for many European governments to "nationalize" different industries. This was particularly prevalent in the United Kingdom, where the steel industry was nationalized, for example. In the early 1980s, France nationalized the banking industry. The opposite of nationalization is privatization.

In the early 1980s, Turkey and Chile were the first capitalist countries to start carrying out mass privatization of government-owned businesses. Under Margaret Thatcher, the United Kingdom pioneered the mass privatization of state industry, including the huge road haulage company (NFC), a health care group (Amersham International), British Telecom, British Petroleum, and British Aerospace.

A country must employ some method to put government-owned businesses into the hands of the private sector; government-owned businesses are not simply given away to the first party who asks. Imagine if the U.S. government said that it wanted to sell the United States Postal Service. How would it do so? One way is to sell it outright, but there might not be any buyers who would be willing to pay to take over such a giant money-losing corporation. An alternative would involve selling shares of stock to anyone who wanted to buy

Privatization
The sale or transfer of state-owned property and businesses to the private sector, in part or in whole. Also refers to *contracting out*—letting private business take over government-provided services such as trash collection.

TABLE 6-3
How Frontier Capitalism Develops

Stage	Characteristics
I	The central government, as the controller of all economic activities, collapses and starts to disappear. The black market, typically involving government enterprises still owned by the state, expands enormously. Many former state factory managers and other bosses become involved in criminal activities using the state's resources. Government corruption flourishes more than before.
II	Small businesses start to flourish. Families pool funds in order to become entrepreneurs. The rules of commerce are not well understood because there is not yet a well-established commercial law system, nor are property rights well defined or protected by the state.
III	The economy is growing, but much of its growth is not measured by government statisticians. Small financial markets, such as stock markets, begin to develop. Foreigners cautiously invest in the new stock markets. The government attempts to develop a clear set of commercial laws.
IV	Foreign corporations are more willing to invest directly in new factories and stores. The state gets serious about selling all businesses that it owns. More resources are devoted to suppressing criminal activity. Commercial law becomes better established and better understood.

them at the stated price. This latter technique is indeed the way in which most privatizations have been carried out in established capitalist countries throughout the world over the past 15 or 20 years.

In the former Soviet Union and in Eastern Europe, alternative systems have been devised. For example, citizens, at various times, have been given vouchers granting them the right to purchase a specified number of shares in particular government-owned companies that were being sold off.

The trend in privatization versus nationalization can be seen in panel (a) of Figure 6-2 on page 124. The cumulative worldwide sales of state-owned enterprises can be seen in panel (b). In Europe, privatization will probably continue at the rate of over $50 billion a year into the next century. Privatization in Latin America will continue much longer. Finally, because privatization in the former Soviet Union and Eastern Europe has in a sense just begun, such wholesale privatization may take a long time indeed.

Political Opposition to Privatization

There is often strong political pressure to slow down or even prevent privatization of state-owned businesses. The political pressure to prevent privatization is derived from simple economics: Managers of state-owned businesses typically have had lifetime job security, better working conditions than they could obtain elsewhere, and little threat of competition. In other words, life for a manager is typically better in a state-owned firm than in that same firm once it has been privatized.

Workers in state-run firms also believe, often rightly, that their lot in life will not be quite so good if the state-owned firm is sold to the private sector. State-owned firms tend to pay their workers higher wages and give them better fringe benefits, including much better pension plans, than similar firms that are privately owned. For example, an examination of state-owned phone companies in France and Germany shows that they have two to three

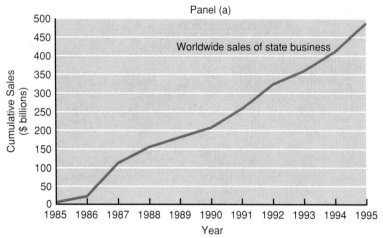

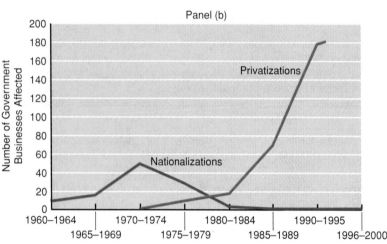

FIGURE 6-2

The Trend Toward Privatization
Privatization worldwide has been on the
upswing since 1985, as shown in panel (a).
Nationalizations (the opposite of privatizations)
reached their peak in about 1970 as is shown
in panel (b).
Source: OECD and *The Economist*, August 21,
1993, p. 19.

times as many workers per telephone customer as the private telephone companies in the
United States. This comparative overuse of labor in state-owned firms is even more obvious in the republics of the former Soviet Union and in Eastern Europe.

Economists cannot say whether privatization of state-owned firms is good or bad.
Rather, economists can simply state that the rigors of a competitive market will generally
cause resources to be used more efficiently after privatization occurs. In the process, however, some managers and workers may be made worse off.

Is There a Right Way to Go About the Transition?

Ever since the fall of the Berlin Wall in 1989, economists have debated whether there is a
"right" way for former socialist and communist countries to move toward capitalist systems. The once-communist nations have, indeed, embarked on a social experiment in how
to move toward a market economy. Basically, they have chosen two methods—a slow one
and a fast one. Romania, Russia, and Ukraine have only gradually privatized their economies, whereas the Czech Republic and, to a lesser extent, Poland and Estonia opted for a
"shock treatment."

The rapid move toward a market economy, though not free of problems, has seemed to
work better than the go-slow approach. The slower the transition occurs, the more the former

entrenched bureaucrats in the state-owned businesses have been able to maintain their power over the use of resources. In the meantime, the state-owned businesses continue to use valuable resources inefficiently in these developing countries.

In contrast, a country like the Czech Republic used a voucher system to privatize over 2,000 state-owned enterprises. All citizens were given vouchers—legal rights evidenced on printed certificates—which could be used to purchase shares of stock in state-owned businesses. A stock market quickly developed in which shares of hundreds of companies are now traded every day. After an initial period of transition to a market economy, the Czech Republic has now achieved one of the lowest unemployment rates in Europe.

We will next examine the current situation of two of the largest countries in the world that are in the throes of frontier capitalism. Both are grappling with the problems of the transition from communism to capitalism.

CONCEPTS IN BRIEF

- Today there are four types of capitalism: consumer, producer, family, and frontier. The last begins when a centralized economy starts collapsing and black markets thrive. Eventually small businesses flourish, and then financial markets develop. Finally, foreign investment is attracted, and state-owned businesses are privatized.

- The development of a well-functioning legal system is one of the most difficult problems for an economy in the frontier capitalism stage. Such economies do not have the laws or courts to handle the new system of property right transfers.

- Privatization, or the turning over to the private sector of state-owned and state-run businesses, is occurring all over the world in all types of economies. There is much political opposition, however, whenever managers in soon-to-be privatized businesses realize that they may face harder times in a private setting.

RUSSIA AND ITS FORMER SATELLITES, YESTERDAY AND TODAY

Russia was the largest republic in the former Soviet Union. The economic system in place was at times called communism and at other times called command socialism. There is no question that it was a command economy in which there was centralized economic leadership and planning. All economies involve planning, of course; the difference is that in capitalist societies, most of the planning is done by private businesses rather than the government. Leaders in the former Soviet Union somehow believed that its economic planners in Moscow could micromanage an economy spanning 11 time zones, involving millions and millions of consumers and producers, and affecting vast quantities of goods and services.

Imagine trying to run a single business that big! No one can. Perhaps more important, state ownership in such a large country resulted in perverse incentives throughout the economy. For example, when the government issued production quotas for glass based on the number of panes, they ended up being almost paper thin and shattering easily. When the government then changed its quotas to weight, the glass panes were so thick that they were useless. In short, former Soviet citizens responded appropriately every time central planners figured out a new way to set production quotas. In the process, untold resources were inefficiently used or completely wasted.

By the time the Soviet Union collapsed in 1991, it consisted of a society in which perhaps 1 or 2 percent of the population (the communists, privileged bureaucrats, athletes, and artists) enjoyed a nice lifestyle and the rest of the citizens were forced to scrape by. The same was true perhaps to an even greater degree in the former East Germany, Romania, Poland, Hungary, Czechoslovakia (now the Czech Republic and Slovakia), and Albania. The standard of living of the average citizen prior to the Soviet Union's breakup was at best a quarter but more realistically one-tenth of that in the United States.

Privatization During Transition

That a former state-owned business in Russia is now privatized does not mean that shareholders control it the way they do in, say, the United States. In the United States, shareholders elect a board of directors, which then chooses upper management. Shareholders can force out directors who have acted improperly and can also show their disapproval by selling their shares of stock and purchasing shares in another company. It will be some time before the same system of control operates on all recently privatized Russian businesses. Many such businesses are actually controlled by their managers and workers and not by shareholders. One can use the analogy of a divorced couple still sharing the same house and the children.

In some former Soviet satellite countries, one arm of government sells a state-owned firm and another reappears as its owner. This has happened a lot in Poland, for example, where the government's Industrial Development Agency is managing one of the 15 funds that were set up to take over 440 formerly state-owned enterprises.

In the businesses that are being run by worker cooperatives, there is little incentive to fire the least efficient workers or to seek more highly qualified workers. Manager-owners do not often do much better. Manager-owners of recently privatized firms in Russia clearly do not want to surrender control.

The Persistence of Old Ways

The more an economy tends toward pure market capitalism, the less place there is for a government elite that is able to usurp economic power and, more important, economic privileges. In Russia today, some of the old Communist Party bases of economic power are being redeveloped. Although newspapers and television stations are now privately owned, their owners are increasingly afraid of angering powerful government interests.

Just a few years ago, President Boris Yeltsin created a new political party named "Our House—Russia." The party was and continues to be backed by wealthy banking and business interests. It consists almost entirely of state bureaucrats and provincial governors and administrators, most of whom are former communists. Prior to the downfall of communism, the political elite were able to use special clinics and hospitals. Today the same persons have the same privileges, although the names of the hospitals have changed. Even a new special food store was built for officials with parliamentary identification cards. Under communism, special food stores served to provide Communist Party elite with low-cost, high-quality food without their having to wait on lines. Why, in Russia's now more capitalistic system, such a special food store has cropped up again remains something of a mystery.

THINKING CRITICALLY ABOUT THE MEDIA

Taking Russia's Pulse

When economists and journalists discuss the transition from the centralized Soviet economy to its current market orientation, they lament the tremendous reduction in national output. Official estimates for the period 1989 to 1995, for example, claim that national output dropped by over 50 percent. True though it may be that output dropped during this time, it is not clear what the actual value of that output was to the population. Much of the reduction was in military hardware, such as missiles. How much did the average citizen lose when that output shrank? Also, fewer television sets and radios were produced during this time period—but the ones produced earlier either never worked properly or tended to explode. Steel mills have been shut down in Russia but they had been using technology that was 45 years old. Further, the official Russian state agency that measures the economy, Goskomstat, has none of the sophistication that the U.S. Department of Commerce and the Bureau of Labor Statistics have for measuring a nation's output. Even if Goskomstat had better computers and more refined techniques, it would still miss a vast off-the-books economy that won't be counted by government statisticians for years to come. All in all, Russia's 150 million people earn more and live better than what Goskomstat statistics say.

The Inevitable Crime Wave

The shift to a market economy in Russia has brought with it a major increase in crime, particularly organized crime. Currently, virtually every small business pays protection money to some gang. Moscow boasts at least a million unregistered firearms, and the country as a whole has over 30 million of them. According to former *Toronto Star* Moscow reporter Stephen Handelman, "The second Russian revolution of this century is awash in corruption, opportunism, and crime." One can compare Russia today with America's Wild West.

One needs to examine the crime statistics more carefully, though, to get a real feeling for what is happening in this nation in transition. Street crime is certainly greater than it used to be under the Soviet regime. But Moscow is still probably safer than New York. With respect to "breaking the law," the legal system is in such a state of flux that probably everyone is breaking the law at one time or another. Because the legal system is in its infancy for facilitating private enterprise, businesspeople have had to resort to extralegal methods to collect debts and enforce contracts. Unfortunately, some of these methods involve firearms and violence.

One can make an analogy with the violence associated with the illegal production and sale of alcoholic beverages during America's experiment with Prohibition (1920–1933) and what is happening in Russia today. The violence associated with the business of illegal booze disappeared with the repeal of Prohibition. It will not disappear so quickly in Russia, but it certainly will eventually fade out as property rights become better established, the legal system increasingly facilitates trade, and the court system gains enough experience to handle legal problems in the business world.

Also, one must look at what used to exist under the old system. Because everything belonged to "the people," there was little in the way of communications, credit, banking, and computerization. Money meant less than did connections and rank in the Communist Party. People who were adept at thriving in such an environment—the Communist Party elite—have had a comparative advantage in the initial stages of transition to a market economy. They maintain the connections with state bureaucrats who controlled resources. It is not surprising that many of those in power today are the same communists who were in power a decade ago.

All of this is simply a transition. The incidence of certain crimes in Russia has actually fallen, as can be seen in Figure 6-3.

- Robbery
- Embezzlement
- Aggravated assault
- Murder
- Rape
- Bribery

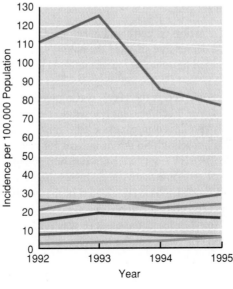

FIGURE 6-3

Crime in Russia

While crime increased after the fall of communism in Russia, its rate has recently stabilized or fallen.

Source: Interior Ministry of Russia.

INTERNATIONAL EXAMPLE
A Booming Business in Facelifts by Russian Plastic Surgeons

One of the beneficiaries of Russia's economic system in transition is the facelift industry. There is as yet no legal procedure in Russia for imposing liability on physicians for malpractice. Consequently, a patient who desires a facelift or other cosmetic surgery has no consent forms to sign, and the physician has no malpractice (liability) insurance to purchase. The result is relatively inexpensive plastic surgery that Germans, Italians, and Americans are taking advantage of. According to one of Russia's best-known plastic surgeons, Igor A. Volf, "Surgeons in the West work in a very rigid frame. They are afraid of being sued by their patients—they fear complications. I do the big, bold operations Western doctors are afraid to do." As word of mouth travels, the demand curve for Russian plastic surgeons is shifting outward to the right.

FOR CRITICAL ANALYSIS: What are the costs that an American contemplating a facelift in Moscow would have to include in making a rational decision about going there? ●

CONCEPTS IN BRIEF

- Russia and its former satellite states in Eastern Europe operated under a system of command socialism with much centralized economic planning. The end result was a declining economy in which a small percentage of the population lived extremely well and the rest very poorly.

- Russia and Eastern Europe are privatizing at varying speeds, depending on the level of political opposition.

- Russia has experienced a crime wave during its transition to capitalism. One can compare this period to America's Wild West and to our period of Prohibition. As property rights and the legal system become more efficient, much of the crime associated with illegal economic activities will probably disappear.

THE PEOPLE'S REPUBLIC OF CHINA

The People's Republic of China remains the largest nation on earth and hence the largest with some form of command socialism. However, a decreasing share of the nation's activity is being guided by government. In fact, China started introducing market reforms in various sectors of the economy well before Russia did.

In 1978, the commune system that had been implemented in the 1950s was replaced by what was known as the *household responsibility system.* Each peasant household became responsible for its own plot of land. Whatever was produced in excess of the minimum obligation to the state remained the property of the household. So the incentives for peasant farmers were quite different from those prior to 1978. Peasants were also encouraged to enrich themselves further by engaging in a variety of economic activities. The results were impressive. Between 1979 and 1984, virtually millions of jobs were created in the urban and rural private sector, and farm productivity increased dramatically.

In the 1980s, the highly centralized planning from Beijing, the capital, was relaxed. Decision-making powers were given to state-owned enterprises at the local level. Indeed,

China had embarked on a gradual sell-off of state-owned enterprises so that the size of the state-run sector, which accounted for 70 percent of industrial production in the mid-1980s, dropped to an estimated 40 percent in 1996. The result was an increase in output. The problem with state-run factories was the **incentive structure.** Managers of those factories never had much incentive to maximize the equivalent of profits. Rather, managers of state-run factories attempted to maximize incomes and benefits for their workers because workers constituted a political constituency that was more important than the politicians at the national level.

Incentive structure
The motivational rewards and costs that individuals face in any given situation. Each economic system has its own incentive structure. The incentive structure is different under a system of private property than under a system of government-owned property, for example.

Two Decades of Economic Reform

Another major economic reform in China began in 1979, when the central government created a special economic zone in Guangdong province, bordering the nation of Hong Kong. In that special zone, the three *P*s of pure capitalism—prices, profits, and private property—have now prevailed for nearly two decades. The result has been economic growth rates that have exceeded those in virtually any other part of the world. Within an area housing less than 1.5 percent of the population, Guangdong province now accounts for about 7 percent of the entire country's industrial output.

Transition Problems in Farming

Even though the Chinese central government was able to increase agricultural production dramatically when it gave peasants the household responsibility system, the agricultural sector has been lagging well behind the industrial sector in recent years. In effect, China has been undergoing an industrial revolution but not an agricultural one. One of the major problems is that peasants do not have legal title to their land. In other words, farmers cannot obtain legal property rights. As a result, the techniques used by agribusiness companies elsewhere in the world cannot be used by most of China's farmers. Peasants, in effect, have their land on loan from the state. The average size of a peasant farm is less than an acre for a family of six. It takes this family about 60 workdays to cultivate this amount of land, whereas a single American farmer can cultivate the same amount of land in about two hours.

Further, there is every incentive for peasant farmers to leave their rural lands and move to the city, where they can earn approximately four times as much income.

THINKING CRITICALLY ABOUT THE MEDIA

268 Million Chinese Unemployed?

"China Sees 268 Million Unemployed in 2000." This was the headline a few years ago, reportedly based on statements by mainland Chinese officials in the Labor Ministry. Imagine that—the number of unemployed in China equaling the entire population of men, women, and children in the United States! A frightening prospect, no doubt, but also pure nonsense. Such a large number of unemployed presupposes that there is no way for them to find jobs of any sort. As China shifts toward a market economy, however, many of the unemployed will be able to find jobs in businesses that the current Chinese leadership cannot even conceive of today. That is what happens in a country in transition toward market capitalism. Of course, during the transition, there will be social and human costs associated with higher-than-normal unemployment rates, but that is statistically a temporary blip, not a long-term trend.

A Major Problem: The Rule of Law

As with virtually all countries experiencing frontier capitalism, China faces the perennial issue of how to establish the rule of law. When no specific property rights exist because resources are owned by "the people," the inevitable result is corruption. As with Russia, there is a sense of the Wild West in China, an atmosphere of lawlessness and unpredictability for anyone doing business. Both the government and the army continue to seek bribes and other favors because those two institutions still control many of the resources and influence the way business is conducted in China.

Only very slowly is China becoming a nation of laws, rather than of men and women. Otherwise stated, only gradually is the institution of a strong legal system being built up in China. The notion of property rights is slow to take in a nation where the communist dogma has denied their legitimacy. A good example is the state-supported bootleg compact disc factories that were first shut down because of international pressure and then reopened a few years ago. That American singers and musicians are being denied royalties seems not to bother some mainland Chinese government officials.

INTERNATIONAL EXAMPLE
A Tale of Two Countries

Approximately 6 million Chinese, most directly from or descended from those on mainland China, live in the state of Hong Kong, a colony leased to the British and scheduled to revert to mainland ownership in mid-1997. A comparison of these two political entities is instructive. During its 99 years as a British colony covering a mere 405 square miles, Hong Kong became the world's eighth-largest trading nation with a higher per capita income than the United Kingdom or France. Total annual output from its 6 million residents exceeded 20 percent of the output of 1.2 billion mainland Chinese. Hong Kong has been the perennial favorite example of economists who wish to show the efficiency of a system following the three *P*s—prices, profits, and private property.

Perhaps more important, Hong Kong demonstrates the benefits of a strong legal system. A *Fortune* magazine survey of 500 corporate executives in 32 countries rated Hong Kong above London and New York as the best city for doing business. Commentators have argued that mainland China does not need Hong Kong's money but rather its rule of law. For decades, these laws have provided businesses with predictable rules governing civil and criminal disputes. Hong Kong has had an independent judicial system, contrary to the one almost completely dominated by the Communist Party on the mainland. Whether the mainland's takeover of Hong Kong results in China's learning from Hong Kong remains to be seen.

FOR CRITICAL ANALYSIS: Reread the discussion of comparative versus absolute advantage in Chapter 2. Hong Kong is basically a barren land with no natural resources. What does this say about absolute versus comparative advantage? ●

The Slow Pace of Privatization

Virtually all state-run companies in China have provided cradle-to-grave social welfare benefits to their workers. The process of privatization, which started gradually years ago, first requires that these companies slowly eliminate many of these social welfare programs. Such programs are one of the reasons why over 50 percent of state-run enterprises are losing money every year. You can see from Figure 6-4 which state-run industrial enterprises are most prevalent. It clearly will be many years before the Chinese government is completely (if ever) out of the petroleum and tobacco businesses. But as Figure 6-5 shows, a growing percentage of firms are escaping from state control.

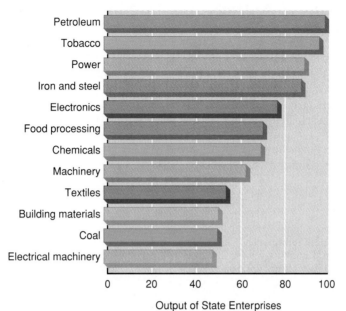

FIGURE 6-4

Relative Importance of Government in China's Industry
The government in China owns most of the oil, tobacco, and power industries, but is shedding itself of other industries.

The trend toward privatization in China is inevitably leading to labor dislocations. As state-run enterprises become privatized, new technology will be introduced that will require fewer labor hours per unit of output. Workers have been and will continue to be laid off in recently privatized firms. Laid-off workers will have to seek employment elsewhere, and in the process unemployment rates will rise, at least temporarily.

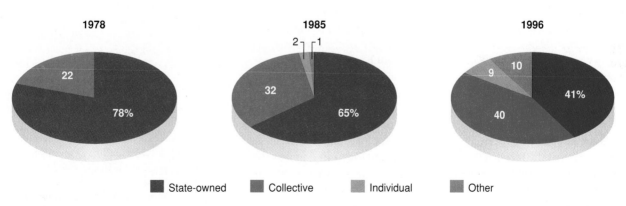

FIGURE 6-5

The Changing Face of China's Business Ownership
State ownership of all industries in China has fallen from 78 percent in 1978 to only 41 percent in 1996.

INTERNATIONAL EXAMPLE
China Eliminates Saturday Work

In 1995, the Chinese government granted its 450 million urban laborers and students Saturdays off. That adds up to about 1.4 billion extra hours of leisure time every week (laborers and students had been putting in a four-hour Saturday workday). The major beneficiaries of this government edict, besides urban laborers and students, seem to be travel agents. They counted the change in work rules as a windfall.

FOR CRITICAL ANALYSIS: What happened to the demand curve for leisure travel after the five-day workweek was instituted? ●

CONCEPTS IN BRIEF

• China started instituting market reforms in 1979 when it created special economic zones in which the three *P*s of capitalism were allowed to work. Problems remain in agriculture because peasant farmers cannot obtain property rights in land.

• The rule of law as capitalist countries know it is coming slowly to China. Government officials sometimes break contract agreements with foreign investors.

• The process of privatization started years ago but is proceeding slowly. The state still owns most of the businesses in oil, tobacco, power, and iron and steel.

FUTURE ECONOMIC POWER SHIFTS

The fact that there are so many economies in transition today is not just a momentary curiosity. It has implications for the future with respect to which nations will become economic powerhouses. Look at the three panels of Figure 6-6. You see in panel (a) that in the mid-1990s, the United States was clearly the world's largest economy. Japan and China were not even half its size. Now look at panel (b), which shows the World Bank's prediction of the largest economies in the year 2020. The leading economic powerhouse then is predicted to be China, with the United States a distant second. (These numbers reflect the total size of the economy, not how rich the average citizen is.) Japan will still be among the top three, but India and Indonesia will have expanded dramatically relative to 1995. Indeed, Asia, including India, will be a major economic power in the year 2020. These developments are reflected in panel (c) of Figure 6-6, where we show the projected shares of world output of today's industrial countries relative to today's developing countries. Realize, however, that the fact that developing Asian countries will dramatically increase the size of their economies does not mean that westerners will be worse off. Rather, the incomes of most westerners will also increase, but not as rapidly. Given that per-person incomes are generally higher in the West than in Asia, westerners will still remain rich by historical standards. The rest of the world is simply catching up with us.

THINKING CRITICALLY ABOUT THE MEDIA

Rich Industrial Nations—Really?

Virtually all news commentators and research organizations continue to classify countries such as the United States, the United Kingdom, and France as the industrial economies. Such an appellation today is a misnomer. In the industrial economies of today, less than one-third of the output is from "industry." Two-thirds of the jobs in so-called industrial economies are from services—doctors, lawyers, computer programmers, and Internet facilitators. Indeed, it might be more appropriate to call the richer countries *knowledge economies* because that is where the primary source of growth will lie—the storage, processing, and distribution of knowledge.

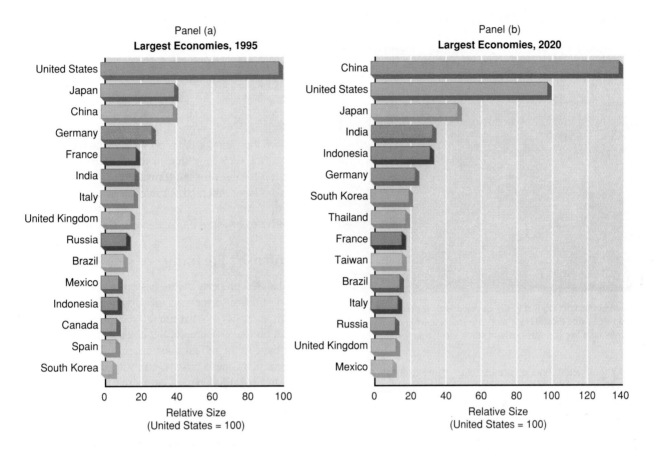

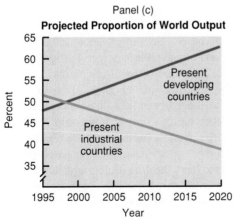

FIGURE 6-6

World Economic Powerhouses, 1995–2020

While the United States is the largest economy today, by 2020, China may be the world's greatest economic power. In any event, the share of world output from developing countries will increase steadily during that same time period.

Source: World Bank, *Global Economic Prospects.*

The Peruvian Transition from No Ownership to Clear Title

Concepts Applied: Property rights, incentives, markets, economies in transition

Formal markets do not easily develop where private ownership does not exist. This is the case in Peru, where farmers till family land for generations without a clear title for that land.

By at least one estimate, over three-quarters of the population of Peru is involved in the "informal society." This term was coined by Peruvian economist Hernando de Soto to emphasize the fact that Peru's official economy is quite small. It turns out that only 20 percent of Peru's land is legally owned. On the remaining 80 percent, which has no true legal ownership, peasant families till the land as they have done for generations.

Constructing *Pueblos Jovenes*

Cities are actually constructed on the unowned land. They are called *pueblos jovenes,* which means "young cities." Sometimes people who have been living there for a long time or who have tilled the land surrounding them try to register the land in their name. The process can take anywhere from six months to two years, though, and costs thousands of dollars in fees, much more than any peasant family is normally able to pay.

No Ownership, No Market, No Incentive

It is difficult, if not impossible, to create markets when ownership is nonexistent. Informal markets do evolve, and that is what has happened throughout Peru. But without specifically defined property rights, individuals cannot exchange land, for example. Consequently, in Peru, for generations, no large-scale farming has occurred, nor have peasant families experienced much incentive to

improve the value of the property on which they farm. It is also not surprising that in the *pueblos jovenes,* construction has been of the flimsiest nature, even by families who have inherited substantial sums of money. If a peasant family doesn't know if it can keep its land, the incentive to invest in it is understandably low.

"Suitcase" Farming

The lack of property rights has created a culture of so-called suitcase farmers in the Upper Huallaga and Rio Apurimac valleys. What the farmers produce, though, is not for normal consumption. It is coca bushes, which provide the raw ingredients for cocaine. Peruvian suitcase farmers plant these bushes, cultivate them, quickly sell them to Colombian buyers, and move off the land.

Enter a New System

Since the beginning of the 1990s, Peru's parliament has passed a spate of new property laws. Today, for a nominal cost, it is possible to register ownership of property in a month or so. So far, at least 150,000 families have obtained title to their land for $11 to $15 per parcel.

For a family to establish title to land, the local leaders in the "informal" neighborhoods have to attest that a family has indeed been using the parcel for generations. If no other family contests ownership of that property, it becomes possible for the family to register ownership.

One group objects to providing well-defined property rights to land: the drug dealers who buy coca plants. They are worried that establishing private property rights to land will discourage the suitcase farmers, leading to a smaller supply of the raw ingredient for cocaine. Not surprisingly, the main office of the Institute for Liberty and Democracy, a group that is helping peasants register their land, has been bombed several times.

FOR CRITICAL ANALYSIS
1. What alternatives would suitcase farmers have if they were given clear ownership rights to the land that they farm?
2. Is it possible to have wealth without legal property rights?

CHAPTER SUMMARY

1. The price system answers the resource allocation and distribution questions relating to what and how much will be produced, how it will be produced, and for whom it will be produced. The question of what to produce is answered by the value people place on a good—the highest price they are willing to pay for it. How goods are produced is determined by competition, which inevitably results in least-cost production techniques. Finally, goods and services are distributed to the individuals who are willing and able to pay for them. This answers the question about for whom goods are produced.

2. Pure capitalism can be defined by the three *P*s: prices, profits, and private property.

3. Communism is an economic system in which, theoretically, individuals would produce according to their abilities and consume according to their needs. Under socialism, the state owns most major capital goods and attempts to redistribute income. Most economies today can be viewed as mixed in that they rely on a combination of private decisions and government controls.

4. Incentives matter in any economic system; consequently, in countries that have had few or unenforced property rights, individuals lacked the incentives to take care of property that wasn't theirs.

5. Today there are four types of capitalism: consumer, producer, family, and frontier. The last emerges when a centralized economy starts collapsing and black markets thrive. Eventually, small businesses flourish and financial markets develop. Finally, foreign investment is attracted, and state-owned businesses are privatized.

6. The development of a well-functioning legal system is one of the most difficult problems for an economy in the frontier capitalism stage. Such economies do not have the laws or courts to handle property right protection and transfers.

7. Privatization, or turning over state-owned or state-run businesses to the private sector is occurring all over the world in all types of economies. There is much political opposition, however, whenever managers in soon-to-be-privatized businesses realize that they may face harder times in a private setting.

8. Russia and its former satellite states in Eastern Europe operated under a system of command socialism with much centralized economic planning. The end result was a declining economy in which a small percentage of the population lived extremely well and the rest very poorly.

9. Russia has experienced a crime wave during its transition to capitalism. One can compare this period to America's Wild West and to our period of Prohibition. As property rights and the legal system become more efficient, much of the crime associated with illegal economic activities probably will disappear.

10. China started instituting true market reforms in 1979, when it created special economic zones in which the three *P*s of capitalism—prices, profits, and private property—were allowed to work. Problems remain in agriculture because peasant farmers cannot obtain property rights to land.

11. The process of privatization in China started years ago but is proceeding slowly. The state still owns most of the businesses in oil, tobacco, power, and iron and steel.

12. The United States and Japan will remain economic powerhouses, but China could take the lead over the next 25 years. Other Asian countries, including Indonesia, India, Taiwan, South Korea, and Thailand, will become economically much stronger than they are today.

DISCUSSION OF PREVIEW QUESTIONS

1. Why does the scarcity problem force all societies to answer the questions *what, how,* and *for whom?* Scarcity exists for a society because people want more than their resources will allow them to have.

Society must decide *what* to produce because of scarcity. But if wants are severely restricted and resources are relatively superabundant, the question of *what* to produce is trivial—society simply produces *everything* that everyone wants. Superabundant resources relative to restricted wants also make the question of *how* to produce trivial. If scarcity doesn't exist, superabundant resources can be combined in *any* manner; waste and efficiency have no meaning without scarcity. Similarly, without scarcity, *for whom* is meaningless; *all* people can consume *all* they want.

2. **How can economies be classified?**

   All societies must resolve the three fundamental economic problems: what, how, and for whom? One way to classify economies is according to the manner in which they answer these questions. In particular, we can classify them according to the degree to which *individuals* privately are allowed to make these decisions. Under pure command socialism, practically all economic decisions are made by a central authority; under pure capitalism, practically all economic decisions are made by private individuals pursuing their own economic self-interest.

3. **Why do we say that *all* economies are mixed economies?**

   No economy in the real world is purely capitalistic. Resource allocation decisions in all economies are made by some combination of private individuals and governments. Even under an idealized capitalistic economy, important roles are played by the government; it is generally agreed that government is required for some income redistribution, national defense, protection of property rights, and so on.

4. **What are the "three *P*s" of pure capitalism?**

   They are prices, profits, and property rights. In a pure capitalist economic system, prices are allowed to change when supply or demand changes. Prices are the signals to all about the relative scarcity of different resources. Profits are not constrained. When profits are relatively great in an industry, more resources flow to it. The converse is also true. Finally, property rights exist and are supported by the legal system.

PROBLEMS

(Answers to the odd-numbered problems appear at the back of the book.)

6-1. Suppose that you are an economic planner and you have been told by your country's political leaders that they want to increase automobile production by 10 percent over last year. What other industries will be affected by this decision?

6-2. Some argue that prices and profits automatically follow from well-established property rights. Explain how this might occur.

6-3. A business has found that it makes the most profits when it produces $172 worth of output of a particular product. It can choose from three possible techniques, A, B, and C, to produce the desired level of output. The table gives the amount of inputs these techniques use along with each input price.

   a. Which technique will the firm choose, and why?

   b. What would the firm's maximum profit be?

   c. If the price of labor increases to $4 per unit, which technique will be chosen, and why? What will happen to profits?

		Production Technique		
Input	Input Unit Price	A (units)	B (units)	C (units)
Land	$10	7	4	1
Labor	2	6	7	18
Capital	15	2	6	3
Entrepreneurship	8	1	3	2

6-4. Answer the questions on the basis of the accompanying graph.

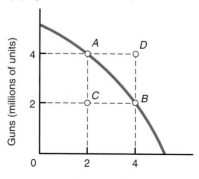

Butter (millions of barrels)

a. A switch to a decentralized, more market-oriented economy might do what to the production possibilities curve, and why?

b. What point on the graph represents an economy with unemployment?

6-5. The table gives the production techniques and input prices for 100 units of product X.

Input	Input Unit Price	Production Technique		
		A (units)	B (units)	C (units)
Labor	$10	6	5	4
Capital	8	5	6	7

a. In a market system, which techniques will be used to produce 100 units of product X?

b. If the market price of a unit of X is $1, which technique will lead to the greatest profit?

c. The output of X is still $1, but the price of labor and capital changes so that labor is $8 and capital is $10. Which production technique will be used?

d. Using the information in (c), what is the potential profit of producing 100 units of X?

6-6. The table gives the production techniques and input prices for one unit of product Y.

Input	Input Unit Price	Production Technique		
		A (units)	B (units)	C (units)
Labor	$10	1	3	2
Capital	5	2	2	4
Land	4	3	1	1

a. If the market price of a unit of product Y is $50, which technique generates the greatest potential profit?

b. If input unit prices change so that labor is $10, capital is $10, and land is $10, which technique will be chosen?

c. Assuming that the unit cost of each input is $10 and the price of a unit of Y is $50, which technique generates the greatest profit?

COMPUTER-ASSISTED INSTRUCTION

The role of prices in communicating information and allocating goods and services are illustrated by examining the ongoing transformation of the economies of Russia and China.

Complete problem and answer appear on disk.

INTERACTING WITH THE INTERNET

Extensive information on Eastern European economic conditions, with an emphasis on financial matters, can be found (for a fee) at

http://www.securities.com/

An excellent source for general information on these and other countries is the CIA's *World Factbook,*

http://www.odci.gov/cia/publications/96fact/index.html

and information on different countries' economic and trade policies can be found at

gopher://gopher.umsl.edu/11/library/govdocs/crpt

A very nice guide with extensive links to trade, economic, and business information for Eastern Europe and the former Soviet Union can be obtained from "REESweb: Russian and East European Studies," sponsored by the University Center for Russian and East European Studies of the University of Pittsburgh. It is located at

http://www.pitt.edu/~cjp/rsecon.html

This is just one section of the university's material on this part of the world.

PART 6

DIMENSIONS OF MICROECONOMICS

The chapters in this book were extracted from the hardbound one-volume edition of *Economics Today*. In previous editions, the hardbound text and the macroeconomics and microeconomics paperbound texts were all numbered individually. Instructors and students who were using different versions of the book (or the software or other supplements) were forced to consult a conversion chart to find their place. Instead, the chapters in all three volumes of this edition are numbered the same—even if there are lapses in sequence—in order to avoid confusion and make the books as easy to use as possible.

CHAPTER 19

CONSUMER CHOICE

Even if you live in the city, you can surely appreciate the existence of the Grand Canyon, the Rocky Mountains, and the great wilderness areas in Alaska and other parts of the country. And even if you have never seen a whale, you may receive some satisfaction from knowing that whales have not been made extinct. Thus when an environmental disaster occurs, such as a huge oil spill, you may feel a certain loss. Should your feelings of loss be taken into account when government officials attempt to determine the policy response to environmental damage? To answer this question, you need to know how consumers make choices and the values they place on those choices.

PREVIEW QUESTIONS

1. What is the law of diminishing marginal utility?

2. How does a consumer maximize total utility?

3. What happens to consumer optimum when price changes?

4. How can the law of diminishing marginal utility account for the law of demand?

Did You Know That . . . in a typical year, an American family spends about 15 percent of its income on food and about the same on housing? Within individual families, however, these relative percentages may be quite different. Some families devote much higher percentages of their income to housing than others. What determines how much each family spends on different items in their budget? One explanation is simply tastes—the values that family members place on different items on which they can spend their income. The saying "You can't argue with tastes" suggests that different individuals have different preferences for how to allocate their limited incomes. Although there is no real theory of what determines people's tastes, we can examine some of the behavior that underlies how consumers react to changes in the prices of the goods and services that they purchase. Recall from Chapter 3 that people generally purchase less at higher prices than at lower prices. This is called the law of demand.

Because the law of demand is important, its derivation is useful because it allows us to arrange the relevant variables, such as price, income, and tastes, in such a way as to understand the real world better and even perhaps generate predictions about it. One way of deriving the law of demand involves an analysis of the logic of consumer choice in a world of limited resources. In this chapter, therefore, we discuss what is called *utility analysis*.

UTILITY THEORY

When you buy something, you do so because of the satisfaction you expect to receive from having and using that good. For everything that you like to have, the more you have of it, the higher the level of satisfaction you receive. Another term that can be used for satisfaction is **utility,** or want-satisfying power. This property is common to all goods that are desired. The concept of utility is purely subjective, however. There is no way that you or I can measure the amount of utility that a consumer might be able to obtain from a particular good, for utility does not imply "useful" or "utilitarian" or "practical." For this reason, there can be no accurate scientific assessment of the utility that someone might receive by consuming a frozen dinner or a movie relative to the utility that another person might receive from that same good or service. Nevertheless, we can infer whether a person receives more utility from consuming one good versus another by that person's behavior. For example, if an individual buys more coffee than tea (when both tea and coffee are priced equally), we are able to say that the individual receives more utility from consuming coffee than from consuming tea.

The utility that individuals receive from consuming a good depends on their tastes and preferences. These tastes and preferences are normally assumed to be given and stable for a given individual. An individual's tastes determine how much utility that individual derives from consuming a good, and this in turn determines how that individual allocates his or her income. People spend a greater proportion of their incomes on goods they like. But we cannot explain why tastes are different between individuals. For example, we cannot explain why some people like yogurt but others do not.

We can analyze in terms of utility the way consumers decide what to buy, just as physicists have analyzed some of their problems in terms of what they call force. No physicist has ever seen a unit of force, and no economist has ever seen a unit of utility. In both cases, however, these concepts have proved useful for analysis.

Throughout this chapter, we will be discussing **utility analysis,** which is the analysis of consumer decision making based on utility maximization.

Utility
The want-satisfying power of a good or service.

Utility analysis
The analysis of consumer decision making based on utility maximization.

Utility and Utils

Util
A representative unit by which utility is measured.

Economists once believed that utility could be measured. In fact, there is a philosophical school of thought based on utility theory called *utilitarianism,* developed by the English philosopher Jeremy Bentham (1748–1832). Bentham held that society should seek the greatest happiness for the greatest number. He sought to apply an arithmetic formula for measuring happiness. He and his followers developed the notion of measurable utility and invented the **util** to measure it. For the moment, we will also assume that we can measure satisfaction using this representative unit. Our assumption will allow us to quantify the way we examine consumer behavior.[1] Thus the first chocolate bar that you eat might yield you 4 utils of satisfaction; the first peanut cluster, 6 utils; and so on. Today, no one really believes that we can actually measure utils, but the ideas forthcoming from such analysis will prove useful in our understanding of the way in which consumers choose among alternatives.

Total and Marginal Utility

Consider the satisfaction, or utility, that you receive each time that you rent and watch a video on your VCR. To make the example straightforward, let's say that there are hundreds of videos to choose from each year and that each of them is of the same quality. Let's say that you normally rent one video per week. You could, of course, rent two, or three, or four per week. Presumably, each time you rent another video per week, you will get additional satisfaction, or utility. The question, though, that we must ask is, given that you are already renting one per week, will the next one rented that week give you the same amount of additional utility?

Marginal utility
The change in total utility due to a one-unit change in the quantity of a good or service consumed.

That additional, or incremental, utility is called **marginal utility,** where *marginal,* as before, means "incremental" or "additional." (Marginal changes also refer to decreases, in which cases we talk about *decremental* changes.) The concept of marginality is important in economics because we make decisions at the margin. At any particular point, we compare additional (marginal) benefits with additional (marginal) costs.

Applying Marginal Analysis to Utility

The specific example presented in Figure 19-1 on page 416 will clarify the distinction between total utility and marginal utility. The table in panel (a) shows the total utility and the marginal utility of watching videos each week. Marginal utility is the difference between total utility derived from one level of consumption and total utility derived from another level of consumption. A simple formula for marginal utility is this:

$$\text{Marginal utility} = \frac{\text{change in total utility}}{\text{change in number of units consumed}}$$

In our example, when a person has already watched two videos in one week and then watches another, total utility increases from 16 utils to 19. Therefore, the marginal utility (of watching one more video after already having watched two in one week) is equal to 3 utils.

---

[1]What follows is typically called *cardinal utility analysis* by economists. It requires cardinal measurement. Numbers such as 1, 2, and 3 are cardinals. We know that 2 is exactly twice as many as 1 and that 3 is exactly three times as many as 1. You will see in Appendix E at the end of this chapter a type of consumer behavior analysis that requires only *ordinal* measurement of utility, meaning ranked or ordered. *First, second,* and *third* are ordinal numbers; nothing can be said about their exact size relationships. We can only talk about their importance relative to each other. Temperature, for example, is an ordinal ranking. One hundred degrees Celsius is not twice as warm as 50 degrees Celsius. All we can say is that 100 degrees Celsius is warmer than 50 degrees Celsius.

Panel (a)

(1) Number of Videos Watched per Week	(2) Total Utility (utils per week)	(3) Marginal Utility (utils per week)
0	0	
		10 (10 − 0)
1	10	
		6 (16 − 10)
2	16	
		3 (19 − 16)
3	19	
		1 (20 − 19)
4	20	
		0 (20 − 20)
5	20	
		−2 (18 − 20)
6	18	

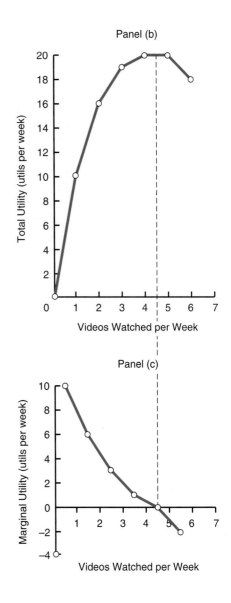

FIGURE 19-1

Total and Marginal Utility of Watching Videos

If we were able to assign specific values to the utility derived from watching videos each week, we could obtain a marginal utility schedule similar in pattern to the one shown in panel (a). In column 1 is the number of videos watched per week; in column 2, the total utility derived from each quantity; and in column 3, the marginal utility derived from each additional quantity, which is defined as the change in total utility due to a change of one unit of watching videos per week. Total utility from panel (a) is plotted in panel (b). Marginal utility is plotted in panel (c), where you see that it reaches zero where total utility hits its maximum at between 4 and 5 units.

GRAPHIC ANALYSIS

We can transfer the information in panel (a) onto a graph, as we do in panels (b) and (c) of Figure 19-1. Total utility, which is represented in column 2 of panel (a), is transferred to panel (b).

Total utility continues to rise until four videos are watched per week. This measure of utility remains at 20 utils through the fifth video, and at the sixth video per week it falls to 18 utils; we assume that at some quantity consumed per unit time period, boredom sets in. This is shown in panel (b).

Marginal Utility

If you look carefully at panels (b) and (c) of Figure 19-1, the notion of marginal utility becomes very clear. In economics, the term *marginal* always refers to a change in the total. The marginal utility of watching three videos per week instead of two videos per week is the increment in total utility and is equal to 3 utils per week. All of the points in panel (c) are taken from column 3 of the table in panel (a). Notice that marginal utility falls throughout the graph. A special point occurs after four videos are watched per week because the total utility curve in panel (b) is unchanged after the consumption of the fourth video. That means that the consumer receives no additional (marginal) utility from watching the fifth video. This is shown in panel (c) as *zero* marginal utility. After that point, marginal utility becomes negative.

In our example, when marginal utility becomes negative, it means that the consumer is fed up with watching videos and would require some form of compensation to watch any more. When marginal utility is negative, an additional unit consumed actually lowers total utility by becoming a nuisance. Rarely does a consumer face a situation of negative marginal utility. Whenever this point is reached, goods become in effect "bads." A rational consumer will stop consuming at the point at which marginal utility becomes negative, even if the good is free.

CONCEPTS IN BRIEF

- Utility is defined as want-satisfying power; it is a power common to all desired goods and services.
- We arbitrarily measure utility in units called utils.
- It is important to distinguish between total utility and marginal utility. Total utility is the total satisfaction derived from the consumption of a given quantity of a good or service. Marginal utility is the *change* in total utility due to a one-unit change in the consumption of the good or service.

Diminishing marginal utility
The principle that as more of any good or service is consumed, its extra benefit declines. Otherwise stated, increases in total utility from the consumption of a good or service become smaller and smaller as more is consumed during a given time period.

DIMINISHING MARGINAL UTILITY

Notice that in panel (c) of Figure 19-1, marginal utility is continuously declining. This property has been named the principle of **diminishing marginal utility.** There is no way that we can prove diminishing marginal utility; nonetheless, economists and others have for years believed strongly in the notion. Diminishing marginal utility has even been called a law. This supposed law concerns a psychological, or subjective, utility that you receive as you consume more and more of a particular good. Stated formally, the law is as follows:

> **As an individual consumes more of a particular commodity, the total level of utility, or satisfaction, derived from that consumption usually increases. Eventually, however, the *rate* at which it increases diminishes as more is consumed.**

Take a hungry individual at a dinner table. The first serving is greatly appreciated, and the individual derives a substantial amount of utility from it. The second serving does not have quite as much impact as the first one, and the third serving is likely to be even less satisfying. This individual experiences diminishing marginal utility of food until he or she stops eating, and this is true for most people. All-you-can-eat restaurants count on this fact; a second helping of ribs may provide some marginal utility, but the third helping would have only a little or even negative marginal utility. The fall in the marginal utility of other goods is even more dramatic.

Consider for a moment the opposite possibility—increasing marginal utility. Under such a situation, the marginal utility after consuming, say, one hamburger would increase. The second hamburger would be more valuable to you, and the third would be even more valuable yet. If increasing marginal utility existed, each of us would consume only one good or service! Rather than observing that "variety is the spice of life," we would see that monotony in consumption was preferred. We do not observe this, and therefore we have great confidence in the concept of diminishing marginal utility.

Consider an example that may affect you or someone you know—having a birthday on or within a few days of December 25. Even if you receive exactly the same number of presents that you would have if your birthday were six months later, your total level of utility, or satisfaction, from your presents will be lower. Why? Because of diminishing marginal utility. Let's say that your relatives and friends all give you compact discs. The total utility you receive from, say, 20 CDs on December 25 is less than if you received 10 in December and 10 on your birthday several months later.

EXAMPLE
Newspaper Vending Machines Versus Candy Vending Machines

Have you ever noticed that newspaper vending machines nearly everywhere in the United States allow you to put in the correct change, lift up the door, and take as many newspapers as you want? Contrast this type of vending machine with candy machines. They are completely locked at all times. You must designate the candy that you wish, normally by using some type of keypad. The candy then drops down to a place where you reach to retrieve it but from which you cannot grab any other candy. The difference between these two types of vending machines is explained by diminishing marginal utility. Newspaper companies dispense newspapers from coin-operated boxes that allow dishonest people to take more copies than they pay for. What would a dishonest person do with more than one copy of a newspaper, however? The marginal utility of a second newspaper is normally zero. The benefit of storing excessive newspapers is usually nil because yesterday's news has no value. But the same analysis does not hold for candy. The marginal utility of a second candy bar is certainly less than the first, but it is normally not zero. Moreover, one can store candy for relatively long periods of time at relatively low cost. Consequently, food vending machine companies have to worry about dishonest users of their machines and must make their machines much more theftproof than newspaper companies do.

FOR CRITICAL ANALYSIS: *Can you think of a circumstance under which a substantial number of newspaper purchasers might be inclined to take more than one newspaper out of a vending machine?* •

OPTIMIZING CONSUMPTION CHOICES

Every consumer has a limited income. Choices must be made. When a consumer has made all of his or her choices about what to buy and in what quantities, and when the total level of satisfaction, or utility, from that set of choices is as great as it can be, we say that the consumer has *optimized*. When the consumer has attained an optimum consumption set of goods and services, we say that he or she has reached **consumer optimum**.[2]

Consumer optimum
A choice of a set of goods and services that maximizes the level of satisfaction for each consumer, subject to limited income.

Consider a simple two-good example. The consumer has to choose between spending income on the rental of videos at $5 each and on purchasing deluxe hamburgers at $3 each. Let's say that the last dollar spent on hamburgers yields 3 utils of utility but the last dollar spent on video rentals yields 10 utils. Wouldn't this consumer increase total utility if some dollars were taken away from hamburger consumption and allocated to video rentals? The answer is yes. Given diminishing marginal utility, more dollars spent on video rentals will reduce marginal utility per last dollar spent, whereas fewer dollars spent on hamburger consumption will increase marginal utility per last dollar spent. The optimum—where total utility is maximized—might occur when the satisfaction per last dollar spent on both hamburgers and video rentals per week is equal for the two goods. Thus the amount of goods consumed depends on the prices of the goods, the income of the consumers, and the marginal utility derived from each good.

Table 19-1 presents information on utility derived from consuming various quantities of videos and hamburgers. Columns 4 and 8 show the marginal utility per dollar spent on

TABLE 19-1
Total and Marginal Utility from Consuming Videos and Hamburgers on an Income of $26

(1) Videos per Period	(2) Total Utility of Videos per Period (utils)	(3) Marginal Utility (utils) MU_v	(4) Marginal Utility per Dollar Spent (MU_v/P_v) (price = $5)	(5) Hamburgers per Period	(6) Total Utility of Hamburgers per Period (utils)	(7) Marginal Utility (utils) MU_h	(8) Marginal Utility per Dollar Spent (MU_h/P_h) (price = $3)
0	0.0	—	—	0	0	—	—
1	50.0	50.0	10.0	1	25	25	8.3
2	95.0	45.0	9.0	2	47	22	7.3
3	135.0	40.0	8.0	3	65	18	6.0
4	171.5	36.5	7.3	4	80	15	5.0
5	200.0	28.5	5.7	5	89	9	3.0

[2]Optimization typically refers to individual decision-making processes. When we deal with many individuals interacting in the marketplace, we talk in terms of an equilibrium in the marketplace. Generally speaking, equilibrium is a property of markets rather than of individual decision making.

videos and hamburgers, respectively. If the prices of both goods are zero, individuals will consume each as long as their respective marginal utility is positive (at least five units of each and probably much more). It is also true that a consumer with infinite income will continue consuming goods until the marginal utility of each is equal to zero. When the price is zero or the consumer's income is infinite, there is no effective constraint on consumption.

Consumer optimum is attained when the marginal utility of the last dollar spent on each good yields the same utility and income is completely exhausted. The individual's income is $26. From columns 4 and 8 of Table 19-1, maximum equal marginal utilities occur at the consumption level of four videos and two hamburgers (the marginal utility per dollar spent equals 7.3). Notice that the marginal utility per dollar spent for both goods is also (approximately) equal at the consumption level of three videos and one hamburger, but here total income is not completely exhausted. Likewise, the marginal utility per dollar spent is (approximately) equal at five videos and three hamburgers, but the expenditures necessary for that level of consumption exceed the individual's income.

Table 19-2 shows the steps taken to arrive at consumer optimum. The first video would yield a marginal utility per dollar of 10, while the first hamburger would yield a marginal utility of only 8.3 per dollar. Because it yields the higher marginal utility per dollar, the video is purchased. This leaves $21 of income. The second video yields a higher marginal utility per dollar (9, versus 8.3 for hamburgers), so it is also purchased, leaving an unspent income of $16. At the third purchase, the first hamburger now yields a higher marginal utility per dollar than the next video (8.3 versus 8), so the first hamburger is purchased. This leaves income of $13 to spend. The process continues until all income is exhausted and the marginal utility per dollar spent is equal for both goods.

To restate, consumer optimum requires the following:

A consumer's money income should be allocated so that the last dollar spent on each good purchased yields the same amount of marginal utility (when all income is spent).

TABLE 19-2

Steps to Consumer Optimum
In each purchase situation described here, the consumer always purchases the good with the higher marginal utility per dollar spent (MU/P). For example, at the time of the third purchase, the marginal utility per last dollar spent on videos is 8, but it is 8.3 for hamburgers, and $16 of income remains, so the next purchase will be a hamburger. Here $P_v = \$5$ and $P_h = \$3$.

	Choices					
	Videos		Hamburgers			
Purchase	Unit	(MU_v/P_v)	Unit	$(MU_h/(P_h)$	Buying Decision	Remaining Income
1	First	10.0	First	8.3	First video	$26 − $5 = $21
2	Second	9.0	First	8.3	Second video	$21 − $5 = $16
3	Third	8.0	First	8.3	First hamburger	$16 − $3 = $13
4	Third	8.0	Second	7.3	Third video	$13 − $5 = $ 8
5	Fourth	7.3	Second	7.3	Fourth video and second hamburger	$ 8 − $5 = $ 3 $ 3 − $3 = $ 0

A Little Math

We can state the rule of consumer optimum in algebraic terms by examining the ratio of marginal utilities and prices of individual products. This is sometimes called the *rule of equal marginal utilities per dollar spent* on a basket of goods. The rule simply states that a consumer maximizes personal satisfaction when allocating money income in such a way that the last dollars spent on good A, good B, good C, and so on, yield equal amounts of marginal utility. Marginal utility (*MU*) from good A is indicated by *MU* of good A. For good B, it is *MU* of good B. Our algebraic formulation of this rule, therefore, becomes

$$\frac{MU \text{ of good A}}{\text{price of good A}} = \frac{MU \text{ of good B}}{\text{price of good B}} = \cdots = \frac{MU \text{ of good Z}}{\text{price of good Z}}$$

The letters A, B, . . . , Z indicate the various goods and services that the consumer might purchase.

We know, then, that the marginal utility of good A divided by the price of good A must equal the marginal utility of any other good divided by its price in order for the consumer to maximize utility. Note, though, that the application of the rule of equal marginal utility per dollar spent is not an explicit or conscious act on the part of consumers. Rather, this is a model of consumer optimum.

HOW A PRICE CHANGE AFFECTS CONSUMER OPTIMUM

Consumption decisions are summarized in the law of demand, which states that the amount purchased is inversely related to price. We can now see why by using the law of diminishing marginal utility.

Purchase decisions are made such that the value of the marginal utility of the last unit purchased and consumed is just equal to the price that had to be paid. No consumer will, when optimizing, buy 10 units of a good per unit time period when the personal valuation placed on the tenth unit is less than the price of the tenth unit.

If we start out at consumer optimum and then observe a price decrease, we can predict that consumers will respond to the price decrease by consuming more. Why? Because before the price change, the marginal utility of the last unit was about equal to the price paid for the last unit. Now, with a lower price, it is possible to consume more than before and still not have the marginal utility be less than the price, because the price has fallen. If the law of diminishing marginal utility holds, the purchase and consumption of additional units will cause marginal utility to fall. Eventually it will fall to the point at which it is equal to the price of the final good consumed. The limit to this increase in consumption is given by the law of diminishing marginal utility. At some point, the marginal utility of an additional unit will be less than what the person would have to give up (price) for that additional unit, and the person will stop buying.

A hypothetical demand curve for video rentals per week for a typical consumer is presented in Figure 19-2 on page 422. At a rental price of $5 per video, the marginal utility of the last video rented per week is MU_1. At a rental price of $4 per video per week, the marginal utility is represented by MU_2. Because of the law of diminishing marginal utility—with the consumption of more videos, the marginal utility of the last unit of these additional videos is lower—MU_2 must be less than MU_1. What has happened is that at a lower price, the number of video rentals per week increased from two to three; marginal utility must have fallen. At a higher consumption rate, the marginal utility falls to meet the lower price for video rentals per week.

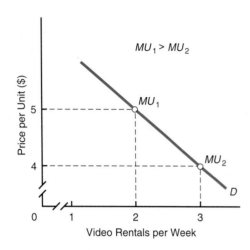

FIGURE 19-2

Video Rental Prices and Marginal Utility
The rate of video rentals per week will increase as long as the marginal utility per last video rental per week exceeds the cost of that rental. A reduction in price from $5 to $4 per video rental causes consumers to increase consumption until marginal utility falls from MU_1 to MU_2 (because of the law of diminishing marginal utility).

The Substitution Effect

What is happening as the price of video rental falls is that consumers are substituting the now relatively cheaper video rentals for other goods and services, such as restaurant meals and live concerts. We call this the **substitution effect** of a change in price of a good because it occurs when consumers substitute relatively cheaper goods for relatively more expensive ones.

We assume that people desire a variety of goods and pursue a variety of goals. That means that few, if any, goods are irreplaceable in meeting demand. We are generally able to substitute one product for another to satisfy demand. This is commonly referred to as the **principle of substitution.**

Let's assume now that there are several goods, not exactly the same, and perhaps even very different from one another, but all serving basically the same purpose. If the relative price of one particular good falls, we will most likely substitute in favor of the lower-priced good and against the other similar goods that we might have been purchasing. Conversely, if the price of that good rises relative to the price of the other similar goods, we will substitute in favor of them and not buy as much of the now higher-priced good.

If the price of some item that you purchase goes down while your money income and all other prices stay the same, your ability to purchase goods goes up. That is to say that your effective **purchasing power** is increased, even though your money income has stayed the same. If you purchase 20 gallons of gas a week at $1.20 per gallon, your total outlay for gas is $24. If the price goes down by 50 percent, to 60 cents a gallon, you would have to spend only $12 a week to purchase the same number of gallons of gas. If your money income and the prices of other goods remain the same, it would be possible for you to continue purchasing 20 gallons of gas a week *and* to purchase more of other goods. You will feel richer and will indeed probably purchase more of a number of goods, including perhaps even more gasoline.

The converse will also be true. When the price of one good you are purchasing goes up, without any other change in prices or income, the purchasing power of your income will drop. You will have to reduce your purchases of either the now higher-priced good or other goods (or a combination).

In general, this **real-income effect** is usually quite small. After all, unless we consider broad categories, such as housing or food, a change in the price of one particular item that

Substitution effect
The tendency of people to substitute cheaper commodities for more expensive commodities.

Principle of substitution
The principle that consumers and producers shift away from goods and resources that become relatively higher priced in favor of goods and resources that are now relatively lower priced.

Purchasing power
The value of money for buying goods and services. If your money income stays the same but the price of one good that you are buying goes up, your effective purchasing power falls and vice versa.

Real-income effect
The change in people's purchasing power that occurs when, other things being constant, the price of one good that they purchase changes. When that price goes up, real income, or purchasing power, falls, and when that price goes down, real income increases.

we purchase will have a relatively small effect on our total purchasing power. Thus we expect the substitution effect usually to be more important than the real-income effect in causing us to purchase more of goods that have become cheaper and less of goods that have become more expensive.

THE DEMAND CURVE REVISITED

Linking the "law" of diminishing marginal utility and the rule of equal marginal utilities per dollar gives us a negative relationship between the quantity demanded of a good or service and its price. As the relative price of video rentals goes up, for example, the quantity demanded will fall; and as the relative price of video rentals goes down, the quantity demanded will rise. Figure 19-2 shows this demand curve for video rentals. As the price of video rentals falls, the consumer can maximize total utility only by renting more videos, and vice versa. In other words, the relationship between price and quantity desired is simply a downward-sloping demand curve. Note, though, that this downward-sloping demand curve (the law of demand) is derived under the assumption of constant tastes and incomes. You must remember that we are keeping these important determining variables constant when we simply look at the relationship between price and quantity demanded.

Marginal Utility, Total Utility, and the Diamond-Water Paradox

Even though water is essential to life and diamonds are not, water is cheap and diamonds are dear. The economist Adam Smith in 1776 called this the "diamond-water paradox." The paradox is easily understood when we make the distinction between total utility and marginal utility. The total utility of water greatly exceeds the total utility derived from diamonds. What determines the price, though, is what happens on the margin. We have relatively few diamonds, so the marginal utility of the last diamond consumed is high. The opposite is true for water. Total utility does not determine what people are willing to pay for a unit of a particular commodity; marginal utility does. Look at the situation graphically in Figure 19-3. We show the demand curve for diamonds, labeled $D_{diamonds}$. The demand curve for water is labeled D_{water}. We plot quantity in terms of kilograms per unit time

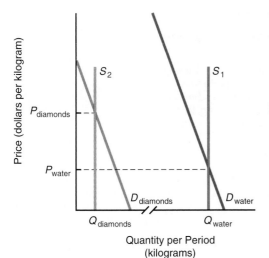

FIGURE 19-3

The Diamond-Water Paradox

We pick kilograms as a common unit of measurement for both water and diamonds. To demonstrate that the demand and supply of water is immense, we have put a break in the horizontal quantity axis. Although the demand for water is much greater than the demand for diamonds, the marginal valuation of water is given by the marginal value placed on the last unit of water consumed. To find that, we must know the supply of water, which is given as S_1. At that supply, the price of water is P_{water}. But the supply for diamonds is given by S_2. At that supply, the price of diamonds is $P_{diamonds}$. The total valuation that consumers place on water is tremendous relative to the total valuation consumers place on diamonds. What is important for price determination, however, is the marginal valuation, or the marginal utility received.

period on the horizontal axis. On the vertical axis we plot price in dollars per kilogram. We use kilograms as our common unit of measurement for water and for diamonds. We could just as well have used gallons, acre-feet, or liters.

Notice that the demand for water is many, many times the demand for diamonds (even though we really don't show this in the diagram). We draw the supply curve of water as S_1 at a quantity of Q_{water}. The supply curve for diamonds is given as S_2 at quantity $Q_{diamonds}$. At the intersection of the supply curve of water with the demand curve of water, the price per kilogram is P_{water}. The intersection of the supply curve of diamonds with the demand curve of diamonds is at $P_{diamonds}$. Notice that $P_{diamonds}$ exceeds P_{water}. Diamonds sell at a higher price than water.

INTERNATIONAL EXAMPLE
The World of Water in Saudi Arabia

The diamond-water paradox deals with the situation in which water, although necessary for life, may be much cheaper than some luxury item. In Saudi Arabia, as you might expect, the contrary can be true. A liter of water costs five times as much as a liter of gasoline, whereas a pair of custom-made British wool dress pants only costs $20. These relative prices are quite different from what we are used to seeing in America. Water costs next to nothing, a liter of gas about 40 cents, and custom-made wool pants at least $200. To understand what has happened in Saudi Arabia, simply substitute gasoline for water and water for diamonds in Figure 19-3.

FOR CRITICAL ANALYSIS: List some of the effects on human behavior that such a high relative price of water would cause. ●

CONCEPTS IN BRIEF

- The law of diminishing marginal utility tells us that each successive marginal unit of a good consumed adds less extra utility.

- Each consumer with a limited income must make a choice about the basket of commodities to purchase; economic theory assumes that the consumer chooses the basket of commodities that yields optimum consumption. The consumer maximizes total utility by equating the marginal utility of the last dollar spent on one good with the marginal utility per last dollar spent on all other goods. That is the state of consumer optimum.

- To remain in consumer optimum, a price decrease requires an increase in consumption; a price increase requires a decrease in consumption.

- Each change in price has a substitution effect and a real-income effect. When price falls, the consumer substitutes in favor of the relatively cheaper good. When price falls, the consumer's real purchasing power increases, causing the consumer to purchase more of most goods. The opposite would occur when price increases. Assuming that the law of diminishing marginal utility holds, the demand curve must slope downward.

Contingent Valuation: Pricing the "Priceless"

Concepts Applied: *Utility, total utility, demand curve*

It is difficult to estimate the dollar amount an average citizen is willing to pay to keep the Grand Canyon's air clean. One way economists attempt to derive the demand for pristine wilderness is to use *contingent valuation.*

Obviously, not everything has a price. That is because not everything is bought and sold in the marketplace. Much of what occurs in the environment is outside of the marketplace. A wilderness area so remote that hardly anyone visits it certainly has a value, but what is it? Just because few people visit doesn't mean it has little worth. If the wilderness were privately owned and the owner received virtually no income from occasional visitors, that does not mean that it has virtually no value.

When Disaster Occurs

When the wilderness area with few visitors is harmed by some disaster of human origin, such as an oil spill, what has been lost? If your house is burned down, you can get a pretty accurate idea of what the insurance company will give you by looking at the housing market for an alternative. Such is not the case with an oil-blighted wilderness area in the far reaches of Alaska.

Nonuse Satisfaction

Even people who never use the wilderness area may place a value on it. They may place a value on the opportunity to preserve the wilderness for their grandchildren and on the mere knowledge that such a pristine wilderness area exists. The question, then, is, how do we get an accurate valuation of these *nonuse* values?

Contingent Valuation

Some economists believe that they can obtain an estimate of the demand curve for a wilderness area, for example, that includes nonuse values by conducting opinion polls. In this technique, called *contingent valuation,* people are asked what they are willing to pay for a particular benefit or what they would accept as compensation for its loss. This technique was used in developing multibillion-dollar damage claims against Exxon after its oil tanker, the *Exxon Valdez,* went aground in Alaska in 1989. In essence, these contingent valuation surveys asked people *not* living in Alaska to place a value on the utility they lost by virtue of the fact that a part of Alaska's pristine beauty was harmed.

Criticisms of Opinion Data

Many economists are critical of opinion surveys conducted to estimate utility. They point out that such estimates of supposed willingness to pay are without strong meaning if individuals don't actually have to make the payments. One opinion survey estimated the average individual's willingness to pay to prevent the extinction of the whooping crane at $149 per year. That comes to almost $30 billion per year for all U.S. adults. Given that there are fewer than 170 whooping cranes in existence, this total represents about $165 million per bird *per year.* There are literally thousands of species that might be protected. Even if households' average willingness to pay is only $10 per year per endangered species, summing that amount over all environmental "goods" would exceed the average family's yearly income many times.

The way in which opinion survey questions are phrased also reveals their weaknesses. In one study, the people interviewed said they would be willing to pay $90 a year to preserve clean air in the Grand Canyon. In a follow-up survey, when they were asked about paying for competing claims of cleaner air in Chicago and the eastern United States as well, they were willing to spend only $16 a year to preserve clean air in the Grand Canyon.

Finally, when people are asked their willingness to accept money in exchange for a harm to a resource rather than their willingness to pay to prevent that identical harm, the dollar values they cite are substantially higher.

FOR CRITICAL ANALYSIS

1. Why can't opinion polls be used effectively to estimate demand curves?

2. How do individuals normally express their perceived level of satisfaction for a good or a service in the marketplace?

CHAPTER SUMMARY

1. As an individual consumes more of a particular commodity, the total level of utility, or satisfaction, derived from that consumption increases. However, the *rate* at which it increases diminishes as more is consumed. This is known as the law of diminishing marginal utility.

2. An individual reaches consumer optimum when the marginal utility per last dollar spent on each commodity consumed is equal to the marginal utility per dollar spent on every other good.

3. When the price of a particular commodity goes up, to get back into an optimum position, the consumer must reduce consumption of the now relatively more expensive commodity. As this consumer moves back up the marginal utility curve, marginal utility increases. A change in price has both a substitution effect and a real-income effect. As the price goes down, for example, the consumer substitutes in favor of the cheaper good, and also as the price goes down, real purchasing power increases, causing a general increase in consumer purchases of most goods and services.

4. It is possible to derive a downward-sloping demand curve by using the principle of diminishing marginal utility.

DISCUSSION OF PREVIEW QUESTIONS

1. **What is the law of diminishing marginal utility?**
The law of diminishing marginal utility states that as an individual consumes more and more units of a commodity per unit of time, eventually the extra benefit derived from consuming successive units will fall. Thus the fourth hamburger consumed in an eight-hour period yields less satisfaction than the third, and the third less than the second. The law is quite general and holds for almost any commodity.

2. **How does a consumer maximize total utility?**
This question deals with the maximization of utility derived not from the consumption of one commodity but from the consumption of all commodities that the individual wants, subject to an income constraint. The rule is that maximization of total utility requires that the last dollar spent on each commodity consumed by the individual have the same marginal utility. Stated differently, the consumer should purchase goods and services up to the point where the consumer's marginal utilities per dollar (marginal utility divided by price) for all commodities are equated and all income is spent (or saved for future spending). For example, assume that you are about to spend all of your income but discover that the marginal utility per dollar's worth for bread will be 10 utils and the marginal utility per dollar's worth of milk will be 30 utils. This means that the last dollar you are going to spend on bread will increase your total utility by 10, whereas the last dollar you are going to spend on milk will increase your total utility by 30. By spending one dollar more on milk and one dollar less on bread, you raise your total utility by about 20 utils, while your total dollar expenditures remain constant. This reallocation causes the marginal utility per dollar's worth of milk to fall and the marginal utility per dollar's worth of bread to rise. To maximize total utility, you will continue to buy more or less of each commodity until the marginal utilities per dollar's worth of all goods you consume are equated.

3. **What happens to consumer optimum when price changes?**
Assume that you have reached an optimum: The marginal utilities per dollar's worth for all the goods you purchase are equated. Assume that the last dollar spent on each of the commodities you purchase increases your total utility by 20 utils. Now suppose that the price of bread falls while all other prices remain constant. Because the price of bread has fallen, the last dollar spent on bread now has a higher marginal utility. This is true because at a lower price

for bread, a $1 bill can purchase a greater quantity of bread. This means that marginal utility per dollar's worth of bread now *exceeds* 20 utils, whereas the marginal utility per dollar's worth of each of the other goods you purchase still equals 20 utils. In short, you are no longer optimizing; your old pattern of expenditures does not maximize your total utility. You can now increase your total utility by purchasing more bread. Note that a reduction in the price of bread (other things held constant) leads to your purchasing more bread per unit of time.

4. How can the law of diminishing marginal utility account for the law of demand?
When a consumer is optimizing, total utility is maximized. An increase in expenditures on any specific commodity will necessarily lead to a reduction in expenditure on another commodity and a reduction

in overall total utility. Why? Because of the law of diminishing marginal utility. For example, suppose that you are maximizing your overall total utility and that the marginal utility per dollar's worth of each commodity you purchase is 20 utils. Suppose that you experiment and spend another dollar on bread—and therefore spend one dollar less on milk. Your total utility must fall because you will receive less than 20 utils for the next dollar's worth of bread, and you lose 20 utils by spending a dollar less on milk. Thus, on net balance, you lose utility. We can see intuitively, then, that because you get less and less additional benefit from consuming more and more bread (or any other commodity), the price of bread (or any other commodity) *must fall* before you will voluntarily purchase more of it. That is how diminishing marginal utility helps explain the law of demand.

PROBLEMS

(Answers to the odd-numbered problems appear at the back of the book.)

19-1. Suppose that you are standing in the checkout line of a grocery store. You have 5 pounds of oranges and three ears of corn. A pound of oranges costs 30 cents; so does an ear of corn. You have $2.40 to spend. You are satisfied that you have reached the highest level of satisfaction, or total utility. Your sister comes along and tries to convince you that you have to put some of the corn back and replace it with oranges. From what you know about utility analysis, how would you explain this disagreement?

19-2. To increase marginal utility, the consumer must decrease consumption (other things being constant). This sounds paradoxical. Why is it a correct statement nonetheless?

19-3. Assume that Alice Warfield's marginal utility is 100 utils for the last hamburger she consumed. If the price of hamburgers is $1 apiece, what is Warfield's marginal utility per dollar's worth of hamburger? What is her marginal utility per dollar's worth if the price is 50 cents per hamburger? If the price is $2? How do we calculate marginal utility per dollar's worth of specific commodities?

19-4. A fall in the price of one good leads to more of that good being consumed, other things remaining constant. How might this increase in consumption be broken down?

19-5. Consider the accompanying table. Following the optimizing rule, how much of each good will be consumed?

Quantity of Good A	Marginal Utility of Good A	Price of Good A	Quantity of Good B	Marginal Utility of Good B	Price of Good B
100	15	$4.51	9	7	$1.69
101	12	4.51	10	5	1.69
102	8	4.51	11	3	1.69
103	6	4.51	12	2	1.69

19-6. If total utility is increasing as more is consumed, what is happening to marginal utility?

19-7. Yesterday you were consuming four eggs and two strips of bacon. Today you are consuming three eggs and three strips of bacon. Your tastes did not change overnight. What might have caused this change? Are you better or worse off?

19-8. The marginal utility of X is five times the marginal utility of Y, but the price of X is only four times the price of Y. How can this disequilibrium be remedied?

19-9. Look at the accompanying table; then answer the questions that follow.

Quantity of X Consumed	Total Utility (utils)
0	0
1	20
2	50
3	70
4	80

a. What is the marginal utility of consuming the first unit of X?
b. What is the marginal utility of consuming the fourth unit of X?
c. When does marginal utility start to diminish?

COMPUTER-ASSISTED INSTRUCTION

The consumer is optimizing when $MU_a/P_a = MU_b/P_b = \cdots = MU_z/P_z$. What does it mean if $MU_a/P_a > MU_b/P_b$? If $MU_a/P_a < MU_b/P_b$? How is a consumer likely to react to such inequalities? Why will the consumer's total utility increase on buying more or less of each good if an inequality exists? Specific calculations shed light on these questions.

Complete problem and answer appear on disk.

MORE ADVANCED CONSUMER CHOICE THEORY

It is possible to analyze consumer choice verbally, as we did for the most part in Chapter 19. The theory of diminishing marginal utility can be fairly well accepted on intuitive grounds and by introspection. If we want to be more formal and perhaps more elegant in our theorizing, however, we can translate our discussion into a graphic analysis with what we call indifference curves and the budget constraint. Here we discuss these terms and their relationship and demonstrate consumer equilibrium in geometric form.

ON BEING INDIFFERENT

What does it mean to be indifferent? It usually means that you don't care one way or the other about something—you are equally disposed to either of two alternatives. With this interpretation in mind, we will turn to two choices, video rentals and restaurant meals. In panel (a) of Figure E-1, we show several combinations of video rentals and restaurant meals per week that a representative consumer considers equally satisfactory. That is to say, for each combination, *A, B, C,* and *D,* this consumer will have exactly the same level of total utility.

The simple numerical example that we have used happens to concern video rentals and restaurant meals per week. This example is used to illustrate general features of indifference curves and related analytical tools that are necessary for deriving the demand curve. Obviously, we could have used any two commodities. Just remember that we are using a *specific* example to illustrate a *general* analysis.

We can plot these combinations graphically in panel (b) of Figure E-1, with restaurant meals per week on the horizontal axis and video rentals per week on the vertical axis. These are our consumer's indifference combinations—the consumer finds each combination as acceptable as the others. When we connect these combinations with a smooth curve, we obtain what is called the consumer's **indifference curve.** Along the indifference curve, every combination of the two goods in question yields the same level of satisfaction. Every point along the

Indifference curve
A curve composed of a set of consumption alternatives, each of which yields the same total amount of satisfaction.

FIGURE E-1

Combinations That Yield Equal Levels of Satisfaction
A, B, C, and *D* represent combinations of video rentals and restaurant meals per week that give an equal level of satisfaction to this consumer. In other words, the consumer is indifferent among these four combinations.

Panel (a)

Combination	Video Rentals per Week	Restaurant Meals per Week
A	1	7
B	2	4
C	3	2
D	4	1

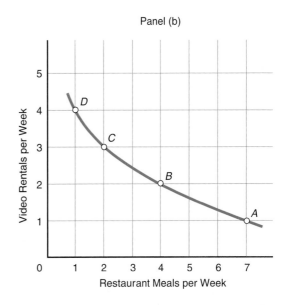

Panel (b)

indifference curve is equally desirable to the consumer. For example, four video rentals per week and one restaurant meal per week will give our representative consumer exactly the same total satisfaction as two video rentals per week and four restaurant meals per week.

PROPERTIES OF INDIFFERENCE CURVES

Indifference curves have special properties relating to their slope and shape.

Downward Slope

The indifference curve shown in panel (b) of Figure E-1 slopes downward; that is, it has a negative slope. Now consider Figure E-2. Here we show two points, A and B. Point A represents four video rentals per week and two restaurant meals per week. Point B represents five video rentals per week and six restaurant meals per week. Clearly, B is always preferred to A because B represents more of everything. If B is always preferred to A, it is impossible for points A and B to be on the same indifference curve because the definition of the indifference curve is a set of combinations of two goods that are equally preferred.

Curvature

The indifference curve that we have drawn in panel (b) of Figure E-1 is special. Notice that it is curved. Why didn't we just draw a straight line, as we have usually done for a demand curve? To find out why we don't posit straight-line indifference curves, consider the implications. We show such a straight-line indifference curve in Figure E-3. Start at point A. The consumer has no restaurant meals and five video rentals per week. Now the consumer wishes to go to point B. He or she is willing to give up only one video rental in order to get one restaurant meal. Now let's assume that the consumer is at point C, consuming one video rental and four restaurant meals per week. If the consumer wants to go to point D, he or she is again willing to give up one video rental in order to get one more restaurant meal per week.

FIGURE E-2

Indifference Curves: Impossibility of an Upward Slope

Point B represents a consumption of more video rentals per week and more restaurant meals per week than point A. B is always preferred to A. Therefore, A and B cannot be on the same indifference curve, which is positively sloped, because an indifference curve shows *equally preferred* combinations of the two goods.

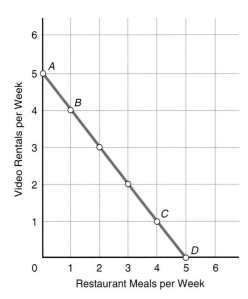

FIGURE E-3

Implications of a Straight-Line Indifference Curve

If the indifference curve is a straight line, the consumer will be willing to give up the same number of video rentals (one for one in this simple example) to get one more restaurant meal per week, whether the consumer has no restaurant meals or a lot of restaurant meals per week. For example, the consumer at point *A* has five video rentals and no restaurant meals per week. He or she is willing to give up one video rental in order to get one restaurant meal per week. At point *C*, however, the consumer has only one video rental and four restaurant meals per week. Because of the straight-line indifference curve, this consumer is willing to give up the last video rental in order to get one more restaurant meal per week, even though he or she already has four.

In other words, no matter how many videos the consumer rents, he or she is willing to give up one video rental to get one restaurant meal per week—which does not seem plausible. Doesn't it make sense to hypothesize that the more videos the consumer rents per week, the less he or she will value an *additional* video rental? Presumably, when the consumer has five video rentals and no restaurant meals per week, he or she should be willing to give up more than one video rental in order to get one restaurant meal. Therefore, a straight-line indifference curve as shown in Figure E-3 no longer seems plausible.

In mathematical jargon, an indifference curve is convex with respect to the origin. Let's look at this in panel (a) of Figure E-1. Starting with combination *A*, the consumer has one video rental but seven restaurant meals per week. To remain indifferent, the consumer would have to be willing to give up three restaurant meals to obtain one more video rental (as shown in combination *B*). However, to go from combination *C* to combination *D*, notice that the consumer would have to be willing to give up only one restaurant meal for an additional video rental per week. The quantity of the substitute considered acceptable changes as the rate of consumption of the original item changes.

Consequently the indifference curve in panel (b) of Figure E-1 will be convex when viewed from the origin.

THE MARGINAL RATE OF SUBSTITUTION

Instead of using marginal utility, we can talk in terms of the marginal rate of substitution between restaurant meals and video rentals per week. We can formally define the consumer's marginal rate of substitution as follows:

> **The marginal rate of substitution is equal to the change in the quantity of one good that just offsets a one-unit change in the consumption of another good, such that total satisfaction remains constant.**

We can see numerically what happens to the marginal rate of substitution in our example if we rearrange panel (a) of Figure E-1 into Table E-1. Here we show restaurant meals

(1) Combination	(2) Restaurant Meals Per Week	(3) Video Rentals Per Week	(4) Marginal Rate of Substitution of Restaurant Meals for Video Rentals
A	7	1	3:1
B	4	2	2:1
C	2	3	1:1
D	1	4	

TABLE E-1

Calculating the Marginal Rate of Substitution
As we move from combination A to combination B, we are still on the same indifference curve. To stay on that curve, the number of restaurant meals decreases by three and the number of video rentals increases by one. The marginal rate of substitution is 3:1. A three-unit decrease in restaurant meals requires an increase in one video rental to leave the consumer's total utility unaltered.

in the second column and video rentals in the third. Now we ask the question, What change in the consumption of video rentals per week will just compensate for a three-unit change in the consumption of restaurant meals per week and leave the consumer's total utility constant? The movement from A to B increases video rental consumption by one. Here the marginal rate of substitution is 3:1—a three-unit decrease in restaurant meals requires an increase of one video rental to leave the consumer's total utility unaltered. Thus the consumer values the three restaurant meals as the equivalent of one video rental. We do this for the rest of the table and find that as restaurant meals decrease further, the marginal rate of substitution goes from 3:1 to 1:1. The marginal rate of substitution of restaurant meals for video rentals per week falls as the consumer obtains more video rentals. That is, the consumer values successive units of video rentals less and less in terms of restaurant meals. The first video rental is valued at three restaurant meals; the last (fourth) video rental is valued at only one restaurant meal. The fact that the marginal rate of substitution falls is sometimes called the *law of substitution*.

In geometric language, the slope of the consumer's indifference curve (actually, the negative of the slope) measures the consumer's marginal rate of substitution. Notice that this marginal rate of substitution is purely subjective or psychological.

THE INDIFFERENCE MAP

Let's now consider the possibility of having both more video rentals *and* more restaurant meals per week. When we do this, we can no longer stay on the same indifference curve that we drew in Figure E-1. That indifference curve was drawn for equally satisfying combinations of video rentals and restaurant meals per week. If the individual can now attain more of both, a new indifference curve will have to be drawn, above and to the right of the one shown in panel (b) of Figure E-1. Alternatively, if the individual faces the possibility of having less of both video rentals and restaurant meals per week, an indifference curve will have to be drawn below and to the left of the one in panel (b) of Figure E-1. We can map out a whole set of indifference curves corresponding to these possibilities.

Figure E-4 shows three possible indifference curves. Indifference curves that are higher than others necessarily imply that for every given quantity of one good, more of the other good can be obtained on a higher indifference curve. Looked at another way, if one goes from curve I_1 to I_2, it is possible to consume the same number of restaurant meals *and* be able to rent more videos per week. This is shown as a movement from point A to point B in Figure E-4. We could do it the other way. When we move from a lower to a higher indif-

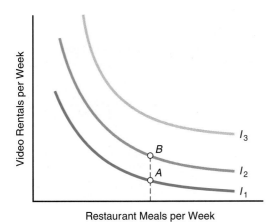

FIGURE E-4
A Set of Indifference Curves
An infinite number of indifference curves can be drawn. We show three possible ones. Realize that a higher indifference curve represents the possibility of higher rates of consumption of both goods. Hence a higher indifference curve is preferred to a lower one because more is preferred to less. Look at points *A* and *B*. Point *B* represents more video rentals than point *A*; therefore, bundles on indifference curve I_2 have to be preferred over bundles on I_1 because the number of restaurant meals per week is the same at points *A* and *B*.

ference curve, it is possible to rent the same number of videos *and* to consume more restaurant meals per week. Thus the higher a consumer is on the indifference map, the greater that consumer's total level of satisfaction.

THE BUDGET CONSTRAINT

Budget Constraint
All of the possible combinations of goods that can be purchased (at fixed prices) with a specific budget.

Our problem here is to find out how to maximize consumer satisfaction. To do so, we must consult not only our *preferences*—given by indifference curves—but also our *market opportunities*—given by our available income and prices, called our **budget constraint.** We might want more of everything, but for any given budget constraint, we have to make choices, or trade-offs, among possible goods. Everyone has a budget constraint; that is, everyone faces a limited consumption potential. How do we show this graphically? We must find the prices of the goods in question and determine the maximum consumption of each allowed by our budget. For example, let's assume that videos rent for $10 apiece and restaurant meals cost $20. Let's also assume that our representative consumer has a total budget of $60 per week. What is the maximum number of videos the consumer can rent? Six. And the maximum number of restaurant meals per week he or she can consume? Three. So now, as shown in Figure E-5, we have two points on our budget line, which is sometimes called the *consumption possibilities curve*. These anchor points of the budget line are obtained by dividing money income by the price of each product. The first point is at *b* on the vertical axis; the second, at *b'* on the horizontal axis. The budget line is linear because prices are given.

Any combination along line *bb'* is possible; in fact, any combination in the colored area is possible. We will assume, however, that the individual consumer completely uses up the available budget, and we will consider as possible only those points along *bb'*.

Slope of the Budget Constraint

The budget constraint is a line that slopes downward from left to right. The slope of that line has a special meaning. Look carefully at the budget line in Figure E-5. Remember from our discussion of graphs in Appendix A that we measure a negative slope by the ratio of the fall in *Y* over the run in *X*. In this case, *Y* is video rentals per week and *X* is restaurant meals per week. In Figure E-5, the fall in *Y* is −2 video rentals per week (a drop from 4 to 2) for a run in *X* of one restaurant meal per week (an increase from 1 to 2); therefore, the slope of

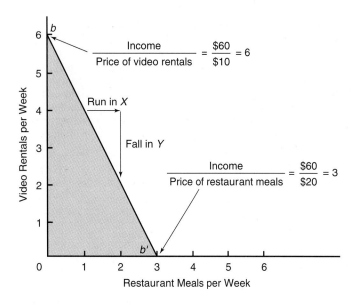

FIGURE E-5

The Budget Constraint
The line *bb'* represents this individual's budget constraint. Assuming that video rentals cost $10 each, restaurant meals cost $20 each, and the individual has a budget of $60 per week, a maximum of six video rentals or three restaurant meals can be bought each week. These two extreme points are connected to form the budget constraint. All combinations within the colored area and on the budget constraint line are feasible.

the budget constraint is $-2/1$, or -2. This slope of the budget constraint represents the rate of exchange between video rentals and restaurant meals; it is the realistic rate of exchange, given their prices.

Now we are ready to determine how the consumer achieves the optimum consumption rate.

CONSUMER OPTIMUM REVISITED

Consumers will try to attain the highest level of total utility possible, given their budget constraints. How can this be shown graphically? We draw a set of indifference curves similar to those in Figure E-4, and we bring in reality—the budget constraint *bb'*. Both are drawn in Figure E-6. Because a higher level of total satisfaction is represented by a higher indifference curve, we know that the consumer will strive to be on the highest indifference

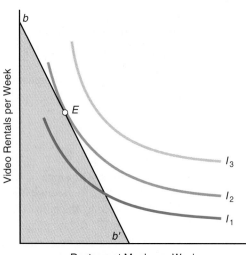

FIGURE E-6

Consumer Optimum
A consumer reaches an optimum when he or she ends up on the highest indifference curve possible, given a limited budget. This occurs at the tangency between an indifference curve and the budget constraint. In this diagram, the tangency is at *E*.

curve possible. However, the consumer cannot get to indifference curve I_3 because the budget will be exhausted before any combination of video rentals and restaurant meals represented on indifference curve I_3 is attained. This consumer can maximize total utility, subject to the budget constraint, only by being at point E on indifference curve I_2 because here the consumer's income is just being exhausted. Mathematically, point E is called the tangency point of the curve I_2 to the straight line bb'.

Consumer optimum is achieved when the marginal rate of substitution (which is subjective) is just equal to the feasible, or realistic, rate of exchange between video rentals and restaurant meals. This realistic rate is the ratio of the two prices of the goods involved. It is represented by the absolute value of the slope of the budget constraint. At point E, the point of tangency between indifference curve I_2 and budget constraint bb', the rate at which the consumer wishes to substitute video rentals for restaurant meals (the numerical value of slope of the indifference curve) is just equal to the rate at which the consumer *can* substitute video rentals for restaurant meals (the slope of the budget line).

EFFECTS OF CHANGES IN INCOME

A change in income will shift the budget constraint bb' in Figure E-6. Consider only increases in income and no changes in price. The budget constraint will shift outward. Each new budget line will be parallel to the original one because we are not allowing a change in the relative prices of video rentals and restaurant meals. We would now like to find out how an individual consumer responds to successive increases in income when relative prices remain constant. We do this in Figure E-7. We start out with an income that is represented by a budget line bb'. Consumer optimum is at point E, where the consumer attains the highest indifference curve I_1, given the budget constraint bb'. Now we let income increase. This is shown by a shift outward in the budget line to cc'. The consumer attains a new optimum at point E'. That is where a higher indifference curve, I_2, is reached. Again, the consumer's income is increased so that the new budget line is dd'. The new optimum now moves to E''. This is where indifference curve I_3 is reached. If we connect the three consumer optimum points, E, E', and E'', we have what is called an income-consumption curve. The **income-consumption curve** shows the optimum consumption points that would occur if income

Income-consumption curve
The set of optimum consumption points that would occur if income were increased, relative prices remaining constant.

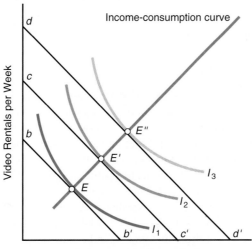

Income-consumption curve

FIGURE E-7

Income-Consumption Curve
We start off with income sufficient to yield budget constraint bb'. The highest attainable indifference curve is I_1, which is just tangent to bb' at E. Next we increase income. The budget line moves outward to cc', which is parallel to bb'. The new highest indifference curve is I_2, which is just tangent to cc' at E'. We increase income again, which is represented by a shift in the budget line to dd'. The new tangency point of the highest indifference curve, I_3, with dd', is at point E''. When we connect these three points, we obtain the income-consumption curve.

Restaurant Meals per Week

Video Rentals per Week

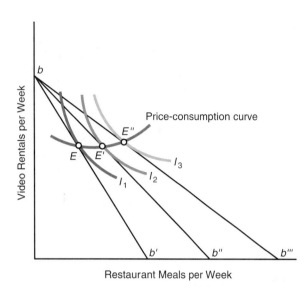

Price-consumption curve

FIGURE E-8

Price-Consumption Curve

As we lower the price of restaurant meals, income measured in terms of restaurant meals per week increases. We show this by rotating the budget constraint from *bb'* to *bb"* and finally to *bb"'*. We then find the highest indifference curve that is attainable for each successive budget constraint. For budget constraint *bb'*, the highest indifference curve is I_1, which is tangent to *bb'* at point *E*. We do this for the next two budget constraints. When we connect the optimum points, *E*, *E'*, and *E"*, we derive the price-consumption curve, which shows the combinations of the two commodities that a consumer will purchase when money income and the price of one commodity remain constant while the other commodity's price changes.

for that consumer were increased continuously, holding the prices of video rentals and restaurant meals constant.

THE PRICE-CONSUMPTION CURVE

In Figure E-8, we hold money income and the price of video rentals constant while we lower the price of restaurant meals. As we keep lowering the price of restaurant meals, the quantity of meals that could be purchased if all income were spent on restaurant meals increases; thus the extreme points for the budget constraint keep moving outward to the right as the price of restaurant meals falls. In other words, the budget line rotates outward from *bb'* to *bb"* and *bb"'*. Each time the price of restaurant meals falls, a new budget line is formed. There has to be a new optimum point. We find it by locating on each new budget line the highest attainable indifference curve. This is shown at points *E, E',* and *E"*. We see that as price decreases for restaurant meals, the consumer purchases more restaurant meals per week. We call the line connecting points *E, E',* and *E"* the **price-consumption curve.** It connects the tangency points of the budget constraints and indifference curves, thus showing the amounts of two goods that a consumer will buy when money income and the price of one commodity are held constant while the price of the remaining good changes.

Price-consumption curve
The set of consumer optimum combinations of two goods that the consumer would choose as the price of one good changes, while money income and the price of the other good remain constant.

DERIVING THE DEMAND CURVE

We are now in a position to derive the demand curve using indifference curve analysis. In panel (a) of Figure E-9, we show what happens when the price of restaurant meals decreases, holding both the price of video rentals and income constant. If the price of restaurant meals decreases, the budget line rotates from *bb'* to *bb"*. The two optimum points are given by the tangency at the highest indifference curve that just touches those two budget lines. This is at *E* and *E'*. But those two points give us two price-quantity pairs. At point *E*, the price of restaurant meals is $20; the quantity demanded is 2. Thus we have one point that we can transfer to panel (b) of Figure E-9. At point *E'*, we have another price-quantity pair. The price has fallen to $10; the quantity demanded has increased to 5. We therefore transfer this other point to panel (b). When we connect these two points (and all the others in between), we derive the demand curve for restaurant meals; it slopes downward.

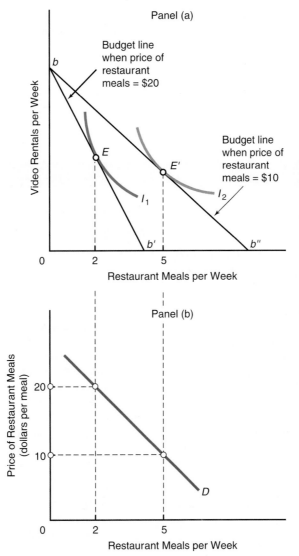

Panel (a)

FIGURE E-9

Deriving the Demand Curve

In panel (a), we show the effects of a decrease in the price of restaurant meals from $20 to $10. At $20, the highest indifference curve touches the budget line bb' at point E. The quantity of restaurant meals consumed is two. We transfer this combination—price, $20; quantity demanded, 2—down to panel (b). Next we decrease the price of restaurant meals to $10. This generates a new budget line, or constraint, which is bb". Consumer optimum is now at E'. The optimum quantity of restaurant meals demanded at a price of $10 is five. We transfer this point—price, $10; quantity demanded, 5—down to panel (b). When we connect these two points, we have a demand curve, D, for restaurant meals.

APPENDIX SUMMARY

1. Along an indifference curve, the consumer experiences equal levels of satisfaction. That is to say, along any indifference curve, every combination of the two goods in question yields exactly the same level of satisfaction.

2. Indifference curves usually slope downward and are usually convex to the origin.

3. To measure the marginal rate of substitution, we find out how much of one good has to be given up in order to allow the consumer to consume one more unit of the other good while still remaining on the same indifference curve. The marginal rate of substitution falls as one moves down an indifference curve.

4. Indifference curves represent preferences. A budget constraint represents opportunities—how much can be purchased with a given level of income. Consumer optimum is obtained when the highest indifference curve is just tangent to the budget constraint line; at

that point, the consumer reaches the highest feasible indifference curve.

5. When income increases, the budget constraint shifts outward to the right, parallel to the previous budget constraint line.

6. As income increases, the consumer optimum moves up to higher and higher indifference curves. When we connect those points with a line, we derive the income-consumption curve.

7. As the price of one good decreases, the budget line rotates. When we connect the tangency points of the highest indifference curves to these new budget lines, we derive the price-consumption curve.

PROBLEMS

(Answers to the odd-numbered problems appear at the back of the book.)

E-1. Suppose that a consumer prefers A to B and B to C but insists that she also prefers C to A. Explain the logical problem here.

E-2. Suppose that you are indifferent among the following three combinations of food (f) and drink (d): 1f and 10d, 2f and 7d, 3f and 2d. Calculate the marginal rate of substitution in consumption between the two goods. Does the substitution of the third f imply a greater sacrifice of d than the second did?

E-3. Construct a budget line from the following information: nominal income of $100 per week; price of beef, P_b, $2 per pound; price of shelter, P_s, $20 per week; all income is spent on beef and shelter. Suppose that your money income remains constant, the price of beef doubles to $4 per pound, and the price of housing falls to $10 per week. Draw the new budget line. Are you now better off or worse off? What do you need to know before deciding?

E-4. Given the following three combinations of goods, $A = 3x + 4y$, $B = 4x + 6y$, and $C = 5x + 4y$, answer the following questions:

  a. Is any one bundle preferred to the other two?
  b. Could a consumer possibly find B and C to be equally acceptable? How about A and C?

E-5. Calculate the marginal rate of substitution of burritos for yogurt for the following consumer's indifference schedule:

Servings of Yogurt per Week	Burritos per Week
10	1
6	2
3	3
1	4

E-6. Assume that you are consuming only yogurt (Y) and gymnasium exercise (G). Each serving of yogurt costs $4, and each visit to the gym costs $8. Given your food and exercise budget, you consume 15 servings of yogurt and five visits to the gym each week. One day, the price of yogurt falls to $3 per serving and the price of gym visits increases to $10. Now you buy 20 servings of yogurt and four gym visits per week.

  a. Draw the old and new budget constraints, and show the two equilibrium bundles of yogurt servings and visits to the gym.
  b. What is your weekly budget for food and exercise?

E-7. Explain why each of the following statements is or is not consistent with our assumptions about consumer preferences.

  a. I can't decide whether to go abroad this summer or to stay at home.
  b. That is mine. You cannot have it. There is nothing you can do to make me change my mind.
  c. I love hot pretzels with mustard at football games. If I had my way, I would never stop eating them.

CHAPTER 20

DEMAND AND SUPPLY ELASTICITY

"Drinking and driving don't mix." Not many people would disagree with this statement. Nonetheless, carnage on America's highways and byways continues year in and year out. About 44,000 men, women, and children die every year in automobile accidents. Nearly half of the victims died because of someone who drank alcohol before getting behind the wheel—in many cases themselves. A disproportionate number of teenagers are involved in alcohol-caused accidents. Would an increase in taxes on beer make a difference? To answer this question, you need to know more about how people respond to changing prices.

PREVIEW QUESTIONS

1. How is total revenue related to the price elasticity of demand?

2. What are the determinants of the price elasticity of demand?

3. What is the income elasticity of demand?

4. What is the price elasticity of supply?

Did You Know That . . . the government predicted it would raise $6 million per year in new revenues from a new 10 percent luxury tax on private airplane and yacht sales a few years ago, but it actually collected only $53,000? How can that be? The answer lies in understanding the relationship between the quantities that people demand at lower prices relative to the quantities that people demand at higher prices. The year during which the 10 percent luxury tax was imposed also saw expensive new yacht sales fall to almost nothing. Clearly, even rich people respond to rising prices, which in this case were caused by a new government tax.

It is not only the government that has to worry about how individuals respond to rising prices; it is perhaps even more important that all businesses take into account consumer response to changing prices. If McDonald's lowers its prices by 10 percent, will fast-food consumers respond by buying so many more Big Macs that the company's revenues will rise? At the other end of the spectrum, can Rolls Royce dealers "get away" with a 2 percent increase in prices? Otherwise stated, will Rolls Royce purchasers respond so little to the relatively small increase in price that the total revenues received for Rolls Royce sales will not fall and may actually rise? The only way to answer these questions is to know how responsive people in the real world will be to changes in prices. Economists have a special name for price responsiveness—*elasticity,* which is the subject of this chapter.

PRICE ELASTICITY

To begin to understand what elasticity is all about, just keep in mind that it means "responsiveness" or "stretchiness." Here we are concerned with the price elasticity of demand and the price elasticity of supply. We wish to know the extent to which a change in the price of, say, petroleum products will cause the quantity demanded and the quantity supplied to change, other things held constant. Let's restrict our discussion at first to the demand side.

Price Elasticity of Demand

We will formally define the **price elasticity of demand,** which we will label E_p, as follows:

$$E_p = \frac{\text{percentage change in quantity demanded}}{\text{percentage change in price}}$$

What will price elasticity of demand tell us? It will tell us the relative amount by which the quantity demanded will change in response to a change in the price of a particular good.

Consider an example in which a 10 percent rise in the price of oil leads to a reduction in quantity demanded of only 1 percent. Putting these numbers into the formula, we find that the price elasticity of demand for oil in this case equals the percentage change in quantity demanded divided by the percentage change in price, or

$$E_p = \frac{-1\%}{+10\%} = -.1$$

Price elasticity of demand (E_p)
The responsiveness of the quantity demanded of a commodity to changes in its price; defined as the percentage change in quantity demanded divided by the percentage change in price.

An elasticity of $-.1$ means that a 1 percent *increase* in the price would lead to a mere .1 percent *decrease* in the quantity demanded. If you were now told, in contrast, that the price elasticity of demand for oil was -1, you would know that a 1 percent increase in the price of oil would lead to a 1 percent decrease in the quantity demanded.

Relative Quantities Only. Notice that in our elasticity formula, we talk about *percentage* changes in quantity demanded divided by *percentage* changes in price. We are therefore not interested in the absolute changes, only in relative amounts. This means that it doesn't matter if we measure price changes in terms of cents, dollars, or hundreds of dollars. It also doesn't matter whether we measure quantity changes in ounces, grams, or pounds. The percentage change will be independent of the units chosen.

POLICY EXAMPLE
Should the U.S. Government Crack Down on Multinational Firms Operating in the United States?

Believe it or not, America is becoming a low-cost manufacturing region. Consequently, foreign companies have shifted production to the United States. The federal government decided that it could raise some additional tax dollars by "cracking down" on foreign companies: During the 1990s, there has been an attempt to increase tax collections from foreign-owned businesses operating in the United States. The policy has not yielded the intended tax revenues sought, however. Rather, it has acted as a disincentive to foreign investment. How much? According to Columbia University economists Jason Cummins and R. Glenn Hubbard, multinationals in any country will decrease their annual rate of investment by 1 to 2 percent for every 1 percent increase in the cost to them of financing their activities. Tax increases in effect increase their cost of capital, and they respond accordingly.

FOR CRITICAL ANALYSIS: What is the approximate price elasticity of demand among multinationals for foreign investment expenditures? ●

Always Negative. The law of demand states that quantity demanded is *inversely* related to the relative price. An increase in the price of a good leads to a decrease in the quantity demanded. If a decrease in the relative price of a good should occur, the quantity demanded would increase by a certain percentage. The point is that price elasticity of demand will always be negative. By convention, *we will ignore the minus sign in our discussion from this point on.*

Basically, the greater the *absolute* price elasticity of demand (disregarding sign), the greater the demand responsiveness to relative price changes—a small change in price has a great impact on quantity demanded. The smaller the absolute price elasticity of demand, the smaller the demand responsiveness to relative price changes—a large change in price has little effect on quantity demanded.

CONCEPTS IN BRIEF

- Elasticity is a measure of the price responsiveness of the quantity demanded and quantity supplied.

- The price elasticity of demand is equal to the percentage change in quantity demanded divided by the percentage change in price.

- Price elasticity of demand is calculated in terms of percentage changes in quantity demanded and in price. Thus it is expressed as a unitless, dimensionless number.

- The law of demand states that quantity demanded and price are inversely related. Therefore, the price elasticity of demand is always negative, because an increase in price will lead to a decrease in quantity demanded and a decrease in price will lead to an increase in quantity demanded. By convention, we ignore the negative sign in discussions of the price elasticity of demand.

Calculating Elasticity

To calculate the price elasticity of demand, we have to compute percentage changes in quantity demanded and in relative price. To obtain the percentage change in quantity demanded, we divide the change in the quantity demanded by the original quantity demanded:

$$\frac{\text{Change in quantity demanded}}{\text{Original quantity demanded}}$$

To find the percentage change in price, we divide the change in price by the original price:

$$\frac{\text{Change in price}}{\text{Original price}}$$

There is an arithmetic problem, though, when we calculate percentage changes in this manner. The percentage change, say, from 2 to 3—50 percent—is not the same as the percentage change from 3 to 2—$33\frac{1}{3}$ percent. In other words, it makes a difference where you start. One way out of this dilemma is simply to use average values.

To compute the price elasticity of demand, we need to deal with the average change in quantity demanded caused by the average change in price. That means that we take the average of the two prices and the two quantities over the range we are considering and compare the change with these averages. For relatively small changes in price, the formula for computing the price elasticity of demand then becomes

$$E_p = \frac{\text{change in quantity}}{\text{sum of quantities}/2} \div \frac{\text{change in price}}{\text{sum of prices}/2}$$

We can rewrite this more simply if we do two things: (1) We can let Q_1 and Q_2 equal the two different quantities demanded before and after the price change and let P_1 and P_2 equal the two different prices. (2) Because we will be dividing a percentage by a percentage, we simply use the ratio, or the decimal form, of the percentages. Therefore,

$$E_p = \frac{\Delta Q}{(Q_1 + Q_2)/2} \div \frac{\Delta P}{(P_1 + P_2)/2}$$

where the Greek letter Δ stands for "change in."

INTERNATIONAL EXAMPLE
The Price Elasticity of Demand for Newspapers

Newspaper owners are always seeking to increase their paper's circulation, not because they want the revenue generated from the sales of the paper, but because the larger the circulation, the more the newspaper can charge for its advertising space. The source of most of a paper's revenues—and profits—comes from its advertisers.

One newspaper owner, Rupert Murdoch, ran an experiment to see how high he could boost sales of a particular newspaper by lowering its price. For one day, he lowered the price of the British daily paper *Today* from 25 pence to 10 pence. According to London's *Financial Times*, the sales of *Today* almost doubled that day, increasing the circulation from

---

590,000 to 1.05 million copies. We can estimate the price elasticity of demand for *Today* by using the formula presented earlier (under the assumption, of course, that all other things were held constant):

$$E_p = \frac{\Delta Q}{(Q_1 + Q_2)/2} \div \frac{\Delta P}{(P_1 + P_2)/2}$$

$$= \frac{1,050,000 - 590,000}{(590,000 + 1,050,000)/2} \div \frac{25 \text{ pence} - 10 \text{ pence}}{(10 \text{ pence} + 25 \text{ pence})/2}$$

$$= \frac{460,000}{820,000} \div \frac{15 \text{ pence}}{17.5 \text{ pence}} = .66$$

The price elasticity of demand of .66 means that a 1 percent decrease in price will lead to a .66 percent increase in quantity demanded.

FOR CRITICAL ANALYSIS: *Would the estimated price elasticity of the* Today *newspaper have been different if we had* not *used the average-values formula? How?* •

PRICE ELASTICITY RANGES

We have names for the varying ranges of price elasticities, depending on whether a 1 percent change in price elicits more or less than a 1 percent change in the quantity demanded.

Elastic demand
A demand relationship in which a given percentage change in price will result in a larger percentage change in quantity demanded. Total expenditures and price changes are inversely related in the elastic region of the demand curve.

Unit elasticity of demand
A demand relationship in which the quantity demanded changes exactly in proportion to the change in price. Total expenditures are invariant to price changes in the unit-elastic region of the demand curve.

Inelastic demand
A demand relationship in which a given percentage change in price will result in a less than proportionate percentage change in the quantity demanded. Total expenditures and price are directly related in the inelastic region of the demand curve.

1. *Elastic demand.* We say that a good has an **elastic demand** whenever the price elasticity of demand is greater than 1. A 1 percent change in price causes a greater than a 1 percent change in the quantity demanded.
2. *Unit elasticity of demand.* In a situation of **unit elasticity of demand,** a 1 percent change in price causes a response of exactly a 1 percent change in the quantity demanded.
3. *Inelastic demand.* In a situation of **inelastic demand,** a 1 percent change in price causes a response of less than a 1 percent change in the quantity demanded. The most extreme inelastic demand is *perfectly inelastic;* no matter what the price, the quantity demanded remains the same, so the price elasticity of demand is zero.

When we say that a commodity's demand is elastic, we are indicating that consumers are relatively responsive to changes in price. When we say that a commodity's demand is inelastic, we are indicating that its consumers are relatively unresponsive to price changes. When economists say that demand is inelastic, it does not mean that quantity demanded is totally unresponsive to price changes. Remember, the law of demand suggests that there will be some responsiveness in quantity demanded to a price change. The question is how much. That's what elasticity attempts to determine.

Extreme Elasticities

There are two extremes in price elasticities of demand. One extreme represents total unresponsiveness of quantity demanded to price changes, which is referred to as

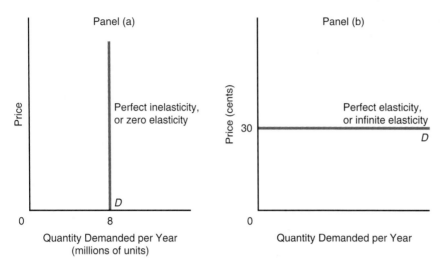

FIGURE 20-1

Extreme Price Elasticities
In panel (a), we show complete price unresponsiveness. The demand curve is vertical at the quantity of 8 million units per year. This means that the price elasticity of demand is zero. In panel (b), we show complete price responsiveness. At a price of 30 cents, in this example, consumers will demand an unlimited quantity of the particular good in question. This is a case of infinite price elasticity of demand.

perfectly inelastic demand, or zero elasticity. The other represents total responsiveness, which is referred to as, infinitely, or **perfectly elastic demand.**

We show perfect inelasticity in panel (a) of Figure 20-1. Notice that the quantity demanded per year is 8 million units, no matter what the price. Hence for any percentage price change, the quantity demanded will remain the same, and thus the change in the quantity demanded will be zero. Look back at our formula for computing elasticity. If the change in the quantity demanded is zero, the numerator is also zero, and a nonzero number divided into zero results in an answer of zero too. Hence there is perfect inelasticity. At the opposite extreme is the situation depicted in panel (b) of Figure 20-1. Here we show that at a price of 30 cents, an unlimited quantity will be demanded. At a price that is only slightly above 30 cents, no quantity will be demanded. There is complete, or infinite, responsiveness here, and hence we call the demand schedule in panel (b) infinitely elastic.

Perfectly inelastic demand
A demand that exhibits zero responsiveness to price changes; no matter what the price is, the quantity demanded remains the same.

Perfectly elastic demand
A demand that has the characteristic that even the slightest increase in price will lead to zero quantity demanded.

CONCEPTS IN BRIEF

- One extreme elasticity occurs when a demand curve is vertical. It has zero price elasticity of demand; it is completely inelastic.

- Another extreme elasticity occurs when a demand curve is horizontal. It has completely elastic demand; its price elasticity of demand is infinite.

ELASTICITY AND TOTAL REVENUES

Suppose that you are in charge of the pricing decision for a cellular telephone service company. How would you know when it is best to raise or not to raise prices? The answer depends in part on the effect of your pricing decision on total revenues, or the total receipts of your company. (The rest of the equation is, of course, your cost structure, a subject we examine in Chapter 22.) It is commonly thought that the way to increase total receipts is to increase price per unit. But is this always the case? Is it possible that a rise in price per unit

THINKING CRITICALLY ABOUT THE MEDIA

For Addicts, Price Does Not Matter?

Both the media and the commonsense definition of a drug addict is a person who has to get a fix "at any price." Consequently, numerous media stories abound about how addicts will do anything they must to get their fixes. The implication is that the price elasticity of demand by addicts for a particular drug is zero—that their demand curves are vertical. There is a problem with this analysis, though. Everyone, addicts included, faces a budget constraint. Consequently, it is impossible for anyone's demand curve to be vertical at *all* prices because he or she could not spend an amount greater than his or her budget constraint.

could lead to a decrease in total revenues? The answers to these questions depend on the price elasticity of demand.

Let's look at Figure 20-2 on page 446. In panel (a), column 1 shows the price of cellular telephone service in dollars per minute, and column 2 represents billions of minutes per year. In column 3, we multiply column 1 times column 2 to derive total revenue because total revenue is always equal to the number of units (quantity) sold times the price per unit, and in column 4, we calculate values of elasticity. Notice what happens to total revenues throughout the schedule. They rise steadily as the price rises from 10 cents to 50 cents per minute; but when the price rises further to 60 cents per minute, total revenues remain constant at $3 billion. At prices per minute higher than 60 cents, total revenues fall as price increases. Indeed, if prices are above 60 cents per minute, total revenues can be increased only by *cutting* prices, not by raising them.

Labeling Elasticity

The relationship between price and quantity on the demand schedule is given in columns 1 and 2 of panel (a) in Figure 20-2. In panel (b), the demand curve, *D*, representing that schedule is drawn. In panel (c), the total revenue curve representing the data in column 3 is drawn. Notice first the level of these curves at small quantities. The demand curve is at a maximum height, but total revenue is zero, which makes sense according to this demand schedule—at a price of $1.10 and above, no units will be purchased, and therefore total revenue will be zero. As price is lowered, we travel down the demand curve, and total revenues increase until price is 60 cents per minute, remain constant from 60 cents to 50 cents per minute, and then fall at lower unit prices. Corresponding to those three sections, demand is elastic, unit-elastic, and inelastic. Hence we have three relationships among the three types of price elasticity and total revenues.

1. *Elastic demand.* A negative relationship exists between small changes in price and changes in total revenues. That is to say, if price is lowered, total revenues will rise when the firm faces demand that is elastic, and if it raises price, total revenues will fall. Consider another example. If the price of Diet Coke were raised by 25 percent and the price of all other soft drinks remained constant, the quantity demanded of Diet Coke would probably fall dramatically. The decrease in quantity demanded due to the increase in the price of Diet Coke would lead in this example to a reduction in the total revenues of the Coca-Cola Company. Therefore, if demand is elastic, price and total revenues will move in *opposite* directions.
2. *Unit-elastic demand.* Changes in price do not change total revenues. When the firm is facing demand that is unit-elastic, if it increases price, total revenues will not change; if it decreases price, total revenues will not change either.
3. *Inelastic demand.* A positive relationship exists between changes in price and total revenues. When the firm is facing demand that is inelastic, if it raises price, total revenues will go up; if it lowers price, total revenues will fall. Consider another example. You have just invented a cure for the common cold that has been approved by the Food and Drug Administration for sale to the public. You are not sure what price you should charge, so you start out with a price of $1 per pill. You sell 20 million pills at that price over a year. The next year, you decide to raise the price by 25 percent, to $1.25. The number of pills you sell drops to 18 million per year. The price increase of 25 percent

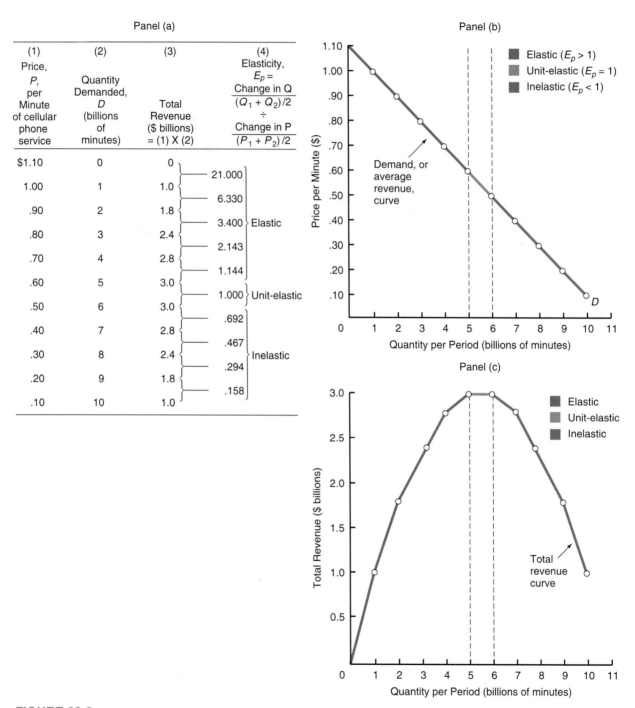

Panel (a)

(1) Price, P, per Minute of cellular phone service	(2) Quantity Demanded, D (billions of minutes)	(3) Total Revenue ($ billions) = (1) X (2)	(4) Elasticity, $E_p =$ $\dfrac{\text{Change in Q}}{(Q_1 + Q_2)/2}$ $\div$ $\dfrac{\text{Change in P}}{(P_1 + P_2)/2}$
$1.10	0	0	
1.00	1	1.0	21.000
.90	2	1.8	6.330
.80	3	2.4	3.400 Elastic
.70	4	2.8	2.143
.60	5	3.0	1.144
.50	6	3.0	1.000 Unit-elastic
.40	7	2.8	.692
.30	8	2.4	.467 Inelastic
.20	9	1.8	.294
.10	10	1.0	.158

FIGURE 20-2

**The Relationship Between Price Elasticity of Demand and Total Revenues for
Cellular Phone Service**

In panel (a), we show the elastic, unit-elastic, and inelastic sections of the demand schedule according to whether a reduction in price increases total revenues, causes them to remain constant, or
causes them to decrease, respectively. In panel (b), we show these regions graphically on the
demand curve. In panel (c), we show them on the total revenue curve.

has led to a 10 percent decrease in quantity demanded. Your total revenues, however, will rise to $22.5 million because of the price increase. We therefore conclude that if demand is inelastic, price and total revenues move in the *same* direction.

The elastic, unit-elastic, and inelastic areas of the demand curve are shown in Figure 20-2. For prices from $1.10 per minute of cellular phone time to 60 cents per minute, as price decreases, total revenues rise from zero to $3 billion. Demand is price-elastic. When price changes from 60 cents to 50 cents, however, total revenues remain constant at $3 billion; demand is unit-elastic. Finally, when price falls from 50 cents to 10 cents, total revenues decrease from $3 billion to $1 billion; demand is inelastic. In panels (b) and (c) of Figure 20-2, we have labeled the sections of the demand curve accordingly, and we have also shown how total revenues first rise, then remain constant, and finally fall.

The relationship between price elasticity of demand and total revenues brings together some important microeconomic concepts. Total revenues, as we have noted, are the product of price per unit times number of units sold. The law of demand states that along a given demand curve, price and quantity changes will move in opposite directions: One increases as the other decreases. Consequently, what happens to the product of price times quantity depends on which of the opposing changes exerts a greater force on total revenues. But this is just what price elasticity of demand is designed to measure—responsiveness of quantity demanded to a change in price. The relationship between price elasticity of demand and total revenues is summarized in Table 20-1.

TABLE 20-1

Relationship Between Price Elasticity of Demand and Total Revenues

Price Elasticity of Demand		Effect of Price Change on Total Revenues (TR)	
		Price Decrease	Price Increase
Inelastic	$(E_p < 1)$	TR ↓	TR ↑
Unit-elastic	$(E_p = 1)$	No change in TR	No change in TR
Elastic	$(E_p > 1)$	TR ↑	TR ↓

INTERNATIONAL EXAMPLE
A Pricing Decision at Disneyland Paris

Several years after it opened with great fanfare, the $4 billion investment in Disneyland Paris (formerly called EuroDisney) was in trouble. In an attempt to improve profits (actually, decrease losses), Disney management decided to lower prices starting in the summer of 1995. Entrance fees during peak periods (April 1 to October 1) dropped from 250 francs (about $50) to 195 francs (about $40). Was this 22 percent reduction in ticket prices a good management strategy for Disney officials? That depends in part on what happened to total revenues. As it turned out, park attendance increased by 700,000 visitors. Thus total revenues increased by more than 22 percent, indicating that the demand for Disneyland Paris is elastic in the price range between $40 to $50.

FOR CRITICAL ANALYSIS: What other factors may have affected attendance at Disneyland Paris? •

CONCEPTS IN BRIEF

- Price elasticity of demand is related to total revenues (and total consumer expenditures).

- When demand is *elastic,* the change in price elicits a change in total revenues (and total consumer expenditures) in the direction opposite that of the price change.

- When demand is *unit-elastic,* a change in price elicits no change in total revenues (or in total consumer expenditures).

- When demand is *inelastic,* a change in price elicits a change in total revenues (and in consumer expenditures) in the same direction as the price change.

DETERMINANTS OF THE PRICE ELASTICITY OF DEMAND

We have learned how to calculate the price elasticity of demand. We know that theoretically, it ranges numerically from zero, completely inelastic, to infinity, completely elastic. What we would like to do now is come up with a list of the determinants of the price elasticity of demand. The price elasticity of demand for a particular commodity at any price depends, at a minimum, on the following:

1. The existence, number, and quality of substitutes
2. The percentage of a consumer's total budget devoted to purchases of that commodity
3. The length of time allowed for adjustment to changes in the price of the commodity

Existence of Substitutes

The closer the substitutes for a particular commodity and the more substitutes there are, the greater will be its price elasticity of demand. At the limit, if there is a perfect substitute, the elasticity of demand for the commodity will be infinity. Thus even the slightest increase in the commodity's price will cause an enormous reduction in the quantity demanded: quantity demanded will fall to zero. We are really talking about two goods that the consumer believes are exactly alike and equally desirable, like dollar bills whose only difference is serial numbers. When we talk about less extreme examples, we can only speak in terms of the number and the similarity of substitutes that are available. Thus we will find that the more narrowly we define a good, the closer and greater will be the number of substitutes available. For example, the demand for a Diet Coke may be highly elastic because consumers can switch to Diet Pepsi. The demand for diet drinks in general, however, is relatively less elastic because there are fewer substitutes.

Share of Budget

We know that the greater the percentage of a total budget spent on the commodity, the greater the person's price elasticity of demand for that commodity. The demand for pepper is thought to be very inelastic merely because individuals spend so little on it relative to their total budgets. In contrast, the demand for things such as transportation and housing is thought to be far more elastic because they occupy a large part of people's budgets—changes in their prices cannot be ignored so easily without sacrificing a lot of other alternative goods that could be purchased.

Consider a numerical example. A household earns $40,000 a year. It purchases $4 of pepper per year and $4,000 of transportation services. Now consider the spending power of this family when the price of pepper and the price of transportation both go up by 100 percent. If the household buys the same amount of pepper, it will now spend $8. It will thus have to reduce other expenditures by $4. This $4 represents only .01 percent of the entire household budget. By contrast, a doubling of transportation costs requires that the family spend $8,000, or $4,000 more on transportation, if it is to purchase the same quantity. That increased expenditure on transportation of $4,000 represents 10 percent of total expenditures that must be switched from other purchases. We would therefore predict that the household will react differently to the doubling of prices for pepper than it will for transportation. It will buy almost the same amount of pepper but will spend significantly less on transportation.

Time for Adjustment

When the price of a commodity changes and that price change persists, more people will learn about it. Further, consumers will be better able to revise their consumption patterns the longer the time period they have to do so. And in fact, the longer the time they do take, the less costly it will be for them to engage in this revision of consumption patterns. Consider a price decrease. The longer the price decrease persists, the greater will be the number of new uses that consumers will discover for the particular commodity, and the greater will be the number of new users of that particular commodity.

It is possible to make a very strong statement about the relationship between the price elasticity of demand and the time allowed for adjustment:

> **The longer any price change persists, the greater the elasticity of demand, other things held constant. Elasticity of demand is greater in the long run than in the short run.**

Let's take an example. Suppose that the price of electricity goes up 50 percent. How do you adjust in the short run? You can turn the lights off more often, you can stop using the stereo as much as you do, and so on. Otherwise it's very difficult to cut back on your consumption of electricity. In the long run, though, you can devise methods to reduce your consumption. Instead of using electric heaters, the next time you have a house built you will install gas heaters. Instead of using an electric stove, the next time you move you will have a gas stove installed. You will purchase fluorescent bulbs because they use less electricity. The more time you have to think about it, the more ways you will find to cut your electricity consumption. We would expect, therefore, that the short-run demand curve for electricity would be relatively inelastic (in the price range around P_e), as demonstrated by D_1 in Figure 20-3 on page 450. However, the long-run demand curve may exhibit much more elasticity (in the neighborhood of P_e), as demonstrated by D_3. Indeed, we can think of an entire family of demand curves such as those depicted in that figure. The short-run demand curve is for the period when there is no time for adjustment. As more time is allowed, the demand curve goes first to D_2 and then all the way to D_3. Thus in the neighborhood of P_e, elasticity differs for each of these curves. It is greater for the less steep curves (but, slope alone does not measure elasticity for the entire curve).

How to Define the Short Run and the Long Run. We've mentioned the short run and the long run. Is the short run one week, two weeks, one month, two months? Is the long run three years, four years, five years? The answer is that there is no single answer. What we mean by the long run is the period of time necessary for consumers to make a full adjustment to a given price change, all other things held constant. In the case of the demand for electricity, the long run will be however long it takes consumers to switch over to cheaper sources of heating, to buy houses that are more energy-efficient, to purchase manufactured appliances that are more energy-efficient, and so on. The long-run elasticity of

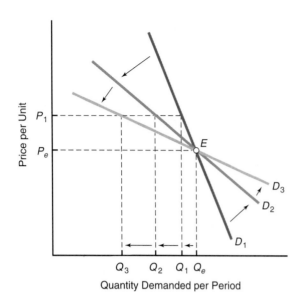

FIGURE 20-3

Short-Run and Long-Run Price Elasticity of Demand

Consider an equilibrium situation in which the market price is P_e and the quantity demanded is Q_e. Then there is a price increase to P_1. In the short run, as evidenced by the demand curve D_1, we move from equilibrium quantity demanded, Q_e, to Q_1. After more time is allowed for adjustment, the demand curve rotates at original price P_e to D_2. Quantity demanded falls again, now to Q_2. After even more time is allowed for adjustment, the demand curve rotates at price P_e to D_3. At the higher price P_1, in the long run, the quantity demanded falls all the way to Q_3.

demand for electricity therefore relates to a period of at least several years. The short run—by default—is any period less than the long run.

EXAMPLE
What Do Real-World Price Elasticities of Demand Look Like?

In Table 20-2, we present demand elasticities for selected goods. None of them is zero, and the largest is 3.8—a far cry from infinity. Remember that even though we are leaving off the negative sign, there is an inverse relationship between price and quantity demanded,

TABLE 20-2

Demand Elasticity for Selected Goods

Here are estimated demand elasticities for selected goods. All of them are negative, although we omit the minus sign. We have given some estimates of the long-run price elasticities of demand. The long run is associated with the time necessary for consumers to adjust fully to any given price change.

Category	Estimated Elasticity	
	Short Run	Long Run
Lamb	2.65	—
Bread	.15	—
Tires and related items	.8	1.2
Auto repair and related services	1.4	2.4
Radio and television repair	.5	3.8
Legitimate theater and opera	.2	.31
Motion pictures	.87	3.7
Foreign travel by U.S. residents	.1	1.8
Taxicabs	.6	—
Local public transportation	.6	1.2
Intercity bus	.2	2.2
Electricity	.1	1.8
Jewelry and watches	.4	.6

and the minus sign is understood. Also remember that these elasticities represent averages over given price ranges. Choosing different price ranges would yield different elasticity estimates for these goods.

Economists have consistently found that estimated price elasticities of demand are greater in the long run than in the short run, as seen in Table 20-2. There you see, for example, in the far-right column that the long-run price elasticity of demand for tires and related items is 1.2, whereas the estimate for the short run is .8. Throughout the table, you see that all estimates of long-run price elasticities of demand exceed their short-run counterparts.

FOR CRITICAL ANALYSIS: Explain the intuitive reasoning behind the difference between long-run and short-run price elasticity of demand. •

CROSS ELASTICITY OF DEMAND

Cross elasticity of demand (E_{xy})
The percentage change in the demand for one good (holding its price constant) divided by the percentage change in the price of a related good.

In Chapter 3, we discussed the effect of a change in the price of one good on the demand for a related good. We defined substitutes and complements in terms of whether a reduction in the price of one caused a decrease or an increase, respectively, in the demand for the other. If the price of compact discs is held constant, the amount of CDs demanded (at any price) will certainly be influenced by the price of a close substitute such as audiocassettes. If the price of stereo speakers is held constant, the amount of stereo speakers demanded (at any price) will certainly be affected by changes in the price of stereo amplifiers.

What we now need to do is come up with a numerical measure of the price responsiveness of demand to the prices of related goods. This is called the **cross elasticity of demand** (E_{xy}), which is defined as the percentage change in the demand for one good divided by the percentage change in the price of the related good. In equation form, the cross elasticity of demand for good X with good Y is

$$E_{xy} = \frac{\text{percentage change in demand for good X}}{\text{percentage change in price of good Y}}$$

Alternatively, the cross elasticity of demand for good Y with good X would use the percentage change in the demand for good Y as the numerator and the percentage change in the price of good X as the denominator.

When two goods are substitutes, the cross elasticity of demand will be positive. For example, when the price of margarine goes up, the demand for butter will rise too as consumers shift away from the now relatively more expensive margarine to butter. A producer of margarine could benefit from a numerical estimate of the cross elasticity of demand between butter and margarine. For example, if the price of butter went up by 10 percent and the margarine producer knew that the cross elasticity of demand was 1, the margarine producer could estimate that the demand for margarine would also go up by 10 percent at any given price. Plans for increasing margarine production could then be made.

When two related goods are complements, the cross elasticity of demand will be negative (and we will not disregard the minus sign). For example, when the price of stereo amplifiers goes up, the demand for stereo speakers will fall. This is because as prices of amplifiers increase, the quantity of amplifiers demanded will naturally decrease. Because amplifiers and stereo speakers are often used together, the demand for speakers is likely to fall. Any manufacturer of stereo speakers must take this into account in making production plans.

If goods are completely unrelated, their cross elasticity of demand will be zero.

POLICY EXAMPLE
Should Public Libraries Be Shut Down?

The public library has been an institution in the United States for years. Most public libraries are paid for out of property taxes. Some policymakers argue that there is no reason to subsidize public libraries anymore. Why? Because individuals are gradually shifting their demand from the use of *physical* public libraries to on-line information services, such as Prodigy, CompuServe, and others available over the Internet. As the price of on-line information has fallen, the demand for traditional library services has dropped. Though no one has calculated the exact cross elasticity of demand for traditional library services, the decrease in usage of such libraries shows that it is significant.

FOR CRITICAL ANALYSIS: Compare your costs of using a library with those for using on-line information services. ●

INCOME ELASTICITY OF DEMAND

In Chapter 3, we discussed the determinants of demand. One of those determinants was income. Briefly, we can apply our understanding of elasticity to the relationship between changes in income and changes in demand. We measure the responsiveness of quantity demanded to income changes by the **income elasticity of demand (E_i):**

$$E_i = \frac{\text{percentage change in demand}}{\text{percentage change in income}}$$

holding relative price constant.

Income elasticity of demand refers to a *horizontal shift* in the demand curve in response to changes in income, whereas price elasticity of demand refers to a movement *along* the curve in response to price changes. Thus income elasticity of demand is calculated at a given price, and price elasticity of demand is calculated at a given income.

A simple example will demonstrate how income elasticity of demand can be computed. Table 20-3 gives the relevant data. The product in question is compact discs. We assume that the price of compact discs remains constant relative to other prices. In period 1, six CDs per month are purchased. Income per month is $400. In period 2, monthly income increases to $600, and the quantity of CDs demanded per month is increased to eight. We can apply the following calculation:

$$E_i = \frac{(8-6)/6}{(600-400)/400} = \frac{1/3}{1/2} = \frac{2}{3} = .667$$

Hence measured income elasticity of demand for CDs for the individual represented in this example is .667. Note that this holds only for the move from six CDs to eight CDs purchased per month. If the situation were reversed, with income decreasing from $600 to

Income elasticity of demand (E_i)
The percentage change in demand for any good, holding its price constant, divided by the percentage change in income; the responsiveness of demand to changes in income, holding the good's relative price constant.

TABLE 20-3

How Income Affects Quantity of CDs Demanded

Period	Number of CDs Demanded per Month	Income per Month
1	6	$400
2	8	600

$400 per month and CDs purchased dropping from eight to six CDs per month, the calculation becomes

$$E_i = \frac{(6-8)/8}{(400-600)/600} = \frac{-2/8}{-1/3} = \frac{-1/4}{-1/3} = \frac{3}{4} = .75$$

In this case, the measured income elasticity of demand is equal to .75.

To get the same income elasticity of demand over the same range of values regardless of direction of change (increase or decrease), we can use the same formula that we used in computing the price elasticity of demand. When doing so, we have:

$$E_i = \frac{\text{change in quantity}}{\text{sum of quantities/2}} \div \frac{\text{change in income}}{\text{sum of incomes/2}}$$

You have just been introduced to three types of elasticities. Two of them—the price elasticity of demand (E_p), and income elasticity (E_i)—are the two most important factors in influencing the quantity demanded for most goods. Reasonably accurate estimates of these can go a long way toward making accurate forecasts of demand for goods or services.

EXAMPLE
Traffic Fatalities, Rising Incomes, and Alcohol Consumption

Economist Christopher Ruhm of the National Bureau of Economic Research discovered that the income elasticity of demand for alcoholic beverages is significant. He found that over a 14-year period, a $1,250 rise in real per capita personal income (expressed in 1996 dollars) increased alcoholic beverage consumption by 1.2 percent. There were also resulting increases in traffic fatalities.

FOR CRITICAL ANALYSIS: A common view is that people turn to drink in times of economic distress. What do the data tell us? •

CONCEPTS IN BRIEF

- Some determinants of price elasticity of demand are (1) the existence, number, and quality of substitutes, (2) the share of the total budget spent on the good in question, and (3) the length of time allowed for adjustment to a change in prices.

- Cross elasticity of demand measures one good's demand responsiveness to another's price changes. For substitutes, it is positive; for complements, it is negative.

- Income elasticity of demand tells you by what percentage demand will change for a particular percentage change in income.

ELASTICITY OF SUPPLY

Price elasticity of supply (E_s)
The responsiveness of the quantity supplied of a commodity to a change in its price; the percentage change in quantity supplied divided by the percentage change in price.

The **price elasticity of supply (E_s)** is defined similarly to the price elasticity of demand. Supply elasticities are generally positive; this is because at higher prices, larger quantities will generally be forthcoming from suppliers. The definition of the price elasticity of supply is as follows:

$$E_s = \frac{\text{percentage change in quantity supplied}}{\text{percentage change in price}}$$

Classifying Supply Elasticities

Just as with demand, there are different types of supply elasticities. They are similar in definition to the types of demand elasticities.

If a 1 percent increase in price elicits a greater than 1 percent increase in the quantity supplied, we say that at the particular price in question on the supply schedule, *supply is elastic*. The most extreme elastic supply is called **perfectly elastic supply**—the slightest reduction in price will cause quantity supplied to fall to zero.

If, conversely, a 1 percent increase in price elicits a less than 1 percent increase in the quantity supplied, we refer to that as an *inelastic supply*. The most extreme inelastic supply is called **perfectly inelastic supply**—no matter what the price, the quantity supplied remains the same.

If the percentage change in the quantity supplied is just equal to the percentage change in the price, we call this *unit-elastic supply*.

We show in Figure 20-4 two supply schedules, S and S'. You can tell at a glance, without reading the labels, which one is infinitely elastic and which one is perfectly inelastic. As you might expect, most supply schedules exhibit elasticities that are somewhere between zero and infinity.

Perfectly elastic supply
A supply characterized by a reduction in quantity supplied to zero when there is the slightest decrease in price.

Perfectly inelastic supply
A supply for which quantity supplied remains constant, no matter what happens to price.

Price Elasticity of Supply and Length of Time for Adjustment

We pointed out earlier that the longer the time period allowed for adjustment, the greater the price elasticity of demand. It turns out that the same proposition applies to supply. The longer the time for adjustment, the more elastic the supply curve. Consider why this is true:

1. The longer the time allowed for adjustment, the more firms are able to figure out ways to increase (or decrease) production in an industry.
2. The longer the time allowed for adjustment, the more resources can flow into (or out of) an industry through expansion (or contraction) of existing firms.

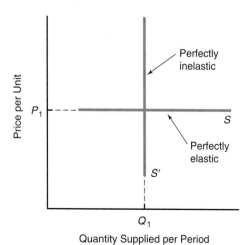

FIGURE 20-4

The Extremes in Supply Curves
Here we have drawn two extremes of supply schedules: S is a perfectly elastic supply curve; S' is a perfectly inelastic one. In the former, an unlimited quantity will be supplied at price P_1. In the latter, no matter what the price, the quantity supplied will be Q_1. An example of S' might be the supply curve for fresh fish on the morning the boats come in.

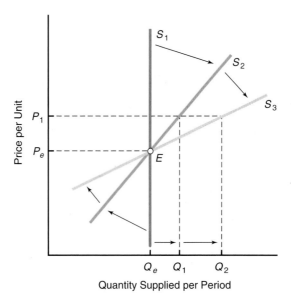

FIGURE 20-5

**Short-Run and Long-Run Price
Elasticity of Supply**
Consider a situation in which the price
is P_e and the quantity supplied is Q_e. In
the short run, we hypothesize a vertical
supply curve, S_1. With the price
increase to P_1, therefore, there will be
no change in the short run in quantity
supplied; it will remain at Q_e. Given
some time for adjustment, the supply
curve will rotate to S_2. The new amount
supplied will increase to Q_1. The long-
run supply curve is shown by S_3. The
amount supplied again increases to Q_2.

We therefore talk about short-run and long-run price elasticities of supply. The short run is
defined as the time period during which full adjustment has not yet taken place. The long
run is the time period during which firms have been able to adjust fully to the change in
price.

Consider an increase in the price of housing. In the very short run, when there is no time
allowed for adjustment, the amount of housing offered for rent or for sale is relatively
inelastic. However, as more time is allowed for adjustment, current owners of the housing
stock can find ways to increase the amount of housing they will offer for rent from given
buildings. The owner of a large house can decide, for example, to have two children move
into one room so that a "new" extra bedroom can be rented out. This can also be done by
the owner of a large house who decides to move into an apartment and rent each floor of
the house to a separate family. Thus the quantity of housing supplied will increase. With
more time, landlords will find it profitable to build new rental units.

We can show a whole set of supply curves similar to the ones we generated for demand.
As Figure 20-5 shows, when nothing can be done in the short run, the supply curve is vertical, S_1. As more time is allowed for adjustment, the supply curve rotates to S_2 and then to
S_3, becoming more elastic as it rotates.

EXAMPLE
The Long-Run Effectiveness of "Sin" Taxes

The government has long regarded alcohol and tobacco as products it
could easily tax heavily. After all, most studies show that the price elasticity of demand is
low for these "sinful" products. That is, the demand curves around the range of prices being
charged for these products have been estimated to be relatively inelastic. Whenever a particular state government started running a budget deficit, it has always felt secure that it
could raise cigarette and alcohol taxes to increase revenues.

The *long-run* demand curves for tobacco and alcohol products, however, may not be so
inelastic. According to Ronald Alt, senior research associate with the Federation of Tax

Administrators in Washington, D.C., "The golden goose of sin taxes is just about cooked." He points out that sin taxes generate much smaller percentages of state revenues than they did 10 or 20 years ago. In 1972, they comprised 25 percent of state budget revenues, whereas today they comprise less than 15 percent. Government officials in New York State agree with Alt. They predicted in 1994 that revenues generated from alcohol taxes would decrease by $7 million and revenues from taxes on tobacco by over $32 million. Other state officials have made similar predictions as well.

Part of the problem with raising taxes on certain products in one state is that residents have the option of purchasing those products in adjoining states that have lower tax rates. For example, smokers in southern New Jersey routinely drive across the border into Delaware to stock up on cigarettes. In New Jersey, the retail price of a pack of cigarettes includes 40 cents plus a sales tax of 6 percent. In Delaware, that same pack is taxed at only 24 cents. Some residents in the high-tax state will buy their cigarettes in the low-tax state. Individual states, therefore, can never hope to obtain as much revenue as they predict when they raise taxes on tobacco and alcohol products.

FOR CRITICAL ANALYSIS: What other factors might be influencing the drop in the revenues collected for "sin" taxes? ●

CONCEPTS IN BRIEF

- Price elasticity of supply is calculated by dividing the percentage change in quantity supplied by the percentage change in price.

- Usually, price elasticities of supply are positive—higher prices yield larger quantities supplied.

- Long-run supply curves are more elastic than short-run supply curves because the longer the time allowed, the more resources can flow into or out of an industry when price changes.

Beer, Taxes, and Teenage Highway Deaths

Concepts Applied: Price elasticity of demand, long run, short run

The laws of supply and demand may be affecting teenage drunk driving more than police realize. The price of liquor has dropped in the past two decades when adjusted for inflation, which would increase the quantity of alcohol demanded according to the supply/demand model.

What is the biggest single cause of death among young people in America today? The answer is automobile accidents, half of which are caused in one way or another by drinking. In response to these statistics, the federal government forced all states to raise their legal drinking age to 21. It did so by threatening to withhold federal highway trust fund monies from states that did not fall in line. Nonetheless, teenagers, through a variety of means, are still able to purchase alcoholic beverages. They do so through older friends and with forged identity cards.

Does Price Matter?

Unless the price elasticity of demand for beer and other alcoholic beverages among teenagers is zero, the quantity demanded will be a function of price. What has happened to beer prices? Look at Figure 20-6 to see the *real* (corrected for inflation) price of beer and hard liquor in America since 1975. Although there has been a slight rise in (real) beer prices since 1990, it is still cheaper than it was two decades ago.

Federal Excise Taxes

Why have the real prices of beer and hard liquor remained so low? Federal excise taxes are based on the *physical quantity* of alcohol, not its wholesale or retail price. Currently, the tax is $2 per liter of pure alcohol for beer and $3.60 per liter of pure alcohol for hard liquor. (Interestingly, these same taxes are $18.20 and $34.50, respectively, in England.) So while the nominal prices of beer and alcoholic beverages have been rising due to inflation, the relative "pain" due to the federal excise tax has fallen.

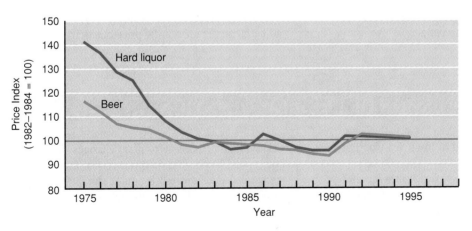

FIGURE 20-6

Alcoholic Drink Prices in the United States
During the late 1970s, the real prices of beer and hard liquor dropped substantially and stayed there
Source: Bureau of Labor Statistics.

Price Responsiveness to Higher Taxes

Economist Michael Grossman of the National Bureau of Economic Research believes that teenagers would have responded to an increase in the federal excise tax on beer. He estimates that if the federal excise tax had simply been increased by the rate of inflation every year since 1951, the number of young "frequent beer drinkers" would have dropped by 20 percent. In one seven-year period, he and his colleagues estimate, 1,660 lives a year would have been saved by a higher federal excise tax on beer.

FOR CRITICAL ANALYSIS
1. What might be the result of a single state's deciding to increase the state tax on beer dramatically?
2. Could this same analysis apply to cigarettes?

CHAPTER SUMMARY

1. Price elasticity of demand is a measure of the percentage change in quantity demanded relative to the percentage change in price, given income, the prices of other goods, and time. Because of the law of demand, price elasticity of demand is always negative.
2. We classify demand as *elastic* if a 1 percent change in price leads to a more than 1 percent change in quantity demanded, *unit-elastic* if it leads to exactly a 1 percent change in quantity demanded, and *inelastic* if it leads to less than a 1 percent change in quantity demanded.
3. When facing a perfectly elastic demand, the slightest increase in price leads to zero quantity demanded; when facing a perfectly inelastic demand, no matter what the price, the quantity demanded remains unchanged. Perfect inelasticity means absolutely no price responsiveness.
4. Price elasticity of demand falls as we move down a straight-line demand curve. It goes from infinity to zero. Elasticity and slope are not equivalent; for example, the slope of a straight-line curve is always constant, whereas elasticity changes as we move along a linear curve. A vertical demand curve is perfectly inelastic; a horizontal demand curve is perfectly elastic.
5. Price elasticity of demand depends on (a) the existence, number, and quality of substitutes, (b) the share of total budget accounted for by the commodity, and (c) the length of time allowed for adjustment to changes in price of the commodity.
6. Cross elasticity of demand measures the responsiveness of the demand for one product, either a substitute or a complement, to changes in the price of another product. When the cross elasticity of demand is negative, the two commodities under study are complements; when the cross elasticity of demand is positive, they are substitutes.
7. Income elasticity of demand is given by the percentage change in demand divided by the percentage change in income, given relative price.
8. Price elasticity of supply is given by the percentage change in quantity supplied divided by the percentage change in price. The greater the time allowed for adjustment, the greater the price elasticity of supply.

DISCUSSION OF PREVIEW QUESTIONS

1. How is total revenue related to the price elasticity of demand?

Total revenue is defined as price times quantity demanded; because price changes lead to changes in quantity demanded, total revenue and elasticity are intimately related. If, over the price range in question, demand is inelastic, this means that buyers are relatively unresponsive to price changes. Intuitively, then, we know that if price rises and quantity demanded does not fall by much, total revenue will rise. Conversely, if price falls and quantity demanded rises only slightly, total revenue will fall. If, over the price range in question, demand is elastic, buyers will be quite responsive to price changes. We can tell intuitively that if price rises and quantity demanded falls greatly, total revenue will fall. Similarly, if price falls and quantity demanded rises greatly, total revenue will rise. Finally, if we are in the range of unit elasticity, given percentage changes in price will lead to equal percentage changes in quantity. Thus total revenue remains unaffected in the unit-elasticity range.

2. What are the determinants of the price elasticity of demand?

Three major determinants of price elasticity of demand are (a) the existence, number, and quality of substitutes, (b) the share of the total budget that the commodity represents, and (c) the length of time buyers have to react to price changes. Clearly, the more substitutes and the better they are, the greater will be the price elasticity of demand. Therefore, the price elasticity of demand rises as we consider the commodities "fruit," then "oranges," then "Sunkist oranges"; more and better substitutes exist for a specific brand of oranges than for the fruit group. Also, when a commodity takes up a small percentage of the consumer budget (other things being constant), we expect the price elasticity of demand to be lower, compared with items important to a budget. Presumably, buyers will have a greater incentive to shop around and seek substitutes for high-cost items than

for low-cost items. Finally, for a given percentage change in price, quantity responsiveness (and therefore elasticity) will increase with the time period allowed for adjustment. With the passage of time, buyers are better able to find and use substitutes.

3. What is the income elasticity of demand?

Income elasticity of demand refers to the responsiveness of buyers to income changes, given relative price. Technically, income elasticity of demand is defined as the percentage change in demand divided by the percentage change in income. The resulting measure is referred to as being income-elastic, unit-elastic, or income-inelastic, depending on whether or not it is greater than, equal to, or less than 1.

4. What is the price elasticity of supply?

Price elasticity of supply refers to the responsiveness of sellers to changes in price. Technically, price elasticity of supply is defined as the percentage change in quantity supplied divided by the percentage change in price. The resulting measure can be greater than, equal to, or less than the number 1—referred to as elastic, unit-elastic, and inelastic price, respectively. The longer the adjustment time, the greater the quantity responsiveness of sellers to given price changes (and hence the greater the price elasticity of supply).

PROBLEMS

(Answers to the odd-numbered problems appear at the back of the book.)

20-1. Use the following hypothetical demand schedule for tea to answer the questions.

Quantity Demanded per Week (ounces)	Price per Ounce	Elasticity
1,000	$ 5	
800	10	
600	15	
400	20	
200	25	

a. Using the demand schedule, determine the elasticity of demand for each price change. (Example: When price changes from $5 to $10, quantity demanded changes from 1,000 to 800 ounces, so the elasticity of demand, using average values, is $\frac{1}{3}$, or .33.)
b. The data given in the demand schedule would plot as a straight-line demand curve. Why is demand more elastic the higher the price?

20-2. Calculate the price elasticity of demand for the product in the table on the next page using average values for the prices and quantities in your formula. Over the price range in question, is this demand schedule inelastic, unit-elastic, or elastic? Is total revenue greater at the lower price or the higher price?

Price per Unit	Quantity Demanded
$4	22
6	18

20-3. Calculate the income elasticity of demand for the product in the following table, using average values for incomes and quantities.

Quantity of VCRs per Year	Per Capita Annual Group Income
1,000	$15,000
2,000	20,000

    a. Is the demand for this product income-elastic or income-inelastic?

    b. Would you consider this commodity a luxury or a necessity?

20-4. Can any demand curve possibly be perfectly inelastic ($E_p = 0$) regardless of price? Explain.

20-5. A new mobile home park charges nothing whatsoever for water used by its inhabitants. Consumption is 100,000 gallons per month. The decision is then made to charge according to how much each mobile home owner uses, at a rate of $10 per 1,000 gallons. Consumption declines to 50,000 gallons per month. What is the difficulty here in accurately estimating the price elasticity of the demand for water by these residents?

20-6. Which of the following cross elasticities of demand would you expect to be positive and which to be negative?

    a. Tennis balls and tennis racquets
    b. Tennis balls and golf balls
    c. Dental services and toothpaste
    d. Dental services and candy
    e. Liquor and ice cubes
    f. Liquor and cocaine

20-7. Suppose that the price of salt rises from 15 cents to 17 cents a pound. The quantity demanded decreases from 525 pounds to 475 pounds per month, and the quantity supplied increases from 525 pounds to 600 pounds per month. (Use averages in calculating elasticities.)

    a. Calculate the price elasticity of demand (E_p) for salt.

    b. Is the demand for salt price-elastic or price-inelastic?

    c. Calculate the elasticity of supply (E_s) for salt.

    d. Is the supply for salt price-elastic or price-inelastic?

20-8. Suppose that an automobile dealer cuts his car prices by 15 percent. He then finds that his car sales revenues have increased by 10 percent.

    a. What can you say about the price elasticity of demand for cars?

    b. What will happen to the dealer's total revenue?

20-9. For any given relative price, would you think that the demand for canal transportation was more or less elastic in 1840 than in 1880? How about the demand for Pony Express messengers before and after the transcontinental telegraph? The demand for rail transportation before and after the Model T Ford? The demand for transatlantic cable-laying equipment before and after communications satellites? The demand for slide rules before and after introduction of the pocket-sized calculator? Why?

COMPUTER-ASSISTED INSTRUCTION

Given a (linear) demand schedule, can you demonstrate that the price elasticity of demand falls as price falls? This problem requires specific calculations of the price elasticity of demand at various prices.

Complete problem and answer appear on disk.

CHAPTER 21

THE FINANCIAL ENVIRONMENT OF BUSINESS

Just about everybody has heard of the great stock market crashes that occurred in October 1929 and in 1987. Throughout its existence, the stock market has had its ups and downs. The evening TV news often broadcasts images of the scene with the closing bell ringing at the New York Stock Exchange, accompanied by wild clapping if "the market" is up. Normally, changes in the stock market are reported by the press as an upward or downward movement in the Dow Jones Industrial Average. Most people talk about "the Dow," but what does it really represent? Before you find out, you need to know more about the financial environment of business.

PREVIEW QUESTIONS

1. What are the main organizational forms that firms take, and what are their advantages and disadvantages?

2. What are corporations' primary sources of financial capital?

3. What are the major differences between stocks and bonds?

4. Is there a world market for U.S. government securities?

Did You Know That . . . every year in the United States, over 2 million new businesses are started? Although most of these involve individuals going into business for themselves, many entrepreneurs raise large sums of money from investors to get under way. These companies turn to financial markets to raise money. They seek **financial capital.**

You've been introduced to the term *physical capital* as one of the five factors of production. In that context, capital consists of the goods that do not directly satisfy human wants but are used to make other goods. *Financial capital* is the money that is made available to purchase capital goods.

Different types of businesses are able to raise financial capital in different ways. Your first step in understanding the firm's financial environment is therefore to understand the way firms are organized.

THE LEGAL ORGANIZATION OF FIRMS

We all know that firms differ from one another. Some sell frozen yogurt, others make automobiles; some advertise, some do not; some have annual sales of a few thousand dollars, others have sales in the billions of dollars. The list of differences is probably endless. Yet for all this diversity, the basic organization of *all* firms can be thought of in terms of a few simple structures, the most important of which are the proprietorship, the partnership, and the corporation.

Proprietorships

The most common form of business organization is the **proprietorship;** as shown in Table 21-1, more than 74 percent of all firms in the United States are proprietorships. Each is owned by a single individual who makes the business decisions, receives all the profits, and is legally responsible for all the debts of the firm. Although proprietorships are numerous, generally they are rather small businesses, with annual sales typically under $50,000. For this reason, even though there are more than 10 million proprietorships in the United States, they account for only about 6 percent of all business revenues.

Advantages of Proprietorships. Proprietorships offer several advantages as a form of business organization. First, they are *easy to form and to dissolve.* In the simplest case, all one must do to start a business is to start working; to dissolve the firm, one simply stops working. Even a more complicated proposition, such as starting a restaurant or a small retail shop, involves only meeting broadly defined health and zoning rules and the payment of a modest business license fee to the local government. To go out of business, one simply

Financial capital
Money used to purchase capital goods such as buildings and equipment.

Proprietorship
A business owned by one individual who makes the business decisions, receives all the profits, and is legally responsible for all the debts of the firm.

TABLE 21-1
Forms of Business Organization

Type of Firm	Percentage of U.S. Firms	Average Size (annual sales in dollars)	Percentage of Total Business Revenues
Proprietorship	74.3	47,569	5.6
Partnership	7.1	384,799	4.0
Corporation	18.6	303,489	90.4

Sources: U.S. Bureau of the Census; *1996 Statistical Abstract.*

locks the front door. The second advantage of the proprietorship is that *all decision-making power resides with the sole proprietor.* The owner decides what and how much will be offered for sale, what the hours of operation will be, and who will perform what tasks. No partners, shareholders, or board of directors need be consulted. The third advantage is that its *profit is taxed only once.* All profit is treated by law as the net income of the proprietor and as such is subject only to personal income taxation.

Disadvantages of Proprietorships. The most important disadvantage of a proprietorship is that the proprietor faces **unlimited liability** *for the debts of the firm.* This means that the owner is personally responsible for all of the firm's debts. Thus the owner's personal assets—home, car, savings account, coin collection—can be subject to seizure by the firm's creditors. The second disadvantage is that it has *limited ability to raise funds,* to expand the business or even simply to help it survive bad times. Because the success of a proprietorship depends so heavily on the good judgment and hard work of but one person—the owner—many lenders are reluctant to lend large sums to a proprietorship. Thus much of the financing of proprietorships often comes from the personal funds of the owner, which helps explain why proprietorships are usually small. The third disadvantage of proprietorships is that they normally *end with the death of the proprietor.* This, of course, creates added uncertainty for prospective lenders or employees, for a freak accident or sudden illness can turn a prosperous firm into a bittersweet memory.

Partnerships

The second important form of business organization is the **partnership.** As shown in Table 21-1, partnerships are far less numerous than proprietorships but tend to be significantly larger, with average sales about eight times greater. A partnership differs from a proprietorship chiefly in that there are two or more co-owners, called partners. They share the responsibilities of operating the firm and its profits, and they are *each* legally responsible for *all* of the debts incurred by the firm. In this sense, a partnership may be viewed as a proprietorship with more than one owner. The partners may contribute equal or different amounts of financial capital to the firm, may have widely different operating responsibilities, and may share the profits in any way they see fit. Not surprisingly, partnerships share many of the advantages and disadvantages of proprietorships.

Advantages of Partnerships. The first advantage of a partnership is that it is *easy to form.* In fact, it is almost as easy as forming a proprietorship, except that it requires two or more participants. Second, partnerships, like proprietorships, often help *reduce the costs of monitoring job performance.* This is particularly true when interpersonal skills are important for successful performance and in lines of business where, even after the fact, it is difficult to measure performance objectively. Thus attorneys and physicians often organize themselves as partnerships. Similarly, in professions such as these, a spectacular success may consist of a greatly reduced jail term for a client or greatly delayed death for a patient. In such circumstances, each partner has far more incentive to monitor his or her own work performance than he or she would as an employee, because the partner shares in the profits of the firm. A third advantage of the partnership is that it *permits more effective specialization* in occupations where, for legal or other reasons, the multiple talents required for success are unlikely to be uniform across individuals. Finally, partnerships share with proprietorships the advantage that the income of the partnership is treated as personal income and thus is subject only to personal taxation.

Unlimited liability
A legal concept whereby the personal assets of the owner of a firm can be seized to pay off the firm's debts.

Partnership
A business owned by two or more co-owners, or partners, who share the responsibilities and the profits of the firm and are individually liable for all of the debts of the partnership.

Disadvantages of Partnerships. Not surprisingly, partnerships also have their disadvantages. First, the *partners each have unlimited liability.* Thus the personal assets of *each* partner are at risk due to debts incurred on behalf of the partnership by *any* of the partners. One partner's poor business judgment may impose substantial losses on all the other partners, a problem the sole proprietor need not worry about. Second, *decision making is generally more costly* in a partnership than in a proprietorship; there are more people involved in making decisions, and they may have differences of opinion that must be resolved before action is possible. Finally, *dissolution of the partnership is generally necessary* when a partner dies or voluntarily withdraws or when one or more partners wish to remove someone from the partnership. As with proprietorships, this creates potential uncertainty for creditors and employees.

Corporations

A **corporation** is a legal entity that may conduct business in its own name just as an individual does. The owners of a corporation are called *shareholders* because they own shares of the profits earned by the firm. By law, shareholders enjoy **limited liability,** which means that if the corporation incurs debts that it cannot pay, creditors have no recourse to the shareholders' personal property. As shown in Table 21-1, corporations are far less numerous than proprietorships, but because of their large size, they are responsible for over 90 percent of all business revenues in the United States. Many, such as Microsoft, IBM, AT&T, and Exxon, are so large that their annual sales are measured in billions of dollars and their names are household words.

Advantages of Corporations. The fact that corporations conduct most of the nation's business suggests that the corporation offers significant advantages as a form of business organization. Perhaps the greatest of these is that the owners of a corporation (the shareholders) enjoy *limited liability.* The liability of shareholders is limited to the value of their shares. The second advantage arises because the law treats it as a legal entity in and of itself; thus the corporation *continues to exist* even if one or more owners of the corporation cease to be owners. A third advantage of the corporation stems from the first two: Corporations are well positioned for *raising large sums of financial capital.* People are able to buy ownership shares or lend money to the corporation knowing that their liability is limited to the amount of money they invest and confident that the corporation's existence does not depend on the life of any one of the firm's owners.

Disadvantages of Corporations. The chief disadvantage of the corporation is the fact that corporate income is subject to *double taxation.* The profits of the corporation are subject first to corporate taxation. Then, if any of the after-tax profits are distributed to shareholders as **dividends,** such payments are treated as personal income to the shareholders and subject to personal taxation. The combined effect is that owners of corporations pay about twice as much in taxes on corporate income as they do on other forms of income.

A second disadvantage of the corporation is that corporations are potentially subject to problems associated with the *separation of ownership and control.* Specifically, it is commonplace for the owners (shareholders) of corporations to have little, if anything, to do with the actual management of the firm. Instead, these tasks are handled by professional managers who may have little or no ownership interest in the firm. The objective of the shareholders is presumably to maximize the value of their holdings. Unless their sole compensation is in the form of shares of stock in the corporation, however, the objective of the managers may differ from this. For example, managers may choose to have more luxurious

Corporation
A legal entity that may conduct business in its own name just as an individual does; the owners of a corporation, called shareholders, own shares of the firm's profits and enjoy the protection of limited liability.

Limited liability
A legal concept whereby the responsibility, or liability, of the owners of a corporation is limited to the value of the shares in the firm that they own.

Dividends
Portion of a corporation's profits paid to its owners (shareholders).

offices than are needed for the efficient operation of the firm. If there are costs to the share-holders in preventing such behavior, the result may be that the market value of the firm is not maximized.

In principle, such problems could arise with a partnership or a proprietorship if the owner or partners hired a manager to take care of day-to-day operations. Nevertheless, the separation of ownership and control is widely regarded as a more important problem for corporations; their attractiveness as a means of raising financial capital from many in-vestors makes them subject to higher costs of agreement among owners with respect to penalties for managers who fail to maximize the value of the firm.

CONCEPTS IN BRIEF

- Proprietorships are the most common form of business organization, comprising more than 74 percent of all firms. Each is owned by a single individual who makes all busi-ness decisions, receives all the profits, and has unlimited liability for the firm's debts.

- Partnerships are much like proprietorships, except that two or more individuals, or partners, share the decisions and the profits of the firm. In addition, each partner has unlimited liability for the debts of the firms.

- Corporations are responsible for the largest share of business revenues. The owners, called shareholders, share in the firm's profits but normally have little responsibility for the firm's day-to-day operations. They enjoy limited liability for the debts of the firm.

METHODS OF CORPORATE FINANCING

When the Dutch East India Company was founded in 1602, it raised financial capital by selling shares of its expected future profits to investors. The investors thus became the own-ers of the company, and their ownership shares eventually became known as "shares of stock," or simply *stocks*. The company also issued notes of indebtedness, which involved borrowing money in return for interest on the funds, plus eventual repayment of the princi-pal amount borrowed. In modern parlance, these notes of indebtedness are called *bonds*. As the company prospered over time, some of its revenues were used to pay lenders the inter-est and principal owed them; of the profits that remained, some were paid to shareholders in the form of dividends, and some were retained by the company for reinvestment in fur-ther enterprises. The methods of financing used by the Dutch East India Company nearly four centuries ago—stocks, bonds, and reinvestment—remain the principal methods of financing for today's corporations.

Share of stock
A legal claim to a share of a corporation's future profits; if it is *common stock*, it incorporates certain voting rights regarding major policy decisions of the corporation; if it is *preferred stock*, its owners are accorded preferential treatment in the payment of dividends.

A **share of stock** in a corporation is simply a legal claim to a share of the corporation's future profits. If there are 100,000 shares of stock in a company and you own 1,000 of them, you own the right to 1 percent of that company's future profits. If the stock you own is *common stock*, you also have the right to vote on major policy decisions affecting the company, such as the selection of the corporation's board of directors. Your 1,000 shares would entitle you to cast 1 percent of the votes on such issues. If the stock you own is *preferred stock*, you also own a share of the future profits of the corporation, but you do *not* have regular voting rights. You do, however, get something in return for giving up your vot-ing rights: preferential treatment in the payment of dividends. Specifically, the owners of preferred stock generally must receive at least a certain amount of dividends in each period before the owners of common stock can receive *any* dividends.

A **bond** is a legal claim against a firm, entitling the owner of the bond to receive a fixed annual *coupon* payment, plus a lump-sum payment at the maturity date of the bond.[1] Bonds are issued in return for funds lent to the firm; the coupon payments represent interest on the amount borrowed by the firm, and the lump-sum payment at maturity of the bond generally equals the amount originally borrowed by the firm. Bonds are *not* claims to the future profits of the firm; legally, bondholders are to be paid whether the firm prospers or not. To help ensure this, bondholders generally must receive their coupon payments each year, and any principal that is due, before *any* shareholders can receive dividend payments.

You can see a comparison of stocks and bonds in Table 21-2.

Reinvestment takes place when the firm uses some of its profits to purchase new capital equipment rather than paying the money out as dividends to shareholders. Although sales of stock are an important source of financing for new firms, reinvestment and borrowing are the principal means of financing for existing firms. Indeed, reinvestment by established firms is such an important source of financing that it dominates the other two sources of corporate finance, amounting to roughly 75 percent of new financial capital for corporations in recent years. Also, small businesses, which are the source of much current growth, usually cannot rely on the stock market to raise investment funds.

Primary and Secondary Financial Markets

Both businesses and investors engage in financial transactions in primary and secondary financial markets.

Primary Markets. If you have ever heard of a "new issue," you are familiar with one aspect of a primary securities market. A **primary market** is one in which newly issued

Bond
A legal claim against a firm, usually entitling the owner of the bond to receive a fixed annual coupon payment, plus a lump-sum payment at the bond's maturity date. Bonds are issued in return for funds lent to the firm.

Reinvestment
Profits (or depreciation reserves) used to purchase new capital equipment.

Primary market
A financial market in which newly issued securities are bought and sold.

TABLE 21-2
The Difference Between Stocks and Bonds

Stocks	Bonds
1. Stocks represent ownership.	1. Bonds represent debt.
2. Common stocks do not have a fixed dividend rate.	2. Interest on bonds must always be paid, whether or not any profit is earned.
3. Stockholders can elect a board of directors, which controls the corporation.	3. Bondholders usually have no voice in or control over management of the corporation.
4. Stocks do not have a maturity date; the corporation does not usually repay the stockholder.	4. Bonds have a maturity date on which the bondholder is to be repaid the face value of the bond.
5. All corporations issue or offer to sell stocks. This is the usual definition of a corporation.	5. Corporations need not issue bonds.
6. Stockholders have a claim against the property and income of a corporation after all creditors' claims have been met.	6. Bondholders have a claim against the property and income of a corporation that must be met before the claims of stockholders.

---

[1]Coupon payments on bonds get their name from the fact that bonds once had coupons attached to them when they were issued. Each year, the owner would clip a coupon off the bond and send it to the issuing firm in return for that year's interest on the bond.

securities are bought and sold. A company that is raising money for the first time goes to the primary market, usually to sell stocks. Corporations can also sell newly issued bonds in primary securities markets. Sometimes you may read about large corporations, such as General Motors, issuing new bonds.

Secondary market
A financial market in which previously issued securities are bought and sold.

Secondary Markets. A **secondary market** is one in which existing securities are exchanged. When you read about what happened on the stock market today, that is information about a secondary market. Secondary markets are important to primary markets because they make stocks and bonds sold in primary markets more liquid. Most of the activities of stockbrokers involve dealings for investors in secondary market transactions. The stockbroker is an intermediary (middleman) who brings together buyers and sellers of various stocks and bonds. In return for the broker's services, which include executing market exchanges for buyers and sellers, the broker receives a commission, or brokerage fee.

THE MARKETS FOR STOCKS AND BONDS

Economists often refer to the "market for wheat" or the "market for labor." For stocks and bonds, there really are markets—centralized, physical locations where exchange takes place. By far the largest and most prestigious of these are the New York Stock Exchange (NYSE) and the New York Bond Exchange, both located in New York City. Numerous other stock and bond markets, or exchanges, are located throughout the United States and in various financial capitals of the world, such as London and Tokyo. Although the exact process by which exchanges are conducted in these markets varies slightly from one to another, the process used on the NYSE is representative of the principles involved.[2]

More than 2,500 stocks are traded on the NYSE, which is sometimes called the "Big Board." Leading brokerage firms—about 600 of them—own seats on the NYSE. These seats, which are actually rights to buy and sell stocks on the floor of the Big Board, are themselves regularly exchanged. In recent years, their value has fluctuated between $350,000 and $1 million each. These prices reflect the fact that stock trades on the NYSE are ultimately handled by the firms owning these seats, and the firms earn commissions on each trade. As trading volume rises, as it did during the 1980s, the value of the seats rises.

The Theory of Efficient Markets

At any point in time, there are tens of thousands, even millions of persons looking for any bit of information that will enable them to forecast correctly the future prices of stocks. Responding to any information that seems useful, these people try to buy low and sell high. The result is that all publicly available information that might be used to forecast stock prices gets taken into account by those with access to the information and the knowledge and ability to learn from it, leaving no

---

[2]A number of stocks and bonds are traded in so-called over-the-counter (OTC) markets, which, although not physically centralized, otherwise operate in much the same way as the NYSE and so are not treated separately in this text.

forecastable profit opportunities. And because so many people are involved in this process, it occurs quite swiftly. Indeed, there is some evidence that *all* information entering the market is fully incorporated into stock prices within less than a minute of its arrival. One view of the stock market is that most public information you will obtain will prove to have little value.

The result of this process is that stock prices tend to follow a *random walk,* which is to say that the best forecast of tomorrow's price is today's price. This is called the **random walk theory.** Although large values of the random component of stock price changes are less likely than small values, nothing else about the magnitude or direction of a stock price change can be predicted. Indeed, the random component of stock prices exhibits behavior much like what would occur if you rolled two dice and subtracted 7 from the resulting score. On average, the dice will show a total of 7, so after you subtract 7, the average result will be zero. It is true that rolling a 12 or a 2 (resulting in a net score of $+5$ or -5) is less likely than rolling an 8 or a 6 (yielding a net score of $+1$ or -1). Nevertheless, positive and negative net scores are equally likely, and the expected net score is zero.

> **Random walk theory**
> The theory that there are no predictable trends in security prices that can be used to "get rich quick."

Inside Information

Isn't there any way to "beat the market"? The answer is yes—but normally only if you have **inside information** that is not available to the public. Suppose that your best friend is in charge of new product development at the country's largest software firm, Microsoft Corporation. Your friend tells you that the company's smartest programmer has just come up with major new software that millions of computer users will want to buy. No one but your friend and the programmer—and now you—is aware of this. You could indeed make money using this information by purchasing shares of Microsoft and then selling them (at a higher price) as soon as the new product is publicly announced. There is one problem: Stock trading based on inside information such as this is illegal, punishable by substantial fines and even imprisonment. So unless you happen to have a stronger than average desire for a long vacation in a federal prison, you might be better off investing in Microsoft after the new program is publicly announced.

> **Inside information**
> Information that is not available to the general public about what is happening in a corporation.

EXAMPLE
How to Read the Financial Press: Stock Prices

Table 21-3, reproduced from the *Wall Street Journal,* contains information about the stocks of four companies. Across the top of the financial page are a series of column headings. Under the heading "Stock" we find the name of the company—in the first row, for example, is Lockheed, the aerospace firm. The two columns to the left of the company's name show the highest and lowest prices at which shares of that company's stock traded during the past 52 weeks. These prices are typically quoted in dollars and eighths of dollars.

Immediately to the right of the company's name you will find the company's *symbol* on the NYSE. This symbol (omitted by some newspapers) is simply the unique identifier used by the exchange when it reports information about the stock. For example, the designation LGN is used by the exchange as the unique identifier for the firm Logicon.

The last four columns of information for each firm summarize the behavior of the firm's stock price on the latest trading day. On this particular day, the highest price at which Lockheed stock traded was $47.375, the lowest price was $46.875, and the last (or closing) price at which it traded was $47.00 per share. The *net change* in the price of Lockheed stock was

TABLE 21-3
Reading Stock Quotes

| 52 Weeks | | Stock | Sym | Div | Yld % | PE | Vol 100s | Hi | Lo | Close | Net Chg |
Hi	Lo										
51	$38\frac{3}{4}$	Lockheed	LK	1.60	3.4	5	2406	$47\frac{3}{8}$	$46\frac{7}{8}$	47	$-\frac{1}{4}$
$44\frac{3}{8}$	$28\frac{1}{8}$	Loctite	LOC	.88	2.0	15	159	$43\frac{1}{2}$	$43\frac{1}{8}$	$43\frac{3}{8}$	$+1\frac{3}{8}$
$100\frac{1}{2}$	62	Loews Cp	LTR	1.00	1.0	8	769	$98\frac{3}{4}$	$97\frac{3}{8}$	$97\frac{3}{8}$	$-1\frac{3}{8}$
$24\frac{7}{8}$	$19\frac{1}{8}$	Logicon	LGN	.36	1.5	12	65	24	$23\frac{3}{4}$	24	$+\frac{1}{4}$

The summary of stock market information presented on the financial pages of many newspapers reveals the following:

52 Weeks Hi/Lo: The highest and lowest prices, in dollars per share, of the stock during the previous 52 weeks.
Stock: The name of the company (frequently abbreviated).
Sym: Highly abbreviated name of the company, as it appears on the stock exchange ticker tape.
Div: Dividend paid, in dollars per share.
Yld %: Yield in percent per year; the dividend divided by the price of the stock.
PE: Price-earnings ratio; the price of the stock divided by the earnings (profits) per share of the company.
Vol 100s: Number of shares traded during the day, in hundreds of shares.
Hi: Highest price at which the stock traded that day.
Lo: Lowest price at which the stock traded that day.
Close: Last price at which the stock traded that day.
Net Chg: Net change in the stock's price from the previous day's closing price.

−$.25, which means that it *closed* the day at a price of 25 cents per share lower than it *closed* the day before.

The dividend column, headed "Div," shows the annual dividend (in dollars and cents) that the company has paid over the preceding year on each share of its stock. In Logicon's case, this amounts to 36 cents a share. If the dividend is divided by the closing price of the stock ($.36 ÷ $24.00), the result is 1.5 percent, which is shown in the yield percentage ("Yld %") column for Logicon. In a sense, the company is paying interest on the stock at a rate of about 1.5 percent. At first glance, this seems like an absurdly low amount; after all, at the time this issue of the *Wall Street Journal* was printed, ordinary checking accounts were paying about 5 percent. The reason people tolerate this seemingly low yield on Logicon (or any other stock) is that they expect that the price of the stock will rise over time, yielding capital gains.

The column heading "PE" stands for *price-earnings ratio*. To obtain the entries for this column, the firm's total earnings (profits) for the year are divided by the number of the firm's shares in existence to give the earnings per share. When the price of the stock is divided by the earnings per share, the result is the price-earnings ratio.

The column to the right of the PE ratio shows the total *volume* of the shares of the stock traded that day, measured in hundreds of shares.

FOR CRITICAL ANALYSIS: Is there necessarily any relationship between the net change in a stock's price and how many shares have been sold on a particular day? ●

CONCEPTS IN BRIEF

- Many economists believe that asset markets, especially the stock market, are efficient, meaning that one cannot make a higher than normal rate of return without having inside information (information that the general public does not possess).

- Stock prices normally follow a random walk, meaning that you cannot predict changes in future stock prices based on information about stock price behavior in the past.

GLOBAL CAPITAL MARKETS

Financial institutions in the United States are tied to the rest of the world via their lending capacities. In addition, integration of all financial markets is increasing. Indeed, recent changes in world finance have been nothing short of remarkable. Distinctions among financial institutions and between financial institutions and nonfinancial institutions have blurred. As the legal barriers that have preserved such distinctions are dismantled, multinational corporations offering a wide array of financial services are becoming dominant worldwide.

Globalizing Financial Markets

The globalization of financial markets is not entirely new. U.S. banks developed worldwide branch networks in the 1960s and 1970s for loans, check clearing, and foreign exchange (currency) trading. Also in the 1970s, firms dealing in U.S. securities (stocks and bonds) expanded their operations in London (on the Eurobond market) and then into other financial centers, including Tokyo. Similarly, foreign firms invaded U.S. shores: first the banks, then securities firms. The "big four" Japanese securities firms now have offices in New York and London.

Money and capital markets today are truly international. Markets for U.S. government securities, interbank lending and borrowing, foreign exchange trading, and common stocks are now trading continuously, in vast quantities, around the clock and around the world.

The World Market for U.S. Government Debt. Trading for U.S. government securities has been described as "the world's fastest-growing 24-hour market." This market was made possible by (1) sophisticated communications and computer technology, (2) deregulation of financial markets in foreign countries to permit such trading, (3) U.S. legislation in 1984 to enable foreign investors to buy U.S. government securities tax-free, and (4) huge annual U.S. government budget deficits, which have poured a steady stream of tradable debt into the world markets.

Other Globalized Markets. Foreign exchange—the buying and selling of foreign currencies—became a 24-hour, worldwide market in the 1970s. Instruments tied to government bonds, foreign exchange, stock market indexes, and commodities (grains, metals, oil) are now traded increasingly in financial futures markets in all the world's major centers of commerce. Most financial firms are coming to the conclusion that to survive as a force in any one of the world's leading financial markets, a firm must have a significant presence in all of them. It is predicted that by the turn of the twenty-first century, between 30 and 50 financial institutions will be at the centers of world finance—New York, London, Tokyo, and Frankfurt—and they will be competing in all those markets to do business with the world's major corporations and portfolio managers. Today, major corporate borrowers throughout the world can choose to borrow from a wide variety of lenders, also located throughout the world. Borrowing on the international capital markets was estimated at $850 billion for the year 1996 for the 24 leading industrialized nations, according to the Organization for Economic Cooperation and Development (OECD).

> **CONCEPTS IN BRIEF**
>
> • Financial markets throughout the world have become increasingly integrated, leading to a global financial market. Interbank lending and borrowing, foreign exchange trading, and common stock sales now occur virtually 24 hours a day throughout the world.
>
> • Many U.S. government or government-guaranteed securities trade 24 hours a day.

PROBLEMS IN CORPORATE GOVERNANCE

Separation of ownership and control
The situation that exists in corporations in which the owners (shareholders) are not the people who control the operation of the corporation (managers). The goals of these two groups are often different.

Many corporations issue stock to raise financial capital that they will use to fund expansion or modernization. The decision to raise capital in this way is ordinarily made not by the owners of the corporation—the holders of its stock—but by the company's managers. This **separation of ownership and control** in corporations leads to incentive problems. Managers may not act in the best interest of shareholders. Further incentive problems arise when corporations borrow money in financial markets. These corporate governance problems have to do with information that is not the same for everyone.

Asymmetric Information: The Perils of Adverse Selection and Moral Hazard

Asymmetric information
Information possessed by one side of a transaction but not the other. The side with more information will be at an advantage.

Adverse selection
The circumstance that arises in financial markets when borrowers who are the worst credit risks are the ones most likely to seek loans.

If you invest in a corporation, you give purchasing power to the managers of that corporation. Those managers have much more information about what is happening to the corporation and its future than you do. The inequality of information between the two parties is called **asymmetric information.** If asymmetric information exists before a transaction takes place, we have a circumstance of **adverse selection.** In financial markets, adverse selection occurs because borrowers who are the worst credit risks (and thus likely to yield the most adverse outcomes) are the ones most likely to seek, and perhaps to receive, loans.

Consider two firms seeking to borrow funds by selling bonds. Suppose that one of the firms, the Dynamic Corporation, is pursuing a project with a small chance of yielding large profits and a large chance of bankruptcy. The other firm, the Reliable Company, intends to invest in a project that is guaranteed to yield the competitive rate of return, thereby ensuring repayment of its debts. Because Dynamic knows the chance is high that it will go bankrupt and never have to pay its debts, it can offer a high interest rate on the bonds it issues. Unless prospective bond purchasers can distinguish perfectly between the two firms' projects, they will select the high-yielding bonds offered by Dynamic and refuse to buy the low-yielding bonds offered by Reliable. Firms like Reliable will be unable to get funding, yet lenders will lose money on firms like Dynamic. Adverse selection thus makes investors less likely to lend to anyone and more inclined to charge higher interest rates when they do lend.

Moral hazard
A problem that occurs because of asymmetric information *after* a transaction occurs. In financial markets, a person to whom money has been lent may indulge in more risky behavior, thereby increasing the probability of default on the debt.

Moral hazard occurs as a result of asymmetric information *after* a transaction occurs. To continue with our example of the Dynamic Corporation, once the firm has sold the bonds, it must choose among alternative strategies in executing its project. Lenders face the hazard that Dynamic may choose strategies contrary to the lenders' well-being and thus immoral from their perspective. Because bondholders are entitled to a fixed amount regardless of the firm's profits, Dynamic has an incentive to select strategies offering a small chance of high profits, thereby enabling the owners to keep the largest amount after paying bondholders. Such strategies are also the riskiest—ones that make it more likely that lenders will not be repaid—so the presence of moral hazard makes lenders less likely to lend to anyone and more inclined to charge higher interest rates when they do lend.

EXAMPLE
Explaining the Success of at Least One Multibillionaire

Multibillionaires are special, and Warren Buffett is one of them. He initially invested $100 and ended up with Berkshire Hathaway, a company with businesses in insurance, candy manufacturing, and newspaper publishing, among others. The company's market value is over $20 billion, though Buffett doesn't own it all. His technique has been an attempt to eliminate the asymmetry problem that is associated with the separation of ownership and control. Buffett invests large sums of money only in businesses that he understands thoroughly. He pays special attention to what management does with excess cash that cannot be properly reinvested inside the corporation. For that is where managers can easily divert funds in ways that do not serve shareholders' best interests. One way of obtaining more information than a typical investor in the companies in which he invests, Buffett has discovered, is becoming a member of the board of directors and befriending the chief executive. He has done so in every enterprise in which he has invested heavily. As a result, he has profited handsomely from his ability to reduce information costs.

FOR CRITICAL ANALYSIS: Is it possible for the average investor to avoid the asymmetric information problem when making an investment decision? ●

The Principal-Agent Problem

A type of moral hazard problem that occurs within firms is called the **principal-agent problem.** The shareholders who own a firm are referred to as *principals,* and the managers who operate the firm are the *agents* of the owners. When the managers do not own all of a firm (as is usually the case), a separation of ownership and control exists, and if the stockholders have less information about the firm's opportunities and risks than the managers do (as is also usually the case), the managers may act in their own self-interests rather than in the interests of the shareholders.

Principal-agent problem
The conflict of interest that occurs when agents—managers of firms—pursue their own objectives to the detriment of the goals of the firms' principals, or owners.

Consider, for example, the choice between two investment projects, one of which involves an enormous amount of work but also promises high profits, while the other requires little effort and promises small returns. Because the managers must do all the work while the shareholders receive all the profits, the managers' incentives are different from those of the shareholders. In this case, the presence of moral hazard will induce the managers to choose the "good life," the easy but low-yielding project—an outcome that fails to maximize the economic value of the firm.

Solving Principal-Agent and Moral Hazard Problems

The dangers associated with asymmetric information are well known to participants in financial markets, who regularly undertake vigorous steps to minimize its costly consequences. For example, research companies such as Standard & Poor's gather financial data and other information about corporations and sell the information to their subscribers. When even this is insufficient to eliminate the dangers of adverse selection, lenders often require that borrowers post **collateral**—assets that the borrower will forfeit in the event that repayment of a debt is not made. A variant of this strategy, designed to reduce moral hazard problems, is called the **incentive-compatible contract:** Lenders make sure that borrowers have a large amount of their own assets at risk so that the incentives of the borrower are compatible with the interests of the lender. Although measures such as these cannot eliminate the losses caused by asymmetric information, they reduce them below what would otherwise be the case.

Collateral
An asset pledged to guarantee the repayment of a loan.

Incentive-compatible contract
A loan contract under which a significant amount of the borrower's assets are at risk, providing an incentive for the borrower to look after the lender's interests.

EXAMPLE
Making Executives Own a Share of the Company

One way to minimize the principal-agent problem is to require that executives own stock in the companies for which they work. An increasing number of corporations are requiring directors and top management to own shares of stock. By the mid-1990s, almost 20 percent of companies surveyed by *Fortune* prepared "guidelines" specifying the amount of stock that executives must own. These include Black & Decker, Union Pacific, and US West. Usually executives are told that they must buy over a period of five years an amount ranging from one to four times their annual salaries.

Do shareholders benefit from top management's owning "a piece of the rock"? One study indicated that companies in which the chief executives had significant ownership experienced a 4 percent higher annual rate of return over a five-year period than similar companies that did not require executives to own stock.

FOR CRITICAL ANALYSIS: Is there any way you can use this information to determine in which corporations you should invest? ●

CONCEPTS IN BRIEF

- When two parties to a transaction have different amounts of information, we call this asymmetric information. Whenever asymmetric information occurs before a transaction takes place, it can result in adverse selection. Adverse selection causes borrowers who are the worst credit risks to be the ones most likely to seek loans.

- When asymmetric information occurs after a transaction, this can cause moral hazard. Lenders often face the hazard that borrowers will choose more risky actions after borrowers have taken out loans.

- The separation of ownership and control in today's large corporations can give rise to the principal-agent problem, whereby the agents (managers) may have interests that differ from those of the principals (shareholders).

- Several methods exist for solving the principal-agent and moral hazard problems. They include requiring lenders to post collateral and devising incentive-compatible contracts in which borrowers have a large amount of their own assets at risk.

What Does the Dow Jones Industrial Average Really Measure?

Concepts Applied: *Stock market, relative changes*

On the trading floor of the New York Stock Exchange, over 2,500 different company stocks are traded every business weekday. The Dow Jones Industrial Average indexes 30 of those companies to describe the market's performance.

Stock prices are in the news frequently. Look at Figure 21-1, which shows the ups and downs of the Dow Jones Industrial Average between 1985 and 1996. It started out in 1985 at less than 1,500 points and ended up in 1996 over 5,000. Its daily changes are tracked by the media, and every slight change seems cause for comment. But few people know what the Dow really represents.

The Dow Is an Index

The Dow Jones Industrial Average was started in 1884 by Charles Dow and Edward Jones, who founded the Dow-Jones Publishing Company. At that time, it was an index that measured changes in the stocks of 11 companies. By 1928, the index increased its coverage to 30 companies, which is where it is today. Those 30 companies are listed in Table 21-4.

Is It Representative?

One would be hard pressed to believe that 30 companies out of the 2,586 on the New York Stock Exchange can be representative. But those 30 companies do represent 25 percent of the exchange's value because they are so large.

Each company's stock is price-weighted in the index. That means that the higher its share price, the more it counts in the calculation.

Which Companies Are Left Out?

As of the mid-1990s, the Dow still did not include Wal-Mart, a company with a market value of over $60 billion and the fifth largest corporation in America, nor did it include Microsoft or Intel, both with market values of around $40 billion.

Don't Be Fooled by the Numbers

While journalists may have a heyday if the Dow falls by, say, 90 points, you need to be more perceptive. When the stock market lost "only" 70 points in the crash of October 1929, it set off a panic. The reason was that the Dow's level at that time was just 343. Hence the Dow had fallen 20 percent in a matter of hours. Today, with the Dow at over 5,000, an equal-sized point drop represents less than a 1.5 percent decline. If you stick with percentage changes, you will see that the daily changes in the Dow are relatively insignificant.

How Useful Is the Dow?

In the final analysis, a stock market index is only as good as its ability to be an accurate barometer of stock market direction. On that account, the Dow Jones Industrial Average, despite its limited base, has been relatively accurate. It certainly has accurately reflected the recessions that occurred in 1960, 1970, and 1973, the two at the beginning of the 1980s, and the one at the beginning of the 1990s. The Dow is also one component of the Index of Leading Economic Indicators compiled by the U.S. Department of Commerce.

FOR CRITICAL ANALYSIS
1. There are several other reputable stock market indexes, such as the S&P 500 and the Russell 2000 (an index with 2,000 stocks). These competitors are rarely cited in the popular press. Why not?
2. Why is the level of the Dow Jones Industrial Average so much higher today than it was during the Great Depression?

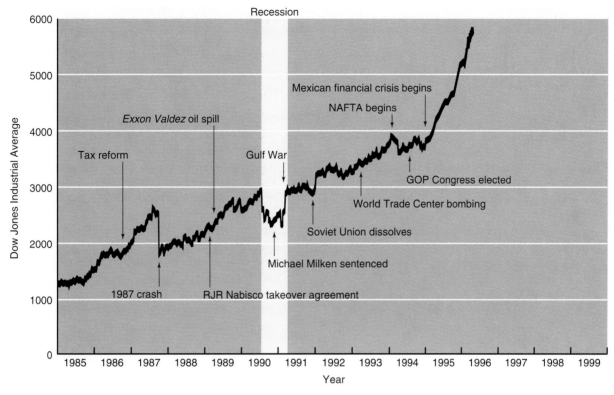

FIGURE 21-1

The Dow Jones Industrial Average Since 1985
The Dow has increased, with occasional stalling, since 1985.

Source: Dow Jones Company.

TABLE 21-4

The 30 Corporations That Make Up the Dow Jones Industrial Average

Allied Signal	Du Pont	3M
Alcoa	Eastman Kodak	J. P. Morgan
American Express	Exxon	Philip Morris
AT&T	General Electric	Procter & Gamble
Bethlehem Steel	General Motors	Sears, Roebuck
Boeing	Goodyear Tire	Texaco
Caterpillar	I.B.M.	Union Carbide
Chevron	International Paper	United Technologies
Coca-Cola	McDonald's	Westinghouse Electric
Walt Disney	Merck & Company	Woolworth

CHAPTER SUMMARY

1. Proprietorships are the most common form of business organization, comprising more than 74 percent of all firms. Each is owned by a single individual who makes all business decisions, receives all the profits, and has unlimited liability for the firm's debts.

2. Partnerships are much like proprietorships, except that two or more individuals, or partners, share the decisions and the profits of the firm; each partner has unlimited liability for the debts of the firm.

3. Corporations are responsible for the largest share of business revenues. The owners, called shareholders, share in the firm's profits but normally have little responsibility for the firm's day-to-day operations. Owners of corporations enjoy limited liability for the debts of the firm.

4. When two parties to a transaction have different amounts of information, we call this asymmetric information. Whenever asymmetric information occurs before a transaction takes place, it can result in adverse selection. Adverse selection causes borrowers who are the worst credit risks to be the ones most likely to seek loans.

5. When asymmetric information occurs after a transaction, this can cause moral hazard. Lenders often face the hazard that borrowers will choose more risky actions after borrowers have taken out loans.

6. The separation of ownership and control in today's large corporation has led to the principal-agent problem, whereby the agents (managers) may have interests that differ from those of the principals (shareholders).

7. Several methods exist for solving the principal-agent and moral hazard problems, including requiring lenders to post collateral and devising incentive-compatible contracts in which borrowers have a large amount of their own assets at risk.

DISCUSSION OF PREVIEW QUESTIONS

1. **What are the main organizational forms that firms take, and what are their advantages and disadvantages?**

The primary organizational forms businesses take are the proprietorship, the partnership, and the corporation. The proprietorship is owned by a single person, the proprietor, who makes the business decisions, is entitled to all the profits, and is subject to unlimited liability—that is, is personally responsible for all debts incurred by the firm. The partnership differs from the proprietorship chiefly in that there are two or more owners, called partners. They share the responsibility for decision making, share the firm's profits, and individually bear unlimited liability for the firm's debts. The net income, or profits, of both proprietorships and partnerships is subject only to personal income taxes. Both types of firms legally cease to exist when the proprietor or a partner gives up ownership or dies. The corporation differs from proprietorships and partnerships in three important dimensions. Owners of corporations enjoy limited liability; that is, their responsibility for the debts of the corporation is limited to the value of their ownership shares. In addition, the income from corporations is subject to double taxation—corporate taxation when income is earned by the corporation and personal taxation when after-tax profits are paid as dividends to the owners. Finally, corporations do not legally cease to exist due to a change of ownership or the death of an owner.

2. **What are corporations' primary sources of financial capital?**

The main sources of financial capital for corporations are stocks, bonds, and reinvestment of profits. Stocks are ownership shares, promising a share of profits, sold to investors. Common stocks also embody voting rights regarding the major decisions of the firm; preferred stocks typically have no voting rights but enjoy priority status in the payment of dividends. Bonds are notes of indebtedness, issued in return for the loan of money. They typically promise to pay interest in the form of annual coupon payments, plus repayment of the original principal amount upon maturity. Bondholders are generally promised payment before any payment of dividends to shareholders, and for this reason bonds are less risky than stocks. Reinvestment involves the purchase of assets by the firm, using retained profits or depreciation reserves it has set aside for this purpose. No new stocks or bonds are issued in the course of reinvestment, although its value is fully reflected in the price of existing shares of stock.

3. **What are the major differences between stocks and bonds?**
Stocks represent ownership in a corporation. They are called equity capital. Bonds represent the debt of a corporation. They are part of the debt capital of a

corporation. Bond owners normally receive a fixed interest payment on a regular basis, whereas owners of stock are not normally guaranteed any dividends. If a corporation goes out of business, bondholders have first priority on whatever value still exists in the entity. Owners of stock get whatever is left over. Finally, if the corporation is very successful, owners of stock can reap the increases in the market value of their shares of stock. In contrast, the market value of corporate bonds is not so closely tied to the profits of a corporation but is rather influenced by how interest rates are changing in the economy in general.

4. **Is there a world market for U.S. government securities?**
Trading in U.S. government securities is one of the fastest-growing 24-hour markets in the world, thanks to sophisticated communications and computer technology. The deregulation of financial markets in foreign countries now permits much more of such trading. Also, since 1984, the United States has allowed foreign investors to buy U.S. government securities tax-free.

PROBLEMS

(Answers to the odd-numbered problems appear at the back of the book.)

21-1. Suppose that federal tax policy were changed to exempt the first $10,000 in dividends each year from personal taxation. How would this affect the choice of organizational form for businesses?

21-2. How would the change in corporate tax policy mentioned in Problem 21-1 affect the method of financing that corporations use?

*21-3. Consider a firm that wishes to borrow $10,000 for one year. Suppose that there is a 20 percent chance

that this firm will go out of business before the end of the year (repaying none of its debts) and an 80 percent chance that it will survive and repay all of its debts. If potential lenders can earn 10 percent per year by lending to other firms that are certain to repay their debts, what rate of interest will the risky firm have to offer if it is to be able to borrow the $10,000?

21-4. Should the government guarantee junk bonds to make sure that the buyers of these bonds do not lose money? What would happen if the government did this?

*This problem is optional; albegra is required.

COMPUTER-ASSISTED INSTRUCTION

Key determinants of the prices of shares of corporate stock are illustrated using numerical problems.

Complete problem and answer appear on disk.

INTERACTING WITH THE INTERNET

An excellent tool for learning about the functioning of financial markets is the Iowa Electronic Markets. It is a registered market that runs on the Internet and is designed to teach the fundamentals of trading in financial markets. To make the learning "real," participants risk their own funds (you can invest quite small amounts). There are two types of markets: political ones, based on the outcome of elections, and financial ones. See

http://www.biz.uiowa.edu/iem/

Two services that provide financial information, some of it free, are QuoteCom at

http://www.quote.com/

and Security APL at

http://www.secapl.com/

The American Stock Exchange can be reached at

http://www.amex.com/

the New York Stock Exchange (still "under construction") at

http://www.nyse.com/

the Chicago Mercantile Exchange at

http://www.interaccess.com/cme/

and the London International Financial Futures and Options Exchange at

http://www.liffe.com/

Not all exchanges offer complete pricing information, but they generally do have extensive material on themselves.

PART 7

MARKET STRUCTURE, RESOURCE ALLOCATION, AND REGULATION

CHAPTER 22

THE FIRM: COST AND OUTPUT DETERMINATION

The lights of Broadway may still beckon both stars and audiences, but Broadway is not what it used to be. At least that is what playwright Neil Simon indicated when he opted for Off-Broadway. Why would America's richest, best-known playwright turn his back on Broadway? To understand this issue, you must learn more about how businesses determine costs, profits, and output.

PREVIEW QUESTIONS

1. How does the economist's definition of profit differ from the accountant's?

2. What distinguishes the long run from the short run?

3. How does the law of diminishing marginal returns account for an *eventually* increasing marginal cost curve for a firm in the short run?

4. Why is the short-run average total cost curve U-shaped?

Did You Know That . . . there are more than 25 steps in the process of manufacturing a simple lead pencil? In the production of an automobile, there are literally thousands. At each step, the manufacturer can have the job done by workers or machines or some combination of the two. The manufacturer must also figure out how much to produce each month. Should a new machine be bought that can replace 10 workers? Should more workers be hired, or should the existing workers be paid overtime? If the price of aluminum is rising, should the company try to make do with plastic? What you will learn about in this chapter is how producers can select the best combination of inputs for any given output that is desired.

Before we look at the firm's costs, we need to define a firm.

THE FIRM

We define a business, or **firm,** as follows:

> **A firm is an organization that brings together factors of production—labor, land, physical capital, human capital, and entrepreneurial skill—to produce a product or service that it hopes can be sold at a profit.**

A typical firm will have an organizational structure consisting of an entrepreneur, managers, and workers. The entrepreneur is the person who takes the risks, mainly of losing his or her personal wealth. In compensation, the entrepreneur will get any profits that are made. Recall from Chapter 2 that entrepreneurs take the initiative in combining land, labor, and capital to produce a good or a service. Entrepreneurs are the ones who innovate in the form of new production and new products. The entrepreneur also decides whom to hire to manage the firm. Some economists maintain that the true quality of an entrepreneur becomes evident with his or her selection of managers. Managers, in turn, decide who should be hired and fired and how the business generally should be set up. The workers ultimately use the other inputs to produce the products or services that are being sold by the firm. Workers and managers are paid contractual wages. They receive a specified amount of income for a specified time period. Entrepreneurs are not paid contractual wages. They receive no reward specified in advance. The entrepreneurs make profits if there are any, for profits accrue to those who are willing to take risks. (Because the entrepreneur gets only what is left over after all expenses are paid, he or she is often referred to as a *residual claimant.* The entrepreneur lays claim to the residual—whatever is left.)

Profit and Costs

Most people think of profit as the difference between the amount of revenues a business takes in and the amount it spends for wages, materials, and so on. In a bookkeeping sense, the following formula could be used:

$$\text{Accounting profits} = \text{total revenues} - \text{explicit costs}$$

where **explicit costs** are expenses that the business managers must take account of because they must actually be paid out by the firm. This definition of profit is known as **accounting profit.** It is appropriate when used by accountants to determine a firm's taxable income. Economists are more interested in how firm managers react not just to changes in explicit costs but also to changes in **implicit costs,** defined as expenses that business managers do not have to pay out of pocket but are costs to the firm nonetheless because they represent an opportunity cost. These are noncash costs—they do not involve any direct cash outlay by the firm and must therefore be measured by the alternative cost principle. That is to say,

Firm
A business organization that employs resources to produce goods or services for profit. A firm normally owns and operates at least one plant in order to produce.

Explicit costs
Costs that business managers must take account of because they must be paid; examples are wages, taxes, and rent.

Accounting profit
Total revenues minus total explicit costs.

Implicit costs
Expenses that managers do not have to pay out of pocket and hence do not normally explicitly calculate, such as the opportunity cost of factors of production that are owned; examples are owner-provided capital and owner-provided labor.

they are measured by what the resources (land, capital) currently used in producing a particular good or service could earn in other uses. Economists therefore use the full opportunity cost of all resources as the figure to subtract from revenues to obtain a definition of profit. Another definition of implicit cost is therefore the opportunity cost of using factors that a producer does not buy or hire but already owns.

Opportunity Cost of Capital

Normal rate of return
The amount that must be paid to an investor to induce investment in a business; also known as the *opportunity cost of capital.*

Firms enter or remain in an industry if they earn, at minimum, a **normal rate of return.** People will not invest their wealth in a business unless they obtain a positive normal (competitive) rate of return—that is, unless their invested wealth pays off. Any business wishing to attract capital must expect to pay at least the same rate of return on that capital as all other businesses (of similar risk) are willing to pay. Put another way, when a firm requires the use of a resource in producing a particular product, it must bid against alternative users of that resource. Thus the firm must offer a price that is at least as much as other users are offering to pay. For example, if individuals can invest their wealth in almost any publishing firm and get a rate of return of 10 percent per year, each firm in the publishing industry must *expect* to pay 10 percent as the normal rate of return to present and future investors. This 10 percent is a *cost to the firm,* the **opportunity cost of capital.** The opportunity cost of capital is the amount of income, or yield, that could have been earned by investing in the next-best alternative. Capital will not stay in firms or industries in which the expected rate of return falls below its opportunity cost, that is, what could be earned elsewhere. If a firm owns some capital equipment, it can either use it or lease it and earn a return. If the firm uses the equipment for production, part of the cost of using that equipment is the forgone revenue that the firm could have earned had it leased out that equipment.

Opportunity cost of capital
The normal rate of return, or the available return on the next-best alternative investment. Economists consider this a cost of production, and it is included in our cost examples.

Opportunity Cost of Owner-Provided Labor and Capital

Single-owner proprietorships often grossly exaggerate their profit rates because they understate the opportunity cost of the labor that the proprietor provides to the business. Here we are referring to the opportunity cost of labor. For example, you may know people who run small grocery stores. These people will sit down at the end of the year and figure out what their "profits" are. They will add up all their sales and subtract what they had to pay to other workers, what they had to pay to their suppliers, what they had to pay in taxes, and so on. The end result they will call "profit." They normally will not, however, have figured into their costs the salary that they could have made if they had worked for somebody else in a similar type of job. By working for themselves, they become residual claimants— they receive what is left after all explicit costs have been accounted for. However, part of the costs should include the salary the owner-operator could have received working for someone else.

Consider a simple example of a skilled auto mechanic working 14 hours a day at his own service station, six days a week. Compare this situation to how much he could earn as a trucking company mechanic 84 hours a week. This self-employed auto mechanic might have an opportunity cost of about $20 an hour. For his 84-hour week in his own service station, he is forfeiting $1,680. Unless his service station shows accounting profits of more than that per week, he is losing money in an economic sense.

Another way of looking at the opportunity cost of running a business is that opportunity cost consists of all explicit and implicit costs. Accountants only take account of explicit costs. Therefore, accounting profit ends up being the residual after only explicit costs are subtracted from total revenues.

This same analysis can apply to owner-provided capital, such as land or buildings. The fact that the owner owns the building or the land with which he or she operates a business does not mean that it is "free." Rather, use of the building and land still has an opportunity cost—the value of the next-best alternative use for those assets.

Accounting Profits Versus Economic Profits

Economic profits
Total revenues minus total opportunity costs of all inputs used, or the total of all implicit and explicit costs.

The term *profits* in economics means the income that entrepreneurs earn, over and above all costs including their own opportunity cost of time, plus the opportunity cost of the capital they have invested in their business. Profits can be regarded as total revenues minus total costs—which is how accountants think of them—but we must now include *all* costs. Our definition of **economic profits** will be the following:

Economic profits = total revenues − total opportunity cost of all inputs used

or

Economic profits = total revenues − (explicit + implicit costs)

Remember that implicit costs include a normal rate of return on invested capital. We show this relationship in Figure 22-1.

THINKING CRITICALLY ABOUT THE MEDIA

Profits Increase by $500 Million!

Headlines like the one on this box make great eyecatchers in a newspaper. But without any other information, being told what the *absolute* profits of some company, such as General Motors or Exxon, are is meaningless. If the total reported yearly profits of Exxon are, say, $1 billion, that can mean that Exxon is doing well or doing abysmally. If the total investment in Exxon is $10 billion, then $1 billion in reported profits represents a 10 percent rate of return. If the investment in Exxon is $50 billion, in contrast, then $1 billion in profits represents only a 2 percent rate of return on investment, which could be considered terrible. Don't be fooled by "huge profits" headlines.

The Goal of the Firm: Profit Maximization

When we examined the theory of consumer demand, utility (or satisfaction) maximization by the individual provided the basis for the analysis. In the theory of the firm and production, *profit maximization* is the underlying hypothesis of our predictive theory. The goal of the firm is to maximize economic profits, and the firm is expected to try to make the positive difference between total revenues and total costs as large as it can.

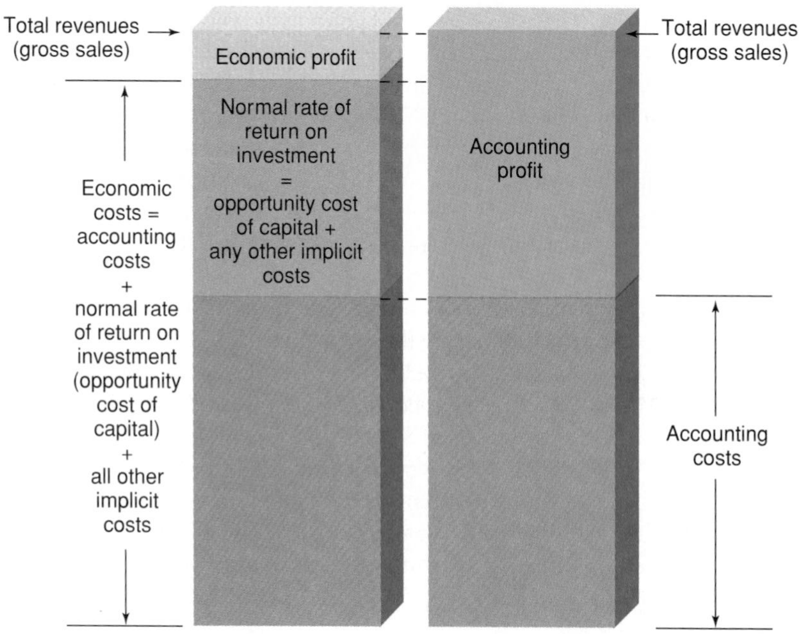

FIGURE 22-1

Simplified View of Economic and Accounting Profit

We see on the right column that accounting profit is the difference between total revenues and total explicit accounting costs. Conversely, we see on the left column that economic profit is equal to total revenues minus economic costs. Economic costs equal explicit accounting costs plus all implicit costs, including a normal rate of return on invested capital.

Our justification for assuming profit maximization by firms is similar to our belief in utility maximization by individuals. To obtain labor, capital, and other resources required to produce commodities, firms must first obtain financing from investors. In general, investors are indifferent about the details of how a firm uses the money they provide. They are most interested in the earnings on this money and the risk of obtaining lower returns or losing the money they have invested. Firms that can provide relatively higher risk-corrected returns will therefore have an advantage in obtaining the financing needed to continue or expand production. Over time we would expect a policy of profit maximization to become the dominant mode of behavior for firms that survive.

CONCEPTS IN BRIEF

- Accounting profits differ from economic profits. Economic profits are defined as total revenues minus total costs, where costs include the full opportunity cost of all of the factors of production plus all other implicit costs.
- Single-owner proprietorships often fail to consider the opportunity cost of the labor services provided by the owner.
- The full opportunity cost of capital invested in a business is generally not included as a cost when accounting profits are calculated. Thus accounting profits often overstate economic profits.
- We assume throughout these chapters that the goal of the firm is to maximize economic profits.

SHORT RUN VERSUS LONG RUN

In Chapter 20, we discussed short-run and long-run price elasticities of supply and demand. For consumers, the long run meant the time period during which all adjustments to a change in price could be made, and anything shorter than that was considered the short run. For suppliers, the long run was the time in which all adjustments could be made, and anything shorter than that was the short run.

Now that we are discussing firms only, we will maintain a similar distinction between the short and the long run, but we will be more specific. In the theory of the firm, the **short run** is defined as any time period that is so short that there is at least one input, such as current **plant size,** that the firm cannot alter.[1] In other words, during the short run, a firm makes do with whatever big machines and factory size it already has, no matter how much more it wants to produce because of increased demand for its product. We consider the plant and heavy equipment, the size or amount of which cannot be varied in the short run, as fixed resources. In agriculture and in some other businesses, land may be a fixed resource.

There are, of course, variable resources that the firm can alter when it wants to change its rate of production. These are called *variable inputs* or *variable factors of production.* Typically, the variable inputs of a firm are its labor and its purchases of raw materials. In the short run, in response to changes in demand, the firm can, by definition, vary only its variable inputs.

The **long run** can now be considered the period of time in which *all* inputs can be varied. Specifically, in the long run, the firm can alter its plant size. How long is the long run? That depends on each individual industry. For Wendy's or McDonald's, the long run may be four

Short run
The time period when at least one input, such as plant size, cannot be changed.

Plant size
The physical size of the factories that a firm owns and operates to produce its output. Plant size can be defined by square footage, maximum physical capacity, and other physical measures.

Long run
The time period in which all factors of production can be varied.

---

[1]There can be many short runs but only one long run. For ease of analysis, in this section we simplify the case to one short run and talk about short-run costs.

or five months, because that is the time it takes to add new franchises. For a steel company, the long run may be several years, because that's how long it takes to plan and build a new plant. An electric utility might need over a decade to build a new plant, for example.

Short run and *long run* in our discussion are in fact management planning terms that apply to decisions made by managers. The firm can operate only in the short run in the sense that decisions must be made in the present. The same analysis applies to your own behavior. You may have many long-run plans about graduate school, vacations, and the like, but you always operate in the short run—you make decisions every day about what you do every day.

THE RELATIONSHIP BETWEEN OUTPUT AND INPUTS

A firm takes numerous inputs, combines them using a technological production process, and ends up with an output. There are, of course, a great many factors of production, or inputs. We classify production inputs into two broad categories (ignoring land)—labor and capital. The relationship between output and these two inputs is as follows:

Output per time period = some function of capital and labor inputs

In simple math, the production relationship can be written $Q = f(K, L)$, where Q = output per time period, K = capital, and L = labor.

We have used the word *production* but have not defined it. **Production** is any process by which resources are transformed into goods or services. Production includes not only making things but also transporting them, retailing, repackaging them, and so on. Notice that if we know that production occurs, we do not necessarily know the value of the output. The production relationship tells nothing about the worth or value of the inputs or the output.

Production
Any activity that results in the conversion of resources into products that can be used in consumption.

INTERNATIONAL EXAMPLE
Europeans Use More Capital

Since 1970, the 15 nations of the European Union (EU) have increased their total annual output of goods and services about as much as the United States. But over this same time period, the EU has dramatically increased the amount of capital relative to the amount of labor it uses in its production processes. Business managers in the EU have substituted capital for labor much more than in the United States because the cost of labor (wages corrected for inflation) has increased by almost 60 percent in the EU but by only 15 percent in the United States.

FOR CRITICAL ANALYSIS: How does a firm decide when to buy more machines? ●

The Production Function: A Numerical Example

The relationship between maximum physical output and the quantity of capital and labor used in the production process is sometimes called a **production function.** The production function is a technological relationship between inputs and output. Firms that are inefficient or wasteful in their use of capital and labor will obtain less output than the production function in theory will show. No firm can obtain more output than the production function shows, however. The production function specifies the maximum possible output that can be produced with a given amount of inputs. It also specifies the minimum amount of inputs necessary to produce a given level of output. The production function depends on the tech-

Production function
The relationship between inputs and output. A production function is a technological, not an economic, relationship.

nology available to the firm. It follows that an improvement in technology that allows the firm to produce more output with the same amount of inputs (or the same output with fewer inputs) results in a new production function.

Look at panel (a) of Figure 22-2. It shows a production function relating total output in column 2 to the quantity of labor measured in workers in column 1. When there are zero

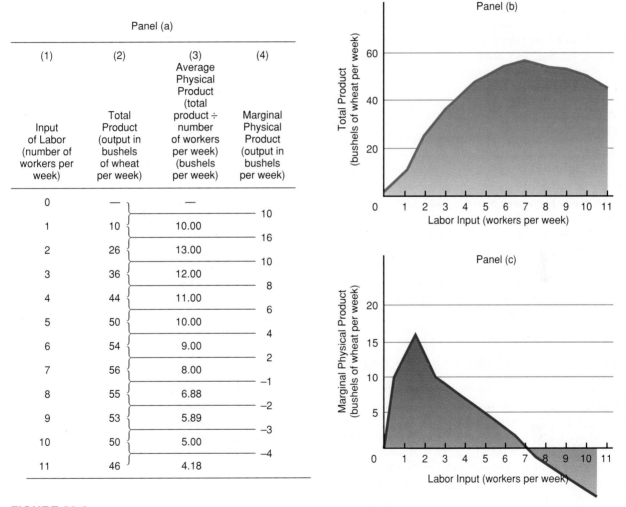

Panel (a)

(1) Input of Labor (number of workers per week)	(2) Total Product (output in bushels of wheat per week)	(3) Average Physical Product (total product ÷ number of workers per week) (bushels per week)	(4) Marginal Physical Product (output in bushels per week)
0	—	—	
			10
1	10	10.00	
			16
2	26	13.00	
			10
3	36	12.00	
			8
4	44	11.00	
			6
5	50	10.00	
			4
6	54	9.00	
			2
7	56	8.00	
			−1
8	55	6.88	
			−2
9	53	5.89	
			−3
10	50	5.00	
			−4
11	46	4.18	

FIGURE 22-2

Diminishing Returns, the Production Function, and Marginal Product: A Hypothetical Case

Marginal product is the addition to the total product that results when one additional worker is hired. Thus the marginal product of the fourth worker is eight bushels of wheat. With four workers, 44 bushels are produced, but with three workers, only 36 are produced; the difference is 8. In panel (b), we plot the numbers from columns 1 and 2 of panel (a). In panel (c), we plot the numbers from columns 1 and 4 of panel (a). When we go from 0 to 1, marginal product is 10. When we go from one worker to two workers, marginal product increases to 16. After two workers, marginal product declines, but it is still positive. Total product (output) reaches its peak at seven workers, so after seven workers marginal product is negative. When we move from seven to eight workers, marginal product becomes −1 bushel.

workers per week of input, there is no output. When there are 5 workers per week of input (given the capital stock), there is a total output of 50 bushels per week. (Ignore for the moment the rest of that panel.) Panel (b) of Figure 22-2 shows this particular hypothetical production function graphically. Note again that it relates to the short run and that it is for an individual firm.

Panel (b) shows a total physical product curve, or the maximum amount of physical output that is possible when we add successive equal-sized units of labor while holding all other inputs constant. The graph of the production function in panel (b) is not a straight line. In fact, it peaks at 7 workers per week and starts to go down. To understand why it starts to go down with an individual firm in the short run, we have to analyze in detail the **law of diminishing (marginal) returns.**

But before that, let's examine the meaning of columns 3 and 4 of panel (a) of Figure 22-2—that is, average and marginal physical product.

Average and Physical Marginal Product

The definition of **average physical product** is straightforward: It is the total product divided by the number of workers expressed in output per week. You can see in column 3 of panel (a) of Figure 22-2 that the average physical product of labor first rises and then steadily falls after two workers are hired.

Remember that *marginal* means "additional." Hence the **marginal physical product** of labor is the change in total product that occurs when a worker joins an existing production process. (The term *physical* here emphasizes the fact that we are measuring in terms of physical units of production, not in dollar terms.) It is also the *change* in total product that occurs when that worker quits or is laid off an existing production process. The marginal physical product of labor therefore refers to the *change in output caused by a one-unit change in the labor input.* (Marginal physical product is also referred to as *marginal productivity* and *marginal return.*)

DIMINISHING MARGINAL RETURNS

The concept of diminishing marginal returns—also known as diminishing marginal product—applies to many situations. If you put a seat belt across your lap, a certain amount of safety is obtained. If you add another seat belt over your shoulder, some additional safety is obtained, but less than when the first belt was secured. When you add a third seat belt over the other shoulder, the amount of *additional* safety obtained is even smaller.

The same analysis holds for firms in their use of productive inputs. When the returns from hiring more workers are diminishing, it does not necessarily mean that more workers won't be hired. In fact, workers will be hired until the returns, in terms of the *value* of the *extra* output produced, are equal to the additional wages that have to be paid for those workers to produce the extra output. Before we get into that decision-making process, let's demonstrate that diminishing returns can be represented graphically and can be used in our analysis of the firm.

Measuring Diminishing Returns

How do we measure diminishing returns? First, we limit the analysis to only one variable factor of production (or input)—let's say the factor is labor. Every other factor of produc-

Law of diminishing (marginal) returns
The observation that after some point, successive equal-sized increases in a variable factor of production, such as labor, added to fixed factors of production, will result in smaller increases in output.

Average physical product
Total product divided by the variable input.

Marginal physical product
The physical output that is due to the addition of one more unit of a variable factor of production; the change in total product occurring when a variable input is increased and all other inputs are held constant; also called *marginal productivity* or *marginal return.*

tion, such as machines, must be held constant. Only in this way can we calculate the marginal returns from using more workers and know when we reach the point of diminishing marginal returns.

The marginal productivity of labor may increase rapidly at the very beginning. A firm starts with no workers, only machines. The firm then hires one worker, who finds it difficult to get the work started. But when the firm hires more workers, each is able to *specialize,* and the marginal productivity of those additional workers may actually be greater than it was with the previous few workers. Beyond some point, however, diminishing returns must set in, *not* because new workers are less qualified, but because each worker has (on average) fewer machines with which to work (remember, all other inputs are fixed). In fact, eventually the firm will become so crowded that workers will start to get in each other's way. At that point, total production declines and marginal physical product becomes negative.

Using these ideas, we can define the law of diminishing returns as follows:

> **As successive equal increases in a variable factor of production are added to fixed factors of production, there will be a point beyond which the extra, or marginal, product that can be attributed to each additional unit of the variable factor of production will decline.**

Note that the law of diminishing returns is a statement about the *physical* relationships between inputs and outputs that we have observed in many firms. If the law of diminishing returns were not a fairly accurate statement about the world, what would stop firms from hiring additional workers forever?

An Example of the Law of Diminishing Returns

Agriculture provides an example of the law of diminishing returns. With a fixed amount of land, fertilizer, and tractors, the addition of more farm workers eventually yields decreasing increases in output. After a while, when all the tractors are being used, additional farm workers will have to start farming manually. They obviously won't be as productive as the first farm workers who manned the tractors. The marginal physical product of an additional farm worker, given a specified amount of capital, must eventually be less than that for the previous workers.

A hypothetical set of numbers illustrating the law of diminishing marginal returns is presented in panel (a) of Figure 22-2. The numbers are presented graphically in panel (c). Marginal productivity (returns from adding more workers) first increases, then decreases, and finally becomes negative.

When one worker is hired, total output goes from 0 to 10. Thus marginal physical product is 10 bushels of wheat per week. When the second worker is hired, total product goes from 10 to 26 bushels of wheat per week. Marginal physical product therefore increases to 16 bushels of wheat per week. When a third worker is hired, total product again increases, from 26 to 36 bushels of wheat per week. This represents a marginal physical product of only 10 bushels of wheat per week. Therefore, the point of diminishing marginal returns occurs after two workers are hired.

Notice that after 7 workers per week, marginal physical product becomes negative. That means that the hiring of an eighth worker would create a situation that reduces total product. Sometimes this is called the *point of saturation,* indicating that given the amount of fixed inputs, there is no further positive use for more of the variable input. We have entered the region of negative marginal returns.

CONCEPTS IN BRIEF

- The technological relationship between output and input is called the production function. It relates output per time period to the several inputs, such as capital and labor.

- After some rate of output, the firm generally experiences diminishing marginal returns.

- The law of diminishing returns states that if all factors of production are held constant except one, equal increments in that one variable factor will eventually yield decreasing increments in output.

SHORT-RUN COSTS TO THE FIRM

You will see that costs are the extension of the production ideas just presented. Let's consider the costs the firm faces in the short run. To make this example simple, assume that there are only two factors of production, capital and labor. Our definition of the short run will be the time during which capital is fixed but labor is variable.

In the short run, a firm incurs certain types of costs. We label all costs incurred **total costs.** Then we break total costs down into total fixed costs and total variable costs, which we will explain shortly. Therefore,

Total costs
The sum of total fixed costs and total variable costs.

$$\text{Total costs (TC)} = \text{total fixed costs (TFC)} + \text{total variable costs (TVC)}$$

Remember that these total costs include both explicit and implicit costs, including the normal rate of return on investment.

After we have looked at the elements of total costs, we will find out how to compute average and marginal costs.

Total Fixed Costs

Let's look at an ongoing business such as Compaq Computer. The decision makers in that corporate giant can look around and see big machines, thousands of parts, huge buildings, and a multitude of other components of plant and equipment that have already been bought and are in place. Compaq has to take account of the technological obsolescence of this equipment, no matter how many computers it produces. The payments on the loans taken out to buy the equipment will all be exactly the same. The opportunity costs of any land that Compaq owns will all be exactly the same. These costs are more or less the same for Compaq no matter how many computers it produces.

We also have to point out that the opportunity cost (or normal rate of return) of capital must be included along with other costs. Remember that we are dealing in the short run, during which capital is fixed. If investors in Compaq Computer have already put $100 million into a new factory addition, the opportunity cost of that capital invested is now, in essence, a *fixed cost*. Why? Because in the short run, nothing can be done about that cost; the investment has already been made. This leads us to a very straightforward definition of fixed costs: All costs that do not vary—that is, all costs that do not depend on the rate of production—are called **fixed costs.**

Fixed costs
Costs that do not vary with output. Fixed costs include such things as rent on a building. These costs are fixed for a certain period of time; in the long run, they are variable.

Let's now take as an example the fixed costs incurred by an assembler of pocket calculators. This firm's total fixed costs will equal the cost of the rent on its equipment and the insurance it has to pay. We see in panel (a) of Figure 22-3 that total fixed costs per day are $10. In panel (b), these total fixed costs are represented by the horizontal line at $10 per day. They are invariant to changes in the output of calculators per day—no matter how many are produced, fixed costs will remain at $10 per day.

Panel (a)

(1)	(2)	(3)	(4)	(5)	(6)	(7)	(8)	(9)
Total Output (Q/day)	Total Fixed Costs (TFC)	Total Variable Costs (TVC)	Total Costs (TC) (4) = (2) + (3)	Average Fixed Costs (AFC) (5) = (2) ÷ (1)	Average Variable Costs (AVC) (6) = (3) ÷ (1)	Average Total Costs (ATC) (7) = (4) ÷ (1)	Total Costs (TC) (4)	Marginal Cost (MC) $(9) = \dfrac{\text{change in (8)}}{\text{change in (1)}}$
0	$10	$ 0	$10	—	—	—	$10	
								$5
1	10	5	15	$10.00	$5.00	$15.00	15	
								3
2	10	8	18	5.00	4.00	9.00	18	
								2
3	10	10	20	3.33	3.33	6.67	20	
								1
4	10	11	21	2.50	2.75	5.25	21	
								2
5	10	13	23	2.00	2.60	4.60	23	
								3
6	10	16	26	1.67	2.67	4.33	26	
								4
7	10	20	30	1.43	2.86	4.28	30	
								5
8	10	25	35	1.25	3.13	4.38	35	
								6
9	10	31	41	1.11	3.44	4.56	41	
								7
10	10	38	48	1.00	3.80	4.80	48	
								8
11	10	46	56	.91	4.18	5.09	56	

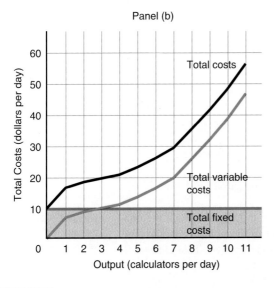

Panel (b)

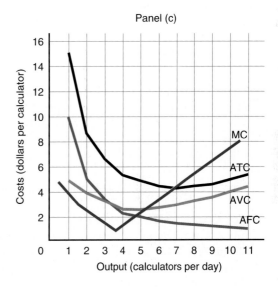

Panel (c)

FIGURE 22-3

Cost of Production: An Example

In panel (a), the derivation of columns 4 through 9 are given in parentheses in each column heading. For example, column 6, average variable costs, is derived by dividing column 3, total variable costs, by column 1, total output per day. Note that marginal cost (MC) in panel (c) intersects average variable costs (AVC) at the latter's minimum point. Also, MC intersects average total costs (ATC) at that latter's minimum point. It is a little more difficult to see that MC equals AVC and ATC at their respective minimum points in panel (a) because we are using discrete one-unit changes. You can see, though, that the marginal cost of going from 4 units per day to 5 units per day is $2 and increases to $3 when we move to 6 units per day. Somewhere in the middle it equals AVC of $2.60, which is in fact the minimum average variable cost. The same analysis holds for ATC, which hits minimum at 7 units per day at $4.28 per unit. MC goes from $4 to $5 and just equals ATC somewhere in between.

Total Variable Costs

Total **variable costs** are costs whose magnitude varies with the rate of production. One obvious variable cost is wages. The more the firm produces, the more labor it has to hire; therefore, the more wages it has to pay. Another variable cost is parts. In the assembly of calculators, for example, microchips must be bought. The more calculators that are made, the more chips must be bought. Part of the rate of depreciation (the rate of wear and tear) on machines that are used in the assembly process can also be considered a variable cost if depreciation depends partly on how long and how intensively the machines are used. Total variable costs are given in panel (a) of Figure 22-3 in column 3. These are translated into the total variable cost curve in panel (b). Notice that the total variable cost curve lies below the total cost curve by the vertical distance of $10. This vertical distance represents, of course, total fixed costs.

Variable costs
Costs that vary with the rate of production. They include wages paid to workers and purchases of materials.

Short-Run Average Cost Curves

In panel (b) of Figure 22-3 we see total costs, total variable costs, and total fixed costs. Now we want to look at average cost. The average cost concept is one in which we are measuring cost per unit of output. It is a matter of simple arithmetic to figure the averages of these three cost concepts. We can define them as follows:

$$\text{Average total costs (ATC)} = \frac{\text{total costs (TC)}}{\text{output } (Q)}$$

$$\text{Average variable costs (AVC)} = \frac{\text{total variable costs (TVC)}}{\text{output } (Q)}$$

$$\text{Average fixed costs (AFC)} = \frac{\text{total fixed costs (TFC)}}{\text{output } (Q)}$$

The arithmetic is done in columns 5, 6, and 7 in panel (a) of Figure 22-3. The numerical results are translated into a graphical format in panel (c). Because total costs (TC) equal variable costs (TVC) plus fixed costs (TFC), the difference between average total costs (ATC) and average variable costs (AVC) will always be identical to average fixed costs (AFC). That means that average total costs and average variable costs move together as output expands.

Now let's see what we can observe about the three average cost curves in Figure 22-3.

Average Fixed Costs (AFC). **Average fixed costs** continue to fall throughout the output range. In fact, if we were to continue the diagram farther to the right, we would find that average fixed costs would get closer and closer to the horizontal axis. That is because total fixed costs remain constant. As we divide this fixed number by a larger and larger number of units of output, the resulting AFC has to become smaller and smaller. In business, this is called "spreading the overhead."

Average fixed costs
Total fixed costs divided by the number of units produced.

Average Variable Costs (AVC). We assume a particular form of the curve for **average variable costs.** The form that it takes is U-shaped: First it falls; then it starts to rise. It is possible for the AVC curve to take other shapes in the long run.

Average variable costs
Total variable costs divided by the number of units produced.

Average Total Costs (ATC). This curve has a shape similar to that of the AVC curve. However, it falls even more dramatically in the beginning and rises more slowly after it has reached a minimum point. It falls and then rises because **average total costs** are the

Average total costs
Total costs divided by the number of units produced; sometimes called *average per-unit total costs.*

summation of the AFC curve and the AVC curve. Thus when AFC and AVC are both falling, ATC must fall too. At some point, however, AVC starts to increase while AFC continues to fall. Once the increase in the AVC curve outweighs the decrease in the AFC curve, the ATC curve will start to increase and will develop its familiar U shape.

Marginal Cost

Marginal costs
The change in total costs due to a one-unit change in production rate.

We have stated repeatedly that the basis of decisions is always on the margin—movement in economics is always determined at the margin. This dictum also holds true within the firm. Firms, according to the analysis we use to predict their behavior, are very interested in their **marginal costs.** Because the term *marginal* means "additional" or "incremental" (or "decremental," too) here, marginal costs refer to costs that result from a one-unit change in the production rate. For example, if the production of 10 calculators per day costs a firm $48 and the production of 11 calculators costs it $56 per day, the marginal cost of producing the eleventh calculator per day is $8.

Marginal costs can be measured by using the formula

$$\text{Marginal cost} = \frac{\text{change in total cost}}{\text{change in output}}$$

We show the marginal costs of calculator production per day in column 9 of panel (a) in Figure 22-3, calculated according to the formula just given. In our example, we have changed output by one unit every time, so we can ignore variations in the denominator in that particular formula.

This marginal cost schedule is shown graphically in panel (c) of Figure 22-3. Just like average variable costs and average total costs, marginal costs first fall and then rise. The U shape of the marginal cost curve is a result of increasing and then diminishing marginal returns. At lower levels of output, the marginal cost curve declines. The reasoning is that as marginal physical product increases with each addition of output, the marginal cost of this last unit of output must fall. Conversely, when diminishing marginal returns set in, marginal physical product decreases (and eventually becomes negative); it follows that the marginal cost of the last unit must rise. These relationships are clearly reflected in the geometry of panels (b) and (c) of Figure 22-3.

In summary:

> As long as marginal physical product rises, marginal cost will fall, and when marginal physical product starts to fall (after reaching the point of diminishing marginal returns), marginal cost will begin to rise.

POLICY EXAMPLE
Can "Three Strikes" Laws Reduce Crime?

Crime and violence have been the top concern of Americans for at least a decade. At both the federal and the state level, politicians have responded with a variety of policies aimed at reducing crime. One popular new law has been labeled "three strikes and you're out." A defendant with a prior conviction for two serious or violent offenses faces mandatory life imprisonment for a third offense.

Such legislation has dramatically affected the marginal cost of violence and murder to potential criminal defendants who have already been convicted of two felonies. Here is what one career criminal, Frank Schweickert, said in a *New York Times* interview: "Before, if I was doing a robbery and getting chased by cops, I'd lay my gun down. . . . But now you are talking about a life sentence. Why isn't it worth doing whatever it takes to get away? If that meant shooting a cop, if that meant shooting a store clerk, if that meant shooting someone innocent in my way, well, they'd have gotten shot. Because what is the worst thing that could happen to me: life imprisonment? If I'm getting a murder sentence anyway, I might as well do whatever it takes to maybe get away." In other words, the "three strikes" legislation has reduced the marginal cost of murder committed while engaging in a criminal activity after two prior felony convictions to zero.

FOR CRITICAL ANALYSIS: *Do criminals subject to the new legislation have to under-stand the concept of marginal cost in order for our theory to predict well? Explain.* •

The Relationship Between Average and Marginal Costs

Let us now examine the relationship between average costs and marginal costs. There is always a definite relationship between averages and marginals. Consider the example of 10 football players with an average weight of 200 pounds. An eleventh player is added. His weight is 250 pounds. That represents the marginal weight. What happens now to the average weight of the team? It must increase. Thus when the marginal player weighs more than the average, the average must increase. Likewise, if the marginal player weighs less than 200 pounds, the average weight will decrease.

There is a similar relationship between average variable costs and marginal costs. When marginal costs are less than average costs, the latter must fall. Conversely, when marginal costs are greater than average costs, the latter must rise. When you think about it, the relationship makes sense. The only way for average variable costs to fall is for the extra cost of the marginal unit produced to be less than the average variable cost of all the preceding units. For example, if the average variable cost for two units of production is $4.00 a unit, the only way for the average variable cost of three units to be less than that of two units is for the variable costs attributable to the last unit—the marginal cost—to be less than the average of the past units. In this particular case, if average variable cost falls to $3.33 a unit, total variable cost for the three units would be three times $3.33, or almost exactly $10.00. Total variable cost for two units is two times $4.00, or $8.00. The marginal cost is therefore $10.00 minus $8.00, or $2.00, which is less than the average variable cost of $3.33.

A similar type of computation can be carried out for rising average variable costs. The only way for average variable costs to rise is for the average variable cost of additional units to be more than that for units already produced. But the incremental cost is the marginal cost. In this particular case, the marginal costs have to be higher than the average variable costs.

There is also a relationship between marginal costs and average total costs. Remember that average total cost is equal to total cost divided by the number of units produced. Remember also that marginal cost does not include any fixed costs. Fixed costs are, by definition, fixed and cannot influence marginal costs. Our example can therefore be repeated substituting *average total cost* for *average variable cost.*

These rising and falling relationships can be seen in Figure 22-3, where MC intersects AVC and ATC at their respective minimum points.

Minimum Cost Points

At what rate of output of calculators per day does our representative firm experience the minimum average total costs? Column 7 in panel (a) of Figure 22-3 shows that the minimum average total cost is $4.28, which occurs at an output rate of seven calculators per day.

We can also find this minimum cost by finding the point in panel (c) of Figure 22-3 at which the marginal cost curve intersects the average total cost curve. This should not be surprising. When marginal cost is below average total cost, average total cost falls. When marginal cost is above average total cost, average total cost rises. At the point where average total cost is neither falling nor rising, marginal cost must then be equal to average total cost. When we represent this graphically, the marginal cost curve will intersect the average total cost curve at the latter's minimum.

The same analysis applies to the intersection of the marginal cost curve and the average variable cost curve. When are average variable costs at a minimum? According to panel (a) of Figure 22-3, average variable costs are at a minimum of $2.60 at an output rate of five calculators per day. This is where the marginal cost curve intersects the average variable cost curve in panel (c) of Figure 22-3.

CONCEPTS IN BRIEF

- Total costs equal total fixed costs plus total variable costs.
- Fixed costs are those that do not vary with the rate of production; variable costs are those that do vary with the rate of production.
- Average total costs equal total costs divided by output (ATC = TC/Q).
- Average variable costs equal total variable costs divided by output (AVC = TVC/Q).
- Average fixed costs equal total fixed costs divided by output (AFC = TFC/Q).
- Marginal cost equals the change in total cost divided by the change in output (MC = ΔTC/ΔQ).
- The marginal cost curve intersects the minimum point of the average total cost curve and the minimum point of the average variable cost curve.

THE RELATIONSHIP BETWEEN DIMINISHING MARGINAL RETURNS AND COST CURVES

There is a unique relationship between output and the shape of the various cost curves we have drawn. Let's consider specifically the relationship between marginal cost and the example of diminishing marginal physical returns in panel (a) of Figure 22-4 on page 496. It turns out that if wage rates are constant, the shape of the marginal cost curve in panel (d) of Figure 22-4 is both a reflection of and a consequence of the law of diminishing returns. Let's assume that each unit of labor can be purchased at a constant price. Further assume that labor is the only variable input. We see that as more workers are hired, marginal physical product first rises and then falls after the point at which diminishing returns are encountered. Thus the marginal cost of each extra unit of output will first fall as long as marginal physical product is rising, and then it will rise as long as marginal physical product is falling. Recall that marginal cost is defined as

$$MC = \frac{\text{change in total cost}}{\text{change in output}}$$

Because the price of labor is assumed to be constant, the change in total cost is simply the constant price of labor, W (we are increasing labor by only one unit). The change in output

Panel (a)

(1) Labor Input	(2) Total Product (number of pairs of shoes sold)	(3) Average Physical Product (pairs per salesperson) (3) = (2) ÷ (1)	(4) Marginal Physical Product	(5) Average Variable Cost (5) = W ($100) ÷ (3)	(6) Marginal Cost (6) = W ($100) ÷ (4)
0	0	—	—	—	—
1	50	50	50	$2.00	$2.00
2	110	55	60	1.82	1.67
3	180	60	70	1.67	1.43
4	240	60	60	1.67	1.67
5	290	58	50	1.72	2.00
6	330	55	40	1.82	2.50
7	360	51	30	1.96	3.33

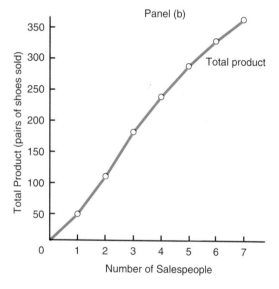

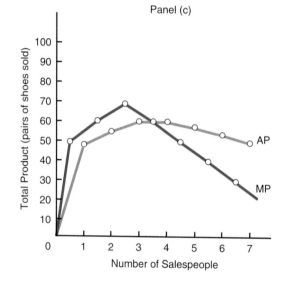

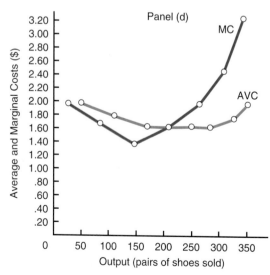

FIGURE 22-4

**The Relationship Between Physical Output
and Costs**

As the number of salespeople increases, the total number of pairs of shoes sold rises, as shown in panels (a)
and (b). In panel (c), marginal product (MP) first rises
and then falls. Average product (AP) follows. The mirror
image of panel (c) is shown in panel (d), in which MC
and AVC first fall and then rise.

is simply the marginal physical product (MPP) of the one-unit increase in labor. Therefore, we see that

$$\text{Marginal cost} = \frac{W}{\text{MPP}}$$

This means that initially, when there are increasing returns, marginal cost falls (we are dividing W by increasingly larger numbers), and later, when diminishing returns set in and marginal physical product is falling, marginal cost must increase (we are dividing W by smaller numbers). As marginal physical product increases, marginal cost decreases, and as marginal physical product decreases, marginal cost must increase. Thus when marginal physical product reaches its maximum, marginal cost necessarily reaches its minimum. To illustrate this, let's return to Figure 22-2 on page 487 and consider specifically panel (a). Assume that a worker is paid $100 a week. When we go from zero labor input to one unit, output increases by 10 bushels of wheat. Each of those 10 bushels of wheat has a marginal cost of $10. Now the second unit of labor is hired, and it too costs $100 per week. Output increases by 16. Thus the marginal cost is $100 ÷ 16 = $6.25. We continue the experiment. We see that the next unit of labor yields only 10 additional bushels of wheat, so marginal cost starts to rise again back to $10. The following unit of labor increases marginal physical product by only 8, so marginal cost becomes $100 ÷ 8 = $12.50.

All of the foregoing can be restated in relatively straightforward terms:

Firms' short-run cost curves are a reflection of the law of diminishing marginal returns. Given any constant price of the variable input, marginal costs decline as long as the marginal product of the variable resource is rising. At the point at which diminishing marginal returns begin, marginal costs begin to rise as the marginal product of the variable input begins to decline.

The result is a marginal cost curve that slopes down, hits a minimum, and then slopes up. The average total cost curve and average variable cost curve are of course affected. They will have their familiar U shape in the short run. Again, to see this, recall that

$$\text{AVC} = \frac{\text{total variable costs}}{\text{total output}}$$

As we move from zero labor input to one unit in panel (a) of Figure 22-2, output increases from zero to 10 bushels. The total variable costs are the price per worker, W ($100), times the number of workers (1). Because the average product of one worker (column 3) is 10, we can write the total product, 10, as the average product, 10, times the number of workers, 1. Thus we see that

$$\text{AVC} = \frac{\$100 \times 1}{10 \times 1} = \frac{\$100}{10} = \frac{W}{\text{AP}}$$

From column 3 in panel (a) of Figure 22-2 we see that the average product increases, reaches a maximum, and then declines. Because AVC = W/AP, average variable cost decreases as average product increases and increases as average product decreases. AVC reaches its minimum when average product reaches its maximum. Furthermore, because ATC = AVC + AFC, the average total cost curve inherits the relationship between the average variable cost and diminishing returns.

To illustrate, consider a shoe store that employs salespeople to sell shoes. Panel (a) of Figure 22-4 presents in column 2 the total number of pairs of shoes sold as the number of salespeople increases. Notice that the total product first increases at an increasing rate and later increases at a decreasing rate. This is reflected in column 4, which shows that the marginal physical product increases at first and then falls. The average physical product too first rises and then falls. The marginal and average physical products are graphed in panel (c) of Figure 22-4. Our immediate interest here is the average variable and marginal costs. Because we can define average variable cost as $100/AP (assuming that the wage paid is constant at $100), as the average product rises from 50 to 55 to 60 pairs of shoes sold, the average variable cost falls from $2.00 to $1.82 to $1.67. Conversely, as average product falls from 60 to 50, average variable cost rises from $1.67 to $2.00. Likewise, because marginal cost can also be defined as W/MPP, we see that as marginal physical product rises from 50 to 70, marginal cost falls from $2.00 to $1.43. As marginal physical product falls to 30, marginal cost rises to $3.33. These relationships are also expressed in panels (b), (c), and (d) of Figure 22-4.

LONG-RUN COST CURVES

The long run is defined as a time period during which full adjustment can be made to any change in the economic environment. Thus in the long run, *all* factors of production are variable. Long-run curves are sometimes called *planning curves,* and the long run is sometimes called the **planning horizon.** We start out our analysis of long-run cost curves by considering a single firm contemplating the construction of a single plant. The firm has three alternative plant sizes from which to choose on the planning horizon. Each particular plant size generates its own short-run average total cost curve. Now that we are talking about the difference between long-run and short-run cost curves, we will label all short-run curves with an *S* and long-run curves with an *L;* short-run average (total) costs will be labeled SAC, and long-run average cost curves will be labeled LAC.

Panel (a) of Figure 22-5 shows three short-run average cost curves for three successively larger plants. Which is the optimal size to build? That depends on the anticipated normal,

Planning horizon
The long run, during which all inputs are variable.

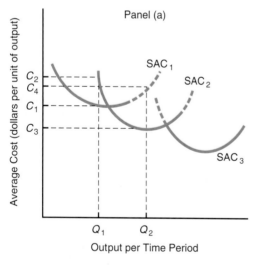

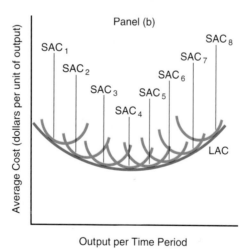

FIGURE 22-5

Preferable Plant Size and the Long-Run Average Cost Curve
If the anticipated permanent rate of output per unit time period is Q_1, the optimal plant to build would be the one corresponding to SAC_1 in panel (a) because average costs are lower. However, if the permanent rate of output increases to Q_2, it will be more profitable to have a plant size corresponding to SAC_2. Unit costs fall to C_3.

If we draw all the possible short-run average cost curves that correspond to different plant sizes and then draw the envelope (a curve tangent to each member of a set of curves) to these various curves, SAC_1–SAC_8, we obtain the long-run average cost curve, or the planning curve, as shown in panel (b).

sustained (permanent) rate of output per time period. Assume for a moment that the anticipated normal, sustained rate is Q_1. If a plant of size 1 is built, the average costs will be C_1. If a plant of size 2 is built, we see on SAC_2 that the average costs will be C_2, which is greater than C_1. Thus if the anticipated rate of output is Q_1, the appropriate plant size is the one from which SAC_1 was derived.

However, if the anticipated permanent rate of output per time period goes from Q_1 to Q_2 and a plant of size 1 had been decided on, average costs would be C_4. If a plant of size 2 had been decided on, average costs would be C_3, which is clearly less than C_4.

In choosing the appropriate plant size for a single-plant firm during the planning horizon, the firm will pick the size whose short-run average cost curve generates an average cost that is lowest for the expected rate of output.

Long-Run Average Cost Curve

Long-run average cost curve
The locus of points representing the minimum unit cost of producing any given rate of output, given current technology and resource prices.

Planning curve
The long-run average cost curve.

If we now assume that the entrepreneur faces an infinite number of choices of plant sizes in the long run, we can conceive of an infinite number of SAC curves similar to the three in panel (a) of Figure 22-5. We are not able, of course, to draw an infinite number; we have drawn quite a few, however, in panel (b) of Figure 22-5. We then draw the "envelope" to all these various short-run average cost curves. The resulting envelope is the **long-run average cost curve.** This long-run average cost curve is sometimes called the **planning curve,** for it represents the various average costs attainable at the planning stage of the firm's decision making. It represents the locus (path) of points giving the least unit cost of producing any given rate of output. Note that the LAC curve is *not* tangent to each individual SAC curve at the latter's minimum points. This is true only at the minimum point of the LAC curve. Then and only then are minimum long-run average costs equal to minimum short-run average costs.

WHY THE LONG-RUN AVERAGE COST CURVE IS U-SHAPED

Economies of scale
Decreases in long-run average costs resulting from increases in output.

Constant returns to scale
No change in long-run average costs when output increases.

Diseconomies of scale
Increases in long-run average costs that occur as output increases.

Notice that the long-run average cost curve, LAC, in panel (b) of Figure 22-5 is U-shaped, similar to the U shape of the short-run average cost curve developed earlier in this chapter. The reason behind the U shape of the two curves is not the same, however. The short-run average cost curve is U-shaped because of the law of diminishing marginal returns. But the law cannot apply to the long run, because in the long run, all factors of production are variable; there is no point of diminishing marginal returns because there is no fixed factor of production. Why, then, do we see the U shape in the long-run average cost curve? The reasoning has to do with economies of scale, constant returns to scale, and diseconomies of scale. When the firm is experiencing **economies of scale,** the long-run average cost curve slopes downward—an increase in scale and production leads to a fall in unit costs. When the firm is experiencing **constant returns to scale,** the long-run average cost curve is at its minimum point, such that an increase in scale and production does not change unit costs. When the firm is experiencing **diseconomies of scale,** the long-run average cost curve slopes upward—an increase in scale and production increases unit costs. These three sections of the long-run average cost curves are broken up into panels (a), (b), and (c) in Figure 22-6 on page 500.

Reasons for Economies of Scale

We shall examine three of the many reasons why a firm might be expected to experience economies of scale: specialization, the dimensional factor, and improved productive equipment.

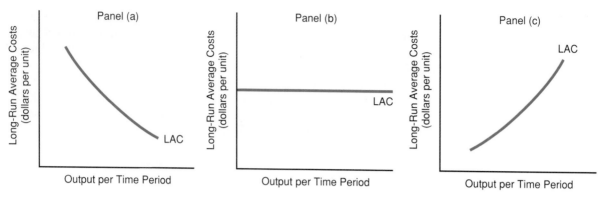

FIGURE 22-6

Economies of Scale, Constant Returns to Scale, and Diseconomies of Scale Shown with the Long-Run Average Cost Curve
Long-run average cost curves will fall when there are economies of scale, as shown in panel (a). They will be constant (flat) when the firm is experiencing constant returns to scale, as shown in panel (b). They will rise when the firm is experiencing diseconomies of scale, as shown in panel (c).

Specialization. As a firm's scale of operation increases, the opportunities for specialization in the use of resource inputs also increase. This is sometimes called *increased division of tasks* or *operations*. Gains from such division of labor or increased specialization are well known. When we consider managerial staffs, we also find that larger enterprises may be able to put together more highly specialized staffs.

Dimensional Factor. Large-scale firms often require proportionately less input per unit of output simply because certain inputs do not have to be physically doubled in order to double the output. Consider the cost of storage of oil. The cost of storage is basically related to the cost of steel that goes into building the storage container; however, the amount of steel required goes up less than in proportion to the volume (storage capacity) of the container (because the volume of a container increases more than proportionately with its surface area).

Improved Productive Equipment. The larger the scale of the enterprise, the more the firm is able to take advantage of larger-volume (output capacity) types of machinery. Small-scale operations may not be able profitably to use large-volume machines that can be more efficient per unit of output. Also, smaller firms often cannot use technologically more advanced machinery because they are unable to spread out the high cost of such sophisticated equipment over a large output.

For any of these reasons, the firm may experience economies of scale, which means that equal percentage increases in output result in a decrease in average cost. Thus output can double, but total costs will less than double; hence average cost falls. Note that the factors listed for causing economies of scale are all *internal* to the firm; they do not depend on what other firms are doing or what is happening in the economy.

EXAMPLE
Goods Versus Ideas

Numerous economic studies have shown that the production of many goods that we consume have constant unit costs once production is under way. Otherwise stated, the production of most goods appears to look like panel (b) in Figure 22-6. Ideas, in contrast, often have exceedingly high costs for the first "unit" of knowledge. Once that first unit is produced, though, both the marginal and average costs for production of additional units is essentially zero. Numerous costs are involved in producing the ideas for new technology. Once those ideas are produced, they can be disseminated electronically on the Internet to everybody in the world at relatively small additional cost.

FOR CRITICAL ANALYSIS: Draw the appropriate long-run average cost curve for ideas. •

Why a Firm Might Experience Diseconomies of Scale

One of the basic reasons that a firm can expect to run into diseconomies of scale is that there are limits to the efficient functioning of management. Moreover, as more workers are hired, a more than proportionate increase in managers and staff people may be needed, and this could cause increased costs per unit. This is so because larger levels of output imply successively larger *plant* size, which in turn implies successively larger *firm* size. Thus as the level of output increases, more people must be hired, and the firm gets bigger. However, as this happens, the support, supervisory, and administrative staff and the general paperwork of the firm all increase. As the layers of supervision grow, the costs of information and communication grow more than proportionately; hence the average unit cost will start to increase.

Some observers of corporate giants claim that many of them are experiencing some diseconomies of scale today. Witness the problems that General Motors and IBM had in the early 1990s. Some analysts say that the financial problems that they have experienced are at least partly a function of their size relative to their smaller, more flexible competitors, who can make decisions more quickly and then take advantage of changing market conditions more rapidly. This seems to be particularly true with IBM. It apparently adapted very slowly to the fact that the large mainframe computer business was declining as micro- and mini-computers became more and more powerful.

MINIMUM EFFICIENT SCALE

Minimum efficient scale (MES)
The lowest rate of output per unit time at which long-run average costs for a particular firm are at a minimum.

Economists and statisticians have obtained actual data on the relationship between changes in all inputs and changes in average cost. It turns out that for many industries, the long-run average cost curve does not resemble that shown in panel (b) of Figure 22-5. Rather, it more closely resembles Figure 22-7 on page 502. What you can observe there is a small portion of declining long-run average costs (economies of scale) and then a wide range of outputs over which the firm experiences relatively constant economies of scale. At the output rate when economies of scale end and constant economies of scale start, the **minimum efficient scale (MES)** for the firm is encountered. It occurs at point *A*. (The point is, of course, approximate. The more smoothly the curve declines into its flat portion, the more approximate will be our estimate of the MES.) The minimum efficient scale will always be the lowest rate of output at which long-run average costs are minimized. In any industry with a long-run average cost curve similar to the one in Figure 22-7, larger firms will have no cost-saving advantage over smaller firms as long as the smaller firms have at least obtained the minimum efficient scale at point *A*.

Among its uses, the minimum efficient scale gives us a rough measure of the degree of competition in an industry. If the MES is small relative to industry demand, the degree of competition in that industry is likely to be high because there is room for many efficiently

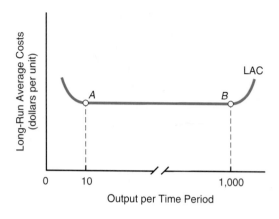

FIGURE 22-7

Minimum Efficient Scale

This long-run average cost curve reaches a minimum point at *A*. After that point, long-run average costs remain horizontal, or constant, and then rise at some later rate of output. Point *A* is called the minimum efficient scale for the firm because that is the point at which it reaches minimum costs. It is the lowest rate of output at which the average long-run costs are minimized.

sized plants. Conversely, when the MES is large relative to industry demand, the degree of competition is likely to be small because there is room for a relatively small number of efficiently sized plants or firms. Looked at another way, if it takes a very large scale of plant to obtain minimum long-run average cost, the output of just a few of these very large firms can fully satisfy total market demand. This means that there isn't room for a large number of smaller plants if maximum efficiency is to be obtained in the industry.

CONCEPTS IN BRIEF

- The long run is often called the planning horizon. The long-run average cost curve is the planning curve. It is found by drawing a line tangent to one point on a series of short-run average cost curves, each corresponding to a different plant size.

- The firm can experience economies of scale, diseconomies of scale, and constant returns to scale, all according to whether the long-run average cost curve slopes downward, slopes upward, or is horizontal (flat). Economies of scale refer to what happens to average cost when all factors of production are increased.

- We observe economies of scale for a number of reasons, among which are specialization, improved productive equipment, and the dimensional factor, because large-scale firms require proportionately less input per unit of output. The firm may experience diseconomies of scale primarily because of limits to the efficient functioning of management.

- The minimum efficient scale occurs at the lowest rate of output at which long-run average costs are minimized.

The Play Must Go On—but Should It Be on Broadway?

Concepts Applied: Costs, profits, normal rate of return, short versus long run

Broadway may offer some of the best theater in the United States, but that does not mean it is also the most profitable venue for theatrical productions. Off-Broadway productions are generally less costly to produce and can return an investor's money faster than Broadway shows can.

It has been well known for years that what Broadway does best is put on plays and musicals that have mass appeal. The playwright with the most mass appeal in America has been Neil Simon, whose plays have been seen on Broadway for nearly three decades. So it came as quite a surprise when Neil Simon started looking for a 500-seat Off-Broadway theater for his comedy *London Suite*. The decision, as it turns out, has nothing to do with an aversion to Broadway. It has to do with basic economics: If the play is successful, how soon will its investors earn back their investment?

Higher Revenues, but Higher Costs, Too

Broadway tickets are more expensive than tickets to Off-Broadway shows. Broadway venues are typically twice as large as their Off-Broadway counterparts. That means that a typical Broadway play can in principle earn more revenues each week—and indeed they usually do. But they also have higher expenses. Even with these higher expenses, it is possible for a Broadway production to make more weekly profit than an Off-Broadway production. Nonetheless, it still sometimes makes business sense to go Off-Broadway.

Some Actual Calculations

The producer of *London Suite,* Emanuel Azenberg, provided the following calculations to the *New York Times.* The assumptions were as follows:

1. The Broadway venue would seat 1,000 and be able to sell tickets at $55 each.
2. The Off-Broadway production would have 500 seats at $40 a ticket.
3. In either production, the average number of seats sold would be 75 percent of capacity.

In Table 22-1, we show the initial investment needed to get to opening night. You can see that for the same play,

TABLE 22-1
Investment in the Play

	Broadway ($ thousands)	Off-Broadway ($ thousands)
Rehearsal salaries	102	63
Advertising	300	121
Administration	235	100
Director and designer fees	126	61
Sets, costumes, and lights	357	87
Labor	175	8
Total investment	1,295	440

TABLE 22-2
Weekly Profits

	Broadway ($ thousands)	Off-Broadway ($ thousands)
Revenues	250	109
Expenses		
Salaries	54	20
Light and sound rental	6	3
Royalties	23	14
Administration and miscellaneous	48	18
Advertising	30	15
Theater rent and house crew	45	12
Total expenses	206	82
Weekly profit	43	27

the initial investment is about three times as much on Broadway as Off-Broadway.

Now let's look at weekly profits in Table 22-2.

Looks Can Be Deceiving

At first blush, it would seem as if the Broadway play is a better deal because it has so much more profit than the Off-Broadway production. But investors do not look at *absolute* profits; they are concerned with the rate of return on their investment. Whereas the weekly profits for the Broadway show are 1.6 times greater than for the Off-

Broadway show, the initial investment for the Broadway show is 2.9 times greater.

Another way to look at this is that it takes 30 weeks for investors to recoup their investment in a Broadway show but only 16 weeks in the Off-Broadway show. And that, of course, occurs only if the play is successful.

FOR CRITICAL ANALYSIS
1. Why should investors be so concerned about how soon their investment is paid back?
2. Why are costs so much higher on Broadway than Off-Broadway?

CHAPTER SUMMARY

1. It is important in economics to distinguish between accounting profits and economic profits. Accounting profits are equal to total revenues minus total explicit costs. Economic profits are equal to total revenues minus total opportunity costs of all factors of production.
2. The short run for the firm is defined as the period during which plant size cannot be altered. The long run is the period during which all factors of production can be varied.
3. Fixed costs are costs that cannot be altered in the short run. Fixed costs are associated with assets that the firm owns that cannot be profitably transferred to another use. Variable costs are associated with input costs that vary as the rate of output varies. Wages are a good example of a variable cost.
4. There are definitional relationships between average, total, and marginal costs:

$$ATC = \frac{TC}{Q}$$

$$AVC = \frac{TVC}{Q}$$

$$AFC = \frac{TFC}{Q}$$

$$MC = \frac{\text{change in TC}}{\text{change in } Q}$$

5. When marginal costs are less than average costs, average costs are falling. When marginal costs are greater than average costs, average costs are rising. The marginal cost curve intersects the average variable cost curve and the average total cost curve at their minimum points.

6. When we hold constant all factors of production except one, an increase in that factor will lead to a change in total physical product. That is how we derive the total physical product curve. The marginal physical product curve is derived from looking at the change in total physical product.

7. After some output rate, firms enter the region of diminishing marginal returns, or diminishing marginal physical product. In other words, after some point, each increment of the variable input will yield a smaller and smaller increment in total output.

8. Given a constant wage rate, the marginal cost curve is the mirror image of the marginal physical product curve. Thus because of the law of diminishing marginal returns, marginal costs will eventually rise.

9. We derive the long-run average cost curve by connecting a smooth line that is just tangent to all of the short-run average cost curves. This long-run average cost curve is sometimes called the planning curve.

10. It is possible for a firm to experience economies of scale, constant returns to scale, or diseconomies of scale, in which case a proportionate increase in *all* inputs will lead, respectively, to decreasing, constant, or increasing average costs. Firms may experience economies of scale because of specialization, the dimensional factor, and the ability to purchase improved productive equipment. Firms may experience diseconomies of scale because of the limitations of efficient management.

11. The long-run average cost curve will be downward-sloping, horizontal, or upward-sloping, depending on whether there are economics of scale, constant returns to scale, or diseconomies of scale.

12. Minimum efficient scale occurs at the lowest rate of output at which long-run average costs are minimized.

DISCUSSION OF PREVIEW QUESTIONS

1. **How does the economist's definition of profit differ from the accountant's?**

   The accountant defines total profits as total revenues minus total costs; the economist defines total profits as total revenues minus total opportunity costs of all inputs used. In other words, the economist takes into account implicit as well as explicit costs; the economist's definition stresses that an opportunity cost exists for all inputs used in the production process. Specifically, the economist estimates the opportunity cost for invested capital, the owner's time, inventories on hand, and so on. Because the economist's definition of costs is more inclusive, accounting profits will exceed economic profits; economic profits exist only when all the opportunity costs are taken into account.

2. **What distinguishes the long run from the short run?**

   The short run is defined as any time period when there is at least one factor of production that a firm cannot vary; in the long run, *all* factors of production can be varied by the firm. Because each industry is likely to be unique in its ability to vary all inputs, the long run differs from industry to industry. Presumably the long run is a lot shorter (in absolute time periods) for firms in the carpentry or plumbing industry than for firms in the automobile or steel industry. In most economic models, labor is usually assumed to be the variable input in the short run, whereas capital is considered to be fixed in the short run; this assumption is fairly descriptive of the real-world situation.

3. **How does the law of diminishing marginal returns account for an *eventually* increasing marginal cost curve for a firm in the short run?**

   Assume that labor is the only variable factor of production. *Eventually,* the law of diminishing returns comes into play (prior to this point, specialization benefits might increase the marginal product of labor), and the marginal product of labor falls. That is, beyond the point of diminishing returns, extra laborers contribute less to total product than immediately preceding laborers do, per unit of time. In effect, this means that if output is to be increased by equal amounts (or equal "batches"), more and more labor time will be required due to its lower marginal product. Later units of output, which are physically identical to earlier units of output, embody more labor time. If wages are constant, later units, which require more worker-hours, have a higher marginal cost. We conclude that beyond the point of diminishing returns, the marginal cost of output rises for the firm in the short run. Prior to the point of diminishing returns, the marginal cost curve falls, due to rising marginal product of labor.

4. Why is the short-run average total cost curve U-shaped?

Average total cost (ATC) equals the sum of average fixed costs (AFC) and average variable costs (AVC); that is, ATC = AFC + AVC. The AFC curve continuously falls because it is derived by dividing a constant number (total fixed costs) by larger and larger numbers (output levels). It falls rapidly at first, then slowly. The AVC curve falls during the early output stages because the benefits of specialization cause the marginal physical product of labor to rise and the marginal cost of output to fall; beyond the point of diminishing returns, the marginal physical product of labor falls, eventually forcing marginal cost to rise above AVC, and therefore AVC rises too. As we go from zero output to higher and higher output levels per unit of time, AFC and AVC both initially fall; therefore, ATC falls too. At some point beyond the point of diminishing marginal returns, AVC rises and outweighs the now slowly falling AFC curve; the net result is that somewhere beyond the point of diminishing marginal returns, the ATC curve rises. Because the ATC curve falls at low output levels and rises at higher output levels, we describe it as U-shaped. Of course, it doesn't look exactly like a *U*, but it is close enough.

PROBLEMS

(Answers to the odd-numbered problems appear at the back of the book.)

22-1. "Now that I have paid off my van, it won't cost me anything except for the running expenses, such as gas, oil, and tune-ups, when I use it." What is wrong with this reasoning?

22-2. Examine this table.

Units of Labor (per eight-hour day)	Marginal Product of Labor (per eight-hour day)
1	2
2	4
3	6
.	.
.	.
.	.
12	20
13	10
14	5
15	3
16	2

a. Suppose that this firm wants to increase output over the short run. How much labor time is required to produce the first unit? The second and third? Do the fourth, fifth, and sixth units of output require more or less labor time than the earlier units?

b. Suppose that we have hired 11 laborers and now want to increase the short-run output in batches of 20. To produce the first batch of 20 (beyond the eleventh laborer), how many labor hours are required? What will the next batch of 20 cost, in labor hours? Do additional batches of 20 cost more or less than earlier batches (beyond the eleventh laborer)?

c. What do parts (a) and (b) imply about the relationship between the marginal product of labor and labor time embodied in equal increments of output?

22-3. Refer to the table in Problem 22-2. Assume that wage rates equal $1 per eight-hour day.

a. By hiring the twelfth unit of labor, what was the cost to the firm of this first batch of 20?

b. What was the marginal cost of output in that range? (Hint: If 20 units cost $1, what did *one* unit cost?)

c. What will the next batch of 10 cost the firm?

d. What is the marginal cost of output over that range?

e. What is happening to the marginal cost of output?

f. How are the marginal product of labor and the marginal cost of output related?

22-4. Your school's basketball team had a foul-shooting average of .800 (80 out of 100) before last night's game, during which they shot 5 for 10 at the foul line.

a. What was their marginal performance last night?

b. What happened to the team's foul-shooting average?

c. Suppose that their foul shooting in the next game is 6 for 10. What is happening to their marginal performance?

d. Now what is the team average foul-shooting percentage?

22-5. Define long-run average total cost. In light of the fact that businesses are operated day to day in the short run, of what use is the concept of long-run average total cost to the entrepreneur?

22-6. A recent college graduate turns down a $20,000-per-year job offer in order to open his own business. He borrows $150,000 to purchase equipment. Total sales during his first year are $250,000. Total labor costs for the first year are $160,000, and raw material costs are equal to $50,000. He pays $15,000 interest on the loan per year. Estimate the economic profit of this business for the first year.

22-7. Examine this table.

Output (units)	Average Fixed Cost	Total Cost
0	—	$200
5	$40	300
10	20	380
20	10	420
40	5	520

a. Find the average variable cost at each level of production.

b. What is the marginal cost of increasing output from 10 to 20 units? From 20 to 40 units?

c. Find the average total cost at each level of production.

22-8. You are given the following graph.

a. At what output level is AVC at a minimum?

b. At what output level is ATC at a minimum?

c. At what output level is MC at a minimum?

d. At what output level do the AVC and MC curves intersect?

e. At what output level do the ATC and MC curves intersect?

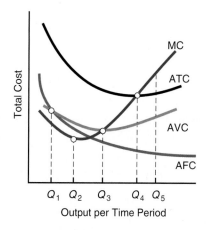

22-9. Fill in the missing values for marginal, average, and total product in the following table. Assume that capital and labor are the only two inputs in the production function and that capital is held fixed.

Units of Labor	Total Product	Marginal Product	Average Product
6	120	—	20
7	147	_____	21
8	_____	23	_____
9	_____	_____	20

COMPUTER-ASSISTED INSTRUCTION

How does the law of diminishing returns affect the marginal product of labor? When the marginal product of labor falls, why does the marginal cost of output rise? Specific calculations are required; such calculations reveal the answers to these important questions.

Complete problem and answer appear on disk.

CHAPTER 23

PERFECT COMPETITION

In small towns across America, local merchants are losing out in the competitive world of retailing. They are falling victim to the aggressive competition of such large-scale chain discounters as Wal-Mart. Typically, when a Wal-Mart comes into a small town, local merchants fear for their businesses—and with good reason. They are often unable to meet the low prices offered by the big discounters. Is this type of competition inevitable, and is there anything that local merchants can do to stop it? An understanding of the model of perfect competition will clarify this issue.

PREVIEW QUESTIONS

1. How much will a perfect competitor produce in the short run?

2. What is the perfectly competitive firm's short-run supply curve?

3. Can a perfectly competitive firm earn economic profits?

4. Why is the perfectly competitive market structure considered economically efficient?

Perfect competition
A market structure in which the
decisions of individual buyers
and sellers have no effect on
market price.

Perfectly competitive firm
A firm that is such a small part
of the total industry that it cannot affect the price of the product it sells.

Price taker
A competitive firm that must
take the price of its product as
given because the firm cannot
influence its price.

Did You Know That . . . in the United States, there are tens of thousands of copy
shops? There are also several thousand desktop publishing companies offering their
services. The number of companies wanting to sell CD-ROM development is much smaller but growing. The number of companies offering to write software applications is somewhere in between, but that is only in the United States. Today, because of the cheapness and
rapidity of modern telecommunications, much of the software code that goes in today's
computer applications programs produced by American companies is written in India and
elsewhere.

Competition is the word that applies to all of these situations. As used in common speech,
competition simply means "rivalry." In perfectly competitive situations, individual buyers
and sellers cannot affect the market price—it is determined by the market forces of demand
and supply. In this chapter we examine what has become known as perfect competition.

CHARACTERISTICS OF A PERFECTLY COMPETITIVE MARKET STRUCTURE

We are interested in studying how a firm acting within a perfectly competitive market structure makes decisions about how much to produce. In a situation of **perfect competition,**
each firm is such a small part that it cannot affect the price of the product in question. That
means that each **perfectly competitive firm** in the industry is a **price taker**—the firm
takes price as a given, something determined *outside* the individual firm.

This definition of a competitive firm is obviously idealized, for in one sense the individual firm *has* to set prices. How can we ever have a situation in which firms regard prices
as set by forces outside their control? The answer is that even though every firm sets its own
prices, a firm in a perfectly competitive situation will find that it will eventually have no
customers at all if it sets its price above the competitive price. The best example is in agriculture. Although the individual farmer can set any price for a bushel of wheat, if that price
doesn't coincide with the market price of a bushel of similar-quality wheat, no one will purchase the wheat at a higher price; nor would the farmer be inclined to reduce revenues by
selling below the market price.

Let's examine the reasons why a firm in a perfectly competitive industry ends up being
a price taker.

1. *There must be a large number of buyers and sellers.* When this is the case, no one buyer
   or one seller has any influence on price.
2. *The product sold by the firms in the industry must be homogeneous.* The product sold
   by each firm in the industry must be a perfect substitute for the product sold by each
   other firm. Buyers must be able to choose from a large number of sellers of a product
   that the buyers believe to be the same.
3. *Any firm can enter or leave the industry without serious impediments.* Firms in a competitive industry cannot be hampered in their ability to get resources or relocate
   resources. They move labor and capital in pursuit of profit-making opportunities to
   whatever business venture gives them their highest expected rate of return on their
   investment.
4. *Both buyers and sellers have equally good information.* Consumers have to be able to
   find out about lower prices charged by competing firms. Firms have to be able to find
   out about cost-saving innovations in order to lower production costs and prices, and
   they have to be able to learn about profitable opportunities in other industries.

INTERNATIONAL EXAMPLE
The Global Coal Market

A good real-world example of perfect competition is the market for coal. Coal is a fossil fuel that started as luxurious vegetation growing in the swamps that covered much of the world about 300 million years ago. Today, coal is found in nearly every region of the world, although the most commercially important deposits are in Asia, Australia, Europe, and North America. Great Britain led the world in coal production until about a century ago.

Throughout the world, coal is produced in literally thousands of different mines. The purchasers of coal, such as steel mills and electric utility generating companies, constantly keep track of the prices of coal output throughout the world. If the price of coal goes up, there are literally thousands of known untapped coal deposits that can be developed. If the price of coal drops, coal mines can be closed. So the market for coal probably conforms as closely as possible to the assumptions underlining the model of perfect competition.

FOR CRITICAL ANALYSIS: There are actually several different grades of coal. Does this seriously violate assumption 2 for a perfectly competitive industry? ●

THE DEMAND CURVE OF THE PERFECT COMPETITOR

When we discussed substitutes in Chapter 20, we pointed out that the more substitutes there were and the more similar they were to the commodity in question, the greater was the price elasticity of demand. Here we assume for the perfectly competitive firm that it is producing a homogeneous commodity that has perfect substitutes. That means that if the individual firm raises its price one penny, it will lose all of its business. This, then, is how we characterize the demand schedule for a perfectly competitive firm: It is the going market price as determined by the forces of market supply and market demand—that is, where the market demand curve intersects the market supply curve. The single-firm demand curve in a perfectly competitive industry is perfectly elastic at the going market price. Remember that with a perfectly elastic demand curve, any increase in price leads to zero quantity demanded.

We show the market demand and supply curves in panel (a) of Figure 23-1. Their intersection occurs at the price of $5. The commodity in question is computer diskettes, and assume for the purposes of this exposition that all diskettes are perfect substitutes for all

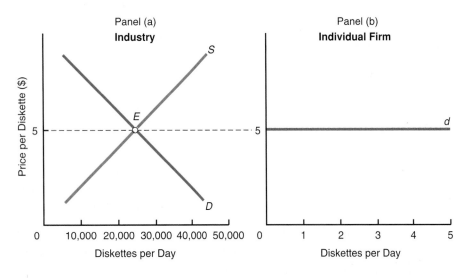

FIGURE 23-1

The Demand Curve for a Diskette Producer
At $5—where market demand, *D*, and market supply, *S*, intersect—the individual firm faces a perfectly elastic demand curve, *d*. If it raises its price even one penny, it will sell no diskettes at all. Notice the difference in the quantities of diskettes represented on the horizontal axis of panels (a) and (b).

others. At the going market price of $5 apiece, a hypothetical individual demand curve for a diskette producer who sells a very, very small part of total industry production is shown in panel (b). At the market price, this firm can sell all the output it wants. At the market price of $5 each, which is where the demand curve for the individual producer lies, consumer demand for the diskettes of that one producer is perfectly elastic. This can be seen by noting that if the firm raises its price, consumers, who are assumed to know that this supplier is charging more than other producers, will buy elsewhere, and the producer in question will have no sales at all. Thus the demand curve for that producer is perfectly elastic. We label the individual producer's demand curve *d*, whereas the *market* demand curve is always labeled *D*.

HOW MUCH SHOULD THE PERFECT COMPETITOR PRODUCE?

As we have shown, a perfect competitor has to accept the price of the product as a given. If the firm raises its price, it sells nothing; if it lowers its price, it makes less money per unit sold than it otherwise could. The firm has one decision left: How much should it produce? We will apply our model of the firm to this question to come up with an answer. We'll use the *profit-maximization model,* which assumes that firms attempt to maximize their total profits—the positive difference between total revenues and total costs.

Total Revenues

Total revenues

The price per unit times the total quantity sold.

Every firm has to consider its *total revenues,* or TR. **Total revenues** are defined as the quantity sold multiplied by the price. (They are the same as total receipts from the sale of output.) The perfect competitor must take the price as a given.

Look at Figure 23-2 on page 512. Much of the information in panel (a) comes from panel (a) of Figure 22-3, but we have added some essential columns for our analysis. Column 3 is the market price, *P*, of $5 per diskette, which is also equal to average revenue (AR) because

$$AR = \frac{TR}{Q} = \frac{PQ}{Q} = P$$

where *Q* stands for quantity. If we assume that all units sell for the same price, it becomes apparent that another name for the demand curve is the *average revenue curve* (this is true regardless of the type of market structure under consideration).

Column 4 shows the total revenues, or TR, as equal to the market price, *P*, times the total output in sales per day, or *Q*. Thus TR = *PQ*. We are assuming that the market supply and demand schedules intersect at a price of $5 and that this price holds for all the firm's production. We are also assuming that because our diskette maker is a small part of the market, it can sell all that it produces at that price. Thus panel (b) of Figure 23-2 shows the total revenue curve as a straight green line. For every unit of sales, total revenue is increased by $5.

Comparing Total Costs with Total Revenues

Total costs are given in column 2 of panel (a) of Figure 23-2 and plotted in panel (b). Remember, the firm's costs always include a normal rate of

Panel (a)

(1) Total Output and Sales per Day (Q)	(2) Total Costs (TC)[*]	(3) Market Price (P)	(4) Total Revenues (TR) (4) = (3) x (1)	(5) Total Profit (TR − TC) (5) = (4) − (2)	(6) Average Total Cost (ATC) (6) = (2) ÷ (1)[*]	(7) Average Variable Cost (AVC)[*]	(8) Marginal Cost (MC) (8) = Change in (2)[*] / Change in (1)	(9) Marginal Revenue (MR) (9) = Change in (4) / Change in (1)
0	$10	$5	$ 0	−$10	—	—		
							$5	$5
1	15	5	5	− 10	$15.00	$5.00		
							3	5
2	18	5	10	− 8	9.00	4.00		
							2	5
3	20	5	15	− 5	6.67	3.33		
							1	5
4	21	5	20	− 1	5.25	2.75		
							2	5
5	23	5	25	2	4.60	2.60		
							3	5
6	26	5	30	4	4.33	2.67		
							4	5
7	30	5	35	5	4.28	2.86		
							5	5
8	35	5	40	5	4.38	3.12		
							6	5
9	41	5	45	4	4.56	3.44		
							7	5
10	48	5	50	2	4.80	3.80		
							8	5
11	56	5	55	− 1	5.09	4.18		

[*]From Figure 22-3.

FIGURE 23-2

Profit Maximization

Profit maximization occurs where marginal revenue equals marginal cost. Panel (a) indicates that this point occurs at a rate of sales of between seven and eight diskettes per day.

In panel (b), we find maximum profits where total revenues exceed total costs by the largest amount. This occurs at a rate of production and sales per day of seven or eight diskettes.

In panel (c), the marginal cost curve, MC, intersects the marginal revenue curve at a rate of output and sales of somewhere between seven and eight diskettes per day.

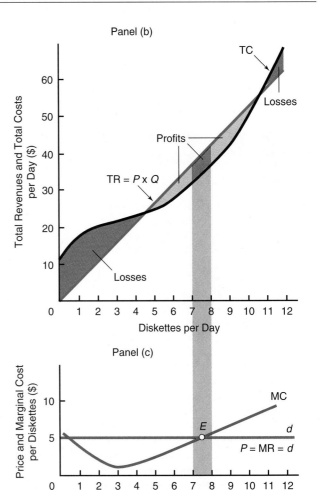

return on investment. So whenever we refer to total costs, we are talking not about accounting costs but about economic costs. When the total cost curve is above the total revenue curve, the firm is experiencing losses. When it is below the total revenue curve, the firm is making profits.

By comparing total costs with total revenues, we can figure out the number of diskettes the individual competitive firm should produce per day. Our analysis rests on the assumption that the firm will attempt to maximize total profits. In panel (a) of Figure 23-2, we see that total profits reach a maximum at a production rate of either seven or eight diskettes per day. We can see this graphically in panel (b) of the figure. The firm will maximize profits where the total revenue curve exceeds the total curve by the greatest amount. That occurs at a rate of output and sales of either seven or eight diskettes per day; this rate is called the **profit-maximizing rate of production.** (If output were continuously divisible or we were dealing with extremely large numbers of diskettes, we would get a unique profit-maximizing output.)

We can also find this profit-maximizing rate of production for the individual competitive firm by looking at marginal revenues and marginal costs.

USING MARGINAL ANALYSIS TO DETERMINE THE PROFIT-MAXIMIZING RATE OF PRODUCTION

It is possible—indeed, preferred—to use marginal analysis to determine the profit-maximizing rate of production. We end up with the same results derived in a different manner, one that focuses more on where decisions are really made—on the margin. Managers examine changes in costs and relate them to changes in revenues. In fact, we almost always compare changes in cost with changes in benefits, where change is occurring at the margin, whether it be with respect to how much more or less to produce, how many more workers to hire or fire, or how much more to study or not study.

Marginal revenue represents the change in total revenues attributable to changing production by one unit of the product in question. Hence a more formal definition of marginal revenue is

$$\text{Marginal revenue} = \frac{\text{change in total revenues}}{\text{change in output}}$$

In a perfectly competitive market, the marginal revenue curve is exactly equivalent to the price line or the individual firm's demand curve because the firm can sell all of its output (production) at the market price. Thus in Figure 23-1, the demand curve, d, for the individual producer is at a price of $5—the price line is coincident with the demand curve. But so is the marginal revenue curve, for marginal revenue in this case also equals $5.

The marginal revenue curve for our competitive diskette producer is shown as a line at $5 in panel (c) of Figure 23-2. Notice again that the marginal revenue curve is equal to the price line, which is equal to the individual firm's demand, or average revenue, curve, d.

When Are Profits Maximized?

Now we add the marginal cost curve, MC, taken from column 8 in panel (a) of Figure 23-2. As shown in panel (c) of that figure, the marginal cost curve first falls and then starts to rise because of the law of diminishing returns, eventually intersecting the marginal revenue curve and then rising above it. Notice that the numbers for both the marginal cost schedule, column 8 in panel (a), and the marginal revenue schedule, column 9 in panel (a), are printed *between* the rows on which the quantities appear. This indicates that we are looking at a *change* between one rate of output and the next.

Profit-maximizing rate of production
The rate of production that maximizes total profits, or the difference between total revenues and total costs; also, the rate of production at which marginal revenue equals marginal cost.

Marginal revenue
The change in total revenues resulting from a change in output (and sale) of one unit of the product in question.

In panel (c), the marginal cost curve intersects the marginal revenue curve somewhere between seven and eight diskettes per day. The firm has an incentive to produce and sell until the amount of the additional revenue received from selling one more diskette just equals the additional costs incurred for producing and selling that diskette. This is how the firm maximizes profit. Whenever marginal cost is less than marginal revenue, the firm will always make more profit by increasing production.

Now consider the possibility of producing at an output rate of 10 diskettes per day. The marginal cost curve at that output rate is higher than the marginal revenue (or *d*) curve. The firm would be spending more to produce that additional output than it would be receiving in revenues; it would be foolish to continue producing at this rate.

But how much should it produce? It should produce at point *E,* where the marginal cost curve intersects the marginal revenue curve from below.[1] The firm should continue production until the cost of increasing output by one more unit is just equal to the revenues obtainable from that extra unit. This is a fundamental rule in economics:

Profit maximization normally occurs at the rate of output at which marginal revenue equals marginal cost.

For a perfectly competitive firm, this is at the intersection of the demand schedule, *d,* and the marginal cost curve, MC. When MR exceeds MC, each additional unit of output adds more to total revenues than to total costs, causing losses to decrease or profits to increase. When MC is greater than MR, each unit produced adds more to total cost than to total revenues, causing profits to decrease or losses to increase. Therefore, profit maximization occurs when MC equals MR. In our particular example, our profit-maximizing, perfectly competitive diskette producer will produce at a rate of either seven or eight diskettes a day. (If we were dealing with a very large rate of output, we would come up with an exact profit-maximizing rate.)

CONCEPTS IN BRIEF

- Four fundamental characteristics of the market in perfect competition are (1) a large number of buyers and sellers, (2) a homogeneous product, (3) unrestrained exit from and entry into the industry by other firms, and (4) good information in the hands of both buyers and sellers.

- A perfectly competitive firm is a price taker. It has no control over price and consequently has to take price as a given, but it can sell all that it wants at the going market price.

- The demand curve for a perfect competitor is a line at the going market price. The demand curve is also the perfect competitor's marginal revenue curve because marginal revenue is defined as the change in total revenue due to a one-unit change in output.

- Profit is maximized at the rate of output where the positive difference between total revenues and total costs is the greatest. This is the same level of output at which marginal revenue equals marginal cost. The perfectly competitive firm produces at an output rate at which marginal cost equals the price per unit of output, because MR $\equiv$ P.

---

[1]The marginal cost curve, MC, also cuts the marginal revenue curve, *d,* from above at an output rate of less than 1 in this example. This intersection should be ignored because it is irrelevant to the firm's decisions.

SHORT-RUN PROFITS

To find what our competitive individual diskette producer is making in terms of profits in the short run, we have to add the average total cost curve to panel (c) of Figure 23-2. We take the information from column 6 in panel (a) and add it to panel (c) to get Figure 23-3. Again the profit-maximizing rate of output is between seven and eight diskettes per day. If we have production and sales of seven diskettes per day, total revenues will be $35 a day. Total costs will be $30 a day, leaving a profit of $5 a day. If the rate of output in sales is eight diskettes per day, total revenues will be $40 and total costs will be $35, again leaving a profit of $5 a day. In Figure 23-3, the lower boundary of the rectangle labeled "Profits" is determined by the intersection of the profit-maximizing quantity line represented by vertical dashes and the average total cost curve. Why? Because the ATC curve gives us the cost per unit, whereas the price ($5), represented by d, gives us the revenue per unit, or average revenue. The difference is profit per unit. So the height of the rectangular box representing profits equals profit per unit, the length equals the amount of units produced, and when we multiply these two quantities, we get total profits. Note, as pointed out earlier, that we are talking about *economic profits* because a normal rate of return on investment is included in the average total cost curve, ATC.

It is certainly possible, also, for the competitive firm to make short-run losses. We give an example in Figure 23-4 on page 516, where we show the firm's demand curve shifting from d_1 to d_2. The going market price has fallen from $5 to $3 per diskette because of changes in market supply or demand conditions (or both). The firm will always do the best it can by producing where marginal revenue equals marginal cost. We see in Figure 23-4 that the marginal revenue (d_2) curve is intersected (from below) by the marginal cost curve at an output rate of about $5\frac{1}{2}$ diskettes per day. The firm is clearly not making profits because average total costs at that output rate are greater than the price of $3 per diskette. The losses are shown in the shaded area. By producing where marginal revenue equals marginal cost, however, the firm is minimizing its losses; that is, losses would be greater at any other output.

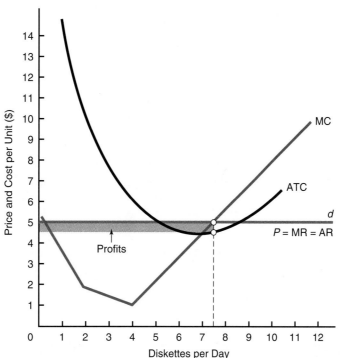

FIGURE 23-3

Measuring Total Profits
Profits are represented by the shaded area. The height of the profit rectangle is given by the difference between average total costs and price ($5), where price is also equal to average revenue. This is found by the vertical difference between the ATC curve and the price, or average revenue, line *d*, at the profit-maximizing rate of output of between seven and eight diskettes per day.

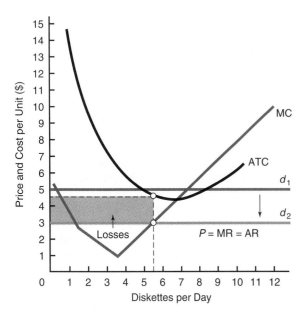

THE SHORT-RUN SHUTDOWN PRICE

In Figure 23-4, the firm is sustaining economic losses. Will it go out of business? In the long run it will, but surprisingly, in the short run the firm will not go out of business, for as long as the loss from staying in business is less than the loss from shutting down, the firm will continue to produce. A firm *goes out of business* when the owners sell its assets to someone else. A firm temporarily *shuts down* when it stops producing, but it still is in business.

Now how can we tell when the firm is sustaining economic losses in the short run and it is still worthwhile not to shut down? The firm must compare the cost of producing (while incurring losses) with the cost of closing down. The cost of staying in production in the short run is given by the total *variable* cost. Looking at the problem on a per-unit basis, as long as average variable cost (AVC) is covered by average revenues (price), the firm is better off continuing to produce. If average variable costs are exceeded even a little bit by the price of the product, staying in production produces some revenues in excess of variable costs that can be applied toward covering fixed costs.

A simple example will demonstrate this situation. The price of a product is $8, and average total costs equal $9 at an output of 100. In this example, average total costs are broken up into average variable costs of $7 and average fixed costs of $2. Total revenues, then, equal $8 × 100, or $800, and total costs equal $9 × 100, or $900. Total losses therefore equal $100. However, this does not mean that the firm will shut down. After all, if it does shut down, it still has fixed costs to pay. And in this case, because average fixed costs equal $2 at an output of 100, the fixed costs are $200. Thus the firm has losses of $100 if it continues to produce, but it has losses of $200 (the fixed costs) if it shuts down. The logic is fairly straightforward:

> **As long as the price per unit sold exceeds the average *variable* cost per unit produced, the firm will be covering at least part of the opportunity cost of the investment in the business—that is, part of its fixed costs.**

Calculating the Short-Run Break-Even Price

Look at demand curve d_1 in Figure 23-5. It just touches the minimum point of the average total cost curve, which, as you will remember, is exactly where the marginal cost curve

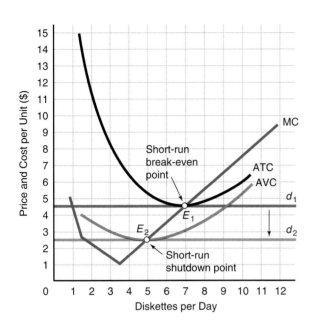

FIGURE 23-5
Short-Run Shutdown and Break-Even Prices
We can find the short-run break-even price and the short-run shutdown price by comparing price with average total costs and average variable costs. If the demand curve is d_1, profit maximization occurs at output E_1, where MC equals marginal revenue (the d curve). Because the ATC curve includes all relevant opportunity costs, point E_1 is the break-even point, and zero economic profits are being made. The firm is earning a normal rate of return. If the demand curve falls to d_2, profit maximization (loss minimization) occurs at the intersection of MC and MR (the d_2 curve), or E_2. Below this price, it does not pay for the firm to continue in operation because its average variable costs are not covered by the price of the product.

Short-run break-even price
The price at which a firm's total revenues equal its total costs. At the break-even price, the firm is just making a normal rate of return on its capital investment. (It is covering its explicit and implicit costs.)

intersects the average total cost curve. At that price, which is about $4.30, the firm will be making exactly zero short-run economic profits. That price is called the **short-run break-even price,** and point E_1 therefore occurs at the short-run break-even price for a competitive firm. It is the point at which marginal revenue, marginal cost, and average total cost are all equal (that is, at which $P = MC$ and $P = ATC$). The break-even price is the one that yields zero short-run economic profits or losses.

Calculating the Short-Run Shutdown Price

To calculate the firm's shutdown price, we must introduce the average variable cost (AVC) to our graph. In Figure 23-5, we have plotted the AVC values from column 7 in panel (a) of Figure 23-2. For the moment, consider two possible demand curves, d_1 and d_2, which are also the firm's respective marginal revenue curves. Therefore, if demand is d_1, the firm will produce at E_1, where that curve intersects the marginal cost curve. If demand falls to d_2, the firm will produce at E_2. The special feature of the hypothetical demand curve, d_2, is that it just touches the average variable cost curve at the latter's minimum point, which is also where the marginal cost curve intersects it. This price is the **short-run shutdown price.**
Why? Below this price, the firm would be paying out more in variable costs than it is receiving in revenues from the sale of its product. Each unit it sold would add to its losses. Clearly, the way to avoid incurring these additional losses, if price falls below the shutdown point, is in fact to shut down operations.

Short-run shutdown price
The price that just covers average variable costs. It occurs just below the intersection of the marginal cost curve and the average variable cost curve.

The intersection of the price line, the marginal cost curve, and the average variable cost curve is labeled E_2. The resulting short-run shutdown price is valid only for the short run because, of course, in the long run the firm will not stay in business at a yield less than a normal rate of return and hence at least zero economic profits.

THE MEANING OF ZERO ECONOMIC PROFITS

The fact that we labeled point E_1 in Figure 23-5 the break-even point may have disturbed you. At point E_1, price is just equal to average total cost. If this is the case, why would a firm continue to produce if it were making no profits whatsoever? If we again make the distinction between accounting profits and economic profits, then at that price the firm has zero economic profits but positive accounting profits. Recall that accounting profits are total revenues minus total explicit costs. What is ignored in such accounting is the reward offered to investors—the opportunity cost of capital—plus all other implicit costs.

In economic analysis, the average total cost curve includes the full opportunity cost of capital. Indeed, the average total cost curve includes the opportunity cost of *all* factors of production used in the production process. At the short-run break-even price, economic profits are, by definition, zero. Accounting profits at that price are not, however, equal to zero; they are positive. Consider an example. A baseball bat manufacturer sells bats at some price. The owners of the firm have supplied all the funds in the business. They have borrowed no money from anyone else, and they explicitly pay the full opportunity cost to all factors of production, including any managerial labor that they themselves contribute to the business. Their salaries show up as a cost in the books and are equal to what they could have earned in the next-best alternative occupation. At the end of the year, the owners find that after they subtract all explicit costs from total revenues, they have earned $100,000. Let's say that their investment was $1 million. Thus the rate of return on that investment is 10 percent per year. We will assume that this turns out to be equal to the rate of return that, on average, all other baseball bat manufacturers make in the industry.

This $100,000, or 10 percent rate of return, is actually, then, a competitive, or normal, rate of return on invested capital in that industry or in other industries with similar risks. If the owners had made only $50,000, or 5 percent on their investment, they would have been able to make higher profits by leaving the industry. The 10 percent rate of return is the opportunity cost of capital. Accountants show it as a profit; economists call it a cost. We include that cost in the average total cost curve, similar to the one shown in Figure 23-5. At the short-run break-even price, average total cost, including this opportunity cost of capital, will just equal that price. The firm will be making zero economic profits but a 10 percent *accounting* rate of return.

Now we are ready to derive the firm's supply curve.

THE PERFECT COMPETITOR'S SHORT-RUN SUPPLY CURVE

What does the supply curve for the individual firm look like? Actually, we have been looking at it all along. We know that when the price of diskettes is $5, the firm will supply seven or eight of them per day. If the price falls to $3, the firm will supply five or six diskettes per day. And if the price falls below $3, the firm will shut down in the short run. Hence in Figure 23-6, the firm's supply curve is the marginal cost curve above the short-run shutdown point. This is shown as the solid part of the marginal cost curve. ***The definition, then, of the individual firm's supply curve in a competitive industry is its marginal cost curve equal to and above the point of intersection with the average variable cost curve.***

The Short-Run Industry Supply Curve

In Chapter 3, we indicated that the market supply curve was the summation of individual supply curves. At the beginning of this chapter, we drew a market supply curve in Figure 23-1. Now we want to derive more precisely a market, or industry, supply curve to reflect individual producer behavior in that industry. First we must ask, What is an industry? It is merely a collection of firms producing a particular product. Therefore, we have a way to figure out the total supply curve of any industry: We add the quantities that each firm will

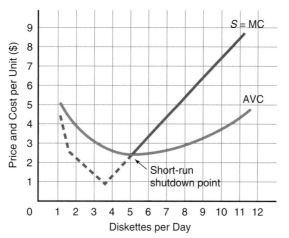

FIGURE 23-6

The Individual Firm's Short-Run Supply Curve
The individual firm's supply curve is the portion of its marginal cost curve above the minimum point on the average variable cost curve.

supply at every possible price. In other words, we sum the individual supply curves of all the competitive firms *horizontally.* The individual supply curves, as we just saw, are simply the marginal cost curves of each firm.

Consider doing this for a hypothetical world in which there are only two diskette producers in the industry, firm A and firm B. These two firms' marginal cost curves are given in panels (a) and (b) of Figure 23-7. The marginal cost curves for the two separate firms are presented as MC_A in panel (a) and MC_B in panel (b). Those two marginal cost curves are drawn only for prices above the minimum average variable cost for each respective firm. Hence we are not including any of the marginal cost curves below minimum average variable cost. In panel (a), for firm A, at price P_1, the quantity supplied would be q_{A1}. At price P_2, the quantity supplied would be q_{A2}. In panel (b), we see the two different quantities that

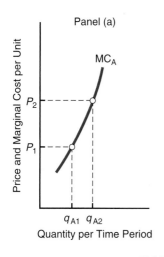

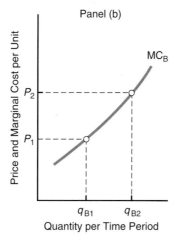

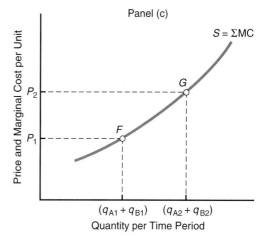

FIGURE 23-7

Deriving the Industry Supply Curve
Marginal cost curves above average minimum variable cost are presented in panels (a) and (b) for firms A and B. We horizontally sum the two quantities supplied, q_{A1} and q_{B1}, at price P_1. This gives us point F in panel (c). We do the same thing for the quantities at price P_2. This gives us point G. When we connect those points, we have the industry supply curve, S, which is the horizontal summation of the firms' marginal cost curves above their respective average minimum costs.

would be supplied by firm B corresponding to those two prices. Now for price P_1 we add horizontally the quantity of q_{A1} and q_{B1}. This gives us one point, F, for our short-run **industry supply curve,** S. We obtain the other point, G, by doing the same horizontal adding of quantities at P_2. When we connect points F and G, we obtain industry supply curve S, which is also marked ΣMC, indicating that it is the horizontal summation of the marginal cost curves (above the respective minimum average variable cost of each firm).[2] Because the law of diminishing returns makes marginal cost curves rise, the short-run supply curve of a perfectly competitive industry must be upward-sloping.

Industry supply curve
The locus of points showing the minimum prices at which given quantities will be forthcoming; also called the *market supply curve.*

Factors That Influence the Industry Supply Curve

As you have just seen, the industry supply curve is the horizontal summation of all of the individual firms' marginal cost curves above their respective minimum average variable cost points. This means that anything that affects the marginal cost curves of the firm will influence the industry supply curve. Therefore, the individual factors that will influence the supply schedule in a competitive industry can be summarized as the factors that cause the variable costs of production to change. These are factors that affect the individual marginal cost curves, such as changes in the individual firm's productivity, in factor costs (wages paid to labor, prices of raw materials, etc.), in taxes, and in anything else that would influence the individual firm's marginal cost curve.

All of these are *ceteris paribus* conditions of supply. Because they affect the position of the marginal cost curve for the individual firm, they affect the position of the industry supply curve. A change in any of these will shift the market supply curve.

CONCEPTS IN BRIEF

- Short-run average profits or average losses are determined by comparing average total costs with price (average revenue) at the profit-maximizing rate of output. In the short run, the perfectly competitive firm can make economic profits or economic losses.

- The competitive firm's short-run break-even output occurs at the minimum point on its average total cost curve, which is where the marginal cost curve intersects the average total cost curve.

- The competitive firm's short-run shutdown output is at the minimum point on its average variable cost curve, which is also where the marginal cost curve intersects the average variable cost curve. Shutdown will occur if price falls below average variable cost.

- The firm will continue production at a price that exceeds average variable costs even though the full opportunity cost of capital is not being met; at least some revenues are going toward paying fixed costs.

- At the short-run break-even price, the firm is making zero economic profits, which means that it is just making a normal rate of return in that industry.

- The firm's short-run supply curve is the portion of its marginal cost curve equal to or above minimum average variable costs. The industry short-run supply curve is a horizontal summation of the individual firms' marginal cost curves above their respective minimum average variable costs.

---

[2] The capital Greek sigma, Σ, is the symbol for summation.

FIGURE 23-8

Industry Demand and Supply Curves and the Individual Firm Demand Curve

The industry demand curve is represented by *D* in panel (a). The short-run industry supply curve is *S* and equal to ΣMC. The intersection of the demand and supply curves at *E* determines the equilibrium or market clearing price at P_e. The individual firm demand curve in panel (b) is set at the market clearing price determined in panel (a). If the producer has a marginal cost curve MC, this producer's individual profit-maximizing output level is at q_e. For AC_1, economic profits are zero; for AC_2, profits are negative; and for AC_3, profits are positive.

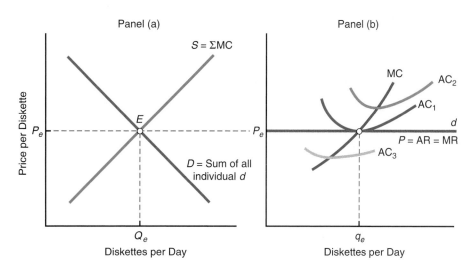

Panel (a)

Panel (b)

COMPETITIVE PRICE DETERMINATION

How is the market, or "going," price established in a competitive market? This price is established by the interaction of all the suppliers (firms) and all the demanders. The market demand schedule, *D*, in panel (a) of Figure 23-8 represents the demand schedule for the entire industry, and the supply schedule, *S*, represents the supply schedule for the entire industry. Price P_e is established by the forces of supply and demand at the intersection of *D* and the short-run industry supply curve, *S*. Even though each individual firm has no control or effect on the price of its product in a competitive industry, the interaction of *all* the producers and buyers determines the price at which the product will be sold. We say that the price P_e and the quantity Q_e in panel (a) of Figure 23-8 constitute the competitive solution to the pricing-quantity problem in that particular industry. It is the equilibrium where quantity demanded equals quantity supplied, and both suppliers and demanders are maximizing. The resulting individual firm demand curve, *d*, is shown in panel (b) of Figure 23-8 at the price P_e.

In a purely competitive industry, the individual producer takes price as a given and chooses the output level that maximizes profits. (This is also the equilibrium level of output from the producer's standpoint.) We see in panel (b) of Figure 23-8 that this is at q_e. If the producer's average costs are given by AC_1, q_e is also the short-run break-even output (see Figure 23-5); if its average costs are given by AC_2, at q_e, AC exceeds price (average revenue), and the firm is incurring losses. Alternatively, if average costs are given by AC_3, the firm will be making economic profits at q_e. In the former case, we would expect, over time, that people will cease production (exit the industry), causing supply to shift inward, whereas in the latter case, we would expect people to enter the industry to take advantage of the economic profits, thereby causing supply to shift outward. We now turn to these long-run considerations.

THE LONG-RUN INDUSTRY SITUATION: EXIT AND ENTRY

In the long run in a competitive situation, firms will be making zero economic profits. In the long run, we surmise that firms in perfect competition will tend to have average total cost curves that just touch the price (marginal revenue) curve, or individual demand curve *d*. How does this occur? It is through an adjustment process that depends on economic profits and losses.

Exit and Entry of Firms

Go back and look at Figures 23-3 and 23-4. The existence of either profits or losses is a signal to owners of capital both within and outside the industry. If the industry is characterized by firms showing economic profits as represented in Figure 23-3, this will signal owners of capital elsewhere in the economy that they, too, should enter this industry. If, by contrast, there are firms in the industry like the ones suffering economic losses represented in Figure 23-4, this signals resource owners outside the industry to stay out. It also signals resource owners within the industry not to reinvest and if possible to leave the industry. It is in this sense that we say that profits direct resources to their highest-valued use. In the long run, capital will flow into industries in which profitability is highest and will flow out of industries in which profitability is lowest.

The price system therefore allocates capital according to the relative expected rates of return on alternative investments. Entry restrictions will thereby hinder economic efficiency, and thus welfare, by not allowing resources to flow to their highest-valued use. Similarly, exit restrictions (such as plant closing laws) will act to trap resources (temporarily) in sectors in which their value is below that in alternative uses. Such laws will also inhibit the ability of firms to respond to changes in the domestic and international marketplace; yet to judge their desirability, we must weigh these factors against the costs to employees and local economies from such sudden economic disruptions.

Not every industry presents an immediate source of opportunity for every firm. In a brief period of time, it may be impossible for a firm that produces tractors to switch to the production of computers, even if there are very large profits to be made. Over the long run, however, we would expect to see such a change, whether or not the tractor producers want to change over to another product. In a market economy, investors supply firms in the more profitable industry with more investment funds, which they take from firms in less profitable industries. (Also, profits give existing firms internal investment funds for expansion.) Consequently, resources needed in the production of more profitable goods, such as labor, will be bid away from lower-valued opportunities. Investors and other suppliers of resources respond to market **signals** about their highest-valued opportunities.

Market adjustment to changes in demand will occur regardless of the wishes of the managers of firms in less profitable markets. They can either attempt to adjust their product line to respond to the new demands, be replaced by managers who are more responsive to new conditions, or see their firms go bankrupt as they find themselves unable to replace worn-out plant and equipment.

In addition, when we say that in a competitive long-run equilibrium situation firms will be making zero economic profits, we must realize that at a particular point in time it would be pure coincidence for a firm to be making *exactly* zero economic profits. Real-world information is not as precise as the curves we use to simplify our analysis. Things change all the time in a dynamic world, and firms, even in a very competitive situation, may for many reasons not be making exactly zero economic profits. We say that there is a *tendency* toward that equilibrium position, but firms are adjusting all the time to changes in their cost curves and in their individual demand curves.

Signals
Compact ways of conveying to economic decision makers information needed to make decisions. A true signal not only conveys information but also provides the incentive to react appropriately. Economic profits and economic losses are such signals.

EXAMPLE
Whittling Away at Apple's Profit Margins

Successful new products yield higher than competitive profits. That, of course, is the incentive that induces firms to introduce new products. Competition, over time, is supposed to cut back gradually on those above-normal profits. This pattern of events occurred with Apple Computer Company. Apple introduced the first truly user-friendly graphics interface computer in the mid-1980s. It offered the first and for several years only mouse-driven machine and programming that used simple icons and pull-down menus to guide users. It chose not to license its operating software technology to anyone else. Consequently, it was able to keep high profit margins, above 50 percent, for the first five years of its sales of Macintosh computers. Then the competing system—IBM and IBM compatibles supported by the Microsoft disk operating system (MS-DOS)—started to get easier to use. Moreover, competition within the IBM-compatible PC market, involving literally hundreds of entrants, kept driving the price of PCs down. Microsoft's introduction of the Windows graphics interface made PCs work more like Macs and further eroded Apple's market position. In the face of declining market share, Apple started reducing its prices and hence its profit margins. By the time the most user-friendly PC operating system, Windows 95, appeared, Apple had lowered its profit margin to less than 25 percent.

FOR CRITICAL ANALYSIS: *Why did Apple lose market share in the personal computer industry?* ●

Long-Run Industry Supply Curves

In panel (a) of Figure 23-8, we drew the summation of all of the portions of the individual firms' marginal cost curve above each firm's respective minimum average variable costs as the upward-sloping supply curve of the entire industry. We should be aware, however, that a relatively steep upward-sloping supply curve may be appropriate only in the short run. After all, one of the prerequisites of a competitive industry is free entry.

Long-run industry supply curve
A market supply curve showing the relationship between price and quantities forthcoming after firms have been allowed the time to enter into or exit from an industry, depending on whether there have been positive or negative economic profits.

Remember that our definition of the long run is a period of time in which adjustments can be made. The **long-run industry supply curve** is a supply curve showing the relationship between quantities supplied by the entire industry at different prices after firms have been allowed to either enter or leave the industry, depending on whether there have been positive or negative economic profits. Also, the long-run industry supply curve is drawn under the assumption that entry and exit have been completed.

The long-run industry supply curve can take one of three shapes, depending on whether input costs stay constant, increase, or decrease as the number of firms in the industry changes. In Chapter 22, we assumed that input prices remained constant to the firm regardless of the firm's rate of output. When we look at the entire industry, when all firms are expanding and new firms are entering, they may simultaneously bid up input prices.

Constant-cost industry
An industry whose total output can be increased without an increase in long-run per-unit costs; an industry whose long-run supply curve is horizontal.

Constant-Cost Industries. In principle, there are small enough industries that use such a small percentage of the total supply of inputs necessary for their production that firms can enter the industry without bidding up input prices. In such a situation, we are dealing with a **constant-cost industry.** Its long-run industry supply curve is therefore horizontal and is represented by S_L in panel (a) of Figure 23-9 on page 524.

We can work through the case in which constant costs prevail. We start out in panel (a) with demand curve D_1 and supply curve S_1. The equilibrium price is P_1. Market demand shifts rightward to D_2. In the short run, the equilibrium price rises to D_2. This generates positive economic profits for existing firms in the industry. Such economic profits induce capital to flow into the industry. The existing firms expand and/or new firms enter. The short-run supply curve shifts outward to S_2. The new intersection with the new demand curve is at E_3. The new equilibrium price is again P_1. The long-run supply curve is obtained by connecting the intersections of the corresponding pairs of demand and supply curves, E_1 and E_3. Labeled S_L, it is horizontal; its slope is zero. In a constant-cost industry, long-run

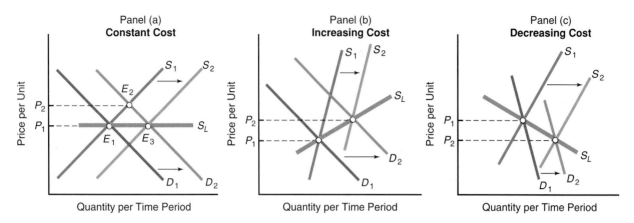

FIGURE 23-9

Constant-Cost, Increasing-Cost, and Decreasing-Cost Industries
In panel (a), we show a situation in which the demand curve shifts from D_1 to D_2. Price increases from P_1 to P_2; however, in time the short-run supply curve shifts outward because positive profits are being earned, and the equilibrium shifts from E_2 to E_3. The market clearing price is again P_1. If we connect points such as E_1 and E_3, we come up with the long-run supply curve S_L. This is a constant-cost industry. In panel (b), costs are increasing for the industry, and therefore the long-run supply curve slopes upward and long-run prices rise from P_1 to P_2. In panel (c), costs are decreasing for the industry as it expands, and therefore the long-run supply curve slopes downward such that long-run prices decline from P_1 to P_2.

supply is perfectly elastic. Any shift in demand is eventually met by an equal shift in supply so that the long-run price is constant at P_1.

Retail trade is often given as an example of such an industry because output can be expanded or contracted without affecting input prices. Banking is another example.

Increasing-Cost Industries. In an **increasing-cost industry,** expansion by existing firms and the addition of new firms cause the price of inputs specialized within that industry to be bid up. As costs of production rise, the ATC curve and the firms' MC curve shift upward, causing short-run supply curves (each firm's marginal cost curve) to shift upward. The result is a long-run industry supply curve that slopes upward, as represented by S_L in panel (b) of Figure 23-9. Examples are residential construction and coal mining—both use specialized inputs that cannot be obtained in ever-increasing quantities without causing their prices to rise.

Increasing-cost industry
An industry in which an increase in industry output is accompanied by an increase in long-run per-unit costs, such that the long-run industry supply curve slopes upward.

Decreasing-Cost Industries. An expansion in the number of firms in an industry can lead to a reduction in input costs and a downward shift in the ATC and MC curves. When this occurs, the long-run industry supply curve will slope downward. An example is given in panel (c) of Figure 23-9. This is a **decreasing-cost industry.**

LONG-RUN EQUILIBRIUM

In the long run, the firm can change the scale of its plant, adjusting its plant size in such a way that it has no further incentive to change. It will do so until profits are maximized. Figure 23-10 shows the long-run equilibrium of the perfectly competitive firm. Given a price

Decreasing-cost industry
An industry in which an increase in output leads to a reduction in long-run per-unit costs, such that the long-run industry supply curve slopes downward.

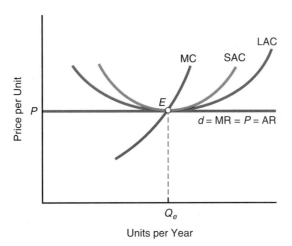

FIGURE 23-10

Long-Run Firm Competitive Equilibrium

In the long run, the firm operates where price, marginal revenue, marginal cost, short-run minimum average cost, and long-run minimum average cost are all equal. This occurs at point E.

of P and a marginal cost curve, MC, the firm produces at output Q_e. Because profits must be zero in the long run, the firm's short-run average costs (SAC) must equal P at Q_e, which occurs at minimum SAC. In addition, because we are in long-run equilibrium, any economies of scale must be exhausted so that we are on the minimum point of the long-run average cost curve (LAC). In other words, the long-run equilibrium position is where "everything is equal," which is at point E in Figure 23-10. There, *price* equals *marginal revenue* equals *marginal cost* equals *average cost* (minimum, short-run, and long-run).

Perfect Competition and Minimum Average Total Cost

Look again at Figure 23-10. In long-run equilibrium, the perfectly competitive firm finds itself producing at output rate Q_e. At that rate of output, the price is just equal to the minimum long-run average cost as well as the minimum short-run average cost. In this sense, perfect competition results in the production of goods and services using the least costly combination of resources. This is an important attribute of a perfectly competitive long-run equilibrium, particularly when we wish to compare the market structure of perfect competition with other market structures that are less than perfectly competitive. We will examine these other market structures in later chapters.

COMPETITIVE PRICING: MARGINAL COST PRICING

In a perfectly competitive industry, each firm produces where its marginal cost curve intersects its marginal revenue (d) curve from below. Thus perfectly competitive firms always sell their goods at a price that just equals marginal cost. This represents an optimal pricing situation because the price that consumers pay reflects the opportunity cost to society of producing the good. Recall that marginal cost is the amount that a firm must spend to purchase the additional resources needed to expand output by one unit. Given competitive markets, the amount paid for a resource will be the same in all of its alternative uses. Thus MC reflects relative resource input use; that is, if the MC of good 1 is twice the MC of good 2, one more unit of good 1 requires twice the resource input of one more unit of good 2. Because under perfect competition, price equals marginal cost, the consumer, in determining allocation of income on purchases on the basis of relative prices, is actually allocating income on the basis of relative resource input use.

Marginal Cost Pricing

The competitive firm produces up to the point at which the market price just equals the marginal cost. Herein lies the element of the optimal nature of a competitive solution. It is called **marginal cost pricing.** The competitive firm sells its product at a price that just equals the cost to society—the opportunity cost—for that is what the marginal cost curve represents. (But note here that it is the self-interest of firm owners that causes price to equal marginal social cost.) In other words, the marginal benefit to consumers, given by the price that they are willing to pay for the last unit of the good purchased, just equals the marginal cost to society of producing the last unit. (If the marginal benefit exceeds the marginal cost ($P > \text{MC}$), too little is being produced in that people value additional units more than the cost to society of producing them; if $P < \text{MC}$, the opposite is true.)

When an individual pays a price equal to the marginal cost of production, the cost to the user of that product is equal to the sacrifice or cost to society of producing that quantity of that good as opposed to more of some other good. (We are assuming that all marginal social costs are accounted for.) The competitive solution, then, is called *efficient,* in the economic sense of the word. Economic efficiency means that it is impossible to increase the output of any good without lowering the *value* of the total output produced in the economy. No juggling of resources, such as labor and capital, will result in an output that is higher in total value than the value of all of the goods and services already being produced. In an efficient situation, it is impossible to make one person better off without making someone else worse off. All resources are used in the most advantageous way possible, and society therefore enjoys an efficient allocation of productive resources. All goods and services are sold at their opportunity cost, and marginal cost pricing prevails throughout.

Marginal cost pricing
A system of pricing in which the price charged is equal to the opportunity cost to society of producing one more unit of the good or service in question. The opportunity cost is the marginal cost to society.

Market Failure

Although perfect competition does offer many desirable results, situations arise when perfectly competitive markets cannot efficiently allocate resources. Either too many or too few resources are used in the production of a good or service. These situations are instances of **market failure.** Externalities and public goods are examples. For reasons discussed in later chapters, perfectly competitive markets cannot efficiently allocate resources in these situations, and alternative allocation mechanisms are called for. Finally, the rate of innovation by perfectly competitive firms may be socially suboptimal, and the distribution of income may differ from what our normative judgment indicates. In all cases, alternative market structures, or government intervention, *may* improve the economic outcome.

Market failure
A situation in which an unrestrained market operation leads to either too few or too many resources going to a specific economic activity.

POLICY EXAMPLE
Can the Government Cure Market Failure Due to Asymmetric Information, or Are Lemons Here to Stay?

One kind of market failure may occur when assumption 4 with respect to perfect competition is violated. Specifically, if information is not the same for buyers and sellers, markets may be dominated by low-quality products. This is a situation of asymmetric information.

Lemons problem
The situation in which consumers, who do not know details about the quality of a product, are willing to pay no more than the price of a low-quality product, even if a higher-quality product at a higher price exists.

It has been called the **lemons problem** because cars, particularly used cars, that turn out to be "bad deals" are called lemons. The potential buyer of a used car has relatively little information about the true quality of the car—its motor, transmission, brakes, and so on. The only way the buyer can find out is to purchase the car and use it for a time. In contrast, the seller usually has much greater information about the quality of the car, for the seller has been using it for some time. The owner of the used car knows whether or not it is a lemon. In situations like this, with asymmetric information between buyer and seller, buyers typically tend to want to pay only a price that reflects the lower quality of the used car in the market, not a price that reflects the higher value of a truly good used car.

From the car seller's point of view, given that the price of used cars will tend to reflect average qualities, all of the owners of known lemons will want to put their cars up for sale. The owners of high-quality used cars will be more reluctant to do so. The logical result of this adverse selection is a disproportionate number of lemons on the used car market and consequently relatively fewer sales than would exist if information were symmetric.

So lemons will be overpriced and great-running used cars will be underpriced. Is there room for government policy to improve this market? Because the government has no better information than used-car buyers, it cannot provide any improved information. What the government has done, though, is require mileage certificates on all used cars and the disclosure of major defects and work that has been performed on them. What the market has done is use brand names both for cars and for firms that sell used cars. Additionally, used-car retailers offer extended warranties.

FOR CRITICAL ANALYSIS: If used-car dealers depend on repeat customers, is the lemons problem reduced or eliminated? ●

CONCEPTS IN BRIEF

- The competitive price is determined by the intersection of the market demand curve and the market supply curve; the market supply curve is equal to the horizontal summation of the portions of the individual marginal cost curves above their respective minimum average variable costs.

- In the long run, competitive firms make zero economic profits because of entry and exit of firms into and out of the industry whenever there are industrywide economic profits or economic losses.

- A constant-cost industry will have a horizontal long-run supply curve. An increasing-cost industry will have a upward-sloping long-run supply curve. A decreasing-cost industry will have a downward-sloping long-run supply curve.

- In the long run, a competitive firm produces where price, marginal revenue, marginal cost, short-run minimum average cost, and long-run minimum average cost are all equal.

- Competitive pricing is essentially marginal cost pricing, and therefore the competitive solution is called efficient because marginal cost represents the social opportunity cost of producing one more unit of the good; when consumers face a price equal to the full opportunity cost of the product they are buying, their purchasing decisions will lead to an efficient use of available resources.

Wal-Mart Versus the Small Shopkeepers

Concepts Applied: *Competition, marginal cost pricing, entry and exit*

Shop owners in small and mid-sized towns usually cannot compete with Wal-Mart's prices and selection. Because there is a belief that many local businesses will go out of business when Wal-Mart enters an area, some towns have decided not to allow the superstore to obtain building permits.

The late Sam Walton started working for J. C. Penney in 1940. He opened the first Wal-Mart in Rogers, Arkansas. Today, the company owns about 2,000 discount stores and over 300 Sam's Wholesale clubs. Sam Walton brought price competition to the small and medium-sized towns of America, towns that had traditionally had only small family-owned specialty stores—usually charging higher prices than stores in big cities.

The Benefits of Buying Large Quantities

One reason that Wal-Mart can offer lower prices than its smaller competitors is because it uses centralized purchasing and orders in tremendous quantities. It therefore often enjoys a lower per-unit cost per item sold than its nondiscount competitors. (It generally has no cost advantage, though, over its discount competitors, such as Kmart.) In other words, the marginal cost of providing its products can be lower than for less efficient, smaller specialty stores, such as local hardware stores. Moreover, its selling costs per unit are often lower because it spreads the overhead for one store over a larger number of stocked items than a small specialty store can.

Small Towns Often Fight Back

When a Wal-Mart comes into a small or medium-sized town, it is often able to sell at a lower price than any of its competitors within the target geographic area. As a consequence, Wal-Mart has driven hundreds of small retailers out of business. In most areas, this has happened without much fuss. But a few localities have fought back.

Anti-Wal-Mart Crusaders Succeed

A few years ago, the New England town of Westford, Massachusetts, decided to fight the entry of a Wal-Mart. The city fathers and mothers of Westford simply would not give Wal-Mart a permit to build. In Greenfield, Massachusetts, voters refused to allow Wal-Mart to build a store in a sandpit a few miles out of town. The goal, according to the townspeople, is to preserve the small-town way of life. Not surprisingly, that means preserving the fortunes of local small downtown retailing merchants.

Reporters from *Newsweek* visited Greenfield. They described their shopping experience as close to dismal. They pointed out that at the local department store, they thought they were back in the 1950s. More important, the *Newsweek* staff did a comparison survey of eight small items on a shopping trip to downtown Greenfield. The results are shown in Table 23-1.

The Cost of Small-Town Charm

Closer examination of the table shows that for this small sample of goods, the residents of Greenfield were paying approximately 35 percent more for maintaining the "charm" of downtown. Economists cannot say whether this is good or bad; they can only point out that the benefits are intangible but the costs are quite obvious—relatively higher prices and hence lower real incomes for the residents of Greenfield, who are deprived of the benefits of a high-volume, low-cost discounter such as Wal-Mart.

Competition theoretically leads to maximum value of output for a given set of inputs over a specific time period. That does not mean that in the process some individ-

TABLE 23-1

The Price of Competition

Item	Retail Price	
	Wal-Mart	**Downtown**
Made in America by Sam Walton	$ 4.48	$ 5.99
Crest Tartar Control Toothpaste, 6.4 oz.	1.23	2.29
Advil, 50 coated 200-mg tablets	3.97	5.57
Johnson's Baby Shampoo, 20 fl. oz.	2.97	4.03
Walt Disney's *Dumbo* video	19.76	24.95
Kodacolor Gold film, 400 ASA, 24 exposures	3.97	6.28
Formula 409 cleaner, 22 fl. oz.	1.97	2.59
Duracell AA alkaline batteries, 2-pack	1.87	2.69

Source: Newsweek, November 8, 1993, p. 57.

uals and businesses will not be hurt. The controversy over allowing Wal-Mart into smaller towns in America simply highlights that there may always be losers when entrepreneurs attempt to force prices down to their marginal cost.

FOR CRITICAL ANALYSIS

1. Why didn't discounters enter small towns in America before the 1950s?

2. To what extent should local merchants who are harmed by the sudden presence of major discounters in their area be compensated by such discounters? Should they be compensated by the residents who will benefit from the lower-priced competitor? Is there ever a valid time when the parties hurt by competition should be compensated by someone?

CHAPTER SUMMARY

1. We define a competitive situation as one in which individual firms cannot affect the price of the product they produce. This is usually when the firm is very small relative to the entire industry. A firm in a perfectly competitive situation is called a price taker; it must take price as a given.

2. The firm's total revenues will equal the price of the product times the quantity sold. Because the competitive firm can sell all it wants at the same price (the "going" price), total revenues equal the going price times the quantity the firm decides to sell.

3. The firm maximizes profits when marginal cost equals marginal revenue. The marginal revenue to the firm is represented by its own perfectly elastic demand curve. This is because marginal revenue is defined as the change in total revenues due to a change in output and sales by one unit. But the competitive firm can sell all it wants at the same price; therefore,

its marginal revenue will equal the price, which will equal its average revenue.

4. A perfectly competitive firm ends up in the long run making zero economic profits. However, it still makes a normal, or competitive, rate of return because that is the opportunity cost of capital. The competitive rate of return on investment is included in the costs as we have defined them for the firm.

5. The firm will always produce along its marginal cost curve unless the price falls below average variable costs; this would be the shutdown price. It occurs at the intersection of the average variable cost curve and the marginal cost curve. Below that price, it is not profitable to stay in production because variable costs will not be completely covered by revenues.

6. The supply curve of the firm is exactly equal to its marginal cost curve above the shutdown price. The supply curve of the industry is equal to the horizontal

summation of all the supply curves of the individual firms. This is a short-run industry supply curve, and it slopes upward.

7. The long-run supply curve will be upward-sloping, horizontal, or downward-sloping, depending on whether the industry is facing increasing, constant, or decreasing costs. The industry may have an upward-sloping long-run supply curve if it faces diseconomies of scale or increasing costs. The industry may have a downward-sloping long-run supply curve if it faces economies of scale or decreasing costs.

DISCUSSION OF PREVIEW QUESTIONS

1. **How much will a perfect competitor produce in the short run?**

A perfect competitor will produce at the profit-maximizing rate of output; it will maximize the positive difference between total revenues and total costs. Another way of viewing this process is through analyzing marginal revenue (MR) and marginal cost (MC). The firm can maximize total profits by producing all outputs for which MR exceeds MC. Thus if MR > MC, the firm will produce the unit in question; if MR < MC, the firm will not produce the unit in question. If MC > MR, the extra cost of producing that unit is greater than the extra revenue that the firm can earn by selling it; producing a unit for which MC > MR leads to a reduction in total profits or an increase in total losses. In short, the perfect competitor will produce up to the output rate at which MR = MC; by doing so, it will have produced all units for which MR > MC, and it will be maximizing total profits.

2. **What is the perfectly competitive firm's short-run supply curve?**

A supply curve indicates the various quantities per unit of time that will be offered, voluntarily, at different prices, other things being constant. Under perfect competition, price (P) equals marginal revenue (MR), and because the profit-maximizing output occurs where P = MC, it follows that any price above MC will induce more output until MC is driven up to equal that price. Thus the marginal cost curve is the firm's short-run supply schedule. We qualify this to note that because the firm has a shutdown point at the minimum average variable cost point, the technical short-run supply curve is the firm's marginal cost curve *above* the minimum average variable cost point.

3. **Can a perfectly competitive firm earn economic profits?**

In the short run, yes; in the long run, no. Though it is possible for a perfectly competitive firm to earn profits in the short run, our assumption of free (unfettered but not costless) entry forces us to conclude that any positive economic (abnormal) profits will be bid away. This will happen because excess profits induce entry into the industry, which amounts to an increase in industry supply. Given demand, an increase in supply will cause market price to fall, thereby shifting the individual firm's demand curve downward. This process continues until economic profits equal zero; free entry allows new entrants to compete away economic profits.

4. **Why is the perfectly competitive market structure considered economically efficient?**

The perfectly competitive market structure is considered economically efficient for two reasons: In the long run, economic profits are zero, and price equals marginal cost. We discuss each in turn. Profits are a signal; if economic profits are positive, the signal is that society wants *more* of this good; if economic profits are negative, this means that society wants *less* of this good; when economic profits are zero, just the "right" quantity of resources is being allocated to the production of a good. Also, the marginal cost of a good represents the social opportunity cost of producing one more unit of that good; the price of a good represents society's marginal valuation of that commodity. When price equals marginal cost, the value to society of the last unit produced (its price) is just offset by what society had to give up in order to get it (its marginal cost). Because under perfect competition, long-run economic profits equal zero and price equals marginal cost, an efficient allocation of resources exists.

PROBLEMS

(Answers to the odd-numbered problems appear at the back of the book.)

23-1. In the accompanying table, we list cost figures for a hypothetical firm. We assume that the firm is selling in a perfectly competitive market. Fill in all the blanks.

Output (units)	Fixed Cost	Average Fixed Cost (AFC)	Variable Cost	Average Variable Cost (AVC)	Total Cost	Average Total Cost (ATC)	Marginal Cost (MC)
1	$100	$_____	$40	$_____	$_____	$_____	$_____
2	100	_____	70	_____	_____	_____	_____
3	100	_____	120	_____	_____	_____	_____
4	100	_____	180	_____	_____	_____	_____
5	100	_____	250	_____	_____	_____	_____
6	100	_____	330	_____	_____	_____	_____

a. How low would the market price of its output have to go before the firm would shut down in the short run?

b. What is the price of its output at which the firm would just break even in the short run? (This is the same price below which the firm would go out of business in the long run.) What output would the firm produce at that price?

c. If the price of its output were $76, what rate of output would the firm produce, and how much profit would it earn?

23-2. Consider the accompanying graph. Then answer the questions.

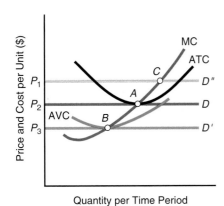

a. Which demand curve indicates that the firm is earning normal profits?

b. Which demand curve indicates that the firm is earning abnormal profits?

c. Which demand curve indicates that the firm is indifferent between shutting down and producing?

d. Which curve is the firm's supply curve?

e. Below which price will the firm shut down?

23-3. In a perfectly competitive market, what is the difference between the demand the industry faces and the demand an individual firm faces?

23-4. Why might a firm continue to produce in the short run, even though the going price is less than its average total cost?

23-5. A firm in a perfectly competitive industry has total revenue of $200,000 per year when producing 2,000 units of output per year.

a. Find the firm's average revenue.

b. Find the firm's marginal revenue.

c. Assuming that the firm is maximizing profits, what is the firm's marginal cost?

d. If the firm is at long-run equilibrium, what are its short-run average costs?

23-6. The accompanying graph is for firm J. Study it; then answer the questions.

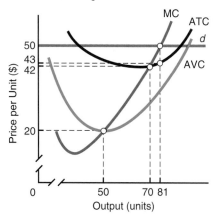

a. How many units will firm J sell in order to maximize profits?

b. What is firm J's total profit from selling the amount of output in part (a)?

c. At what price will firm J shut down in the short run?

d. If the cost curves shown represent production at the optimal long-run plant size, at what price will firm J shut down in the long run?

23-7. You have a friend who earns $25,000 a year working for a collection agency. In a savings and loan account she has $200,000 that she inherited. She is earning 6 percent per year on that money. She quits her job and buys a car wash with the $200,000. At the end of one year, she shows you her tax return. It indicates that the car wash had a pretax profit of $40,000. "What do you think about that?" she remarks. What is your answer?

COMPUTER-ASSISTED INSTRUCTION

Why do perfect competitors choose to produce at an output rate at which MR equals MC? What are the consequences for them if they fail to follow this rule?

Complete problem and answer appear on disk.

CHAPTER 24

MONOPOLY

Your genes make up your heredity constitution. Genes occur in strands of genetic material called chromosomes. Each gene carries a genetic code that is the chemical equation which translates hereditary information into proteins. Scientists are identifying new genes on a regular basis now. The discovery of new gene data has led and will continue to lead to the development of drugs necessary for the prevention, treatment, and cure of many life-threatening diseases—pretty important stuff, to be sure. Much of the information relating to these new genetic data is owned by one Anglo-American drug company, SmithKline Beecham. Does this drug company therefore have market power? To answer this question, you need to study the theory and reality of monopoly.

PREVIEW QUESTIONS

PREVIEW QUESTIONS

1. For the monopolist, marginal revenue is less than selling price. Why?

2. What is the profit-maximizing rate of output for the monopolist?

3. What are some common misconceptions about monopolists?

4. What is the cost to society of monopoly?

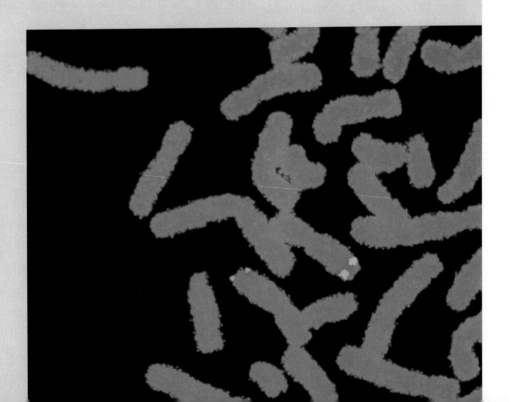

Did You Know That . . . the Central Selling Organization (CSO), a marketing group based in London, sells about 80 percent of the world's rough-cut diamonds each year, collecting handling fees of about 12 percent? The CSO is owned by South Africa's De Beers, the world's largest diamond mining company, controlled by Harry Oppenheimer. In any given year, the CSO sells between $4 and $5 billion in diamonds, making around $400 million a year in profits. It spends relatively little each year on advertising—"A diamond is forever." For all intents and purposes, there is one seller of rough-cut diamonds in the world, and you can be certain that the principal seller attempts to extract the maximum amount of profit possible under the circumstances.

Single sellers of goods and services exist all around you. The company that sells food in your school cafeteria has most probably been granted the exclusive right to do so by your college or university. The ski resort that offers you food at the top of the mountain does not allow anyone else to open a restaurant next to it. When you run a business that is the only one of its type in a particular location, you can usually charge a higher price per constant-quality unit than when there is intense competition. In this chapter you will read more about situations in which competition is restricted. We call these situations *monopoly*.

DEFINITION OF A MONOPOLIST

The word *monopoly* probably brings to mind notions of a business that gouges the consumer, sells faulty products, gets unconscionably rich, and other negative thoughts. But if we are to succeed in analyzing and predicting the behavior of noncompetitive firms, we will have to be more objective in our definition. Although most monopolies in the United States are relatively large, our definition will be equally applicable to small businesses: A **monopolist** is the *single supplier* of a good or service for which there is no close substitute.

In a monopoly market structure, the firm (the monopolist) and the industry are one and the same. Occasionally there may be a problem in identifying an industry and therefore determining if a monopoly exists. For example, should we think of aluminum and steel as separate industries, or should we define the industry in terms of basic metals? Our answer depends on the extent to which aluminum and steel can be substituted in the production of a wide range of products.

As we shall see in this chapter, a seller prefers to have a monopoly than to face competitors. In general, we think of monopoly prices as being higher than prices under perfect competition and of monopoly profits as being higher than profits under perfect competition (which are, in the long run, merely equivalent to a normal rate of return). How does a firm obtain a monopoly in an industry? Basically, there must be *barriers to entry* that enable firms to receive monopoly profits in the long run. Barriers to entry are restrictions on who can start a business or who can stay in a business.

Monopolist

A single supplier that comprises its entire industry for a good or service for which there is no close substitute.

BARRIERS TO ENTRY

For any amount of monopoly power to continue to exist in the long run, the market must be closed to entry in some way. Either legal means or certain aspects of the industry's technical or cost structure may prevent entry. We will discuss several of the barriers to entry that have allowed firms to reap monopoly profits in the long run (even if they are not pure monopolists in the technical sense).

Ownership of Resources Without Close Substitutes

Preventing a newcomer from entering an industry is often difficult. Indeed, some economists contend that no monopoly acting without government support has been able to prevent entry into the industry unless that monopoly has had the control of some essential natural resource. Consider the possibility of one firm's owning the entire supply of a raw material input that is essential to the production of a particular commodity. The exclusive ownership of such a vital resource serves as a barrier to entry until an alternative source of the raw material input is found or an alternative technology not requiring the raw material in question is developed. A good example of control over a vital input is the Aluminum Company of America (Alcoa), a firm that prior to World War II controlled the world's bauxite, the essential raw material in the production of aluminum. Such a situation is rare, though, and is ordinarily temporary.

Problems in Raising Adequate Capital

Certain industries require a large initial capital investment. The firms already in the industry can, according to some economists, obtain monopoly profits in the long run because no competitors can raise the large amount of capital needed to enter the industry. This is called the "imperfect" capital market argument employed to explain long-run, relatively high rates of return in certain industries. These industries are generally ones in which large fixed costs must be incurred merely to start production. Their fixed costs are generally for expensive machines necessary to the production process.

EXAMPLE
"Intel Inside"

Many observers of today's high-stakes high-technology world argue that the world's largest manufacturer of microprocessors, Intel, is a monopoly. They point out that to compete effectively with Intel, a potential adversary would have to invest billions of dollars. Intel provides the critical microprocessor chip that goes into the majority of the world's personal computers. Each new generation of microprocessor quickly becomes the industry standard for all IBM-compatible personal computers. Apple computers for years used a Motorola-made chip. In an attempt to fight back against Intel, Apple, Motorola, and IBM formed an alliance that did develop the Power PC microprocessor. So far, though, it has not made serious inroads into Intel's market. A few companies have attempted to clone Intel's chips, but they have not been very successful for both legal and technical reasons.

FOR CRITICAL ANALYSIS: Intel spends billions of dollars developing each new generation of microprocessor. Would it spend more or less if it had a smaller share of the microprocessor market? •

Economies of Scale

Sometimes it is not profitable for more than one firm to exist in an industry. This is so if one firm would have to produce such a large quantity in order to realize lower unit costs that there would not be sufficient demand to warrant a second producer of the same product. Such a situation may arise because of a phenomenon we discussed in Chapter 22, economies of scale. When economies of scale exist, total costs increase less than proportionately to the increase in output. That is, proportional increases in output yield proportionately smaller

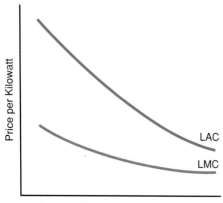

FIGURE 24-1

The Cost Curves That Might Lead to a Natural Monopoly: The Case of Electricity
Whenever long-run average costs are falling, so, too, will be long-run marginal costs. Also, long-run marginal costs (LMC) will always be below long-run average costs (LAC). A natural monopoly might arise in such a situation. The first firm to establish the low unit cost capacity would be able to take advantage of the lower average total cost curve. This firm would drive out all rivals by charging a lower price than the others could sustain at their higher average costs.

increases in total costs, and per-unit costs drop. The advantage in economies of scale lies in the fact that larger firms (with larger output) have lower costs that enable them to charge lower prices, and that drives smaller firms out of business.

When economies of scale occur over a wide range of outputs, a **natural monopoly** may develop. The natural monopoly is the firm that first takes advantage of persistent declining long-run average costs as scale increases. The natural monopolist is able to underprice its competitors and eventually force all of them out of the market.

In Figure 24-1, we have drawn a downward-sloping long-run average cost curve (LAC). Recall that when average costs are falling, marginal costs are less than average costs. We can apply the same analysis in the long run. When the long-run average cost curve (LAC) is falling, the long-run marginal cost curve (LMC) will be below the LAC.

In our example, long-run average costs are falling over such a large range of production rates that we would expect only one firm to survive in such an industry. That firm would be the natural monopolist. It would be the first one to take advantage of the decreasing average costs; that is, it would construct the large-scale facilities first. As its average costs fell, it would lower prices and get an increasingly larger share of the market. Once that firm had driven all other firms out of the industry, it would set its price to maximize profits.

Natural monopoly

A monopoly that arises from the peculiar production characteristics in an industry. It usually arises when there are large economies of scale relative to the industry's demand such that one firm can produce at a lower average cost than can be achieved by multiple firms.

Legal or Governmental Restrictions

Governments and legislatures can also erect barriers to entry. These include licenses, franchises, patents, tariffs, and specific regulations that tend to limit entry.

Licenses, Franchises, and Certificates of Convenience. In many industries, it is illegal to enter without a government license, or a "certificate of convenience and public necessity." For example, in many states you cannot form an electrical utility to compete with the electrical utility already operating in your area. You would first have to obtain a certificate of convenience and public necessity from the appropriate authority, which is usually the state's public utility commission. However, public utility commissions rarely, if ever, issue a certificate to a group of investors who want to compete directly in the same geographic area with an existing electrical utility; hence entry into the industry in a particular geographic area is prohibited, and long-run monopoly profits could conceivably be earned by the electrical utility already serving the area.

To enter interstate (and also many intrastate) markets for pipelines, television and radio broadcasting, and transmission of natural gas, to cite a few such industries, it is often necessary to obtain similar permits. Because these franchises or licenses are restricted, long-run monopoly profits might be earned by the firms already in the industry.

POLICY EXAMPLE
Should the U.S. Postal Service Remain a Monopoly—or Does It Matter?

The U.S. Postal Service (USPS) has been granted a monopoly on first-class mail by the government. For years, would-be competitors have tried to get Congress to repeal the laws shielding the USPS from outside competitors. The Postal Service has argued that because it is a natural monopoly—economies of scale exist—low-cost delivery is possible only with its coverage of the entire U.S. market. This policy debate is losing its significance today because of modern technology and other factors. Any monopoly power that the USPS had with respect to parcel delivery has been whittled away by the more efficient and cheaper United Parcel Service. For urgent delivery, Federal Express, Airborne, and others have further eroded the USPS monopoly. In the 1990s, technology has perhaps rendered the most fatal blow to the USPS's monopoly position. The fax machine is usually cheaper and certainly faster than sending a letter domestically or internationally. Now that fax modems are routinely installed in all new personal computers, faxing may become ubiquitous. So, too, may the use of electronic mail. With over 40 million users of the Internet active today, e-mail offers an almost free substitute for mailing a letter. There is now even a substitute for certified mail in the form of recorded certified phone messages (the service is called Certi-Call).

FOR CRITICAL ANALYSIS: *In what ways might the USPS slow down the erosion of its monopoly position?* ●

Patents. A patent is issued to an inventor to provide protection from having the invention copied or stolen for a period of 17 years. Suppose that engineers working for Ford Motor Company discover a way to build an engine that requires half the parts of a regular engine and weighs only half as much. If Ford is successful in obtaining a patent on this discovery, it can (in principle) prevent others from copying it. The patent holder has a monopoly. However, it is the patent holder's responsibility to defend the patent. That means that Ford—like other patent owners—must expend resources to prevent others from imitating its invention. If in fact the costs of enforcing a particular patent are greater than the benefits, the patent may not bestow any monopoly profits on its owner. The policing costs would be just too high.

EXAMPLE
Patents as Intellectual Property

A patent may bestow on its owner a monopoly for a given time period. So, too, may copyrights. Trademarks don't actually bestow monopoly power, but they do in certain cases have extreme value. Coca-Cola can exploit its trademark by licensing it for clothes and paraphernalia. So, too, can Harley-Davidson. Both of those companies have done so. Copyrights, trademarks, patents, and the like are all part of what is known as intellectual property. Songs, music, computer programs, and designs are all intellectual property. Indeed, some economists believe that the world value of intellectual property now exceeds the value of physical property, such as real estate, buildings, and equipment. Not surprisingly, in the corporate world, when a business buys another business, the acquiring company's lawyers have to worry a great deal about the acquired company's intellectual property portfolio. What intellectual property rights in terms of patents, trademarks, and copyrights does the soon-to-be-acquired company actually own?

FOR CRITICAL ANALYSIS: Why doesn't the ownership of a well-known trademark bestow true monopoly power on its owner? ●

Tariffs. **Tariffs** are special taxes that are imposed on certain imported goods. Tariffs have the effect of making imports relatively more expensive than their domestic counterparts so that consumers switch to the relatively cheaper domestically made products. If the tariffs are high enough, imports become overpriced, and domestic producers gain monopoly advantage as the sole suppliers. Many countries have tried this protectionist strategy by using high tariffs to shut out foreign competitors.

Tariffs
Taxes on imported goods.

Regulations. During much of the twentieth century, government regulation of the American economy has increased, especially along the dimensions of safety and quality. For example, pharmaceutical quality-control regulations enforced by the Food and Drug Administration may require that each pharmaceutical company install a $2 million computerized testing machine that requires elaborate monitoring and maintenance. Presumably, this large fixed cost can be spread over a larger number of units of output by larger firms than by smaller firms, thereby putting the smaller firms at a competitive disadvantage. It will also deter entry to the extent that the scale of operation of a potential entrant must be sufficiently large to cover the average fixed costs of the required equipment. We examine regulation in more detail in Chapter 26.

Cartels

"Being the only game in town" is preferable because such a monopoly position normally allows the monopolist to charge higher prices and make greater profits. Not surprisingly, manufacturers and sellers have often attempted to form an organization (which often is international) that acts as one. This is called a **cartel.** Cartels are an attempt by their members to earn higher than competitive profits. They set common prices and output quotas for their members. The key to the success of a cartel is keeping one member from competing against other members by expanding production and thereby lowering price. Apparently, one of the most successful international cartels ever was the Organization of Petroleum Exporting Countries (OPEC), an association of the world's largest oil-producing countries, including Saudi Arabia, which at times has accounted for a significant percentage of the world's crude oil output. OPEC effectively organized a significant cutback on the production of crude oil in the wake of the so-called Yom Kippur War in the Middle East in 1973. Within one year, the spot price of crude oil jumped from $2.12 to $7.61 per barrel on the world market. By the early 1980s, the price had risen to over $30.
   Most cartels have not as much success.

Cartel
An association of producers in an industry that agree to set common prices and output quotas to prevent competition.

INTERNATIONAL EXAMPLE
"We're Just Trying to Keep the Market Stable"

The stated goal of most international cartels is keeping markets "stable." In reality, cartel members are seeking higher prices (and profits) for their product. But to achieve their aims, the producing countries have to be willing to withhold some of their production from the world market. In this way, the world price of a commodity does not fall if world production increases.

Nowhere are international cartels as prevalent as in the market for commodities. The International Coffee Organization lasted 30 years until the United States pulled out; it was succeeded by the Association of Coffee Producing Countries. Cocoa has the International Cocoa Organization. There is even an ostrich cartel called the Little Karoo Agricultural Cooperative.

The U.S. government has at times sanctioned the equivalent of a cartel. A meeting in Washington, D.C., involving executives from a dozen global aluminum producers and government officials representing the United States, the European Union, and four other nations ultimately resulted in an agreement by all those attending to reduce aluminum production. All such reductions were voluntary except by Russia. In exchange for cutting primary aluminum production by 500,000 tons over a two-year period, Russia received the promise of $250 million of U.S. taxpayers' money for equity investments. U.S. government officials claim that "the markets are still open" nonetheless.

FOR CRITICAL ANALYSIS: The price of gasoline today (corrected for inflation) is about 50 percent of what it was in 1984. What does that tell you about the long-run effectiveness of global cartels? •

CONCEPTS IN BRIEF

- A monopolist is defined as a single seller of a product or a good for which there is no good close substitute.

- To maintain a monopoly, there must be barriers to entry. Barriers to entry include ownership of resources without close substitutes; large capital requirements in order to enter the industry; economies of scale; legally required licenses, franchises, and certificates of convenience; patents; tariffs; and safety and quality regulations.

THE DEMAND CURVE A MONOPOLIST FACES

A *pure monopolist* is the sole supplier of *one* product, good, or service. A pure monopolist faces a demand curve that is the demand curve for the entire market for that good.

The monopolist faces the industry demand curve because the monopolist is the entire industry.

Because the monopolist faces the industry demand curve, which is by definition downward-sloping, its decision-making process with respect to how much to produce is not the same as for a perfect competitor. When a monopolist changes output, it does not automatically receive the same price per unit that it did before the change.

Profits to Be Made from Increasing Production

How do firms benefit from changing production rates? What happens to price in each case? Let's first review the situation among perfect competitors.

Marginal Revenue for the Perfect Competitor. Recall that a competitive firm has a perfectly elastic demand curve. That is because the competitive firm is such a small part of the market that it cannot influence the price of its product. It is a *price taker.* If the forces of supply and demand establish that the price per constant-quality pair of shoes is $50, the individual firm can sell all the pairs of shoes it wants to produce at $50 per pair. The average revenue is $50, the price is $50, and the marginal revenue is also $50.

Let us again define marginal revenue:

Marginal revenue equals the change in total revenue due to a one-unit change in the quantity produced and sold.

In the case of a competitive industry, each time a single firm changes production by one unit, total revenue changes by the going price, and price is always the same. Marginal revenue never changes; it always equals price, or average revenue. Average revenue was defined as total revenue divided by quantity demanded, or

$$\text{Average revenue} = \frac{\text{TR}}{Q} = \frac{PQ}{Q} = P$$

Marginal Revenue for the Monopolist. What about a monopoly firm? Because a monopoly is the entire industry, the monopoly firm's demand curve is the market demand curve. The market demand curve slopes downward, just like the other demand curves that we have seen. Therefore, to sell more of a particular product, given the industry demand curve, the monopoly firm must lower the price. Thus the monopoly firm moves *down* the demand curve. If all buyers are to be charged the same price, the monopoly must lower the price on all units sold in order to sell more. It cannot just lower the price on the *last* unit sold in any given time period in order to sell a larger quantity.

Put yourself in the shoes of a monopoly ferryboat owner. You have a government-bestowed franchise, and no one can compete with you. Your ferryboat goes between two islands. If you are charging $1 per crossing, a certain quantity of your services will be demanded. Let's say that you are ferrying 100 people a day each way at that price. If you decide that you would like to ferry more individuals, you must lower your price to all individuals—you must move *down* the existing demand curve for ferrying services. To calculate the marginal revenue of your change in price, you must first calculate the total revenues you received at $1 per passenger per crossing and then calculate the total revenues you would receive at, say, 90 cents per passenger per crossing.

It is sometimes useful to compare monopoly markets with perfectly competitive markets. The only way the monopolist can increase sales is by getting consumers to spend more of their incomes on the monopolist's product and less on all other products combined. Thus the monopolist is constrained by the entire market demand curve for its product. We see this in Figure 24-2, which compares the demand curves of the perfect competitor and the monopolist.

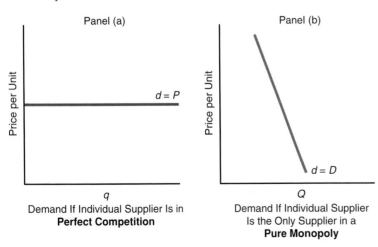

FIGURE 24-2

Demand Curves for the Perfect Competitor and the Monopolist
The perfect competitor in panel (a) faces a perfectly elastic demand curve, *d.* The monopolist in panel (b) faces the entire industry demand curve, which slopes downward.

Here we see the fundamental difference between the monopolist and the competitor. The competitor doesn't have to worry about lowering price to sell more. In a purely competitive situation, the competitive firm accounts for such a small part of the market that it can sell its entire output, whatever that may be, at the same price. The monopolist cannot. The more the monopolist wants to sell, the lower the price it has to charge on the last unit (and on *all* units put on the market for sale). Obviously, the extra revenues the monopolist receives from selling one more unit are going to be smaller than the extra revenues received from selling the next-to-last unit. The monopolist has to lower the price on the last unit to sell it because it is facing a downward-sloping demand curve and the only way to move down the demand curve is to lower the price on all units.

The Monopolist's Marginal Revenue: Less than Price

An essential point is that for the monopolist, marginal revenue is always less than price. To understand why, look at Figure 24-3, which shows a unit increase in sales due to a reduction in the price of a commodity from P_1 to P_2. After all, the only way that sales can increase, given a downward-sloping demand curve, is for the price to fall. Price P_2 is the price received for the last unit. Thus price P_2 times the last unit sold represents what is received from the last unit sold. That is equal to the vertical column (area A). Area A is one unit wide by P_2 high.

But price times the last unit sold is *not* the addition to *total* revenues received from selling that last unit. Why? Because price had to be reduced on all previous units sold (Q) in order to sell the larger quantity $Q + 1$. The reduction in price is represented by the vertical distance from P_1 to P_2 on the vertical axis. We must therefore subtract area B from area A to come up with the *change* in total revenues due to a one-unit increase in sales. Clearly, the change in total revenues—that is, marginal revenue—must be less than price because marginal revenue is always the difference between areas A and B in Figure 24-3. For example, if the initial price is $8 and quantity demanded is 3, to increase quantity to 4 units, it is necessary to decrease price to $7, not just for the fourth unit, but on all three previous units as well. Thus at a price of $7, marginal revenue is $7 − $3 = $4 because there is a $1 per unit price reduction on three previous units. Hence marginal revenue, $4, is less than price, $7.

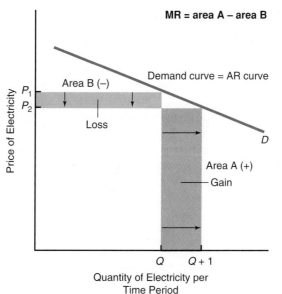

MR = area A – area B

FIGURE 24-3

Marginal Revenue: Always Less than Price

The price received for the last unit sold is equal to P_2. The revenues received from selling this last unit are equal to P_2 times one unit, or the area of the vertical column. However, if a single price is being charged for all units, total revenues do not go up by the amount of the area represented by that column. The price had to be reduced on all the previous Q units that were being sold at price P_1. Thus we must subtract area B—the rectangle between P_1 and P_2 from the origin to Q—from area A in order to derive marginal revenue. Marginal revenue is therefore always less than price.

ELASTICITY AND MONOPOLY

The monopolist faces a downward-sloping demand curve (its average revenue curve). That means that it cannot charge just *any* price with no changes in quantity (a common misconception) because, depending on the price charged, a different quantity will be demanded.

Earlier we defined a monopolist as the single seller of a well-defined good or service with no *close* substitute. This does not mean, however, that the demand curve for a monopoly is vertical or exhibits zero price elasticity of demand. (Indeed, as we shall see, the profit-maximizing monopolist will never operate in a price range in which demand is inelastic.) After all, consumers have limited incomes and alternative wants. The downward slope of a monopolist's demand curve occurs because individuals compare the marginal satisfaction they will receive to the cost of the commodity to be purchased. Take the example of telephone service. Even if miraculously there were absolutely no substitute whatsoever for telephone service, the market demand curve would still slope downward. At lower prices, people will add more phones and separate lines for different family members.

Furthermore, the demand curve for telephone service slopes downward because there are at least several *imperfect* substitutes, such as letters, telegrams, in-person conversations, and CB and VHF-FM radios. Thus even though we defined a monopolist as a single seller of a commodity with no *close* substitute, we can talk about the range of *imperfect* substitutes. The more such imperfect substitutes there are, the more elastic will be the monopolist's demand curve, all other things held constant.

CONCEPTS IN BRIEF

- The monopolist estimates its marginal revenue curve, where marginal revenue is defined as the change in total revenues due to a one-unit change in quantity sold.

- For the perfect competitor, price equals marginal revenue equals average revenue. For the monopolist, price is always greater than marginal revenue. For the monopolist, marginal revenue is always less than price because price must be reduced on all units to sell more.

- The price elasticity of demand for the monopolist depends on the number and similarity of substitutes. The more numerous and more similar the substitutes, the greater the price elasticity of demand of the monopolist's demand curve.

COSTS AND MONOPOLY PROFIT MAXIMIZATION

To find out the rate of output at which the perfect competitor would maximize profits, we had to add cost data. We will do the same thing now for the monopolist. We assume that profit maximization is the goal of the pure monopolist, just as for the perfect competitor. The perfect competitor, however, has only to decide on the profit-maximizing rate of output because price was given. The competitor is a price taker. For the pure monopolist, we must seek a profit-maximizing *price-output combination* because the monopolist is a **price searcher.** We can determine this profit-maximizing price-output combination with either of two equivalent approaches—by looking at total revenues and total costs or by looking at marginal revenues and marginal costs. We shall examine both approaches.

Price searcher
A firm that must determine the price-output combination that maximizes profit because it faces a downward-sloping demand curve.

The Total Revenues–Total Costs Approach

We show hypothetical demand (rate of output and price per unit), revenues, costs, and other data in panel (a) of Figure 24-4. In column 3, we see total revenues for our hypothetical

Panel (a)

(1) Output (units)	(2) Price per Unit	(3) Total Revenues (TR) (3) = (2) x (1)	(4) Total Costs (TC)	(5) Total Profit (5) = (3) – (4)	(6) Marginal Cost (MC)	(7) Marginal Revenue (MR)
0	$8.00	$ .00	$10.00	–$10.00		
					$4.00	$7.80
1	7.80	7.80	14.00	– 6.20		
					3.50	7.40
2	7.60	15.20	17.50	– 2.30		
					3.25	7.00
3	7.40	22.20	20.75	1.45		
					3.05	6.60
4	7.20	28.80	23.80	5.00		
					2.90	6.20
5	7.00	35.00	26.70	8.30		
					2.80	5.80
6	6.80	40.80	29.50	11.30		
					2.75	5.40
7	6.60	46.20	32.25	13.95		
					2.85	5.00
8	6.40	51.20	35.10	16.10		
					3.20	4.60
9	6.20	55.80	38.30	17.50		
					4.00	4.20
10	6.00	60.00	42.30	17.70		
					6.00	3.80
11	5.80	63.80	48.30	15.50		
					9.00	3.40
12	5.60	67.20	57.30	9.90		

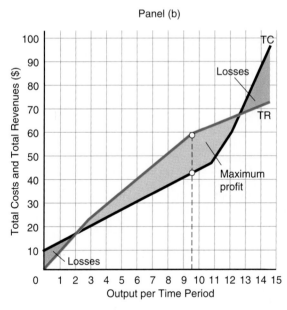

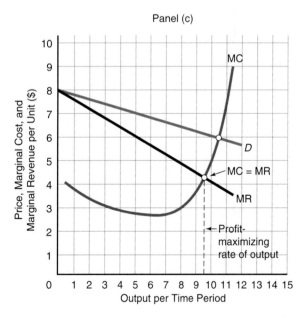

FIGURE 24-4
Monopoly Costs, Revenues, and Profits
In panel (a), we give hypothetical demand (rate of output and price per unit), revenues, costs, and other relevant data. As shown in panel (b), the monopolist maximizes profits where the positive difference between TR and TC is greatest. This is at an output rate of between 9 and 10. Put another way, profit maximization occurs where marginal revenue equals marginal cost, as shown in panel (c). This is at the same output rate of between 9 and 10. (The MC curve must cut the MR curve from below.)

monopolist, and in column 4, we see total costs. We can transfer these two columns to panel (b). The only difference between the total revenue and total cost diagram in panel (b) and the one we showed for a perfect competitor in Chapter 23 is that the total revenue line is no longer straight. Rather, it curves. For any given demand curve, in order to sell more, the monopolist must lower the price. Thus, the basic difference between a monopolist and a perfect competitor has to do with the demand curve for the two types of firms. Monopoly market power is derived from facing a downward-sloping demand curve.

Profit maximization involves maximizing the positive difference between total revenues and total costs. This occurs at an output rate of between 9 and 10 units.

The Marginal Revenue–Marginal Cost Approach

Profit maximization will also occur where marginal revenue equals marginal cost. This is as true for a monopolist as it is for a perfect competitor (but the monopolist will charge a higher price). When we transfer marginal cost and marginal revenue information from columns 6 and 7 in panel (a) of Figure 24-4 to panel (c), we see that marginal revenue equals marginal cost at an output rate of between 9 and 10 units. Profit maximization occurs at the same output as in panel (b).

Why Produce Where Marginal Revenue Equals Marginal Cost? If the monopolist goes past the point where marginal revenue equals marginal cost, marginal cost will exceed marginal revenue. That is, the incremental cost of producing any more units will exceed the incremental revenue. It just wouldn't be worthwhile, as was true also in perfect competition. But if the monopolist produces less than that, it is also not making maximum profits. Look at output rate Q_1 in Figure 24-5. Here the monopolist's marginal revenue is at A, but marginal cost is at B. Marginal revenue exceeds marginal cost on the last unit sold; the profit for that *particular* unit, Q_1, is equal to the vertical difference between A

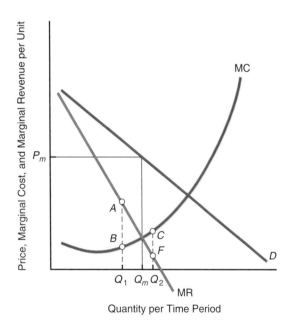

FIGURE 24-5

Maximizing Profits
The profit-maximizing production rate is Q_m, and the profit-maximizing price is P_m. The monopolist would be unwise to produce at the rate Q_1 because here marginal revenue would be Q_1A and marginal costs would be Q_1B. Marginal revenue exceeds marginal cost. The firm will keep producing until the point Q_m, where marginal revenue just equals marginal cost. It would be foolish to produce at the rate Q_2, for here marginal cost exceeds marginal revenue. It behooves the monopolist to cut production back to Q_m.

and B, or the difference between marginal revenue and marginal cost. The monopolist would be foolish to stop at output rate Q_1 because if output is expanded, marginal revenue will still exceed marginal cost, and therefore total profits will rise. In fact, the profit-maximizing monopolist will continue to expand output and sales until marginal revenue equals marginal cost, which is at output rate Q_m. The monopolist won't produce at rate Q_2 because here, as we see, marginal costs are C and marginal revenues are F. The difference between C and F represents the *reduction* in total profits from producing that additional unit. Total profits will rise as the monopolist reduces its rate of output back toward Q_m.

What Price to Charge for Output?

How does the monopolist set prices? We know the quantity is set at the point at which marginal revenue equals marginal cost. The monopolist then finds out how much can be charged—how much the market will bear—for that particular quantity, Q_m, in Figure 24-5. We know that the demand curve is defined as showing the *maximum* price for which a given quantity can be sold. That means that our monopolist knows that to sell Q_m, it can charge only P_m because that is the price at which that specific quantity, Q_m, is demanded. This price is found by drawing a vertical line from the quantity, Q_m, to the market demand curve. Where that line hits the market demand curve, the price is determined. We find that price by drawing a horizontal line from the demand curve over to the price axis; that gives us the profit-maximizing price, P_m.

In our detailed numerical example, at a profit-maximizing rate of output of a little less than 10 in Figure 24-4, the firm can charge a maximum price of about $6 and still sell all the goods produced, all at the same price.

The basic procedure for finding the profit-maximizing short-run price-quantity combination for the monopolist is first to determine the profit-maximizing rate of output, by either the total revenue–total cost method or the marginal revenue–marginal cost method, and then to determine by use of the demand curve, D, the maximum price that can be charged to sell that output.

Don't get the impression that just because we are able to draw an exact demand curve in Figure 24-4 and Figure 24-5, real-world monopolists have such perfect information. The process of price searching by a less than perfect competitor is just that—a process. A monopolist can only estimate the actual demand curve and therefore can only make an educated guess when it sets its profit-maximizing price. This is not a problem for the perfect competitor because price is given already by the intersection of market demand and market supply. The monopolist, in contrast, reaches the profit-maximizing output-price combination by trial and error.

CALCULATING MONOPOLY PROFIT

We have talked about the monopolist's profit, but we have yet to indicate how much profit the monopolist makes. We have actually shown total profits in column 5 of panel (a) in Figure 24-4. We can also find total profits by adding an average total cost curve to panel (c) of

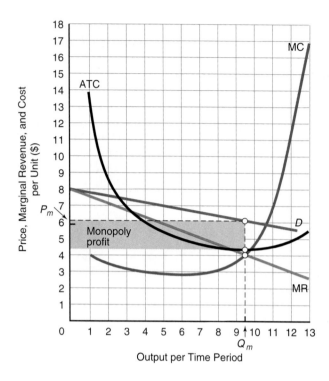

FIGURE 24-6

Monopoly Profit

We find monopoly profit by subtracting total costs from total revenues at an output rate of almost 10, labeled Q_m, which is the profit-maximizing rate of output for the monopolist. The profit-maximizing price is therefore about $6 and is labeled P_m. Monopoly profit is given by the shaded area, which is equal to total revenues (P × Q) minus total costs (ATC × Q). This diagram is similar to panel (c) of Figure 24-4, with the short-run average total cost curve (ATC) added.

that figure. We do that in Figure 24-6. When we add the average total cost curve, we find that the profit that a monopolist makes is equal to the shaded area [or total revenues minus total costs (ATC × Q)]. Given the demand curve and a uniform pricing system (i.e., all units sold at the same price), there is no way for a monopolist to make greater profits than those shown by the shaded area. The monopolist is maximizing profits where marginal cost equals marginal revenue. If the monopolist produces less than that, it will be forfeiting some profits. If the monopolist produces more than that, it will be forfeiting some profits.

The same is true of a perfect competitor. The competitor produces where marginal revenues equal marginal costs because it produces at the point where the marginal cost curve intersects the perfectly elastic firm demand curve. The perfectly elastic firm demand curve represents the marginal revenue curve for the pure competitor, for the same average revenues are obtained on all the units sold. Perfect competitors maximize profits at MR = MC, as do pure monopolists. But the perfect competitor makes no true economic profits in the long run; rather, all it makes is a normal, competitive rate of return.

In Chapter 23, we talked about companies experiencing short-run economic profits because they had, for example, invented something new. Competition, though, gradually eroded those higher than normal profits. The fact that a firm experiences higher than normal profits today does not mean that it has a monopoly forever. Try as companies may, keeping competitors away is never easy.

No Guarantee of Profits

The term *monopoly* conjures up the notion of a greedy firm ripping off the public and making exorbitant profits. However, the mere existence of a monopoly does not guarantee high

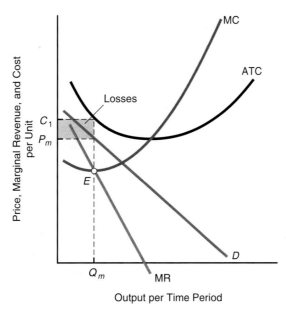

FIGURE 24-7

Monopolies: Not Always Profitable

Some monopolists face the situation shown here. The average total cost curve, ATC, is everywhere above the average revenue, or demand, curve, D. In the short run, the monopolist will produce where MC = MR at point E. Output Q_m will be sold at price P_m, but cost per unit is C_1. Losses are the shaded rectangle. Eventually, the monopolist will go out of business.

profits. Numerous monopolies have gone bankrupt. Figure 24-7 shows the monopolist's demand curve as D and the resultant marginal revenue curve as MR. It does not matter at what rate of output this particular monopolist operates; total costs cannot be covered. Look at the position of the average total cost curve. It lies everywhere above D (the average revenue curve). Thus there is no price-output combination that will allow the monopolist even to cover costs, much less earn profits. This monopolist will, in the short run, suffer economic losses as shown by the shaded area. The graph in Figure 24-7 depicts a situation for millions of typical monopolies that exist; they are called inventions. The owner of a patented invention or discovery has a pure legal monopoly, but the demand and cost curves may be such that production is not profitable. Every year at inventors' conventions, one can see many inventions that have never been put into production because they were deemed "uneconomic" by potential producers and users.

CONCEPTS IN BRIEF

- The basic difference between a monopolist and a perfect competitor is that a monopolist faces a downward-sloping demand curve, and therefore marginal revenue is less than price.

- The monopolist must choose the profit-maximizing price-output combination—the output at which marginal revenue equals marginal cost and the highest price possible as given by the demand curve for that particular output rate.

- Monopoly short-run profits are found by looking at average total costs compared to price per unit. This difference multiplied by quantity sold at that price determines monopoly profit.

- A monopolist does not necessarily earn a profit. If the average total cost curve lies entirely above the demand curve for a monopoly, production will not be profitable.

ON MAKING HIGHER PROFITS: PRICE DISCRIMINATION

In a perfectly competitive market, each buyer is charged the same price for every unit of the particular commodity (corrected for differential transportation charges). Because the product is homogeneous and we also assume full knowledge on the part of the buyers, a difference in price cannot exist. Any seller of the product who tried to charge a price higher than the going market price would find that no one would purchase it from that seller.

In this chapter we have assumed until now that the monopolist charged all consumers the same price for all units. A monopolist, however, may be able to charge different people different prices or different unit prices for successive units sought by a given buyer. When there is no cost difference, either one or a combination of these strategies is called **price discrimination.** A firm will engage in price discrimination whenever feasible to increase profits. A price-discriminating firm is able to charge some customers more than other customers.

It must be made clear at the outset that charging different prices to different people or for different units that reflect differences in the cost of service to those particular people does not amount to price discrimination. This is **price differentiation:** differences in price that reflect differences in marginal cost.

We can also say that a uniform price does not necessarily indicate an absence of price discrimination. Charging all customers the same price when production costs vary by customer is actually a case of price discrimination.

Price discrimination
Selling a given product at more than one price, with the price difference being unrelated to differences in cost.

Price differentiation
Establishing different prices for similar products to reflect differences in marginal cost in providing those commodities to different groups of buyers.

Necessary Conditions for Price Discrimination

Four conditions are necessary for price discrimination to exist:

1. The firm must face a downward-sloping demand curve.
2. The firm must be able to separate markets at a reasonable cost.
3. The buyers in the various markets must have different price elasticities of demand.
4. The firm must be able to prevent resale of the product or service.

For example, charging students a lower price than nonstudents for a movie can be done relatively easily. The cost of checking student IDs is apparently not significant. Also, it is fairly easy to make sure that students do not resell their tickets to nonstudents.

INTERNATIONAL EXAMPLE
Fuji Film Price Discrimination

For years, Kodak argued that the Japanese film company, Fuji, was "dumping" its film in the United States. In effect, Kodak was arguing that Fuji was price-discriminating. Because, according to Kodak, Fuji had effectively blocked Kodak from successfully competing in Japan, Fuji faced a less elastic demand for film in Japan than it did in the United States, where Kodak dominated the market. Panel (a) of Figure 24-8 shows the relatively inelastic demand curve, D_J, that Fuji faces domestically. In the United States, Fuji faces a relatively elastic demand curve, D_{US}. For the sake of simplicity, marginal cost is assumed to be constant for Fuji. At profit maximization, marginal revenue must equal marginal cost. Here we have a common marginal cost, MC. There are two sets of marginal revenue curves, however—MR_J and MR_{US}. For profit maximization, $MR_J = MR_{US} = MC$. (In essence, it is as if the Fuji film sold in Japan and in the United States

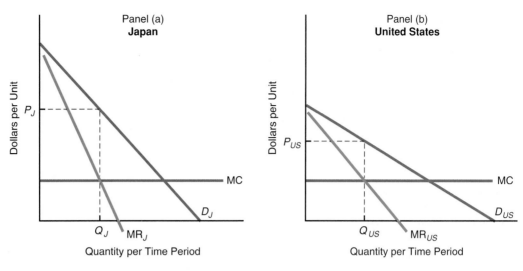

FIGURE 24-8

Price Discrimination in Film by Fuji

The Japanese film industry is protected from foreign competition and therefore faces a relatively inelastic demand curve, D_J, in panel (a). In the United States, as shown in panel (b), the industry faces competition such that its demand curve, D_{US}, is more elastic. (For simplicity, the marginal cost curve is assumed to be horizontal.) Profit maximization occurs in each market where MC = MR. In Japan, that is at Q_J, at which point film can be sold at a price of P_J. In the United States, profit maximization occurs at Q_{US}, at which point film can be sold at a price of P_{US}. Prices charged in Japan for the same film are higher than prices charged in the United States.

were two different goods having exactly the same marginal cost to produce.) The market for Fuji film in Japan is given in panel (a) of Figure 24-8. MC = MR at Q_J, sold at price P_J. Buyers of Fuji film in the United States have a more elastic demand because of competition from Kodak. They ended up paying only P_{US} for quantity Q_{US}. P_{US} is lower than P_J. (This analysis is no longer accurate because through legal maneuverings, Kodak forced Fuji to raise its film prices in the United States.)

FOR CRITICAL ANALYSIS: Assuming that price discrimination was being undertaken by Fuji, who was benefiting? ●

THE SOCIAL COST OF MONOPOLIES

Let's run a little experiment. We will start with a purely competitive industry with numerous firms, each one unable to affect the price of its product. The supply curve of the industry is equal to the horizontal sum of the marginal cost curves of the individual producers above their respective minimum average variable costs. In panel (a) of Figure 24-9 on page 550, we show the market demand curve and the market supply curve in a perfectly competitive situation. The competitive price in equilibrium is equal to P_e, and the equilibrium quantity at that price is equal to Q_e. Each individual competitor faces a demand curve (not shown) that is coincident with the price line P_e. No individual supplier faces the market demand curve, D.

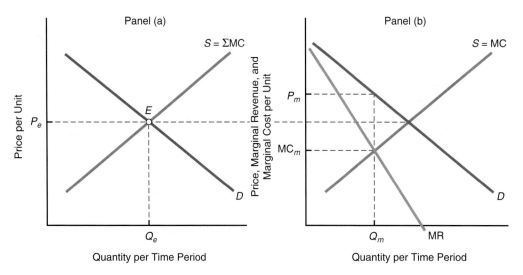

FIGURE 24-9

The Effects of Monopolizing an Industry

In panel (a), we show a competitive situation in which equilibrium is established at the intersection of D and S at point E. The equilibrium price would be P_e, and the equilibrium quantity would be Q_e. Each individual competitive producer faces a demand curve that is a horizontal line at the market clearing price, P_e. What happens if the industry is suddenly monopolized? We assume that the costs stay the same; the only thing that changes is that the monopolist now faces the entire downward-sloping demand curve. In panel (b), we draw the marginal revenue curve. Marginal cost is S because that is the horizontal summation of all the individual marginal cost curves. The monopolist therefore produces at Q_m and charges price P_m. P_m in panel (b) is higher than P_e in panel (a), and Q_m is less than Q_e. We see, then, that a monopolist charges a higher price and produces less than an industry in a competitive situation.

Now let's assume that a monopolist comes in and buys up every single competitor in the industry. In so doing, we'll assume that the monopolist does not affect any of the marginal cost curves or demand. We can therefore redraw D and S in panel (b) of Figure 24-9, exactly the same as in panel (a).

How does this monopolist decide how much to charge and how much to produce? If the monopolist is profit-maximizing, it is going to look at the marginal revenue curve and produce at the output where marginal revenue equals marginal cost. But what is the marginal cost curve in panel (b) of Figure 24-9? It is merely S because we said that S was equal to the horizontal summation of the portions of the individual marginal cost curves above each firm's respective minimum average variable cost. The monopolist therefore produces quantity Q_m and sells it at price P_m. Notice that Q_m is less than Q_e and that P_m is greater than P_e. A monopolist therefore produces a smaller quantity and sells it at a higher price. This is the reason usually given when economists criticize monopolists. Monopolists raise the price and restrict production, compared to a competitive situation. For a monopolist's product, consumers are forced to pay a price that exceeds the marginal cost of production. Resources are misallocated in such a situation—too few resources are being used in the monopolist's industry, and too many are used elsewhere.

Notice from Figure 24-9 that by setting MR = MC, the monopolist produces at a rate of output where $P > MC$ (compare P_m to MC_m). The marginal cost of a commodity (MC) represents what society had to give up in order to obtain the last unit produced. Price, by contrast, represents what buyers are willing to pay to acquire that last unit. Thus the price of a good represents society's valuation of the last unit produced. The monopoly outcome of $P > MC$ means that the value to society of the last unit produced is greater than its cost (MC); hence not enough of the good is being produced. As we have pointed out before, these differences between monopoly and competition arise not because of differences in costs but rather because of differences in the demand curves the individual firms face. The monopolist has monopoly power because it faces a downward-sloping demand curve. The individual perfect competitor faces a perfectly elastic demand curve.

Before we leave the topic of the cost to society of monopolies, we must repeat that our analysis is based on a heroic assumption. That assumption is that the monopolization of the perfectly competitive industry does not change the cost structure. If monopolization results in higher marginal cost, the cost to society is even greater. Conversely, if monopolization results in cost savings, the cost, if any, to society is less than we infer from our analysis. Indeed, we could have presented a hypothetical example in which monopolization led to such a dramatic reduction in average cost that society actually benefited. Such a situation is a possibility in industries in which economies of scale exist for a very great range of outputs.

CONCEPTS IN BRIEF

- Four conditions are necessary for price discrimination: (1) The firm must face a downward-sloping demand curve, (2) the firm must be able to distinguish markets, (3) buyers in different markets must have different price elasticities of demand, and (4) resale of the product or service must be preventable.

- A monopolist can make higher profits if it can price-discriminate. Price discrimination requires that two or more identifiable classes of buyers exist whose price elasticities of demand for the product or service are different and that these two classes of buyers can be distinguished at little cost.

- Price differentiation should not be confused with price discrimination. The former occurs when differences in price reflect differences in marginal cost.

- Monopoly results in a lower quantity being sold because the price is higher than it would be in an ideal perfectly competitive industry in which the cost curves were essentially the same as the monopolist's.

The Right to Develop Drugs Based on Genetic Data

Concepts Applied: *Market power, price searcher, monopoly*

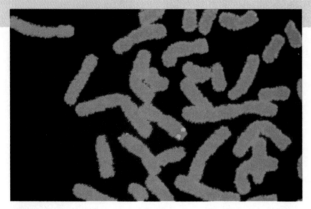

The pharmaceutical company SmithKline Beecham has a monopoly over much of the information about the genes in human chromosomes. SmithKline recoups its huge investment in gene research by licensing the information to other companies.

The pharmaceutical company SmithKline Beecham, through a research pact with Human Genome Sciences, Inc., claims to have isolated almost 50,000 human genes. Roche Holding of Switzerland and Glaxo Holdings of England have formed similar alliances, but none has been as successful as SmithKline. The question for each company is whether it should use its successful gene discoveries in developing its own drugs or sell or license the genetic sequences to other drug companies.

The Controversy

Because the area in question relates to health care, there is a controversy. Does not SmithKline owe to humanity the valuable information it has? A few years ago, academic researchers called on SmithKline to make public its information on the molecular arrangement of a gene. The molecular sequence is the biological blueprint of a gene. Therefore, knowledge of it allows a company to make a drug that will enhance or block the gene's functioning in order to treat a disease. Researchers have already learned the molecular sequence for the gene that causes breast cancer, the gene that causes obesity, and the gene that causes type II (non-insulin-dependent) diabetes.

Monopoly Returns Needed

According to George Poste, SmithKline's research director, his company is not about to publish the initial information on the molecular arrangement of a gene. "The more people who get access to sequence data, the greater the number of competitors we have." After all, SmithKline paid $125 million for its association with Human Genome, Inc. SmithKline wants to make at least a normal rate of return on that investment.

The New Market in Genes

SmithKline decided to sell the rights to genes rather than exploit the new information itself in the form of new drugs. The firm decided that even large pharmaceutical companies can handle only a small percentage of the genetic data that are available. SmithKline believes that it can earn higher profits by obtaining licensing royalties on the new drugs based on its genetic discoveries than by developing them itself. Presumably, it charges higher than its marginal cost at all times. After all, it is in a classic monopoly position. It owns the rights to the genetic data. If it were to charge marginal cost, that would be effectively zero. That is the nature of many discoveries today. There are huge initial costs for the first unit but zero marginal costs for each additional unit. SmithKline could pass on genetic data over the Internet essentially free, if it so chose.

FOR CRITICAL ANALYSIS

1. It is "bad" for the economy that SmithKline is not charging a price equal to marginal cost for its genetic data discoveries?
2. Does SmithKline have a pure monopoly with respect to genetic data?

CHAPTER SUMMARY

1. We formally define a monopolist as the single supplier of a product or service with no close substitute. A monopolist faces the entire industry demand curve because the monopolist *is* the industry. Pure monopolists are rare.

2. A monopolist can usually remain a monopolist only if other firms are prevented from entering the industry and sharing in the monopoly profits. One barrier to entry is government restrictions. Patents are another.

3. A monopoly could arise because of firm economies of scale, which are defined as a situation in which an increase in output leads to a more than proportionate decrease in average total costs. If this were the case, average total costs would be falling as production increased. The first company to produce a great deal and take advantage of firm economies of scale could conceivably lower price and drive everyone else out of the industry. This would be a natural monopolist.

4. Health and quality regulations can be a barrier to entry because the increased fixed costs put smaller firms at a competitive disadvantage.

5. The marginal revenue that a monopolist receives is defined in the same way as the marginal revenue that a competitor receives. Nevertheless, because the monopolist faces the industry demand curve, it must lower price to increase sales, not only on the last unit sold, but also on all the preceding units. The monopolist's marginal revenue is therefore equal to the price received on the last unit sold minus the reduction in price on all the previous units times the number of previous units sold.

6. The profit-maximizing price that the monopolist charges is the maximum price that it can get away with while still selling everything produced up to the point where marginal revenue equals marginal cost.

We find this price by extending a vertical line from the intersection of the marginal revenue curve and the marginal cost curve up to the demand curve and then over to the vertical axis, which measures price.

7. Total profits are total revenues minus total costs. Total revenues are equal to the price of the product (the profit-maximizing price) times the quantity produced (the quantity found at the intersection of the marginal revenue and marginal cost curves). Total costs are equal to the quantity produced times average total costs. The difference between these total costs and total revenues is profits.

8. It can be shown that a competitive industry, if monopolized, will end up charging a higher price for its product but supplying a lower quantity of it. That is why monopolies are considered "bad" in an economic analysis. The monopolist will restrict production and increase price.

9. If a monopolist can effectively separate demanders into groups according to their demand elasticities, it can become a price-discriminating monopolist. (Resale between groups that were charged different prices must be prevented.) Price discrimination should not be confused with price differentiation, which occurs when differences in price reflect differences in marginal cost.

10. Four conditions are necessary for price discrimination to exist: (1) The firm must face a downward-sloping demand curve, (2) the firm must be able to distinguish markets, (3) buyers in different markets must have different price elasticities of demand, and (4) the firm must be able to prevent resale of the product.

11. Monopoly involves costs to society because the higher price leads to a reduction in output and consumption of the monopolized good.

DISCUSSION OF PREVIEW QUESTIONS

1. For the monopolist, marginal revenue is less than selling price. Why?

In the perfectly competitive model, the firm's selling price equals its marginal revenue (MR) because the firm can sell all it wants to sell at the going market price. This is not the case for the monopolist, which, as the sole supplier, faces the (downward-sloping) demand curve for the product. Thus the monopolist can sell more only by lowering price on all units sold per time period, assuming that it can't discriminate on price. Thus the monopolist's marginal revenue will equal price (which it gains from selling one more unit) *minus* the revenue that it loses from selling previously produced units at a lower price.

2. **What is the profit-maximizing rate of output for the monopolist?**

A monopolist will produce up to the point where marginal cost (MC) equals marginal revenue (MR). For example, if the output rate for the monopolist at which MR = MC is 80,000 units per week and MR is falling while MC is rising, any output beyond 80,000 units will have MC > MR; to produce units beyond 80,000 units will lower total profits. To produce at a rate less than 80,000 units per week would mean that not all the outputs at which MR > MC will be produced; hence total profits would not be maximized. Total profits are maximized at the output rate where MR = MC because all outputs for which MR > MC will be produced.

3. **What are some common misconceptions about monopolists?**

Many people think that a monopolist charges the highest price possible. This is untrue; the monopolist tries to maximize *total profits*, not price. The monopolist produces where MR = MC and *then* charges the highest price consistent with that output rate. Note that a monopolist can't charge any price *and* sell any amount; it must choose a price and have the amount that it can sell be determined by the demand curve, or it must choose an output rate (where MR = MC) and have selling price determined by where that quantity intersects the demand curve. Another common misconception is that a monopolist must earn economic profits. This is not the case. To take an extreme example, if the monopolist's average cost curve lies above the demand curve, the monopolist will be suffering economic losses.

4. **What is the cost to society of monopoly?**

Because barriers to entry exist under monopoly, a monopolist could theoretically earn economic profits in the long run. Because profits are a signal that society wants more resources in that area, a misallocation of resources could exist; not enough resources flow to production of the monopolized commodity. Also, because the monopolist's selling price (P) exceeds its marginal revenue (MR) and the profit-maximizing output rate is where MR = MC (marginal cost), $P >$ MR = MC, or simply $P >$ MC (unlike under the perfectly competitive market structure, where $P =$ MC). The marginal cost of the commodity reflects what society had to give up in order to get the last unit produced, and price is what buyers have to pay in order to get it. Because $P >$ MC under monopoly, buyers must pay *more* to get this commodity than they must give up in order to get it; hence not enough of this commodity is produced. In short, under monopoly, price is higher and output is less than under perfect competition.

PROBLEMS

(Answers to the odd-numbered problems appear at the back of the book.)

24-1. Use the graph to answer the questions.

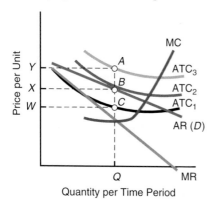

Quantity per Time Period

a. Suppose that a monopolist faces ATC_1. Define the rectangle that shows the monopolist's total costs at output rate Q. Also define the rectangle showing total revenue. Is the monopolist showing an economic loss, break-even (normal profit), or an economic profit? What is the significance of the MC = MR output?

b. Suppose that the monopolist faces ATC_2. Define the rectangle that shows the monopolist's total costs at output rate Q. Also define the rectangle showing total revenue. Is the monopolist showing an economic loss, break-even (normal profit), or an economic profit? What is the significance of the MC = MR output?

c. Suppose that the monopolist faces ATC_3. Define the rectangle that shows the monopolist's total costs at output rate Q. Also define the rectangle showing total revenue. Is the monopolist showing an economic loss, break-even (normal profit), or an economic profit? What is the significance of the MC = MR output?

24-2. Suppose that a monopolist faces the following demand schedule. Compute marginal revenue.

Price	Quantity Demanded	Marginal Revenue
$1,000	1	$_____
920	2	_____
840	3	_____
760	4	_____
680	5	_____
600	6	_____
520	7	_____
440	8	_____
350	9	_____
260	10	_____

24-3. State the necessary conditions for price discrimination. Then discuss how they might apply to the medical services of a physician.

24-4. In the text, we indicated that a monopolist will produce at the rate of output at which MR = MC and will then charge the highest price consistent with that output level. What conditions would exist if the monopolist charged a lower price? A higher price?

24-5. Summarize the relationship between price elasticity of demand and marginal revenue.

24-6. Explain why a monopolist will never set a price (and produce the corresponding output) at which the demand is price-inelastic.

24-7. Examine the revenue and cost figures for a monopoly firm in the table at the bottom of the page.

a. Fill in the empty columns.
b. At what rate(s) of output would the firm operate at a loss?
c. At what rate(s) of output would the firm break even?
d. At what rate(s) of output would the firm be maximizing its profits, and what would those profits be?

24-8. Answer the questions based on the accompanying graph for a monopolist.

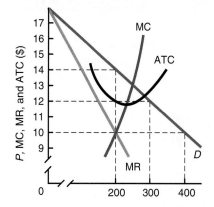

a. If this firm is a profit maximizer, how much output will it produce?
b. At what price will the firm sell its output?
c. How much profit or loss will this firm realize?
d. ATC is at its minimum at what cost per unit?

Price	Quantity Demanded	Total Revenue	Marginal Revenue	Total Cost	Marginal Cost	Profit or Loss
$20	0	$_____	$_____	$ 4	$_____	$_____
16	1	_____	_____	10	_____	_____
12	2	_____	_____	14	_____	_____
10	3	_____	_____	20	_____	_____
7	4	_____	_____	28	_____	_____
4	5	_____	_____	40	_____	_____
0	6	_____	_____	54	_____	_____

24-9. Examine this information for a monopoly product.

Price	Quantity
$10.00	1,000
8.00	2,000
6.00	3,000
4.00	4,000
2.00	5,000
.50	6,000

   a. Calculate total revenue.
   b. Calculate marginal revenue.

   c. What is the maximum output that the producer of this product would ever produce?
   d. Why would this firm never produce more than the output amount in part (c)?

24-10. Suppose that a single-price monopolist and a comparable perfectly competitive industry experience a cost increase that causes average and marginal cost curves to shift upward by 10 percent. Will the resulting increase in market price be greater or less for the monopolist than for the perfectly competitive industry?

COMPUTER-ASSISTED INSTRUCTION

Monopolists follow the rule of producing at a quantity at which MR = MC, yet the outcome differs somewhat from that under competition. Here we find out why, and we explore the consequences for the monopolist if it deviates from this rule.

Complete problem and answer appear on disk.

CHAPTER 25

MONOPOLISTIC COMPETITION, OLIGOPOLY, AND STRATEGIC BEHAVIOR

Growth in the telecommunications industry is explosive. One of the key players in this industry is the federal government through the Federal Communications Commission (FCC). The FCC controls how the electromagnetic spectrum is used. As recently as the early 1990s, the FCC gave away rights to cellular licenses. By the mid-1990s, the FCC had switched to a different method—the auction—to determine which companies would own certain new frequencies that had been opened up. In the process, the U.S. Treasury picked up quite a few billion dollars and telecommunication companies learned a lot about how to behave strategically. To understand strategic behavior, you need to learn more about markets that are not perfectly competitive but at the same time are not pure monopolies.

PREVIEW QUESTIONS

1. What are the characteristics of the monopolistically competitive market structure?

2. How does the monopolistic competitor determine the equilibrium price-output combination?

3. How does the monopolistically competitive market structure differ from that of perfect competition?

4. What are the characteristics of the oligopolistic market structure?

557

Did You Know That ... the so-called father of the modern department store, John
Wanamaker, once said, "Half the money I spend on advertising is wasted. The trouble
is, I don't know which half"? Obviously, American businesses do not know either, for they
continue to advertise more each year. Total advertising expenditures amount to billions of
dollars every year. The number of ads popping up on the Internet's World Wide Web shows
that American businesses will leave no stone unturned in their quest to let people know
about their existence, what they have to sell, how they sell it, where it can be bought, and
at what price.

Advertising did not show up in our analysis of perfect competition. Nonetheless, it plays
a large role in industries that cannot be described as perfectly competitive but cannot be
described as pure monopolies either. A combination of consumers' preferences for variety
and competition among producers has led to similar but *differentiated* products in the marketplace. This situation has been described as *monopolistic competition*, the subject of the
first part of this chapter. In the second part of the chapter, we look at how firms that are neither perfect competitors nor pure monopolists make strategic decisions. Such decisions do
not exist for pure monopolists, who do not have to worry about actual competitors. And
clearly, perfect competitors cannot make any strategic decisions, for they must take the
market price as given. We call firms that have the ability to make strategic decisions
oligopolies, which we will define more formally later in this chapter.

MONOPOLISTIC COMPETITION

In the 1920s and 1930s, economists became increasingly aware that there were many
industries for which both the perfectly competitive model and the pure monopoly model
did not apply and did not seem to yield very accurate predictions. Theoretical and empirical research was instituted to develop some sort of middle ground. Two separately developed models of **monopolistic competition** resulted. At Harvard, Edward Chamberlin published *The Theory of Monopolistic Competition* in 1933. The same year, Britain's Joan
Robinson published *The Economics of Imperfect Competition*. In this chapter we will outline the theory as presented by Chamberlin.

Chamberlin defined monopolistic competition as a market structure in which there is a
relatively large number of producers offering similar but differentiated products. Monopolistic competition therefore has the following features:

Monopolistic competition
A market situation in which a
large number of firms produce
similar but not identical products. Entry into the industry is
relatively easy.

1. Significant numbers of sellers in a highly competitive market
2. Differentiated products
3. Sales promotion and advertising
4. Easy entry of new firms in the long run

Even a cursory look at the American economy leads to the conclusion that monopolistic
competition is the dominant form of market structure in the United States. Indeed, that is
true of all developed economies.

Number of Firms

In a perfectly competitive situation, there is an extremely large number of firms; in pure
monopoly, there is only one. In monopolistic competition, there is a large number of firms,
but not as many as in perfect competition. This fact has several important implications for
a monopolistically competitive industry.

1. *Small share of market.* With so many firms, each firm has a relatively small share of the total market. Thus it has only a very small amount of control over the market clearing price.
2. *Lack of collusion.* With so many firms, it is very difficult for all of them to get together to collude—to cooperate in setting a pure monopoly price (and output). Price rigging in a monopolistically competitive industry is virtually impossible. Also, barriers to entry are minor, and the flow of new firms into the industry makes collusive agreements less likely. The large number of firms makes the monitoring and detection of cheating very costly and extremely difficult. This difficulty is compounded by differentiated products and high rates of innovation; collusive agreements are easier for a homogeneous product than for heterogeneous ones.
3. *Independence.* Because there are so many firms, each one acts independently of the others. No firm attempts to take into account the reaction of all of its rival firms—that would be impossible with so many rivals. Rivals' reactions to output and price changes are largely ignored.

Product Differentiation

Product differentiation

The distinguishing of products by brand name, color, and other minor attributes. Product differentiation occurs in other than perfectly competitive markets in which products are, in theory, homogeneous, such as wheat or corn.

Perhaps the most important feature of the monopolistically competitive market is **product differentiation.** We can say that each individual manufacturer of a product has an absolute monopoly over its own product, which is slightly differentiated from other similar products. This means that the firm has some control over the price it charges. Unlike the perfectly competitive firm, it faces a downward-sloping demand curve.

Consider the abundance of brand names for toothpaste, soap, gasoline, vitamins, shampoo, and most other consumer goods and a great many services. We are not obliged to buy just one type of television set, just one type of jeans, or just one type of footwear. There are usually a number of similar but differentiated products from which to choose. One reason is that the greater a firm's success at product differentiation, the greater the firm's pricing options.

Each separate differentiated product has numerous similar substitutes. This clearly has an impact on the price elasticity of demand for the individual firm. Recall that one determinant of price elasticity of demand is the availability of substitutes: The greater the number of substitutes available, other things being equal, the greater the price elasticity of demand. If the consumer has a vast array of alternatives that are just about as good as the product under study, a relatively small increase in the price of that product will lead many consumers to switch to one of the many close substitutes. Thus the ability of a firm to raise the price above the price of *close* substitutes is very small. The result of this is that even though the demand curve slopes downward, it does so only slightly. In other words, it is relatively elastic (over that price range) compared to a monopolist's demand curve. In the extreme case, with perfect competition, the substitutes are perfect because we are dealing with only one particular undifferentiated product. In that case, the individual firm has a perfectly elastic demand curve.

Ease of Entry

For any current monopolistic competitor, potential competition is always lurking in the background. The easier—that is, the less costly—entry is, the more a current monopolistic competitor must worry about losing business.

A good example of a monopolistically competitive industry is the computer software industry. Many small firms provide different programs for many applications. The fixed capital costs required to enter this industry are small; all you need are skilled programmers. In addition, there are few legal restrictions. The firms in this industry also engage in extensive advertising in over 150 computer publications.

Sales Promotion and Advertising

Monopolistic competition differs from perfect competition in that no individual firm in a perfectly competitive market will advertise. A perfectly competitive firm, by definition, can sell all that it wants to sell at the going market price anyway. Why, then, would it spend even one penny on advertising? Furthermore, by definition, the perfect competitor is selling a product that is identical to the product that all other firms in the industry are selling. Any advertisement that induces consumers to buy more of that product will, in effect, be helping all the competitors, too. A perfect competitor therefore cannot be expected to incur any advertising costs (except for all firms in an industry collectively agreeing to advertise to urge the public to buy more beef or drink more milk).

But because the monopolistic competitor has at least *some* monopoly power, advertising may result in increased profits. Advertising is used to increase demand and to differentiate one's product. How much advertising should be undertaken? It should be carried to the point at which the additional revenue from one more dollar of advertising just equals that one dollar of marginal cost.

Advertising as Signaling Behavior. Recall from Chapter 23 that signals are compact gestures or actions that convey information. For example, high profits in an industry are signals that resources should flow to that industry. Individual companies can explicitly engage in signaling behavior. They do so by establishing brand names or trademarks, and then promoting them heavily. This is a signal to prospective consumers that this is a company that plans to stay in business. Before the modern age of advertising, banks in America faced a problem of signaling their soundness. They chose to make the bank building large, imposing, and constructed out of marble and granite. Stone communicated permanence. The effect was to give the bank's customers confidence that they were not doing business with a fly-by-night operation.

When Dell Computer advertises its brand name heavily, it incurs substantial costs. The only way it can recoup those costs is by selling lots of Dell computers over a long period of time. Thus heavy advertising of its brand name is a signal to personal computer buyers that Dell is interested in each customer's repeat business.

But what about advertising that does not seem to convey any information, not even about price? What good is an advertisement for, say, Wal-Mart that simply states, "We give you value that you can count on"?

EXAMPLE
Can Advertising Lead to Efficiency?

Advertising budgets by major retailers may just seem like an added expense, not a step on the road to economic efficiency. According to research by economists Kyle Bagwell of Northwestern University and Garey Ramey of the University of California at San Diego, just the opposite is true. When retailers advertise heavily, they increase the number of shoppers that come to their store. Such increased traffic allows retailers to offer a wider selection of goods, to invest in cost-reduction technology (such as computerized inventory and satellite communications), and to exploit manufacturers' quantity discounts. Such cost reductions can help explain the success of Wal-Mart, Circuit City, and Home Depot. Consequently, Bagwell and Ramey conclude that advertising can help promote efficiency even if it provides no "hard" information. Advertising signals to consumers where they can find big-company, low-priced, high-variety stores.

FOR CRITICAL ANALYSIS: Which is true, then: "We are bigger because we are better" or "We are better because we are bigger"? ●

CONCEPTS IN BRIEF

- Monopolistic competition is a market structure that lies between pure monopoly and perfect competition.

- A monopolistically competitive market structure has (1) a large number of sellers, (2) differentiated products, (3) advertising, and (4) easy entry of firms in the long run.

- Because of the large number of firms, each has a small share of the market, making collusion difficult; the firms are independent.

PRICE AND OUTPUT FOR THE MONOPOLISTIC COMPETITOR

Now that we are aware of the assumptions underlying the monopolistic competition model, we can analyze the price and output behavior of each firm in a monopolistically competitive industry. We assume in the analysis that follows that the desired product type and quality have been chosen. We further assume that the budget and the type of promotional activity have already been chosen and do not change.

The Individual Firm's Demand and Cost Curves

Because the individual firm is not a perfect competitor, its demand curve slopes downward, as is shown in all three panels of Figure 25-1 on page 562. Hence it faces a marginal revenue curve that is also downward-sloping and below the demand curve. To find the profit-maximizing rate of output and the profit-maximizing price, we go to the output where the marginal cost curve intersects the marginal revenue curve from below. That gives us the profit-maximizing output rate. Then we draw a vertical line up to the demand curve. That gives us the price that can be charged to sell exactly that quantity produced. This is what we have done in Figure 25-1. In each panel, a marginal cost curve intersects the marginal revenue curve at E. The profit-maximizing rate of output is q_e, and the profit-maximizing price is P.

Short-Run Equilibrium

In the short run, it is possible for a monopolistic competitor to make economic profits— profits over and above the normal rate of return or beyond what is necessary to keep that firm in that industry. We show such a situation in panel (a) of Figure 25-1. The average total

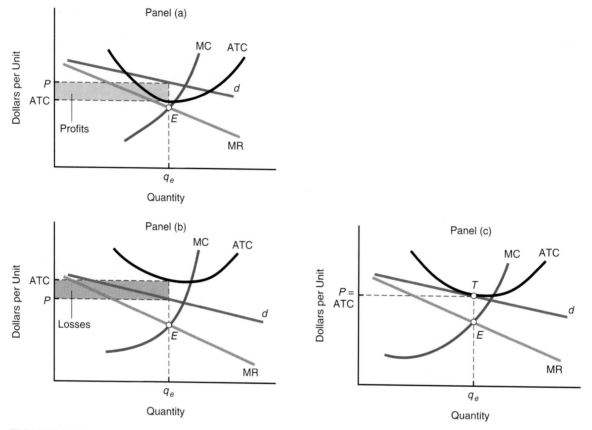

FIGURE 25-1

Short-Run and Long-Run Equilibrium with Monopolistic Competition
In panel (a), the typical monopolistic competitor is shown making economic profits. If that were the situation, there would be entry into the industry, forcing the demand curve for the individual monopolistic competitor leftward. Eventually, firms would find themselves in the situation depicted in panel (c), where zero economic profits are being made. In panel (b), the typical firm is in a monopolistically competitive industry making economic losses. If that were the case, firms would leave the industry. Each remaining firm's demand curve would shift outward to the right. Eventually, the typical firm would find itself in the situation depicted in panel (c).

cost curve is drawn in below the demand curve, d, at the profit-maximizing rate of output, q_e. Economic profits are shown by the shaded rectangle in that panel.

Losses in the short run are clearly also possible. They are presented in panel (b) of Figure 25-1. Here the average total cost curve lies everywhere above the individual firm's demand curve, d. The losses are marked as the shaded rectangle.

Just as with any market structure or any firm, in the short run it is possible to observe either economic profits or economic losses. (In the long run such is not the case with monopolistic competition, however.) In either case, the price does not equal marginal cost but rather is above it. Therefore, there is some misallocation of resources, a topic that we will discuss later in this chapter.

The Long Run: Zero Economic Profits

The long run is where the similarity between perfect competition and monopolistic competition becomes more obvious. In the long run, because so many firms produce substitutes for the product in question, any economic profits will disappear with competition. They will be reduced to zero either through entry by new firms seeing a chance to make a higher rate of return than elsewhere or by changes in product quality and advertising outlays by existing firms in the industry. (Profitable products will be imitated by other firms.) As for economic losses in the short run, they will disappear in the long run because the firms that suffer them will leave the industry. They will go into another business where the expected rate of return is at least normal. Panels (a) and (b) of Figure 25-1 therefore represent only short-run situations for a monopolistically competitive firm. In the long run, the average total cost curve will just touch the individual firm's demand curve *d* at the particular price that is profit-maximizing for that particular firm. This is shown in panel (c) of Figure 25-1.

A word of warning: This is an idealized, long-run equilibrium situation for each firm in the industry. It does not mean that even in the long run we will observe every single firm in a monopolistically competitive industry making *exactly* zero economic profits or *just* a normal rate of return. We live in a dynamic world. All we are saying is that if this model is correct, the rate of return will *tend toward* normal—economic profits will *tend toward* zero.

COMPARING PERFECT COMPETITION WITH MONOPOLISTIC COMPETITION

If both the monopolistic competitor and the perfect competitor make zero economic profits in the long run, how are they different? The answer lies in the fact that the demand curve for the individual perfect competitor is perfectly elastic. Such is not the case for the individual monopolistic competitor; its demand curve is less than perfectly elastic. This firm has some control over price. Price elasticity of demand is not infinite.

We see the two situations in Figure 25-2 on page 564. Both panels show average total costs just touching the respective demand curves at the particular price at which the firm is selling the product. Notice, however, that the perfect competitor's average total costs are at a minimum. This is not the case with the monopolistic competitor. The equilibrium rate of output is to the left of the minimum point on the average total cost curve where price is greater than marginal cost. The monopolistic competitor cannot expand output to the point of minimum costs without lowering price, and then marginal cost would exceed marginal revenue. A monopolistic competitor at profit maximization charges a price that exceeds marginal cost. In this respect it is similar to the monopolist.

It has consequently been argued that monopolistic competition involves waste because minimum average total costs are not achieved and price exceeds marginal cost. There are too many firms, each with excess capacity, producing too little output. According to critics of monopolistic competition, society's resources are being wasted.

Chamberlin had an answer to this criticism. He contended that the difference between the average cost of production for a monopolistically competitive firm in an open market and the minimum average total cost represented what he called the cost of producing

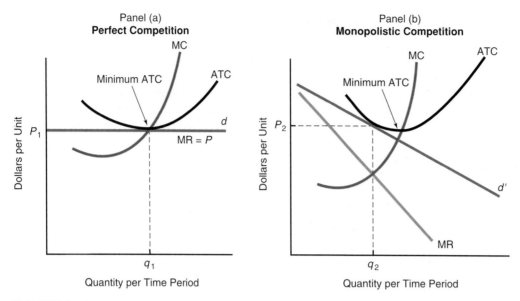

FIGURE 25-2

Comparison of the Perfect Competitor with the Monopolistic Competitor

In panel (a), the perfectly competitive firm has zero economic profits in the long run. The price is set equal to marginal cost, and the price is P_1. The firm's demand curve is just tangent to the minimum point on its average total cost curve, which means that the firm is operating at an optimum rate of production. With the monopolistically competitive firm in panel (b), there are also zero economic profits in the long run. The price is greater than marginal cost; the monopolistically competitive firm does not find itself at the minimum point on its average total cost curve. It is operating at a rate of output to the left of the minimum point on the ATC curve.

"differentness." Chamberlin did not consider this difference in cost between perfect competition and monopolistic competition a waste. In fact, he argued that it is rational for consumers to have a taste for differentiation; consumers willingly accept the resultant increased production costs in return for choice and variety of output.

CONCEPTS IN BRIEF

- In the short run, it is possible for monopolistically competitive firms to make economic profits or economic losses.

- In the long run, monopolistically competitive firms will make zero economic profits—that is, they will make a normal rate of return.

- Because the monopolistic competitor faces a downward-sloping demand curve, it does not produce at the minimum point on its average total cost curve. Hence we say that a monopolistic competitor has higher average total costs per unit than a perfect competitor would have.

- Chamberlin argued that the difference between the average cost of production for a monopolistically competitive firm and the minimum average total cost at which a competitive firm would produce is the cost of producing "differentness."

OLIGOPOLY

There is another market structure that we have yet to discuss, and it is an important one indeed. It involves a situation in which a few large firms dominate an entire industry. They are not competitive in the sense that we have used the term; they are not even monopolistically competitive. And because there are several of them, a pure monopoly does not exist. We call such a situation an **oligopoly,** which consists of a small number of interdependent sellers. Each firm in the industry knows that other firms will react to its changes in prices, quantities, and qualities. An oligopoly market structure can exist for either a homogeneous or a differentiated product.

Oligopoly
A market situation in which there are very few sellers. Each seller knows that the other sellers will react to its changes in prices and quantities.

Characteristics of Oligopoly

Oligopoly is characterized by the small number of interdependent firms that constitute the entire market.

Small Number of Firms. How many is "a small number of firms"? More than two but less than 100? The question is not easy to answer. Basically, though, oligopoly exists when a handful of firms dominate the industry enough to set prices. The top few firms in the industry account for an overwhelming percentage of total industry output.

Oligopolies usually involve three to five big companies dominating the industry. Between World War II and the 1970s, the U.S. automobile industry was dominated by three firms—General Motors, Chrysler, and Ford. Chewing-gum manufacturing and coin-operated amusement games are dominated by four large firms.

Strategic dependence
A situation in which one firm's actions with respect to price, quality, advertising, and related changes may be strategically countered by the reactions of one or more other firms in the industry. Such dependence can exist only when there are a limited number of major firms in an industry.

Interdependence. All markets and all firms are, in a sense, interdependent. But only when a few large firms dominate an industry does the question of **strategic dependence** of one on the others' actions arise. The firms must recognize that they are interdependent. Any action on the part of one firm with respect to output, price, quality, or product differentiation will cause a reaction on the part of other firms. A model of such mutual interdependence is difficult to build, but examples are not hard to find in the real world. Oligopolists in the cigarette industry, for example, are constantly reacting to each other.

Recall that in the model of perfect competition, each firm ignores the reactions of other firms because each firm is able to sell all that it wants at the going market price. At the other extreme, the pure monopolist does not have to worry about the reaction of current rivals because there are none. In an oligopolistic market structure, the managers of firms are like generals in a war: *They must attempt to predict the reaction of rival firms.* It is a strategic game.

Why Oligopoly Occurs

Why are some industries dominated by a few large firms? What causes an industry that might otherwise be competitive to tend toward oligopoly? We can provide some partial answers here.

Economies of Scale. Perhaps the strongest reason that has been offered for the existence of oligopoly is economies of scale. Recall that economies of scale are defined as a situation in which a doubling of output results in less than a doubling of total costs. When economies of scale exist, the firm's average total cost curve will slope downward as the firm produces more and more output. Average total cost can be reduced by continuing to expand the scale of operation. Smaller firms in such a situation will have a tendency to be inefficient. Their average total costs will be greater than those incurred by a large firm. Little by little, they will go out of business or be absorbed into the larger firm.

Barriers to Entry. It is possible that certain barriers to entry have prevented more competition in oligopolistic industries. They include legal barriers, such as patents, and control and ownership over critical supplies. Indeed, we can find periods in the past when firms maintained market power because they were able not only to erect a barrier to entry but also to keep it in place year after year. In principle, the chemical, electronics, and aluminum industries have been at one time or another either monopolistic or oligopolistic because of the ownership of patents and the control of strategic inputs by specific firms.

Oligopoly by Merger. Another reason that oligopolistic market structures may sometimes develop is that firms merge. A merger is the joining of two or more firms under single ownership or control. The merged firm naturally becomes larger, enjoys greater economies of scale as output increases, and may ultimately have a greater ability to control the market price for its product.

There are two types of mergers, horizontal and vertical. A **horizontal merger** involves firms selling a similar product. If two shoe manufacturing firms merge, that is a horizontal merger. If a group of firms, all producing steel, merge into one, that is also a horizontal merger. A **vertical merger** occurs when one firm merges with either a firm from which it purchases an input or a firm to which it sells its output. Vertical mergers occur, for example, when a coal-using electrical utility purchases a coal-mining firm or when a shoe manufacturer purchases retail shoe outlets. (Obviously, vertical mergers cannot create oligopoly as we have defined it.)

We have been talking about oligopoly in a theoretical manner until now. It is time to look at the actual picture of oligopolies in the United States.

Measuring Industry Concentration

As we have stated, oligopoly is a situation in which a few interdependent firms control a large part of total output in an industry. This has been called *industry concentration*. Before we show the concentration statistics in the United States, let's determine how industry concentration can be measured.

Concentration Ratio. The most popular way to compute industry concentration is to determine the percentage of total sales or production accounted for by the top four or top eight firms in an industry. This gives the four- or eight-firm **concentration ratio.** An example of an industry with 25 firms is given in Table 25-1. We can see in that table that the four largest firms account for almost 90 percent of total output in the hypothetical industry. That is an example of an oligopoly.

U.S. Concentration Ratios. Table 25-2 shows the four-firm *domestic* concentration ratios for various industries. Is there any way that we can show or determine which indus-

---

THINKING CRITICALLY ABOUT THE MEDIA

The "Big Three"

Media references to the automobile industry often make mention of "Detroit" or the "Big Three," referring to Ford, General Motors, and Chrysler. Indeed, the "Big Three" do account for about 90 percent of the value of total *domestic* shipments of motor vehicles. Thus it would seem that automobile manufacturing is a classic case of an oligopoly. Thirty years ago that was true; today it is not. The "Big Three" can no longer concern themselves merely with one another's reactions; they now have to worry about Toyota, Nissan, BMW, and a dozen other foreign competitors. Imports now account for almost 30 percent of total new car sales in the United States. The "Big Three" would love to be pure oligopolists in the U.S. market again, but increasing world trade has made that impossible.

Horizontal merger
The joining of firms that are producing or selling a similar product.

Vertical merger
The joining of a firm with another to which it sells an output or from which it buys an input.

Concentration ratio
The percentage of all sales contributed by the leading four or leading eight firms in an industry; sometimes called the *industry concentration ratio*.

TABLE 25-1
Computing the Four-Firm Concentration Ratio

Firm	Annual Sales ($ Millions)	
1	150	
2	100	= 400 Total number of Firms in industry = 25
3	80	
4	70	
5 through 25	50	
Total	450	

Four-firm concentration ratio $= \dfrac{400}{450} = 88.9\%$

tries to classify as oligopolistic? There is no definite answer. If we arbitrarily picked a four-firm concentration ratio of 75 percent, we could indicate that tobacco products, soft drinks, breakfast cereals, and domestic motor vehicles were oligopolistic. But we would always be dealing with an arbitrary definition.

The concept of an industry is necessarily arbitrary. As a consequence, concentration ratios rise as we narrow the definition of an industry and fall as we broaden it. Thus we must be certain that we are satisfied with the measurement of the industry under study before we jump to conclusions about whether the industry is too concentrated as evidenced by a high measured concentration ratio.

Oligopoly, Efficiency, and Resource Allocation

Although oligopoly is not the dominant form of market structure in the United States, oligopolistic industries do exist. To the extent that oligopolies have market power, they lead to resource misallocations, just as monopolies do. Oligopolies charge prices that exceed marginal cost. But what about oligopolies that occur because of economies of scale? One could argue that consumers end up paying lower prices than if the industry were composed of numerous smaller firms.

TABLE 25-2
Four-Firm Domestic Concentration Ratios for Selected U.S. Industries

Industry	Percentage of Value of Total Domestic Shipments Accounted For by the Top Four Firms
Domestic motor vehicles	90
Breakfast cereals	87
Soft drinks	85
Tobacco products	82
Primary aluminum	74
Transportation equipment	52
Petroleum and coal products	30
Printing and publishing	7

Source: U.S. Bureau of the Census.

All in all, there is no definite evidence of serious resource misallocation in the United States because of oligopolies. In any event, the more U.S. firms face competition from the rest of the world, the less any current oligopoly will be able to exercise market power.

CONCEPTS IN BRIEF

- An oligopoly is a market situation in which there are a small number of interdependent sellers.

- Oligopoly may result from (1) economies of scale, (2) barriers to entry, and (3) mergers.

- Horizontal mergers involve the joining of firms selling a similar product.

- Vertical mergers involve the merging of one firm either with the supplier of an input or the purchaser of its output.

- Industry concentration can be measured by the percentage of total sales accounted for by the top four or top eight firms.

STRATEGIC BEHAVIOR AND GAME THEORY

At this point, we should be able to show oligopoly price and output determination in the way we showed it for perfect competition, pure monopoly, and monopolistic competition, but we cannot. Whenever there are relatively few firms competing in an industry, each can and does react to the price, quantity, quality, and product innovations that the others undertake. In other words, each oligopolist has a **reaction function.** Oligopolistic competitors are interdependent. Consequently, the decision makers in such firms must employ strategies. And we must be able to model their strategic behavior if we wish to predict how prices and outputs are determined in oligopolistic market structures. In general, we can think of reactions of other firms to one firm's actions as part of a *game* that is played by all firms in the industry. Not surprisingly, economists have developed **game theory** models to describe firms' rational interactions. Game theory is the analytical framework in which two or more individuals, companies, or nations compete for certain payoffs that depend on the strategy that the others employ. Poker is such a game situation because it involves a strategy of bluffing.

Some Basic Notions About Game Theory

Games can be either cooperative or noncooperative. If firms get together to collude or form a cartel, that is considered a **cooperative game.** Whenever it is too costly for firms to negotiate such collusive agreements and to enforce them, they are in a **noncooperative game** situation. Most strategic behavior in the marketplace would be described as a noncooperative game.

Games can be classified by whether the payoffs are negative, zero, or positive. A **zero-sum game** is one in which one player's losses are offset by another player's gains; at any time, sum totals are zero. If two retailers have an absolutely fixed total number of customers, the customers that one retailer wins over are exactly equal to the customers that the other retailer loses. A **negative-sum game** is one in which players as a group lose at the end of the game (although one perhaps by more than the other, and it's possible for one or more

---

Reaction function
The manner in which one oligopolist reacts to a change in price, output, or quality made by another oligopolist in the industry.

Game theory
A way of describing the various possible outcomes in any situation involving two or more interacting individuals when those individuals are aware of the interactive nature of their situation and plan accordingly. The plans made by these individuals are known as *game strategies.*

Cooperative game
A game in which the players explicitly collude to make themselves better off. As applied to firms, it involves companies colluding in order to make higher than competitive rates of return.

Noncooperative game
A game in which the players neither negotiate nor collude in any way. As applied to firms in an industry, this is the common situation in which there are relatively few firms and each has some ability to change price.

Zero-sum game
A game in which any gains within the group are exactly offset by equal losses by the end of the game.

Negative-sum game
A game in which players as a group lose at the end of the game.

Positive-sum game
A game in which players as a group are better off at the end of the game.

Strategy
Any rule that is used to make a choice, such as "Always pick heads"; any potential choice that can be made by players in a game.

Dominant strategies
Strategies that always yield the highest benefit. Regardless of what other players do, a dominant strategy will yield the most benefit for the player using it.

Prisoners' dilemma
A famous strategic game in which two prisoners have a choice between confessing and not confessing to a crime. If neither confesses, they serve a minimum sentence. If both confess, they serve a maximum sentence. If one confesses and the other doesn't, the one who confesses goes free. The dominant strategy is always to confess.

Payoff matrix
A matrix of outcomes, or consequences, of the strategies available to the players in a game.

players to win). A **positive-sum game** is one in which players as a group end up better off. Some economists describe all voluntary exchanges as positive-sum games. After an exchange, both the buyer and the seller are better off than they were prior to the exchange.

Strategies in Noncooperative Games. Players, such as decision makers in oligopolistic firms, have to devise a **strategy,** which is defined as a rule used to make a choice. The goal of the decision maker is of course to devise a strategy that is more successful than alternative strategies. Whenever a firm's decision makers can come up with certain strategies that are generally successful no matter what actions competitors take, these are called **dominant strategies.** The dominant strategy always yields the unique best action for the decision maker no matter what action the other "players" undertake. Relatively few business decision makers over a long period of time have successfully devised dominant strategies. We know this by observation: Few firms in oligopolistic industries have maintained relatively high profits consistently over time.

EXAMPLE
The Prisoners' Dilemma

One real-world example of simple game theory involves what happens when two people, both involved in a bank robbery, are later caught. What should they do when questioned by police? The result has been called the **prisoners' dilemma.** The two suspects, Sam and Carol, are interrogated separately and confronted with alternative potential imprisonments. The interrogator indirectly indicates to Sam and Carol the following:

1. If both confess to the bank robbery, they will both go to jail for five years.
2. If neither confesses, they will each be given a sentence of two years on a lesser charge.
3. If one prisoner turns state's evidence and confesses, that prisoner goes free and the other one, who did not confess, will serve 10 years on bank robbery charges.

You can see the prisoners' alternatives in the **payoff matrix** in Figure 25-3. The two possibilities for each prisoner are "confess" and "don't confess." There are four possibilities:

1. Both confess.
2. Neither confesses.
3. Sam confesses (turns state's evidence) but Carol doesn't.
4. Carol confesses (turns state's evidence) but Sam doesn't.

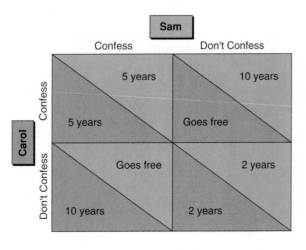

FIGURE 25-3

The Prisoners' Dilemma Payoff Matrix
Regardless of what the other prisoner does, each person is better off if he or she confesses. So confessing is the dominant strategy and each ends up behind bars for five years.

In Figure 25-3, all of Sam's possible outcomes are shown on the upper half of each rectangle, and all of Carol's possible outcomes are shown on the lower half.

By looking at the payoff matrix, you can see that if Carol confesses, Sam's best strategy is to confess also—he'll get only 5 years instead of 10. Conversely, if Sam confesses, Carol's best strategy is also to confess—she'll get 5 years instead of 10. Now let's say that Sam is being interrogated and Carol doesn't confess. Sam's best strategy is still to confess, because then he goes free instead of serving two years. Conversely, if Carol is being interrogated, her best strategy is still to confess even if Sam hasn't. She'll go free instead of serving 10 years. To confess is a dominant strategy for Sam. To confess is also a dominant strategy for Carol. The situation is exactly symmetrical. So this is the prisoners' dilemma. The prisoners know that both prisoners will be better off if neither confesses. Yet it is in each individual prisoner's interest to confess, even though the *collective* outcome of each prisoner's pursuing his or her own interest is inferior for both.

FOR CRITICAL ANALYSIS: Can you apply the prisoners' dilemma to the firms in a two-firm industry that agree to split the market? (Hint: Think about the payoff to cheating on the market-splitting agreement.) ●

Applying Game Theory to Pricing Strategies

We can apply game strategy to two firms—oligopolists—that have to decide on their pricing strategy. Each can choose either a high or a low price. Their payoff matrix is shown in Figure 25-4. If they each choose high prices, they can each make $6 million, but if they each choose low prices, they will only make $4 million each. If one sets a high price and the other a low one, the low-priced firm will make $8 million, but the high-priced firm will only make $2 million. As in the prisoners' dilemma, in the absence of collusion, they will end up choosing low prices.

Opportunistic Behavior

In the prisoners' dilemma, it was clear that cooperative behavior—both parties standing firm without admitting to anything—leads to the best outcome for both players. But each prisoner (player) stands to gain by cheating. Such action is called **opportunistic behavior.** Our daily economic activities involve the equivalent of the prisoners' dilemma all the time. We

Opportunistic behavior
Actions that ignore the possible long-run benefits of cooperation and focus solely on short-run gains.

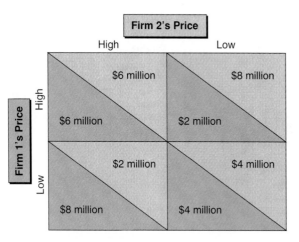

FIGURE 25-4

Game Theory and Pricing Strategies
This payoff matrix shows that if both oligopolists choose a high price, each makes $6 million. If they both choose a low price, each makes $4 million. If one chooses a low price and the other doesn't, the low-priced firm will make $8 million. Unless they collude, however, they will end up at the low-priced solution.

could engage in opportunistic behavior. You could write a check for a purchase knowing that it is going to bounce because you have just closed that bank account. When you agree to perform a specific task for pay, you could perform your work in a substandard way. When you go to buy an item, the seller might be able to cheat you by selling you a defective item.

In short, if all of us—sellers and buyers—engaged in opportunistic behavior all of the time, we would always end up in the bottom right-hand box of the prisoners' dilemma payoff matrix in Figure 25-3. We would constantly be acting in a world of noncooperative behavior. That is not the world in which most of us live, however. Why not? Because most of us engage in *repeat transactions.* Manufacturers would like us to keep purchasing their products. Sellers would like us to keep coming back to their stores. As a seller of labor services, each of us would like to keep our jobs, get promotions, or be hired away by another firm at a higher wage rate. We engage in a **tit-for-tat strategic behavior.** In tit-for-tat strategy, manufacturers and sellers continue to guarantee their merchandise, in spite of cheating by a small percentage of consumers.

Tit-for-tat strategic behavior
In game theory, cooperation that continues so long as the other players continue to cooperate.

INTERNATIONAL EXAMPLE
Collapsing Oil Prices

Sometimes, the tit-for-tat strategy is costly to market participants. Recall from Chapter 24 that the Organization of Petroleum Exporting Countries (OPEC) is a global cartel whose members control much of the world's output of crude oil. Under the terms of the tit-for-tat strategy, each OPEC member continues to cooperate as long as the other members do likewise. If anyone cheats on the cartel, the appropriate tit-for-tat response is to cut the price of crude oil and keep cutting prices until the original cheater reverts to the higher price previously agreed on by the cartel members. Saudi Arabia, the largest oil-producing member of OPEC, appears to have followed this strategy. It has effectively said to other members of OPEC, "If you adhere to your agreed-on production limits, so shall we; but if you expand production beyond those limits, so shall we." Sometimes Saudi Arabia has difficulty knowing whether an OPEC member has cheated. When Iraq and Iran were at war in the 1980s, both depended on oil production to finance their defense expenditures. Saudi Arabia thought they were both cheating on the OPEC agreements by expanding production. They claimed otherwise, but Saudi Arabia responded tit-for-tat by hiking production. Prices collapsed: In just one year (1985 to 1986), crude oil prices plunged from $24.10 to $12.50 per barrel.

FOR CRITICAL ANALYSIS: Why would you expect a major crude oil producer, such as Saudi Arabia, to take the lead in enforcing a tit-for-tat strategy? ●

PRICE RIGIDITY AND THE KINKED DEMAND CURVE

Let's hypothesize that the decision makers in an oligopolistic firm assume that rivals will react in the following way: They will match all price decreases (in order not to be undersold) but not price increases (because they want to capture more business). There is no collusion. The implications of this reaction function are rigid prices and a kinked demand curve.

Nature of the Kinked Demand Curve

In Figure 25-5, we draw a kinked demand curve, which is implicit in the assumption that oligopolists match price decreases but not price increases. We start off at a given price of

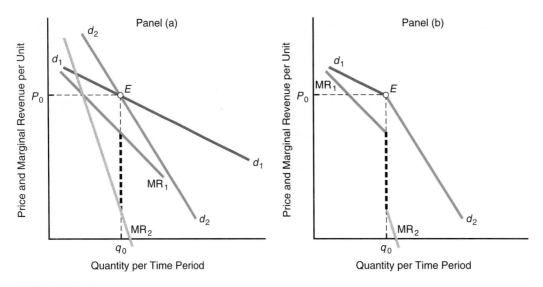

FIGURE 25-5

The Kinked Demand Curve

If the oligopolist firm assumes that rivals will not match price changes, it faces demand curve $d_1 d_1$ and marginal revenue curve MR_1. If it assumes that rivals will match price changes, it faces demand curve $d_2 d_2$ and marginal revenue curve MR_2. If the oligopolist believes that rivals will not react to price increases but will react to price decreases, at prices above P_0 it faces demand curve $d_1 d_1$ and at prices below P_0 it faces the other demand curve, $d_2 d_2$. The overall demand curve will therefore have a kink, as is seen in panel (b) at price P_0. The marginal revenue curve will have a vertical break, as shown by the dashed line in panel (b).

P_0 and assume that the quantity demanded at the price for this individual oligopolist is q_0. The starting price of P_0 is usually the stable market price. If the oligopolist assumes that rivals will not react, it faces demand curve $d_1 d_1$ with marginal revenue curve MR_1. Conversely, if it assumes that rivals will react, it faces demand curve $d_2 d_2$ with marginal revenue curve MR_2. More than likely, the oligopoly firm will assume that if it lowers price, rivals will react by matching that reduction to avoid losing their respective shares of the market. The oligopolist that initially lowers its price will not greatly increase its quantity demanded. So when it lowers its price, it believes that it will face demand curve $d_2 d_2$. But if it increases price above P_0, rivals will probably not follow suit. Thus a higher price than P_0 will cause quantity demanded to decrease rapidly. The demand schedule to the left of and above point E will be relatively elastic, as represented by $d_1 d_1$. At prices above P_0, the relevant demand curve is $d_1 d_1$, whereas below price P_0, the relevant demand curve will be $d_2 d_2$. Consequently, at point E there will be a *kink* in the resulting demand curve. This is shown in panel (b) of Figure 25-5, where the demand curve is labeled $d_1 d_2$. The resulting marginal revenue curve is labeled $MR_1 MR_2$. It has a discontinuous portion, or gap, represented by the boldfaced dashed vertical lines in both panels.

Price Rigidity

The kinked demand curve analysis may help explain why price changes might be infrequent in an oligopolistic industry without collusion. Each oligopolist can see only harm in a price change: If price is increased, the oligopolist will lose many of its customers to rivals who do not raise their prices. That is to say, the oligopolist moves up from point E along demand curve d_1 in panel (b) of Figure 25-5. However, if an oligopolist lowers its price, given that rivals will lower their prices too, its sales will not increase very much. Moving down from point E in panel (b) of Figure 25-5, we see that the demand curve is relatively inelastic. If the elasticity is less than 1, total revenues will fall rather than rise with the lowering of price. Given that the production of a larger output will increase total costs, the oligopolist's profits will fall. The lowering of price by the oligopolist might start a *price war* in which its rival firms will charge an even lower price.

The theoretical reason for price inflexibility under the kinked demand curve model has to do with the discontinuous portion of the marginal revenue curve shown in panel (b) of Figure 25-5, which we reproduce in Figure 25-6. Assume that marginal cost is represented by MC. The profit-maximizing rate of output is q_0, which can be sold at a price of P_0. Now assume that the marginal cost curve rises to MC'. What will happen to the profit-maximizing rate of output? Nothing. Both quantity and price will remain the same for this oligopolist.

Remember that the profit-maximizing rate of output is where marginal revenue equals marginal cost. The shift in the marginal cost curve to MC' does not change the profit-maximizing rate of output in Figure 25-6 because MC' still cuts the marginal revenue curve in the latter's discontinuous portion. Thus the equality between marginal revenue and marginal cost still holds at output rate q_0 even when the marginal cost curve shifts upward. What will happen when marginal costs fall to MC"? Nothing. This oligopolist will continue to produce at a rate of output q_0 and charge a price of P_0. Whenever the marginal cost curve cuts the discontinuous portion of the marginal revenue curve, fluctuations (within limits) in marginal cost will not affect output or price because the profit-maximizing condition MR = MC will hold. The result is that even when firms in an oligopolistic industry such as this experience increases or decreases in costs, their prices do not change as long as MC cuts MR in the discontinuous portion. Hence prices are seen to be rigid in oligopolistic industries if oligopolists react the way we assume they do in this model.

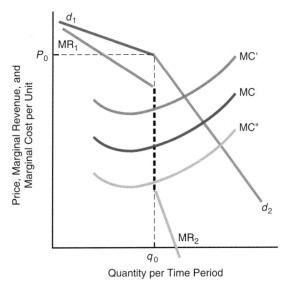

FIGURE 25-6

Changes in Cost May Not Alter the Profit-Maximizing Price and Output

As long as the marginal cost curve intersects the marginal revenue curve in the latter's discontinuous portion, the profit-maximizing price P_0 (and output q_0) will remain unchanged even with changes in MC. (However, the firm's rate of profit will change.)

Criticisms of the Kinked Demand Curve

One of the criticisms directed against the kinked demand curve is that we have no idea how the existing price, P_0, came to be. If every oligopolistic firm faced a kinked demand curve, it would not pay for it to change prices. The problem is that the kinked demand curve does not show us how demand and supply originally determine the going price of an oligopolist's product.

As far as the evidence goes, it is not encouraging. Oligopoly prices do not appear to be as rigid, particularly in the upward direction, as the kinked demand curve theory implies. During the 1970s and early 1980s, when prices in the economy were rising overall, oligopolistic producers increased their prices frequently. Evidence of price changes during the Great Depression showed that oligopolies changed prices much more frequently than monopolies.

EXAMPLE
Do Pet Products Have Nine Lives?

A. J. Heinz's Pet Products Company knows all about the kinked demand curve. It makes 9-Lives cat food. To meet increased competition (at lower prices) from Nestlé, Quaker, Grand Metropolitan, and Mars, Heinz dropped prices by over 22 percent on the wholesale price of a case of 9-Lives. Finally, it had "had enough." It decided to buck the trend by *raising* prices. The result? A disaster, because none of Heinz's four major competitors increased their prices. Heinz's market share dropped from 23 percent to 15 percent almost overnight.

FOR CRITICAL ANALYSIS: What does Heinz's experience with 9-Lives perhaps suggest about the price elasticity of demand for its product? ●

CONCEPTS IN BRIEF

- Each oligopolist has a reaction function because oligopolistic competitors are interdependent. They must therefore engage in strategic behavior. One way to model this behavior is to use game theory.

- Games can be either cooperative or noncooperative. A cartel is cooperative. When a cartel breaks down and its members start cheating, the industry becomes a noncooperative game. In a zero-sum game, one player's losses are exactly offset by another player's gains. In a negative-sum game, all players collectively lose, perhaps one more than the others. In a positive-sum game, the players as a group end up better off.

- Decision makers in oligopolistic firms must devise a strategy. A dominant strategy is one that is generally successful no matter what actions competitors take.

- The kinked demand curve oligopoly model predicts that major shifts in marginal cost will cause any change in industry price.

STRATEGIC BEHAVIOR WITH IMPLICIT COLLUSION: A MODEL OF PRICE LEADERSHIP

What if oligopolists do not actually collude to raise prices and share markets but do so implicitly? There are no formal cartel arrangements and no formal meetings. Nonetheless, there is *tacit collusion*. One example of this is the model of **price leadership**.

Price leadership
A practice in many oligopolistic industries in which the largest firm publishes its price list ahead of its competitors, who then match those announced prices. Also called *parallel pricing*.

In this model, the basic assumption is that the dominant firm, usually the biggest, sets the price and allows other firms to sell all they can at that price. The dominant firm then sells the rest. The dominant firm always makes the first move in a price leadership model. By definition, price leadership requires that one firm be the leader. Because of laws against collusion, firms in an industry cannot communicate this directly. That is why it is often natural for the largest firm to become the price leader. In the automobile industry during the period of General Motors' dominance (until the 1980s), that company was traditionally the price leader. At various times in the breakfast food industry, Kellogg was the price leader. Some observers have argued that Harvard University was the price leader among Ivy League schools. In the banking industry, various dominant banks have been price leaders in announcing changes in the prime rate, the interest rate charged on loans offered to the best credit risks. One day a large New York–based bank, such as Chase Manhattan, would announce an increase or decrease in its prime rate. Five or six hours later, all other banks would announce the same change in their prime rate.

Price Wars

Price war

A pricing campaign designed to drive competing firms out of a market by repeatedly cutting prices.

Price leadership may not always work. If the price leader ends up much better off than the firms that follow, the followers may in fact not set prices according to those set by the dominant firm. The result may be a **price war.** The dominant firm lowers its prices a little bit, but the other firms lower theirs even more. Price wars have occurred in many industries. Supermarkets within a given locale often engage in price wars, especially during holiday periods. One may offer turkeys at so much per pound on Wednesday; competing stores cut their price on turkeys on Thursday, so the first store cuts its price even more on Friday. We see price wars virtually every year in the airline industry.

EXAMPLE
Cigarette Price Wars

Price wars occur commonly between long-distance telephone companies, between airlines, and between the makers of cigarettes, soft drinks, computer disc drives, diapers, frozen dinners, and personal computer hardware and software. They do not always lead to the desired result for the company that started the price war. Consider the case of Philip Morris, which cut the price of Marlboro cigarettes by 40 cents a pack to about $1.80. Its main competitor, RJR Nabisco, matched the price cut for Camels. Philip Morris claimed victory because Marlboro's market share increased from 22.1 percent to 27.3 percent. But the domestic operating profits for both companies plummeted in the process; so, too, did the trading value of their stocks. According to business consultants Mike Marn and Robert Garda of the McKinsey Company, the reason is that most companies are unable to offset lower prices with higher volume because variable costs do not start falling until sales increase by about 20 percent. When Philip Morris cut its prices by 18 percent, unit sales increased by only 12.5 percent and profits fell by 25 percent.

FOR CRITICAL ANALYSIS: *How do price wars fit into the tit-for-tat strategic behavior of game theory?* ●

DETERRING ENTRY INTO AN INDUSTRY

Some economists believe that all decision making by existing firms in a stable industry involves some type of game playing. An important part of game playing does not have to do with how existing competitors might react to a decision by others. Rather, it has to do with how *potential* competitors might react. Strategic decision making requires that existing firms in an industry come up with strategies to deter entrance into that industry. One important way is, of course, to get a local, state, or federal government to restrict entry. Another way is to adopt certain pricing and investment strategies that may deter entry.

Increasing Entry Costs

One **entry deterrence strategy** is to raise the cost of entry by a new firm. The threat of a price war is one technique. To sustain a long price war, existing firms might invest in excess capacity so that they can expand output if necessary. When existing firms invest in excess capacity, they are signaling potential competitors that they will engage in a price war.

> **Entry deterrence strategy**
> Any strategy undertaken by firms in an industry, either individually or together, with the intent or effect of raising the cost of entry into the industry by a new firm.

Another way that existing domestic firms can raise the entry cost of foreign firms is by getting the U.S. government to pass stringent environmental or health and safety standards. These typically raise costs more for foreign producers, often in developing countries, than for domestic producers.

Limit-Pricing Strategies

If existing firms make it clear to potential competitors that the existing firms will not change their output rate after entry, this is a signal. It tells potential firms that the existing firm will simply lower its market price (moving down the firm demand curve) until it sells the same quantity as before the new entry came into the industry. The existing firms limit their price to be above competitive prices, but if there is a new entrant, the new limit price will be below the one at which the new firm can make a profit. This is called the **limit-pricing model.**

> **Limit-pricing model**
> A model that hypothesizes that a group of colluding sellers will set the highest common price that they believe they can charge without new firms seeking to enter that industry in search of relatively high profits.

Raising Customers' Switching Costs

If an existing firm can make it more costly for customers to switch from its product or service to a competitor's, the existing firm can deter entry. There are a host of ways in which existing firms can raise customers' switching costs. Makers of computer equipment have in the past produced operating systems and software that would not run on competitors' computers. Any customer wanting to change from one computer system to another faced a high switching cost.

EXAMPLE
High Switching Costs in the Credit World

One way banks keep their customers is by raising the cost of switching to a different bank. A few years ago, Security Pacific National Bank (now part of Bank of America) offered to rebate the points borrowers paid on mortgages after five years. Each point is equal to 1 percent of the loan amount and is a premium paid for obtaining a lower mortgage rate. Three points on a $100,000 loan would equal $3,000. Even though interest rates fell sharply after this program was launched, few customers at Security Pacific moved their mortgages to banks charging lower rates. After all, to refinance a mortgage at another bank before the end of the five-year period meant that the customer would lose out on the rebate.

Another example of high switching costs in the credit world involves the General Motors credit card, which offers a 5 percent rebate toward a new GM car (to a maximum of $5,000). If you have used this card for several years and have not yet accumulated $5,000 toward the purchase of a new General Motors vehicle, there is little chance you will switch to Citibank's Ford rebate card.

FOR CRITICAL ANALYSIS: What other credit card systems are in effect that raise switching costs across credit cards? ●

CONCEPTS IN BRIEF

- One type of strategic behavior involving implicit collusion is price leadership. The dominant firm is assumed to set the price and then allows other firms to sell all that they want to sell at that price. Whatever is left over is sold by the dominant firm. The dominant firm always makes the first move in a price leadership model. If the nondominant firms decide to compete, they may start a price war.

- One strategic decision may be to attempt to raise the cost of entry of new firms into an industry. The threat of a price war is one technique. Another is to lobby the federal government to pass stringent environmental or health and safety standards in an attempt to keep out foreign competition.

- If existing firms limit prices to a level above competitive prices before entry but are willing to reduce it, this is called a limit-pricing model.

- Another way to raise the cost to new firms is to make it more costly for customers to switch from one product or service to a competitor's.

COMPARING MARKET STRUCTURES

Now that we have looked at perfect competition, pure monopoly, monopolistic competition, and oligopoly, we are in a position to compare the attributes of these four different market structures. We do this in summary form in Table 25-3, in which we compare the number of sellers, their ability to set price, and whether product differentiation exists, and we give some examples of each of the four market structures.

TABLE 25-3
Comparing Market Structures

Market Structure	Number of Sellers	Unrestricted Entry and Exit	Ability to Set Price	Long-Run Economic Profits Possible	Product Differentiation	Nonprice Competition	Examples
Perfect competition	Numerous	Yes	None	No	None	None	Agriculture, coal
Monopolistic competition	Many	Yes	Some	Not for most firms	Considerable	Yes	Toothpaste, toilet paper, soap, retail trade
Oligopoly	Few	Partial	Some	Yes	Frequent	Yes	Cigarettes, steel
Pure monopoly	One	No (for entry)	Considerable	Yes	None (product is unique)	Yes	Electric company, local telephone company

Game Theory: The New Business Tool in Telecommunications

Concepts Applied: *Game theory, strategic behavior, supply and demand*

The electronic frequencies used in pagers and cellular phones are becoming more valuable as the wireless services market explodes. In two recent auctions of these frequencies run by the FCC, telecommunications companies paid more than $8 billion for licenses.

Parts of the electromagnetic spectrum are becoming more and more valuable. As digital technology becomes more reliable and cheaper to use, telecommunications companies are willing to pay more for the rights to use part of the electromagnetic spectrum. The Federal Communications Commission (FCC), under the authorization of Congress, started using a sophisticated auction method to "sell" parts of the spectrum. In a normal auction, bidders submit price offers in sealed envelopes, which are opened on a specific date, and the contract is awarded to the highest bidder. But more efficient results can be obtained using game theory. The parties who truly value certain frequencies for certain purposes are able to acquire them, and as an added benefit, the U.S. Treasury obtains more revenues.

Using Game Theory to Devise the Best Auction

The rules of the FCC auction for new licenses, developed with the help of economists specializing in game theory, consisted of the following:

1. Bidding is open, so every bidder knows what every other contender is bidding.

2. All licenses are offered simultaneously.
3. After all bids have been studied, another round of bidding occurs.
4. Bidders are allowed to change what they are bidding on, such as telecommunications services in Los Angeles or New York. Bidders are also allowed to combine licenses to create large territories.
5. The bidding continues until there are no higher bids.

What Determines Geographic Values?

Not every telecommunications firm will value different geographic areas the same. If you already own the rights to offer paging services in New York City, you will be willing to pay more to get those same rights in nearby New Jersey. If you are a telephone company already in a geographic area, you will be willing to bid more for the rights to a new paging service in that same area than a newcomer that does not already have service trucks and office buildings.

War Rooms

Each time the FCC has opened bidding for a new part of the electromagnetic spectrum in different geographic areas, potential bidders have set up "war rooms" to do competitor analyses—strategic modeling—to determine how much to bid and how. Each team studied the ability of competing companies to take on the extra debt to pay for purchase of the new licenses. Some teams even looked into the personal quirks and needs of the chief executive officers of other bidding companies. Some teams decided to signal to other players that they were willing to spend whatever it would take to gain the licenses in a specific geographic area. Pacific Telesis did this in one auction by taking out full-page newspaper ads months before the auction declaring its belief that it had great strategic advantages in California and stating, "We're determined to win the wireless licenses here."

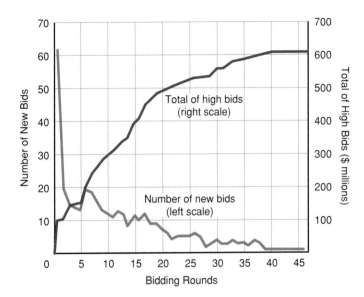

FIGURE 25-7
Bidding for FCC Licenses
When the FCC in July 1994 allowed for continuous new bids for new frequencies, it received fewer and fewer new bids over time, but the government's total take continued to rise. The bidding stopped after 46 rounds. The federal government received over $600 million.
Source: Peter C. Cranton, University of Maryland.

The Results

Figure 25-7 shows the results of the first auction based on game theory that the FCC held in July 1994. This auction was for narrowband personal communication services, such as pagers. The FCC (U.S. taxpayers) obtained $617 million.

The second such auction lasted three months, ending in the summer of 1995 after 112 rounds of bidding. The FCC's take: $7.7 billion.

FOR CRITICAL ANALYSIS

1. What alternative ways are there to sell parts of the electromagnetic spectrum to telecommunications firms?
2. What benefit did PacTel believe it would obtain by incurring advertising costs to announce its intentions to bid high for licenses in California?

CHAPTER SUMMARY

1. Numerous market situations lie between the extremes of pure competition and pure monopoly. Monopolistic competition and oligopoly are two of these situations.
2. Monopolistic competition is a theory developed by Edward Chamberlin of Harvard University in 1933. It refers to a market composed of specific product groups in which the different companies involved have slight monopoly powers because each has a product slightly different from the others. Examples of product groups might include the toothpaste and soap industries. The monopolistic competitor ends up with zero economic profits because there is free entry into the industry. However, according to Chamberlin, the monopolistic competitor does not produce where

price equals marginal costs and therefore does not produce at the minimum point on the average total cost curve.

3. Advertising occurs in industries in which the firms are not pure price takers. The basic goal of advertisers is to increase demand for their product.
4. In the short run, it is possible for a monopolistic competitor to make economic profits or economic losses. In the long run, monopolistic competitors make zero economic profits (that is, they make just the normal rate of return).
5. When we compare monopolistic competition with perfect competition, we find that the monopolistic competitor does not produce where average total costs are at a minimum, whereas the perfect competitor does.

6. Oligopoly is a market situation in which there are just a few firms. Each firm knows that its rivals will react to a change in price. Oligopolies are usually defined as industries in which the four-firm concentration ratio is relatively high.

7. Oligopolies are characterized by relatively high barriers to entry, interdependence, product differentiation, and growth through merger.

8. Each oligopolist has a reaction function because oligopolistic competitors are interdependent and must therefore engage in strategic behavior. One way to model this behavior is to use game theory.

9. Games can be either cooperative or noncooperative. A cartel is cooperative. When a cartel breaks down and its members start cheating, the industry becomes a noncooperative game. In a zero-sum game, one player's losses are exactly offset by another player's gains. In a negative-sum game, players as a group lose, perhaps one more than the others. In a positive-sum game, players as a group end up better off.

10. The kinked demand curve oligopoly model indicates that prices will be relatively rigid unless demand or cost conditions change substantially.

11. Price leadership is strategic behavior that involves implicit collusion. The dominant firm is assumed to set the price and then allows other firms to sell all that they want to sell at that price. Whatever is left over is sold by the dominant firm. The dominant firm always makes the first move. If the nondominant firms decide to compete, they may start a price war.

12. One strategic decision may be to attempt to raise the cost of entry of new firms into an industry. The threat of a price war is one technique. Another is to lobby the federal government to pass stringent environmental or health and safety standards in an attempt to keep out foreign competition. A third is to make it more costly for customers to switch from one product or service to a competitor's.

DISCUSSION OF PREVIEW QUESTIONS

1. What are the characteristics of the monopolistically competitive market structure?

The monopolistically competitive market structure lies between the extremes of monopoly and perfect competition, but closer to the latter. Under monopolistic competition, there are a large number of sellers, each with a small market share, acting independently of one another, producing a differentiated product. This product differentiation is advertised; advertising emphasizes product differences or, on occasion, "creates" differences.

2. How does the monopolistic competitor determine the equilibrium price-output combination?

The monopolistic competitor has some control over price; it faces a downward-sloping demand curve. The monopolistic competitor must lower price in order to increase sales; the marginal revenue curve for the monopolistic competitor is therefore downward-sloping. In equilibrium, the profit-maximizing rate of output will therefore be where the upward-sloping (increasing) marginal cost curve intersects the downward-sloping (decreasing) marginal revenue curve. The output rate being thus established, price is set at the corresponding market clearing level. Any other output rate would lead to a reduction in total profits.

3. How does the monopolistically competitive market structure differ from that of perfect competition?

Like the perfect competitor, the monopolistic competitor acts independently of its competitors and is able to earn economic profits only in the short run; competition from entrants eliminates long-run economic profits under both market structures. Yet an important difference exists in the two models: The perfect competitor faces a perfectly elastic demand curve, whereas the monopolistic competitor faces a downward-sloping demand curve. Because economic profits must equal zero in the long run, the demand (average revenue) curve must be tangent to the average total cost (ATC) curve in both models. Under perfect competition, a perfectly elastic demand curve can only be tangent to a U-shaped ATC curve at the latter's minimum point (where its slope is zero). Under monopolistic competition, the demand curve must be tangent to the firm's ATC somewhere to the *left* of the ATC's minimum point. Thus under perfect competition, long-run equilibrium will be at minimum ATC, whereas under monopolistic competition, long-run equilibrium will be at a higher ATC—and at a lower output rate.

4. What are the characteristics of the oligopolistic market structure?

Like the monopolistically competitive market structure, oligopoly lies between the extremes of perfect competition and monopoly. However, oligopoly is closer to being unique; under oligopoly, a small number of firms dominate the market, and the firms cannot act independently. An oligopolist must take into account the reactions of its rivals when it sets policy; this interdependence makes the oligopoly model unique. It also makes the price-output decision a complex one for the oligopolists—and hence for economists who analyze this market structure. It is believed that oligopolies emerge because great economies of scale, in conjunction with a limited market demand, allow the few largest to drive out competitors. Also, oligopolies may arise because of barriers to entry and mergers.

PROBLEMS

(Answers to the odd-numbered problems appear at the back of the book.)

25-1. Suppose that you own a monopolistically competitive firm that sells automobile tune-ups at a price of $25 each. You are currently selling 100 per week. As the owner-operator, you initiate an ad campaign on a local AM radio station. You promise to smooth out any ill-running car at a price of $25. The result is that you end up tuning 140 cars per week. What is the "marginal revenue" of this ad campaign? What additional information do you need to determine whether your profits have risen?

25-2. The graph depicts long-run equilibrium for a monopolistic competitor.

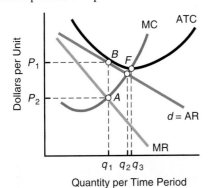

Quantity per Time Period

a. Which output rate represents equilibrium?
b. Which price represents equilibrium?
c. Which labeled point indicates that economic profits are zero?
d. Which labeled point indicates minimum ATC?
e. Is ATC at the equilibrium output rate above or at minimum ATC?
f. Is the equilibrium price greater than, less than, or equal to the marginal cost of producing at the equilibrium output rate?

25-3. The table indicates some information for industry A.

Firm	Annual Sales ($ millions)
1	200
2	150
3	100
4	75
5 through 30	300

a. What is the four-firm concentration ratio for this industry (with just 30 firms)?
b. Assume that industry A is the steel industry. What would happen to the concentration index if we redefined industry A as the cold rolled-steel industry? As the metals industry?

25-4. Explain how, in the long run, any economic profits will be eliminated in a monopolistically competitive industry.

25-5. Explain why an oligopolist's demand curve might be kinked.

25-6. The table on the following page gives some cost and demand data for an oligopolistic industry. There are five firms. Assume that each one faces the same long-run total cost curve and that each firm knows that any change in price will be matched by all other firms in the industry.

a. Fill in the blanks.
b. What will the profit-maximizing rate of output be for each firm?
c. What price will be charged for this output?
d. What will the profits be for each of the five firms?

Price	Quantity Demanded	Total Revenue	Marginal Revenue	Quantity Demanded ÷ Number of Firms	Total Revenue ÷ Number of Firms	Marginal Revenue ÷ Number of Firms	Individual Firm Quantity Supplied	Long-Run Total Costs	Long-Run Marginal Costs
$20	5	$_____	$_____	_____	_____	_____	1	$20	$_____
18	10	_____	_____	_____	_____	_____	2	30	_____
16	15	_____	_____	_____	_____	_____	3	36	_____
14	20	_____	_____	_____	_____	_____	4	44	_____
12	25	_____	_____	_____	_____	_____	5	60	_____

25-7. Suppose that you run a movie theater. At your price of $5 per person, you sell 5,000 tickets per week. Without changing your price, you initiate a $1,000-per-week advertising campaign. Assuming that all your nonadvertising costs are totally unrelated to the number of weekly viewers you have, how much additional revenue must you generate to justify continuation of the ad campaign? How many more customers would this require?

25-8. Study the accompanying graph for a firm in an oligopolistic industry.

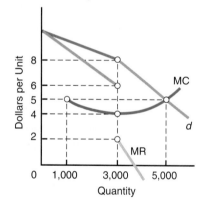

a. How much will this oligopolistic firm produce?
b. At what price will the firm sell this output?
c. How much can marginal cost vary without causing a change in price?

25-9. There are only two firms in an industry. They collude to share the market equally. They jointly set a monopoly price and split the quantity demanded at that price. Here are their options.

a. They continue to collude (no cheating) and make $10 million each in profits.
b. One firm cheats on the agreement, but the other firm doesn't. The firm that cheats makes $12 million a year in profit, whereas the firm that doesn't cheat makes $7 million in profit.
c. They both cheat and each one makes $6 million a year in profit.

Construct a payoff matrix for these two firms. How does this situation relate to the prisoners' dilemma?

COMPUTER-ASSISTED INSTRUCTION

Given a table with relevant information, can you determine an industry's four-firm concentration ratio? Does this ratio overstate or understate the true concentration of that industry? Specific calculations reveal some interesting answers about the usefulness of concentration ratios.

Complete problem and answer appear on disk.

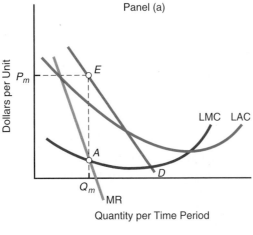

Panel (a)

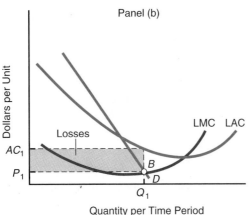

Panel (b)

FIGURE 26-1

Profit Maximization and Regulation Through Marginal Cost Pricing
The profit-maximizing natural monopolist here would produce at the point in panel (a) where marginal costs equal marginal revenue—that is, at point A, which gives the quantity of production Q_m. The price charged would be P_m. If a regulatory commission attempted to regulate natural monopolies so that price equaled long-run marginal cost, the commission would make the monopolist set production at the point where the marginal cost curve intersects the demand schedule. This is shown in panel (b). The quantity produced would be Q_1, and the price would be P_1. However, average costs at Q_1 are equal to AC_1. Losses would ensue, equal to the shaded area. It would be self-defeating for a regulatory commission to force a natural monopolist to produce at an output rate at which $MC = P$ without subsidizing some of its costs because losses would eventually drive the natural monopolist out of business.

looked at all of the upward-sloping portions of actual and potential firms' marginal cost curves above their respective average variable costs. We then summed all of these portions of the firms' supply curves; that gave us the industry supply curve. We assume that a regulatory commission forces the natural monopolist to engage in marginal cost pricing and hence to produce at quantity Q_1 and to sell the product at price P_1. How large will the monopolist's profits be? Profits, of course, are the *positive* difference between total revenues and total costs. In this case, total revenues equal P_1 times Q_1, and total costs equal average costs times the number of units produced. At Q_1, average cost is equal to AC_1. Average costs are higher than the price that the regulatory commission forces our natural monopolist to charge. Profits turn out to be losses and are equal to the shaded area in panel (b) of Figure 26-1. Thus regulation that forces a natural monopolist to produce and price as if it were in a competitive situation would also force that monopolist into negative profits, or losses. Obviously, the monopolist would rather go out of business than be subject to such regulation.

As a practical matter, then, regulators can't force a natural monopolist to engage in marginal cost pricing. Consequently, regulation of natural monopolies has often taken the form of allowing the regulated natural monopolist to set price where LAC intersects D in panel (b) of Figure 26-1. This is called *average cost pricing*. Average cost includes what the regulators deem a "fair" rate of return on investment.

INTERNATIONAL EXAMPLE
European Post Offices: Natural Monopolies and How to Evade Them

Both in the United States and in the European Union (EU), the postal service has been a legal monopoly. Governments have argued that their post offices are natural monopolies because of economies of scale. In Europe, governments set the postal price at P_m, as in panel (a) of Figure 26-1, rather than P_1, as in panel (b).

Enter third-party mail handlers as a way to erode such monopoly power. In the Netherlands, the government-owned telecommunications company Koninklijke PTT Nederland formed an international mail joint venture with KLM Royal Dutch Airlines called Interpost. Interpost's foreign mail rates, especially to the United States and Asia, are sometimes as low as one-fourth of what a German or French person would have to pay. Third-party mail handlers are now picking up bulk mail in countries surrounding the Netherlands, trucking it in, and then letting Interpost send it out.

A similar activity is occurring as a way to avoid state-owned telephone companies in the EU. People in Europe can now call computers in the United States, then hang up, and the computer calls back. An open line is established, thereby allowing the European to call U.S. numbers (and elsewhere) as if the caller were in America. The savings sometimes exceeds 70 percent.

FOR CRITICAL ANALYSIS: *If postal services are natural monopolies, why do we need laws preventing private firms from competing with them?* •

CONCEPTS IN BRIEF

- A natural monopoly arises when one firm can produce all of an industry's output at a lower per-unit cost than other firms.

- The first firm to take advantage of the declining long-run average cost curve can undercut the prices of all other sellers, forcing them out of business, thereby obtaining a natural monopoly.

- A natural monopolist allowed to maximize profit will set quantity where marginal revenue equals long-run marginal cost. Price is determined from the demand curve at that quantity.

- A natural monopolist that is forced to set price equal to long-run marginal cost will sustain losses.

REGULATION

The U.S. government began regulating social and economic activity early in the nation's history, but the amount of government regulation has increased in the twentieth century. There are three types of government regulation:

1. Regulation of natural monopolies
2. Regulation of inherently competitive industries
3. Regulation for public welfare across all industries, or so-called social regulation

For example, various state commissions regulate the rates and quality of service of electric power companies, which are considered natural monopolies. Trucking and interstate moving companies are inherently competitive industries but have nonetheless been made subject to government regulation in the past. And federal and state governments impose occupational, health, and safety rules on a wide variety of employers.

Objectives of Economic Regulation

Economic regulation is typically intended to control the prices that regulated enterprises are allowed to charge. Various public utility commissions throughout the United States regulate the rates (prices) of electrical utility companies and some telephone operating companies. This has usually been called rate regulation. The goal of rate regulation has, in principle, been the prevention of both monopoly profits and predatory competition.

Two traditional methods of rate regulation have involved cost-of-service regulation and rate-of-return regulation. A regulatory commission using **cost-of-service regulation** allows the regulated companies to charge only prices that reflect the actual average cost of providing the services to the customer. In a somewhat similar vein, regulatory commissions using the **rate-of-return regulation** method allow regulated companies to set prices that ensure a normal, or competitive, rate of return on the investment in the business. We implied these two types of regulation when discussing panel (b) of Figure 26-1. If the long-run average cost curve in that figure includes a competitive rate of return on investment, regulating the price at AC_1 is an example of rate-of-return regulation.

A major problem with regulating monopolies concerns the quality of the service or product involved. Consider the many facets of telephone service: getting a dial tone, hearing other voices clearly, getting the operator to answer quickly, having out-of-order telephone lines repaired rapidly, putting through a long-distance call quickly and efficiently—the list goes on and on. But regulation of a telephone company usually dealt with the prices charged for telephone service. Of course, regulators were concerned with the quality of service, but how could that be measured? Indeed, it cannot be measured very easily. Therefore, it is extremely difficult for any type of regulation to be successful in regulating the *price per constant-quality unit.* Certainly, it is possible to regulate the price per unit, but we don't really know that the quality remains unchanged when the price is not allowed to rise "enough." Thus if regulation doesn't allow prices to rise, quality of service may be lowered, thereby raising the price per constant-quality unit.

Cost-of-service regulation
Regulation based on allowing prices to reflect only the actual cost of production and no monopoly profits.

Rate-of-return regulation
Regulation that seeks to keep the rate of return in the industry at a competitive level by not allowing excessive prices to be charged.

POLICY EXAMPLE
Can the FCC Effectively Regulate Cable TV?

In 1992, Congress passed the Cable Reregulation Act. The genesis of the act was the feeling that consumers were receiving a monthly "zapping" from the cable industry. Immediately after the passage of the act, the FCC decided that cable companies needed to roll back their rates by 7 percent. The FCC announced that it was going to engage in cost-of-service rate regulation. Could the FCC ever succeed in so doing? The answer is probably no, because it would have to value the assets of 11,000 different cable systems. Few of those assets are the same, and most of them are intangible (nonphysical). Pity the poor regulators. (The Telecommunications Act of 1996 eliminated this issue.)

FOR CRITICAL ANALYSIS: What type of competition do even monopoly cable systems face? ●

Social Regulation

As mentioned, social regulation reflects concern for public welfare across all industries. In other words, regulation is focused on the impact of production on the environment and society, the working conditions under which goods and services are produced, and sometimes the physical attributes of goods. The aim is a better quality of life for all through a less polluted environment, better working conditions, and safer and better products. For example, the Food and Drug Administration (FDA) attempts to protect against impure and unsafe foods, drugs, cosmetics, and other potentially hazardous products; the Consumer Product Safety Commission (CPSC) specifies minimum standards for consumer products in an attempt to reduce "unreasonable" risks of injury; the Environmental Protection Agency (EPA) watches over the amount of pollutants released into the environment; the Occupational Safety and Health Administration (OSHA) attempts to protect workers against work-related injuries and illnesses; and the Equal Employment Opportunity Commission (EEOC) seeks to provide fair access to jobs.

Table 26-1 lists some major federal regulatory agencies and their areas of concern. Although most people agree with the idea behind such social regulation, many disagree on whether we have too much regulation—whether it costs us more than the benefits we receive. Some contend that the costs that firms incur in abiding by regulations run into the hundreds of billions of dollars per year. The result is higher production costs, which are then passed on to consumers. Also, the resources invested in complying with regulatory measures could be invested in other uses. Furthermore, extensive regulation may have an anticompetitive effect because it may represent a relatively greater burden for smaller firms than for larger ones.

But the *potential* benefits of more social regulation are many. For example, the water we drink in some cities is known to be contaminated with cancer-causing chemicals; air pollution from emissions and toxic wastes from production processes cause many illnesses. Some contaminated areas have been cleaned up, but many other problem areas remain.

The benefits of social regulation may not be easy to measure and may accrue to society for a long time. Furthermore, it is difficult to put a dollar value on safer working conditions

TABLE 26-1

Some Federal Regulatory Agencies

Agency	Jurisdiction	Date Formed	Major Regulatory Functions
Federal Communications Commission (FCC)	Product markets	1934	Regulates broadcasting, telephone, and other communication services.
Federal Trade Commission (FTC)	Product Markets	1914	Responsible for preventing businesses from engaging in unfair trade practices and in monopolistic actions, as well as protecting consumer rights.
Equal Employment Opportunity Commission (EEOC)	Labor markets	1964	Investigates complaints of discrimination based on race, religion, sex, or age in hiring, promotion, firing, wages, testing, and all other conditions of employment.
Securities and Exchange Commission (SEC)	Financial markets	1934	Regulates all public securities markets to promote full disclosure.
Environmental Protection Agency (EPA)	Environment	1970	Develops and enforces environmental standards for air, water, toxic waste, and noise.
Occupational Safety and Health Administration (OSHA)	Health and safety	1970	Regulates workplace safety and health conditions.

and a cleaner environment. In any case, the debate goes on. However, it should be pointed out that the controversy is generally not about whether we should have social regulation but about when and how it is being done and whether we take *all* of the costs and benefits into account. For example, is regulation best carried out by federal, state, or local authorities? Is a specific regulation economically justified through a complete cost-benefit analysis?

Creative Response and Feedback Effects: Results of Regulation

Creative response
Behavior on the part of a firm that allows it to comply with the letter of the law but violate the spirit, significantly lessening the law's effects.

Regulated firms commonly try to avoid the effects of regulation whenever they can. In other words, the firms engage in **creative response,** which is a response to a regulation that conforms to the letter of the law but undermines its spirit. Take state laws requiring male-female pay-equity: The wages of women must be on a par with those paid to males who are performing the same tasks. Employers that pay the same wages to both males and females are clearly not in violation of the law. However, wages are only one component of total employee compensation. Another component is fringe benefits, such as on-the-job training. Because on-the-job training is difficult to observe from outside the firm, employers could offer less on-the-job training to women and still not be in technical violation of pay-equity laws. This unobservable difference would mean that males were able to acquire skills that could raise their future income even though current wages among males and females were equal, in compliance with the law.

Individuals have a type of creative response that has been labeled a *feedback effect*. Regulation may alter individuals' behavior after the regulation has been put into effect. If regulation requires fluoridated water, then parents know that their children's teeth have significant protection against tooth decay. Consequently, the feedback effect on parents' behavior is that they may be less concerned about how many sweets their children eat.

EXAMPLE
The Effectiveness of Auto Safety Regulation

A good example of the feedback effect has to do with automotive safety regulation. Since the 1960s, the federal government has required automobile manufacturers to make cars increasingly safer. Some of the earlier requirements involved nonprotruding door handles, collapsible steering columns, and shatterproof glass. More recent requirements involve I-beams in the doors, better seat belts, and airbags. The desired result was fewer injuries and deaths for drivers involved in accidents. According to economist Sam Peltzman, however, due to the feedback effect, drivers have gradually started driving more recklessly. Automobiles with more safety features have been involved in a disproportionate number of accidents.

FOR CRITICAL ANALYSIS: The feedback effect has also been called the law of unintended consequences. Why? ●

EXPLAINING REGULATORS' BEHAVIOR

Regulation has usually been defended by contending that government regulatory agencies are needed to correct market imperfections. We are dealing with a nonmarket situation because regulators are paid by the government and their decisions are not determined or constrained by the market. A number of theories have been put forward to describe the behavior of regulators. These theories can help us understand how regulation has often harmed consumers through higher prices and less choice and benefited producers through higher profits and fewer competitive forces. Two of the best-known theories of regulatory behavior are the *capture hypothesis* and the *share-the-gains, share-the-pains theory.*

The Capture Hypothesis

It has been observed that with the passage of time, regulators often end up adopting the views of the regulated. According to the **capture hypothesis,**[1] no matter what the reason for a regulatory agency's having been set up, it will eventually be captured by the special interests of the industry that is being regulated. Consider the reasons.

Who knows best about the industry that is being regulated? The people already in the industry. Who, then, will be asked to regulate the industry? Again, people who have been in the industry. And people who used to be in the industry have allegiances and friendships with others in the industry.

Also consider that whenever regulatory hearings are held, the affected consumer groups will have much less information about the industry than the people already in the industry, the producers. Additionally, the cost to any one consumer to show up at a regulatory hearing to express concern about a change in the rate structure will certainly exceed any perceived benefit that that consumer could obtain from going to the rate-making hearing.

Because they have little incentive to do so, consumers and taxpayers will not be well organized, nor will they be greatly concerned with regulatory actions. But the special interests of the industry are going to be well organized and well defined. Political entrepreneurs within the regulatory agency see little payoff in supporting the views of consumers and taxpayers anyway. After all, few consumers understand the benefits deriving from regulatory agency actions. Moreover, how much could a consumer directly benefit someone who works in an agency? Regulators have the most incentive to support the position of a well-organized special-interest group within the industry that is being regulated.

Capture hypothesis
A theory of regulatory behavior that predicts that the regulators will eventually be captured by the special interests of the industry being regulated.

"Share the Gains, Share the Pains"

A somewhat different view of regulators' behavior is given in the **share-the-gains, share-the-pains theory.**[2] This theory looks at the specific aims of the regulators. It posits that a regulator simply wants to continue in the job. To do so, the regulator must obtain the approval of both the legislators who established and oversee the regulatory agency and the industry that is being regulated. A third group that must be taken into account is, of course, the customers of the industry.

Under the capture hypothesis, only the special interests of the industry being regulated had to be taken into account by the regulators. The share-the-gains, share-the-pains model contends that such a position is too risky because customers who are really hurt by improper regulation will complain to legislators, who might fire the regulators. Thus each regulator has to attach some weight to these three separate groups. What happens if there is an abrupt increase in fuel costs for electrical utilities? The capture theory would predict that regulators would relatively quickly allow for a rate increase in order to maintain the profits of the industry. The share-the-gains, share-the-pains theory, however, would predict that there will be an adjustment in rates, but not as quickly or as completely as the capture theory would predict. The regulatory agency is not completely captured by the industry; it has to take account of legislators and consumers.

Share-the-gains, share-the-pains theory
A theory of regulatory behavior in which the regulators must take account of the demands of three groups: legislators, who established and who oversee the regulatory agency; members of the regulated industry; and consumers of the regulated industry's products or services.

---

[1]See George Stigler, *The Citizen and the State: Essays on Regulation* (Chicago: University of Chicago Press, 1975).

[2]See Sam Peltzman, "Towards a More General Theory of Regulation," *Journal of Law and Economics,* 19 (1976), pp. 211–240.

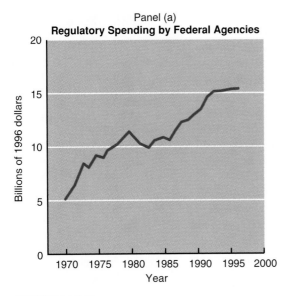

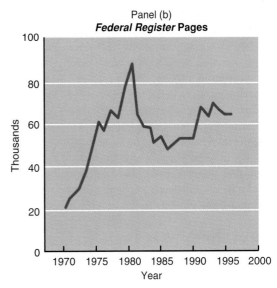

FIGURE 26-2

Regulation on the Rise

In panel (a), federal government regulatory spending is shown to exceed $16 billion per year today. State and local spending is not shown. In panel (b), the number of pages in the *Federal Register* per year has been rising since about 1990.

Sources: Institute for University Studies; *Federal Register,* various issues.

THE COSTS OF REGULATION

There is no truly accurate way to measure the costs of regulation. Panel (a) of Figure 26-2 shows regulatory spending in 1996 dollars. Except in the years 1981–1985, regulatory spending by federal agencies has increased. This is consistent with what has happened to the number of pages in the *Federal Register,* which publishes all the new federal regulatory rules; you can see that in panel (b). But actual direct costs to taxpayers are only a small part of the overall cost of regulation. Pharmaceutical-manufacturing safety standards raise the price of drugs. Automobile safety standards raise the price of cars. Environmental controls on manufacturing raise the price of manufactured goods. All of these increased prices add to the cost of regulation. According to economist Thomas Hopkins at the Rochester Institute of Technology, the economic cost of environmental and safety regulation exceeds $200 billion a year. When he adds the cost of all other kinds of regulations, he comes up with a grand total of over $600 billion a year, or about 8 percent of each year's total income in this country. Not surprisingly, the increasing cost of regulation on occasion has brought about cries for deregulation.

DEREGULATION

Deregulation
The elimination or phasing out of regulations on economic activity.

Regulation increased substantially during the 1970s. By the end of that decade, numerous proposals for **deregulation**—the removal of old regulations—had been made. Most deregulation proposals and actions since then have been aimed at industries in which price competition and entry competition by new firms continued to be thwarted by the regulators. The Air Deregulation Act of 1978 eliminated the Civil Aeronautics Board and allowed comptetition among the airlines themselves to control fares and routes flown. In 1980, the Interstate Commerce Commission's power over interstate trucking rates and routes was virtually eliminated, and the same occurred for buses in 1982. Savings account interest rates were deregulated in 1980. Railroad pricing was made more flexible during the same year.

Even prior to this spate of deregulatory acts by Congress, the Federal Communications Commission (FCC) had started in 1972 to deregulate the television broadcast industry. The result has been an increased number of channels, more direct satellite broadcasting, and more cable television transmissions. (Further deregulation occurred in 1996.) In 1975, the Securities and Exchange Commission (SEC) deregulated brokerage fees charged by brokers on the New York Stock Exchange.

Short-Run Versus Long-Run Effects of Deregulation

The short-run effects of deregulation are not the same as the long-run effects. In the short run, a regulated industry that becomes deregulated may experience numerous temporary adjustments. One is the inevitable shakeout of higher-cost producers with the concomitant removal of excess monopoly profits. Another is the sometimes dramatic displacement of workers who have labored long and hard in the formerly regulated industry. The level of service for some consumers may fall; for example, after the deregulation of the telephone industry, some aspects of telephone service decreased in quality. When airlines were deregulated, service to some small cities was eliminated or became more expensive. The power of unions in the formerly regulated industry may decrease. And bankruptcies may cause disruptions, particularly in the local economy where the headquarters of the formerly regulated firm are located.

Proponents of deregulation, or at least of less regulation, contend that there are long-run, permanent benefits. These include lower prices that are closer to marginal cost. Furthermore, fewer monopoly profits are made in the deregulated industry. Such proponents argue that deregulation has had positive *net* benefits.

Deregulation and Contestable Markets

A major argument in favor of deregulation is that when government-imposed barriers to entry are removed, competition will cause firms to enter markets that previously had only a few firms with market power due to those entry barriers. Potential competitors will become actual competitors, and prices will fall toward a competitive level. Recently, this argument has been bolstered by a relatively new model of efficient firm behavior that predicts competitive prices in spite of a lack of a large number of firms. This model is called the **theory of contestable markets.** Under the theory of contestable markets, most of the outcomes predicted by the theory of perfect competition will occur in certain industries with relatively few firms. Specifically, where the theory of contestable markets is applicable, the few firms may still produce the output at which price equals marginal cost in both the short run and the long run. These firms will receive zero economic profits in the long run.

Unconstrained and Relatively Costless Entry and Exit. For a market to be perfectly contestable, firms must be able to enter and leave the industry easily. Freedom of entry and exit implies an absence of nonprice constraints and of serious fixed costs associated with a potential competitor's decision to enter a contestable market. Such an absence of impor-

---

THINKING CRITICALLY ABOUT THE MEDIA

Deregulation of Airlines and Safety

Every time there is a major commercial airline crash that involves death and injury, the media have a field day. Some journalists have even argued that such airline crashes are due to deregulation of the airline industry. Though it may be true that there are more airlines fatalities today than prior to deregulation in 1978, airline safety has increased significantly. Lower airline prices, coupled with increasing population, have caused airline traffic to increase dramatically. Even if a larger number of accidents seem to be occurring, the number of *fatal accidents per 100,000 departures* has decreased almost 75 percent since 1978.

Theory of contestable markets
A hypothesis concerning pricing behavior that holds that even though there are only a few firms in an industry, they are forced to price their products more or less competitively because of the ease of entry by outsiders. The key aspect of a contestable market is relatively costless entry into and exit from the industry.

tant fixed costs results if the firm need buy no specific durable inputs in order to enter, if it uses up all such inputs it does purchase, or if all of its specific durable inputs are salable upon exit without any losses beyond those normally incurred from depreciation. The important issue is whether or not a potential entrant can easily get his or her investment out at any time in the future.

The mathematical model of perfect contestability is complex, but the underlying logic is straightforward. As long as conditions for free entry prevail, any excess profits, or any inefficiencies on the part of incumbent firms, will serve as an inducement for potential entrants to enter. By entering, new firms can temporarily profit at no risk to themselves from the less than competitive situation in the industry. Once competitive conditions are again restored, these firms will leave the industry just as quickly.

Benefits of Contestable Markets. Contestable markets have several desirable characteristics. One has to do with profits. Profits that exceed the opportunity cost of capital will not exist in the long run because of freedom of entry, just as in a perfectly competitive industry. The elimination of "excess" profits can occur even with only a couple of firms in an industry. The threat of entry will cause them to expand output to eliminate excess profit.

Also, firms that have cost curves that are higher than those of the most efficient firms will find that they cannot compete. These firms will be replaced by entrants whose cost curves are consistent with the most efficient technology. In other words, in contestable markets, there will be no cost inefficiencies in the long run.

Rethinking Regulation Using Cost-Benefit Analysis

Rather than considering deregulation as the only solution to "too much" regulation, some economists argue that regulation should simply be put to a cost-benefit test. Specifically, the cost of existing and proposed regulations should be compared to the benefits. Unless it can be demonstrated that regulations generate net positive benefits (benefits greater than costs), such regulations should not be in effect.

CONCEPTS IN BRIEF

- It is difficult to regulate the price per constant-quality unit because it is difficult to measure all dimensions of quality.

- The capture hypothesis holds that regulatory agencies will eventually be captured by special interests of the industry. This is because consumers are a diffuse group who individually are not affected greatly by regulation, whereas industry groups are well focused and know that large amounts of potential profits are at stake and depend on the outcome of regulatory proceedings.

- In the share-the-gains, share-the-pains theory of regulation, regulators must take account of the interests of three groups: the industry, legislators, and consumers.

- The 1970s and 1980s were periods of deregulation during which formerly regulated industries became much more competitive. The short-run effects of deregulation in some industries were numerous bankruptcies and disrupted service. The long-run results in many deregulated industries included better service, more variety, and lower costs. One argument in favor of deregulation involves the theory of contestable markets—if entry and exit are relatively costless, the number of firms in an industry is irrelevant in terms of determining whether consumers pay competitive prices.

ANTITRUST POLICY

It is the expressed aim of our government to foster competition in the economy. To this end, numerous attempts have been made to legislate against business practices that seemingly destroy the competitive nature of the system. This is the general idea behind antitrust legislation: If the courts can prevent collusion among sellers of a product, monopoly prices will not result; there will be no restriction of output if the members of an industry are not allowed to join together in restraint of trade. Remember that the competitive solution to the price-quantity problem is one in which the price of the item produced is equal to its marginal social opportunity cost. Also, no *economic* profits are made in the long run.

The Sherman Antitrust Act of 1890

The Sherman Antitrust Act was passed in 1890. It was the first attempt by the federal government to control the growth of monopoly in the United States. The most important provisions of that act are as follows:

> *Section 1:* Every contract, combination in the form of trust or otherwise, or conspiracy, in restraint of trade or commerce among the several states, or with foreign nations, is hereby declared to be illegal.

> *Section 2:* Every person who shall monopolize, or attempt to monopolize, or combine or conspire with any other person or persons to monopolize any part of the trade or commerce . . . shall be guilty of a misdemeanor.[3]

Notice how vague this act really is. No definition is given for the terms *restraint of trade* or *monopolization.* Despite this vagueness, however, the act was used to prosecute the infamous Standard Oil trust of New Jersey. Standard Oil of New Jersey was charged with violations of Sections 1 and 2 of the Sherman Antitrust Act. This was in 1906, when Standard Oil controlled over 80 percent of the nation's oil-refining capacity. Among other things, Standard Oil was accused of both predatory price cutting to drive rivals out of business and obtaining preferential price treatment from the railroads for transporting Standard Oil products, thus allowing Standard to sell at lower prices.

Standard Oil was convicted in a district court. The company then appealed to the Supreme Court, which ruled that Standard's control of and power over the oil market created "a *prima facie* presumption of intent and purpose to maintain dominancy . . . not as a result from normal methods of industrial development, but by means of combination." Here the word *combination* meant taking over other businesses and obtaining preferential price treatment from railroads. The Supreme Court forced Standard Oil of New Jersey to break up into many smaller companies.

The Clayton Act of 1914

The Sherman Act was so vague that in 1914 a new law was passed to sharpen its antitrust provisions. This law was called the Clayton Act. It prohibited or limited a number of very specific business practices, which again were felt to be "unreasonable" attempts at restraining trade or commerce. Section 2 of that act made it illegal to "discriminate in price between different purchasers" except in cases in which the differences are due to actual dif-

---

[3] This is now a felony.

ferences in selling or transportation costs. Section 3 stated that producers cannot sell goods "on the condition, agreement or understanding that the . . . purchaser thereof shall not use or deal in the goods . . . of a competitor or competitors of the seller." And Section 7 provided that corporations cannot hold stock in another company if the effect "may be to substantially lessen competition."

The Federal Trade Commission Act of 1914 and Its 1938 Amendment

The Federal Trade Commission Act was designed to stipulate acceptable competitive behavior. In particular, it was supposed to prevent cutthroat pricing—excessively aggressive competition, which would tend to eliminate too many competitors. One of the basic features of the act was the creation of the Federal Trade Commission (FTC), charged with the power to investigate unfair competitive practices. The FTC can do this on its own or at the request of firms that feel they have been wronged. It can issue cease and desist orders where "unfair methods of competition in commerce" are discovered. In 1938, the Wheeler-Lea Act amended the 1914 act. The amendment expressly prohibits "unfair or deceptive acts or practices in commerce." Pursuant to that act, the FTC engages in what it sees as a battle against false or misleading advertising, as well as the misrepresentation of goods and services for sale in the marketplace.

The Robinson-Patman Act of 1936

In 1936, Section 2 of the Clayton Act was amended by the Robinson-Patman Act. The Robinson-Patman Act was aimed at preventing producers from driving out smaller competitors by means of selected discriminatory price cuts. The act has often been referred to as the "Chain Store Act" because it was meant to protect *independent* retailers and wholesalers from "unfair discrimination" by chain stores.

The act was the natural outgrowth of increasing competition that independents faced when chain stores and mass distributors started to develop after World War I. The essential provisions of the act are as follows:

1. It was made illegal to pay brokerage fees unless an independent broker was employed.
2. It was made illegal to offer concessions, such as discounts, free advertising, or promotional allowances, to one buyer of a firm's product if the firm did not offer the same concessions to all buyers of that product.
3. Other forms of discrimination, such as quantity discounts, were also made illegal whenever they "substantially" lessened competition.
4. It was made illegal to charge lower prices in one location than in another or to sell at "unreasonably low prices" if such marketing techniques were designed to "destroy competition or eliminate a competitor."

POLICY EXAMPLE
Should Wal-Mart Be Forced to Raise Prices?

The issue of predatory pricing gained national prominence when three independent pharmacies filed suit against Wal-Mart in an Arkansas court. Independent retailers in small towns across the country have long accused Wal-Mart of selling goods below cost to drive them out of business. The three pharmacies that brought suit against

Wal-Mart claimed that it was engaging in predatory pricing by selling as many as 200 items below cost at its store in Conway, Arkansas. Wal-Mart responded that it makes its pricing decisions based on how much competition it faces: more competition, lower prices. Wal-Mart attorneys pointed out that when Wal-Mart entered the Conway business area, there were 12 pharmacies, all of which remain in existence today, plus two new ones. The number of pharmacists in the county increased from 38 to 58.

A local judge found Wal-Mart guilty; on appeal, Wal-Mart prevailed.

FOR CRITICAL ANALYSIS: Supermarkets routinely advertise "loss leaders" such as turkeys at Thanksgiving that are priced below cost. Is there any difference between spending on loss leaders and simply spending more on traditional types of advertising? ●

Exemptions from Antitrust Laws

Numerous laws exempt the following industries and business practices from antitrust legislation:

1. All labor unions
2. Public utilities—electric, gas, and telephone companies
3. Professional baseball
4. Cooperative activities among American exporters
5. Hospitals
6. Public transit and water systems
7. Suppliers of military equipment
8. Joint publishing arrangement in a single city by two or more newspapers

POLICY EXAMPLE
Should Baseball Be Exempt from Antitrust Laws?

When the baseball strike in the mid-1990s destroyed one entire season, members of Congress threatened to "do something." Specifically, they wanted to pass legislation to eliminate professional baseball's exemption from antitrust laws. The exemption dates back to 1922 when the U.S. Supreme Court said that even though the clubs were located "in different cities and for the most part different states" and that "constantly repeated traveling on the part of the clubs" was required, the primary business of the clubs was "giving exhibitions of baseball which are purely state affairs." According to the Supreme Court, neither the interstate exhibition nor the interstate travel of the clubs' members (baseball players and managers) "truly involves interstate commerce." Therefore, they were not within the reach of U.S. antitrust laws.

Under modern interpretations of what constitutes interstate commerce, the 1922 decision would be considered in error. Nonetheless, professional baseball continues to retain its extraordinary status as the only professional sport exempt from antitrust laws.

FOR CRITICAL ANALYSIS: Who would lose if baseball became subject to federal antitrust laws? ●

THE ENFORCEMENT OF ANTITRUST LAWS

Monopolization
The possession of monopoly power in the relevant market and the willful acquisition or maintenance of that power, as distinguished from growth or development as a consequence of a superior product, business acumen, or historical accident.

Most antitrust enforcement today is based on the Sherman Act. The Supreme Court has defined the offense of **monopolization** as involving the following elements: "(1) the possession of monopoly power in the relevant market and (2) the willful acquisition or maintenance of that power, as distinguished from growth or development as a consequence of a superior product, business acumen, or historical accident."

Monopoly Power and the Relevant Market

The Sherman Act does not define monopoly. Monopoly clearly is not a single entity. Also, monopoly is not a function of size alone. For example, a "mom and pop" grocery store located in an isolated desert town is a monopolist in at least one sense.

Market share test
The percentage of a market that a particular firm controls, used as the primary measure of monopoly power.

As difficult as it is to define market power precisely, it is even more difficult to measure it. As a workable proxy, courts often look to the firm's percentage share of the "relevant market." This is the so-called **market share test.** A firm is generally considered to have monopoly power if its share of the relevant market is 70 percent or more. This is not an absolute dictum, however. It is only a loose rule of thumb; in some cases, a smaller share may be held to constitute monopoly power.

The relevant market consists of two elements: a relevant product market and a relevant geographic market. What should the relevant product market include? It must include all products produced by different firms that have identical attributes, such as sugar. Yet products that are not identical may sometimes be substituted for one another. Coffee may be substituted for tea, for example. In defining the relevant product market, the key issue is the degree of interchangeability between products. If one product is a sufficient substitute for another, the two products are considered to be part of the same product market.

The second component of the relevant market is the geographic boundaries of the market. For products that are sold nationwide, the geographic boundaries of the market encompass the entire United States. If a producer and its competitors sell in only a limited area (one in which customers have no access to other sources of the product), the geographic market is limited to that area. A national firm may thus compete in several distinct areas and have monopoly power in one area but not in another.

CONCEPTS IN BRIEF

- The first national antitrust law was the Sherman Antitrust Act, passed in 1890, which made illegal every contract and combination in the form of a trust in restraint of trade.

- The Clayton Act made price discrimination and interlocking directorates illegal.

- The Federal Trade Commission Act of 1914 established the Federal Trade Commission. The Wheeler-Lea Act of 1938 amended the 1914 act to prohibit "unfair or deceptive acts or practices in commerce."

- The Robinson-Patman Act of 1936 was aimed at preventing large producers from driving out small competitors by means of selective discriminatory price cuts.

ISSUES AND APPLICATIONS

Should Microsoft Be Broken Up?

Concepts Applied: *Antitrust policies, market power, monopoly, relevant market, potential competition, marginal cost*

The Justice Department's antitrust division has been conducting a series of investigations into software giant Microsoft. The government has already stopped Microsoft from purchasing Intuit and enforced several licensing contracts with computer manufacturers.

Nowhere in the Sherman Antitrust Act or other antitrust laws will you find that it is illegal to be big and successful. Rather, to be in violation of antitrust laws, a business has to act in restraint of trade or attempt to monopolize an industry. Getting big through being more efficient is not necessarily an attempt to monopolize.

Microsoft Corporation currently has its operating systems in four-fifths of the world's personal computers. Microsoft has also developed application software, such as Word for word processing. Some critics of Microsoft argue that it is so big and powerful, it should be broken up into an operating system company and an applications company. Apparently, that is the philosophy underpinning the U.S. Justice Department's most recent actions.

Nix on the Microsoft–Intuit Deal

Microsoft chairman Bill Gates knows that telecommunications is expanding rapidly. He made an offer to buy the biggest home accounting and banking software company, Intuit. The U.S. Justice Department antitrust division nixed the deal. Why? Because the merger of one dominant market player with another dominant market player seemed to spell monopoly. Intuit, with its Quicken program, did have 7 million household users. But that left the rest of the nation's computer owners up for grabs. Also, the real profit will not be made in selling accounting and

banking programs but in obtaining transactions fees from people who use such programs to make on-line connections to their banks. Consequently, the true potential competitors are Visa, MasterCard, AT&T, Sprint, MCI, TV cable companies, and regional phone companies. When viewed in this light, Microsoft does not look so big.

Should Microsoft Be Prevented from Bundling Programs?

Gates's latest operating system, Windows 95, is estimated to be installed in about 16 million PCs as of the end of 1996. The marginal cost of installing Internet access software, banking software, spreadsheet software, and other programs is virtually zero. Such "bundled" software may, according to critics of Microsoft, pose an unfair competitive threat to providers of similar applications programs. The process of bundling, though, was started many years ago. More and more applications programs are adding more and more features all the time. Moreover, there are still 70,000 software companies competing for PC owners' business.

Tomorrow's Technology Is Unknown

When all is said and done, we don't really know what tomorrow's technology will be. The U.S. Justice Department spent eight years trying to prosecute IBM for antitrust violations. By the time the government dropped its case, the PC revolution had occurred and IBM no longer had as much market power. The same may ultimately be the case with Microsoft. No one knows what types of computer and telecommunications systems will dominate a decade from now. Fast-changing technology may overcome any monopolistic advantage that one company has.

FOR CRITICAL ANALYSIS
1. Consumers can interact with banks and retailers via the phone system. What other possibilities may exist for such interactivity?
2. Microsoft freely supplies the technical details that rival software suppliers need to write software that can work on the Microsoft operating system. Why would Microsoft help competitors write competing software?

CHAPTER SUMMARY

1. Regulation may be applied to a natural monopoly, which arises when, for example, the average total cost curve falls over a very large range of production rates. In such a situation, only one firm can survive. It will be the firm that can expand production and sales faster than the others to take advantage of the falling average total costs. If regulation seeks to force the natural monopolist to produce at the point where the marginal cost curve (supply curve in the competitive case) intersects the demand curve, the natural monopolist will incur losses, because when average total costs are falling, marginal costs are below average total costs. The regulators face a dilemma.

2. There are several ways of regulating monopolies, the most common ones being on a cost-of-service basis or a rate-of-return basis. Under cost-of-service regulation, the regulated monopolies are allowed to charge prices that reflect only reasonable costs. Under rate-of-return regulation, the regulated monopolies are allowed to set rates so as to make a competitive rate of return for the equity shareholders. Supposedly, no monopoly profits can therefore be earned.

3. The capture hypothesis predicts that because of the diffuse interests of consumers as compared to the well-focused interests of industry members, regulators will eventually be captured by those whom they regulate.

4. The share-the-gains, share-the-pains theory predicts that regulators must take account not only of the desires of members of the industry but also of the wishes of legislators and consumers.

5. The 1970s and 1980s were periods of deregulation during which formerly regulated industries became much more competitive. The short-run effects of deregulation in some industries were numerous bankruptcies and disrupted service. The long-run results in many deregulated industries included better service, more variety, and lower costs.

6. One argument in favor of deregulation involves the theory of contestable markets—if entry and exit are relatively costless, the number of firms in an industry is irrelevant in terms of determining whether consumers pay competitive prices.

7. Some economists argue that all actual and proposed regulation be subject to strict cost-benefit analysis.

8. Antitrust legislation is designed to obviate the need for regulation. The major antitrust acts are the Sherman, Clayton, and Robinson-Patman acts.

DISCUSSION OF PREVIEW QUESTIONS

1. **What is a natural monopoly, and how does one arise?**

   A natural monopoly is a situation in which the long-run average cost curve falls persistently as output expands. Thus the natural monopolist is a firm that by expanding is able to charge a price lower than its competitors can, thereby eliminating them. A natural monopolist arises due to tremendous economies of scale; expanding output causes ATC to fall.

2. **If natural monopolies are required to price at marginal cost, what problem emerges?**

   We have noted in earlier chapters that efficiency requires that people pay the marginal cost for a good

or a service. If regulators grant a firm monopoly privileges (recognizing it as a natural monopoly and regulating it to keep it in line) but force it to price at its marginal cost of production, a problem emerges. Because long-run ATC is persistently falling, it follows that long-run marginal cost must be below long-run ATC. Forcing a firm to charge a price equal to marginal cost implies that average revenue = price = marginal cost < average total cost (AR = P = MC < ATC). It follows that AR < ATC, and therefore the regulated natural monopolist would experience *negative* economic profits. In that case, it would shut down unless subsidized. In short, forcing a regulated natural monopolist to price at marginal cost may be socially beneficial, but such a policy requires that the natural monopolist be subsidized to cover the resulting economic losses to the firm.

3. What are some means of regulating a natural monopoly?

Two important means of regulating a natural monopoly are cost of service and rate of return. Cost-of-service regulation aims at requiring a natural monopolist to price at levels that would result from a more competitive situation. In effect, the natural monopolist is required to charge the average cost of providing the service in question, thereby ensuring zero economic profits. The rate-of-return form of regulation in effect allows a natural monopolist to price at rates that permit it an *overall* "normal" rate of return, because the natural monopolist will remain in operation only if it earns at least a normal return on invested capital.

4. Why have economists been reevaluating the government's role as an economic regulator?

Presumably, regulation is an attempt to prevent monopoly abuses and to simulate a competitive market structure where one would not otherwise exist. Yet much academic research indicates that this is not the case; regulated industries apparently behave more like monopolies than the overall manufacturing sector does. Some analysts have claimed that the regulated firms sooner or later "capture" the regulatory agencies; before long, regulated industries have the protection and sanction of the regulatory bodies! Hence many economists favor deregulation—at least of the older variety of regulation, as existed in the airline, interstate transport, and communications industries. The consensus is less clear regarding regulation by the newer agencies such as the Environmental Protection Agency (EPA) and the Occupational Safety and Health Administration (OSHA).

PROBLEMS

(Answers to the odd-numbered problems appear at the back of the book.)

26-1. The accompanying graph depicts a situation for a monopolist.

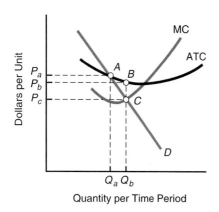

Quantity per Time Period

    a. If this monopolist were required to price at marginal cost, what would the quantity and price be?

    b. What rectangle would indicate total economic losses if this monopolist were required to price at marginal cost?

26-2. "The elimination of all tariffs would dissipate more monopoly power than any other single government action." What do tariffs (taxes on imported goods only) have to do with monopoly power?

26-3. Assume that you are in charge of enforcing the Occupational Safety and Health Act. If you are not constrained to consider the costs of new regulations that increase worker health and safety, what *will* constrain your behavior, if anything? If you now must consider the costs of your new rules, how might you go about your job?

26-4. Would you expect to find more or less corruption of government officials in a regulatory agency that auctioned off "certificates of convenience" or in one that rationed them according to nonfinancial criteria? Why?

26-5. Why is the right of free entry insufficient to prevent sustained economic profits within a natural monopoly?

26-6. Suppose that you own the only natural mineral spring spa in your state. Why would we *not* expect to see the state government regulating the price you charge?

26-7. "Philosophically, I am vehemently opposed to government interference in the marketplace. As the owner of a liquor store, however, I can tell you that deregulation will be bad for the citizenry. You would not want a liquor store on every corner, would you?" Why would you predict that a liquor store owner would defend regulation of the liquor industry in this way?

26-8. The federal government brought an antitrust suit against IBM in 1982. Eventually the case was dismissed as being "without merit." In the beginning of the 1990s, IBM layed off thousands of its workers. What has happened since the time IBM was being prosecuted as a monopoly and today, when it is suffering hard financial times?

COMPUTER-ASSISTED INSTRUCTION

How do natural monopolies arise? This problem relates economies of scale and profit-maximizing behavior to the formation of natural monopolies.

INTERACTING WITH THE INTERNET

The Federal Trade Commission (FTC) is located at
    http://www.ftc.gov/
and the Antitrust Division of the Department of Justice is at
    http://gopher.usdoj.gov/atr/atr.htm
    A good general overview on antitrust issues, with many links to other sources, can be found on the "Antitrust Policy Page" at
    http://www.vanderbilt.edu/Owen/froeb/antitrust/antitrust.html

PART 8

PRODUCTIVE FACTORS, POVERTY, THE ENVIRONMENT, AND INTEREST GROUPS

CHAPTER 27

LABOR DEMAND AND SUPPLY

Except for a relatively small Native American population, North America has been peopled by immigrants for hundreds of years. Indeed, most Americans are proud of their foreign origins, be they Asian, European, African, Latin American, or Middle Eastern. Immigration today, nonetheless, has become a major policy issue. In particular, some politicians and labor unions argue that current immigration is hurting the U.S. economy and is thus pushing down the wages of nonimmigrant U.S. workers. Before you can analyze this issue, you need to know about the basic model of labor demand and supply.

PREVIEW QUESTIONS

1. When hiring labor, what general rule will be followed by employers who wish to maximize profits?

2. What is the profit-maximizing rate of employment for a perfectly competitive firm?

3. What is the profit-maximizing rate of employment for an imperfectly competitive firm?

4. How is an industry wage rate determined?

Did You Know That . . . during the first half of the 1990s, the chief executive of Walt Disney, Michael D. Eisner, was paid by that corporation a total of $235,204,000? That comes out to an average of $47 million a year. In contrast, if you are a typical college or university student, the most you can hope to make during the first year after receiving a B.A. or B.S. is between $25,000 and $50,000, or approximately one one-thousandth of Eisner's average annual salary. Leaving aside whether he is worth it, to understand why firms pay different workers different wages requires an understanding of the demand for and supply of labor.

A firm's demand for inputs can be studied in much the same manner as we studied the demand for output in different market situations. Again, various market situations will be examined. Our analysis will always end with the same commonsense conclusion: A firm will hire employees up to the point beyond which it isn't profitable to hire any more. It will hire employees to the point at which the marginal benefit of hiring a worker will just equal the marginal cost. Basically, in every profit-maximizing situation, it is most profitable to carry out an activity up to the point at which the marginal benefit equals the marginal cost. Remembering that guideline will help you in analyzing decision making at the firm level. We will start our analysis under the assumption that the market for input factors is perfectly competitive. We will further assume that the output market is perfectly competitive. This provides a benchmark against which to compare other situations in which labor markets or product markets are not perfectly competitive.

COMPETITION IN THE PRODUCT MARKET

Let's take as our example a compact disc (CD) manufacturing firm that is in competition with many companies selling the same kind of product. Assume that the laborers hired by our CD manufacturing firm do not need any special skills. This firm sells its product in a perfectly competitive market. A CD manufacturer also buys labor (its variable input) in a perfectly competitive market. A firm that hires labor under perfectly competitive conditions hires only a minuscule proportion of all the workers who are potentially available to the firm. By "potentially available" we mean all the workers in a given geographic area who possess the skills demanded by our perfect competitor. In such a market, it is always possible for the individual firm to pick up extra workers without having to offer a higher wage. Thus the supply of labor to the firm is perfectly elastic—that is, represented by a horizontal line at the going wage rate established by the forces of supply and demand in the entire labor market. The firm is a price taker in the labor market.

MARGINAL PHYSICAL PRODUCT

Look at panel (a) of Figure 27-1. In column 1, we show the number of workers per week that the firm can hire. In column 2, we show total physical product (TPP) per week, the total *physical* production that different quantities of the labor input (in combination with a fixed amount of other inputs) will generate in a week's time. In column 3, we show the additional output gained when a CD manufacturing company adds workers to its existing manufacturing facility. This column, the **marginal physical product (MPP) of labor,** represents the extra (additional) output attributed to employing additional units of the variable input factor. If this firm adds a seventh worker, the MPP is 118. The law of diminishing marginal returns predicts that additional units of a variable factor will, after some point, cause the MPP to decline, other things being held constant.

Marginal physical product (MPP) of labor
The change in output resulting from the addition of one more worker. The MPP of the worker equals the change in total output accounted for by hiring the worker, holding all other factors of production constant.

FIGURE 27-1

Marginal Revenue Product

In panel (a), column 4 shows marginal revenue product (MRP), which is the amount of additional revenue the firm receives for the sale of that additional output. Marginal revenue product is simply the amount of money the additional worker brings in—the combination of that worker's contribution to production and the revenue that that production will bring to the firm. For this perfectly competitive firm, marginal revenue is equal to the price of the product, or $6 per unit. At a weekly wage of $498, the profit-maximizing employer will pay for only 12 workers because then the marginal revenue product is just equal to the wage rate or weekly salary.

Panel (a)

(1) Labor Input (workers per week)	(2) Total Physical Product (TPP) CDs per Week	(3) Marginal Physical Product (MPP) CDs per Week	(4) Marginal Revenue (MR = P = $6 net) x MPP = Marginal Revenue Product (MRP) ($ per additional worker)	(5) Wage Rate ($ per week) = Marginal Factor Cost (MFC) = Change in Total Costs Change in Labor
6	882			
		118	708	498
7	1,000			
		111	666	498
8	1,111			
		104	624	498
9	1,215			
		97	582	498
10	1,312			
		90	540	498
11	1,402			
		83	498	498
12	1,485			
		76	456	498
13	1,561			

In panel (b), we find the number of workers the firm will want to hire by observing the wage rate that is established by the forces of supply and demand in the entire labor market. We show that this employer is hiring labor in a perfectly competitive labor market and therefore faces a perfectly elastic supply curve represented by *s* at $498 per week. As in all other situations, we basically have a supply and demand model; in this example, the demand curve is represented by MRP, and the supply curve is *s*. Equilibrium occurs at their intersection.

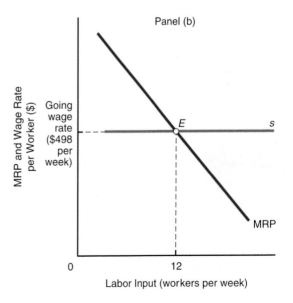

Why the Decline in MPP?

We are assuming all other nonlabor factors of production are held constant. So if our CD manufacturing firm wants to add one more worker to its production line, it has to crowd all the existing workers a little closer together because it does not increase its capital stock (the production equipment). Therefore, as we add more workers, each one has a smaller and smaller fraction of the available capital stock with which to work. If one worker uses one machine, adding another worker usually won't double the output because the machine can run only so fast and for so many hours per day. In other words, MPP declines because of the law of diminishing marginal returns.

Marginal Revenue Product

We now need to translate into a dollar value the physical product that results from hiring an additional worker. This is done by multiplying the marginal physical product by the marginal revenue of the firm. Because our CD firm is selling its product in a perfectly competitive market, marginal revenue is equal to the price of the product. If the seventh worker's MPP is 118 and the marginal revenue is $6 per CD, the **marginal revenue product (MRP)** is $708 (118 × $6). The MRP is shown in column 4 of panel (a) of Figure 27-1. *The marginal revenue product represents the worker's contribution to the firm's total revenues.*

Marginal revenue product (MRP)
The marginal physical product (MPP) times marginal revenue. The MRP gives the additional revenue obtained from a one-unit change in labor input.

When a firm operates in a competitive product market, the marginal physical product times the product price is also sometimes referred to as the *value of marginal product (VMP)*. Because price and marginal revenue are the same for a perfectly competitive firm, the VMP is also the MRP.

In column 5 of panel (a) of Figure 27-1, we show the wage rate, or *marginal factor cost,* of each worker. The marginal cost of workers is the extra cost incurred in employing that factor of production. We call that cost the **marginal factor cost (MFC).** Otherwise stated,

Marginal factor cost (MFC)
The cost of using an additional unit of an input. For example, if a firm can hire all the workers it wants at the going wage rate, the marginal factor cost of labor is the wage rate.

$$\text{Marginal factor cost} \equiv \frac{\text{change in total cost}}{\text{change in amount of resource used}}$$

Because each worker is paid the same competitively determined wage of $498 per week, the MFC is the same for all workers. And because the firm is buying labor in a perfectly competitive labor market, the wage rate of $498 per week really represents the firm's supply curve of labor. That curve is perfectly elastic because the firm can purchase all labor at the same wage rate, considering that it is a minuscule part of the entire labor-purchasing market. (Recall the definition of perfect competition.) We show this perfectly elastic supply curve as *s* in panel (b) of Figure 27-1.

EXAMPLE
Does Attractiveness Lead to Higher Marginal Revenue Product?

Economist Daniel Hamermesh of the University of Texas (Austin) and Jeff Biddle of Michigan State University discovered that "plain-looking" people earn 5 to 10 percent less than people of "average" looks, who in turn earn 5 percent less than those who are considered "good-looking." Surprisingly, their research showed that the "looks effect" on wages was greater for men than for women. This wage differential related to appearance is not, contrary to popular belief, evident only in modeling, acting, or working directly with the public. Looks seem to account for higher earnings in jobs such as bricklaying, factory work, and telemarketing.

According to Hamermesh and Biddle, part of the wage differential may be created by the fact that attractiveness leads to higher marginal revenue product. More attractive individuals may have higher self-esteem, which in turn causes them to be more productive on the job.

FOR CRITICAL ANALYSIS: What are some of the other possible reasons that more attractive people tend to earn more? ●

General Rule for Hiring

Virtually every optimizing rule in economics involves comparing marginal benefits with marginal cost. The general rule, therefore, for the hiring decision of a firm is this:

> **The firm hires workers up to the point at which the additional cost associated with hiring the last worker is equal to the additional revenue generated by that worker.**

In a perfectly competitive situation, this is the point at which the wage rate just equals the marginal revenue product. If the firm hired more workers, the additional wages would not be covered by additional increases in total revenue. If the firm hired fewer workers, it would be forfeiting the contributions that those workers could make to total profits.

Therefore, referring to columns 4 and 5 in panel (a) of Figure 27-1, we see that this firm would certainly employ the seventh worker, because the MRP is $708 while the MFC is only $498. The firm would continue to employ workers up to the point at which MFC = MRP because as workers are added, they contribute more to revenue than to cost.

The MRP Curve: Demand for Labor

We can also use panel (b) of Figure 27-1 to find how many workers our firm should hire. First, we draw a straight line across from the going wage rate, which is determined by demand and supply in the labor market. The straight line is labeled *s* to indicate that it is the supply curve of labor for the *individual* firm purchasing labor in a perfectly competitive labor market. That firm can purchase all the labor it wants of equal quality at $498 per worker. This perfectly elastic supply curve, *s,* intersects the marginal revenue product curve at 12 workers per week. At the intersection, *E,* the wage rate is equal to the marginal revenue product. Equilibrium for the firm is obtained when the firm's demand curve for labor, which turns out to be its MRP curve, intersects the firm's supply curve for labor, shown as *s.* The firm in our example would not hire the thirteenth worker, who will add only $456 to revenue but $498 to cost. If the price of labor should fall to, say, $456 per worker, it would become profitable for the firm to hire an additional worker; there is an increase in the quantity of labor demanded as the wage decreases.

DERIVED DEMAND

Derived demand

Input factor demand derived from demand for the final product being produced.

We have identified an individual firm's demand for labor curve as its MRP curve. Under conditions of perfect competition in both product and labor markets, MRP is determined by multiplying MPP times the product's price. This suggests that the demand for labor is a **derived demand.** That is to say that our CD firm does not want to purchase the services of labor just for the services themselves. Factors of production are rented or purchased not because they give any intrinsic satisfaction to the firms' owners but because they can be used to manufacture output that is expected to be sold for profit.

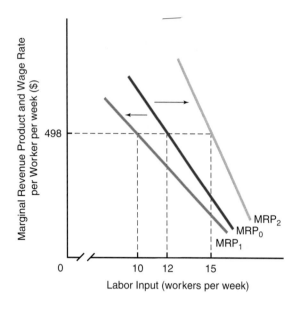

FIGURE 27-2

Demand for Labor, a Derived Demand

The demand for labor is derived from the demand for the final product being produced. Therefore, the marginal revenue product curve will shift whenever the price of the product changes. If we start with the marginal revenue product curve MRP at the going wage rate of $498 per week, 12 workers will be hired. If the price of CDs goes down, the marginal product curve will shift to MRP_1, and the number of workers hired will fall to 10. If the price of CDs goes up, the marginal revenue product curve will shift to MRP_2, and the number of workers hired will increase to 15.

We know that an increase in the market demand for a given product raises the product's price (all other things held constant), which in turn increases the marginal revenue product, or demand for the resource. Figure 27-2 illustrates the effective role played by changes in product demand in a perfectly competitive product market. The MRP curve shifts whenever there is a change in the price of the final product that the workers are making. If, for example, the market price of CDs goes down, the MRP curve will shift downward to the left from MRP_0 to MRP_1. We know that $MRP \equiv MPP \times MR$. If marginal revenue (here the output price) falls, so, too, does the demand for labor; at the same going wage rate, the firm will hire fewer workers. This is because at various levels of labor use, the marginal revenue product of labor falls so that at the initial equilibrium, the price of labor (here the MFC) becomes greater than MRP. Thus the firm would reduce the number of workers hired. Conversely, if the marginal revenue (output price) rises, the demand for labor will also rise, and the firm will want to hire more workers at each and every possible wage rate.

We just pointed out that $MRP \equiv MPP \times MR$. Clearly, then, a change in marginal productivity, or in the marginal physical product of labor, will shift the MRP curve. If the marginal productivity of labor decreases, the MRP curve, or demand curve, for labor will shift inward to the left. Again, this is because at every quantity of labor used, the MRP will be lower. A lower quantity of labor will be demanded at every possible wage rate.

THE MARKET DEMAND FOR LABOR

The downward-sloping portion of each individual firm's marginal revenue product curve is also its demand curve for the one variable factor of production—in our example, labor. When we go to the entire market for a particular type of labor in a particular industry, we find that quantity of labor demanded will vary as the wage rate changes. Given that the market demand curve for labor is made up of the individual firm demand curve for labor, we can safely assume that the market demand curve for labor will look like D in panel (b) of Figure 27-3: It will slope downward. That market demand curve for labor in the CD industry shows the quantities of labor demanded by all of the firms in the industry at various wage rates.

It is important to note that the market demand curve for labor is not a simple horizontal summation of the labor demand curves of all individual firms. Remember that the demand

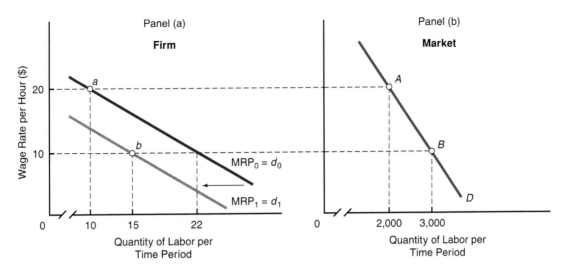

FIGURE 27-3

Derivation of the Market Demand Curve for Labor

The market demand curve for labor is not simply the horizontal summation of each individual firm's demand curve for labor. If wage rates fall from $20 to $10, all firms will increase employment and therefore output, causing the price of the product to fall. This causes the marginal revenue product curve of each firm to shift inward, as from d_0 to d_1 in panel (a). The resulting market demand curve, D, in panel (b) is therefore less elastic than it would be if output price remained constant.

for labor is a derived demand. Even if we hold labor productivity constant, the demand for labor still depends on both the wage rate and the price of the final output. Assume that we start at a wage rate of $20 per hour and employment level 10 in panel (a) of Figure 27-3. If we sum all such employment levels—point a in panel (a)—across firms, we get a market quantity demanded of 2,000—point A in panel (b)—at the wage rate of $20. A decrease in the wage rate to $10 per hour induces individual firms' employment level to increase toward a quantity demanded of 22. As all firms simultaneously increase employment, however, there is a shift in the product supply curve such that output increases. Hence the price of the product must fall. The fall in the output price in turn causes a downward shift of each firm's MRP curve (d_0) to MRP_1 (d_1) in panel (a). Thus each firm's employment of labor increases to 15 rather than to 22 at the wage rate of $10 per hour. A summation of all such employment levels gives us 3,000—point B—in panel (b).

DETERMINANTS OF DEMAND ELASTICITY FOR INPUTS

Just as we were able to discuss the price elasticity of demand for different commodities in Chapter 20, we can discuss the price elasticity of demand for inputs. The price elasticity of demand for labor is defined in a manner similar to the price elasticity of demand for goods: the percentage change in quantity demanded divided by the percentage change in the price of labor. When the numerical value of this ratio is less than 1, it is inelastic; when it is 1, unit-elastic; and when it is greater than 1, elastic.

There are four principal determinants of the price elasticity of demand for an input. The price elasticity of demand for a variable input will be greater:

1. The greater the price elasticity of demand for the final product
2. The easier it is for a particular variable input to be substituted for by other inputs

3. The larger the proportion of total costs accounted for by a particular variable input
4. The longer the time period being considered

Consider some examples. An individual radish farmer faces an extremely elastic demand for radishes, given the existence of many competing radish growers. If the farmer's laborers tried to obtain a significant wage increase, the farmer couldn't pass on the resultant higher costs to radish buyers. So any wage increase to the individual radish farmer would lead to a large reduction in the quantity of labor demanded.

Clearly, the easier it is for a producer to switch to using another factor of production, the more responsive that producer will be to an increase in an input's price. If plastic and aluminum can easily be substituted in the production of, say, car bumpers, then a price rise in aluminum will cause automakers to reduce greatly their quantity of aluminum demanded.

When a particular input's costs account for a very large share of total costs, any increase in that input's price will affect total costs relatively more. If labor costs are 80 percent of total costs, a company will cut back on employment more aggressively than if labor costs were only 8 percent of total costs, for any given wage increase.

Finally, over longer periods, firms have more time to figure out ways to economize on the use of inputs whose prices have gone up. Furthermore, over time, technological change will allow for easier substitution in favor of relatively cheaper inputs and against inputs whose prices went up. At first, a pay raise obtained by a strong telephone company union may not result in many layoffs, but over time, the telephone company will use new technology to replace many of the now more expensive workers.

CONCEPTS IN BRIEF

- The change in total output due to a one-unit change in one variable input, holding all other inputs constant, is called the marginal physical product (MPP). When we multiply marginal physical product times marginal revenue, we obtain the marginal revenue product (MRP).

- A firm will hire workers up to the point at which the additional cost of hiring one more worker is equal to the additional revenues generated. For the individual firm, therefore, its MRP of labor curve is also its demand for labor curve.

- The demand for labor is a derived demand, derived from the demand for final output. Therefore, if the price of final output changes, this will cause a shift in the MRP curve (which is also the firm's demand for labor curve).

- Input price elasticity of demand depends on final product elasticity, the ease of other input substitution, the relative importance of the input's cost in total costs, and the time allowed for adjustment.

WAGE DETERMINATION

Having developed the demand curve for labor (and all other variable inputs) in a particular industry, let's turn to the labor supply curve. By adding supply to the analysis, we can come up with the equilibrium wage rate that workers earn in an industry. We can think in terms of a supply curve for labor that slopes upward in a particular industry. At higher wage rates, more workers will want to enter that particular industry. The individual firm, however, does not face the entire *market* supply curve. Rather, in a perfectly competitive case, the indi-

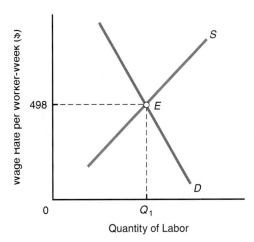

FIGURE 27-4

The Equilibrium Wage Rate and the CD Industry

The industry demand curve for labor is *D*. We put in a hypothetical upward-sloping labor supply curve for the CD industry, *S*. The intersection is at point *E*, giving an equilibrium wage rate of $498 per week and an equilibrium quantity of labor demanded of Q_1. At a price above $498 per week, there will be an excess quantity of workers supplied. At a price below $498 per week, there will be an excess quantity of workers demanded.

vidual firm is such a small part of the market that it can hire all the workers that it wants at the going wage rate. We say, therefore, that the industry faces an upward-sloping supply curve but that the individual *firm* faces a perfectly elastic supply curve for labor.

The demand curve for labor in the CD industry is *D* in Figure 27-4, and the supply curve of labor is *S*. The equilibrium wage rate of $498 a week is established at the intersection of the two curves. The quantity of workers both supplied and demanded at that rate is Q_1. If for some reason the wage rate fell to $400 a week, in our hypothetical example, there would be an excess number of workers demanded at that wage rate. Conversely, if the wage rate rose to $600 a week, there would be an excess quantity of workers supplied at that wage rate.

We have just found the equilibrium wage rate for the entire CD industry. The individual firm must take that equilibrium wage rate as given in the competitive model used here because the individual firm is a very small part of the total demand for labor. Thus each firm purchasing labor in a perfectly competitive market can purchase all of the input it wants at the going market price.

POLICY EXAMPLE

Should the Minimum Wage Be Raised to Help Young People?

The equilibrium wage rate model shown in Figure 27-4 does not apply when the government sets a minimum wage rate below which employers are not allowed to pay workers and workers are not allowed to offer their services. Recall from Chapter 4 that in general, a minimum wage (if set above equilibrium) creates an excess quantity of labor supplied (a surplus) at that legal minimum. Thus young people probably would not be helped by an increase in minimum wages. Look at Figure 27-5 on page 614. There you see the unemployment rate for young people ages 16 to 19. As the minimum wage was raised starting in 1990, so did the rate of unemployment increase for young people. It started falling again only around 1992. Why? In part because what is important is the real, inflation-corrected minimum wage rate. In real terms, the minimum wage dropped to its lowest point in 45 years in 1989. Then it rose until 1992 and started falling again, exactly coincident with the reduction in the unemployment rate for young people. So to answer the policy question, raising the minimum wage probably would not help young people as a group, although it might help some young people who retain their jobs at the higher wage rate.

FIGURE 27-5

Teenage Unemployment and the Real Minimum Wage

Although the nominal minimum wage trends up, the real (inflation-corrected) minimum wage reached its peak in the late 1960s. The teenage unemployment rate is closely correlated with changes in the *real* minimum wage.

Source: U.S. Department of Labor, Bureau of Labor Statistics.

FOR CRITICAL ANALYSIS: Why are young people most affected by changes in the minimum wage? (Hint: Which workers have the lowest MRP?) ●

ALTERNATIVE THEORIES OF WAGE DETERMINATION: EFFICIENCY WAGES AND INSIDERS VERSUS OUTSIDERS

The relatively straightforward analysis of the supply and demand of labor just presented may not fully explain the equilibrium level of wages under certain circumstances. There are two important alternative theories of wage determination that may apply to at least some parts of the economy. We analyze those two theories now.

Efficiency Wages

Let's say that in the CD industry, employers can hire as many workers as they want at the equilibrium weekly wage rate of $498. Associated with that weekly wage rate is a specified amount of employment in each firm. Within each firm, though, there is turnover. Some workers quit to go on to other jobs. Turnover costs are significant. Workers have to be trained. What if a firm, even though it could hire workers at $498 a week, offered employment at $600 a week? Several things might occur. First, current employees would have less desire to look elsewhere to find better jobs. There would be less turnover. Second, those workers who applied for openings might be of higher quality, being attracted by the higher wage rate. Third, workers on the job might actually become more productive because they do not want to lose their jobs. They know that alternative competitive wages are $498 a week.

The higher-than-competitive wage rates offered by such a firm have been designated **efficiency wages.** The underlying assumption is that firms operate more efficiently if they pay their workers a higher wage rate.

Insiders and Outsiders

A related view of the labor market involves the notion of insiders within a firm. The insiders are those current employees who have the "inside track" and can maintain their posi-

Efficiency wages

Wages set above competitive levels to increase labor productivity and profits by enhancing the efficiency of the firm through lower turnover, ease of attracting higher-quality workers, and better efforts by workers.

tions because the firm would have to incur costs to replace them. These employee insiders are therefore able to exercise some control over the terms under which new employees (outsiders) are hired by the firm. They keep other potential workers out by not allowing them to offer themselves for work at a lower real wage rate than that being earned by the insiders. As pointed out earlier, the costs of hiring and firing workers are significant. Indeed, the cost of firing one worker may sometimes be relatively high: termination wages, retraining payments, and litigation if the worker believes termination was unjustified. All such costs might contribute to the development of insider-dominated labor markets. They contain significant barriers to entry by outsiders.

Insider-outsider theory
A theory of labor markets in which workers who are already employed have an influence on wage bargaining in such a way that outsiders who are willing to work for lower real wages cannot get a job.

So the **insider-outsider theory** predicts that wages may remain higher than the standard supply and demand model would predict even though outsiders are willing to work at lower real wages.

EXAMPLE
Competing for the Boss's Job

Although efficiency wage theory and the insider-outsider theory may explain wages that are somewhat above a competitive level, they have a harder time explaining really big differences in wages within a firm's management structure. CEOs tend to make many times more than vice-presidents do. Senior vice-presidents often make double what a regular vice-president makes. According to one theory, corporations create these big salary differentials, *not* in an attempt to reward the recipients, but rather to create a structure of powerful incentives to get people in the organization to work harder. Pay is based on *relative* performance, relative to one's peers within the management organization. The pay of a vice-president is not what motivates that vice-president; it is the pay of the CEO, to whose job the vice-president aspires. Economists Edward Lazer of Stanford University and Sherwin Rosen of the University of Chicago call this concept *tournament theory.* They argue that vice-presidents and others under them are involved in a series of tournaments. The winner of each tournament moves up to the next higher level. All aspire to the highest level, that of the CEO.

FOR CRITICAL ANALYSIS: If luck plays an unusually large role in a vice-president's rise to the top, will the pay differential between vice-presidents and the CEO have to be relatively large or small compared to a situation in which luck is not important? ●

SHIFTS IN THE MARKET DEMAND FOR AND SUPPLY OF LABOR

Just as we discussed shifts in the supply curve and the demand curve for various products in Chapter 3, we can discuss the effects of shifts in supply and demand in labor markets.

Reasons for Labor Demand Curve Shifts

Many factors can cause the demand curve for labor to shift. We have already discussed a number of them. Clearly, because the demand for labor or any other variable input is a derived demand, the labor demand curve will shift if there is a shift in the demand for the final product. There are two other important determinants of the position of the demand curve for labor: changes in labor's productivity and changes in the price of related factors of production (substitutes and complements).

Changes in Demand for Final Product. The demand for labor or any other variable input is derived from the demand for the final product. The marginal revenue product is equal to marginal physical product times marginal revenue. Therefore, any change in the price of the final product will change MRP. This happened when we derived the market demand for labor. The general rule of thumb is as follows:

> **A change in the demand for the final product that labor (or any other variable input) is producing will shift the market demand curve for labor in the same direction.**

Changes in Labor Productivity. The second part of the MRP equation is MPP, which relates to labor productivity. We can surmise, then, that, other things being equal,

> **A change in labor productivity will shift the market labor demand curve in the same direction.**

Labor productivity can increase because labor has more capital or land to work with, because of technological improvements, or because labor's quality has improved. Such considerations explain why the real standard of living of workers in the United States is higher than in most countries. American workers generally work with a larger capital stock, have more natural resources, are in better physical condition, and are better trained than workers in many countries. Hence the demand for labor in America is, other things held constant, greater. Conversely, labor is relatively scarcer in the United States than it is in many other countries. One result of relatively greater demand and relatively smaller supply is a relatively higher wage rate.

EXAMPLE
Does It Pay to Study?

One way to increase labor productivity is to increase skill level. One way to do that, of course, is to go to college. Is there a big payoff? According to a recent study of identical twins carried out by economists Orley Ashenfelter and Alan Krueger, the answer is a resounding yes. They studied the earning patterns of more than 250 identical twins. In this manner, they were able to hold constant heredity, early home life, and so on. They focused on differences in the number of years of schooling. They discovered that each additional year of schooling increased wages almost 16 percent. Four years of college yielded a 67 percent increase in monthly wages compared to no college.

Some economists believe that a college degree is part of **labor market signaling.** Employers do not have much information about the future productivity of job applicants. Typically, the only way to find out is to observe someone working. Employers attempt to reduce the number of bad choices that they might make by using a job applicant's amount of higher education as a signal. According to the labor market signaling theory, even if higher education does not change productivity, it acts as an effective signal of greater individual abilities.

Labor market signaling
The process by which a potential worker's acquisition of credentials, such as a degree, is used by the employer to predict future productivity.

FOR CRITICAL ANALYSIS: Why does studying identical twins' earnings hold constant many of the factors that can determine differences in wages? •

Change in the Price of Related Factors. Labor is not the only resource used. Some resources are substitutes and some are complements. If we hold output constant, we have the following general rule:

> **A change in the price of a substitute input will cause the demand for labor to change in the same direction. This is typically called the *substitution effect*.**

Panel (a)

(1) Labor Input workers per week)	(2) Total Physical Product (TPP) CDs per week	(3) Marginal Physical Product (MPP) CDs per week	(4) Price of Product (P)	(5) Total Revenue (TR) = (2) x (4)	(6) Marginal Revenue Product (MRP$_m$) = $\frac{\text{Change in (5)}}{\text{Change in (1)}}$
7	1,000		$8.00	$ 8,000.00	
		111			$665.80
8	1,111		7.80	8,665.80	
		104			568.20
9	1,215		7.60	9,234.00	
		97			474.80
10	1,312		7.40	9,708.80	
		90			385.60
11	1,402		7.20	10,094.40	
		83			300.60
12	1,485		7.00	10,395.00	
		76			219.80
13	1,561		6.80	10,614.80	

FIGURE 27-6

A Monopolist's Marginal Revenue Product
The monopolist hires just enough workers to make marginal revenue product equal to the going wage rate. If the going wage rate is $498 per week, as shown by the labor supply curve, s, the monopolist would want to hire between 9 and 10 workers per week. That is the profit-maximizing amount of labor. The MRP curve for the perfect competitor from Figure 27-1 is also plotted (MRP$_c$). The monopolist's MRP curve will always be less elastic than it would be if marginal revenue were constant.

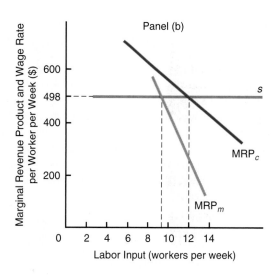

Product," gives the monopolistic firm a quantitative notion of how profitable additional workers and additional production actually are. The marginal revenue product curve for this monopolist has been plotted in panel (b) of the figure. To emphasize the steeper slope of the monopolist's MRP curve, MRP$_m$, the MRP curve for the perfect competitor in Figure 27-1, labeled MRP$_c$, has been plotted on the same graph.

Why does MRP$_m$ represent the monopolist's input demand curve? As always, our profit-maximizing monopolist will continue to hire labor as long as additional profits result. Profits are made as long as the additional cost of more workers is outweighed by the additional revenues made from selling the output of those workers. When the wage rate equals these additional revenues, the monopolist stops hiring. That is, it stops hiring when the wage rate is equal to the marginal revenue product because additional workers would add more to cost than to revenue.

Why the Monopolist Hires Fewer Workers

Because we have used the same numbers as in Figure 27-1, we can see that the monopolist hires fewer worker-weeks than the perfect competitor. That is to say, if we could magically change the CD industry in our example from one in which there is perfect competition in the output market to one in which there is monopoly in the output market, the amount of employment would fall. Why? Because the monopolist must take account of the declining product price that must be charged in order to sell a larger number of CDs. Remember that every firm hires up to the point at which marginal benefit equals marginal cost. The marginal benefit to the monopolist of hiring an additional worker is not simply the additional output times the price of the product. Rather, the monopolist faces a reduction in the price charged on all units sold in order to be able to sell more. So the monopolist ends up hiring fewer workers than all of the perfect competitors taken together, assuming that all other factors remain the same for the two hypothetical examples. But this should not come as a surprise. In considering product markets, by implication we saw that a monopolized CD industry would produce less output than a competitive one. Therefore, the monopolized CD industry would want fewer workers.

OTHER FACTORS OF PRODUCTION

The analysis in this chapter has been given in terms of the demand for the variable input labor. The same analysis holds for any other variable factor input. We could have talked about the demand for fertilizer or the demand for the services of tractors by a farmer instead of the demand for labor and reached the same conclusions. The entrepreneur will hire or buy any variable input up to the point at which its price equals the marginal revenue product.

A further question remains: How much of each variable factor should the firm use when all the variable factors are combined to produce the product? We can answer this question by looking at either the profit-maximizing side of the question or the cost-minimizing side.[1]

Profit Maximization Revisited

If a firm wants to maximize profits, how much of each factor should be hired (or bought)? As we just saw, the firm will never hire a factor of production unless the marginal benefit from hiring that factor is at least equal to the marginal cost. What is the marginal benefit? As we have pointed out several times, the marginal benefit is the change in total revenues due to a one-unit change in use of the variable input. What is the marginal cost? In the case of a firm buying in a competitive market, it is the price of the variable factor—the wage rate if we are referring to labor.

---

[1]Many economic problems involving maximization of profit or other economic variables have *duals,* or precise restatements, in terms of *minimization* rather than maximization. The problem "How do we maximize our output, given fixed resources?" for example, is the dual of the problem "How do we minimize our cost, given fixed output?" Noneconomists sometimes confuse their discussions of economic issues by mistakenly believing that a problem and its dual are two problems rather than one. Asking, for example, "How can we maximize our profits while minimizing our costs?" makes about as much sense as asking, "How can we cross the street while getting to the other side?"

Capital Substitution Threatens Jobs

Every time there is an improvement in capital productivity, the media figure out ways to discuss the resultant loss of employment because of capital substitution. In the absence of restrictions in the labor market, though, capital substitution simply means that in a particular firm or industry, more capital is used and less labor. There are two additional factors to consider: (1) What about the workers used to make the additional capital? Won't there be increases in employment in the capital-producing industries? (2) The economy is not just machines versus workers. Even though the number of employees in manufacturing in the United States has dropped because of capital substitution, the number of employees in service industries, such as software programming, has greatly increased. The U.S. economy has added over 50 million jobs since 1970 despite machines having replaced many workers.

The profit-maximizing combination of resources for the firm will be where, in a perfectly competitive situation,

$$\text{MRP of labor} = \text{price of labor (wage rate)}$$
$$\text{MRP of land} = \text{price of land (rental rate per unit)}$$
$$\text{MRP of capital} = \text{price of capital (cost per unit of service)}$$

Alternatively, we can express this profit-maximizing rule as

$$\frac{\text{MRP of labor}}{\text{Price of labor}} = \frac{\text{MRP of land}}{\text{price of land}} = \frac{\text{MRP of capital}}{\text{price of capital}}$$

The marginal revenue product of each of a firm's resources must be exactly equal to its price. If the MRP of labor were \$20 and its price were only \$15, the firm would be underemploying labor.

Cost Minimization

From the cost minimization point of view, how can the firm minimize its total costs for a given output? Assume that you are an entrepreneur attempting to minimize costs. Consider a hypothetical situation in which if you spend \$1 more on labor, you would get 20 more units of output, but if you spend \$1 more on machines, you would get only 10 more units of output. What would you want to do in such a situation? Most likely you would wish to hire more workers or sell off some of your machines, for you are not getting as much output per last dollar spent on machines as you are per last dollar spent on labor. You would want to employ factors of production so that the marginal products per last dollar spent on each are equal. Thus the least-cost, or cost minimization, rule will be as follows:

> **To minimize total costs for a particular rate of production, the firm will hire factors of production up to the point at which the marginal physical product per last dollar spent on each factor of production is equalized.**

That is,

$$\frac{\text{MPP of labor}}{\text{Price of labor (wage rate)}} = \frac{\text{MPP of capital}}{\text{price of capital (cost per unit of service)}} = \frac{\text{MPP of land}}{\text{price of land (rental rate per unit)}}$$

All we are saying here is that the profit-maximizing firm will always use *all* resources in such combinations that cost will be minimized for any given output rate. This is commonly called the *least-cost combination of resources*. There is an exact relationship between the profit-maximizing combination of resources and the least-cost combination of resources. In other words, either rule can be used to yield the same cost-minimizing rate of use of each variable resource.[2]

---

[2]This can be proved as follows: Profit maximization requires that the price of every input must equal that input's marginal revenue product (the general case). Let i be the input. Then $P_i = \text{MRP}_i$. But MRP_i is equal to marginal revenue times marginal physical product of the input. Therefore, $P_i = \text{MR} \times \text{MPP}_i$. If we divide both sides by MPP_i, we get $P_i/\text{MPP}_i = \text{MR}$. If we take the reciprocal, we obtain $\text{MPP}_i/P_i = 1/\text{MR}$. That is another way of stating our cost minimization rule.

EXAMPLE
Cost Minimization and the Substitution of Software for Labor

The computer revolution, while it is increasing employment in one sector of the economy, may at the same time be decreasing the use of labor in other sectors. In particular, accounting software (capital) is replacing certified public accountants (labor) at an increasing rate. Accounting software has become more numerous, less costly, easier to use, and more sophisticated in the past several years. Nonetheless, the number of certified accountants has risen virtually every year since 1970. A prediction would be that the relative salaries of CPAs should therefore fall in the future (all other things held constant).

The same analysis holds for attorneys. Legal software has proliferated, gotten more sophisticated, dropped in price, and become easier to use. Consequently, paralegals are now able to do many of the jobs that lawyers used to do. Not surprisingly, the paralegal profession is expanding rapidly, while the growth in the number of attorneys is starting to slow down.

FOR CRITICAL ANALYSIS: Can you apply the same analysis to physicians? •

CONCEPTS IN BRIEF

- When a firm sells its output in a monopoly market, marginal revenue is less than price.

- Just as the MRP is the perfectly competitive firm's input demand curve, the MRP is also the monopolist's demand curve.

- For a less than perfectly competitive firm, the profit-maximizing combination of factors will occur where each factor is used up to the point where its MRP is equal to its unit price.

- To minimize total costs for a given output, the profit-maximizing firm will hire each factor of production up to the point where the marginal physical product per last dollar spent on each factor is equal to the marginal physical product per last dollar spent on each of the other factors of production.

Are Immigrants Pushing Down U.S. Wages?

Concepts Applied: *Demand for and supply of labor, shifts in the supply curve of labor, real wages, productivity*

The percentage of U.S. population that is immigrants is rising. Nonetheless, the belief that immigrants abuse the welfare system and contribute to higher unemployment rates for native American workers is not well documented.

Immigration has been on the upsurge since the 1930s, as you can see in panel (a) of Figure 27-7. But immigrants as a percentage of the population are still much less than they were 100 years ago, as can be seen in panel (b) of the figure. Thus any notion that immigration is posing an increased threat to American culture certainly does not stand up to the facts.

A Worldwide Phenomenon

Immigration into the United States, whether legal or illegal, is just a small part of a worldwide phenomenon of human migration. Today, at least 100 million people live outside the country in which they were born. Most of this migration is not to the richer industrialized countries. Consequently, by 2000, fully 17 of the world's biggest cities will be in the developing world with Mexico City, Mexico (26 million), and São Paulo, Brazil (22 million), in first and second place, respectively. New York City will rank fifth.

Just because human migration occurs everywhere does not mean that it is "good" for the U.S. economy.

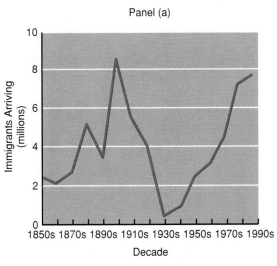

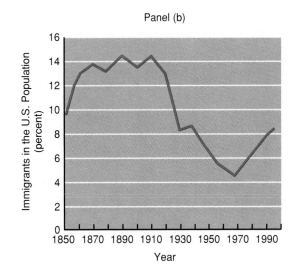

FIGURE 27-7

Immigrants in America
Since the 1850s, the rate of immigrant arrivals peaked in the 1900–1910 period but has almost returned to that high level today, as is seen in panel (a). Nonetheless, the percentage of the U.S. population that is foreign-born is still lower than it was from the 1850s to the 1920s, as is seen in panel (b).
Sources: U.S. Census Bureau; U.S. Immigration and Naturalization Service.

623

Costs and Benefits of Immigration

At least a million—and possibly several million—legal and illegal immigrants arrive and remain in the United States every year. One of the basic criticisms of immigrants is that they use the welfare system more than in proportion to their numbers. This particular issue was argued by proponents of Proposition 187, which won 60 percent of the vote in California only to be thrown out by the courts. Proposition 187 would have made illegal immigrants ineligible for public health services (except for emergency care), attendance at public schools and at state colleges and universities, and most welfare programs.

Although some data show that the percentage of immigrant households on welfare is greater than "native" households, the numbers are suspect. After all, immigrants usually arrive when they are young and healthy. Consequently, they generally need fewer welfare services than native-born families. More important, because they are young, they do not receive Medicare and Social Security, two of the greatest expenditures of the federal government. Moreover, according to economist Julian Simon at the University of Maryland, the typical immigrant family contributes $2,500 more in taxes per year than it obtains in services.

Employment and Wages

Another major question with respect to immigration is whether immigrants will force down wages and create unemployment. According to numerous studies, there is virtually no statistically significant change in unemployment rates when immigration increases.

The data on wage rates are inconclusive. While immigrants definitely increase the supply curve of labor, they mainly affect specific parts of the labor market, and then for only a short time. On an empirical basis, given that America has been peopled by immigrants since the beginning and that real wage rates have been rising more or less steadily, immigration cannot have reduced real wage rates. What has happened is that all labor has become increasingly productive in spite of large increases in the labor force due to both native births and net immigration.

FOR CRITICAL ANALYSIS

1. Nobel Prize laureate Gary Becker has argued that the U.S. government should sell visas at, say, $50,000 each. What would be the costs and benefits of such a policy?
2. "Most new arrivals compete for low-skilled jobs with other immigrants, not with the native-born." If this quote is correct, how does it affect the argument against immigration?

CHAPTER SUMMARY

1. In a competitive situation in which the firm is a very small part of the entire product and labor market, the firm will want to hire workers up to the point at which the marginal revenue product just equals the going wage rate.
2. The marginal revenue product curve for the individual competitive firm is the input demand curve. The competitive firm hires up to the point at which the wage rate equals the MRP.
3. The summation of all the MRP curves does not equal the market demand curve for labor. The market demand curve for labor is less elastic than the sum of the MRP curves because as more workers are hired,

output is increased and the price of the product must fall, lowering the MRP.
4. The demand for labor is derived from the demand for the product produced.
5. The elasticity of demand for an input is a function of several determinants, including the elasticity of demand for the final product. Moreover, the price elasticity of demand for a variable input will usually be larger in the long run than it is in the short run because there is time for adjustment.
6. The firm buying labor in a perfectly competitive labor market faces a perfectly elastic supply curve at the going wage rate because the firm can hire all it

wants at that wage rate. The industry supply curve of labor slopes upward.

7. Efficiency wage theory predicts that wages paid above market wages may lead to high productivity because of lower turnover rates and better work effort by existing workers.

8. The demand curve for labor will shift if (a) the demand for final product shifts, (b) labor productivity changes, or (c) the price of a substitute or a complementary factor of production changes.

9. The MRP curve is also the monopolist's input demand curve. Because marginal revenue is less than the price of the product for a monopolist, the monopolist's input demand curve is steeper.

10. A firm minimizes total costs by equating the ratio of marginal physical product of labor divided by the price of labor with the ratio of marginal physical product of machines to the price of capital with all other such ratios for all the different factors of production. This is the mirror of profit maximization.

DISCUSSION OF PREVIEW QUESTIONS

1. **When hiring labor, what general rule will be followed by employers who wish to maximize profits?**
Employers who wish to maximize total profits will hire labor (or any other factor of production) up to the point at which the marginal cost of doing so equals the marginal benefit, MB. In that way, they will have used up all instances in which the marginal benefit of hiring labor exceeds the marginal cost, MC, of hiring labor. If MB > MC, they will hire more labor; if MB < MC, they will hire less; when MB = MC, they will be maximizing total profits.

2. **What is the profit-maximizing rate of employment for a perfectly competitive firm?**
The perfectly competitive firm will accept prevailing wage rates; it can hire as much labor as it wishes at the going rate. It follows that the MC of hiring labor to the perfectly competitive firm is a constant that is equal to the prevailing wage rate; $MC = W$, where W is the market wage rate. The MB of hiring labor is the value of the marginal product of an additional unit of labor. The perfectly competitive firm will maximize total profits by hiring labor up to the point at which it drives the MRP down to equal the constant wage rate: $MRP = W$. This is also how the firm minimizes costs for a given output.

3. **What is the profit-maximizing rate of employment for an imperfectly competitive firm?**
For an imperfectly competitive firm, $P > MR$. Thus in the short run the marginal benefit of hiring addi-

tional units of labor falls for two reasons: (a) The law of diminishing returns causes marginal physical product to diminish, and (b) to increase sales, price must fall—on previously produced units as well as the new one. Thus the MB of hiring labor equals the *marginal revenue* times the marginal physical product of labor: $MB = MRP = MR \times MPP$.

By assumption, the imperfectly competitive firm is a competitor in the input markets, so in hiring labor it (like the perfect competitor) faces a constant marginal cost equal to the going wage rate; $MC = W$ for the imperfectly competitive firm too. What about the profit-maximizing rate of employment for the imperfectly competitive firm? It hires up to the point at which it drives down the marginal revenue product of labor ($MRP = MR \times MPP$) until it equals the going wage rate; $MRP = W$ is the equilibrium condition in this model.

4. **How is an industry wage rate determined?**
Wage rates are a price; they are the price of labor. As such, wage rates are determined like all prices, by the forces of supply and demand. The market, or industry, wage rate will be determined by the point of intersection of the industry supply of labor curve and the industry demand for labor curve. At the point of intersection, the quantity of labor supplied equals the quantity of labor demanded, and equilibrium exists; both buyers and sellers are able to realize their intentions.

PROBLEMS

(Answers to the odd-numbered problems appear at the back of the book.)

27-1. Assume that the product in the table is sold by a perfectly competitive firm for $2 per unit.

    a. Use the information in the table to derive a demand schedule for labor.

    b. What is the most that this firm would be willing to pay each worker if five workers were hired?

    c. If the going salary for this quality labor is $200 per week, how many workers will be hired?

Quantity of Labor	Total Product per Week	MPP	MRP
1	250	_____	$_____
2	450	_____	_____
3	600	_____	_____
4	700	_____	_____
5	750	_____	_____
6	750	_____	_____

27-2. The table presents some production function data for a firm in which the only variable input is capital; the labor input is fixed. First fill in the other columns. What quantity of capital will the firm use if the price of capital is $90 per machine-week? If the price of capital is $300 per machine-week, what quantity of capital will the firm use? Explain.

27-3. The accompanying graph indicates labor supply and demand in the construction industry.

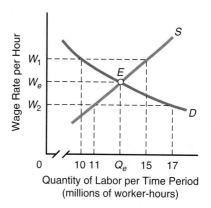

    a. When wage rates are W_1 per hour, how many worker-hours do workers intend to offer per unit?

    b. How much do businesses intend to buy at this wage rate?

    c. Which group can realize its intentions, and which can't?

    d. What forces will be set in motion at wage rate W_1, given a free market for labor?

27-4. Using the graph in Problem 27-3, answer the following questions.

    a. At wage rate W_2, how many worker-hours do workers intend to offer?

Quantity of Capital (machine-weeks)	Total Product per Week	Marginal Product of Capital per Week	Marginal Revenue (product price) per Unit	Marginal Revenue Product per Week
0	0	_____	$10	$_____
1	25	_____	10	_____
2	45	_____	10	_____
3	60	_____	10	_____
4	70	_____	10	_____
5	75	_____	10	_____

b. At W_2, how many worker-hours do businesses intend to purchase?

c. Which group can realize its intentions, and which can't?

d. What forces will be set in motion at W_2 if a free market for labor exists in this industry?

e. What will the equilibrium wage rate be?

27-5. The price elasticity of demand for the final output product directly affects the elasticity of demand for the input factor. Why?

27-6. Suppose that you are seeking to maximize output for a given outlay. If the marginal physical product of input x is 10 and that of input y is 20, and the prices of the two inputs are $3 and $7, respectively, how should you alter your input mix in order to increase output and profit?

27-7. Suppose that you are a monopolist and labor is the only variable input you employ. You are currently producing 150 units of output and selling them for $20 apiece. You are considering the possibility of hiring an additional full-time employee. You estimate that daily output would increase to 160 units if you hired this additional person and that you would be able to sell all of those units at a price of $19 each. What is the MRP of labor (per worker-day)? Assuming that you take the price of labor as a given, what is the maximum daily wage that would make it in your interest to hire this additional employee?

27-8. When there is only one variable input, how does a monopoly seller's demand for that input differ from that of a perfectly competitive seller?

27-9. Assume that you have graduated from college. You decide to look for a job rather than go for further schooling. Indicate how the following criteria might affect the salary that you will receive and the type of job you may end up taking after you graduate.

a. You want to stay near your family, so you do not consider moving out of your immediate geographic area to find a job.

b. You look only for jobs that allow you to apply the knowledge and skills you have learned in your college major.

c. You now live in the city but decide that you will only work in a rural area.

COMPUTER-ASSISTED INSTRUCTION

We explore the foundations of the demand for and the supply of labor, along the way demonstrating the consequences of the minimum wage.

Complete problem and answer appear on disk.

CHAPTER 28

UNIONS AND LABOR MARKET MONOPOLY POWER

The average major-league baseball player today earns about $1.2 million a year. The average professional football player earns about $680,000 a year. The average professional basketball player earns about $2 million a year. At the same time, professional sports team owners continue to buy and sell professional franchises for tens and hundreds of millions of dollars.

For many years, players' salaries grew relatively slowly. Only since 1989 have they increased significantly. To understand the market for professional sports league players, you have to acquire an understanding of various restrictions in the labor market.

PREVIEW QUESTIONS

1. What are the major types of unions?

2. What do unions seek to maximize?

3. Do unions help workers?

4. What is a monopsonist and how does one determine its profit-maximizing employment rate?

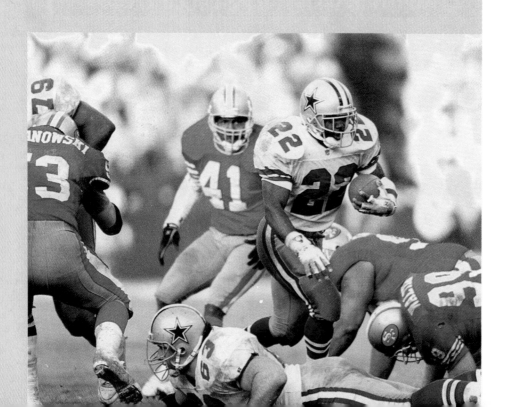

Labor unions
Worker organizations that seek to secure economic improvements for their members; they also seek to improve the safety, health, and other benefits (such as job security) of their members.

Craft unions
Labor unions composed of workers who engage in a particular trade or skill, such as baking, carpentry, or plumbing.

Collective bargaining
Bargaining between the management of a company or of a group of companies and the management of a union or a group of unions for the purpose of setting a mutually agreeable contract on wages, fringe benefits, and working conditions for all employees in all the unions involved.

Did You Know That . . . in 1971, some 2.5 million workers were involved in strikes, but in the past few years, fewer than 250,000 have been involved? More than 12 times the number of workdays were lost to strikes in the 1950s than are lost to them today. The labor landscape has been changing in the United States. That does not mean that concerted activity on the part of groups of workers is insignificant in our economy, though. Some workers are able to earn more than they would in a competitive labor market because they have obtained a type of monopoly power. These are members of effective **labor unions,** workers' organizations that seek to secure economic improvements for their members. In forming unions, a certain monopoly element enters into the supply of labor equation. That is because we can no longer talk about a perfectly competitive labor supply situation when active and effective unions bargain as a single entity with management. The entire supply of a particular group of workers is controlled by a single source. Later in the chapter, we will examine the converse—a single employer who is the sole user of a particular group of workers.

THE AMERICAN LABOR MOVEMENT

The American labor movement started with local **craft unions.** These were groups of workers in individual trades, such as shoemaking, printing, or baking. Initially, in the United States, laborers struggled for the right to band together to bargain as a unit. In the years between the Civil War and the Great Depression (1861–1930s), the Knights of Labor, an organized group of both skilled and unskilled workers, demanded an eight-hour workday, equal pay for women and men, and the replacement of free enterprise with the socialist system. In 1886, a dissident group from the Knights of Labor formed the American Federation of Labor (AFL) under the leadership of Samuel Gompers. Until World War I, the government supported business's opposition to unions by offering the use of police personnel to break strikes. During World War I, the image of the unions improved and membership increased to more than 5 million. But after the war, the government decided to stop protecting labor's right to organize. Membership began to fall.

Then came the Great Depression. Franklin Roosevelt's National Industrial Recovery Act of 1933 gave labor the federal right to bargain collectively, but that act was declared unconstitutional. The 1935 National Labor Relations Act (NLRA), otherwise known as the Wagner Act, took its place. The NLRA guaranteed workers the right to start unions, to engage in **collective bargaining** (bargaining between management and representatives of all union members), and to be members in any union that was started.

INTERNATIONAL EXAMPLE
European Merchant Guilds, the Original Craft Unions

The origin of today's modern craft unions is found in a type of association that flourished in continental Europe and England during the Middle Ages. Around the eleventh century, merchants started traveling from market to market in a caravan to protect themselves from bandits. The members of the caravan elected a leader whose rules they pledged to obey. The name of such a caravan was *Gilde* in the Germanic countries of Europe. When the members of the caravan returned home, they frequently stayed in close association. They soon found it beneficial to seek exclusive rights to a particular trade from a feudal lord or, later, from the city government itself. Soon merchant guilds obtained a monopoly over an industry and its related commerce in a city. It supervised the crafts and the wholesale and retail selling of commodities manufactured in that city. Nonmember merchants were not allowed to sell goods at retail and were subject to many restrictions from which members of the guild were exempt.

FOR CRITICAL ANALYSIS: Analyze the medieval guild in terms of the insider-outsider theory presented in Chapter 27. ●

Industrial Unions

In 1938, the Congress of Industrial Organizations (CIO) was formed by John L. Lewis, the president of the United Mine Workers. Prior to the formation of the CIO, most labor organizations were craft unions. The CIO was composed of **industrial unions** such as the Knights of Labor—unions with membership from an entire industry such as steel or automobiles. In 1955, the CIO and the AFL merged. Organized labor's failure to grow at a continuing rapid rate caused leadership in both associations to seek the merger.

Three important industrial unions declared in the summer of 1995 that they, too, planned to merge. By the beginning of the twenty-first century, the United Auto Workers, the United Steelworkers of America, and the International Association of Machinists will have formed a single industrial union with nearly 2 million members.

Congressional Control over Labor Unions

Since the Great Depression, Congress has occasionally altered the relationship between labor and management through significant legislation. One of the most important pieces of legislation was the Taft-Hartley Act of 1947 (the Labor Management Relations Act). Among other things, it allows individual states to pass their own **right-to-work laws.** A right-to-work law makes it illegal for union membership to be a requirement for continued employment in any establishment.

More specifically, the act makes a **closed shop** illegal; a closed shop requires union membership before employment can be obtained. A **union shop,** however, is legal; a union shop does not require membership as a prerequisite for employment, but it can, and usually does, require that workers join the union after a specified amount of time on the job. (Even a union shop is illegal in states with right-to-work laws.)

Jurisdictional disputes, sympathy strikes, and secondary boycotts are made illegal by this act as well. A **jurisdictional dispute** involves two or more unions fighting (and striking) over which should have control in a particular jurisdiction. For example, should a carpenter working for a steel manufacturer be part of the steelworkers' union or the carpenters' union? A **sympathy strike** occurs when one union strikes in sympathy with another union's cause or strike. For example, if the retail clerks' union in an area is striking grocery stores, Teamsters may refuse to deliver products to those stores in sympathy with the retail clerks' demands for higher wages or better working conditions. A **secondary boycott** is the boycotting of a company that deals with a struck company. For example, if union workers strike a baking company, the boycotting of grocery stores that continue to sell that company's products is a secondary boycott. The secondary boycott brings pressure on third parties to force them to stop dealing with an employer who is being struck.

In general, the Taft-Hartley Act outlawed unfair labor practices of unions, such as make-work rules and forcing unwilling workers to join a particular union. Perhaps the most famous aspect of the Taft-Hartley Act is its provision that the president can obtain a court

Industrial unions
Labor unions that consist of workers from a particular industry, such as automobile manufacturing or steel manufacturing.

Right-to-work laws
Laws that make it illegal to require union membership as a condition of continuing employment in a particular firm.

Closed shop
A business enterprise in which employees must belong to the union before they can be hired and must remain in the union after they are hired.

Union shop
A business enterprise that allows the hiring of nonunion members, conditional on their joining the union by some specified date after employment begins.

Jurisdictional dispute
A dispute involving two or more unions over which should have control of a particular jurisdiction, such as a particular craft or skill or a particular firm or industry.

Sympathy strike
A strike by a union in sympathy with another union's strike or cause.

Secondary boycott
A boycott of companies or products sold by companies that are dealing with a company being struck.

injunction that will stop a strike for an 80-day cooling-off period if the strike is expected to imperil the nation's safety or health.

The Current Status of Labor Unions

If you look at Figure 28-1, you can see that organized labor's heyday occurred from the 1940s through the 1970s. Since then, union membership has fallen almost every year. Currently, it is hovering around 15 percent of the civilian labor force. If you remove labor unions in the public sector—federal, state, and local government workers—private sector union membership in the United States is only about 11 percent of the civilian labor force.

Part of the explanation for the decline in union membership has to do with the shift away from manufacturing. Unions were always strongest in so-called blue-collar jobs. In 1948, workers in goods-producing industries, transportation, and utilities constituted 51.2 percent of private nonagricultural employment. Today that number is only 25 percent. Manufacturing jobs account for only 16 percent of all employment. In addition, persistent illegal immigration has weakened the power of unions. Much of the unskilled and typically nonunionized work in the United States is done by foreign-born workers, some of whom are undocumented. They are unlikely targets for union organizers.

FIGURE 28-1

Decline in Union Membership

Numerically, union membership in the United States has increased dramatically since the 1930s, but as a percentage of the labor force, union membership peaked around 1960 and has been falling ever since. Most recently, the absolute number of union members has also diminished.

Sources: L. Davis et al., *American Economic Growth* (New York: HarperCollins, 1972), p. 220; U.S. Department of Labor, Bureau of Labor Statistics. 1996 data estimated.

The deregulation of certain industries has also led to a decline in unionism. More intense competition in formally regulated industries, such as the airlines, has led to a movement toward nonunionized labor. Finally, increased labor force participation by women has led to a decline in union importance. Women have traditionally been less inclined to join unions than their male counterparts.

INTERNATIONAL EXAMPLE
Europe's Management-Labor Councils

Unionization rates are much higher in the European Union (EU) than in the United States, averaging 48 percent. Perhaps more important, most EU countries have institutionalized the concept of *management-labor councils*. In Germany, legislation dating back to the early 1950s created such councils, requiring that management and labor reach decisions jointly and unanimously. German management-labor councils use up a significant amount of management time. At H. C. Asmussen, a small German distilling company with 300 workers, there are five work councils, some of which meet weekly.

On a pan-European basis, an EU directive has forced 1,500 of the European Union's largest companies to set up Europe-wide worker-management consultative committees. In the United States, no such legislation exists, although there is a management desire to create more "quality circles" (to improve quality and to reduce costs) that involve workers and management. These are often used as a threat to unions or even a substitute for them. In fact, some American unions have succeeded in getting the federal government, through the National Labor Relations Board, to disband such quality circles.

FOR CRITICAL ANALYSIS: Why do you think American unions might be against quality circles involving management and workers? •

CONCEPTS IN BRIEF

- The American Federation of Labor (AFL), composed of craft unions, was formed in 1886 under the leadership of Samuel Gompers. Membership increased until after World War I, at which time the government temporarily stopped protecting labor's right to organize.

- During the Great Depression, legislation was passed that allowed for collective bargaining. The National Labor Relations Act of 1935 guaranteed workers the right to start unions. The Congress of Industrial Organizations (CIO), composed of industrial unions, was formed during the Great Depression.

UNIONS AND COLLECTIVE BARGAINING CONTRACTS

Unions can be regarded as setters of minimum wages. Through collective bargaining, unions establish minimum wages below which no individual worker can offer his or her services. Each year, collective bargaining contracts covering wages as well as working conditions and fringe benefits for about 8 million workers are negotiated. Union negotiators act as agents for all members of the bargaining unit. They bargain with management about the provisions of a labor contract. Once union representatives believe that they have an acceptable collective contract, they will submit it to a vote of the union members. If approved by the members, the contract sets wage rates, maximum workdays, working conditions, fringe benefits, and other matters, usually for the next two or three years. Typically, collective bargaining contracts between management and the union apply also to nonunion members who are employed by the firm or the industry.

Strike: The Ultimate Bargaining Tool

Whenever union-management negotiations break down, union negotiators may turn to their ultimate bargaining tool, the threat or the reality of a strike. The first recorded strike in U.S. history occurred shortly after the Revolutionary War, when Philadelphia printers walked out in 1786 over a demand for a weekly minimum wage of $6. Strikes make headlines, but in only 4 percent of all labor-management disputes does a strike occur before the contract is signed. In the other 96 percent of cases, contracts are signed without much public fanfare.

The purpose of a strike is to impose costs on recalcitrant management to force its acceptance of the union's proposed contract terms. Strikes disrupt production and interfere with a company's or an industry's ability to sell goods and services. The strike works both ways, though. Workers draw no wages while on strike (they may be partly compensated out of union strike funds). Striking union workers may also be eligible to draw state unemployment benefits.

The impact of a strike is closely related to the ability of striking unions to prevent nonstriking (and perhaps nonunion) employees from continuing to work for the targeted company or industry. Therefore, steps are usually taken to prevent others from working for the employer. **Strikebreakers** can effectively destroy whatever bargaining power rests behind a strike. Numerous methods have been used to prevent strikebreakers from breaking strikes. Violence has been known to erupt, almost always in connection with attempts to prevent strikebreaking.

Strikebreakers
Temporary or permanent workers hired by a company to replace union members who are striking.

EXAMPLE
Strikes in Professional Sports

Twice in the past two decades, professional baseball players have gone on strike. In 1994, virtually the entire season was lost. At the start of the following season, professional baseball team owners hired replacement players at much lower salaries. The same action was taken by professional football team owners during the NFL strike in 1987. For three games, substitute football players, alongside regular team players who "crossed the picket line," courageously attempted to play professional football. The results were not quite what fans were used to seeing—and therein lies the rub. Compare this situation with one in which a shoemaking factory suffers a strike. Strikebreakers (substitute "players") can learn the strikers' jobs relatively quickly; the skills involved are not too difficult. But in professional sports, it is hard, if not impossible, to duplicate the skills of the best players. Therefore, professional league players are not so easily replaced. Moreover, current professional sports management cannot figure out ways to automate sports as, say, the telephone industry has done in order to weaken the power of unions in that industry.

FOR CRITICAL ANALYSIS: Who benefited from the strikes in professional football and professional baseball? •

UNION GOALS

We have already pointed out that one of the goals of unions is to set minimum wages. In many situations, any wage rate set higher than a competitive market clearing wage rate will reduce total employment in that market. This can be seen in Figure 28-2. We have a competitive market for labor. The market demand curve is D, and the market supply curve is S. The market clearing wage rate will be W_e; the equilibrium quantity of labor will be Q_e. If the union establishes by collective bargaining a minimum wage rate that exceeds W_e, an excess quantity of labor will be supplied (assuming no change in the labor demand schedule). If the minimum wage established by union collective bargaining is W_U, the quantity supplied would be Q_S; the quantity demanded would be Q_D. The difference is the excess quantity supplied, or surplus. Hence the following point becomes clear:

> **One of the major roles of a union that establishes a wage rate above the market clearing wage rate is to ration available jobs among the excess number of workers who wish to work in unionized industries.**

Note also that the surplus of labor is equivalent to a shortage of jobs at wage rates above equilibrium.

The union may use a system of seniority, a lengthening of the apprenticeship period to discourage potential members from joining, and other such rationing methods. This has the effect of shifting the supply of labor curve to the left in order to support the higher wage, W_U.

There is a trade-off here that any union's leadership must face: Higher wages inevitably mean a reduction in total employment, as more persons are seeking a smaller number of positions. (Moreover, at higher wages, more workers will seek to enter the industry, thereby adding to the surplus that occurs because of the union contract.) Facing higher wages, management may replace part of the workforce with machinery.

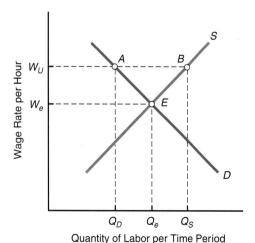

FIGURE 28-2

Unions Must Ration Jobs
If the union succeeds in obtaining wage rate W_U, the quantity of labor demanded will be Q_D, but the quantity of labor supplied will be Q_S. The union must ration a limited number of jobs to a greater number of workers; the surplus of labor is equivalent to a shortage of jobs at that wage rate.

Union Strategies

If we view unions as monopoly sellers of a service, we can identify three different wage and employment strategies that they use: ensuring employment for all members of the union, maximizing aggregate income workers, and maximizing wage rates for some workers.

Employing All Members in the Union. Assume that the union has Q_1 workers. If it faces a labor demand curve such as D in Figure 28-3, the only way it can "sell" all of those workers' services is to accept a wage rate of W_1. This is similar to any other demand curve. The demand curve tells the maximum price that can be charged to sell any particular quantity of a good or service. Here the service happens to be labor.

Maximizing Member Income. If the union is interested in maximizing the gross income of its members, it will normally want a smaller membership than Q_1—namely, Q_2 workers, all employed and paid a wage rate of W_2. The aggregate income to all members of the union is represented by the wages of only the ones who work. Total income earned by union members is maximized where the price elasticity of demand is numerically equal to 1. That occurs where marginal revenue equals zero. In Figure 28-3, marginal revenue equals zero at a quantity of labor Q_2. So we know that if the union obtains a wage rate equal to W_2, and therefore Q_2 workers are demanded, the total income to the union membership will be maximized. In other words, $Q_2 \times W_2$ (the shaded area) will be greater than any other combination of wage rates and quantities of union workers demanded. It is, for example, greater than $Q_1 \times W_1$. Note that in this situation, if the union started out with Q_1 members, there would be $Q_1 - Q_2$ members out of *union* work at the wage rate W_2. (Those out of union work either remain unemployed or go to other industries, which has a depressing effect on wages in nonunion industries due to the increase in supply of nonunion workers there.)

Maximizing Wage Rates for Certain Workers. Assume that the union wants to maximize the wage for some of its workers—perhaps those with the most seniority. If it wanted to keep a quantity of Q_3 workers employed, it would seek to obtain a wage rate of W_3. This would require deciding which workers should be unemployed and which workers should work and for how long each week or each year they should be employed.

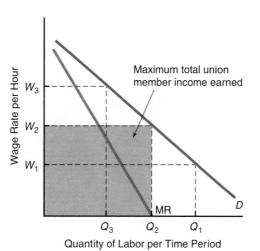

FIGURE 28-3

What Do Unions Maximize?
Assume that the union wants to employ all its Q_1 members. It will attempt to get wage rate W_1. If the union wants to maximize total wage receipts (income), it will do so at wage rate W_2, where the elasticity of the demand for labor is equal to 1. (The shaded area represents the maximum total income that the union would earn at W_2.) If the union wants to maximize the wage rate for a given number of workers, say, Q_3, it will set the wage rate at W_3.

Limiting Entry over Time

One way to raise wage rates without specifically setting wages is for unions to limit the size of their membership to the size of their employed workforce when the union was first organized. No workers are put out of work at the time the union is formed. Over time, as the demand for labor in the industry increases, there is no net increase in union membership, so larger wage increases are obtained than would otherwise be the case. We see this in Figure 28-4. Union members freeze entry into their union, thereby obtaining a wage rate of $16 per hour instead of allowing a wage rate of $15 per hour with no restriction on labor supply.

Altering the Demand for Union Labor

Another way in which unions can increase wages is to shift the demand curve for labor outward to the right. This approach compares favorably with the supply restriction approach because it increases both wage rates and employment level. The demand for union labor can be increased by increasing worker productivity, increasing the demand for union-made goods, and decreasing the demand for non-union-made goods.

Increasing Worker Productivity. Supporters of unions have argued that unions provide a good system of industrial jurisprudence. The presence of unions may induce workers to feel that they are working in fair and just circumstances. If so, they work harder, increasing labor productivity. Productivity is also increased when unions resolve differences and reduce conflicts between workers and management, thereby providing a smoother administrative environment.

Increasing Demand for Union-Made Goods. Because the demand for labor is a derived demand, a rise in the demand for products produced by union labor will increase the demand for union labor itself. One way in which unions attempt to increase the demand for union labor–produced products is by advertising "Look for the union label."

Decreasing the Demand for Non-Union-Made Goods. When the demand for goods that are competing with (or are substitutes for) union-made goods is reduced, consumers

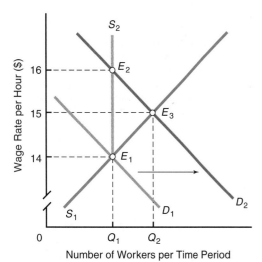

FIGURE 28-4

Restricting Supply over Time
When the union was formed, it didn't affect wage rates or employment, which remained at $14 and Q_1 (the equilibrium wage rate and quantity). However, as demand increased—that is, as the demand schedule shifted outward to D_2 from D_1—the union restricted membership to its original level of Q_1. The new supply curve is S_1S_2, which intersects D_2 at E_2, or at a wage rate of $16. Without the union, equilibrium would be at E_3 with a wage rate of $15 and employment of Q_2.

shift to union-made goods, increasing the demand. A good example is when various unions campaign against imports; restrictions on imported cars are supported by the United Auto Workers as strongly as the Textile Workers Unions support restrictions on imported textile goods. The result is greater demand for goods "made in the USA," which in turn presumably increases the demand for American union (and nonunion) labor.

HAVE UNIONS RAISED WAGES?

We have seen that unions are able to raise the wages of their members if they are successful at limiting the supply of labor in a particular industry. They are also able to raise wages above what wages would otherwise be to the extent that they can shift the demand for union labor outward to the right. This can be done using the methods we have just discussed, including collective bargaining agreements that require specified workers for any given job—for example, by requiring a pilot, a copilot, and an engineer in the cockpit of a jet airplane even if an engineer is not needed on short flights. Economists have done extensive research to determine the actual increase in union wages relative to nonunion wages. They have found that in certain industries, such as construction, and in certain occupations, such as commercial airline pilot, the union wage differential can be 50 percent or more. That is to say, unions have been able in some industries and occupations to raise wage rates 50 percent or more above what they would be in the absence of unions.

In addition, the union wage differential appears to increase during recessions. This is because unions often, through collective bargaining, have longer-term contracts than nonunion workers so that they do not have to renegotiate wage rates, even when overall demand in the economy falls.

On average, unions appear to be able to raise the wage rates of their members relative to nonunion members by 10 to 20 percent. Note, though, that when unions increase wages beyond what productivity increases would permit, some union members will be laid off. A redistribution of income from low- to high-seniority union workers is not equivalent to higher wages for *all* union members.

CAN UNIONS INCREASE PRODUCTIVITY?

A traditional view of union behavior is that unions decrease productivity by artificially shifting the demand curve for union labor outward through excessive staffing and make-work requirements. For example, some economists have traditionally felt that unions tend to bargain for excessive use of workers, as when requiring an engineer on all flights. This is referred to as **featherbedding.** Many painters' unions, for example, resisted the use of paint sprayers and required that their members use only brushes. They even specified the maximum width of the brush. Moreover, whenever a union strikes, productivity drops, and this reduction in productivity in one sector of the economy can spill over into other sectors.

This traditional view against unions has recently been countered by a view that unions can actually increase productivity. The new labor economists contend that unions act as a collective voice for their members. In the absence of a collective voice, any dissatisfied worker either simply remains at a job and works in a disgruntled manner or quits. But unions, as a collective voice, can listen to worker grievances on an individual basis and then apply pressure on the employer to change working conditions and other things. The individual worker does not run the risk of being singled out by the employer and harassed. Also, the individual worker doesn't have to spend time trying to convince the employer that some change in the working arrangement should be made. Given that unions provide this

Featherbedding
Any practice that forces employers to use more labor than they would otherwise or to use existing labor in an inefficient manner.

collective voice, worker turnover in unionized industries should be less, and this should contribute to productivity. Indeed, there is strong evidence that worker turnover is reduced when unions are present. Of course, this evidence may also be consistent with the fact that wage rates are so attractive to union members that they will not quit unless working conditions become truly intolerable.

THE BENEFITS OF LABOR UNIONS

It should by now be clear that there are two opposing views about unions. One portrays them as monopolies whose main effect is to raise the wage rate of high-seniority members at the expense of low-seniority members. The other contends that they can increase labor productivity through a variety of means. Harvard economists Richard B. Freeman and James L. Medoff argue that the truth is somewhere in between. They came up with the following conclusions:

1. Unionism probably raises social efficiency, thereby contradicting the traditional monopoly interpretation of what unions do. Even though unionism reduces employment in the unionized sector, it does permit labor to develop and implement workplace practices that are more valuable to workers. In some settings, unionism is associated with increased productivity.
2. Unions appear to reduce wage inequality.
3. Unions seem to reduce profits.
4. Internally, unions provide a political voice for all workers, and unions have been effective in promoting general social legislation.
5. Unions tend to increase the stability of the workforce by providing services, such as arbitration proceedings and grievance procedures.

Freeman and Medoff take a positive view of unionism. But their critics point out that they may have overlooked the fact that many of the benefits that unions provide do not require that unions engage in restrictive labor practices, such as the closed shop. Unions could still do positive things for workers without restricting the labor market.

CONCEPTS IN BRIEF

- When unions raise wage rates above market clearing prices, they face the problem of rationing a restricted number of jobs to a more than willing supply of workers.
- Unions may pursue any one of three goals: (1) to employ all members in the union, (2) to maximize total income of the union's workers, or (3) to maximize wages for certain, usually high-seniority, workers.
- Unions can increase the wage rate of members by engaging in practices that shift the union labor supply curve inward or shift the demand curve for union labor outward (or both).
- Some economists believe that unions can increase productivity by acting as a collective voice for their members, thereby freeing members from the task of convincing their employers that some change in working arrangements should be made. Unions may reduce turnover, thus improving productivity.

MONOPSONY: A BUYER'S MONOPOLY

Let's assume that a firm is a perfect competitor in the product market. The firm cannot alter the price of the product it sells, and it faces a perfectly elastic demand curve for its product. We also assume that the firm is the only buyer of a particular input. Although this situation may not occur often, it is useful to consider. Let's think in terms of a factory town, like those dominated by textile mills or in the mining industry. One company not only hires the workers but also owns the businesses in the community, owns the apartments that workers live in, and hires the clerks, waiters, and all other personnel. This buyer of labor is called a **monopsonist,** the single buyer.

Monopsonist
A single buyer.

What does an upward-sloping supply curve mean to a monopsonist in terms of the costs of hiring extra workers? It means that if the monopsonist wants to hire more workers, it has to offer higher wages. Our monopsonist firm cannot hire all the labor it wants at the going wage rate. If it wants to hire more workers, it has to raise wage rates, including the wage of all its current workers (assuming a non-wage-discriminating monopsonist). It therefore has to take account of these increased costs when deciding how many more workers to hire.

EXAMPLE
Monopsony in College Sports

How many times have you read stories about colleges and universities violating National Collegiate Athletic Association (NCAA) rules? If you keep up with the sports press, these stories about alleged violations occur every year. About 600 four-year colleges and universities belong to the NCAA, which controls more than 20 sports. In effect, the NCAA operates an intercollegiate cartel that is dominated by universities that operate big-time athletic programs. It operates as a cartel with monopsony (and monopoly) power in four ways:

1. It regulates the number of student athletes that universities can recruit.
2. It often fixes the prices that the university charges for tickets to important intercollegiate sporting events.
3. It sets the prices (wages) and the conditions under which the universities can recruit these student athletes.
4. It enforces its regulations and rules with sanctions and penalties.

The NCAA rules and regulations expressly prohibit bidding for college athletes in an overt manner. Rather, the NCAA requires that all athletes be paid the same for tuition, fees, room, board, and books. Moreover, the NCAA limits the number of athletic scholarships that can be given by a particular university. These rules are ostensibly to prevent the richest universities from "hiring" the best student athletes.

Not surprisingly, from the very beginning of the NCAA, individual universities and colleges have attempted to cheat on the rules in order to attract better athletes. The original agreement among the colleges was to pay no wages. Almost immediately after this agreement was put into effect, colleges switched to offering athletic scholarships, jobs, free room and board, travel expenses, and other enticements. It was not unusual for athletes to be paid $10 an hour to rake leaves when the going wage rate for such work was only $5 an hour. Finally, the NCAA had to agree to permit wages up to a certain amount per year.

If all universities had to offer exactly the same money wages and fringe benefits, the academically less distinguished colleges in metropolitan areas (with a large potential number of ticket-buying fans) would have the most inducement to violate the NCAA agreements (to compensate for the lower market value of their degrees). They would figure out all sorts of techniques to get the best student athletes. Indeed, such schools have in fact cheated more than other universities and colleges, and their violations have been detected and punished with a greater relative frequency than those of other colleges and universities.

FOR CRITICAL ANALYSIS: College and university administrators argue that the NCAA rules are necessary to "keep business out of higher education." How can one argue that college athletics is related to academics? •

Marginal Factor Cost

The monopsonist faces an upward-sloping supply curve of the input in question because as the only buyer, it faces the entire market supply curve. Each time the monopsonist buyer of labor, for example, wishes to hire more workers, it must raise wage rates. Thus the marginal cost of another unit of labor is rising. In fact, the marginal cost of increasing its workforce will always be greater than the wage rate. This is because in the situation in which the monopsonist pays the same wage rate to everyone in order to obtain another unit of labor, the higher wage rate has to be offered not only to the last worker but also to all its other workers. We call the additional cost to the monopsonist of hiring one more worker the marginal factor cost (MFC).

The marginal factor cost for the last worker is therefore his or her wages plus the increase in the wages of all other existing workers. As we pointed out in Chapter 27, marginal factor cost is equal to the change in total variable cost due to a one-unit change in the one variable factor of production—in this case, labor. In Chapter 27, marginal factor cost was simply the competitive wage rate because the employer could hire all workers at the same wage rate.

Derivation of a Marginal Factor Cost Curve

Panel (a) of Figure 28-5 shows the quantity of labor purchased, the wage rate per hour, the total cost of the quantity of labor purchased per hour, and the marginal factor cost per hour for the additional labor bought.

We translate the columns from panel (a) to the graph in panel (b) of the figure. We show the supply curve as *S*, which is taken from columns 1 and 2. (Note that this is the same as the *average* factor cost curve; hence you can view Figure 28-5 as showing the relationship between average factor cost and marginal factor cost.) The marginal factor cost curve (MFC) is taken from columns 1 and 4. The MFC curve must be above the supply curve whenever the supply curve is upward-sloping. If the supply curve is upward-sloping, the firm must pay a higher wage rate in order to attract a larger amount of labor. This higher wage rate must be paid to all workers; thus the increase in total costs due to an increase in the labor input will exceed the wage rate. Note that in a perfectly competitive input market, the supply curve is perfectly elastic and the marginal factor cost curve is identical to the supply curve.

Employment and Wages Under Monopsony

To determine the number of workers that a monopsonist desires to hire, we compare the marginal benefit to the marginal cost of each hiring decision. The marginal cost is the mar-

Panel (a)

(1) Quantity of Labor Supplied to Management	(2) Required Hourly Wage Rate	(3) Total Wage Bill (3) = (1) x (2)	(4) Marginal Factor Cost $(MFC) = \dfrac{\text{Change in (3)}}{\text{Change in (1)}}$
0	—	—	
			$1.00
1	$1.00	$1.00	
			3.00
2	2.00	4.00	
			3.20
3	2.40	7.20	
			4.00
4	2.80	11.20	
			6.80
5	3.60	18.00	
			7.20
6	4.20	25.20	

FIGURE 28-5

Derivation of a Marginal Factor Cost Curve

The supply curve, S, in panel (b) is taken from columns 1 and 2 of panel (a). The marginal factor cost curve (MFC) is taken from columns 1 and 4. It is the increase in the total wage bill resulting from a one-unit increase in labor input.

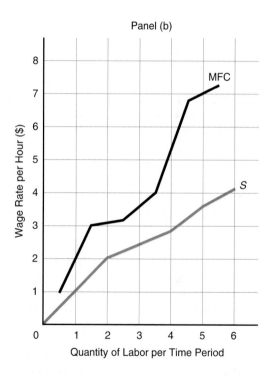

Panel (b)

ginal factor cost curve, and the marginal benefit is the marginal revenue product curve. In Figure 28-6 on page 642, we assume competition in the output market and monopsony in the input market. A monopsonist finds its profit-maximizing quantity of labor demanded at *E*, where the marginal revenue product is just equal to the marginal factor cost.

How much is the firm going to pay these workers? In a nonmonopsonistic situation it would face a given wage rate in the labor market, but because it is a monopsonist, it faces the entire supply curve, *S*.

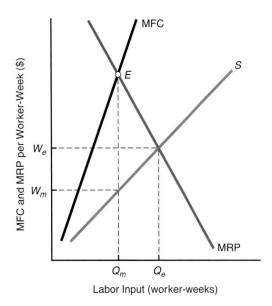

FIGURE 28-6

Marginal Factor Cost Curve for a Monopsonist

The monopsonist firm looks at a marginal cost curve, MFC, that slopes upward and is above its labor supply curve, S. The marginal benefit of hiring additional workers is given by the firm's MRP curve. The intersection of MFC with MRP, at point E, determines the number of workers hired. The firm hires Q_m workers but has to pay them only W_m in order to attract them. Compare this with the competitive solution, in which the wage rate would have to be W_e and the quantity of labor would be Q_e.

A monopsonist faces an *upward-sloping* supply curve for labor. Firms do not usually face the market supply curve; most firms can hire all the workers they want at the going wage rate and thus usually face a perfectly elastic supply curve for each factor of production. The market supply curve, however, slopes upward.

The monopsonist therefore sets the wage rate so that it will get exactly the quantity, Q_m, supplied to it by its "captive" labor force. We find that wage rate is W_m. There is no reason to pay the workers any more than W_m because at that wage rate, the firm can get exactly the quantity it wants. The actual quantity used is established at the intersection of the marginal factor cost curve and the marginal revenue product curve for labor—that is, at the point at which the marginal revenue from expanding employment just equals the marginal cost of doing so.

Notice that the profit-maximizing wage rate paid to workers (W_m) is lower than the marginal revenue product. That is to say that workers are paid a wage that is less than their contribution to the monopsonist's revenues. This is sometimes referred to as **monopsonistic exploitation** of labor. The monopsonist is able to do this because each individual worker has little power in bargaining for a higher wage. The organization of workers into a union, though, creates a monopoly supplier of labor, which gives the union some power to bargain for higher wages.

What happens when a monopsonist meets a monopolist? This is the situation called **bilateral monopoly,** defined as a market structure in which a single buyer faces a single seller. An example is a state education employer facing a single teachers' union in the labor market. Another example is a professional players' union facing an organized group of team owners. Such bilateral monopoly situations have indeed occurred in professional baseball and football. To analyze bilateral monopoly, we would have to look at the interaction of both sides, buyer and seller. The price outcome turns out to be indeterminate.

Monopsonistic exploitation

Exploitation due to monopsony power. It leads to a price for the variable input that is less than its marginal revenue product. Monopsonistic exploitation is the difference between marginal revenue product and the wage rate.

Bilateral monopoly

A market structure consisting of a monopolist and a monopsonist.

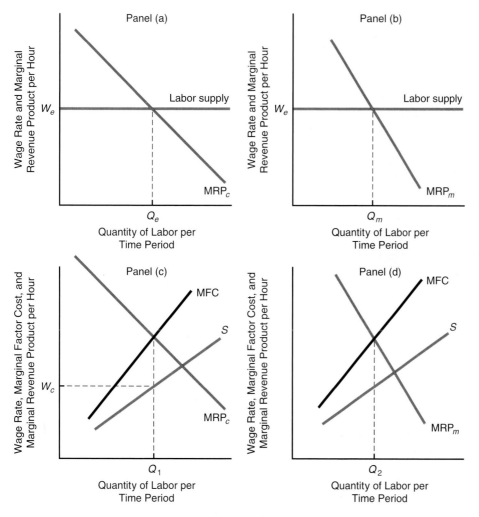

FIGURE 28-7

Summary of Pricing and Employment Under Various Market Conditions

In panel (a), the firm operates in perfect competition in both input and output markets. It purchases labor up to the point where the going rate W_e is equal to MRP_c. It hires quantity Q_e of labor. In panel (b), the firm is a perfect competitor in the input market but has a monopoly in the output market. It purchases labor up to the point where W_e is equal to MRP_m. It hires a smaller quantity of labor, Q_m, than in panel (a). In panel (c), the firm is a monopsonist in the input market and a perfect competitor in the output market. It hires labor up to the point where $MFC = MRP_c$. It will hire quantity Q_1 and pay wage rate W_c. Panel (d) shows bilateral monopoly. The wage outcome is indeterminate.

We have studied the pricing of labor in various situations, including perfect competition in both the output and input markets and monopoly in both the output and input markets. Figure 28-7 shows four possible situations graphically.

CONCEPTS IN BRIEF

• A monopsonist is a single buyer. The monopsonist faces an upward-sloping supply curve of labor.

• Because the monopsonist faces an upward-sloping supply curve of labor, the marginal factor cost of increasing the labor input by one unit is greater than the wage rate. Thus the marginal factor cost curve always lies above the supply curve.

• A monopsonist will hire workers up to the point at which marginal factor cost equals marginal revenue product. Then the monopsonist will find what minimal wage is necessary to attract that number of workers. This is taken from the supply curve.

Pro Sports Means Big Bucks

Concepts Applied: *Monopoly, monopsony, bilateral monopoly, collusion, marginal revenue product, marginal factor cost*

Professional sports players, such as the Dallas Cowboys' Emmitt Smith (22), make multimillion-dollar salaries. Sports players of the past, however, were not as fortunate, earning as a group millions less than their marginal revenue product in the 1960s and 1970s.

A year does not go by without a headline in the sports news that involves multimillion-dollar figures—either a new contract for a professional player that breaks all records or a team franchise that was just sold for $140 million. For many years, though, the big dollar figures were all on the side of the team owners. For many years, professional players faced classic monopsony power by team owners.

The Era of Monopsony Power

Through a variety of restrictions, professional team owners in baseball, basketball, and football acted in concert as single buyers of the labor services of players. The result was salaries below players' marginal revenue product. Economists Lawrence Kahn and Peter Sherer of the University of Illinois estimated that a popular NBA star, such as Wilt Chamberlain, could have earned about $3 million per year (in 1996 dollars) in the early 1970s had he been able to sell his services to the highest bidder. Instead he was paid about $1.7 million (in 1996 dollars). A similar

study done by Gerald Scully found that star hitters in baseball were paid almost $3 million per year less than their marginal revenue product in the late 1960s.

Look at Figure 28-8. In panel (a), you see what happened to baseball players' income during a four-year period of strong collusion by baseball team owners. In panel (b), you see what happened to profits during the same period.

The Era of Bilateral Monopoly

Through a variety of successful court cases and the formation of stronger and stronger players' unions, professional sports has become more of a bilateral monopoly situation. The wage rate is now higher than under pure monopsony, but it is theoretically indeterminate because it depends on the respective bargaining power of the two opposing sides. Strikes in professional baseball and football resulted when bargaining did not yield satisfactory results for both sides.

Taxpayers' Dollars, Too

One little-known fact concerning both high salaries for professional sports players and large profits for owners of professional teams is that both phenomena are in part the result of taxpayer subsidization. Taxpayers do not give money directly to baseball, football, and basketball players or to team owners. Rather, taxpayers give them money indirectly by subsidizing new stadiums. Just consider that in 1950, not a single stadium for baseball's National League was owned by the public; today, more than 80 percent of the league's stadiums are publicly owned. For the American League, the comparable numbers are 12 percent in 1950 and almost 90 percent today. In the National Football League, 36 percent of stadiums were publicly owned in 1950; today that number is 96 percent. For basketball, the number went from 46 to 76 percent and for hockey, from 0 to 52 percent.

Here are some of the sums that taxpayers have transferred:

Camden Yards, Baltimore: $200 million
Comiskey Park, Chicago: $135 million
Jacobs Field, Cleveland: $236 million
Ball Park, Arlington, Texas: $135 million

All in all, just since 1992, about $1.5 billion of taxpayers' money has been spent on professional sports sta-diums, with another $2 billion under construction today and plans for yet another $5 billion by 2000.

In essence, taxpayers, whether they are fans or not, are subsidizing professional sports.

FOR CRITICAL ANALYSIS
1. What arguments are there to justify subsidizing professional sports?
2. What is the difference between a monopoly and a bilateral monopoly?

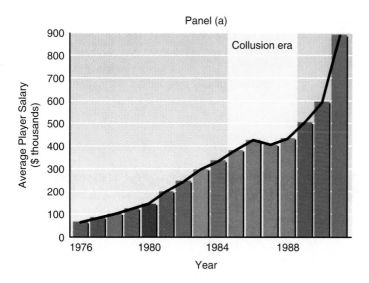

FIGURE 28-8

The Effect of Monopsony Power on Baseball Players' Salaries and the Incomes of Team Owners
The salaries of professional baseball players remained almost flat from 1985 through 1988, the four years during which team owners successfully colluded, as shown in panel (a). In panel (b), you see that team owners experienced rising net incomes during that same period.
Source: National League.

CHAPTER SUMMARY

1. The American labor movement started with local craft unions but was very small until the twentieth century. Important organizations in the history of labor in the United States are the Knights of Labor, the American Federation of Labor, and the Congress of Industrial Organizations.

2. The Great Depression facilitated passage of the National Industrial Recovery Act. This act established the right of labor to bargain collectively. It was later supplanted by the Wagner Act.

3. Unions raise union wage rates relative to nonunion wages. The union wage differential increases during recessions because of the longer-term nature of union collective bargaining contracts.

4. Because unions act as a collective voice for individual employees, they may increase productivity by reducing the time that employees spend trying to alter unproductive working arrangements. Unions may also increase productivity by reducing turnover.

5. Monopsony is a situation in which there is only one buyer of a particular input. The single buyer faces an upward-sloping supply curve and must therefore pay higher wage rates to attract additional workers. The single buyer faces a marginal factor cost curve that is upward-sloping and above the supply curve. The buyer hires workers up to the point at which the marginal revenue product equals the marginal factor cost. Then the labor buyer will find out how low a wage rate can be paid to get that many workers.

6. When a single buyer faces a single seller, a situation of bilateral monopsony exists.

DISCUSSION OF PREVIEW QUESTIONS

1. What are the major types of unions?

The earliest, and one of the most important forms today, is the craft union, which is an organization of skilled laborers. Another major type is the industrial union, in which all or most laborers in an industry, such as the steelworkers or mineworkers, unite.

2. What do unions seek to maximize?

Unions do not have unlimited power; in the United States, the rules that have evolved declare that unions can set wage rates *or* the number of laborers who will be employed, but not both. Consequently, a trade-off exists for union leaders: If they maximize wages, some members will become unemployed; if they maximize employment, wages will be relatively low. Union leaders often decide to maximize wages for a given number of workers—presumably the higher-seniority workers. Each union reaches its own decision as to how to resolve the trade-off.

3. Do unions help workers?

If unions are to be considered effective, they must increase real wage rates *above* productivity increas-es; after all, market forces will increase real wage rates at the rate of productivity change. Yet if real wage rates are increased more rapidly than the rate of productivity increases, unions will cause reduced employment; hence some laborers will be helped (those who retain their jobs at above-productivity wage levels), and some will be hurt (those who lose their jobs). The evidence is that unions are neither a necessary nor a sufficient condition for high real wages. Wages in the United States were relatively high before the U.S. labor movement. Moreover, labor's overall share of national income has not changed significantly since the 1930s, although *union* labor's share may have increased relative to nonunion labor's share.

4. What is a monopsonist, and how does one determine its profit-maximizing employment rate?

A monopsonist is a single buyer. A monopsonist hires labor up to the point at which the marginal benefit of doing so equals the marginal cost of doing so. The marginal benefit of hiring labor is labor's marginal revenue product: MB = MRP of labor. The marginal cost of hiring labor must reflect the fact that the monopsonist faces the industry labor supply schedule; hence the monopsonist must increase wage rates in order to hire more labor. Of course, it must increase wage rates for all the labor that it hires, not just the marginal laborer. Thus the MC of hiring labor for a monopsonist (the marginal factor cost, MFC)

will be greater than the wage rate. Since the profit-maximizing employment rate is generally where MB = MC, the monopsonist will hire labor up to the point where MRP = MFC. It then pays the lowest wage rate required to attract that quantity of labor. This wage rate will be below the MRP of labor.

PROBLEMS

(Answers to the odd-numbered problems appear at the back of the book.)

28-1. The accompanying graph indicates a monopsonistic firm that is also a perfect competitor in the product market.

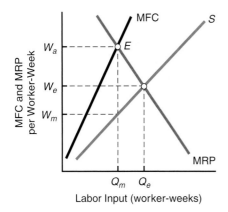

a. What does MRP stand for?
b. Which is the supply of labor curve?
c. How many laborers will this firm voluntarily hire?
d. Given the profit-maximizing employment rate, what is the lowest wage rate that this firm can offer to get this quantity of labor?

28-2. Does a perfectly competitive firm have to worry about the impact of its own demand for labor on the going wage rate?

28-3. Give examples of perfectly competitive sellers having monopsony power in the input market.

28-4. Suppose that you operate a firm that sells its output in a perfectly competitive market. However, you are the only employer in your island economy. You are currently employing 10 full-time employees at a wage rate of $50 per person per day, and you are producing 100 units of output per day. Labor is your only variable input. The market price of your output is $8 per unit. You estimate that daily output would rise to 108 units per day if you increased your workforce to 11 people. To attract the eleventh worker, you would have to pay a wage rate of $52 to all employees. Should you expand your workforce?

28-5. Imagine yourself managing a plant that is a monopsony buyer of its sole input and is also the monopoly seller of its output. You are currently employing 30 people, producing 20 units of output per day, and selling them for $100 apiece. Your current wage rate is $60 per day. You estimate that you would have to raise your wage scale for all workers to $61 per day in order to attract one more person to your firm. The 31 employees would be able to produce 21 units of output per day, which you would be able to sell at $99.50 apiece. Should you hire the thirty-first employee?

28-6. If a union, in its collective bargaining, sets a wage rate that maximizes total union members' income, will all union members be employed? Explain your answer.

28-7. Why will a union never want to bargain collectively for a wage rate that would exist with perfect competition in the labor market?

28-8. "The states that have right-to-work laws deprive workers from enjoying the full benefits of unions." What arguments can be used to support this statement? To deny its validity?

28-9. The marginal factor cost curve faced by a firm buying an input in a perfectly competitive market is identical to its supply curve for that input. Why is this not true for a monopsonist? Explain your answer.

COMPUTER-ASSISTED INSTRUCTION

How does the behavior of monopsonists differ from the behavior of competitive purchasers of labor? What are the consequences of these differences?

Complete problem and answer appear on disk.

INTERACTING WITH THE INTERNET

The AFL-CIO has a substantial amount of material on the organization and issues important to it at **http://www.aflcio.org/**

CHAPTER 29

RENT, INTEREST, AND PROFITS

Do you know what the odds of winning the lottery are? They are the same as the odds of a poker player drawing four royal flushes in a row, all in spades, and then getting up from the card table and meeting four total strangers who were born on the exact same day. Nonetheless, lottomania continues in most of the United States. Of course, somebody has to win. Somebody does, virtually every week. The announced awards, though, constitute a form of false advertising. To understand why, you have to know how to value money that you receive in the future. You will learn about this in the process of studying rent, interest, and profits in this chapter.

PREVIEW QUESTIONS

1. What is rent?

2. What is interest?

3. What is the economic function of interest rates?

4. What is the economic function of profits?

Did You Know That . . . in America, presumably one of the most industrialized countries in the world today, compensation for labor services makes up over 70 percent of national income every year? But what about the other 30 percent? It consists of compensation to the owners of the other factors of production that you read about in Part 1: land, capital, and entrepreneurship. Somebody owns the real estate downtown for which the monthly commercial rents are higher for one square foot than you might pay to rent a whole apartment. Land, obviously, is a factor of production, and it has a market clearing price. Businesses also have to use capital. Compensation for that capital is interest, and it, too, has a market clearing level. Finally, some of you may have entrepreneurial ability that you offer to the marketplace. Your compensation is called profit. In this chapter you will also learn about the sources and functions of profit.

RENT

When you hear the term *rent,* you are accustomed to having it mean the payment made to property owners for the use of land or apartments. The term *rent* has a different meaning in economics. **Economic rent** is payment to the owner of a resource in excess of its opportunity cost—the payment that would be necessary to call forth production of that amount of the resource. Economists originally used the term *rent* to designate payment for the use of land. What was thought to be important about land was that its supply is completely inelastic. Hence the supply curve for land is a vertical line; no matter what the prevailing market price for land, the quantity supplied will remain the same.

Economic rent
A payment for the use of any resource over and above its opportunity cost.

Determining Land Rent

The concept of economic rent is associated with the British economist David Ricardo (1772–1823). He looked at two plots of land on which grain was growing, one of which happened to be more fertile than the other. The owners of these two plots sold the grain that came from their land, but the one who owned the more fertile land grew more grain and therefore made more profits. According to Ricardo, the owner of the fertile land was receiving economic rents that were due not to the landowner's hard work or ingenuity but rather to an accident of nature. Ricardo asked his readers to imagine another scenario, that of walking up a hill that starts out flat with no rocks and then becomes steeper and rockier. The value of the land falls as one walks up the hill. If a different person owns the top of the hill than the bottom, the highland owner will receive very little in payment from, say, a farmer who wants to cultivate land for wheat production.

Here is how Ricardo analyzed economic rent for land. He first simplified his model by assuming that all land is equally productive. Then Ricardo assumed that the quantity of land in a country is *fixed.* Graphically, then, in terms of supply and demand, we draw the supply curve of land vertically (zero price elasticity). In Figure 29-1, the supply curve of land is represented by S. If the demand curve is D_1, it intersects the supply curve, S, at price P_1. The entire amount of revenues obtained, $P_1 \times Q_1$, is labeled "Economic rent." If the demand for land increased to D_2, the equilibrium price would rise to P_2. Additions to economic rent are labeled "More economic rent." Notice that the quantity of land remains insensitive to the change in price. Another way of stating this is that the supply curve is perfectly inelastic.

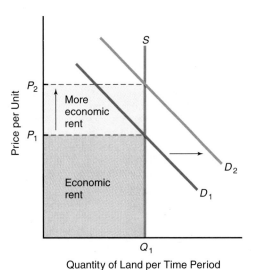

FIGURE 29-1

Economic Rent

If indeed the supply curve of land were completely price-inelastic in the long run, it would be depicted by S. At the quantity in existence, Q_1, any and all revenues are economic rent. If demand is D_1, the price will be P_1; if demand is D_2, price will rise to P_2. Economic rent would be $P_1 \times Q_1$ and $P_2 \times Q_1$, respectively.

ECONOMIC RENT TO LABOR

Land and natural resources are not the only factors of production to which the analysis of economic rent can be applied. In fact, the analysis is probably more often applicable to labor. Here is a list of people who provide different labor services, some of whom probably receive large amounts of economic rent:

> Professional sports superstars
> Rock stars
> Movie stars
> World-class models
> Successful inventors and innovators
> World-famous opera stars

Just apply the definition of economic rent to the phenomenal earnings that these people make. They would undoubtedly work for much, much less than they earn. Therefore, much of their earnings constitutes economic rent (but not all, as we shall see). Economic rent occurs because specific resources cannot be replicated exactly. No one can duplicate today's most highly paid entertainment figures, and therefore they receive economic rent.

Economic Rent and the Allocation of Resources

If an extremely highly paid movie star would make the same number of movies at half his or her current annual earnings, does that mean that 50 percent of his or her income is unnecessary? To answer the question, consider first why the superstar gets such a high income. The answer can be found in Figure 29-1. Substitute *entertainment activities of the superstars* for the word *land*. The high "price" received by the superstar is due to the demand for his or her services. If Kevin Costner announces that he will work for a measly $1 million a movie and do two movies a year, how is he going to know which production

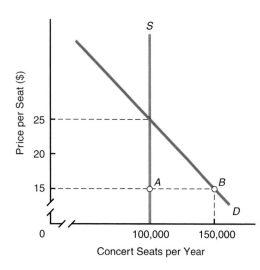

FIGURE 29-2

The Allocative Function of Rent

If the performer agrees to give five concerts a year "at any price" and there are 20,000 seats in each concert hall, the supply curve of concerts, S, is vertical at 100,000 seats per year. The demand curve is given by D. The performer wants a price of only $15 to be charged. At that price, the quantity of seats demanded per year is 150,000. The excess quantity demanded is equal to the horizontal distance between points A and B, or 50,000 seats per year.

company values his services the most highly? Costner and other movie stars let the market decide where their resources should be used. In this sense, we can say the following:

Economic rent allocates resources to their highest-valued use.

Otherwise stated, economic rent directs resources to the people who can most efficiently use them.

A common counterexample involves rock stars who claim that their tickets are overpriced. Consequently, they agree to perform, say, five concerts with all tickets being sold at the same price, $15. Assume that a star performs these concerts in halls with 20,000 seats. A total of 100,000 individuals per year will be able to see this particular performer. This is represented by point A in Figure 29-2. By assumption, this performer is still receiving some economic rent because we are assuming that the supply curve of concerts is vertical at 100,000 seats per year. At a price per ticket of $15, however, the annual quantity of seats demanded will be 150,000, represented by point B. The difference between points A and B is the excess quantity of tickets demanded at the below-market-clearing price of $15 a seat. The *additional* economic rent that could be earned by this performer by charging the clearing price of $25 per seat in this graph would serve as the rationing device that would make the quantity demanded equal to the quantity supplied.

In such situations, which are fairly common, part of the economic rent that could have been earned is dissipated—it is captured, for example, by radio station owners in the form of promotional gains when they are allowed to give away a certain number of tickets on the air (even if they have to pay $15 per ticket) because the tickets are worth $25. Ticket holders who resell tickets at higher prices ("scalpers") also capture part of the rent. Conceivably, at 100,000 seats per year, this performer could charge the market clearing price of $25 per ticket and give away to charity the portion of the economic rent ($10 per ticket) that would be dissipated. In such a manner, the performer could make sure that the recipients of the rent are worthy in his or her own esteem.

EXAMPLE

Economic Rent and the Superstar Income Earners

Everybody knows that big-time entertainers make big bucks. Just consider Table 29-1, which lists some of the top income-earning entertainers in America today as estimated by *Forbes* magazine. The difficult question here is how much of those millions

TABLE 29-1
Superstar Earnings

Name	Occupation	Earnings (annual)
Steven Spielberg	Director/producer, founding partner of DreamWorks studio	$285,000,000
Oprah Winfrey	Television talk show host	146,000,000
The Beatles	Rock band	130,000,000
The Rolling Stones	Rock band	121,000,000
The Eagles	Rock band	95,000,000
David Copperfield	Magician	81,000,000
Pink Floyd	Rock band	70,000,000
Michael Jackson	Pop singer	67,000,000
Barbra Streisand	Actor/director/producer/pop singer	63,000,000
Sylvester Stallone	Actor/producer	58,000,000

Source: Fortune, 1996.

of dollars can be called economic rent. Whereas a relatively new superstar entertainer would certainly work for much less than he or she earns, the same may not necessarily be true for superstar entertainers who have been doing the same thing year in and year out for several decades. In other words, given their already extremely high accumulated wealth and their presumably more jaded outlook about their work, perhaps they would work very little if they were not paid tens of millions of dollars a year.

FOR CRITICAL ANALYSIS: Even if some superstar entertainers would work for less, what forces cause them to make so much income anyway? ●

Taxing Away Economic Rent

Some people have argued in favor of imposing high taxes on economic rent. For example, drug companies that have developed *successful* patented drugs make large amounts of economic rent during the life of the patent. That is to say, the marginal cost of production is much less than the price charged. If the government taxed this economic rent completely, those successful drugs already on the market would in fact stay on the market. But there would be long-run consequences. Drug companies would invest fewer resources in discovering new successful drugs. So economic rent is typically a *short-run* phenomenon. In the long run, it constitutes a source of reward for risk taking in society. This is true not only in the drug business but also in entertainment and professional sports.

CONCEPTS IN BRIEF

• Economic rent is defined as payment for a factor of production that is completely inelastic in supply. It is payment for a resource over and above what is necessary to keep that resource in existence at its current level in the long run.

• Economic rent serves an allocative function by guiding available supply to the most efficient use.

Interest
The payment for current rather than future command over resources; the cost of obtaining credit. Also, the return paid to owners of capital.

INTEREST

The term **interest** is used to mean two different things: (1) the price paid by debtors to creditors for the use of loanable funds and (2) the market return earned by (nonfinancial) capital as a factor of production. Owners of capital, whether directly or indirectly, obtain interest income. Often businesses go to credit markets to obtain so-called money capital in order to invest in physical capital from which they hope to make a satisfactory return. In other words, in our complicated society, the production of capital goods often occurs because of the existence of credit markets in which borrowing and lending take place. For the moment, we will look only at the credit market.

Interest and Credit

When you obtain credit, you actually obtain money to have command over resources today. We can say, then, that interest is the payment for current rather than future command over resources. Thus interest is the payment for obtaining credit. If you borrow $100 from me, you have command over $100 worth of goods and services today. I no longer have that command. You promise to pay me back $100 plus interest at some future date. The interest that you pay is usually expressed as a percentage of the total loan calculated on an annual basis. If at the end of one year you pay me back $110, the annual interest is $10 ÷ $100, or 10 percent. When you go out into the marketplace to obtain credit, you will find that the interest rate charged differs greatly. A loan to buy a house (a mortgage) may cost you 7 to 10 percent annual interest. An installment loan to buy an automobile may cost you 9 to 14 percent annual interest. The federal government, when it wishes to obtain credit (issues U.S. Treasury securities), may have to pay only 3 to 8 percent annual interest. Variations in the rate of annual interest that must be paid for credit depend on the following factors.

1. *Length of loan.* In some (but not all) cases, the longer the loan will be outstanding, other things being equal, the greater will be the interest rate charged.
2. *Risk.* The greater the risk of nonrepayment of the loan, other things being equal, the greater the interest rate charged. Risk is assessed on the basis of the creditworthiness of the borrower and whether the borrower provides collateral for the loan. Collateral consists of any asset that will automatically become the property of the lender should the borrower fail to comply with the loan agreement.
3. *Handling charges.* It takes resources to set up a loan. Papers have to be filled out and filed, credit references have to be checked, collateral has to be examined, and so on. The larger the amount of the loan, the smaller the handling (or administrative) charges as a percentage of the total loan. Therefore, we would predict that, other things being equal, the larger the loan, the lower the interest rate.

What Determines Interest Rates?

The overall level of interest rates can be described as the price paid for loanable funds. As with all commodities, price is determined by the interaction of supply and demand. Let's first look at the supply of loanable funds and then at the demand for them.

The Supply of Loanable Funds. The supply of loanable funds (credit available) depends on individuals' willingness to save.[1] When you save, you exchange rights to current consumption for rights to future consumption. The more current consumption you give up, the more valuable is a marginal unit of present consumption in comparison with future consumption.

Recall from our discussion of diminishing marginal utility that the more of something you have, the less you value an additional unit. Conversely, the less of something you have, the more you value an additional unit. Thus when you give up current consumption of a

---

[1] Actually, the supply of loanable funds also depends on business and government saving and on the behavior of the monetary authorities and the banking system. For simplicity of discussion, we ignore these components here.

good—that is, have less of it—you value an additional unit more. The more you save today, the more utility you attach to your last unit of today's consumption. So to be induced to save more—to consume less—you have to be offered a bigger and bigger reward to match the marginal utility of current consumption you will give up by saving. Because of this, if society wants to induce people to save more, it must offer a higher rate of interest. Hence we expect that the supply curve of loanable funds will slope upward. At higher rates of interest, savers will be willing to offer more current consumption to borrowers, other things being constant.[2] When the income of individuals increases or when there is a change in individual preferences toward more saving, the supply curve of loanable funds will shift outward to the right, and vice versa.

The Demand for Loanable Funds. There are three major sources of the demand for loanable funds:

1. Households that want loanable funds for the purchase of services and nondurable goods, as well as consumer durables such as automobiles and homes
2. Businesses that want loanable funds to make investments
3. Governments that want loanable funds, usually to cover deficits—the excess of government spending over tax revenues

We will ignore the government's demand for loanable funds and consider only consumers and businesses.

Loans are taken out both by consumers and by businesses. It is useful for us to separate the motives underlying the demand for loans by these two groups of individuals. We will therefore treat consumption loans and investment loans separately. In the discussion that follows, we will assume that there is no inflation—that is, that there is no persistent increase in the overall level of prices.

Consumer Demand for Loanable Funds. In general, consumers demand loanable funds because they tend to prefer earlier consumption to later consumption. That is to say, people subjectively value goods obtained immediately more than the same goods of the same quality obtained later on. Consider that sometimes an individual household's present income falls below the average income level expected over a lifetime. Individuals may go to the credit market to borrow whenever they perceive a temporary dip in their current income—assuming that they expect their income to go back to normal later on. Furthermore, by borrowing, they can spread out purchases more evenly during their lifetimes. In so doing, they're able to increase their lifetime total utility.

Consumers' demand for loanable funds will be inversely related to the cost of borrowing—the rate of interest. Why? For the same reason that all demand curves slope downward: A higher rate of interest means a higher cost of borrowing, and a higher cost of borrowing must be weighed against alternative uses of limited income. At higher costs of borrowing, consumers will forgo current consumption.

POLICY EXAMPLE
Should Rent-to-Own Stores Be Regulated?

A growing number of consumers are implicitly borrowing money by dealing with rent-to-own stores that offer them television sets and refrigerators for low weekly payments. At the end of a very long period, they end up owning the item. For example, a consumer can rent a television for $12 a week and at the end of 91 weeks will own it.

---

[2]A complete discussion would include the income effect: At higher interest rates, households receive a higher yield on savings, permitting them to save less to achieve any given target.

Some investigators claim that because the TV is worth only $125 new, consumers are pay-ing over 300 percent annual interest. The U.S. Public Interest Research Group found many cases in which refrigerators with a cash price of $350 ended up costing $1,172 to a cus-tomer buying them from a rent-to-own store. Pennsylvania passed legislation to put in an 18 percent cap on the implicit annual interest rate. Because the number of rent-to-own stores nationwide has increased from 3,000 in 1983 to almost 9,000 today, empirically we know that a consumer demand exists for their services. Typically, the people who use them do not qualify for normal consumer credit. That is why they end up paying such implicitly high interest rates.

FOR CRITICAL ANALYSIS: What do you think happened to the growth in rent-to-own stores after the Pennsylvania legislation was passed? •

Business Demand for Loanable Funds.   Businesses demand loanable funds to make in-vestments that they believe will increase productivity or profit. Whenever a business be-lieves that by making an investment, it can increase revenues (net of other costs) by more than the cost of capital, it will make the investment. Businesses compare the interest rate they must pay in the loanable funds market with the interest rate they think they can earn by investing. This comparison helps them decide whether to invest.

In any event, we hypothesize that the demand curve for loanable funds by firms for investment purposes will be negatively sloped. At higher interest rates, fewer investment projects will make economic sense to businesses because the cost of capital (loanable funds) will exceed the net revenues derivable from the capital investment. Conversely, at lower rates of interest, more investment projects will be undertaken because the cost of cap-ital will be less than the expected rate of return on the capital investment.

The Equilibrium Rate of Interest

When we add together the demand for loanable funds by households and businesses (and government in more complex models), we obtain a demand curve for loanable funds, as given in Figure 29-3. The supply curve is S. The equilibrium rate of interest is i_e.

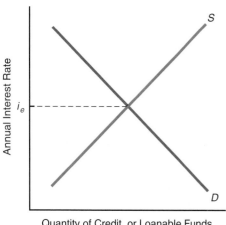

Quantity of Credit, or Loanable Funds,
per Time Period

FIGURE 29-3

The Supply of and Demand for Loanable Funds

We draw D as the demand curve for all loanable funds by households and businesses (and gov-ernments). It slopes downward. S is the supply curve of credit, or loanable funds. It slopes upward. The intersection of S and D gives the equilibrium rate of interest at i_e.

INTERNATIONAL EXAMPLE
One Consequence of Privatizing Italian Banks: Loan Sharking

Until 1994, almost all Italian banks were government-owned, and loans usually were decided on political grounds. When the Italian government got out of some of the banking business, though, the newly privatized bank loan officers lacked the skills and experience necessary to judge whether a potential borrower was a good or a bad credit risk. Consequently, during this interim period after privatization, many small businesspersons in Italy were turned away when they sought loans. Bank loan officers steered them to "loan sharks." Many such lenders operate in violation of Italian law and end up charging borrowers 300 to 500 percent per year, well above the posted "equilibrium" interest rate at the nation's biggest banks.

FOR CRITICAL ANALYSIS: Who typically ends up agreeing to the high interest rates charged by loan sharks? ●

Real Versus Nominal Interest Rates

Nominal rate of interest
The market rate of interest expressed in today's dollars.

We have been assuming that there is no inflation. In a world of inflation—a persistent rise in an average of all prices—the **nominal rate of interest** will be higher than it would be in a world with no inflation. Basically, nominal, or market, rates of interest rise to take account of the anticipated rate of inflation. If, for example, there is no inflation and no inflation is expected, the nominal rate of interest might be 5 percent for home mortgages. If the rate of inflation goes to 10 percent a year and stays there, everybody will anticipate that inflation rate. The nominal rate of interest will rise to about 15 percent to take account of the anticipated rate of inflation. If the interest rate did not rise to 15 percent, the interest earned at 5 percent would be worth less in the future because inflation would have eroded its purchasing power. We can therefore say that the nominal, or market, rate of interest is approximately equal to the real rate of interest plus the anticipated rate of inflation, or

$$i_n = i_r + \text{anticipated rate of inflation}$$

Real rate of interest
The nominal rate of interest minus the anticipated rate of inflation.

where i_n equals the nominal rate of interest and i_r equals the real rate of interest. In short, you can expect to see high nominal rates of interest in periods of high or rising inflation rates. The **real rate of interest** may not necessarily be high, though. We must first correct the nominal rate of interest for the anticipated rate of inflation before determining whether the real interest rate is in fact higher than normal.

The Allocative Role of Interest

Back in Chapters 4 and 6, we talked about the price system and the role that prices play in the allocation of resources. Interest is a price that allocates loanable funds (credit) to consumers and to businesses. Within the business sector, interest allocates loanable funds to different firms and therefore to different investment projects. Investment, or capital, projects with rates of return higher than the market rate of interest in the credit market will be undertaken, given an unrestricted market for loanable funds. For example, if the expected rate of return on the purchase of a new factory in some industry is 15 percent and loanable funds can be acquired for 11 percent, the investment project may proceed. If, however, that same project had an expected rate of return of only 9 percent, it would not be undertaken. In sum, the interest rate allocates loanable funds to industries whose investments yield the highest returns—where resources will be the most productive.

It is important to realize that the interest rate performs the function of allocating money capital (loanable funds) and that this ultimately allocates real physical capital to various firms for investment projects.

Interest Rates and Present Value

Businesses make investments in which they often incur large costs today but don't make any profits until some time in the future. Somehow they have to be able to compare their investment cost today with a stream of future profits. How can they relate present cost to future benefits?

Interest rates are used to link the present with the future. After all, if you have to pay $110 at the end of the year when you borrow $100, that 10 percent interest rate gives you a measure of the premium on the earlier availability of goods and services. If you want to have things today, you have to pay the 10 percent interest rate in order to have current purchasing power.

The question could be put this way: What is the present value (the value today) of $110 that you could receive one year from now? That depends on the market rate of interest, or the rate of interest that you could earn in some appropriate savings institution, such as in a savings account. To make the arithmetic simple, let's assume that the rate of interest is 10 percent. Now you can figure out the **present value** of $110 to be received one year from now. You figure it out by asking the question, How much money must I put aside today at the market interest rate of 10 percent to receive $110 one year from now? Mathematically, we represent this equation as

$$(1 + .1)PV_1 = \$110$$

where PV_1 is the sum that you must set aside now.

Let's solve this simple equation to obtain PV_1:

$$PV_1 = \frac{\$110}{1.1} = \$100$$

That is to say, $100 will accumulate to $110 at the end of one year with a market rate of interest of 10 percent. Thus the present value of $110 one year from now, using a rate of interest of 10 percent, is $100. The formula for present value of any sums to be received one year from now thus becomes

$$PV_1 = \frac{FV_1}{1 + i}$$

where

PV_1 = present value of a sum one year hence
FV_1 = future sum of money paid or received one year hence
i = market rate of interest

Present Values for More Distant Periods. The present-value formula for figuring out today's worth of dollars to be received at a future date can now easily be seen. How much would have to be put in the same savings account today to have $110 two years from now if the account pays a rate of 10 percent per year compounded annually?

After one year, the sum that would have to be set aside, which we will call PV_2, would have grown to $PV_2 \times 1.1$. This amount during the second year would increase to $PV_2 \times 1.1 \times 1.1$, or $PV_2 \times (1.1)^2$. To find the PV_2 that would grow to $110 over two years, let

$$PV_2 \times (1.1)^2 = \$110$$

THINKING CRITICALLY ABOUT THE MEDIA

Those Astronomical Interest Rates

The media have a field day when they analyze economic statistics in particular developing countries. You may have read a story about double- and triple-digit interest rates in such countries as Brazil, Argentina, and Russia. The problem with such stories is that they ignore the difference between nominal and real interest rates. Almost always, astronomically high interest rates are due to people's expectations of very high rates of inflation. Consequently, even with double- and triple-digit nominal interest rates in certain countries, *real* interest rates may be quite low.

Present value
The value of a future amount expressed in today's dollars; the most that someone would pay today to receive a certain sum at some point in the future.

TABLE 29-2

Present Value of a Future Dollar

This table shows how much a dollar received at the end of a certain number of years in the future is worth today. For example, at 5 percent a year, a dollar to be received 20 years in the future is worth 37.7 cents; if received in 50 years, it isn't even worth a dime today. To find out how much $10,000 would be worth a certain number of years from now, just multiply the figures in the table by 10,000. For example, $10,000 received at the end of 10 years discounted at a 5 percent rate of interest would have a present value of $6,140.

Year	Compounded Annual Interest Rate				
	3%	5%	8%	10%	20%
1	.971	.952	.926	.909	.833
2	.943	.907	.857	.826	.694
3	.915	.864	.794	.751	.578
4	.889	.823	.735	.683	.482
5	.863	.784	.681	.620	.402
6	.838	.746	.630	.564	.335
7	.813	.711	.583	.513	.279
8	.789	.677	.540	.466	.233
9	.766	.645	.500	.424	.194
10	.744	.614	.463	.385	.162
15	.642	.481	.315	.239	.0649
20	.554	.377	.215	.148	.0261
25	.478	.295	.146	.0923	.0105
30	.412	.231	.0994	.0573	.00421
40	.307	.142	.0460	.0221	.000680
50	.228	.087	.0213	.00852	.000109

and solve for PV_2:

$$PV_2 = \frac{\$110}{(1.1)^2} = \$90.91$$

Thus the present value of $110 to be paid or received two years hence, discounted at an interest rate of 10 percent per year compounded annually, is equal to $90.91. In other words, $90.91 put into a savings account yielding 10 percent per year compounded interest would accumulate to $110 in two years.

The General Formula for Discounting. The general formula for **discounting** becomes

Discounting
The method by which the present value of a future sum or a future stream of sums is obtained.

$$PV_t = \frac{FV_t}{(1 + i)^t}$$

where t refers to the number of periods in the future the money is to be paid or received.

Table 29-2 gives the present value of $1 to be received in future years at various interest rates. The interest rate used to derive the present value is called the **rate of discount.**

Rate of discount
The rate of interest used to discount future sums back to present value.

INTERNATIONAL EXAMPLE
Viager, or Betting on an Early Death (Someone Else's)

In France, it is possible to make a legal bet on when someone is going to die. It is done through a real estate transaction called *viager,* the right for someone to receive periodic payments until his or her death. Apartments and houses are sold via the system of *viager* in the following manner: Typically, a senior citizen agrees to transfer ownership of the apartment or house in which he or she is living upon his or her death. In exchange for the future right to own the real estate, the purchaser agrees to pay a specified amount every month until the occupant-owner's death. In essence, then, the future owner is looking at the present value of a stream of payments coupled with the current occupant-owner's life expectancy. Under a fair *viager* contract, the present value of the purchase price is approximately equal to the market price of the real estate. If the occupant-owner dies earlier than anticipated, though, the purchaser pays less. The converse is almost always true also.

FOR CRITICAL ANALYSIS: How does present value enter in to the market for the purchase of life insurance policies from terminally ill people suffering from AIDS and cancer? How does this relate to a viager *contract?* •

CONCEPTS IN BRIEF

- Interest is the price paid for the use of capital. It is also the cost of obtaining credit. In the credit market, the rate of interest paid depends on the length of the loan, the risk, and the handling charges, among other things.

- The interest rate is determined by the intersection of the supply curve of credit, or loanable funds, and the demand curve for credit, or loanable funds. The major sources for the demand for loanable funds are households, businesses, and governments.

- Nominal, or market, interest rates include a factor to take account of the anticipated rate of inflation. Therefore, during periods of high anticipated inflation, nominal interest rates will be relatively high.

- Payments received or costs incurred in the future are worth less than those received or incurred today. The present value of any future sum is lower the farther it occurs in the future and the greater the discount rate used.

PROFITS

In Chapter 2, we identified entrepreneurship, or entrepreneurial talent, as a factor of production. Profit is the reward that this factor earns. You may recall that entrepreneurship involves engaging in the risk of starting new businesses. In a sense, then, nothing can be produced without an input of entrepreneurial skills.

Until now, we have been able to talk about the demand for and supply of labor, land, and capital. We can't talk as easily about the demand for and supply of entrepreneurship. For one thing, we have no way to quantify entrepreneurship. What measure should we use? We do know that entrepreneurship exists. We cannot, however, easily present a supply and demand analysis to show the market clearing price per unit of entrepreneurship. We must use a different approach, focusing on the reward for entrepreneurship—profit. First we will determine what profit is *not*. Then we will examine the sources of true, or economic, profit. Finally, we will look at the functions of profits in a market system.

Distinguishing Between Economic Profit and Business, or Accounting, Profit

In our discussion of rent, we had to make a distinction between the common notions of rent and the economist's concept of economic rent. We must do the same thing when we refer to profit. We always have to distinguish between **economic profit** and **accounting profit.** The accountant calculates profit for a business as the difference between total explicit revenues and total explicit costs. Consider an extreme example. You are given a large farm as part of your inheritance. All of the land, fertilizer, seed, machinery, and tools has been fully paid for by your deceased relative. You take over the farm and work on it diligently with

Economic profit
The difference between total revenues and the opportunity cost of all factors of production.

Accounting profit
Total revenues minus total explicit costs.

half a dozen workers. At the end of the year, you sell the output for $1 million. Your accountant then subtracts your actual ("explicit") expenses, mainly the wages you paid.

The difference is called profit, but it is not economic profit. Why? Because no accounting was taken of the *implicit* costs of using the land, seed, tools, and machinery. The only explicit cost considered was the workers' wages. But as long as the land could be rented out, the seed could be sold, and the tools and machinery could be leased, there was an opportunity cost to using them. To derive the economic profit that you might have earned last year from the farm, you must subtract from total revenues the full opportunity cost of all factors of production used (which will include both implicit and explicit costs).

In summary, then, accounting profit is used mainly to define taxable income and, as such, may include some returns to both the owner's labor and capital. Economic profit, by contrast, represents a return over and above the opportunity cost of all resources (including a normal return on the owner's entrepreneurial abilities).

When viewed in this light, it is possible for economic profit to be negative, even if accounting profit is positive. Turning to our farming example again, what if the opportunity cost of using all of the resources turned out to be $1.1 million? The economic profit would have been −$100,000. You would have suffered economic losses.

In sum, the businessperson's accounting definition and the economist's economic definition of profit usually do not coincide. Economic profit is a residual. It is whatever remains after all economic, or opportunity, costs have been taken into account.

Explanations of Economic Profit

Alternative explanations of profit are numerous. Let us examine a few of them: restrictions on entry, innovation, and reward for bearing uninsurable risks.

Restrictions on Entry. We pointed out in Chapter 24 that monopoly profits—a special form of economic profits—are possible when there are barriers to entry, and these profits are often called monopoly rents by economists. Entry restrictions exist in many industries, including taxicabs, cable television franchises, and prescription drugs and eyeglasses. Basically, monopoly profits are built into the value of the business that owns the particular right to have the monopoly.

Innovation. A number of economists have maintained that economic profits are created by innovation, which is defined as the creation of a new organizational strategy, a new marketing strategy, or a new product. This source of economic profit was popularized by Harvard economics professor Joseph Schumpeter (1883–1950). The innovator creates new economic profit opportunities through innovation. The successful innovator obtains a temporary monopoly position, garnering temporary economic profits. When other firms catch up, those temporary economic profits disappear.

Reward for Bearing Uninsurable Risks

There are risks in life, including those involved in any business venture. Many of these risks can be insured, however. You can insure against the risk of losing your house to fire, flood, hurricane, or earthquake. You can do the same if you own a business. You can insure against the risk of theft also. Insurance companies are willing to sell you such insurance because they can predict relatively accurately what percentage of a class of insured assets will suffer losses each year. They charge each insured person or business enough to pay for those fully anticipated losses and to make a normal rate of return.

But there are risks that cannot be insured. If you and a group of your friends get together and pool your resources to start a new business, no amount of statistical calculations can accurately predict whether your business will still be running a year from now or 10 years from now. Consequently, you can't, when you start your business, buy insurance against losing money, bad management, miscalculations about the size of the market, aggressive competition by big corporations, and the like. Entrepreneurs therefore incur uninsurable risks. According to a theory of profits advanced by economist Frank H. Knight (1885–1973), this is the origin of economic profit.

The Function of Economic Profit

In a market economy, the expectation of profits induces firms to discover new products, new production techniques, and new marketing techniques—literally all the new ways to make higher profits. Profits in this sense spur innovation and investment.

Profits also cause resources to move from lower-valued to higher-valued uses. Prices and sales are dictated by the consumer. If the demand curve is close to the origin, there will be few sales and few profits, if any. The lack of profits therefore means that there is insufficient demand to cover the opportunity cost of production. In the quest for higher profits, businesses will take resources out of areas in which either accounting losses or lower than normal rates of return are being made and put them into areas in which there is an expectation of higher profits. The profit reward is an inducement for an industry to expand when demand and supply conditions warrant it. Conversely, the existence of economic losses indicates that resources in the particular industry are not valued as highly as they might be elsewhere. These resources therefore move out of that industry, or at least no further resources are invested in it. Therefore, resources follow the businessperson's quest for higher profits. Profits allocate resources, just as wages and interest do.

CONCEPTS IN BRIEF

- Profit is the reward for entrepreneurial talent, a factor of production.

- It is necessary to distinguish between accounting profit and economic profit. Accounting profit is measured by the difference between total revenues and all explicit costs. Economic profit is measured by the difference between total revenues and the total of all opportunity costs of all factors of production.

- Theories of why profits exist include restriction on entry, innovation, and payment to entrepreneurs for taking uninsurable risks.

- The function of profits in a market economy is to allocate scarce resources. Resources will flow to wherever profits are highest.

A Million-Dollar Jackpot Doesn't Make a Millionaire

Concept Applied: *Present value*

Americans purchase billions of dollars worth of lottery tickets every year. However, winners receive substantially less than the announced jackpot. Payments spread out over 20 years or more significantly decrease the present value of the jackpot.

Every year, over a million Americans in 36 states and the District of Columbia play the lottery. We purchase collectively about $35 billion worth of tickets in this relatively newly legalized form of gambling. Sometimes the winners are not happy, though.

Suing the Lottery

When Michael Ondrish won the lottery in Arizona, he thought he was an instant millionaire. He discovered, though, that instead, the state of Arizona was going to pay him $50,000 a year for 20 years (a grand total of $1 million). He went to court charging fraud and deception. In the state advertisement for the lottery, it never mentioned the 20-year payment system. The court went along with the state lottery in arguing that if Ondrish did not like what he won, he could return his ticket and be repaid the dollar that he spent on it.

Present Value Is What Counts

In reality, though, the millions of dollars of jackpots that are advertised by states running lotteries are not really the millions they claim to be. Let's see why. You win a $15 million state lottery jackpot. Rather than handing you a check for $15 million, the state typically pays you your winnings in installments of, say, $750,000 each over 20 years. Is $750,000 each year for 20 years worth $15 million today? It is true that the $750,000 per year for 20 years does add up to $15 million. But if you were given $15 million all at once, you could invest it at the market rate of interest today and it would be worth considerably more 20 years from now.

Thus in actuality, 20 annual payments of $750,000 are worth much less than $15 million. At an interest rate of 10 percent, they are worth only $6,385,500. You can use Table 29-2 to actually calculate the present value of each $750,000 payment at the end of each year in the future. We can also view this by looking at the value of each of the $750,000 payments. The last installment of $750,000 in the twentieth year is worth a mere $111,750 today, discounted at 10 percent. If we used a higher discount rate, it would be worth even less in present value.

Now you can see why the state prefers to pay out winnings in installments rather than in a lump sum.

FOR CRITICAL ANALYSIS

1. How do income taxes affect the validity of advertising about lotteries?
2. If the chances of winning the lottery are so low, as pointed out in the first page of this chapter, why do more than 100 million people play it every year?

CHAPTER SUMMARY

1. Resources that have a fixed supply are paid what is called economic rent. We therefore define economic rent as the payment over and above what is necessary to keep a resource of constant quality and quantity in supply at its current level.

2. Resource owners (including labor owners) of factors with inelastic supply earn economic rent because competition among potential users of those resources bids up the price offered.

3. Interest can be defined as the payment for command over resources today rather than in the future. Interest is typically seen as the payment for credit, but it can also be considered the payment for the use of capital. Interest charged depends on length of loan, risk, and handling charges.

4. The equilibrium rate of interest is determined by the intersection of the demand for credit, or loanable funds, and the supply of credit, or loanable funds.

5. The nominal rate of interest includes a factor that takes account of the anticipated rate of inflation. In periods of high anticipated inflation, nominal, or market, interest rates will be high. Real interest rates may not actually be higher, however, because they are defined as the nominal rate of interest minus the anticipated rate of inflation.

6. The present value of any sum in the future is less than that same sum today. Present value decreases as the sum is paid or obtained further and further in the future and as the rate of discount increases.

7. Frank Knight believed that profit was a payment to entrepreneurs for undertaking risks that are uninsurable. Other reasons why profit exists include restrictions on entry and reward for innovation.

DISCUSSION OF PREVIEW QUESTIONS

1. What is rent?

Rent is payment for the use of land. Economists have long played with the notion that land is completely inelastic in supply, although this is a debatable issue and depends on various definitions. Modern economists now refer to a payment to any factor of production that is in excess of opportunity cost as economic rent. For instance, from society's point of view, the total supply of land is fixed. Also, athletes and entertainers presumably earn economic rent: Beyond some "normal" income, the opportunity cost to superstars of performing is zero; hence "abnormal" income is not necessary to induce them to perform. Note that we usually discuss positively sloped supply schedules indicating that higher relative prices are necessary to induce increased quantity supplied. This is not the case with economic rent.

2. What is interest?

On the most obvious level, interest is a payment for the use of money. On another level, interest can be considered payment for obtaining credit; by borrowing, people (consumers or businesses) obtain command over resources now rather than in the future. Those who wish to make purchases now instead of later are allowed to do so even if they do not currently earn purchasing power. They do so by borrowing, and interest is the price they must pay for the privilege of making expenditures now instead of later.

3. What is the economic function of interest rates?

Interest rates are the price of credit, and like all prices, interest rates play an allocative role. That is, interest is a rationing device. We have said that interest is the price of credit; this credit is allocated to the households and businesses that are willing to pay the highest price (interest rate). Such is the rationing function of credit. On a more fundamental level, we can see that something other than scarce loanable funds is allocated. After all, businesses don't borrow money simply for the privilege of paying interest! The key to understanding what *physical* resources are being allocated is to follow the money: On what do businesses spend this borrowed money? The answer is for the most part, capital goods. Thus the interest rate plays the crucial role of allocating scarce capital goods; the firms that are willing to pay the highest interest rates will be the ones that will be able to purchase the most scarce capital goods. Firms putting capital to the most profitable uses will be able to pay the highest interest rates (and be most acceptable to lenders) and will therefore receive disproportionately greater quantities of new capital. Interest rates help bring about this capital rationing scheme in a market economy.

4. What is the economic function of profits?

Profit is the return on entrepreneurial talent or the price paid to risk takers. Profits also play a rationing role in society. Profits (in conjunction with interest rates) perform the all-important function of deciding which industries (and which firms within an industry) expand and which are forced to contract. Profitable firms can reinvest profits (and offer to pay higher interest rates), while unprofitable firms are forced to contract or go bankrupt. In short, businesses' quests for profits assure that scarce resources flow from less profitable to more profitable uses; profits help society decide which firms are to expand and which are to contract.

PROBLEMS

(Answers to the odd-numbered problems appear at the back of the book.)

29-1. "All revenues obtained by the Italian government from Renaissance art museums are economic rent." Is this statement true or false, and why?

29-2. Some people argue that the extraordinary earnings of entertainment and sports superstars are not economic rent at all but merely the cost of ensuring that a steady stream of would-be stars and starlets continues to flow into the sports and entertainment fields. How would the argument go?

29-3. "If employers paid marginal revenue product (MRP) to each of their inputs, there would be no profits left over." Is this statement true or false, and why?

29-4. The accompanying graph shows the supply of and demand for land. The vertical axis is the price per year received by landowners for permitting the land to be used by farmers.

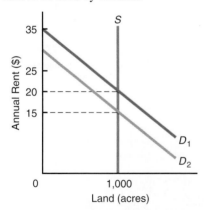

a. Assume that the demand curve for land is D_1. How much economic rent is received by landowners?

b. Now assume that the demand curve for land falls to D_2. How much economic rent is received now?

29-5. The graph shows the demand for and supply of loanable funds.

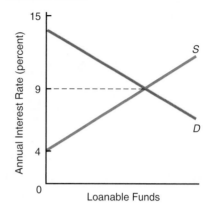

a. What is the equilibrium interest rate?

b. If the supply of loanable funds decreases, what will happen to the equilibrium interest rate?

c. If anticipated inflation is 4 percent for the year, what is the real equilibrium interest rate?

29-6. Make a list of risks that you might face in your life that you believe are insurable. Now make a list of risks that you believe are uninsurable. What is the general distinction between these lists?

29-7. Why do you think that the interest rate you have to pay on an automobile loan is greater than what you have to pay for a loan on a house? Why is the interest rate charged for a loan to purchase a used car usually more than for a loan to purchase a new car?

29-8. At the beginning of the 1980s, virtually all interest rates were much higher than they are in the 1990s. What do you think the major difference is between these two periods that might have caused interest rates to fall so dramatically?

29-9. Assume that everybody has perfect information about all events in the future. What would you expect to happen to economic profits in such a world?

COMPUTER-ASSISTED INSTRUCTION

We explore the many implications of the fact that differently dated goods are fundamentally different commodities.

Complete problem and answer appear on disk.

CHAPTER 30

INCOME, POVERTY, AND HEALTH CARE

By some measures, America remains the richest nation on earth, not only in terms of total annual national income, but also in terms of average annual income per person. Notwithstanding such riches, there are over 100 federal antipoverty programs, including 12 different programs to provide food to the needy and 7 housing programs. Total social welfare spending by federal, state, and local governments for every family of four below the poverty level exceeds $25,000 per year. Nonetheless, officially measured poverty, if anything, is stable or slightly on the rise. Can anything be done to reform our welfare system? To answer this question, you need to know more about the distribution of income, the facts about poverty, and health care problems in this nation.

PREVIEW QUESTIONS

1. What is a Lorenz curve, and what does it measure?

2. What has been happening to the distribution of income in the United States?

3. What is the difference between income and wealth?

4. Why do people earn different incomes?

Distribution of income
The way income is allocated
among the population.

Did You Know That . . . 2.3 million U.S. households are worth more than $1 million? That constitutes 2.4 percent of all American households. When you go further up the ladder, there are only 400 households that are worth $260 million or more, or just 0.0004 percent. Some companies have a disproportionate share of millionaires, particularly new ones. Microsoft reportedly has 2,000 millionaires among its 16,000 employees. Its founder and CEO, William Gates, at last count was worth $12 billion. At the same time, there are over 13 million people officially defined as living below the poverty line. Why do some people earn more income than others? Why is the **distribution of income** the way it is? Economists have devised various theories to explain this distribution. We will present some of these theories in this chapter. We will also present some of the more obvious institutional reasons why income is not distributed equally in the United States as well as what can be done about health care.

INCOME

Income provides each of us with the means of consuming and saving. Income can be derived from a payment for labor services or a payment for ownership of one of the other factors of production besides labor—land, physical capital, human capital, and entrepreneurship. In addition, individuals obtain spendable income from gifts and government transfers. (Some individuals also obtain income by stealing, but we will not treat this matter here.) Right now, let us examine how money income is distributed across classes of income earners within the United States.

Lorenz curve
A geometric representation of
the distribution of income. A
Lorenz curve that is perfectly
straight represents complete
income equality. The more
bowed a Lorenz curve, the
more unequally income is
distributed.

Measuring Income Distribution: The Lorenz Curve

We can represent the distribution of money income graphically with what is known as the **Lorenz curve,** named after a U.S.-born statistician, Max Otto Lorenz, who proposed it in 1905. The Lorenz curve shows what portion of total money income is accounted for by different proportions of the nation's households. Look at Figure 30-1. On the horizontal axis,

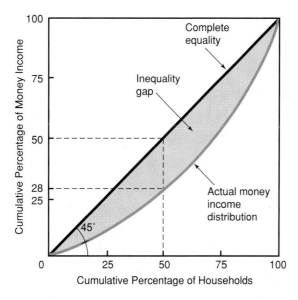

FIGURE 30-1

The Lorenz Curve
The horizontal axis measures the cumulative percentage of households from 0 to 100 percent. The vertical axis measures the cumulative percentage of money income from 0 to 100. A straight line at a 45-degree angle cuts the box in half and represents a line of complete income equality, along which 25 percent of the families get 25 percent of the money income, 50 percent get 50 percent, and so on. The Lorenz curve, showing actual money income distribution, is not a straight line but rather a curved line as shown. The difference between complete money income equality and the Lorenz curve is the inequality gap.

we measure the *cumulative* percentage of households, lowest-income households first. Starting at the left corner, there are zero households; at the right corner, we have 100 percent of households; and in the middle, we have 50 percent of households. The vertical axis represents the cumulative percentage of money income. The 45-degree line represents complete equality: 50 percent of the households obtain 50 percent of total income, 60 percent of the households obtain 60 percent of total income, and so on. Of course, in no real-world situation is there such complete equality of income; no actual Lorenz curve would be a straight line. Rather, it would be some curved line, like the one labeled "Actual money income distribution" in Figure 30-1. For example, the bottom 50 percent of households in the United States receive about 28 percent of total money income.

In Figure 30-2, we again show the actual money income distribution Lorenz curve, and we also compare it to the distribution of money income in 1929. Since that year, the Lorenz curve has become less bowed; that is, it has moved closer to the line of complete equality.

Criticisms of the Lorenz Curve. In recent years, economists have placed less and less emphasis on the shape of the Lorenz curve as an indication of the degree of income inequality in a country. There are five basic reasons why the Lorenz curve has been criticized:

1. The Lorenz curve is typically presented in terms of the distribution of *money* income only. It does not include **income in kind,** such as government-provided food stamps, education, or housing aid, and goods or services produced and consumed in the home or on the farm.
2. The Lorenz curve does not account for differences in the size of households or the number of wage earners they contain.
3. It does not account for age differences. Even if all families in the United States had exactly the same *lifetime* incomes, chances are that young families would have lower incomes, middle-aged families would have relatively high incomes, and retired families would have low incomes. Because the Lorenz curve is drawn at a moment in time, it could never tell us anything about the inequality of *lifetime* income.
4. The Lorenz curve ordinarily reflects money income *before* taxes.
5. It does not measure unreported income from the underground economy, a substantial source of income for some individuals.

Income in kind
Income received in the form of goods and services, such as housing or medical care; to be contrasted with money income, which is simply income in dollars, or general purchasing power, that can be used to buy *any* goods and services.

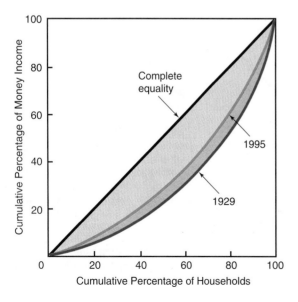

FIGURE 30-2

Lorenz Curves of Income Distribution, 1929 and 1995
Since 1929, the Lorenz curve has moved slightly inward toward the straight line of perfect income equality.
Source: U.S. Department of Commerce.

TABLE 30-1

Percentage Share of Money Income for Households Before Direct Taxes

Income Group	1994	1973	1960	1947
Lowest fifth	4.7	5.5	4.8	5.1
Second fifth	10.8	11.9	12.2	11.8
Third fifth	17.3	17.5	17.8	16.7
Fourth fifth	24.3	24.0	24.0	23.2
Highest fifth	42.9	41.1	41.3	43.3

Source: U.S. Bureau of the Census.
Note: Figures may not sum to 100 percent due to rounding.

Income Distribution in the United States

We could talk about the percentage of income earners within specific income classes—those earning between $20,001 and $30,000 per year, those earning between $30,001 and $40,000 per year, and so on. The problem with this type of analysis is that we live in a growing economy. Income, with some exceptions, is going up all the time. If we wish to make comparisons of the relative share of total income going to different income classes, we cannot look at specific amounts of money income. Instead, we talk about a distribution of income over five groups. Then we can talk about how much the bottom fifth (or quintile) makes compared with the top fifth, and so on. In Table 30-1, we see the percentage share of income for households before direct taxes. The table groups households according to whether they are in the lowest 20 percent of the income distribution, the second lowest 20 percent, and so on. We see that in 1994, the lowest 20 percent had a combined money income of 4.7 percent of the total money income of the entire population. This is a little less than the lowest 20 percent had at the end of World War II. Accordingly, the conclusion has been drawn that there have been only slight changes in the distribution of money income. Indeed, considering that the definition of money income used by the U.S. Bureau of the Census includes only wage and salary income, income from self-employment, interest and dividends, and such government transfer payments as Social Security and unemployment compensation, we have to agree that the distribution of money income has not changed. *Money* income, however, understates *total* income for individuals who receive in-kind transfers from the government in the form of food stamps, public housing, education, and so on. In particular, since World War II, the share of total income—money income plus in-kind benefits—going to the bottom 20 percent of households has probably more than doubled.

INTERNATIONAL EXAMPLE
Relative Income Inequality Throughout the Richest Countries

The United States wins again—it has, according to the World Bank, the greatest amount of income inequality of any of the major industrialized countries. Look at Figure 30-3 on page 670. There you see the ratio of income of the richest 20 percent of households to the poorest 20 percent of households. Should something be done about such income inequality?

Public attitudes toward the government's role in reducing income inequality differ dramatically in the United States and elsewhere. Whereas fewer than 30 percent of Americans believe that government should reduce income differentials, between 60 and 80 percent of Britons, Germans, Italians, and Austrians believe it is the government's job.

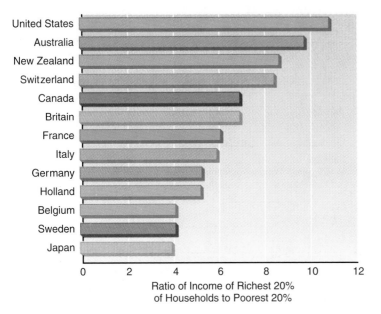

FIGURE 30-3

Relative Income Inequality in the World

The United States has greater income inequality than other developed countries.

Source: World Bank.

FOR CRITICAL ANALYSIS: *Does it matter whether the same families stay in the lowest fifth of income earners over time? Otherwise stated, do we need to know anything about mobility across income groups?* ●

The Distribution of Wealth

We have been referring to the distribution of income in the United States. We must realize that income—a flow—can be viewed as a return on wealth (both human and nonhuman)—a stock. A discussion of the distribution of income in the United States is not the same thing as a discussion of the distribution of wealth. A complete concept of wealth would include tangible objects, such as buildings, machinery, land, cars, and houses—nonhuman wealth—as well as people who have skills, knowledge, initiative, talents, and so on—human wealth. The total of human and nonhuman wealth in the United States makes up our nation's capital stock. (Note that the terms *wealth* and *capital* are often used only with reference to nonhuman wealth.) The capital stock consists of anything that can generate utility to individuals in the future. A fresh ripe tomato is not part of our capital stock. It has to be eaten before it turns rotten, and once it has been eaten, it can no longer generate satisfaction.

Figure 30-4 shows that the richest 10 percent of U.S. households hold about two-thirds of all wealth. The problem with those data, gathered by the Federal Reserve System, is that they do not include many important assets. The first of these is workers' claims on private pension plans, which equal at least $4 trillion according to economist Lawrence B. Lindsey. If you add the value of these pensions, household wealth increases by almost a quarter, meaning that the majority of U.S. house-

THINKING CRITICALLY ABOUT THE MEDIA

Increasing Income Inequality and Working Spouses

The media have been having a field day pointing out that the United States has the greatest income inequality in the industrialized world. Underlying the statistics, though, is a little-known fact: Income inequality is measured with respect to *households*. No distinction is made between one- and two-earner households. If two $80,000-a-year lawyers marry, their household income is now $160,000, and they have moved into a higher income group. Not surprisingly, most single tax returns show smaller earnings than joint returns of married couples. In 1969, some 48 percent of working-age married couples had two earners; today that figure is 72 percent. Consequently, part of the reported increase in income inequality in the United States is simply due to an increase in the number of working spouses.

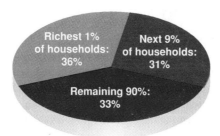

FIGURE 30-4
Measured Total Wealth Distribution
The top 10 percent of households have 67 percent of all measured wealth.
Source: Board of Governors of the Federal Reserve.

holds belong to the middle class. Also omitted is future Social Security liabilities, estimated at about $13 trillion. Again, most of this is "owned" by the middle class.

EXAMPLE
Are We Running to Stay in Place?

There are a lot of statistics around that can show that the typical working person in the United States has not experienced an increase in standard of living since 1970. If we correct take-home wages for inflation, that is an accurate statement. Indeed, the secretary of labor has frequently announced that real wages have actually *fallen* since 1973. There are at least two problems with such statements, though. The first concerns total compensation. Compensation of workers does not consist solely of wages. Whereas in 1970, nonsalary benefits (medical care, insurance, pension payments, and so on) amounted to 24 percent of wages, they now come to around 40 percent. Second, even if after-tax real wages have not increased, the typical American household is at least 20 percent better off than in 1970. Why? Because more households have a second breadwinner. Furthermore, fewer babies are being born, so expenses per household are lower.

One other piece of data is telling: Virtually every measure of consumption per capita is growing, year in and year out. Consequently, the majority of Americans continue to experience increases in their standard of living as measured by their actual purchases of goods and services.

FOR CRITICAL ANALYSIS: Why might an individual be most concerned about total compensation? ●

CONCEPTS IN BRIEF

• The Lorenz curve graphically represents the distribution of income. If it is a straight line, there is complete equality of income. The more it is bowed, the more inequality of income exists.

• The distribution of wealth is not the same as the distribution of income. Wealth includes assets such as houses, stocks, and bonds. Although the apparent distribution of wealth seems to be more concentrated at the top, the data used are not very accurate, and most summary statistics fail to take account of workers' claims on private and public pensions, which are substantial.

DETERMINANTS OF INCOME DIFFERENCES

We know that there are income differences—that is not in dispute. A more important question is why these differences in income occur, for if we know why income differences occur, perhaps we can change public policy, particularly with respect to helping people in the lowest income classes climb the income ladder. What is more, if we know the reasons for income differences, we can ascertain whether any of these determinants have changed over time. We will look at four income difference determinants: age, marginal productivity, inheritance, and discrimination.

Age

Age turns out to be a determinant of income because with age comes, usually, more education, more training, and more experience. It is not surprising that within every class of income earners, there seem to be regular cycles of earning behavior. Most individuals earn more when they are middle-aged than when they are younger or older. We call this the **age-earnings cycle.**

The Age-Earnings Cycle. Every occupation has its own age-earnings cycle, and every individual will probably experience some variation from the average. Nonetheless, we can characterize the typical age-earnings cycle graphically in Figure 30-5. Here we see that at age 18, income is relatively low. Income gradually rises until it peaks at about age 50. Then it falls until retirement, when it becomes zero (that is, currently earned income becomes zero, although retirement payments may then commence). The reason for such a regular cycle in earnings is fairly straightforward.

When individuals start working at a young age, they typically have no work-related experience. Their ability to produce is less than that of more seasoned workers—that is, their productivity is lower. As they become older, they obtain more training and accumulate more experience. Their productivity rises, and they are therefore paid more. They also generally start to work longer hours. As the age of 50 approaches, the productivity of individual workers usually peaks. So, too, do the number of hours per week that are worked. After this peak in the age-earnings cycle, the detrimental effects of aging—decreases in stamina, strength, reaction time, and the like—usually outweigh any increases in training

Age-earnings cycle
The regular earnings profile of an individual throughout his or her lifetime. The age-earnings cycle usually starts with a low income, builds gradually to a peak at around age 50, and then gradually curves down until it approaches zero at retirement.

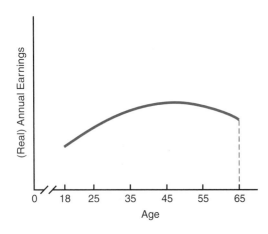

FIGURE 30-5

Typical Age-Earnings Profile
Within every class of income earners there is usually a typical age-earnings profile. Earnings are lowest when starting work at age 18, reach their peak at around age 50, and then taper off until retirement around age 65, when they become zero for most people. The rise in earnings up to age 50 is usually due to increased experience, longer working hours, and better training and schooling. (We abstract from economywide productivity changes that would shift the entire curve upward.)

or experience. Also, hours worked usually start to fall for older people. Finally, as a person reaches retirement, both productivity and hours worked diminish rather drastically.

Note that general increases in overall productivity for the entire workforce will result in an upward shift in the typical age-earnings profile given in Figure 30-5. Thus even at the end of the age-earnings cycle, when just about to retire, the worker would not receive a really low wage compared with the starting wage 45 years earlier. The wage would be higher due to factors that contribute to rising real wages for everyone, regardless of the stage in the age-earnings cycle.

Now we have some idea why specific individuals earn different incomes at different times in their lives, but we have yet to explain why different people are paid different amounts of money for their labor. One way to explain this is to recall the marginal productivity theory developed in Chapter 27.

Marginal Productivity

When trying to determine how many workers a firm would hire, we had to construct a marginal revenue product curve. We found that as more workers were hired, the marginal revenue product fell due to diminishing marginal returns. If the forces of demand and supply established a certain wage rate, workers would be hired until their marginal physical product times marginal revenue was equal to the going wage rate. Then the hiring would stop. This analysis suggests what workers can expect to be paid in the labor market: They can each expect to be paid their marginal revenue product (assuming that there are low-cost information flows and that the labor and product markets are competitive).

In a competitive situation, with mobility of labor resources (at least on the margin), workers who are being paid less than their marginal revenue product will be bid away to better employment opportunities. Either they will seek better employment themselves, or other employers will offer them a slightly higher wage rate. This process will continue until each worker is being paid his or her marginal revenue product.

You may balk at the suggestion that people are paid their marginal revenue product because you may personally know individuals whose MRP is more or less than what they are being paid. Such a situation may, in fact, exist because we do not live in a world of perfect information or in a world with perfectly competitive input and output markets. Employers cannot always seek out the most productive employees available. It takes resources to research the past records of potential employees, their training, their education, and their abilities. Nonetheless, competition creates a tendency toward equality of wages and MRP.

Determinants of Marginal Productivity. If we accept marginal revenue product theory, we have a way to find out how people can earn higher incomes. If they can increase the value of their marginal physical product, they can expect to be paid more. Some of the determinants of marginal physical product are talent, education, experience, and training. Most of these are means by which marginal physical product can be increased. Let's examine them in greater detail.

Talent. This factor is the easiest to explain but difficult to acquire if you don't have it. Innate abilities and attributes can be very strong, if not overwhelming, determinants of a person's potential productivity. Strength, coordination, and mental alertness are facets of nonacquired human capital and thus have some bearing on the ability to earn income.

Someone who is extremely tall has a better chance of being a basketball player than someone who is short. A person born with a superior talent for abstract thinking has a better chance of making a relatively higher income as a mathematician or a physicist than someone who is not born with that talent.

Experience. Additional experience at particular tasks is another way to increase productivity. Experience can be linked to the well-known *learning curve* that applies when the same task is done over and over. The worker repeating a task becomes more efficient: The worker can do the same task in less time or in the same amount of time but better. Take an example of a person going to work on an automobile assembly line. At first she is able to fasten only three bolts every two minutes. Then the worker becomes more adept and can fasten four bolts in the same time plus insert a rubber guard on the bumper. After a few more weeks, another task can be added. Experience allows this individual to improve her productivity. The more effectively people learn to do something, the quicker they can do it and the more efficient they are. Hence we would expect experience to lead to higher productivity. And we would expect people with more experience to be paid more than those with less experience. More experience, however, does not guarantee a higher wage rate. The *demand* for a person's services must also exist. Spending a long time to become a first-rate archer in modern society would probably add very little to a person's income. Experience has value only if the output is demanded by society.

Training. Training is similar to experience but is more formal. Much of a person's increased productivity is due to on-the-job training. Many companies have training programs for new workers. On-the-job training is perhaps responsible for as much of an increase in productivity as is formal education beyond grade school.

EXAMPLE
Economists, Aging, and Productivity

Do the actions of professional economists fit the model that predicts a decrease in productivity after some peak at around age 50? Yes, according to University of Texas economist Daniel Hamermesh. One measure of productivity of economics professors is the number of articles they publish in professional journals. Whereas the over-50 economists constitute 30 percent of the profession, they contribute a mere 6 percent of the articles published in leading economics journals. Whereas 56 percent of economists between ages 36 and 50 submit articles on a regular basis, only 14 percent of economists over 50 do so.

FOR CRITICAL ANALYSIS: Why should we predict that an economist closer to retirement will submit fewer professional journal articles than a younger economist? (Hint: Normally, professors who have tenure can't be fired.) ●

Investment in Human Capital. Investment in human capital is just like investment in any other thing. If you invest in yourself by going to college, rather than going to work after high school and earning more current income, you will presumably be rewarded in the future with a higher income or a more interesting job (or both). This is exactly the motivation that underlies the decision of many college-bound students to obtain a formal higher education. Undoubtedly there would be students going to school even if the rate of return on formal education were zero or negative. But we do expect that the higher the rate of return on investing in ourselves, the more such investment there will be. U.S. Labor Department data demonstrate conclusively that, on average, high school graduates make more than grade school graduates and that college graduates make more than high school graduates. The estimated annual income of a full-time worker with four years of college in the mid-1990s was about $50,000. That person's high school counterpart was estimated to earn only $30,000, which gives a "college premium" of about 67 percent. Generally, the rate of return on investment in human capital is on a par with the rate of return on investment in other areas.

To figure out the rate of return on an investment in a college education, we first have to figure out the marginal costs of going to school. The main cost is not what you have to pay for books, fees, and tuition but rather the income you forgo. *The main cost of education is the income forgone—the opportunity cost of not working.* In addition, the direct expenses of college must be paid for. Not all students forgo all income during their college years. Many work part time. Taking account of those who work part time and those who are supported by state tuition grants and other scholarships, the average rate of return on going to college is somewhere between 8 and 12 percent. This is not a bad rate. Of course, this type of computation does leave out all the consumption benefits you get from attending college. Also omitted from the calculations is the change in personality after going to college. You undoubtedly come out a different person. Most people who go through college feel that they have improved themselves both culturally and intellectually in addition to having increased their potential marginal revenue product so that they can make more income. How do we measure the benefit from expanding our horizons and our desire to experience different things in life? This is not easy to measure, and such nonmoney benefits from investing in human capital are not included in normal calculations.

Inheritance

It is not unusual to inherit cash, jewelry, stocks, bonds, homes, or other real estate. Yet only about 10 percent of income inequality in the United States can be traced to differences in wealth that was inherited. If for some reason the government confiscated all property that had been inherited, there would be very little measured change in the distribution of income in the United States. In any event, at both federal and state levels of taxation, substantial inheritance taxes are levied on the estates of relatively wealthy deceased Americans (although there are some legally valid ways to avoid certain estate taxes).

Discrimination

Economic discrimination occurs whenever workers with the same marginal revenue product receive unequal pay due to some noneconomic factor such as their race, sex, or age. Alternatively, it occurs when there is unequal access to labor markets. It is possible—and indeed quite obvious—that discrimination affects the distribution of income. Certain groups in our society are not paid wages at rates comparable to those received by other groups, even when we correct for productivity. Differences in income remain between whites and nonwhites and between men and women. For example, the median income of black families is about 60 percent that of white families. The median wage rate of women is about 70 percent that of men. Some people argue that all of these differences are due to discrimination against nonwhites and against women. We cannot simply accept *any* differences in income as due to discrimination, though. What we need to do is discover why differences in income between groups exist and then determine if factors other than discrimination in the labor market can explain them. The unexplained part of income differences can rightfully be considered the result of discrimination.

Access to Education. African Americans and other minorities have faced discrimination in the acquisition of human capital. The amount and quality of schooling offered black Americans has generally been inferior to that offered whites. Even if minorities attend school as long as whites, their scholastic achievement can be lower because they are typically allotted fewer school resources than their white counterparts. Nonwhite urban individuals are more likely to live in lower-income areas, which have fewer resources to allocate to education due to the lower tax base. One study showed that nonwhite urban males receive between 23 and 27 percent less income than white urban males because of lower-quality education. This would mean that even if employment discrimination were substantially reduced, we would still expect to see a difference between white and nonwhite income because of the low quality of schooling received by the nonwhites and the resulting lower level of productivity. We say, therefore, that among other things, African Americans and certain other minority groups, such as Hispanics, suffer from too small an investment in human capital. Even when this difference in human capital is taken into account, however, there still appears to be an income differential that cannot be explained. The unexplained income differential between whites and blacks is often attributed to discrimination in the labor market. Because no better explanation is offered, we will stick with the notion that discrimination in the labor market does indeed exist.

> ### THINKING CRITICALLY ABOUT THE MEDIA
>
> #### Bad News—and Plenty of It
>
> The media seem addicted to bad news, particularly with respect to the income and job gains of minorities and women. The reality is somewhat better, however. While it is still true that college-educated African-American males earn only 72 percent of what their white counterparts earn, 28 percent have executive, or administrative, or managerial jobs versus 30 percent of non-Hispanic whites. While it is still true that first-generation Hispanic immigrants have relatively low incomes, second-generation Mexican Americans earn almost identical wages to similarly educated non-Hispanic whites. Although women still earn less than men, in one generation they have gone from only low-level jobs to making up 40 percent of medical and law students, administrators, managers, executives, and Ph.D. candidates. Today, women make up almost 60 percent of public officials in America. Of course, the most elite jobs—senior managers in the top Fortune 500 companies— are still male-dominated. Consequently, many women are starting their own businesses.
>
> The race and gender employment situation is not all roses, but it may not be as bad as the media tell us it is.

The Doctrine of Comparable Worth. Discrimination against women can occur because of barriers to entry in higher-paying occupations and because of discrimination in the acquisition of human capital, just as has occurred for African Americans. Consider the distribution of highest-paying and lowest-paying occupations. The lowest-paying jobs are dominated by females, both white and nonwhite. For example, the proportion of women in secretarial, clerical, janitorial, and food service jobs ranges from 70 percent (food service) to 97 percent (secretarial). Proponents of the **comparable-worth doctrine** feel that female secretaries, janitors, and food service workers should be making salaries comparable to those of male truck drivers or construction workers, assuming that the levels of skill and responsibility in these jobs are comparable. These advocates also believe that a comparable-worth policy would benefit the economy overall. They contend that adjusting the wages of workers in female-dominated jobs upward would create a move toward more efficient and less discriminatory labor markets.

Comparable-worth doctrine
The belief that women should receive the same wages as men if the levels of skill and responsibility in their jobs are equivalent.

THEORIES OF DESIRED INCOME DISTRIBUTION

We have talked about the factors affecting the distribution of income, but we have not yet mentioned the normative issue of how income *ought* to be distributed. This, of course, requires a value judgment. We are talking about the problem of economic justice. We can never completely resolve this problem because there are always going to be conflicting values. It is impossible to give all people what each thinks is just. Nonetheless, two particular normative standards for the distribution of income have been popular with economists. These are income distribution based on productivity and income distribution based on equality.

Productivity

The *productivity standard* for the distribution of income can be stated simply as "To each according to what he or she produces." This is also called the *contributive standard* because it is based on the principle of rewarding according to the contribution to society's total output. It is also sometimes referred to as the *merit standard* and is one of the oldest concepts of justice. People are rewarded according to merit, and merit is judged by one's ability to produce what is considered useful by society.

However, just as any standard is a value judgment, so is the productivity standard. It is rooted in the capitalist ethic and has been attacked vigorously by some economists and philosophers, including Karl Marx, who felt that people should be rewarded according to need and not according to productivity.

We measure a person's productive contribution in a capitalist system by the market value of that person's output. We have already referred to this as the marginal revenue product theory of wage determination.

Do not immediately jump to the conclusion that in a world of income distribution determined by productivity, society will necessarily allow the aged, the infirm, and the disabled to die of starvation because they are unproductive. In the United States today, the productivity standard is mixed with a standard based on people's "needs" so that the aged, the disabled, the involuntarily unemployed, the very young, and other unproductive (in the market sense of the word) members of the economy are provided for through private and public transfers.

Equality

The *egalitarian principle* of income distribution is simply "To each exactly the same." Everyone would have exactly the same amount of income. This criterion of income distribution has been debated as far back as biblical times. This system of income distribution has been considered equitable, meaning that presumably everybody is dealt with fairly and equally. There are problems, however, with an income distribution that is completely equal.

Some jobs are more unpleasant or more dangerous than others. Should the people undertaking these jobs be paid exactly the same as everyone else? Indeed, under an equal distribution of income, what incentive would there be for individuals to take risky, hazardous, or unpleasant jobs at all? What about overtime? Who would be willing to work overtime without additional pay? There is another problem: If everyone earned the same income, what incentive would there be for individuals to invest in their own human capital—a costly and time-consuming process?

Just consider the incentive structure within a corporation. Recall from Chapter 27 that much of the pay differential between, say, the CEO and all of the vice-presidents is meant to create competition among the vice-presidents for the CEO's job. The result is higher productivity. If all incomes were the same, much of this competition would disappear, and productivity would fall.

There is some evidence that differences in income lead to higher rates of economic growth. Future generations are therefore made better off. Elimination of income differences may reduce the rate of economic growth and cause future generations to be poorer than they otherwise might have been.

CONCEPTS IN BRIEF

- Most people follow an age-earnings cycle in which they earn relatively small incomes when they first start working, increase their incomes until about age 50, and then slowly experience a decrease in their real incomes as they approach retirement.

- If we accept the marginal revenue product theory of wages, workers can expect to be paid their marginal revenue product. However, full adjustment is never obtained, so some workers may be paid more or less than their MRP.

- Marginal physical productivity depends on talent, education, experience, and training.

- Going to school and receiving on-the-job training can be considered an investment in human capital. The main cost of education is the opportunity cost of not working.

- Discrimination is most easily observed in various groups' access to high-paying jobs and to quality education. Minorities and women are disproportionately underrepresented in high-paying jobs. Also, minorities sometimes do not receive access to higher education of the same quality offered to majority-group members.

- Proponents of the comparable-worth doctrine contend that disparate jobs can be compared by examining efforts, skill, and educational training and that wages should therefore be paid on the basis of this comparable worth.

- Two normative standards for income distribution are income distribution based on productivity and income distribution based on equality.

POVERTY AND ATTEMPTS TO ELIMINATE IT

Throughout the history of the world, mass poverty has been accepted as inevitable. However, this nation and others, particularly in the Western world, have sustained enough economic growth in the past several hundred years so that *mass* poverty can no longer be said to be a problem for these fortunate countries. As a matter of fact, the residual of poverty in the United States strikes us as bizarre, an anomaly. How can there still be so much poverty in a nation of such abundance? Having talked about the determinants of the distribution of income, we now have at least some ideas of why some people are destined to remain low-income earners throughout their lives.

There are methods of transferring income from the relatively well-to-do to the relatively poor, and as a nation we have been using them for a long time. Today, we have a vast array of welfare programs set up for the purpose of redistributing income. However, we know that these programs have not been entirely successful. Are there alternatives to our

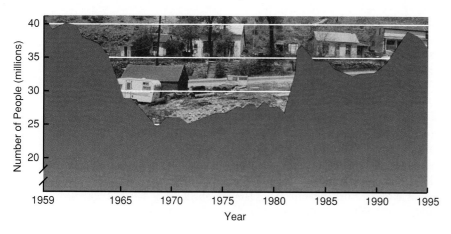

FIGURE 30-6

Official Number of Poor in the United States

The number of individuals classified as poor fell steadily from 1959 through 1969. From 1970 to 1981, the number stayed about the same. It then increased during the 1981–1982 recession, dropped off for a while, and has risen again in the 1990s.

Source: U.S. Department of Labor.

current welfare system? Is there a better method of helping the poor? Before we answer these questions, let's look at the concept of poverty in more detail and at the characteristics of the poor.

We see in Figure 30-6 that the number of individuals classified as poor fell steadily from 1959 to 1969. For a few years, the number of poor leveled off until the recession of 1981–1982. The number then fell, only to rise again during the recession of the early 1990s.

 INTERNATIONAL EXAMPLE
Poverty Worldwide and How to Cure It: Suggestions from the UN Summit

For seven days in 1995, delegations from 140 countries gathered in Copenhagen for the United Nations' World Summit for Social Development. According to the UN, 1.3 billion people live in poverty throughout the world. The attendees agreed to a document that commits them to the goal of "eradicating poverty in the world." Nobel Prize–winning economist James Tobin offered one solution: Tax speculative international currency transactions to raise $50 billion a year for the United Nations to support development programs. The delegates also argued for a "20-20 compact." Donor nations should agree to direct 20 percent of their foreign aid to alleviate poverty in less developed countries, and recipient countries should direct 20 percent of their national budgets to the same programs.

FOR CRITICAL ANALYSIS: If economist Tobin's idea were put into practice, who would collect the tax, given that the United Nations does not have taxing power? ●

Defining Poverty

The threshold income level, which is used to determine who falls into the poverty category, was originally based on the cost of a nutritionally adequate food plan designed by the U.S. Department of Agriculture for emergency or temporary use. The threshold was determined by multiplying the food plan cost by 3 on the assumption that food expenses comprise approximately one-third of a poor family's income. Annual revisions of the threshold level were based only on price changes in the food budget. In 1969, a federal interagency committee looked at the calculations of the threshold and decided to set new standards, with adjustments made on the basis of changes in the Consumer Price Index. For example, in 1996, the official poverty level for an urban family of four was around $16,000. It goes up each year to reflect whatever inflation has occurred.

Absolute Poverty

Because the low-income threshold is an absolute measure, we know that if it never changes in real terms, we will reduce poverty even if we do nothing. How can that be? The reasoning is straightforward. Real incomes in the United States have been growing at a compounded annual rate of almost 2 percent per capita for at least the past century and at about 2.5 percent since World War II. If we define the poverty line at a specific real level, more and more individuals will make incomes that exceed that poverty line. Thus in absolute terms, we will eliminate poverty (assuming continued per capita growth and no change in income distribution).

Relative Poverty

Be careful with this analysis, however. Poverty has generally been defined in relative terms; that is, it is defined in terms of the income levels of individuals or families relative to the rest of the population. As long as the distribution of income is not perfectly equal, there will always be some people who make less income than others, even if their relatively low income is high by historical standards. Thus in a relative sense, the problem of poverty will always exist, although it can be reduced. In any given year, for example, the absolute poverty level *officially* decided on by the U.S. government is far above the average income in many countries in the world.

Transfer Payments as Income

The official poverty level is based on pretax income, including cash but not in-kind subsidies—food stamps, housing vouchers, and the like. If we correct poverty levels for such benefits, the percentage of the population that is below the poverty line drops dramatically. Some economists argue that the way the official poverty level is calculated makes no sense in a nation that redistributed over $800 billion in cash and noncash transfers in 1996.

Furthermore, some of the nation's official poor partake in the informal, or underground, sectors of the economy without reporting their income from these sources. And some of the officially defined poor obtain benefits from owning their own home (40 percent of all poor households do own their own homes). Look at Figure 30-7 for two different views of what has happened to the relative position of this nation's poor. The graph shows the ratio of the top fifth of the nation's households to the bottom fifth of the nation's households. If we look only at measured income, it appears that the poor are getting relatively poorer compared to the rich (the top line). If we compare household spending (consumption), a different picture emerges. The nation's poorest households are in fact holding their own.

Attacks on Poverty: Major Income Maintenance Programs

There are a variety of income maintenance programs designed to help the poor. We examine a few of them here.

Social Security. For the retired, the unemployed, and the disabled, social insurance programs provide income payments in prescribed situations. The best known is Social Secu-

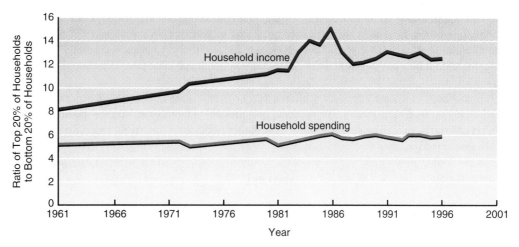

FIGURE 30-7

Relative Poverty: Comparing Household Incomes and Household Spending

This graph shows, on the vertical axis, the ratio of the top 20 percent of income-earning households to the bottom 20 percent. If measured household income is used, there appears to be increasing income inequality, particularly during the early to mid-1980s. If we look at household *spending*, though, inequality appears to remain constant.

Sources: U.S. Bureau of Labor Statistics; U.S. Bureau of the Census.

rity, which includes what has been called old-age, survivors', and disability insurance (OASDI). This is essentially a program of compulsory saving financed from compulsory payroll taxes levied on both employers and employees. Workers pay for Social Security while working and receive the benefits after retirement. The benefit payments are usually made to people who have reached retirement age. When the insured worker dies, benefits accrue to the survivors, including widows and children. Special benefits provide for disabled workers. Over 90 percent of all employed persons in the United States are covered by OASDI. Social Security was originally designed as a social insurance program that workers paid for themselves and under which they received benefits that varied with the size of past contributions. Today, it is simply an intergenerational income transfer that is only vaguely related to past earnings. It transfers income from Americans who work—the young through the middle-aged—to those who do not work—older retired persons.

In 1996, more than 49 million people were receiving OASDI checks averaging about $713 a month. Benefit payments from OASDI redistribute income to some degree. However, benefit payments are not based on recipient need. Participants' contributions give them the right to benefits even if they would be financially secure without them. Social Security is not really an insurance program because people are not guaranteed that the benefits they receive will be in line with the contributions they have made. It is not a personal savings account. The benefits are legislated by Congress. In the future, Congress may not be as sympathetic toward older people as it is today. It could (and probably will have to) legislate for lower real levels of benefits instead of higher ones.

Supplemental Security Income (SSI) and Aid to Families with Dependent Children (AFDC). Many people who are poor but do not qualify for Social Security benefits are assisted through other programs. The federally financed and administered Supplemental Security Income (SSI) program was instituted in 1974. The purpose of SSI is to establish a nationwide minimum income for the aged, the blind, and the disabled. SSI has become one of the fastest-growing transfer programs in America. Whereas in 1974 less than $8 billion was spent, the prediction for 1999 is $35.4 billion. Americans currently eligible for SSI include children and individuals claiming mental disabilities, including drug addicts and alcoholics.

Aid to Families with Dependent Children (AFDC) is a state-administered program, financed in part by federal grants. The program provides aid to families in which dependent children do not have the financial support of the father because of desertion, disability, or death. (Some critics argue that AFDC provides an incentive for fathers to desert their families because that may be the only way for a family to receive such payments.) The projected expenditures for AFDC are $26.6 billion in 1999.

Food Stamps. Food stamps are government-issued coupons that can be used to purchase food. The food stamp program was started in 1964, seemingly, in retrospect, mainly to shore up the nation's agricultural sector by increasing demand for food through retail channels. In 1964, some 367,000 Americans were receiving food stamps. In 1996, the estimate is over 28 million recipients. The annual cost has jumped from $860,000 to more than $29 billion. In 1996, almost one in every nine citizens (including children) was using food stamps. The food stamp program has become a major part of the welfare system in the United States. The program has also become a method of promoting better nutrition among the poor.

The Earned Income Tax Credit Program (EITC). In 1975, the EITC was created to provide rebates of Social Security taxes to low-income workers. Over one-fifth of all tax returns claim an earned-income tax credit. In some states, such as Mississippi, as well as the District of Columbia, nearly half of all families are eligible for EITC. The program works as follows: Households with a reported income of less than $25,300 (exclusive of welfare payments) receive EITC benefits up to $2,528. There is a catch, though. Those with earnings between $8,425 and $11,000 get a flat $2,528. But families earning between $11,000 and $25,300 get penalized 17.68 cents for every dollar they earn above $11,000. This constitutes a punitive tax. Thus the EITC discourages work by a low- or moderate-income earner more than it rewards work. In particular, it discourages low-income earners from taking on a second job. The General Accounting Office estimates that hours worked by working wives in EITC-beneficiary households have consequently decreased by 10 percent. The average EITC recipient works 1,300 hours compared to a normal work year of 2,000 hours.

No Apparent Reduction in Poverty Rates

In spite of the numerous programs in existence and the hundreds of billions of dollars transferred to the poor, the officially defined rate of poverty in the United States has shown no long-run tendency to decline. From 1945 until the early 1970s, the percentage of Americans in poverty fell steadily every year. It reached a low of around 11 percent in 1973, shot back up beyond 15 percent in 1983, fell steadily to 13.1 percent in 1990, and has been rising ever since. Why this has happened is a real puzzlement. Since the War on Poverty was launched under President Lyndon B. Johnson in 1965, nearly $4 trillion has been transferred to the poor, and yet more Americans are poor today than ever before. Is there a way that we can reform welfare to improve the situation? We attempt to shed some light on this question in the Issues and Applications section at the end of this chapter.

CONCEPTS IN BRIEF

- If poverty is defined in absolute terms, economic growth eventually decreases the number of officially defined poor. If poverty is defined relatively, however, we will never eliminate it.

- Major attacks on poverty have been social insurance programs in the form of Social Security, Supplemental Security Income, Aid to Families with Dependent Children, the earned-income tax credit, and food stamps.

- Although the relative lot of the poor measured by household income seems to have worsened, household spending by the bottom 20 percent of households compared to the top 20 percentile has shown little change since the 1960s.

HEALTH CARE

It may seem strange to be reading about health care in a chapter on the distribution of income and poverty. Yet health care is in fact intimately related to those two topics. For example, sometimes people become poor because they do not have adequate health insurance (or have none at all), fall ill, and deplete all of their wealth on care. Moreover, sometimes individuals remain in certain jobs simply because their employer's health care package seems so good that they are afraid to change jobs and risk not being covered by health care insurance in the process. Finally, as you will see, much of the cause of the increased health care spending in America can be attributed to a change in the incentives that Americans face.

America's Health Care Situation

Spending for health care is estimated to account for 15 percent of the total annual income created in the U.S. economy. You can see from Figure 30-8 that in 1965, about 6 percent of annual income was spent on health care, but that percentage has been growing steadily ever since. Per capita spending on health care is greater in the United States than anywhere else in the world today. On a per capita basis, we spend more than twice as much as citizens of

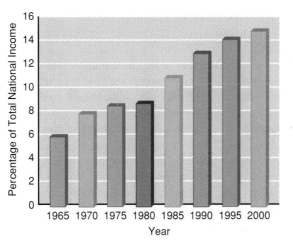

FIGURE 30-8

Percentage of Total National Income Spent on Health Care in the United States
Sources: U.S. Department of Commerce; U.S. Department of Health and Human Services.

Luxembourg, Austria, Australia, Japan, and Denmark. We spend almost three times as much on a per capita basis as citizens of Spain and Ireland.

Why Have Health Care Costs Risen So Much?   There are numerous explanations for why health care costs have risen so much. At least one has to do with changing demographics: The U.S. population is getting older.

The Age–Health Care Expenditure Equation.   The top 5 percent of health care users incur over 50 percent of all health costs. The bottom 70 percent of health care users account for only 10 percent of health care expenditures. Not surprisingly, the elderly make up most of the top users of health care services. Nursing home expenditures are made primarily by people older than 70. The use of hospitals is also dominated by the aged.

The U.S. population is aging steadily. More than 12 percent of the current 265 million Americans are over 65. It is estimated that by the year 2035, senior citizens will comprise about 22 percent of our population. This aging population stimulates the demand for health care. The elderly consume more than four times the per capita health care services that the rest of the population uses. In short, whatever the demand for health care services is today, it is likely to be considerably higher in the future as the U.S. population ages.

New Technologies.   Another reason that health care costs have risen so dramatically is high technology. A CT (computerized tomography) scanner costs around $1 million. An MRI (magnetic resonance imaging) scanner can cost over $2 million. A PET (positron emission tomography) scanner costs around $4 million. All of these machines became increasingly available in the 1980s and 1990s and are desired throughout the country. Typical fees for procedures using them range from $300 to $500 for a CT scan to as high as $2,000 for a PET scan. The development of new technologies that help physicians and hospitals prolong human life is an ongoing process in an ever-advancing industry. New procedures at even higher prices can be expected in the future.

Third-Party Financing.   Currently, government spending on health care constitutes over 40 percent of total health care spending (of which the *federal* government pays about 70 percent). Private insurance accounts for a little over 35 percent of payments for health care. The remainder—less than 20 percent—is paid directly by individuals. Figure 30-9 shows the change in the payment scheme for medical care in the United States since 1930. Medicare and Medicaid are the main sources of hospital and other medical benefits to 35 million Americans, most of whom are over 65. Medicaid—the joint state-federal program—provides long-term health care, particularly for people living in nursing homes. Medicare, Medicaid, and private insurance companies are considered **third parties** in the medical care equation. Caregivers and patients are the two primary parties. When third parties step in to pay for medical care, the quantity demanded for those services increases. For example, when Medicare and Medicaid went into effect in the 1960s, the volume of federal government–reimbursed medical services increased by more than 65 percent.

The availability of third-party payments for costly medical care has generated increases in the availability of hospital beds. Between 1974 and 1996, the number of hospital beds increased by over 50 percent. Present occupancy rates are only around 65 percent.

THINKING CRITICALLY ABOUT THE MEDIA

The Difference Between Medical Care Expenditures and Medical Care Costs

For years, the media, as well as politicians around the country, have repeatedly decried rising medical care expenditures in the United States. In reality, the actual *cost* of being cured for a particular disease has been falling since 1900. Medical care expenditures have increased because medical progress now allows us to cure—sometimes at a very high price—more and more diseases and disorders. Back when these maladies were considered incurable, no effort was made to cure them and little was spent on treatment. That is why health care costs seemed so much lower then.

Third parties
Parties who are not directly involved in a given activity or transaction. For example, in the relationship between caregivers and patients, fees may be paid by third parties (insurance companies, government).

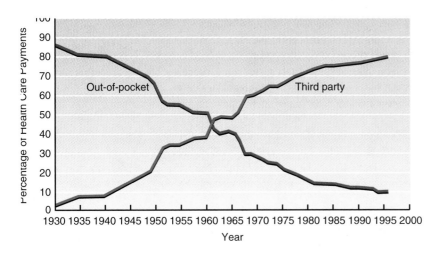

FIGURE 30-9
Third Party Versus Out-of-Pocket Health Care Payments
Out-of-pocket payments for health care services have been falling steadily since the 1930s. In contrast, third-party payments for health care have risen to the point that they account for over 80 percent of all such outlays today.
Sources: Health Care Financing Administration; U.S. Department of Health and Human Services.

Price, Quantity Demanded, and the Question of Moral Hazard. While some people may think that the demand for health care is insensitive to price changes, theory clearly indicates otherwise. Look at Figure 30-10. There you see a hypothetical demand curve for health care services. To the extent that third parties—whether government or private insurance—pay for health care, the out-of-pocket cost, or net price, to the individual will drop. In an extreme example, all medical expenses are paid for by third parties so that the price is zero in Figure 30-10 and the quantity demanded is many times what it would be at a higher price.

One of the issues here has to do with the problem of moral hazard. Consider two individuals with two different health insurance policies. The first policy pays for all medical expenses, but in the second the individual has to pay the first $1,000 a year (this amount is known as the *deductible*). Will the behavior of the two individuals be different? Generally, the answer is yes. The individual with no deductible may be more likely to seek treatment for health problems after they develop rather than try to avoid them and will generally expect medical attention on a more regular basis. In contrast, the individual who faces the first $1,000 of medical expenses each year will tend to engage in more wellness activities and will be less inclined to seek medical care for minor problems. The moral hazard here is that the individual with the zero deductible for medical care expenses may engage in a lifestyle that is less healthful than will the individual with the $1,000 deductible.

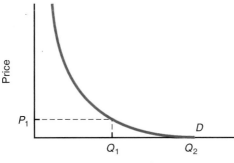

FIGURE 30-10
The Demand for Health Care Services
At price P_1, the quantity of health care services demanded per year would hypothetically be Q_1. If the price falls to zero (third-party payment with zero deductible), the quantity demanded expands to Q_2.

Moral Hazard as It Affects Physicians and Hospitals. The issue of moral hazard also has a direct effect on the behavior of physicians and hospital administrators. Due to third-party payments, patients rarely have to worry about the expense of operations and other medical procedures. As a consequence, both physicians and hospitals order more procedures. Physicians are typically reimbursed on the basis of medical procedures; thus they have no financial interest in trying to keep hospital costs down. Indeed, many have an incentive to raise costs.

Such actions are most evident with terminally ill patients. A physician may order a CT scan and other costly procedures for a terminally ill patient. The physician knows that Medicare or some other type of insurance will pay. Then the physician can charge a fee for analyzing the CT scan. Fully 30 percent of Medicare expenditures are for Americans who are in the last six months of their lives.

Rising Medicare expenditures are one of the most serious problems facing the federal government today. The number of beneficiaries has increased from 19.1 million in 1966 (first year of operation) to an estimated 40 million in 1996. Figure 30-11 shows that federal spending on Medicare has been growing at over 10 percent a year, adjusted for inflation.

Is National Health Insurance the Answer?

Proponents of a national health care system believe that the current system relies too heavily on private insurers. They argue in favor of a Canadian-style system. In Canada, the government sets the fees that are paid to each doctor for seeing a patient and prohibits private practice. The Canadian government also imposes a cap on the incomes that any doctor can receive in a given year. The Canadian federal government provides a specified amount of funding to hospitals, leaving it to them to decide how to allocate the funds. If we were to follow the Canadian model, the average American would receive fewer health services than at present. Hospital stays would be longer, but there would be fewer tests and procedures. Today, there is no discernible difference in infant mortality or life expectancy between the United States and Canada. If we switched to using the Canadian health care system model, we would hence not expect to see any change in those two statistics.

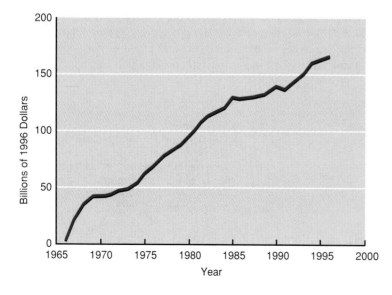

FIGURE 30-11

Federal Medicare Spending

Federal spending on Medicare has increased about 10 percent a year, after adjusting for inflation, since its inception in 1966.

Sources: Economic Report of the President; U.S. Bureau of Labor Statistics.

Alternatives to a national health care policy involve some type of national health insurance, perhaps offered only to people who qualify on the basis of low annual income. A number of politicians have offered variations on such a program. The over 20 million Americans who have no health insurance at some time during each year would certainly benefit. The share of annual national income that goes to health care expenditures would rise, however. Also, the federal budget deficit might increase by another $30 billion to $50 billion (or more) per year to pay for the program.

INTERNATIONAL EXAMPLE
Deterioration in the United Kingdom's National Health Care System

Many countries now have single-payer health care systems that in essence offer "free" universal health care. The United Kingdom's National Health Care Services (NHS) has been in existence since 1948. Once touted as one of the world's best national health care systems, both the system and the services it offers have deteriorated dramatically. In 1948, there were 10 hospital beds for every 1,000 people; today there are only 5 per 1,000. Since 1948, about 50 percent of that nation's hospitals have closed for "efficiency" reasons. The UK now has a lower hospital bed supply than any other Western European country except Portugal and Spain. Even its two most prestigious teaching hospitals are scheduled to close.

Because hospital bed space is limited, currently more than 1 million British subjects are on a waiting list for hospital admission. Many others who need medical care are not on the list because they are so discouraged by the long wait that they simply choose not to seek medical treatment. In some London hospitals, it is common for patients to wait more than 12 hours to see a doctor.

Despite all of the hospital closings and the decline in medical personnel, employment by the National Health Care system has skyrocketed. In 1948, there were .73 staff for each hospital bed; today there are 3.1. The additional staff do not deal directly with the treatment of patients, though. Rather they have become part of the NHS bureaucracy, which requires that a department or committee be established for every new area of medicine or research that develops. The NHS consists of a bureaucratic network unknown in the decentralized system in the United States.

FOR CRITICAL ANALYSIS: Why have so many hospitals been closed in the United Kingdom? ●

Countering the Moral Hazard Problem: A Medical Savings Account

Medical savings accounts (MSAs)
A tax-exempt health care account to which individuals would pay into on a regular basis and from which medical care expenses could be paid.

As an alternative to a massive redesign of the United States' health care industry, a number of experts, as well as members of Congress, have offered the idea of **medical savings accounts (MSAs).** MSAs allow individuals to save money in a tax-exempt account. Each individual would be able to use that money to pay routine medical expenses. In addition, the individual or family could purchase relatively inexpensive catastrophic health insurance to protect against major medical expenditures. The existence of MSAs would relieve employers from having to provide high-cost full-coverage (zero-deductible) insurance for their employees. Employer health insurance plans would simply be catastrophic insurance policies with, say, a $3,000 deductible. The payment for deductible health care expenses would be covered by the MSA paid into individually by each worker.

Benefits of MSAs. Note two aspects of MSAs:

1. Contributors who do not spend all the money on medical care get to keep whatever is left in the plan plus interest. In essence, then, MSAs serve as a supplemental retirement plan.

2. The moral hazard problem is reduced significantly. Because individuals ultimately pay for their own minor medical expenses, they no longer have the incentive to seek medical care as frequently for minor problems. In contrast, they do have an incentive to engage in wellness activities, such as reducing smoking, drinking, and obesity. Also, there would be a reestablishment of the physician-patient relationship due to the absence of third-party payers for up to $3,000 a year in medical expenses. Physicians could not routinely order expensive tests without first consulting with the patient.

Critics' Responses. Some critics argue that because individuals get to keep whatever they don't spend from their MSAs, they will forgo necessary visits to medical care facilities and may develop more serious medical problems as a consequence.

Other critics argue that MSAs would sabotage managed care plans, which are growing in importance today. Under managed care plans, deductibles are either reduced or eliminated completely. In exchange, managed health care plan participants are extremely limited in physician choice. Just the opposite would occur with MSAs—high deductibles and unlimited choice of physicians.

CONCEPTS IN BRIEF

- Health care costs have risen because (1) our population has been getting older and the elderly use more health care services, (2) new technologies and medicine cost more, and (3) third-party financing—private and government-sponsored health insurance—reduces the incentive for individuals to reduce their spending on health care services.

- National health insurance has been proposed as an answer to our current problems, but it does little to alter the reasons why health care costs continue to rise.

- An alternative to a national health care program might be medical savings accounts, which allow individuals to set aside money that is tax exempt, to be used only for medical care. Whatever is left over becomes a type of retirement account.

Making Sense of Welfare Reform

Concepts Applied: *Demand curve, moral hazard, marginal tax rate*

As long as most welfare programs continue to be "means-tested," recipients will face higher marginal tax rates than even the nation's highest-paid individuals. While welfare recipients are often criticized for being lazy, high implicit marginal tax rates and low-paying public service jobs provide little incentive for them to enter the workforce.

At least one presidential candidate in the past 20 years has said he will change "welfare as we know it." The fact is, so far, all welfare programs taken as a group continue to work as they always have. The results are not encouraging. Figure 30-12 on page 690 shows that the official poverty rate dropped steadily from 1950 into the early 1970s but has remained constant or been rising since then. During the same time period, welfare spending has increased dramatically.

Implicit Marginal Tax Rates Reduce Work Incentives

The fact is that most welfare programs are "means-tested." When a person's income (means) increases by a certain amount, welfare benefits are reduced or eliminated. The result is an implicitly extremely high marginal tax rate. Consider a typical person receiving food stamps, AFDC payments, and Medicaid for a total of $950 per month. If that same person takes a minimum wage job and earns, say, $820 a month, food stamps are reduced by $125 a month and AFDC payments are eliminated completely. That person has to pay taxes of about $60 a month, and if

there are job-related expenses such as transportation of $100 a month, the net increase in real take-home pay is about $60. Nationwide, it has been estimated that a welfare mother without work experience will end up making a net wage of only $1.50 per hour if she chooses to leave welfare to go to work. In other words, so long as welfare programs are means-tested, welfare recipients will face much higher marginal tax rates than even America's highest-income-earning individuals.

A series of controlled experiments in Seattle and Denver revealed that every dollar of guaranteed income reduced labor earnings by 80 percent. Guaranteed incomes reduced the number of hours worked by an average of 40 percent for unmarried young people.

"Workfare"

Welfare reform has often been couched in terms of *workfare*—the requirement that welfare recipients perform public service jobs in exchange for benefits. At the basis of the workfare concept is the strange and inappropriate view of welfare recipients that they are looking for a free ride and might even be lazy. A more accurate view is that welfare recipients are acting rationally in the face of high implicit marginal income tax rates. Moreover, low-pay public service jobs hardly offer the earnings differential needed to convince welfare recipients to abandon welfare.

Despite the fact that workfare proposals for welfare reform play into the public's feeling that no one should "get something for nothing," such programs are not free. Each public service job, according to the Congressional Budget Office, costs $3,500 a year to monitor. If it involves mothers, an additional $3,000 per year has to be anted up for child care costs.

What About Job Training?

Some people argue that the way to reduce welfare spending is through government-provided job-training programs. The Department of Education currently offers 59 such programs, and the Department of Labor offers 34. Almost every other government agency offers at least

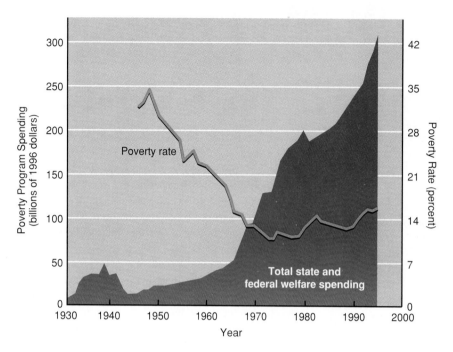

FIGURE 30-12

Welfare Spending and the Poverty Rate
Welfare spending has increased dramatically since the late 1960s. Nonetheless, the measured poverty rate has remained relatively stable.
Sources: U.S. Department of Commerce and Department of Health and Human Services.

one training program. Statistical evidence of the results of such job-training programs is not encouraging. Approximately two-thirds of long-time welfare recipients quit the jobs they obtain after such training programs in about five months and return to the welfare rolls. In addition, some job-training programs actually encourage people to go on welfare. One such program was offered by President Clinton. In that plan, job training was to be made available only to people on welfare. Had it been enacted, it would have become rational for low-income working individuals to quit working and enter the welfare system.

How to Analyze All Welfare Reform Proposals

Basically, all welfare reform proposals must be analyzed using the following rule of thumb: Low-income or no-income individuals in America respond to incentives. As long as programs to transfer income, in cash or in kind, present individuals benefiting from them with high implicit marginal tax rates, there will be disincentives to enter the labor force.

FOR CRITICAL ANALYSIS

1. Examine Figure 30-12 again. Offer an explanation of why the official poverty rate has not fallen in spite of substantial increases in social welfare spending.
2. If you divide the total number of the officially poor into the total amount of social welfare spending, you get about $25,000 per family of four, well above the poverty line. Why are there so many people still below the poverty line nonetheless?

CHAPTER SUMMARY

1. We can represent the distribution of income graphically with a Lorenz curve. The extent to which the line is bowed from a straight line shows how unequal the distribution of income is.

2. The distribution of pretax money income in the United States has remained fairly constant since World War II. The lowest fifth of income earners still receive only about 5 percent of total pretax money

income, while the top fifth of income earners receive about 40 percent.

3. The distribution of wealth is not the same as the distribution of income. Wealth includes assets such as houses, stocks, and bonds. Though the apparent distribution of wealth seems to be more concentrated at the top, the data used are not very accurate, nor do most summary statistics take account of workers' claims on private and public pensions.

4. Most individuals face a particular age-earnings cycle. Earnings are lowest when starting out to work at age 18 to 24. They gradually rise and peak at about age 50, then fall until retirement age. They go up usually because of increased experience, increased training, and longer working hours.

5. The marginal productivity theory of the distribution of income indicates that workers can expect to be paid their marginal revenue product. The marginal physical product is determined largely by talent, education, experience, and training.

6. Discrimination is usually defined as a situation in which a certain group is paid a lower wage than other groups for the same work. It also exists in hiring and promotions.

7. One way to invest in your own human capital is to go to college. The investment usually pays off; the rate of return is somewhere between 8 and 12 percent.

8. A definition of poverty made in relative terms means that there will always be poor in our society because the distribution of income will never be exactly equal.

9. The major income maintenance programs are Social Security (OASDI), Aid to Families with Dependent Children (AFDC), Supplemental Security Income (SSI), and the Earned Income Tax Credit Program (EITC).

10. The costs of medical care have risen because the U.S. population has been getting older and the elderly use more health care services, new technologies and medicine cost more, and third-party financing (health insurance) lessens the incentive to reduce spending on health care services.

DISCUSSION OF PREVIEW QUESTIONS

1. **What is a Lorenz curve, and what does it measure?**
A Lorenz curve indicates the portion of total money income accounted for by given proportions of a nation's households. It is a measure of income inequality that can be found by plotting the cumulative percentage of money income on the y axis and the percentage of households on the x axis. Two major problems with using the Lorenz curve to measure income equality are that it typically does not take into account income in kind, such as food stamps and housing aid, and that it does not account for differences in household size (and effort) or age. Adjustments for these would undoubtedly reduce the degree of measured income inequality in the United States.

2. **What has been happening to the distribution of income in the United States?**
Since World War II, the distribution of *money* income has not changed significantly, but the distribution of *total* income—which includes in-kind government transfers—has changed a great deal. Since the 1960s, *total* income inequality has been reduced significantly. The fact that more (total) income equality has been achieved in the United States in recent years is of tremendous importance, yet few people seem to be aware of this fact.

3. **What is the difference between income and wealth?**
Income is a *flow* concept and as such is measured per unit of time; we usually state that a person's income is X dollars *per year.* Wealth is a *stock* concept; as such, it is measured at a given point in time. We usually say that a person's wealth is $200,000 or $1 million. If people save out of a given income, it is possible for their wealth to be rising while their income is constant. Technically, a person's wealth may be defined as the value of his or her assets (human and

nonhuman) minus his or her liabilities (wealth being equivalent to net worth) at some point in time.

4. Why do people earn different incomes?

The major theory to account for income differentials in market economies is the marginal productivity theory. This theory says that laborers (as well as other resources) tend to be paid the value of their marginal revenue product. Laborers who are paid less than their MRP will go to other employers who will gladly pay them more (it will be profitable for them to do

so); laborers who are being paid more than their MRP may well lose their jobs (at least in the private sector). Thus productivity differences due to age, talent (intelligence, aptitudes, coordination), experience, and training can account for income differences. Of course, imperfect markets can potentially lead to income differences, at a given productivity, due to exploitation and discrimination. Income differences can also be accounted for by differences in nonhuman wealth—individuals can earn income on their property holdings.

PROBLEMS

(Answers to the odd-numbered problems appear at the back of the book.)

30-1. It is often observed that black Americans, on average, earn less than whites. What are some possible reasons for these differences?

30-2. The accompanying graph shows Lorenz curves for two countries.

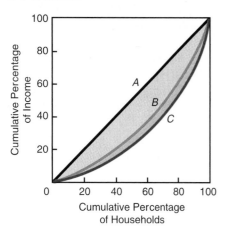

a. Which line indicates complete equality of income?
b. Which line indicates the most income inequality?
c. One country's "income inequality" is described by line *B*. Suppose that this country's income is to be adjusted for age and other variables such

that income on the *y* axis reflects *lifetime* income instead of income in a given year. Would the new, adjusted Lorenz curve move inward toward *A* or outward toward *C?*

30-3. What are two common normative standards of income distribution?

30-4. What does it mean when we say that some welfare recipients face a 120 percent marginal tax rate if they choose to go to work?

30-5. How might a program that truly made every household's income equal affect economy efficiency?

30-6. "Universal access" to health insurance has been a rallying cry for some people who wish to reform our current system. Under universal access, anyone who applies for insurance must be given it at the same rate that everybody else is paying. What might be some of the problems with such a system? (Hint: Would individuals want to join health insurance plans immediately or wait until they are sick with some long-term illness?)

30-7. What incentives do hospitals face when the federal and state governments pay for patients' health care? What incentives do government bureaucrats who work in the health care area face? What incentives do patients face when the government pays for their health care?

COMPUTER-ASSISTED INSTRUCTION

Many people believe that there is too much income inequality in the United States—that is, that the rich earn too much and the poor earn too little. This problem shows that the normal method of measuring income inequality is biased; it overstates true income inequality.

Complete problem and answer appear on disk.

INTERACTING WITH THE INTERNET

An excellent source for all sorts of statistics on the United States is the Census Bureau's site at
http://www.census.gov/
The holdings are quite extensive, so it may take a bit of effort to find what you want. Material includes the *Statistical Abstract of the United States*, providing details from the 1990 census, and the *County and City Data Book*, offering material on poverty. For nonmacroeconomic statistical material on the United States, you should check here first.

The Department of Health and Human Services is located at
http://www.os.dhhs.gov/
There you can find a number of links to its various agencies (such as the National Center for Health Statistics) and information about their programs.

CHAPTER 31

ENVIRONMENTAL ECONOMICS

If you are like most people, you eat some fish and other seafood on a regular basis. Throughout the United States and the world, fish stocks in the wild are dwindling. According to the Food and Agricultural Organization of the United Nations, 70 percent of the world's fisheries are near collapse or already completely depleted. Haddock has virtually disappeared from New England's coastal waters. There are no more large flounder or cod. Why did this problem occur, and is there a technological solution to it today? To answer these questions, you need to know more about environmental economics.

PREVIEW QUESTIONS

1. What is a negative externality?

2. How can poorly defined property rights create negative externalities?

3. If property rights are poorly defined, *must* negative externalities arise?

4. What is the optimal quantity of pollution?

Did You Know That... plants pollute? That's right, plants generate toxins as nature's attempt at protecting them from being eaten. Many of these toxins are known carcinogens. There are, for example, more known carcinogens in that cup of coffee you drink than in all of the pesticide residue on food that you consume in one year. Brussel sprouts, broccoli, mushrooms, potatoes, parsnips, and pears all contain natural carcinogens. When you think of pollution, nonetheless, you are probably thinking of smelly, foul, ugly air emanating from smokestacks across America, oil spills fouling pristine waters and killing wildlife, and other natural resources being ruined. Today, the American public, in general, appears to be willing to pay more to keep the environment "in good shape." But what does that mean?

As you might expect, after having read the previous chapters in this textbook, the economic way of thinking about the environment has a lot to do with costs. But of course your view of how to clean up the environment has a lot to do with costs also. Are you willing to give up driving your car in order to have a cleaner environment? Or would you pay $4 for a gallon of gas to help clean up the environment? In a phrase, how much of your current standard of living are you willing to give up to help the environment? The economic way of looking at ecological issues is often viewed as antienvironmental. But this is not so. Economists want to help citizens and policymakers opt for informed policies that have the maximum possible *net* benefits (benefits minus costs). As you will see, every decision in favor of "the environment" involves a trade-off.

PRIVATE VERSUS SOCIAL COSTS

Human actions often give rise to unwanted side effects—the destruction of our environment is one. Human actions generate pollutants that go into the air and the water. The question that is often asked is, Why can individuals and businesses continue to create pollution without necessarily paying directly for the negative consequences?

Until now, we've been dealing with situations in which the costs of an individual's actions are borne directly by the individual. When a business has to pay wages to workers, it knows exactly what its labor costs are. When it has to buy materials or build a plant, it knows quite well what these will cost. An individual who has to pay for car repairs or a theater ticket knows exactly what the cost will be. These costs are what we term *private costs*. **Private costs** are borne solely by the individuals who incur them. They are *internal* in the sense that the firm or household must explicitly take account of them.

What about a situation in which a business dumps the waste products from its production process into a nearby river or in which an individual litters a public park or beach? Obviously, a cost is involved in these actions. When the firm pollutes the water, people downstream suffer the consequences. They may not want to swim in or drink the polluted water. They may also be unable to catch as many fish as before because of the pollution. In the case of littering, the people who come along after our litterer has cluttered the park or the beach are the ones who bear the costs. The cost of these actions is borne by people other than those who commit the actions. The creator of the cost is not the sole bearer. The costs are not internalized by the individual or firm; they are external. When we add *external* costs to *internal*, or private, costs, we get **social costs.** Pollution problems—indeed, all problems pertaining to the environment—may be viewed as situations in which social costs exceed private costs. Because some economic participants don't pay the full social costs of their actions but rather only the smaller private costs, their actions are socially "unacceptable." In such situations in which there is a divergence between social and private costs, we

Private costs

Costs borne solely by the individuals who incur them. Also called *internal costs.*

Social costs

The full costs borne by society whenever a resource use occurs. Social costs can be measured by adding private, or internal, costs to external costs.

therefore see "too much" steel production, automobile driving, and beach littering, to pick only a few of the many possible examples.

The Costs of Polluted Air

Why is the air in cities so polluted from automobile exhaust fumes? When automobile drivers step into their cars, they bear only the private costs of driving. That is, they must pay for the gas, maintenance, depreciation, and insurance on their automobiles. However, they cause an additional cost, that of air pollution, which they are not forced to take account of when they make the decision to drive. Air pollution is a cost because it causes harm to individuals—burning eyes, respiratory ailments, and dirtier clothes, cars, and buildings. The air pollution created by automobile exhaust is a cost that individual operators of automobiles do not yet bear directly. The social cost of driving includes all the private costs plus at least the cost of air pollution, which society bears. Decisions made only on the basis of private costs lead to too much automobile driving or, alternatively, to too little money spent on the reduction of automobile pollution for a given amount of driving. Clean air is a scarce resource used by automobile drivers free of charge. They will use more of it than they would if they had to pay the full social costs.

EXTERNALITIES

When a private cost differs from a social cost, we say that there is an **externality** because individual decision makers are not paying (internalizing) all the costs. (We briefly covered this topic in Chapter 5.) Some of these costs remain external to the decision-making process. Remember that the full cost of using a scarce resource is borne one way or another by all who live in the society. That is, society must pay the full opportunity cost of any activity that uses scarce resources. The individual decision maker is the firm or the customer, and external costs and benefits will not enter into that individual's or firm's decision-making processes.

We might want to view the problem as it is presented in Figure 31-1. Here we have the market demand curve, D, for the product X and the supply curve, S_1, for product X. The

Externality
A situation in which a private cost diverges from a social cost; a situation in which the costs of an action are not fully borne by the two parties engaged in exchange or by an individual engaging in a scarce-resource-using activity. (Also applies to benefits.)

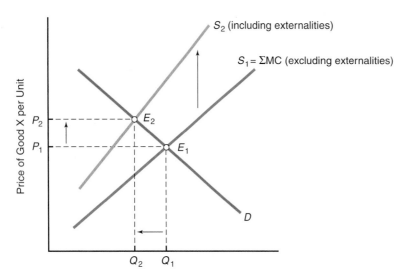

FIGURE 31-1

Reckoning with Full Social Costs
The supply curve, S_1, is equal to the horizontal summation (Σ) of the individual marginal cost curves above the respective minimum average variable costs of all the firms producing good X. These individual marginal cost curves include only internal, or private, costs. If the external costs were included and added to the private costs, we would have social costs. The supply curve would shift upward to S_2. In the uncorrected situation, the equilibrium price would be P_1 and the equilibrium quantity would be Q_1. In the corrected situation, the equilibrium price would rise to P_2 and the equilibrium quantity would fall to Q_2.

supply curve, S_1, includes only internal, or private, costs. The intersection of the demand and supply curves as drawn will be at price P_1 and quantity Q_1 (at E_1). However, we will assume that the production of good X involves externalities that the private firms did not take into account. Those externalities could be air pollution, water pollution, scenery destruction, or anything of that nature.

We know that the social costs of producing product X exceed the private costs. We show this by drawing curve S_2. It is above the original supply curve S_1 because it includes the full social costs of producing the product. If firms could be made to bear these costs, the price would be P_2 and the quantity Q_2 (at E_2). The inclusion of external costs in the decision-making process leads to a higher-priced product and a decline in quantity produced. Thus we see that when social costs are not being fully borne by the creators of those costs, the quantity produced is "excessive," because the price is too low.

CORRECTING FOR EXTERNALITIES

We can see here an easy method for reducing pollution and environmental degradation. Somehow the signals in the economy must be changed so that decision makers will take into account *all* the costs of their actions. In the case of automobile pollution, we might want to devise some method by which motorists are taxed according to the amount of pollution they cause. In the case of a firm, we might want to devise a system whereby businesses are taxed according to the amount of pollution for which they are responsible. In this manner, they would have an incentive to install pollution abatement equipment.

The Polluters' Choice

Facing an additional cost of polluting, firms will be induced to (1) install pollution abatement equipment or otherwise change production techniques so as to reduce the amount of pollution, (2) reduce pollution-causing activity, or (3) simply pay the price to pollute. The relative costs and benefits of each option for each polluter will determine which one or combination will be chosen. Allowing the choice is the efficient way to decide who pollutes and who doesn't. In principle, each polluter faces the full social cost of its actions and makes a production decision accordingly.

Is a Uniform Tax Appropriate?

It may not be appropriate to levy a *uniform* tax according to physical quantities of pollution. After all, we're talking about social costs. Such costs are not necessarily the same everywhere in the United States for the same action.

Essentially, we must establish the amount of the *economic damages* rather than the amount of the physical pollution. A polluting electrical plant in New York City will cause much more damage than the same plant in Remote, Montana. There are already innumerable demands on the air in New York City, so the pollution from smokestacks will not be cleansed away naturally. Millions of people will breathe the polluted air and thereby incur the costs of sore throats, sickness, emphysema, and even early death. Buildings will become dirtier faster because of the pollution, as will cars and clothes. A given quantity of pollution will cause more harm in concentrated urban environments than it will in less dense rural environments. If we were to establish some form of taxation to align private costs with social costs and to force people to internalize externalities, we would somehow have to come up with a measure of *economic* costs instead of *physical* quantities. But the tax, in any event, would fall on the private sector and modify private-sector economic agents' behavior. Therefore, because the economic cost for the same physical quantity of pollution would be different in different locations according to population density, the natural formation of mountains and rivers, and so forth, so-called optimal taxes on pollution would vary from location to location. (Nonetheless, a uniform tax might make sense when administrative costs, particularly the cost of ascertaining the actual economic costs, are relatively high.)

 INTERNATIONAL EXAMPLE
The Black Sea Becomes the Dead Sea: The Results of Externalities

The Black Sea is one of the dirtiest bodies of water in the world because for nearly 30 years it has been the dumping ground for half of Europe—the repository of phosphorus, inorganic nitrogen, DDT, and mercury, all generated by the 165 million people living around it. Only 5 out of 26 species of fish that lived in the sea in the 1960s remain. Because of pollution, the 42,000 square miles of oyster and blue mussel fields now yield one-tenth of their previous output. Cholera outbreaks have occurred routinely because raw sewage enters the Black Sea virtually everywhere. Prior to the breakup of the Soviet Union, there was virtually no concern for environmental degradation of the Black Sea. Currently, Russia, Georgia, Ukraine, Bulgaria, Romania, and Turkey have agreed to control maritime pollution. Because the cleanup will cost billions, such cleanup will not occur very rapidly in these developing countries.

FOR CRITICAL ANALYSIS: If the Black Sea were surrounded by just one country, could its degradation be more easily controlled? Why or why not? ●

CONCEPTS IN BRIEF

- Private costs are costs that are borne directly by consumers and producers when they engage in any resource-using activity.

- Social costs are private costs plus any other costs that are external to the decision maker. For example, the social costs of driving include all the private costs plus any pollution and congestion caused.

- When private costs differ from social costs, externalities exist because individual decision makers are not internalizing all the costs that society is bearing.

- When social costs exceed private costs, we say that there are externalities.

POLLUTION

The term *pollution* is used quite loosely and can refer to a variety of by-products of any activity. Industrial pollution involves mainly air and water but can also include noise and such concepts as aesthetic pollution, as when a landscape is altered in a negative way. For the most part, we will be analyzing the most common forms, air and water pollution.

When asked how much pollution there should be in the economy, many people will respond, "None." But if we ask those same people how much starvation or deprivation of consumer products should exist in the economy, many will again say, "None." Growing and distributing food or producing consumer products creates pollution, however. In effect,

The World's Ecology Is Being Destroyed—or Is It?

Most media reports about the ecology are negative. There are some encouraging signs nonetheless. As a result of forest management, for example, wooded areas in Vermont, Massachusetts, and Connecticut have increased from 35 percent of total landmass in the mid-eighteenth century to almost 60 percent today. The number of bird species has not plummeted as predicted. Smog has dissipated in many U.S. cities. And there has been virtually no degradation of pristine rivers by *new* water pollution sources in the United States in recent years.

therefore, there is no correct answer to how much pollution should be in an economy because when we ask how much pollution there *should* be, we are entering the realm of normative economics. We are asking people to express values. There is no way to disprove somebody's value system scientifically. One way we can approach a discussion of the "correct" amount of pollution would be to set up the same type of marginal analysis we used in our discussion of a firm's employment and output decisions. That is to say, we should pursue measures to reduce pollution only up to the point at which the marginal benefit from further reduction equals the marginal cost of further reduction.

Look at Figure 31-2. On the horizontal axis, we show the degree of cleanliness of the air. A vertical line is drawn at 100 percent cleanliness—the air cannot become any cleaner. Consider the benefits of obtaining a greater degree of air cleanliness. These benefits are represented by the marginal benefit curve, which slopes downward because of the law of diminishing marginal utility.

When the air is very dirty, the marginal benefit from air that is a little cleaner appears to be relatively high, as shown on the vertical axis. As the air becomes cleaner and cleaner, however, the marginal benefit of a little bit more air cleanliness falls.

Consider the marginal cost of pollution abatement—that is, the marginal cost of obtaining cleaner air. In the 1960s, automobiles had no pollution abatement devices. Eliminating only 20 percent of the pollutants emitted by internal-combustion engines entailed a relatively small cost per unit of pollution removed. The cost of eliminating the next 20 percent rose, though. Finally, as we now get to the upper limits of removal of pollutants from the emissions of internal-combustion engines, we find that the elimination of one more percentage point of the amount of pollutants becomes astronomically expensive. To go from 97 percent cleanliness to 98 percent cleanliness involves a marginal cost that is many times greater than going from 10 percent cleanliness to 11 percent cleanliness.

It is realistic, therefore, to draw the marginal cost of pollution abatement as an upward-sloping curve, as shown in Figure 31-2. (The marginal cost curve slopes up because of the law of diminishing returns.)

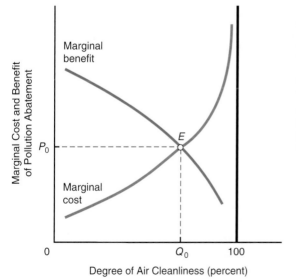

FIGURE 31-2

The Optimal Quantity of Air Pollution
As we attempt to get a greater degree of air cleanliness, the marginal cost rises until even the slightest attempt at increasing air cleanliness leads to a very high marginal cost, as can be seen at the upper right of the graph. Conversely, the marginal benefit curve slopes downward: The more pure air we have, the less we value an additional unit of pure air. Marginal cost and marginal benefit intersect at point E. The optimal degree of air cleanliness is something less than 100 percent at Q_0. The price that we should pay for the last unit of air cleanup is no greater than P_0, for that is where marginal cost equals marginal benefit.

The Optimal Quantity of Pollution

The **optimal quantity of pollution** is defined as the level of pollution at which the marginal benefit equals the marginal cost of obtaining clean air. This occurs at the intersection of the marginal benefit curve and the marginal cost curve in Figure 31-2, at point E, which is analytically exactly the same as for every other economic activity. If we increased pollution control by one more unit greater than Q_0, the marginal cost of that small increase in the degree of air cleanliness would be greater than the marginal benefit to society.

As is usually the case in economic analysis, the optimal quantity of just about anything occurs when marginal cost equals marginal benefit. That is, the optimal quantity of pollution occurs at the point at which the marginal cost of reducing (or abating) pollution is just equal to the marginal benefit of doing so. The marginal cost of pollution abatement rises as more and more abatement is achieved (as the environment becomes cleaner and cleaner, the *extra* cost of cleansing rises). The state of technology is such that early units of pollution abatement are easily achieved (at low cost), but attaining higher and higher levels of environmental quality becomes progressively more difficult (as the extra cost rises to prohibitive levels). At the same time, the marginal benefits of a cleaner and cleaner environment fall; the marginal benefit of pollution abatement declines as the concept of a cleaner and cleaner environment moves from human life-support requirements to recreation to beauty to a perfectly pure environment. The point at which the increasing marginal cost of pollution abatement equals the decreasing marginal benefit of pollution abatement defines the (theoretical) optimal quantity of pollution.

Recognizing that the optimal quantity of pollution is not zero becomes easier when we realize that it takes scarce resources to reduce pollution. It follows that a trade-off exists between producing a cleaner environment and producing other goods and services. In that sense, nature's ability to cleanse itself is a resource that can be analyzed like any other resource, and a cleaner environment must take its place with other societal wants.

Optimal quantity of pollution
The level of pollution for which the marginal benefit of one additional unit of clean air just equals the marginal cost of that additional unit of clean air.

CONCEPTS IN BRIEF

- The marginal cost of cleaning up the environment rises as we get closer to 100 percent cleanliness. Indeed, it rises at an increasing rate.

- The marginal benefit of environmental cleanliness falls as we have more of it.

- The optimal quantity of pollution is the quantity at which the marginal cost of cleanup equals the marginal benefit of cleanup.

- Pollution abatement is a trade-off. We trade off goods and services for cleaner air and water, and vice versa.

COMMON PROPERTY

In most cases, you do not have **private property rights**—exclusive ownership rights—to the air surrounding you, nor does anyone else. Air is a **common property**—nonexclusive—resource. Therein lies the crux of the problem. When no one owns a particular resource, no one has any incentive (conscience aside) to consider misuse of that resource. If one person decides not to pollute the air, there normally will be no significant effect on the total level of pollution. If one person decides not to pollute the ocean, there will still be approximately the same amount of ocean pollution—provided, of course, that the individual was previously responsible for only a small part of the total amount of ocean pollution.

Private property rights
Exclusive rights of ownership that allow the use, transfer, and exchange of property.

Common property
Property that is owned by everyone and therefore by no one. Air and water are examples of common property resources.

Basically, pollution occurs where we have poorly defined private property rights, as in air and common bodies of water. We do not, for example, have a visual pollution problem in people's attics. That is their own property, which they choose to keep as clean as they want, given their preferences for cleanliness as weighed against the costs of keeping the attic neat and tidy.

Where private property rights exist, individuals have legal recourse to any damages sustained through the misuse of their property. When private property rights are well defined, the use of property—that is, the use of resources—will generally involve contracting between the owners of those resources. If you own land, you might contract with another person who wants to use your land for raising cows. The contract would most likely be written in the form of a lease agreement.

INTERNATIONAL POLICY EXAMPLE
Should Ivory Imports Be Banned Worldwide?

Not many years ago, an important government official in Kenya burned 2,500 elephant tusks worth an estimated $4 million. He wanted to dramatize the plight of the African elephant, which poachers have been killing in order to sell their ivory. This "white gold" is worth about $100 per pound on the international market. At the beginning of the 1990s, the Convention on International Trade and Endangered Species prohibited all trade in ivory. Zimbabwe refuses to accept the import ban. Rather, it passed ownership of much of its elephant population to different tribes. The tribes charge relatively high prices to trophy hunters. Because they retain the benefits from taking care of the elephants and preventing poaching, the elephant population in Zimbabwe is growing rapidly. Elsewhere in Africa, poaching is on the upsurge because the ban on the ivory trade has caused an increase in its price. The problem of elephant extinction is due mainly to the common property nature of elephants in Africa.

FOR CRITICAL ANALYSIS: Alligators in Florida and Louisiana can be raised on special farms. The Florida Alligator Farmers Association has argued that "if people want to protect the alligator, the best thing they can do is buy an alligator handbag." Analyze this statement. •

Voluntary Agreements and Transactions Costs

Is it possible for externalities to be internalized via voluntary agreement? Take a simple example. You live in a house with a nice view of a lake. The family living below you plants a tree. The tree grows so tall that it eventually starts to cut off your view. In most cities, no one has property rights to views; therefore, you cannot usually go to court to obtain relief. You do have the option of contracting with your neighbor, however.

Voluntary Agreements: Contracting. You have the option of paying your neighbors (contracting) to cut back the tree. You could start out with an offer of a small amount and keep going up until your neighbors agree or until you reach your limit. Your limit will equal the value you place on having an unobstructed view of the lake. Your neighbors will be willing if the payment is at least equal to the reduction in their intrinsic property value due to a stunted tree. Your offering the payment makes your neighbors aware of the social cost of their actions. The social cost here is equal to the care of the tree plus the cost suffered by you from an impeded view of the lake.

In essence, then, your offer of money income to your neighbors indicates to them that there is an opportunity cost to their actions. If they don't comply, they forfeit the money that you are offering them. The point here is that *opportunity cost always exists, whoever has property rights.* Therefore, we would expect under some circumstances that voluntary contracting will occur to internalize externalities.[1] The question is, When will voluntary agreements occur?

Transaction Costs. One major condition for the outcome just outlined above is that the **transaction costs**—all costs associated with making and enforcing agreements—must be low relative to the expected benefits of reaching an agreement. (We already looked at this topic briefly in Chapter 4.) If we expand our example to a much larger one such as air pollution, the transaction costs of numerous homeowners trying to reach agreements with the individuals and companies that create the pollution are relatively high. Consequently, we don't expect voluntary contracting to be an effective way to internalize the externality of air pollution.

Transaction costs
All costs associated with making, reaching, and enforcing agreements.

Changing Property Rights

In considering the problem of property rights, we can approach it by assuming that initially in a society, many property rights and many resources are not defined. But this situation does not cause a problem so long as no one cares to use the resources for which there are no property rights or so long as enough of these resources are available that people can have as much as they want at a zero price. Only when and if a use is found for a resource or the supply of a resource is inadequate at a zero price does a problem develop. The problem requires that something be done about deciding property rights. If not, the resource will be wasted and possibly even destroyed. Property rights can be assigned to individuals who will then assert control; or they may be assigned to government, which can maintain and preserve the resource, charge for its use, or implement some other rationing device. What we have seen with common property such as air and water is that governments have indeed attempted to take over the control of those resources so that they cannot be wasted or destroyed.

Another way of viewing the pollution problem is to argue that property rights are "sacred" and that there are property rights in every resource that exists. We can then say that each individual does not have the right to act on anything that is not his or her property. Hence no individual has the right to pollute because that amounts to using property that the individual does not specifically own.

Clearly, we must fill the gap between private costs and true social costs in situations in which we have to make up somehow for the fact that property rights are not well defined or assigned. There are three ways to fill this gap: taxation, subsidization, and regulation. Government is involved in all three. Unfortunately, government does not have perfect information and may not pick the appropriate tax, subsidy, or type of regulation. We also have to consider cases in which taxes are hard to enforce or subsidies are difficult to give out to "worthy" recipients. In such cases, outright prohibition of the polluting activity may be the optimal solution to a particular pollution problem. For example, if it is difficult to monitor the level of a particular type of pollution that even in small quantities can cause severe environmental damage, outright prohibition of such pollution may be the only alternative.

---

[1]This analysis is known as the *Coase theorem,* named after its originator, Ronald Coase, who demonstrated that negative or positive externalities do not necessarily require government intervention in situations in which property rights are defined and enforceable and transaction costs are relatively low.

Are There Alternatives to Pollution-Causing Resource Use?

Some people cannot understand why, if pollution is bad, we still use pollution-causing resources such as coal and oil to generate electricity. Why don't we forgo the use of such polluting resources and opt for one that apparently is pollution free, such as solar energy? Contrary to some people's beliefs, there is no nationwide or worldwide conspiracy to prevent us from shifting to solar power. The plain fact is that the cost of generating solar power in most circumstances is much higher than generating that same power through conventional means. We do not yet have the technology that allows us the luxury of driving solar-powered cars. Moreover, with current technology, the solar panels necessary to generate the electricity for the average town would cover massive sections of the countryside, and the manufacturing of those solar panels would itself generate pollution.

WILD SPECIES, COMMON PROPERTY, AND TRADE-OFFS

One of the most distressing common property problems concerns endangered species, usually in the wild. No one is too concerned about the quantity of dogs, cats, cattle, sheep, and horses. The reason is that virtually all of those species are private property. Spotted owls, bighorn mountain sheep, condors, and the like are typically common property. No one has a vested interest in making sure that they perpetuate in good health.

The federal government passed the Endangered Species Act in an attempt to prevent species from dying out. Initially, few individuals were affected by the rulings of the Interior Department with respect to which species were listed as endangered. Eventually, however, as more and more species were put on the endangered list, a trade-off became apparent. Nationwide, the trade-off was brought to the public's attention when the spotted owl was declared an endangered species in the Pacific Northwest. Ultimately, thousands of logging jobs were lost when the courts upheld the ban on logging in the areas presumed to be the spotted owl's natural habitat. Then another small bird, the marbled murrelet, was found in an ancient forest, causing the Pacific Lumber Company to cut back its logging practices. In 1995, the U.S. Supreme Court ruled that the federal government did have the right to regulate activities on private land in order to save endangered species.

The issues are not straightforward. Today, the earth has only .02 percent of all of the species that have ever lived. Every year, 1,000 to 3,000 new species are discovered and classified. Estimates of how many species are actually dying out vary from a high of 50,000 a year to a low of one every four years.

EXAMPLE
The Demand for Steel and Spotted Owls

Normally one does not associate spotted owls with steel. But when the federal government greatly reduced the amount of forest land that could be harvested in deference to the spotted owl's natural habitat, wood prices skyrocketed. In March 1992, the cost was $320 per thousand board-feet for house-framing lumber. By March 1994, it had jumped to $447, thereby adding $5,000 to the cost of the average new home. The result has been a greater interest in wood substitutes, including steel studs and frames. In one year, Tristeel Structures in Corinth, Texas, sold four times as many steel-framed houses as the previous year. Nationwide, the year after the spotted owl controversy, steel-framed housing starts increased by a factor of 30.

FOR CRITICAL ANALYSIS: Is steel a renewable or a nonrenewable resource, and does it matter? ●

CONCEPTS IN BRIEF

- A common property resource is one that no one owns—or, otherwise stated, that everyone owns.

- Common property exists when property rights are indefinite or nonexistent.

- When no property rights exist, pollution occurs because no one individual or firm has a sufficient economic incentive to care for the common property in question, be it air, water, or scenery.

- Private costs will not equal social costs when common property is at issue unless only a few individuals are involved and they are able to contract among themselves.

RECYCLING

As part of the overall ecology movement, there has been a major push to save scarce resources via recycling. **Recycling** involves reusing paper products, plastics, glass, and metals rather than putting them into solid waste dumps. Many cities have instituted mandatory recycling programs.

Recycling
The reuse of raw materials derived from manufactured products.

The benefits of recycling are straightforward. Fewer *natural* resources are used. But some economists argue that recycling does not necessarily save *total* resources. For example, recycling paper products may not necessarily save trees, according to A. Clark Wiseman, an economist for Resources for the Future in Washington, D.C. He argues that an increase in paper recycling will eventually lead to a reduction in the demand for virgin paper and thus for trees. Because most trees are planted specifically to produce paper, a reduction in the demand for trees will mean that certain land now used to grow trees will be put to other uses. The end result may be smaller rather than larger forests, a result that is probably not desired in the long run.

Recycling's Invisible Costs

The recycling of paper can also pollute. Used paper has ink on it that has to be removed during the recycling process. According to the National Wildlife Federation, the product of 100 tons of deinked (bleached) fiber generates 40 tons of sludge. This sludge has to be disposed of, usually in a landfill. A lot of recycled paper companies, however, are beginning to produce unbleached paper. In general, recycling does create waste that has to be disposed of.

There is also an issue involved in the use of resources. Recycling requires human effort. The labor resources involved in recycling are often many times more costly than the potential savings in scarce resources not used. That means that net resource use, counting all resources, may sometimes be greater with recycling than without it.

Landfills

One of the arguments in favor of recycling is to avoid a solid waste "crisis." Some people believe that we are running out of solid waste dump sites in the United States. This is perhaps true in and near major cities, and indeed the most populated areas of the country might ultimately benefit from recycling programs. In the rest of the United States, however, the data do not seem to indicate that we are running out of solid waste landfill sites. Throughout the United States, the disposal price per ton of city garbage has actually fallen. Prices vary, of course, for the 180 million tons of trash generated each year. In San Jose, California, it costs $10 a ton to dump, whereas in Morris County, New Jersey, it costs $131 a ton.

Currently, municipalities burn about 16 percent of their solid waste and recycle a few percentage points more. The amount of solid waste dumped in landfills estimated for 1996 is 125 million tons. By 2000, it is expected to drop to 100 million tons even as total trash output rises above 200 million tons. In all likelihood, partly because of recycling efforts, the cost of solid waste disposal will continue to drop as the supply curve of solid waste disposal shifts outward faster than the demand curve. Thus in some instances the use of recycling to reduce solid waste disposal ends up costing society more resources because simply throwing waste into a landfill may be less costly.

INTERNATIONAL POLICY EXAMPLE
Can Citizens Recycle Too Much? The Case of Germany

Recycling is popular throughout the European Union, but the Germans have raised it to an art form. Germany has a law requiring that manufacturers or retailers take back their packaging or ensure that 80 percent of it is collected rather than thrown away. What is collected must be recycled or reused. The law covers about 40 percent of the country's garbage. The problem is that German consumers responded more enthusiastically than anticipated: So much plastic packaging has been collected that German recyclers do not have the capacity to use it all. Consequently, Germany has been exporting its recyclable waste to neighboring Belgium, France, and the Netherlands. France threatened to curb its imports of German recyclable trash. Belgium even argued in front of the European Parliament that Germany was engaging in unfair competition. In the meantime, the company in charge of recycling Germany's trash, Duales System Deutschland, is losing hundreds of millions of dollars a year. Considering that it costs $2,000 a ton to recycle plastic and that the price of petroleum (the main ingredient in plastic) is relatively low, the future of recycling in Germany does not look bright.

FOR CRITICAL ANALYSIS: How is it possible to recycle "too much"? ●

Should We Save Scarce Resources?

Periodically, the call for recycling focuses on the necessity of saving scarce resources because "we are running out." There is little evidence to back up this claim because virtually every natural resource has fallen in price (corrected for inflation) over the past several decades. In 1980, economist Julian Simon made a $1,000 bet with well-known environmentalist Paul Erlich. Simon bet $200 per resource that any five natural resources that Erlich picked would decline in price (corrected for inflation) by the end of the 1980s. Simon won. (When Simon asked Erlich to renew the bet for $20,000 for the 1990s, Erlich declined.) During the 1980s, the price of virtually every natural resource fell (corrected for

THINKING CRITICALLY ABOUT THE MEDIA

We Are Running Out of Everything!

It is going to be a world with no more oil, natural gas, copper, or zinc. At least that is the impression one gets these days from the media. In reality, as Yale University economist William Nordhaus has discovered, the real (inflation-corrected) prices for most nonrenewable resources have fallen over the past 125 years. Real energy prices have dropped an average of 1.6 percent per year; major mineral prices have dropped 1.3 to 2.9 percent a year; even the price of land has dropped .8 percent per year. Unless supply and demand analysis is no longer valid, those numbers indicate that the supply of nonrenewable resources is increasing faster than the demand.

inflation), and so did the price of every agricultural commodity. The same was true for every forest product. Though few people remember the dire predictions of the 1970s, many noneconomists throughout the world argued at that time that the world's oil reserves were vanishing. If this were true, the pretax, inflation-corrected price of gasoline would not be the same today as it was in the late 1940s (which it is).

In spite of predictions in the early 1980s by World Watch Institute president Lester Brown, real food prices did not rise. Indeed, the real price of food fell by more than 30 percent for the major agricultural commodities during the 1980s. A casual knowledge of supply and demand tells you that since demand for food did not decrease, supply must have increased faster than demand.

With respect to the forests, at least in the United States and Western Europe, there are more forests today than there were 100 years ago. In this country, the major problems of deforestation seem to be on land owned by the United States Forest Service for which private timber companies are paid almost $1 billion a year in subsidies to cut down trees.

CONCEPTS IN BRIEF

- Recycling involves reusing paper, glass, and other materials rather than putting them into solid waste dumps. Recycling does have a cost both in the resources used for recycling and in the pollution created during recycling, such as the sludge from deinking paper for reuse.

- Landfills are an alternative to recycling. Expansion of these solid waste disposal sites is outpacing demand increases.

- Resources may not be getting scarcer. The inflation-corrected price of most resources has been falling for decades.

Technology to the Rescue of Dwindling Fish Stocks

Concepts Applied: Marginal cost, marginal benefit, common property, social cost, private cost, opportunity cost

Overfishing has caused the worldwide stock of fish to be severely limited, and in some cases, totally depleted. Attempts to remedy this problem have come in the form of government imposition of limiting-access schemes in which catch limits are set.

Overfishing is a common property problem. An individual who fishes for a living will fish until the marginal benefit equals the marginal cost. That individual considers only his or her actual private costs when computing marginal cost. These include the opportunity cost of investing in equipment, depreciation, and supplies, as well as the individual's opportunity cost of time. What the private fisher does not take into account is the potential cost to society if common property fishing grounds are overfished. The result has been called the "tragedy of the commons." The tragedy occurs because of the overuse of the common property resource. In the case of fish, there is strong evidence that the tragedy of the commons has occurred. Some solutions have already been tried.

Limited-Access Schemes

Some governments, such as New Zealand, have instituted limited-access schemes in which officials set annual catch limits. The right to a percentage of that catch is privately owned and can be traded. Once instituted in New Zealand, according to economist Michael De Alessi, fishers began to practice conservation and limit their harvest.

Similar systems have been instituted in Alaska for the Pacific whiting.

Technology and Private Ownership

The tragedy of the commons with respect to fishing involves common property ownership of most migratory species. The territorial waters of the United States extend over a million square miles of ocean. Thus it has never seemed possible for anybody to "own" migratory schools of fish. Today, this is now feasible due to branding technologies, including sonar. Scientists at Cornell University have used the Integrated Underseas Surveillance System to track a single blue whale for over 40 days without the use of radio beacons. Because constant monitoring is now technologically feasible, at least with whales, it is possible to enforce private property rights in that species if we so choose.

Satellite technologies allow for the tagging and monitoring of certain species of sea life. Branding fish is another possibility. Fish packers might then compensate fish "ranchers" according to how much of each branded fish was packed. According to economist De Alessi, it is now possible for autonomous underwater vehicles actually to "corral" schools of certain types of fish like herds of sheep. This might be feasible for very expensive fish such as giant bluefin tuna, which routinely fetch up to thousands of dollars each in Tokyo.

Using sonar and satellites, it is also possible to create a "virtual fence." Satellites can provide information on ship location and ship activity even to the extent of knowing when a ship has lowered a net. Boats that are fishing illegally could be identified.

FOR CRITICAL ANALYSIS
1. In the American West a century ago, land expanses were great and fencing material was relatively expensive. How did cattlemen solve the problem of intermingling herds?
2. What are some currently available ways to solve the fish stock depletion problem without using sophisticated new technologies?

707

CHAPTER SUMMARY

1. In some situations, there are social costs that do not equal private costs—that is, there are costs to society that exceed the cost to the individual. These costs may include air and water pollution, for which private individuals do not have to pay. Society, however, does bear the costs of these externalities. Few individuals or firms voluntarily consider social costs.

2. One way to analyze the problem of pollution is to look at it as an externality. Individual decision makers do not take account of the negative externalities they impose on the rest of society. In such a situation, they produce "too much" pollution and "too many" polluting goods.

3. It might be possible to ameliorate the situation by imposing a tax on polluters. The tax, however, should be dependent on the extent of the economic damages created rather than on the physical quantity of pollution. This tax will therefore be different for the same level of physical pollution in different parts of the country because the economic damage differs, depending on location, population density, and other factors.

4. The optimal quantity of pollution is the quantity at which the marginal cost of cleanup equals the marginal benefit of cleanup. Pollution abatement is a trade-off. We trade off goods and services for cleaner air and water, and vice versa.

5. Another way of looking at the externality problem is to realize that it involves the lack of definite property rights. No one owns common property resources such as air and water, and therefore no one takes account of the long-run pernicious effects of excessive pollution.

6. There are alternatives to pollution-causing resource use—for example, solar energy. We do not use solar energy because it is too expensive relative to conventional alternatives and because the creation of solar panels would generate pollution.

7. Recycling involves reusing paper, glass, and other materials rather than putting them into solid waste dumps. Recycling does have a cost both in the resources used for recycling and in the pollution created during recycling. Landfills are an alternative to recycling. These solid waste disposal sites are being expanded faster than the demand for them.

8. Resources may not be getting scarcer. The inflation-corrected price of most resources has been falling for decades.

DISCUSSION OF PREVIEW QUESTIONS

1. What is a negative externality?

A negative externality exists if the social costs exceed the private costs of some activity; if parties not involved in that activity are adversely affected, negative externalities are said to exist. Pollution is an example of a negative externality; for example, transactions between automobile producers and users impose costs in the form of pollution on people who neither produce nor consume the autos.

2. How can poorly defined property rights create negative externalities?

Nature's ability to cleanse itself can be considered a scarce resource, and as such, it behooves society to use this resource efficiently. However, if everyone owns natural resources, in effect *no one* owns them. Consequently, people will use natural resources, for good or for ill, as though they were free. Of course, excessive use of natural resources eventually impairs nature's ability to cleanse itself; enter the concept of pollution (an accumulation of unwanted matter). Now the marginal cost to *private* polluters is still zero (or nearly zero), whereas the cost to society of using this (now scarce) resource is positive. In short, third parties are adversely affected when pollution results from the production and consumption of goods that lead to waste, which creates pollution.

3. If property rights are poorly defined, *must* negative externalities arise?

No. If contracting costs are small and enforcement is relatively easy, voluntary contracts will arise and the full opportunity costs of actions will be accounted for. That is, when transaction costs are small, private and social costs will converge, as the parties affected contract with the parties creating the additional costs, and externalities will disappear. What is interesting is that regardless of how property rights are assigned, resources will be allocated in the same way. Of course, the specific assignment of property rights does affect the distribution of wealth, even though resource allocation is independent of the specific property right assignment; what is important for efficient resource allocation is that *someone* have property rights. It should be noted that, unfortunately, the main externalities, such as air and water pollution, are very complex, contracting costs are very high, and enforcement is difficult. As a consequence, free market solutions are not likely to emerge—indeed, they have not.

4. What is the optimal quantity of pollution?
The optimal quantity of pollution cannot be zero because at 100 percent cleanliness, the marginal cost

of pollution abatement would greatly exceed the marginal benefit. We would have too much pollution abatement; we would be using resources in a socially suboptimal manner. That means that the resources being used in pollution abatement would have a higher value elsewhere in society.

We live in a world of scarce resources. If the value we receive from spending one more dollar on cleaning up the environment is less than the value we would receive by spending that dollar on something else—such as cancer research—we are not allocating our resources efficiently if we still choose to spend that dollar on pollution abatement.

PROBLEMS

(Answers to the odd-numbered problems appear at the back of the book.)

31-1. Construct a typical supply and demand graph. Show the initial equilibrium price and quantity. Assume that the good causes negative externalities to third parties (persons not involved in the transactions). Revise the graph to compensate for that fact. How does the revised situation compare with the original?

31-2. Construct a second supply and demand graph for any product. Show the equilibrium price and quantity. Assuming that the good generates external benefits, modify the diagram to allow for them. Show the new equilibrium price and quantity. How does the revised situation compare with the original?

31-3. Suppose that polluters are to be charged by government agencies for the privilege of polluting.
   a. How should the price be set?
   b. Which firms will treat waste, and which will pay to pollute?
   c. Is it possible that some firms will be forced to close down because they now have to pay to pollute? Why might this result be good?
   d. If producers are charged to pollute, they will pass this cost on to buyers in the form of higher prices. Why might this be good?

31-4. Why has the free market not developed contractual arrangements to eliminate excess air pollution in major U.S. cities?

31-5. What is the problem with common property resources?

31-6. The accompanying graph shows external costs arising from the production of good Y.

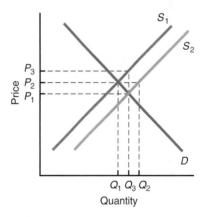

   a. Which curve includes only the private costs of producing good Y?
   b. Which supply curve includes the external costs of producing good Y?
   c. How much of good Y is produced and at what price?
   d. Who bears the cost of producing the amount of good Y in part (c)?
   e. If external costs are included, how much of good Y should be produced, and at what price should it be sold?

710 PART 8 • PRODUCTIVE FACTORS, POVERTY, THE ENVIRONMENT, AND INTEREST GROUPS

31-7. The table shows the costs and benefits of removing air pollution.

Annual Units of Pollution	Annual Total Air Pollution Damage	Annual Total Costs of Air Pollution Reduction
0	$ 0	$410
1	30	260
2	70	160
3	150	80
4	270	20
5	430	0

a. Find the marginal benefits of pollution reduction.
b. Find the marginal costs of pollution reduction.
c. Assume that society is currently allowing 5 units of air pollution per year. If pollution is reduced to 3 units, what is the net gain or loss to society?
d. Suppose that all air pollution is eliminated. What would be the net gain or loss to society?
e. If air pollution were regulated efficiently, how many units of air pollution would be allowed each year?

31-8. Examine this marginal cost and marginal benefit schedule for air cleanliness:

Quantity (%)	Marginal Benefit	Marginal Cost
0	$50,000	$ 5,000
20	45,000	10,000
40	35,000	15,000
60	25,000	25,000
80	10,000	40,000
100	0	∞

a. Graph the marginal benefit and marginal cost curves.
b. What is the optimal degree of air cleanliness?
c. How much will the optimal amount of air cleanliness cost?
d. What is the optimal amount of air pollution?
e. Would we want a level of zero pollution? Why or why not?

31-9. Explain why it is possible to have too little pollution. What might government do to cause private individuals and businesses to generate too little pollution?

COMPUTER-ASSISTED INSTRUCTION

Environmental problems almost always involve externalities. You are asked to examine some of them in this exercise.

Complete problem and answer appear on disk.

INTERACTING WITH THE INTERNET

The Environmental Protection Agency (EPA) is located at
   http://www.epa.gov/
It has general information about the agency and material on its programs, initiatives, rules, regulations, and legislation. It also has "Citizen Information," which describes the role individuals can play in environmental issues. An organization that takes an economist's view toward environmental issues is Resources for the Future at
   http://www.rff.org/
So does the Political Economy Research Center (PERC) at
   http://www.perc.org/

CHAPTER 32

PUBLIC CHOICE: THE ECONOMICS OF INTEREST GROUPS

If you are a typical consumer of food products, you account for some of the 16 billion pounds of sugar eaten in one form or another in this country each year. Did you know, though, that the domestic price of sugar in the United States is approximately twice the world price? Not only that, sugar farmers are provided with low-cost loans from the U.S. Treasury. The sugar industry's sweet deal with the federal government is coming under attack, however, from a coalition of big sugar buyers. To understand how interest groups operate in our political system, you need to know more about the theory of public choice.

PREVIEW QUESTIONS

1. What is the essence of the public-choice model?

2. Why can private choice indicate intensity of wants but public choice cannot?

3. How can logrolling enable legislators to indicate the intensity of their wants?

4. When do distributional coalitions emerge?

711

Did You Know That . . . more than 1,200 organizations whose names begin with the word *National* are listed in the Washington, D.C., telephone directory? Another 600 begin with the word *American* or *Americans*. At least 10,000 separate groups exist for the purpose of influencing government policies, and an estimated 80,000 persons are engaged in lobbying in the nation's capital at this very instant. Perhaps without realizing it, you have been introduced to a number of important **interest groups** in the last few chapters: unions, health care professionals, medical insurance companies, poverty workers, and environmentalists. What these diverse groups have in common is that they often seek to influence government legislation and change the flow of resources in our economy.

Another interest group that has had great success in influencing government is agriculture, to which you were first introduced in Chapter 4. Throughout this chapter, we will use agriculture as a key example to explain the economics of interest groups. This analysis can be subsumed under what economists call the *theory of public choice*.

COLLECTIVE DECISION MAKING: THE THEORY OF PUBLIC CHOICE

The public sector has a vast influence on the American economy. Yet the economic model used until now has applied only to the behavior of the private sector—firms and households. Such a model does not adequately explain the behavior of the public sector. We shall attempt to do so now.

Governments consist of individuals. No government actually thinks and acts; rather, government actions are the result of decision making by individuals in their roles as elected representatives, appointed officials, and salaried bureaucrats. Therefore, to understand how government works, we must examine the incentives for the people in government as well as those who would like to be in government—avowed candidates or would-be candidates for elective or appointed positions—and special-interest lobbyists attempting to get government to do something. At issue is the analysis of **collective decision making.** Collective decision making involves the actions of voters, politicians, political parties, interest groups, and many other groups and individuals. The analysis of collective decision making is usually called the **theory of public choice.** It has been given this name because it involves hypotheses about how choices are made in the public sector, as opposed to the private sector. The foundation of public-choice theory is the assumption that individuals will act within the political process to maximize their *individual* (not collective) well-being. In that sense, the theory is similar to our analysis of the market economy, in which we also assume that individuals are motivated by self-interest.

To understand public-choice theory, it is necessary to point out other similarities between the private market sector and the public, or government, sector; then we will look at the differences.

Similarities in Market and Public-Sector Decision Making

In addition to the similar assumption of self-interest being the motivating force in both sectors, there are other similarities.

Scarcity. At any given moment, the amount of resources is fixed. This means that for the private and the public sectors combined, there is a scarcity constraint. Everything that is

Interest group
Any group that seeks to cause government to change spending in a way that will benefit the group's members or to undertake any other action that will improve their lot. Also called a *special-interest group*.

Collective decision making
How voters, politicians, and other interested parties act and how these actions influence nonmarket decisions.

Theory of public choice
The study of collective decision making.

spent by all levels of government, plus everything that is spent by the private sector, must add up to the total income available at any point in time. Hence every government action has an opportunity cost, just as in the market sector.

Competition. Although we typically think of competition as a private market phenomenon, it is also present in collective action. Given the scarcity constraint government also faces, bureaucrats, appointed officials, and elected representatives will always be in competition for available government funds. Furthermore, the individuals within any government agency or institution will act as individuals do in the private sector: They will try to obtain higher wages, better working conditions, and higher job-level classifications. They will compete and act in their own, not society's, interest.

Similarity of Individuals. Contrary to popular belief, there are not two types of individuals, those who work in the private sector and those who work in the public sector; rather, individuals working in similar positions can be considered similar. The difference, as we shall see, is that the individuals in government face a different **incentive structure** than those in the private sector. For example, the costs and benefits of being efficient or inefficient differ when one goes from the private to the public sector.

Incentive structure
The system of rewards and punishments individuals face with respect to their own actions.

One approach to predicting government bureaucratic behavior is to ask what incentives bureaucrats face. Take the United States Postal Service as an example. The bureaucrats running that government corporation are human beings with IQs not dissimilar to those possessed by workers in similar positions at Microsoft or American Airlines. Yet the Postal Service does not function like either of these companies. The difference can be explained, at least in part, in terms of the incentives provided for managers in the two types of institutions. When the bureaucratic managers and workers at Microsoft make incorrect decisions, work slowly, produce shoddy products, and are generally "inefficient," the profitability of the company declines. The owners—millions of shareholders—express their displeasure by selling some of their shares of company stock. The market value, as tracked on the stock exchange, falls. But what about the U.S. Postal Service? If a manager, a worker, or a bureaucrat in the Postal Service gives shoddy service, there is no straightforward mechanism by which the organization's owners—the taxpayers—can express their dissatisfaction. Despite the Postal Service's status as a "government corporation," taxpayers as shareholders do not really own shares of stock in the organization that they can sell.

The key, then, to understanding purported inefficiency in the government bureaucracy is not found in an examination of people and personalities but rather in an examination of incentives and institutional arrangements.

Differences Between Market and Collective Decision Making

There are probably more dissimilarities between the market sector and the public sector than there are similarities.

Government, or political, goods
Goods (and services) provided by the public sector; they can be either private or public goods.

Government Goods at Zero Price. The majority of goods that governments produce are furnished to the ultimate consumers without direct money charge. **Government, or political, goods** can be either private goods or public goods. The fact that they are furnished to the ultimate consumer free of charge does *not* mean that the cost to society of those goods is zero, however; it only means that the price *charged* is zero. The full opportunity cost to society is the value of the resources used in the production of goods produced and provided by the government.

For example, none of us pays directly for each unit of consumption of defense or police protection. Rather, we pay for all these things indirectly through the taxes that support our governments—federal, state, and local. This special feature of government can be looked at in a different way. There is no longer a one-to-one relationship between the consumption of a government-provided good and the payment for that good. Consumers who pay taxes collectively pay for every political good, but the individual consumer may not be able to see the relationship between the taxes that he or she pays and the consumption of the good. Indeed, most taxpayers will find that their tax bill is the same whether or not they consume, or even like, government-provided goods.

Use of Force. All governments are able to engage in the legal use of force in their regulation of economic affairs. For example, governments can exercise the use of *expropriation,* which means that if you refuse to pay your taxes, your bank account and other assets may be seized by the Internal Revenue Service. In fact, you have no choice in the matter of paying taxes to governments. Collectively, we decide the total size of government through the political process, but individually we cannot determine how much service we pay for just for ourselves during any one year.

Voting Versus Spending. In the private market sector, a dollar voting system is in effect. This dollar voting system is not equivalent to the voting system in the public sector. There are, at minimum, three differences:

1. In a political system, one person gets one vote, whereas in the market system, the dollars one spends count as votes.
2. The political system is run by **majority rule,** whereas the market system is run by **proportional rule.**
3. The spending of dollars can indicate intensity of want, whereas because of the all-or-nothing nature of political voting, a vote cannot.

Ultimately, the main distinction between political votes and dollar votes here is that political outcomes may differ from economic outcomes. Remember that economic efficiency is a situation in which, given the prevailing distribution of income, consumers get the economic goods they want. There is no corresponding situation using political voting. Thus we can never assume that a political voting process will lead to the same decisions that a dollar voting process will lead to in the marketplace.

Indeed, consider the dilemma every voter faces. Usually a voter is not asked to decide on a single issue (although this happens); rather, a voter is asked to choose among candidates who present a large number of issues and state a position on each of them. Just consider the average U.S. senator who has to vote on several thousand different issues during a six-year term. When you vote for that senator, you are voting for a person who must make thousands of decisions during the next six years.

Political Participants: The Iron Triangle

In the private marketplace, we often focus on the behavior of the three key group participants: consumers, employees, and owners of businesses. In the political marketplace, these three groups correspond to constituents, bureaucrats, and members of Congress. As an example, let's consider the three groups that are involved in the agricultural industry. The principal constituents (consumers of Department of Agriculture subsidies and rules) are, of

Majority rule
A collective decision-making system in which group decisions are made on the basis of 50.1 percent of the vote. In other words, whatever more than half of the electorate votes for, the entire electorate has to accept.

Proportional rule
A decision-making system in which actions are based on the proportion of the "votes" cast and are in proportion to them. In a market system, if 10 percent of the "dollar votes" are cast for blue cars, 10 percent of the output will be blue cars.

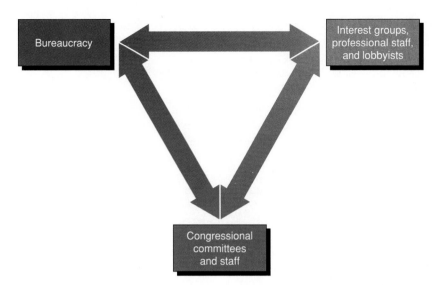

FIGURE 32-1

The Iron Triangle

The "iron triangle" is an alliance of mutual benefit among some unit within the bureaucracy, its interest or client group, and committees or subcommittees of Congress and their staff members.

course, the various interest groups that farmers have set up. These include the American Farm Bureau Federation, the National Cattlemen's Association, the National Milk Producers' Association, the Corn Growers' Association, and the Citrus Growers' Association.

The bureaucrats are within the Department of Agriculture, consisting of over 110,000 individuals who work directly for the federal government and many thousands more who work as contractors, subcontractors, or consultants to the department.

Finally, members of Congress in essence act as venture capitalists who provide the funding (via taxation) for agricultural spending programs and give overall directions to them. Within Congress, there are two major congressional committees concerned with agriculture: the House Committee on Agriculture and the Senate Committee on Agriculture, Nutrition, and Forestry. Each has seven subcommittees.

The relationship among these three groups has been said to form an "iron triangle," as shown in Figure 32-1.

EXAMPLE
Farmers Take the Bureaucracy into Their Own Hands

Since 1933, farmer-elected, farmer-member county committees, along with local employees of the Agricultural Department, both run and receive subsidies from the federal government. According to the Environmental Working Group in Washington, D.C., over 20 percent of county employees of the Agricultural Department receive direct payments from the department as part of the farm program (to which you were first introduced in Chapter 4 using the example of price supports). The average member of the farmer-elected county committees receives almost $40,000 a year, while county employees of the Agricultural Department receive about $52,000 a year. As one example, county employees in agricultural department offices in Iowa during one 10-year period received $32 million in payments from the federal government, more than those in any other state.

FOR CRITICAL ANALYSIS: The way farm subsidies are given out has been compared to permitting welfare recipients to form neighborhood committees and run their own welfare programs, deciding how much each person should get every year. Is this analogy fair? •

CONCEPTS IN BRIEF

- The theory of public choice analyzes how collective decision making is carried out in the public sector. It uses economic analysis to evaluate the operation of democratic government and assumes the self-interest of all political participants.

- Both the market sector and the public sector face scarcity, feature competition, and contain similar individuals.

- Collective decision making differs from market decision making in that many government, or political, goods are provided at zero price, collective action may involve the use of force, and political voting may lead to different results than dollar voting.

- The "iron triangle" of political participants is made up of constituents, bureaucrats, and members of Congress.

THE ECONOMICS OF INTEREST GROUPS: CONCENTRATION OF BENEFITS AND DISPERSION OF COSTS

At the heart of how interest groups influence government in our democratic system is who benefits and who pays for government actions. By definition, interest groups represent relatively well defined groups of individuals or businesses that know what is in their own best interest. Whenever an interest group can obtain more government funding for its activities, its members experience increases in economic welfare. Taxpayers, in contrast, may end up *individually* paying very little for the concentrated benefits that go to the interest group. Thus the costs for many government actions are dispersed among all potential voters.

Distributional Coalitions

Concentrated groups in our democratic society succeed in transferring income to themselves from everybody else through what is known as **distributional coalitions.** These coalitions are small groups that gain much individually at the expense of many individuals who lose much collectively, but little individually, from the special privileges granted members of the coalition. Most collective action—action designed to influence public officials—takes place in small homogeneous groups rather than large diverse groups. Normally, individuals with a common interest will not voluntarily combine and act to further their common interest unless each individual has an incentive to participate in such collective action. Members of distributional coalitions have an incentive to act collectively to induce the median *legislator* to vote in a way that is not consistent with the interests of the median *constituent.*

Distributional coalitions
Associations such as cartels, unions, and cooperatives that are formed to gain special government privileges in order to redistribute wealth by taking small amounts from each of many people and giving large amounts to each of only a few.

EXAMPLE
Why Dairy Farmers Have Been Subsidized So Much

One clear-cut, tightly knit, homogeneous small group of individuals is dairy farmers. An examination of how much dairy farmers benefited in one state, Florida, is illustrative. In a recent year, Florida dairy farmers received $40.3 million in price support payments. Almost 100 percent went to 177 farmers. Each received an average payment in one year of $226,700. In the extreme, if the cost of these payments were borne solely by the residents of Florida, each resident in the state would pay $3.35. How much effort will the residents of Florida make—in other words, what is the value of the resources that they will spend—so as *not* to pay that $3.35 a year? At best they would pay $3.34. At worst, they would pay nothing—why should they take the effort? The 177 Florida dairy farmers, however, each have a great incentive to ensure that their payments from the federal government continue. The residents of the state have no incentive to try to stop these payments.

FOR CRITICAL ANALYSIS: There is a lobbying group aimed at helping the general public. It is called Common Cause. How much success do you think Common Cause can have? •

Logrolling

Logrolling
The practice of exchanging political favors by elected representatives. Typically, one elected official agrees to vote for the policy of another official in exchange for the vote of the latter in favor of the former's desired policy.

Sometimes even lobbying or well-placed campaign contributions are not sufficient to get the programs that distributional coalitions want. In such cases, **logrolling** has been an effective tool. This practice involves an exchange of votes among legislators: Representative A votes for a program that benefits representative B's constituents in return for B's vote on a program that benefits A's constituents. One official may want the continuation of an army base in his hometown while another may want a new dam to be built in her home state, and so it goes. You vote for my army base, and I'll vote for your dam.

One of the major benefits of logrolling is that it allows an elected representative to demonstrate his or her *intensity* of preference, which presumably reflects the intensity of preferences of the constituents. For example, if a representative knows that it is extremely important for his constituents to keep the army base in his hometown, he may be willing to vote for a larger number of pet projects of other representatives to make sure that his pet project is passed. The problem, of course, is that typically—and our example fits perfectly—elected representatives care about geographic representation. *We have a geographically based political system.* The legislator has an incentive to represent local interests in the national legislature (Congress). The broader national issues typically suffer. National legislation becomes the vehicle for local support. The result is what is often known as "pork barrel" legislation that benefits very specific local areas.

EXAMPLE
Logrolling with Food Stamps

A classic example of logrolling as a device to facilitate the redistribution of wealth is found in government programs for "feeding the hungry." Legislators from rural farming regions and lawmakers representing low-income urban areas have forged an effective alliance to promote subsidized food distribution to the poor. Urban legislators get cheap food for their constituents, and rural legislators obtained a convenient means of disposing of the surpluses that were generated by past agricultural price supports.

Supporters of subsidized food distribution have been particularly successful in promoting and expanding the food stamp program. Indeed, according to the U.S. Senate Committee on Agriculture, the program "has been used in legislative strategy to entice urban legislators who might not otherwise support costly farm price support programs to do so in exchange for rural support for the food stamp program." This process began with the Food Stamp Act of 1964, which laid the foundation for the present-day system. In 1968, the timing of food stamp legislation was tied to the legislative cycle of the farm bill—presumably to facilitate enforcement of logrolling deals made between rural and urban legislators. In 1970, federal expenditures on food stamps were doubled, then doubled again in 1971. By this time, legislating against hunger had become a favorite activity in Congress, spurred by the rural-urban coalition of farm representatives and legislators from low-income districts.

FOR CRITICAL ANALYSIS: Why do legislators end up supporting welfare transfers in kind rather than in cash? Would recipients prefer cash or in-kind benefits? ●

CONCEPTS IN BRIEF

- Distributional coalitions, which are associations such as unions and farmers' cooperatives, are formed to gain special government privileges for their members. The members of these coalitions tend to gain a great deal individually, at the expense of the many, who lose much collectively but little individually.

- Logrolling is the exchange of votes among elected representatives, such as occurs when farm representatives agree to vote for food stamps for the poor in return for urban representatives' votes for farm subsidies.

THE ROLE OF BUREAUCRATS

Programs require people to operate them. This is manifested in government today in the form of well-established bureaucracies, in which **bureaucrats** (nonelected officials) work. Bureaucracies can exert great influence on matters concerning themselves—the amount of funding granted them and the activities in which they engage. In the political marketplace, well-organized bureaucracies can even influence the expression of public demand itself. In many cases, they organize the clientele (interest groups), coach that clientele on what is appropriate, and stick up for the "rights" of the clientele. Farm and welfare programs are good examples.

Bureaucrats
Nonelected government officials who are responsible for the day-to-day operation of government and the observance of its regulations and laws.

Gauging Bureaucratic Performance

It is tempting, but incorrect, to think of bureaucrats as mere "technocrats," executors of orders and channels of information, in this process. They have at least two incentives to make government programs larger and more resistant to attack than we might otherwise expect. First, society has decided that in general, government should not be run on a profit-making basis. Measures of performance other than bottom-line profits must be devised. In the private market, successful firms typically expand to serve more customers; although this growth is often incidental to the underlying profitability, the two frequently go hand in hand. In parallel, performance in government is often measured by the number of clients served, and rewards are distributed accordingly. As a result, bureaucrats have an incentive to expand the size of their clientele—not because it is more profitable (beneficial) to society but because that is how *bureaucrats'* rewards are structured.

In general, performance measures that are not based on long-run profitability are less effective at gauging true performance. This makes it potentially easier for the government bureaucrat to *appear* to perform well, collect rewards for measured performance, and then leave for greener pastures. To avoid this, a much larger proportion of the rewards given bureaucrats are valuable only as long as they continue being bureaucrats—large staffs, expensive offices, generous pensions, and the like. Instead of getting large current salaries (which can be saved for a rainy day), they get rewards that disappear if their jobs disappear. Naturally, this increases the incentives of bureaucrats to make sure that their jobs don't disappear.

Rational Ignorance

At this point you may well be wondering, How do these guys get away with it? The answer lies in *rational ignorance* on the part of voters, ignorance that is carefully cultivated by the members of distributional coalitions.

On most issues, there is little incentive for the individual voter to expend resources to determine how to vote. Moreover, the ordinary course of living provides most individuals with enough knowledge to decide whether they should invest in learning more about a given issue. For example, suppose that American voters were asked to decide if the sign marking the entrance to an obscure national park should be enlarged. Most voters would decide that the potential costs and benefits of this decision were negligible: The new sign is unlikely to be the size of the state of Rhode Island, and anybody who has even *heard* of the national park in question probably already has a pretty good idea of its location. Thus most voters would choose to remain rationally ignorant about the *exact* costs and benefits of enlarging the sign, implying that (1) many will choose not to vote at all and (2) those who do vote will simply flip a coin or cast their ballot based on some other, perhaps ideological, grounds.

Why Be Rationally Ignorant? For most political decisions, majority rule prevails. Only a coalition of voters representing slightly more than 50 percent of those who vote is needed. Whenever a vote is taken, the result is going to involve costs and benefits. Voters, then, must evaluate their share of the costs and benefits of any budgetary expenditure. Voters, however, are not perfectly informed. That is one of the crucial characteristics of the real world—information is a resource that is costly to obtain. Rational voters will, in fact, decide to remain at some level of ignorance about government programs because the benefits from obtaining more information may not be worth the cost, given each individual voter's extremely limited impact on the outcome of an election. For the same reason, voters will fail to inform themselves about taxes or other revenue sources to pay for proposed expenditures because they know that for any specific expenditure program, the cost to them individually will be small. At this point it might be useful to contrast this situation with what exists in the nonpolitical private market sector of the economy. In the private market sector, the individual chooses a mix of purchases and bears fully the direct and indirect consequences of this selection (ignoring for the moment the problem of externalities).

The Costs and Benefits of Voting. Voters' incentives to remain rationally ignorant about most issues are compounded by other factors. First, even if the *total* costs or benefits of a political decision are large, the costs or benefits to any *individual* voter are likely to be small. We saw this earlier with price support payments for Florida dairy farmers. Even though these payments cost Floridians as a group roughly $40 million, the cost to any individual in the state is unlikely to be much more than about $3.35. Because individual benefits (to non–dairy farmers) are unlikely to be much different, most Floridians will not bother to find out whether or not it is in their interest to favor price supports for milk (and the tax costs are actually spread among all Americans).

Why Not Vote the Rascals Out? Each time a legislator votes in favor of an interest group at the expense of the general public (and this happens almost all the time), it would seem that voters have an incentive to "vote the rascal out." The problem is that even if the legislator's constituents as a group suffer substantial costs due to dairy price supports, the loss suffered by any individual constituent is quite small. In the case of dairy price supports, few nonfarmer constituents are likely to vote against the legislator just because he or she voted in favor of dairy price supports. A constituent's vote on a legislative candidate depends on the entire *package* of positions adopted by the legislator; for nonfarmers, the issue of price supports is a trivial component of that package. Moreover, campaign contributions from farmers enable the legislator to inform constituents of his or her supportive votes on other issues of more importance to nonfarmers—education, perhaps, or child care. This typically more than offsets any votes lost due to the legislator's support for farm subsidies. Thus the activities of distributional coalitions (interest groups) create a gap between the self-interest of the median *legislator* and the self-interest of the median *constituent*. For this reason, farm subsidies and other special-interest legislation that might not be enacted if all citizens voted on the issue may still be enacted when only legislators vote.

THE ECONOMICS OF INTEREST GROUPS IN ACTION: MORE ON AGRICULTURE

The proportion of the U.S. population living on farms has dropped from 43.8 percent in 1880 to about 1.8 percent today. Although food is essential for life, citizens of the United States, a relatively wealthy nation, spend less than 10 percent of their incomes on food. The 1,925,000 farms in the United States are able to satisfy not only Americans' demand for food but also the demand by other countries' citizens in terms of food exports. The average farming family currently earns over $50,000 a year, of which $30,000 is from nonfarm activities. Each year, the federal government spends about $30,000 per farm on U.S. Department of Agriculture programs. You were introduced to one of those programs (phased out for the most part in 1996), price supports, in Chapter 4.

The Economics and Politics of Price Supports

Traditionally, advocates of price supports argued that it was a method to guarantee a decent income for low-income farmers. More recently, it also was argued that the price support program helped keep small farmers in business, thus preventing agribusinesses from taking over all agricultural production. In fact, these political justifications made no economic sense.

Historically, the benefits of price support programs were skewed toward the owners of very large farms. The benefits of the price support programs were proportional to output:

Population Outgrowing Farmland

The media, without any critical comment, dutifully reported the outcome of several studies purporting to show that population is outgrowing farmland and therefore not everybody will have enough to eat in the not-too-distant future. One such report was generated by Population Action International. Another report with a similar conclusion was generated by the World Bank's Consultative Group on International Agricultural Research. Interestingly, economics was named the "dismal science" because the Reverend Thomas Malthus predicted the same thing in 1798. Just as his prediction was wildly off base, so, too, are those of the present-day Malthusians. Indeed, just the opposite has occurred: World food prices, corrected for inflation, have been following a general trend downward for the past 150 years. Because of improving technology, farm productivity has increased and continues to increase even faster than population.

Big farms with large incomes produce more output and therefore received more subsidies. The 15,000 largest farms in America account for more than 25 percent of all farm profits. The 125,000 largest farms obtain over 60 percent of all farm profits.

Price supports also failed to slow the move toward larger farms. Price support subsidies were made on a *per-bushel* basis, not on a *per-farm* basis. Thus the price support system provided no advantage to growing crops on small farms rather than large farms. If other factors make it more efficient to grow food on large farms, that is where it will be grown, whether there are price supports or not. Perhaps recognizing this, Congress responded by imposing upper limits on the total cash payment that any given farmer could receive. These limits, however, were easily and routinely avoided by the owners of large farms, who, for example, "leased" portions of their land to numerous tenants, each of whom qualified individually for the full allowable payment. Thus the limits had little practical impact.

There is one further point: *All* of the benefits derived from price support subsidies ultimately accrued to *landowners* on whose land price-supported crops could be grown. When price supports were announced and put into effect, the value of land rose to reflect the full value of the future price support subsidies. Thus the original landowners, rather than operators of farms, captured the benefit of the subsidies. Most of the benefits of the farm programs were capitalized into the value of the farmland. So much for helping the poor and the landless!

Acreage Restrictions

The politicians who introduced price supports realized that farmers would respond to higher prices with higher production and that the government would be stuck with the resulting surpluses. So from the beginning, *acreage restrictions* were imposed on farmers who participated in the price support programs. Farmers agreeing to acreage restrictions, or *acreage allotment programs,* as they are called, consented to reduce the number of acres they planted. There were no direct payments to the farmers for abiding by their acreage allotments; the program was merely the implicit entry fee for farmers who wished to take advantage of the price supports.

When the government required that land be removed from production, this caused a reduction in the supply of the crop. Nevertheless, if farmers were required to reduce the amount of land they used by, say, 20 percent, output at any given price did not fall by 20 percent because farmers withdrew their *least productive* land from use. Moreover, they figured out new ways of squeezing just a little more production from any given amount of land. They could still expand output by using other factors of production, such as fertilizer and machinery. To get any given level of output, they had to use more of these nonfixed inputs than they ordinarily would because they were not allowed to expand their usage of land. Thus the marginal cost of production was higher than it would have been in the absence of the acreage restriction.

The net effects of the acreage restrictions were thus twofold. First, crop surpluses were reduced but not eliminated. Second, the restrictions led to an inefficient use of resources, not from the standpoint of the farmers, for they produced at the lowest possible cost given the acreage restriction, but from the standpoint of society. Because the most efficient means of production (more land) was not permitted, more expensive inputs had to be used.

Target Prices and Deficiency Payments

Starting in 1973, government policy toward agriculture added a new twist: the **target price.** Target prices differed from price supports in that the government guaranteed that the farmer would *receive* at least the target price but permitted the price *paid* by consumers to fluctuate, depending on how much of the crop was produced. Instead of buying and storing commodities, the government simply sent a cash payment to farmers if the price paid by consumers was less than the target price. For example, if the target price for wheat was $4.50 per bushel and the price paid by consumers was $3.50, farmers received **deficiency payments** equal to the $1 difference multiplied by the number of bushels they sold on the open market. A deficiency payment, then, was simply another way to pay a subsidy to farmers without having the government actually purchase and store their crops.

The Freedom to Farm Act of 1996

For most crops, price supports, acreage restrictions, targets prices, and deficiency payments were eliminated in 1996. You can be sure, though, that farmers were not left out in the cold to battle the free market. Indeed, projected guaranteed federal government payments to farmers through the year 2002 actually exceed projected payments that would have occurred under the old agriculture subsidy programs. The new legislation also retains some "conservation" aspects, that is, paying some farmers to keep land as wildlife habitats. Additionally, price-support programs for sugar and peanuts were retained. So, in a nutshell, most farmers will be able to respond to worldwide market forces while at the same time receiving guaranteed subsidies for several years to come. Perhaps in the long run taxpayers and food consumers will be better off—provided of course that the old program isn't reinstituted after 2002.

Target price
A price set by the government for specific agricultural products. If the market clearing price was below the target price, a *deficiency payment*, equal to the difference between the market price and the target price, was given to farmers for each unit of the good they produce.

Deficiency payment
A direct subsidy paid to farmers equal to the amount of a crop they produced multiplied by the difference between the target price for that good and its market price.

CONCEPTS IN BRIEF

- Because price supports benefited farmers directly in proportion to the amount of farm goods they produce, owners of large farms received the bulk of the payments. Also, because the payments were tied to output and not farms, price supports did not help keep small farmers in business in preference to large farmers.

- The ultimate beneficiaries of price supports were the owners of farmland, for the price of this land rose whenever price supports were increased.

- Target prices were an attempt by the government to avoid the surpluses caused by price supports. The government set a target price, which it guaranteed that farmers would receive for their crops, but it allowed the market price to adjust to clear the market. If the market price was less than the target price, farmers received deficiency payments equal to the difference multiplied by the amount of the crop they produced.

- Target prices reduced surpluses, but they also made it more obvious that the government was making direct subsidy payments to farmers.

THE COST OF AGRICULTURAL PROGRAMS

During the late 1980s and early 1990s, government agricultural programs such as price supports and deficiency payments produced direct cash benefits to farmers worth about $25 billion per year. The combined cost to taxpayers and consumers of providing these benefits averaged about $31 billion per year. The difference—about $6 billion per year—is the efficiency loss, or waste, caused by these programs. After Social Security, government programs to subsidize farmers have been the single largest and most expensive system of income transfers in the United States. Indeed, the cost of farm subsidies has exceeded the *combined* cost of welfare payments (Aid to Families with Dependent Children) and unemployment insurance payments.

To put these numbers in some perspective, recall that there are about 2 million farmers in this country. Thus government agricultural programs produce *direct* cash benefits to the average farmer of $12,000 per year. Paying these subsidies costs each person in the United States about $125 per year. For the typical family of four, this amounts to $500 per year—$400 in higher taxes and $100 in higher food bills. The benefits, meanwhile, accrue somewhat differently. Approximately two-thirds of all farm aid has gone to farms with annual sales in excess of $100,000, and payments to farms with sales in excess of $500,000 average nearly $40,000 per farm each year. Indeed, 15 percent of all federal farm payments have gone to farmers with a net worth exceeding $1 million. It is little surprise that farm programs have been dubbed "welfare for the rich."

INTERNATIONAL EXAMPLE
Agriculture and an Effective Interest Group

The United States is not alone in having agriculture constitute an effective interest group. Figure 32-2 shows farm support costs in various countries. One of the most aggressive farm support programs is in the European Union. It is called the common

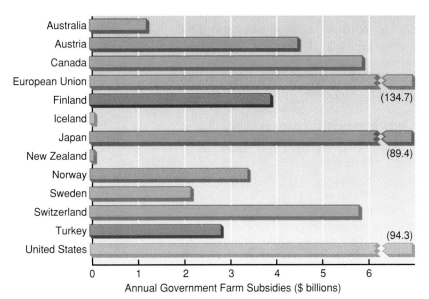

FIGURE 32-2

Farm Subsidies Around the World, 1995

Of the major economies today, only Iceland and New Zealand do not subsidize their farmers very much. The United States, the European Union, and Japan take the lead.

Source: Organization for Economic Cooperation and Development.

agricultural policy (CAP). CAP imposes annual costs of $1,500 in taxes and higher prices a year on the average European family of four. Even though the European Commission has routinely called for the gradual reduction in subsidies to agriculture in Europe, EU farmers have succeeded in preventing almost all such retrenchments.

Most farm subsidy programs worldwide are aimed at maintaining jobs in the agricultural sector. Ironically, in countries where farm subsidies are the most generous—the EU, Japan, and Norway—the most agricultural jobs have been lost as a share of total employment, not the fewest. Low-subsidy, high-efficiency New Zealand and Australia have done a better job at keeping farmers at work.

FOR CRITICAL ANALYSIS: Why have farmers around the world been so effective in obtaining subsidies for their industry?   ●

The Estimated Benefits of Undistorted Agricultural Trade

In an open economy with undistorted agricultural trade, the industrially advanced economies would benefit—over and above the savings in reduced subsidies—to the tune of about $38 billion per year each. The major beneficiaries would be Japan, the European Union, and the United States. These numbers alone suggest that there must be pressure to open up world agricultural markets and to reduce farm subsidies. The future is not so rosy, however.

The cost of farming programs continues to be spread out among all consumers. Moreover, the cost per consumer in countries that become richer, all other things held constant, is falling. This is because food constitutes a declining share in the family budget as families get richer. Moreover, because of increases in farm productivity, the trend is toward lower (inflation-corrected) prices for food. Hence farmers can still maintain their relatively high subsidy levels while nonfarmers see food prices falling.

Perhaps more important, on the producer side, as the number of farmers decreases, the benefits of farm programs are more highly concentrated. This means that lobbying efforts become more efficient to undertake. In other words, as the number of farmers decreases, protection becomes relatively cheaper to obtain. Furthermore, the declining number of farmers and farms, particularly in the industrialized world, elicits a kind of sympathy. France is a particularly good example. Surveys continually show that the average French citizen believes that rural life would disappear without farm subsidies. And the French are apparently willing to continue paying those farm subsidies. Farm subsidies, though, in France and elsewhere, cannot stop the exodus from the farms. In France, for example, 3 percent of farmers and farmhands quit every year.

We can conclude that in spite of the pressures in an open economy to reduce farm subsidies throughout the world, they are not going to disappear overnight.

CONCEPTS IN BRIEF

- Voters may be rationally ignorant about many election issues because the cost of obtaining more information may outweigh the benefits of doing so. Distributional coalitions attempt to promote rational ignorance for their own benefit by hiding the true costs of the programs they favor.

• Bureaucrats often exert great influence on the course of policy because they are in charge of the day-to-day operation of current policy and provide much of the information needed to formulate future policy. Bureaucracies often organize their clientele, coach clients on what is appropriate, and stick up for their rights.

POLITICAL RENT SEEKING

Governments have the ability to bestow large monetary benefits on individuals and firms. Government can do this, for example, by picking one defense firm to become a monopoly supplier of a particular type of armament. In the past, the federal government has routinely given a monopoly to specific parts of the electromagnetic spectrum for radio and TV. In most states, the government makes it illegal for a competing electric company to go into business. In virtually all states, the government has made it illegal for individuals to practice law without a license, thereby restricting supply in the legal profession. The same is true for the medical profession.

In short, there are potentially large profits to be captured by getting the government to create a monopoly for you. We would expect, therefore, that individuals will expend resources to capture such profits. Indeed, an army of lawyers, business executives, and expert witnesses crowd the halls of Congress and the courtrooms, attempting to obtain government-bestowed monopolies, trying to prevent competition when a monopoly already exists, and engaging in various other endeavors that allow them to control a source of monopoly profits. Put yourself in the place of a monopolist who has been given monopoly power through some act of Congress. Let's say that you are making monopoly profits—profits over and above what you would make in a competitive industry—of $1 million per year. Wouldn't you be willing to spend a quarter of that million dollars a year on a lobbying effort to make sure that Congress does not change the law to allow competition in your industry? Indeed, you might spend considerably more than that to protect your $1 million annual monopoly profit. From a use-of-resources point of view, the resources that you spend in protecting your monopoly do not yield any true social product.

Of course, not all benefits from government action involve creating or maintaining monopolies. Rather, you have seen in this chapter that government actions can benefit industries through direct payments, such as agricultural subsidies. When interest groups make an attempt to influence and manipulate public policy for their own gain, they are engaged in what is known as **rent seeking.** This inelegant term comes from the economist's view of rent to which you were introduced in Chapter 29. Remember that economic rent is defined as the amount of payment to a resource over and above what is necessary to keep it in its current use and quality. Thus rent seeking involves individuals expending resources to capture economic rent that can be created by government actions. Part of the gains from getting government to benefit a particular interest group are therefore dissipated through rent-seeking activities. Those resources involve payments to lobbyists, lawyers, and accountants and occasionally direct bribes to politicians. Because the use of those resources is simply to obtain a *transfer* within society, we say that they are wasted and that inefficiency results. The problem is that in a democratic society, it is difficult to find a way around such inefficiencies. The First Amendment to the U.S. Constitution guarantees freedom of speech. By any measure, lobbying activities are speech.

Rent seeking
The use of resources in an attempt to get government to bestow a benefit on an interest group.

Big Sugar's Sweet Deal

Concepts Applied: Imports, exports, subsidies, interest groups, coalitions

The government has imposed quotas on sugar imports to protect U.S. farmers and thereby caused the market price for sugar to remain at twice the world average. Candy and beverage companies have joined together to lobby against these quotas.

The sugar wars started in earnest when congressional budget cutters started targeting agricultural programs in the mid-1990s. Whether the sugar industry's sweet deal will be soured by the time you read this is unknowable, for it remained intact even after heavy political pressure to eliminate it in the 104th Congress. Here is how the deal works.

Restricting Sugar Imports

Low-cost imports of sugar (at the world price) are restricted by the federal government, which sets sugar import quotas annually. Sugar consumption in the United States is about 16 billion pounds a year, but annual domestic production is only 15.5 billion pounds. The remaining 500 million pounds are imported. Without the import quotas, the domestic price of sugar would immediately fall to the world price, and the annual quantity of sugar demanded would increase to about 18 billion pounds. At least an additional 2 billion pounds would have to be imported.

The major beneficiaries of import quota restrictions on sugar are sugarbeet and sugarcane growers. Sugar import quotas create a transfer: Each family of four annually transfers about $400 to the 11,400 sugarbeet and sugarcane growers in this country. That is, each U.S. family is paying that much more for food products using sugar because the U.S. price is about twice the world price of sugar.

Other Direct and Indirect Subsidies from the Federal Government

In addition to benefiting from import restrictions, sugar growers obtained low-cost loans from the U.S. Treasury. They also obtain guarantees of a price considerably higher than the world's market price. The total cost to American consumers is about $1.5 billion a year.

Another Interest Group Fights Back

Major users of sugar, such as Coca-Cola, Hershey, Nabisco, and Kraft, have teamed up with consumer groups and environmentalists to fight "big sugar." They formed the Coalition to End Welfare for Big Sugar. They have run ads to attack the subsidy.

In response, sugar growers have increased their campaign contributions to influential congressional candidates and current House and Senate agricultural committee members. Since 1979, these two groups have obtained over $15 million in perfectly legal contributions from big sugar growers.

Substitutes Do Exist

Major users of sugar have done more than try to fight sugar subsidies in Congress. They have searched for and found sugar substitutes. The most often used substitute is high-fructose corn syrup. Use of that substitute 20 years ago was less than 1 billion pounds per year. Today, it exceeds 17 billion pounds.

FOR CRITICAL ANALYSIS

1. Sugar growers argue that they need their subsidies and import quotas because otherwise they would face subsidized European competition. Analyze this argument.

2. Hershey Foods exports worldwide. What alternative does Hershey have that will allow it to avoid high sugar prices in the United States?

CHAPTER SUMMARY

1. Public-choice economics examines motives behind political entrepreneurs and the outcomes of political actions. Public-choice theory predicts that participants in the political marketplace, such as politicians, act so as to maximize their own self-interest rather than the public interest.

2. The market sector and the public sector both face scarcity, feature competition, and contain similar individuals. They differ in that many government, or political, goods are provided at zero price, collective action may involve the use of force, and political voting can lead to different results than dollar voting.

3. Distributional coalitions, which are associations such as unions and farmers' cooperatives, are formed to gain special government privileges for their members. The members of these coalitions tend to gain a great deal individually, at the expense of the many, who lose much collectively but little individually. Distributional coalitions have played a major role in the growth of government in the twentieth century.

4. Logrolling is the exchange of votes among elected representatives, such as occurs when farm representatives agree to vote for food stamps for the poor in return for urban representatives' votes for farm subsidies.

5. Bureaucrats often exert great influence on the course of policy because they are in charge of the day-to-day operation of current policy and provide much of the information needed to formulate future policy. Bureaucracies often organize their clientele, coach clients on what is appropriate, and stick up for their rights.

6. Voters may be rationally ignorant about many election issues because the cost of obtaining more information may outweigh the benefits of doing so. Distributional coalitions attempt to promote rational ignorance for their own benefit by hiding the costs of the programs they favor.

7. Because price supports were tied to the volume of production, richer farmers received the bulk of the subsidies that resulted from price supports. Also, because price supports were paid without regard to the size of farms, they generally did not help keep smaller farmers in business.

8. Acreage restrictions were an attempt to reduce surpluses by requiring farmers to stop cultivating part of their land in return for price support subsidies. When they participated in acreage restriction programs, farmers put aside their least productive land and increased the use of nonland inputs on the remaining land in cultivation. These practices tended to offset the surplus-reducing intent of these programs.

9. Target prices avoided surpluses by making deficiency payments to farmers to make up for the difference between the government-established target price and the market clearing price.

DISCUSSION OF PREVIEW QUESTIONS

1. **What is the essence of the public-choice model?**
   The essence of the public-choice model is that politicians, bureaucrats, and voters will act so as to maximize *their own* self-interest (or economic well-being) rather than the community's. In other words, because such people are human, they are subject to the same

motivations and drives as the rest of us. They will usually make decisions in terms of what benefits them, not society as a whole. Such an assumption permits economists to apply economic maximization principles to voters, candidates, elected officials, and policymakers.

2. Why can private choice indicate intensity of wants but public choice cannot?

If Ronald loves pasta, he can freely spend a high percentage of his income on it. The fact that he does spend a high percentage of his income on pasta and a zero percentage of his income on rice indicates the intensity of his wants. He can allocate his "dollar votes" in such a way as to reveal his preferences—and maximize his utility. In a "one-person, one-vote" situation, however, Ronald has only *one* vote. He must choose among different candidates, each of whom offers a platform of many publicly provided goods. Ronald's vote "buys" both the services he wants and the services he does not want.

3. How can logrolling enable legislators to indicate the intensity of their wants?

Logrolling is a procedure in which legislators can trade votes. If your legislator is in an oil-producing state, she presumably has an intense desire to vote for bills that promote the interests of the oil industry. Legislators, however, also have only one vote per bill. By trading her vote on issues that she (and her constituents) are not concerned with, she can induce other legislators to vote for the pro-oil bill. Such vote trading, in effect, gives her more than one vote on this bill—and no vote on other bills.

4. When do distributional coalitions emerge?

Distributional coalitions emerge when it is possible for a small group to benefit hugely at the expense of a large group that pays *individually* relatively small amounts. For example, assume that 10,000 honey producers value government price supports at $100 million; assume also that the cost of the program to the rest of society is about 1 cent per person in taxes and 2 cents per pound more in the price for honey. Honey producers will find it profitable to form a distributional coalition, which will contribute to a politician's campaign for election or reelection. Taxpayers and honey consumers will not find it beneficial to form a counterforce to that distributional coalition.

PROBLEMS

(Answers to the odd-numbered problems appear at the back of the book.)

32-1. The existence of information and transactions costs has many implications in economics. What are some of these implications in the context of issues discussed in this chapter?

32-2. Suppose that a government program that subsidizes a certain group in America ends up generating $200,000 per year in additional income to each member of the group. The average income in America for a family of four is about $45,000 per year, and the official poverty line is much less than that. How could you explain the continued success of such a program? Under what circumstances might such a program be terminated?

32-3. A favorite presidential campaign theme in recent years has been to reduce the size, complexity, and bureaucratic nature of the federal government. Nonetheless, the size of the federal government, however measured, continues to increase. Use the theory of public choice to explain why.

32-4. Civics textbooks often claim that voting is one of the most precious and important responsibilities of citizens living in a democracy. Yet if it is raining hard on election day, the percentage of eligible voters that actually votes usually falls. What does this tell you about the public's view of its voting responsibility?

32-5. Term limits have been declared unconstitutional at the federal level, yet many states impose term limits on their state legislatures. Use the theory of public choice to explain how such term limits might change the relationship among the participants in the political marketplace.

32-6. Suppose that you see a distinct problem in our country that needs solving. You decide to run for office and learn everything you can about the problem so that you are an expert in how government can solve it. You don't know much else about other problems or issues. How successful might you be in your campaign to be a "niche" politician? Explain.

32-7. Some people maintain that unless farmers are subsidized, many will leave the farms, a small number of farms will take over the industry (creating an oligopolistic market structure), and prices will rise correspondingly. Currently, about 1.9 million farms are in existence in the United States, and 20 percent of these farms account for 80 percent of the value of total farm output.

a. What is the number of farms accounting for this 80 percent of output?
b. In light of this fact, is it likely that an oligopoly, defined as a market structure with only a few firms accounting for most production and sales, will arise in the agricultural industry in the United States?

32-8. Farmers are usually required to put aside some land to take part in government programs. The objective is for farm output to be reduced. How might this objective not be achieved?

32-9. Explain how the theory of public choice predicts the persistence of agricultural subsidies in the face of a declining farm population.

32-10. Assume that farmers are poor. What is the difference between a general income redistribution program that would give poor farmers income directly and a farming subsidy program that pays them so much per unit of farm product output?

32-11. Outline what would occur if Congress eliminated all farm subsidies tomorrow. How would these events change if Congress instead indicated that it would eliminate all farm programs in 20 years?

COMPUTER-ASSISTED INSTRUCTION

Some people contend that we have had enormous food surpluses in the United States because our farmers are so efficient that they can produce more than we can eat. If that is so, how did this situation come about? Analyzing it requires the proper interpretation of graphs. Analysis reveals that food surpluses are due not to efficiency but to government price supports above the equilibrium.

Complete problem and answer appear on disk.

PART 9

GLOBAL ECONOMICS

CHAPTER 33

COMPARATIVE ADVANTAGE AND THE OPEN ECONOMY

If you use a VCR, camcorder, camera, or pocket calculator, chances are it was made in Japan. In the 1950s, "made in Japan" was synonymous with low quality; today, the opposite is true. The Japanese dominate consumer electronics. And their cars are often favored over American counterparts. It is indeed due to the rising share of Japanese car imports that the United States has on several occasions been willing to threaten a trade war with Japan. To understand why, you need to know about international trade, comparative advantage, and protectionism.

Did **You Know That...** Boeing's latest airplane and the world's largest twin-engine jetliner, the 777, is made in Everett, Washington, but its parts come from 13 other countries, including Australia (rudder and elevators), Brazil (wingtips and dorsal fins), France (landing gears), Ireland (landing gear doors), Italy (wing outboard flaps), and Great Britain (flight computers and engines)? Japan provides 20 percent of the structure, including most of the fuselage.

The story of the Boeing 777 is repeated in the automobile industry. Parts from literally all over the world end up in cars "made in America." The running shoes you buy, the sheets you sleep on, and the clothes you put on your back are often wholly or partly produced outside the United States. Clearly, international trade today affects you whether you are aware of it or not. We are entering an age of a truly global economy. Learning about international trade is simply learning about everyday life.

THE WORLDWIDE IMPORTANCE OF INTERNATIONAL TRADE

Look at panel (a) of Figure 33-1. Since the end of World War II, world output of goods and services (world gross domestic product, or GDP) has increased almost every year until the present, when it is almost six times what it was. Look at the top line in panel (a). World trade has increased to almost 13 times what it was in 1950.

The United States figured prominently in this expansion of world trade. In panel (b) of Figure 33-1, you see imports and exports expressed as a percentage of total annual yearly

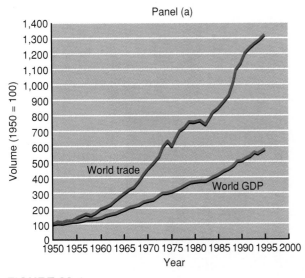
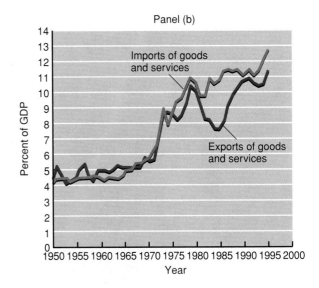

FIGURE 33-1

The Growth of World Trade

In panel (a), you can see the growth in world trade in relative terms because we use an index of 100 to represent real world trade in 1950. By the mid-1990s, that index had increased to over 1,300. At the same time, the index of world GDP (annual world income) had gone up to only around 600. World trade is clearly on the rise: Both imports and exports, expressed as a percentage of annual national income (GDP) in panel (b), have been rising.

Sources: Steven Husted and Michael Melvin, *International Economics,* 3d ed. (New York: HarperCollins, 1995), p. 11, used with permission; *International Trade;* Federal Reserve System; and U.S. Department of Commerce.

income (GDP). Whereas imports added up to barely 4 percent of annual national income in 1950, today they account for over 12 percent. International trade has definitely become more important to the economy of the United States.

INTERNATIONAL EXAMPLE
The Importance of International Trade in Various Countries

Whereas both imports and exports in the United States each account for more than 10 percent of total annual national income, in some countries the figure is much greater (see Table 33-1).

Another way to understand the worldwide importance of international trade is to look at trade flows on the world map in Figure 33-2 on page 736

TABLE 33-1

Importance of Imports in Selected Countries

Country	Imports as a Percentage of Annual National Income
Luxembourg	95.0
Netherlands	58.0
Norway	30.0
Canada	23.5
Germany	23.0
United Kingdom	21.0
China	19.0
France	18.4
Japan	6.8

Source: International Monetary Fund.

FOR CRITICAL ANALYSIS: The yearly volume of imports in Hong Kong exceeds Hong Kong's total national income by several times. How is that possible? (Hint: Is there another reason to import a good besides wanting to consume it?) •

WHY WE TRADE: COMPARATIVE ADVANTAGE AND EXHAUSTING MUTUAL GAINS FROM EXCHANGE

You have already been introduced to the concept of specialization and mutual gains from trade in Chapter 2. These concepts are worth repeating because they are essential to understanding why the world is better off because of more international trade. The best way to understand the gains from trade among nations is first to understand the output gains from specialization between individuals.

The Output Gains from Specialization

Suppose that a creative advertising specialist can come up with two pages of ad copy (written words) an hour or generate one computerized art rendering per hour. At the same time, a computer artist can write one page of ad copy per hour or complete one computerized art

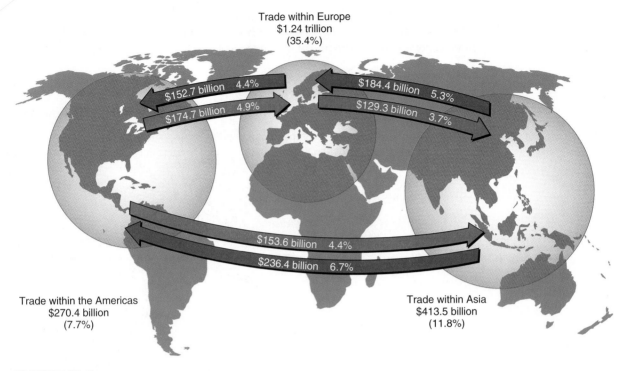

FIGURE 33-2

World Trade Flows

International merchandise trade amounts to over $3 trillion worldwide. The percentage figures show the proportion of trade flowing in the various directions.

Source: World Trade Organization (data are for 1995).

rendering per hour. Here the ad specialist can come up with more pages of ad copy per hour than the computer specialist and seemingly is just as good as the computer specialist at doing computerized art renderings. Is there any reason for the creative specialist and the computer specialist to "trade"? The answer is yes, because such trading will lead to higher output.

Consider the scenario of no trading. Assume that during each eight-hour day, the ad specialist and the computer whiz devote half of their day to writing ad copy and half to computerized art rendering. The ad specialist would create eight pages of ad copy (4 hours × 2) and four computerized art renderings (4 × 1). During that same period, the computer specialist would create four pages of ad copy (4 × 1) and four computerized art renderings (4 × 1). Each day, the combined output for the ad specialist and the computer specialist would be 12 pages of ad copy and eight computerized art renderings.

If the ad specialist specialized only in writing ad copy and the computer whiz specialized only in creating computerized art renderings, their combined output would rise to 16 pages of ad copy (8 × 2) and eight computerized art renderings (8 × 1). Overall, production would increase by four pages of ad copy per day.

The creative advertising employee has a comparative advantage in writing ad copy, and the computer specialist has a comparative advantage in doing computerized art renderings. **Comparative advantage** involves the ability to produce something at a lower opportunity cost compared to other producers, as we pointed out in Chapter 2.

Comparative advantage
The ability to produce a good or service at a lower opportunity cost compared to other producers.

TABLE 33-2	Product	United States (worker-days)	France (worker-days)
Comparative Costs of Production	Wine (1 liter)	1	1
	Beer (1 liter)	1	2

Specialization Among Nations

To demonstrate the concept of comparative advantage for nations, let's take the example of France and the United States. In Table 33-2, we show the comparative costs of production of wine and beer in terms of worker-days. This is a simple two-country, two-commodity world in which we assume that labor is the only factor of production. As you can see from the table, in the United States, it takes one worker-day to produce 1 liter of wine, and the same is true for 1 liter of beer. In France, it takes one worker-day to produce 1 liter of wine but two worker-days for 1 liter of beer. In this sense, Americans appear to be just as good at producing wine as the French and actually have an **absolute advantage** in producing beer.

Absolute advantage
The ability to produce more output from given inputs of resources than other producers can.

Trade will still take place, however, which may seem paradoxical. How can trade take place if we can produce both goods at least as cheaply as the French can? Why don't we just produce both ourselves? To understand why, let's assume first that there is no trade and no specialization and that the workforce in each country consists of 200 workers. These 200 workers are divided equally in the production of wine and beer. We see in Table 33-3 that 100 liters of wine and 100 liters of beer are produced per day in the United States. In France, 100 liters of wine and 50 liters of beer are produced per day. The total daily world production in our two-country world is 200 liters of wine and 150 liters of beer.

Now the countries specialize. What can France produce more cheaply? Look at the comparative costs of production expressed in worker-days in Table 33-2. What is the cost of producing 1 liter more of wine? One worker-day. What is the cost of producing 1 liter more of beer? Two worker-days. We can say, then, that in France the opportunity cost of producing wine is less than that of producing beer. France will specialize in the activity that has the lower opportunity cost. In other words, France will specialize in its comparative advantage, which is the production of wine.

According to Table 33-4 on page 738, after specialization, the United States produces 200 liters of beer and France produces 200 liters of wine. Notice that the total world production per day has gone up from 200 liters of wine and 150 liters of beer to 200 liters of wine and 200 liters of beer per day. This was done without any increased use of resources. The gain, 50 "free" liters of beer, results from a more efficient allocation of resources worldwide. World output is greater when countries specialize in producing the goods in

TABLE 33-3		United States		France		
Daily World Output Before Specialization	Product	Workers	Output (liters)	Workers	Output (liters)	World Output (liters)
It is assumed that 200 workers are available in each country.	Wine	100	100	100	100	200
	Beer	100	100	100	50	150

Product	United States		France		World Output (liters)
	Workers	Output (liters)	Workers	Output (liters)	
Wine	—	—	200	200	200
Beer	200	200	—	—	200

TABLE 33-4

Daily World Output After Specialization
It is assumed that 200 workers are available in each country.

which they have a comparative advantage and then engage in foreign trade. Another way of looking at this is to consider the choice between two ways of producing a good. Obviously, each country would choose the less costly production process. One way of "producing" a good is to import it, so if in fact the imported good is cheaper than the domestically produced good, we will "produce" it by importing it. Not everybody, of course, is better off when free trade occurs. In our example, U.S. wine makers and French beer makers are worse off because those two *domestic* industries have disappeared.

Some people are worried that the United States (or any country, for that matter) might someday "run out of exports" because of overaggressive foreign competition. The analysis of comparative advantage tells us the contrary. No matter how much other countries compete for our business, the United States (or any other country) will always have a comparative advantage in something that it can export. In 10 or 20 years, that something may not be what we export today, but it will be exportable nonetheless because we will have a comparative advantage in producing it.

Other Benefits from International Trade: The Transmission of Ideas

Beyond the fact that comparative advantage generally results in an overall increase in the output of goods produced and consumed, there is another benefit to international trade. International trade bestows benefits on countries through the international transmission of ideas. According to economic historians, international trade has been the principal means by which new goods, services, and processes have spread around the world. For example, coffee was initially grown in Arabia near the Red Sea. Around A.D. 675, it began to be roasted and consumed as a beverage. Eventually, it was exported to other parts of the world, and the Dutch started cultivating it in their colonies during the seventeenth century and the French in the eighteenth century. The lowly potato is native to the Peruvian Andes. In the sixteenth century, it was brought to Europe by Spanish explorers. Thereafter, its cultivation and consumption spread rapidly. It became part of the American agricultural scene in the early eighteenth century.

All of the *intellectual property* that has been introduced throughout the world is a result of international trade. This includes new music, such as rock and roll in the 1950s and hip-hop and grunge in the 1990s. It includes the software applications that are common for computer users everywhere.

New processes have been transmitted through international trade. One of those involves the Japanese manufacturing innovation which emphasized redesigning the system rather than running the existing system in the best possible way. Inventories were reduced to just-in-time levels by reengineering machine setup methods. Just-in-time inventory control is now common in American factories.

INTERNATIONAL EXAMPLE
International Trade and the Alphabet

Even the alphabetic system of writing that appears to be the source of most alphabets in the world today was spread through international trade. According to some scholars, the Phoenicians, who lived on the long, narrow strip of Mediterranean coast north of Israel from the ninth century B.C. to around 300 B.C., created the first true alphabet. Presumably, they developed the alphabet to keep international trading records on their ships rather than having to take along highly trained scribes.

FOR CRITICAL ANALYSIS: Before alphabets were used, how might have people communicated in written form? ●

THE RELATIONSHIP BETWEEN IMPORTS AND EXPORTS

The basic proposition in understanding all of international trade is this:

In the long run, imports are paid for by exports.[1]

The reason that imports are ultimately paid for by exports is that foreigners want something in exchange for the goods that are shipped to the United States. For the most part, they want goods made in the United States. From this truism comes a remarkable corollary:

Any restriction of imports ultimately reduces exports.

This is a shocking revelation to many people who want to restrict foreign competition to protect domestic jobs. Although it is possible to protect certain U.S. jobs by restricting foreign competition, it is impossible to make *everyone* better off by imposing import restrictions. Why? Because ultimately such restrictions lead to a reduction in employment in the export industries of the nation.

Think of exports as simply another way of producing goods. International trade is merely an economic activity like all others; it is a production process that transforms exports into imports.

INTERNATIONAL EXAMPLE
The Importation of Priests into Spain

Imports affect not only goods but also services and the movement of labor. In Spain, some 3,000 priests retire each year, but barely 250 young men are ordained to replace them. Over 70 percent of the priests in Spain are now over the age of 50. The Spanish church estimates that by 2005, the number of priests will have fallen to half the 20,441 who were active in Spain in 1990. The Spanish church has had to seek young seminarians from Latin America under what it calls Operation Moses. It is currently subsidizing the travel and training of an increasing number of young Latin Americans to take over where native Spaniards have been before.

FOR CRITICAL ANALYSIS: How might the Spanish Catholic church induce more native Spaniards to become priests? ●

---

[1]We have to modify this rule by adding that in the short run, imports can also be paid for by the sale (or export) of real and financial assets, such as land, stocks, and bonds, or through an extension of credit from other countries.

INTERNATIONAL COMPETITIVENESS

"The United States is falling behind." "We need to stay competitive internationally." These and similar statements are often heard in government circles when the subject of international trade comes up. There are two problems with this issue. The first has to do with a simple definition. What does "global competitiveness" really mean? When one company competes against another, it is in competition. Is the United States like one big corporation, in competition with other countries? Certainly not. The standard of living in each country is almost solely a function of how well the economy functions *within that country,* not relative to other countries.

Another problem arises with respect to the real world. According to the Institute for Management Development in Lausanne, Switzerland, the United States continues to lead the pack in world competitiveness, ahead of Japan, Hong Kong, Germany, and the rest of the European Union. According to the report, America's top-class ranking is due to the rapid U.S. economic recovery from its 1990–1991 recession, widespread entrepreneurship, and a decade of economic restructuring. Other factors include America's sophisticated financial system and large investments in scientific research.

> ## THINKING CRITICALLY ABOUT THE MEDIA
>
> ### Foreigners' Productivity Improvements
>
> With so much emphasis on America's competitiveness in the global economy, the media fail to understand a basic tenet: International trade is not a zero-sum game. If other countries in the world increase their productivity faster than in America, so be it. A more productive Germany will of course have more products to sell in the United States. At the same time, though, Germany will represent a bigger market for America's exports. In other words, a successful European or Asian economy can become successful without that success being at the expense of the United States. In fact, such successful economies are likely to help us by providing us with larger markets (and by selling us their own goods of higher quality at lower prices).

CONCEPTS IN BRIEF

- Countries can be better off materially if they specialize in producing goods for which they have a comparative advantage.

- It is important to distinguish between absolute and comparative advantage; the former refers to the ability to produce a unit of output with fewer physical units of input; the latter refers to producing output that has the lowest opportunity cost for a nation.

- Different nations will always have different comparative advantages because of differing opportunity costs due to different resource mixes.

ARGUMENTS AGAINST FREE TRADE

Numerous arguments are raised against free trade. They mainly point out the costs of trade; they do not consider the benefits or the possible alternatives for reducing the costs of free trade while still reaping benefits.

The Infant Industry Argument

A nation may feel that if a particular industry were allowed to develop domestically, it could eventually become efficient enough to compete effectively in the world market. Therefore, if some restrictions were placed on imports, domestic producers would be given the time needed to develop their efficiency to the point where they would be able to compete in the domestic market without any restrictions on imports. In graphic terminology, we would expect that if the protected industry truly does experience improvements in production techniques or technological breakthroughs toward greater efficiency in the future, the supply

Infant industry argument
The contention that tariffs should be imposed to protect from import competition an industry that is trying to get started. Presumably, after the industry becomes technologically efficient, the tariff can be lifted.

curve will shift outward to the right so that the domestic industry can produce larger quantities of each and every price. This **infant industry argument** has some merit in the short run and has been used to protect a number of industries in their infancy around the world. Such a policy can be abused, however. Often the protective import-restricting arrangements remain even after the infant has matured. If other countries can still produce more cheaply, the people who benefit from this type of situation are obviously the stockholders (and specialized factors of production that will earn economic rents) in the industry that is still being protected from world competition. The people who lose out are the consumers, who must pay a price higher than the world price for the product in question. In any event, it is very difficult to know beforehand which industries will eventually survive. In other words, we cannot predict very well the specific infant industries that should be protected. Note that when we talk about which industry "should be" protected, we are in the realm of normative economics. We are making a value judgment, a subjective statement of what *ought to be*.

 EXAMPLE
An Infant Industry Blossoms Due to Protection from Foreign Imports: The Case of Marijuana

Marijuana was made illegal in the United States in the 1930s, but just as for many other outlawed drugs, a market for it remained. Until about 25 years ago, virtually all the marijuana consumed in the United States was imported. Today, earnings from the burgeoning and increasingly high-tech "pot" industry are estimated at $35 billion a year, making it the nation's biggest cash crop (compared to corn at $15 billion). Starting with President Richard Nixon in the 1970s, the federal government has in effect ended up protecting the domestic marijuana industry from imports by declaring a war on drugs. Given virtually no foreign competition, the American marijuana industry expanded and invested millions in developing both more productive and more potent seeds as well as more efficient growing technologies. Domestic marijuana growers now dominate the high end of a market in which consumers pay $300 to $500 an ounce for a reengineered home-grown product. New growing technologies allow domestic producers, using high-intensity sodium lights, carbon dioxide, and advances in genetics, to produce a kilogram of the potent sinsemilla variety every two months in a space no bigger than a phone booth.

FOR CRITICAL ANALYSIS: What has spurred domestic producers to develop highly productive indoor growing methods? •

Countering Foreign Subsidies and Dumping

Another strong argument against unrestricted foreign trade has to do with countering other nations' subsidies to their own producers. When a foreign government subsidizes its producers, our producers claim that they cannot compete fairly with these subsidized foreigners. To the extent that such subsidies fluctuate, it can be argued that unrestricted free trade will seriously disrupt domestic producers. They will not know when foreign governments are going to subsidize their producers and when they are not. Our competing industries will be expanding and contracting too frequently.

Dumping
Selling a good or a service abroad at a price below its cost of production or below the price charged in the home market.

The phenomenon called *dumping* is also used as an argument against unrestricted trade. **Dumping** occurs when a producer sells its products abroad at a price below its cost of production or below the price that is charged in the home market. Although cries of dumping against foreign producers are often heard, they typically occur only when the foreign nation is in the throes of a serious recession. The foreign producer does not want to slow down its production at home. Because it anticipates an end to the recession and doesn't want to hold large inventories, it dumps its products abroad at prices below its costs. This does, in fact, disrupt international trade. It also creates instability in domestic production and therefore may impair commercial well-being at home.

POLICY EXAMPLE
How Should Antidumping Laws Be Administered?

It is one thing to pass a law against dumping but quite another to administer it. Current antidumping laws are the bailiwick of the Import Administration, in the U.S. Commerce Department. With its $30 million annual budget and 300 employees, it routinely decides which products should be targeted for antidumping duties, whether they be Chinese garlic or Colombian flowers. Once a decision has been made by the Import Administration, there is virtually no way to reverse it. The manner in which this government agency operates is patently unfair to our trading partners. When a U.S. company or industry files a dumping case against a foreign company, the Import Administration requires that the foreign company answer impossibly long questionnaires in a relatively short period of time. Most foreigners cannot respond by the deadline, at which point the Import Administration slaps on the highest possible duties.

FOR CRITICAL ANALYSIS: The Institute for International Economics estimates that the Import Administration's actions cost American consumers at least $2.6 billion per year. How do consumers suffer? •

Protecting American Jobs

Perhaps the argument used most often against free trade is that unrestrained competition from other countries will eliminate American jobs because other countries have lower-cost labor than we do. (Less restrictive environmental standards in other countries might also lower their costs relative to ours.) This is a compelling argument, particularly for politicians from areas that might be threatened by foreign competition. For example, a representative from an area with shoe factories would certainly be upset about the possibility of constituents' losing their jobs because of competition from lower-priced shoe manufacturers in Brazil and Italy. But of course this argument against free trade is equally applicable to trade between the states.

Economists David Gould, G. L. Woodbridge, and Roy Ruffin examined the data on the relationship between increases in imports and the rate of unemployment. Their conclusion was that there is no causal link between the two. Indeed, in half the cases they studied, when imports increased, unemployment fell.

Another issue has to do with the cost of protecting American jobs by restricting international trade. The Institute for International Economics examined just the restrictions on foreign textiles and apparel goods. U.S. consumers pay $9 billion a year more to protect jobs in those industries. That comes out to $50,000 a year for each job saved in an industry in which the average job pays only $20,000 a year. Similar studies have yielded similar results: Restrictions on the imports of Japanese cars have cost $160,000 *per year* for every job saved in the auto industry. Every

THINKING CRITICALLY ABOUT THE MEDIA

Unfair Competition from Low-Wage Countries

Protectionists are able to get the media to carry stories about how low-wage countries are stealing American jobs. The facts are exactly the opposite. The highest-labor-cost country in the world is Germany, and it is also the largest exporter in the world. The United States, Japan, France, and the United Kingdom also have relatively high labor costs, and they, too, are some of the world's biggest exporters. If the low-wage myth were true, the United States would never be able to compete with, say, Mexican labor. Yet the reality is that the United States exports much more to Mexico than it imports. Finally, both the World Bank and the Organization for Economic Cooperation and Development have done exhaustive studies on the issue. Their conclusion is that there is no evidence that trade with low-wage countries results in large-scale job losses to industrial countries. The real competition for American manufacturing comes from high-wage countries, such as Germany and Japan.

job preserved in the glass industry has cost $200,000 each and every year. Every job preserved in the U.S. steel industry has cost an astounding $750,000 per year.

In the long run, the industries that have had the most protection—textiles, clothing, and iron and steel—have seen the most dramatic reductions in employment in the United States.

CONCEPTS IN BRIEF

- The infant industry argument against free trade contends that new industries should be protected against world competition so that they can become technologically efficient in the long run.

- Unrestricted foreign trade may allow foreign governments to subsidize exports or foreign producers to engage in dumping—selling products in other countries below their cost of production. To the extent that foreign export subsidies and dumping create more instability in domestic production, they may impair our well-being.

WAYS TO RESTRICT FOREIGN TRADE

There are many ways in which international trade can be stopped or at least stifled. These include quotas and taxes (the latter are usually called *tariffs* when applied to internationally traded items). Let's talk first about quotas.

Quotas

Quota system
A government-imposed restriction on the quantity of a specific good that another country is allowed to sell in the United States. In other words, quotas are restrictions on imports. These restrictions are usually applied to one or several specific countries.

Under the **quota system,** individual countries or groups of foreign producers are restricted to a certain amount of trade. An import quota specifies the maximum amount of a commodity that may be imported during a specified period of time. For example, the government might not allow more than 50 million barrels of foreign crude oil to enter the United States in a particular year.

Consider the example of quotas on textiles. Figure 33-3 presents the demand and the supply curves for imported textiles. In an unrestricted import market, the equilibrium quantity

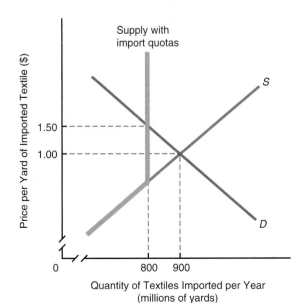

FIGURE 33-3

The Effect of Quotas on Textile Imports
Without restrictions, 900 million yards of textiles would be imported each year into the United States at the world price of $1.00 per yard. If the federal government imposes a quota of only 800 million yards, the effective supply curve becomes vertical at that quantity. It intersects the demand curve at the new equilibrium price of $1.50 per yard.

imported is 900 million yards at a price of $1 per yard (expressed in constant-quality units). When an import quota is imposed, the supply curve is no longer *S*. Rather, the supply curve becomes vertical at some amount less than the equilibrium quantity—here, 800 million yards per year. The price to the American consumer increases from $1.00 to $1.50. The domestic suppliers of textiles obviously benefit by an increase in revenues because they can now charge a higher price.

POLICY EXAMPLE
Is America Being "Fair" in Its Textile Trade Wars?

Textiles provide a real-world example of quotas in action. On the one hand, the federal government claims to be in favor of freer trade; on the other hand, it routinely imposes stricter quotas on textile imports. Take Kenya, a country to which the United States has given over $1 billion in foreign aid since 1980. The goal was to help Kenya develop its private sector. Kenya's textile industry did develop, and it started exporting pillowcases and shirts. Then the U.S. Commerce Department turned around and determined that the United States should reduce imports of Kenyan pillowcases by 1,565,616 in 1995.

A similar example involves Egyptian shirts. The United States has given Egypt over $30 billion in foreign aid since 1980, partly in the hope that it would develop its private sector. In the mid-1990s, the Commerce Department announced plans to impose import quotas on shirts manufactured in Egypt. The list continues: import quotas on men's shirts from El Salvador, on silk-blend men's and boys' coats and jackets from Hong Kong, on shirts made in Kuwait, on men's and women's coats produced in Oman, and on cotton shirts made in Pakistan.

FOR CRITICAL ANALYSIS: Who benefits from quotas on foreign-made textiles? •

Voluntary Quotas. Quotas do not have to be explicit and defined by law. They can be "voluntary." Such a quota is called a **voluntary restraint agreement (VRA).** In the early 1980s, the United States asked Japan voluntarily to restrain its exports to the United States. The Japanese government did so, limiting itself to exporting 2.8 million Japanese automobiles. Today, there are VRAs on machine tools and textiles.

The opposite of a VRA is a **voluntary import expansion (VIE).** Under a VIE, a foreign government agrees to have its companies import more foreign goods from another country. The United States almost started a major international trade war with Japan in 1995 over just such an issue. The U.S. government wanted Japanese automobile manufacturers voluntarily to increase their imports of U.S.-made automobile parts.

Voluntary restraint agreement (VRA)
An official agreement with another country that "voluntarily" restricts the quantity of its exports to the United States.

Voluntary import expansion (VIE)
An official agreement with another country in which it agrees to import more from the United States.

Tariffs

We can analyze tariffs by using standard supply and demand diagrams. Let's use as our commodity laptop computers, some of which are made in Japan and some of which are made domestically. In panel (a) of Figure 33-4, you see the demand and supply of Japanese laptops. The equilibrium price is $1,000 per constant-quality unit, and the equilibrium quantity is 10 million per year. In panel (b), you see the same equilibrium price of $1,000, and the *domestic* equilibrium quantity is 5 million units per year.

Now a tariff of $500 is imposed on all imported Japanese laptops. The supply curve shifts upward by $500 to S_2. For purchasers of Japanese laptops, the price increases to

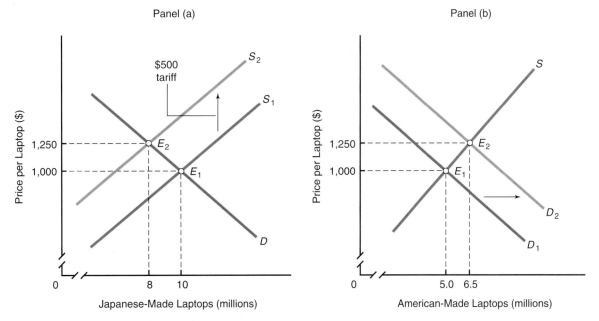

FIGURE 33-4

The Effect of a Tariff on Japanese-Made Laptop Computers

Without a tariff, the United States buys 10 million Japanese laptops per year at an average price of $1,000, as shown in panel (a). American producers sell 5 million domestically made laptops, also at $1,000 each, as shown in panel (b). A $500-per-laptop tariff will shift the Japanese import supply curve to S_2 in panel (a), so that the new equilibrium is at E_2, with price $1,250 and quantity sold reduced to 8 million per year. The demand curve for American-made laptops (for which there is no tariff) shifts to D_2 in panel (b). Sales increase to 6.5 million per year.

$1,250. The quantity demanded falls to 8 million per year. In panel (b), you see that at the higher price of imported Japanese laptops, the demand curve for American-made laptops shifts outward to the right to D_2. The equilibrium price increases to $1,250, but the equilibrium quantity increases to 6.5 million units per year. So the tariff benefits domestic laptop producers because it increases the demand for their products due to the higher price of a close substitute, Japanese laptops. This causes a redistribution of income from American consumers of laptops to American producers of laptops.

Tariffs in the United States. In Figure 33-5 on page 746, we see that tariffs on all imported goods have varied widely. The highest rates in the twentieth century occurred with the passage of the Smoot-Hawley Tariff in 1930.

POLICY EXAMPLE
Did the Smoot-Hawley Tariff Worsen the Great Depression?

By 1930, the unemployment rate had almost doubled in a year. Congress and President Hoover wanted to do something that would help stimulate U.S. production and reduce unemployment. The result was the Smoot-Hawley Tariff, which set tariff schedules for over 20,000 products, raising duties on imports by an average of 52 percent. This attempt to improve the domestic economy at the expense of foreign economies backfired. Each trading partner of the United States in turn imposed its own high tariffs, including the United Kingdom, the Netherlands, France, and Switzerland. The result was a massive reduction in international trade by an incredible 64 percent in three years. Some believe that the ensuing world Great Depression was partially caused by such tariffs.

FOR CRITICAL ANALYSIS: The Smoot-Hawley Tariff has been labeled a "beggar thy neighbor" policy. Explain why. ●

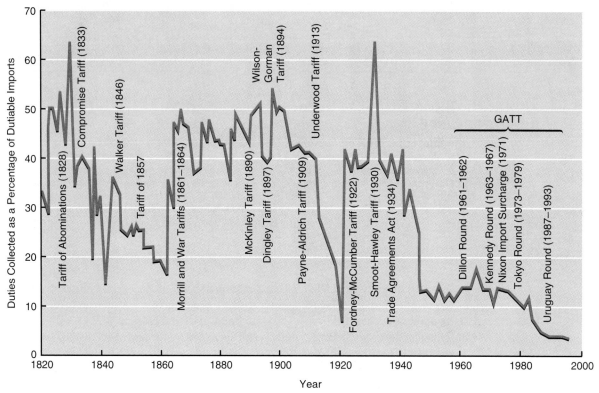

FIGURE 33-5

Tariff Rates in the United States Since 1820

Tariff rates in the United States have bounced around like a football; indeed, in Congress, tariffs are a political football. Import-competing industries prefer high tariffs. In the twentieth century, the highest tariff we have had was the Smoot-Hawley Tariff of 1930, which was almost as high as the "tariff of abominations" in 1828.

Source: U.S. Department of Commerce.

Current Tariff Laws. The Trade Expansion Act of 1962 gave the president the authority to reduce tariffs by up to 50 percent. Subsequently, tariffs were reduced by about 35 percent. In 1974, the Trade Reform Act allowed the president to reduce tariffs further. In 1984, the Trade and Tariff Act resulted in the lowest tariff rates ever. All such trade agreement obligations of the United States are carried out under the auspices of the **General Agreement on Tariffs and Trade (GATT),** which was signed in 1947. Member nations of GATT account for more than 85 percent of world trade. As you can see in Figure 33-5, there have been a number of rounds of negotiations to reduce tariffs since the early 1960s. The latest round was called the Uruguay Round because that is where the meetings were held.

General Agreement on Tariffs and Trade (GATT)
An international agreement established in 1947 to further world trade by reducing barriers and tariffs.

The World Trade Organization (WTO)

The Uruguay Round of the General Agreement on Tariffs and Trade (GATT) was ratified by 117 nations at the end of 1993. A year later, in a special session of Congress, the entire treaty was ratified. As of January 1, 1995, the new **World Trade Organization (WTO)** replaced GATT.

The ratification of GATT by the United States will result in a roughly 40 percent cut in tariffs worldwide. Agricultural subsidies will be reduced and perhaps eventually eliminated. Protection for patents will be extended worldwide. The WTO will have arbitration boards to settle international disputes over trade issues. No country has a veto. A country that loses a WTO ruling has to comply or face trade sanction by the country that wins arbitration.

In short, the passage of GATT and the creation of the WTO constitute the furthest-reaching global trade agreement in history. Advanced technologies in particular will benefit from the worldwide extension of the protection of patents. Copyrights on books and recordings will be protected from piracy better than ever before. Protectionist rules, such as "local content" requirements that force foreign firms to use locally produced inputs, will be eliminated. Also, other countries will have to treat American service suppliers no less favorably than they treat their own service suppliers.

World Trade Organization (WTO)
The successor organization to GATT, it handles all trade disputes among its 117 member nations.

CONCEPTS IN BRIEF

- One means of restricting foreign trade is a quota system. Beneficiaries of quotas are the importers who get the quota rights and the domestic producers of the restricted good.

- Another means of restricting imports is a tariff, which is a tax on imports only. An import tariff benefits import-competing industries and harms consumers by raising prices.

- The main international institution created to improve trade among nations is the General Agreement on Tariffs and Trade (GATT). The latest round of trade talks under GATT, the Uruguay Round, led to the creation of the World Trade Organization.

Waging the Second War on Japan

Concepts Applied: *Comparative advantage, specialization, competitiveness, protectionism, benefits from trade*

American cars may not be selling well in Japan, but that probably has little to do with Japanese import restrictions. German car manufacturers have thrived in Japan by heavily investing in car dealerships and new models.

The facts seem simple enough. For many years, the value of goods imported from Japan has exceeded the value of goods exported to Japan. "Japan bashers" use this information to argue that Japan does not provide a "level" playing field with respect to international trade.

Japanese Restrictions on Imports

As proof that the Japanese are unfair when it comes to international trade, proponents of getting tough with Japan point out that (1) many Japanese markets are completely closed to foreign competition, (2) Japanese government officials routinely take months to examine American imports for safety and quality (in particular, American automobiles), and (3) Japan's business system is not conducive to American suppliers "breaking in."

The *Keiretsu*

It is true that the Japanese have a corporate system that is different from that in the United States. One major difference is the existence in Japan of the *keiretsu*, a grouping arrangement that links companies together. Even in the absence of tariffs on auto parts, American auto part manufacturers cannot crack the tight links that automakers, such as Nissan and Toyota, maintain with their *keiretsu*

suppliers. Many of these links go back decades and today are reinforced by cross-ownership of shares. It is not atypical for Nissan to send its own managers to a supplier to get operations in order.

The Problem with Focusing on Automobiles

The United States' focus on the success of the Japanese automobile industry is inconsistent with our ideas of a market economy that rewards performance. Economist William Kline uses the following analogy: It would be the same as convicting Michael Jordan of being unfairly compensated in basketball but not in baseball. Why? Because when Michael Jordan plays basketball, he earns many times more than when he plays baseball. The reason, of course, is that Michael Jordan is relatively much better at playing basketball.

The same is true for Japanese automobile producers. The reason there is such a large difference between the sales of Japanese cars in Japan and competing U.S. imports there is that Japanese automobile producers make a better product. According to Kline, there is virtually no evidence that Japanese consumers buy Japanese cars because of trade barriers that keep out U.S. imports. German automakers are doing quite well in Japan because they have invested in their own dealer networks and started producing right-hand-drive cars years ago, something U.S. automakers started doing only recently.

What About "Fairness"?

Even if we assume that the Japanese restrict American imports, that still does not mean we should engage in a trade war with Japan by setting up a system of impediments to Japanese imports. Americans do not lose because of imports and gain from exports. As long as Americans continue to obtain Japanese goods on cheaper terms than by producing them ourselves, Americans will gain. It does not matter why we are getting Japanese goods on cheaper terms.

"We Don't Need Trading Partners like That"

On occasion, American politicians declare that "we don't need that kind of trade" whenever they look at the fact that Americans import more from Japan than Americans export to Japan. This assumption is equivalent to saying that you should not continue trading with your hairstylist, accountant, lawyer, or butcher. After all, you are buying more from all of them than they are buying from you.

FOR CRITICAL ANALYSIS

1. Recently, U.S. mail-order companies, such as L. L. Bean, have started sending thousands of catalogs to consumers in Japan and obtaining orders from them. What do you think accounts, at least in part, for the new success of American mail-order companies in that country?
2. For the world as a whole during any one-year period, what has to be true about the value of total world imports relative to the value of total world exports?

CHAPTER SUMMARY

1. It is important to distinguish between absolute and comparative advantage. A person or country that can do everything "better" (with higher labor productivity) than every other person or country has an absolute advantage in everything. Nevertheless, trade will still be advantageous if people will specialize in the things that they do *relatively* best, exploiting their respective comparative advantage.

2. Along with the gains, there are costs from trade. Certain industries and their employees may be hurt if trade is opened up.

3. An import quota restricts the quantity of imports coming into the country. It therefore raises the price. Consumers always lose.

4. When governments impose "voluntary" quotas, they are called voluntary restraint agreements (VRAs).

5. An import tariff raises the domestic price of foreign produced goods. It therefore allows domestic producers to raise their own prices. The result is a higher price to consumers, a lower quantity of imports, and a lower volume of international trade.

6. The main international institution created to improve trade among nations was the General Agreement on Tariffs and Trade (GATT), replaced in 1993 by the World Trade Organization (WTO).

DISCUSSION OF PREVIEW QUESTIONS

1. Is international trade important to the United States?

The direct impact of international trade on the United States, as measured by the ratio of exports to GDP, is relatively small compared with many other nations. Yet it is hard to imagine what life would be like without international trade. Initially, many prices would rise rapidly, but eventually domestic production would begin on many goods we presently import. However, consider life without imports of coffee, tea, bananas, and foreign wines, motorcycles, automobiles, televisions, VCRs, and hundreds of other goods from food and clothing to electronics—not to mention vital imports such as bauxite, chromium, cobalt, nickel, platinum, and tin.

2. What is the relationship between imports and exports?

Because foreigners eventually want real goods and services as payment for the real goods and services they export to other countries, ultimately each country pays for its imports with its exports. Hence on a worldwide basis, the value of imports must equal the value of exports.

3. **What is the ultimate effect of a restriction on imports?**

Because each country must pay for its imports with its exports, any restriction on imports must ultimately lead to a reduction in exports. So even though restrictions on imports because of tariffs or quotas may benefit workers and business owners in the protected domestic industry, such protection will harm workers and business owners in the export sector in general.

4. **What are some arguments against free trade?**

The infant industry argument maintains that new industries developing domestically need protection from foreign competitors until they are mature enough themselves to compete with foreigners, at which time protection will be removed. One problem with this argument is that it is difficult to tell when maturity has been reached, and domestic industries will fight against weaning. Moreover, this argument is hardly relevant to most U.S. industries. It is also alleged (and is true to a large extent) that free trade leads to instability for specific domestic industries as comparative advantage changes in a dynamic world. Nations that have traditionally held a comparative advantage in the production of some goods occasionally lose that advantage (while gaining others). Regional hardships are a result, and protection of domestic jobs is demanded.

PROBLEMS

(Answers to the odd-numbered problems appear at the back of the book.)

33-1. Examine the hypothetical table of worker-hours required to produce caviar and wheat in the United States and in Russia.

Product	United States	Russia
Caviar (ounce)	6 worker-hours	9 worker-hours
Wheat (bushel)	3 worker-hours	6 worker-hours

    a. What is the opportunity cost to the United States of producing one ounce of caviar per time period? What is the opportunity cost to the United States of producing one bushel of wheat?

    b. What is the opportunity cost to Russia of producing one ounce of caviar per time period? What is the opportunity cost to Russia of producing one bushel of wheat?

    c. The United States has a comparative advantage in what? Russia has a comparative advantage in what?

33-2. Study the hypothetical table of worker-hours required to produce coffee and beans in Colombia and Turkey.

Product	Colombia	Turkey
Coffee (pound)	2 worker-hours	1 worker-hour
Beans (pound)	6 worker-hours	2 worker-hours

    a. What is the opportunity cost to Colombia of producing one pound of coffee? One pound of beans?

    b. What is the opportunity cost to Turkey of producing one pound of coffee? One pound of beans?

    c. Colombia has a comparative advantage in what? Turkey has a comparative advantage in what?

33-3. Assume that the United States can produce *everything* with fewer labor-hours than any other country on earth. Even under this extreme assumption, why would the United States still trade with other countries?

33-4. Examine the hypothetical table of worker-hours required to produce cheese and cloth in two countries, A and B.

Product	Country A	Country B
Cheese (pound)	$\frac{2}{3}$ worker-hours	2 worker-hours
Cloth (yard)	$\frac{1}{2}$ worker-hours	1 worker-hour

a. What is the opportunity cost to country A of producing one pound of cheese? One yard of cloth?

b. What is the opportunity cost to country B of producing one pound of cheese? One yard of cloth?

c. Country A has a comparative advantage in what?

d. Country B has a comparative advantage in what?

33-5. The use of tariffs and quotas to restrict imports results in higher prices and is successful in reducing imports. In what way is using a tariff different from using a quota?

33-6. Two countries, Austral Land and Boreal Land, have the following production opportunities shown in the graphs.

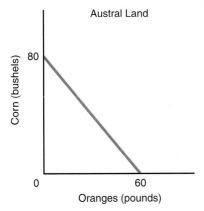

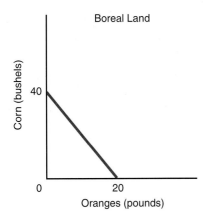

a. Who has an absolute advantage in corn? In oranges?

b. Who has a comparative advantage in corn? In oranges?

c. Should Boreal Land export at all? If so, which good should it export?

d. What is Austral Land's opportunity cost of oranges in terms of corn? What is Boreal Land's opportunity cost of corn in terms of oranges?

33-7. The accompanying graph gives the supply and demand for grapes. S and D are the United States' supply and demand curves, respectively. Assume that the world price of grapes is 50 cents per pound.

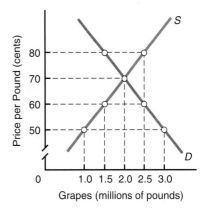

a. How many pounds are produced domestically? How many pounds are imported?

b. Suppose that the United States imposes a 10-cent-per-pound tariff. How many pounds would now be produced domestically? How many pounds would be imported? What are the U.S. government's revenues?

c. Suppose now that the government imposes a 20-cent-per-pound tariff. What price can domestic growers now receive for their grapes? How many pounds will domestic growers produce? How many pounds will be imported? What are government revenues?

33-8. If free trade is so obviously beneficial, why are there so many restrictions on international trade? (Hint: Review the theory presented in Chapter 32.)

33-9. Explain why an increase in taxes on imports (tariffs) will reduce exports.

33-10. Assume that a country with whom the United States is trading imposes restrictions on U.S.-made imports into that country. Will the United States be better off by simultaneously imposing restrictions on the other country's imports into the United States? Why or why not?

COMPUTER-ASSISTED INSTRUCTION

We show that the combination of specialization and exchange is the next best thing to a free lunch.

Complete problem and answer appear on disk.

INTERACTING WITH THE INTERNET

The text of the GATT agreement can be found at
   http://ananse.irv.uit.no/trade_law/gatt/nav/toc.html
and the text of NAFTA at
   gopher://cyfer.esusda.gov/11/ace/policy/nafta
and
   gopher://wiretap.spies.com/11/Gov/NAFTA
Find links to sites with pro and con material on NAFTA at
   **http://www.yahoo.com/Business_and_Economy/Trade/North_American_Free_Trade_
      Agreement__NAFTA/**
   A very good source for general information on the nations of the world is the CIA's *World Factbook* at
   http://www.odci.gov/cia/publications/95fact/index.html
Information on different countries' economic and trade policies can be found at
   gopher://UMSLVMA.UMSL.EDU:70/11/LIBRARY/GOVDOCS/CRPT

CHAPTER 34

EXCHANGE RATES AND THE BALANCE OF PAYMENTS

If you talk to Americans who traveled to Europe in the mid-1980s, they will probably regale you with stories of how cheap their trip was. If you go to Europe today, the stories will be quite different—more like cries of outrage at having been gouged by shopkeepers and restaurateurs. What difference does a decade make? Well, when you are talking about the dollar, a lot. Today, in some countries, such as Germany and Japan, the dollar buys barely half what it did in 1985. Should we be worrying about a weaker dollar? To answer this question, you need to know about international financial transactions and the determinants of foreign exchange rates.

PREVIEW QUESTIONS

1. What is the difference between the balance of trade and the balance of payments?

2. What is a foreign exchange rate?

3. What is a flexible exchange rate system?

4. What is the gold standard?

Did You Know That . . . every day, around the clock, over $1 trillion of foreign currencies are traded? Along with that trading come news headlines, such as "The dollar weakened today," "The dollar is clearly overvalued," "The dollar is under attack," and "Members of the Group of Seven agreed to prevent the dollar from rising." If you are confused by such newspaper headlines, join the crowd. Surprisingly, though, if you regard the dollar, the pound, the deutsche mark, the yen, and the franc as assets that are subject to the laws of supply and demand, the world of international finance can be quickly demystified. Perhaps the first step is to examine the meaning of the terms used with respect to America's international financial transactions during any one-year period.

THE BALANCE OF PAYMENTS AND INTERNATIONAL CAPITAL MOVEMENTS

Governments typically keep track of each year's economic activities by calculating the gross domestic product—the total of expenditures on all newly produced final domestic goods and services—and its components. In the world of international trade also, a summary information system has been developed. It relates to the balance of trade and the balance of payments. The **balance of trade** refers specifically to exports and imports of *goods and services* as discussed in Chapter 33. When international trade is in balance, the value of exports equals the value of imports.

The **balance of payments** is a more general concept that expresses the total of all economic transactions between two nations, usually for a period of one year. Each country's balance of payments summarizes information about that country's exports, imports, earnings by domestic residents on assets located abroad, earnings on domestic assets owned by foreign residents, international capital movements, and official transactions by central banks and governments. In essence, then, the balance of payments is a record of all the transactions between households, firms, and government of one country and the rest of the world. Any transaction that leads to a *payment* by a country's residents (or government) is a deficit item, identified by a negative sign (−) when we examine the actual numbers that might be in Table 34-1. Any transaction that leads to a *receipt* by a country's residents (or government) is a surplus item and is identified by a plus sign (+) when actual numbers are considered. Table 34-1 gives a listing of the surplus and deficit items on international accounts.

Balance of trade
The value of goods and services bought and sold in the world market.

Balance of payments
A summary record of a country's economic transactions with foreign residents and governments over a year.

TABLE 34-1

Surplus (+) and Deficit (−) Items on the International Accounts

Surplus Items (+)	Deficit Items (−)
Exports of merchandise	Imports of merchandise
Private and governmental gifts from foreigners	Private and governmental gifts to foreigners
Foreign use of domestically owned transportation	Use of foreign-owned transportation
Foreign tourists' expenditures in this country	Tourism expenditures abroad
Foreign military spending in this country	Military spending abroad
Interest and dividend receipts from foreigners	Interest and dividends paid to foreigners
Sales of domestic assets to foreigners	Purchases of foreign assets
Funds deposited in this country by foreigners	Funds placed in foreign depository institutions
Sales of gold to foreigners	Purchases of gold from foreigners
Sales of domestic currency to foreigners	Purchases of foreign currency

Accounting Identities

Accounting identities
Statements that certain numerical measurements are equal by accepted definition (for example, "assets equal liabilities plus stockholders' equity").

Accounting identities—definitions of equivalent values—exist for financial institutions and other businesses. We begin with simple accounting identities that must hold for families and then go on to describe international accounting identities.

If a family unit is spending more than its current income, such a situation necessarily implies that the family unit must be doing one of the following:

1. Drawing down its wealth. The family must reduce its money holdings, or it must sell stocks, bonds, or other assets.
2. Borrowing.
3. Receiving gifts from friends or relatives.
4. Receiving public transfers from a government, which obtained the funds by taxing others. (A transfer is a payment, in money or in goods or services, made without receiving goods or services in return.)

In effect, we can use this information to derive an identity: If a family unit is currently spending more than it is earning, it must draw on previously acquired wealth, borrow, or receive either private or public aid. Similarly, an identity exists for a family unit that is currently spending less than it is earning: It must increase its wealth by increasing its money holdings or by lending and acquiring other financial assets, or it must pay taxes or bestow gifts on others. When we consider businesses and governments, each unit in each group faces its own identities or constraints; thus, net lending by households must equal net borrowing by businesses and governments.

Even though our individual family unit's accounts must balance, in the sense that the identity discussed previously must hold, sometimes the item that brings about the balance cannot continue indefinitely. *If family expenditures exceed family income and this situation is financed by borrowing, the household may be considered to be in disequilibrium because such a situation cannot continue indefinitely.* If such a deficit is financed by drawing on previously accumulated assets, the family may also be in disequilibrium because it cannot continue indefinitely to draw on its wealth; eventually, it will become impossible for that family to continue such a lifestyle. (Of course, if the family members are retired, they may well be in equilibrium by drawing on previously acquired assets to finance current deficits; this example illustrates that it is necessary to understand circumstances fully before pronouncing an economic unit in disequilibrium.)

Individual households, businesses, and governments, as well as the entire group of households, businesses, and governments, must eventually reach equilibrium. Certain economic adjustment mechanisms have evolved to ensure equilibrium. Deficit households must eventually increase their incomes or decrease their expenditures. They will find that they have to pay higher interest rates if they wish to borrow to finance their deficits. Eventually their credit sources will dry up, and they will be forced into equilibrium. Businesses, on occasion, must lower costs and/or prices—or go bankrupt—to reach equilibrium.

When nations trade or interact, certain identities or constraints must also hold. Nations buy goods from people in other nations; they also lend to and present gifts to people in other nations. If a nation interacts with others, an accounting identity ensures a balance (but not an equilibrium, as will soon become clear). Let's look at the three categories of balance of payments transactions: current account transactions, capital account transactions, and official reserve account transactions.

Current Account Transactions

During any designated period, all payments and gifts that are related to the purchase or sale of both goods and services constitute the current account in international trade. The three major types of current account transactions are the exchange of merchandise goods, the exchange of services, and unilateral transfers.

Merchandise Trade Transactions. The largest portion of any nation's balance of payments current account is typically the importing and exporting of merchandise goods. During 1996, for example, as can be seen in lines 1 and 2 of Table 34-2, the United States exported $609.6 billion of merchandise and imported $770.8 billion. The balance of merchandise trade is defined as the difference between the value of merchandise exports and the value of merchandise imports. For 1996, the United States had a balance of merchandise trade deficit because the value of its merchandise imports exceeded the value of its merchandise exports. This deficit amounted to $161.2 billion (line 3).

Service Exports and Imports. The balance of (merchandise) trade has to do with tangible items—you can feel them, touch them, and see them. Service exports and imports have to do with invisible or intangible items that are bought and sold, such as shipping, insurance, tourist expenditures, and banking services. Also, income earned by foreigners on U.S. investments and income earned by Americans on foreign investments are part of service imports and exports. As can be seen in lines 4 and 5 of Table 34-2, in 1996, service exports were $220.4 bil-

---

THINKING CRITICALLY ABOUT THE MEDIA

Perhaps the Trade Situation Isn't So Bad After All

Virtually every month, there appears a spate of articles and TV sound bites about America's trade deficit. The official numbers may be in error, however, for they ignore the multinational nature of modern firms. American international trade figures exclude sales in other countries for subsidiaries of American-owned companies. Because of a host of other problems, some government economists believe that they are underestimating the value of U.S. exports by as much as 10 percent. Economist Paul Krugman of Stanford University agrees. When he added up the value of world exports and compared it with the value of world imports, he found that the planet Earth had a trade deficit of $100 billion! Perhaps we are trading with aliens and don't know it.

TABLE 34-2

U.S. Balance of Payments Account, 1996 (in Billions of Dollars)

Current Account		
(1) Exports of goods	+609.6	
(2) Imports of goods	−770.8	
(3) Balance of trade		−161.2
(4) Exports of services	+220.4	
(5) Imports of services	−151.6	
(6) Balance of services		+68.8
(7) Balance on goods and services [(3) + (6)]		−92.4
(8) Net unilateral transfers	−30.7	
(9) Balance on current account		−123.1
Capital Account		
(10) U.S. capital going abroad	−314.8	
(11) Foreign capital coming into the United States	+431.5[a]	
(12) Balance on capital account [(10) + (11)]		+116.7
(13) Balance on current account plus balance on capital account [(9) + (12)]		−6.4
(14) Official transactions		+6.4
(15) Total (balance)		$00.0

Sources: U.S. Department of Commerce, Bureau of Economic Analysis; U.S. Department of the Treasury.

[a]Includes a $24 billion statistical discrepancy, probably unaccounted capital inflows, many of which relate to the illegal drug trade.

lion and service imports were $151.6 billion. Thus the balance of services was about $68.8 billion in 1996 (line 6). Exports constitute receipts or inflows into the United States and are positive; imports constitute payments abroad or outflows of money and are negative.

When we combine the balance of merchandise trade with the balance of services, we obtain a balance on goods and services equal to −$92.4 billion in 1996 (line 7).

Unilateral Transfers. Americans give gifts to relatives and others abroad. The federal government grants gifts to foreign nations. Foreigners give gifts to Americans, and some foreign governments have granted money to the U.S. government. In the current account, we see that net unilateral transfers—the total amount of gifts given by Americans minus the total amount received by Americans from abroad—came to −$30.7 billion in 1996 (line 8). The fact that there is a minus sign before the number for unilateral transfers means that Americans gave more to foreigners than foreigners gave to Americans.

Balancing the Current Account. The balance on current account tracks the value of a country's exports of goods and services (including military receipts plus income on investments abroad) and transfer payments (private and government) relative to the value of that country's import of goods and services (including military payments) and transfer payments (private and government). In 1996, it was a *negative* $123.1 billion.

If exports exceed imports, a current account surplus is said to exist; if imports exceed exports, a current account deficit is said to exist. A current account deficit means that we are importing more than we are exporting. Such a deficit must be paid for by the export of money or money equivalent, which means a capital account surplus.

Capital Account Transactions

In world markets, it is possible to buy and sell not only goods and services but also real and financial assets. This is what the capital accounts are concerned with in international transactions. Capital account transactions occur because of foreign investments—either foreigners investing in the United States or Americans investing in other countries. The purchase of shares of stock on the London stock market by an American causes an outflow of funds. The building of a Japanese automobile factory in the United States causes an inflow of funds. Any time foreigners buy U.S. government securities, that is an inflow of funds. Any time Americans buy foreign government securities, there is an outflow of funds. Loans to and from foreigners cause outflows and inflows.

Line 10 of Table 34-2 indicates that in 1996, the value of private and government capital going out of the United States was −$314.8 billion, and line 11 shows that the value of private and government capital coming into the United States (including a statistical discrepancy) was $431.5 billion. U.S. capital going abroad constitutes payments or outflows and is therefore negative. Foreign capital coming into the United States constitutes receipts or inflows and is therefore positive. Thus there was a positive net capital movement of $116.7 billion into the United States (line 12). This is also called the balance on capital account.

There is a relationship between the current account and the capital account, assuming no interventions by the central banks of nations. *The current account and the capital account must sum to zero. Stated differently, the current account deficit equals the capital account surplus. Any nation experiencing a current account deficit, such as the United States, must also be running a capital account surplus.*

EXAMPLE
Does America's Continuing Trade Deficit Mean It Has a Weak Economy?

The current account in the United States has been in deficit continuously since the early 1980s. This is not something new. During the 1880s, the United States had many years of current account deficits. They were equally matched by capital account surpluses, as the rest of the world sent capital to the United States to finance the building of the railroads and the development of the trans-Mississippi West. By the early 1900s, the United States accumulated a long string of current account surpluses. By World War I, Americans had repaid all their external debt and had become a net creditor. In 1980, the United States was in fact the world's largest creditor. By 1986, it was the world's largest debtor nation. This can be seen in Figure 34-1. Whenever America is in deficit in its current account, it is in surplus in its capital account.

Contrary to popular belief, the United States does not necessarily have a trade deficit because it is a weak economy and cannot compete in world markets. Rather, the United States appears to be a good place to invest capital because there are strong prospects for growth and investment opportunities. So long as foreigners wish to invest more in the United

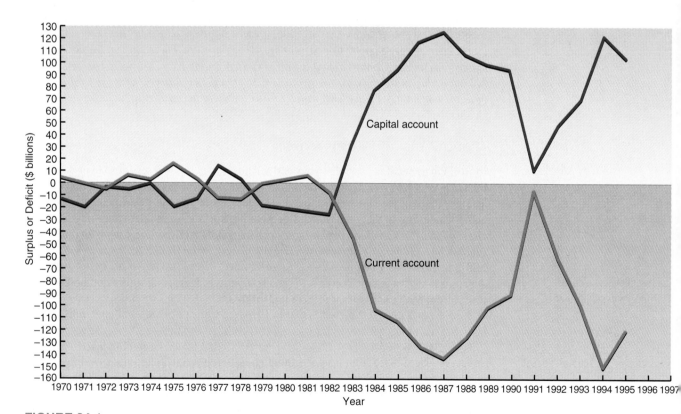

FIGURE 34-1

The Relationship Between the Current Account and the Capital Account
To some extent, the capital account is the mirror image of the current account. We can see this in the years since 1970. When the current account was in surplus, the capital account was in deficit. When the current account was in deficit, the capital account was in surplus. Indeed, virtually the only time foreigners can invest in America is when the current account is in deficit.

Sources: International Monetary Fund;: *Economic Indicators.*

States than Americans wish to invest abroad, there will always be a deficit in our current account balance. Americans are the beneficiaries of international capital flows.

FOR CRITICAL ANALYSIS: Why are politicians, nonetheless, so worried about the international trade deficit? ●

Official Reserve Account Transactions

The third type of balance of payments transaction concerns official reserve assets, which consist of the following:

Special drawing rights (SDRs)
Reserve assets created by the International Monetary Fund that countries can use to settle international payments.

1. Foreign currencies
2. Gold
3. **Special drawing rights (SDRs),** which are reserve assets that the International Monetary Fund created to be used by countries to settle international payment obligations
4. The reserve position in the International Monetary Fund
5. Financial assets held by an official agency, such as the U.S. Treasury Department

To consider how official reserve account transactions occur, look again at Table 34-2. The surplus in our capital account was +$116.7 billion. But the deficit in our current account was −$123.1 billion, so we had a net deficit on the combined accounts (line 13) of −$6.4 billion. In other words, the United States obtained less in foreign money in all its international transactions than it used. How is this deficiency made up? By our central bank drawing down its existing balances of foreign monies, or the +$6.4 billion in official transactions shown on line 14 in Table 34-2. You might ask why there is a plus sign on line 14. The answer is because this represents a *supply* (an inflow) of foreign exchange into our international transactions.

The balance (line 15) in Table 34-2 is zero, as it must be with double-entry bookkeeping. Our balance of payments deficit is measured by the official transactions figure on line 14. (This does not mean we are in equilibrium, though.)

THINKING CRITICALLY ABOUT THE MEDIA

Developing Countries Are Getting All the Capital

Many developing countries are growing more rapidly than the developed countries. Several reports have been commented on by the media in recent years in which it is argued that developing economies are "sucking up" all the world's capital. Let's put the numbers in context. About $60 billion a year of capital moves from advanced to developing countries. All of the countries in the world, in contrast, invest over $4 trillion a year. So such capital flows represent only 1.5 percent of total world investment. What's to worry?

What Affects the Balance of Payments?

A major factor affecting our balance of payments is our rate of inflation relative to that of our trading partners. Assume that the rate of inflation in the United States and in France is equal. All of a sudden, our inflation rate increases. The French will find that American products are becoming more expensive, and we will export fewer of them to France. Americans will find French products relatively cheaper, and we will import more. The converse will occur if our rate of inflation suddenly falls relative to that of France. All other things held constant, whenever our rate of inflation exceeds that of our trading partners, we expect to see a "worsening" of our balance of trade and payments. Conversely, when our rate of inflation is less than that of our trading partners, other things being constant, we expect to see an "improvement" in our balance of trade and payments.

Another important factor that sometimes influences our balance of payments is our relative political stability. Political instability causes *capital flight:* Owners of capital in countries anticipating or experiencing political instability will often move assets to countries that are politically stable, such as the United States. Hence our balance of payments is likely to improve whenever political instability looms in other nations in the world.

CONCEPTS IN BRIEF

- The balance of payments reflects the value of all transactions in international trade, including goods, services, financial assets, and gifts.

- The merchandise trade balance gives us the difference between exports and imports of tangible items. Merchandise trade transactions are represented by exports and imports of tangible items.

- Service exports and imports relate to the trade of intangible items, such as shipping, insurance, and tourist expenditures. They include income earned by foreigners on U.S. investments and income earned by Americans on foreign investments.

- Unilateral transfers involve international private gifts and federal government grants or gifts to foreign nations.

- When we add the balance of merchandise trade plus the balance of services and take account of net unilateral transfers, we come up with the balance on current account, which is a summary statistic taking into account the three transactions that form the current account transactions.

- There are also capital account transactions that relate to the buying and selling of financial and real assets. Foreign capital is always entering the United States, and American capital is always flowing abroad. The difference is called the balance on capital account.

- Another type of balance of payments transaction concerns the official reserve assets of individual countries, or what is often simply called official transactions. By standard accounting convention, official transactions are exactly equal to but opposite in sign to the balance of payments of the United States.

- Our balance of trade can be affected by our relative rate of inflation and by political instability elsewhere compared to the stability that exists in the United States.

DETERMINING FOREIGN EXCHANGE RATES

When you buy foreign products, such as French wine, you have dollars with which to pay the French winemaker. The French winemaker, however, cannot pay workers in dollars. The workers are French, they live in France, and they must have francs to buy goods and services in that country. There must therefore be some way of exchanging dollars for the francs that the winemaker will accept. That exchange occurs in a **foreign exchange market,** which in this case specializes in exchanging francs and dollars. (When you obtain foreign currencies at a bank or an airport currency exchange, you are participating in the foreign exchange market.)

Foreign exchange market
The market for buying and selling foreign currencies.

The particular exchange rate between francs and dollars that would prevail depends on the current demand for and supply of francs and dollars. In a sense, then, our analysis of the exchange rate between dollars and francs will be familiar, for we have used supply and demand throughout this book. If it costs you 20 cents to buy one franc, that is the **foreign exchange rate** determined by the current demand for and supply of francs in the foreign exchange market. The French person going to the foreign exchange market would need five francs to buy one dollar. (Our numbers are, of course, hypothetical.)

Foreign exchange rate
The price of one currency in terms of another.

We will continue our example in which the only two countries in the world are France and the United States. Now let's consider what determines the demand for and supply of foreign currency in the foreign exchange market.

Demand for and Supply of Foreign Currency

You wish to buy some French Bordeaux wine. To do so, you must have French francs. You go to the foreign exchange market (or your American bank). Your desire to buy the French wine therefore causes you to offer (supply) dollars to the foreign exchange market. Your demand for French francs is equivalent to your supply of American dollars to the foreign exchange market. Indeed:

> **Every U.S. transaction concerning the importation of foreign goods constitutes a supply of dollars and a demand for some foreign currency, and the opposite is true for export transactions.**

In this case, this import transaction constitutes a demand for French francs.

In our example, we will assume that only two goods are being traded, French wine and American jeans. The American demand for French wine creates a supply of dollars and a demand for francs in the foreign exchange market. Similarly, the French demand for American jeans creates a supply of francs and a demand for dollars in the foreign exchange market. In the situation of **flexible exchange rates,** the supply of and demand for dollars and francs in the foreign exchange market will determine the equilibrium foreign exchange rate. The equilibrium exchange rate will tell us how many francs a dollar can be exchanged for—that is, the dollar price of francs—or how many dollars (or fractions of a dollar) a franc can be exchanged for—the franc price of dollars.

Flexible exchange rates
Exchange rates that are allowed to fluctuate in the open market in response to changes in supply and demand. Sometimes called *floating exchange rates.*

The Equilibrium Foreign Exchange Rate

To determine the equilibrium foreign exchange rate, we have to find out what determines the demand for and supply of foreign exchange. We will ignore for the moment any speculative aspect of buying foreign exchange; that is, we assume that there are no individuals who wish to buy francs simply because they think that their price will go up in the future.

The idea of an exchange rate is no different from the idea of paying a certain price for something you want to buy. If you like coffee, you know you have to pay about 75 cents a cup. If the price went up to $2.50, you would probably buy fewer cups. If the price went down to 5 cents, you might buy more. In other words, the demand curve for cups of coffee, expressed in terms of dollars, slopes downward following the law of demand. The demand curve for francs slopes downward also, and we will see why.

Demand Schedule for French Francs. Let's think more closely about the demand schedule for francs. Let's say that it costs you 20 cents to purchase one franc; that is the exchange rate between dollars and francs. If tomorrow you had to pay 25 cents for the same franc, the exchange rate would have changed. Looking at such an increase with respect to the franc, we would say that there has been an **appreciation** in the value of the franc in the foreign exchange market. But this increase in the value of the franc means that there has been a **depreciation** in the value of the dollar in the foreign exchange market. The dollar used to buy five francs; tomorrow, the dollar will be able to buy only four francs at a price of 25 cents per franc. If the dollar price of francs rises, you will probably demand fewer francs. Why? The answer lies in looking at the reason you demand francs in the first place.

You demand francs in order to buy French wine. Your demand curve for French wine, we will assume, follows the law of demand and therefore slopes downward. If it costs you more American dollars to buy the same quantity of French wine, presumably you will not buy the same quantity; your quantity demanded will be less. We say that your demand for French francs is *derived from* your demand for French wine. In panel (a) of Figure 34-2, we present the hypothetical demand schedule for French wine in the United States by a representative wine drinker. In panel (b), we show graphically the American demand curve for French wine in terms of American dollars taken from panel (a).

Let us assume that the price per liter of French wine in France is 20 francs. Given that price, we can find the number of francs required to purchase up to 4 liters of French wine. That information is given in panel (c) of Figure 34-2. If one liter requires 20 francs, 4 liters require 80 francs. Now we have enough information to determine the derived demand curve for French francs. If one franc costs 20 cents, a bottle of wine would cost $4 (20 francs per bottle × 20 cents per franc = $4 per bottle). At $4 per bottle, the typical representative American wine drinker would, we see from panel (a) of Figure 34-2, demand 4 liters. From panel (c) we see that 80 francs would be demanded to buy the 4 liters of wine. We show this quantity demanded in panel (d). In panel (e), we draw the derived demand curve for francs. Now consider what happens if the price of francs goes up to 30 cents. A bottle of French wine costing 20 francs in France would now cost $6. From panel (a) we see that at $6 per liter, 3 liters will be imported from France into the United States by our representative domestic wine drinker. From panel (c) we see that 3 liters would require 60 francs to be purchased; thus in panels (d) and (e) we see that at a price of one franc per 30 cents, the quantity demanded will be 60 francs. We continue similar calculations all the way up to a price of 50 cents per franc. At that price a bottle of French wine costing 20 francs in France would cost $10, and our representative wine drinker would import only one bottle.

Downward-Sloping Derived Demand.   As can be expected, as the price of francs falls, the quantity demanded will rise. The only difference here from the standard demand analysis developed in Chapter 3 and used throughout this text is that the demand for francs is derived from the demand for a final product—French wine in our example.

Supply of French Francs.   The supply of French francs is a derived supply in that it is derived from a French person's demand for American jeans. We could go through an example similar to the one for wine to come up with a supply schedule of French francs in France. It slopes upward. Obviously, the French want dollars in order to purchase American goods. In principle, the French will be willing to supply more francs when the dollar price of francs goes up because they can then buy more American goods with the same quantity of francs; that is, the franc would be worth more in exchange for American goods than when the dollar price for francs was lower. Let's take an example. Suppose a pair of jeans in the United States costs $10. If the exchange rate is 25 cents for one franc, the French have to come up with 40 francs (= $10 at 25 cents per franc) to buy one pair of

Appreciation
An increase in the value of a currency in terms of other currencies.

Depreciation
A decrease in the value of a currency in terms of other currencies.

Panel (a)
**Demand Schedule for French Wine in the
United States per Week**

Price per Liter	Quantity Demanded (liters)
$10	1
8	2
6	3
4	4

Panel (b)
American Demand Curve for French Wine

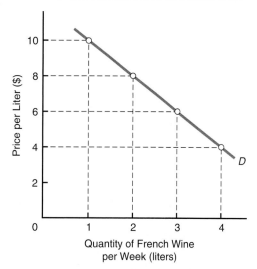

Panel (c)
**Francs Required to Purchase
Quantity Demanded (at *P* = 20 francs per liter)**

Quantity Demanded (liters)	Francs Required
1	20
2	40
3	60
4	80

Panel (d)
**Derived Demand Schedule for Francs in the
United States with Which to Pay for Imports of Wine**

Dollar Price of One Franc	Dollar Price of Wine	Quantity of Wine Demanded (liters)	Quantity of Francs Demanded per Week
$ .50	$10	1	20
.40	8	2	40
.30	6	3	60
.20	4	4	80

FIGURE 34-2

Deriving the Demand for French Francs
In panel (a), we show the demand schedule for French wine in the United States, expressed in terms of dollars per liter. In panel (b), we show the demand curve, *D,* which slopes downward. In panel (c), we show the number of francs required to purchase up to 4 liters of wine. If the price per liter of wine in France is 20 francs, we can now find the quantity of francs needed to pay for the various quantities demanded. In panel (d), we see the derived demand for francs in the United States in order to purchase the various quantities of wine given in panel (a). The resultant demand curve, D_1, is shown in panel (e). It is the American derived demand for francs.

Panel (e)
American Derived Demand for Francs

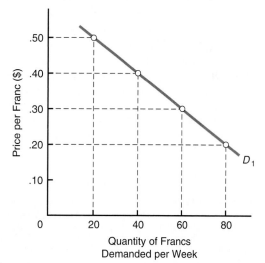

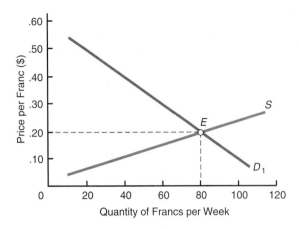

FIGURE 34-3

The Equilibrium Exchange Rate for Two Individuals
The derived demand curve for French francs is taken from panel (e) of Figure 34-2. The derived supply curve, S, results from the representative French purchaser of American jeans, who supplies francs to the foreign exchange market when demanding U.S. dollars in order to buy American jeans. D_1 and S intersect at E. The equilibrium exchange rate is 20 cents per franc.

jeans. If, however, the exchange rate goes up to 50 cents for one franc, the French must come up with only 20 francs (= $10 at 50 cents per franc) to buy a pair of American jeans. At a lower price (in francs) of American jeans, the French will demand a larger quantity. In other words, as the price of French francs goes up in terms of dollars, the quantity of American jeans demanded will go up, and hence the quantity of French francs supplied will go up. Therefore, the supply schedule of foreign currency (francs) will slope upward.[1]

We could easily work through a detailed numerical example to show that the supply curve of French francs slopes upward. Rather than do that, we will simply draw it as upward-sloping in Figure 34-3. In our hypothetical example, assuming that there is only one wine drinker in America and one demander of jeans in France, the equilibrium exchange rate will be set at 20 cents per franc, or 5 francs to one dollar. Let us now look at the aggregate demand for and supply of French francs. We take all demanders of French wine and all demanders of American jeans and put their demands for and supplies of francs together into one diagram. Thus we are showing an aggregate version of the demand for and supply of French francs. The horizontal axis in Figure 34-4 represents a quantity of foreign exchange—the number of francs per year. The vertical axis represents the exchange rate—the price of foreign currency (francs) expressed in dollars (per franc). Thus at the foreign currency price of 25 cents per franc, you know that it will cost you 25 cents to buy one franc. At the foreign currency price of 20 cents per franc, you know that it will cost you 20 cents to buy one franc. The equilibrium is again established at 20 cents for one franc. This equilibrium is not established because Americans like to buy francs or because the French like to buy dollars. Rather, the equilibrium exchange rate depends on how many pairs of jeans the French want and how much French wine the Americans want (given their respective incomes, their tastes, and the relative price of wine and jeans).[2]

A Shift in Demand. Assume that a successful advertising campaign by American wine importers has caused the American demand (curve) for French wine to double. Americans

---

[1] Actually, the supply schedule of foreign currency will be upward-sloping if we assume that the demand for American imported jeans on the part of the French is price-elastic. If the demand schedule for jeans is price-inelastic, the supply schedule will be negatively sloped. In the case of unit elasticity of demand, the supply schedule for francs will be a vertical line. Throughout the rest of this chapter, we will assume that demand is price-elastic. Remember that the price elasticity of demand tells us whether or not total expenditures by jeans purchasers in France will rise or fall when the French franc drops in value. In the long run, it is quite realistic to think that the price elasticity of demand for imports is numerically greater than 1 anyway.

[2] Remember that we are dealing with a two-country world in which we are considering only the exchange of American jeans and French wine. In the real world, more than just goods and services are exchanged among countries. Some Americans buy French financial assets; some French buy American financial assets. We are ignoring such transactions for the moment.

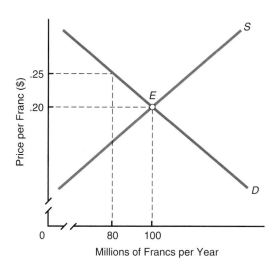

FIGURE 34-4

Aggregate Demand for and Supply of French Francs
The aggregate supply curve for French francs results from the total French demand for American jeans. The demand curve, *D*, slopes downward like most demand curves, and the supply curve, *S*, slopes upward. The foreign exchange price, or the U.S. dollar price of francs, is given on the vertical axis. The number of francs, in millions, is represented on the horizontal axis. If the foreign exchange rate is 25 cents—that is, if it takes 25 cents to buy one franc—Americans will demand 80 million francs. The equilibrium exchange rate is at the intersection of *D* and *S*. The equilibrium exchange rate is 20 cents. At this point, 100 million French francs are both demanded and supplied each year.

demand twice as much wine at all prices. Their demand curve for French wine has shifted outward to the right.

The increased demand for French wine can be translated into an increased demand for francs. All Americans clamoring for bottles of French wine will supply more dollars to the foreign exchange market while demanding more French francs to pay for the wine. Figure 34-5 presents a new demand schedule, D_2, for French francs; this demand schedule is to the right of and outward from the original demand schedule. If the French do not change their desire for American jeans, the supply schedule for French francs will remain stable. A new equilibrium will be established at a higher exchange rate. In our particular example, the new equilibrium is established at an exchange rate of 30 cents per franc. It now takes 30 cents to buy one French franc, whereas it took 20 cents before. This is translated as an increase in the price of French wine to Americans and as a decrease in the price of American jeans to the French. (Otherwise stated, there has been a decline in the foreign exchange value of the dollar.)

A Shift in Supply. We just assumed that Americans' preference for French wine had shifted. Because the demand for French francs is a derived demand by Americans for

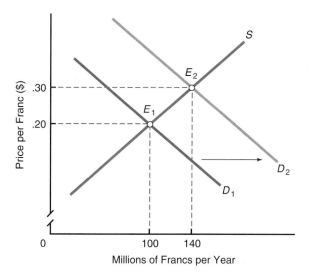

FIGURE 34-5

A Shift in the Demand Schedule
The demand schedule for French wine shifts to the right, causing the derived demand schedule for francs to shift to the right also. We have shown this as a shift from D_1 to D_2. We have assumed that the French supply schedule for francs has remained stable—that is, French demand for American jeans has remained constant. The old equilibrium foreign exchange rate was 20 cents. The new equilibrium exchange rate will be E_2; it will now cost 30 cents to buy one franc. The higher price of francs will be translated into a higher U.S. dollar price for French wine and a lower French franc price for American jeans.

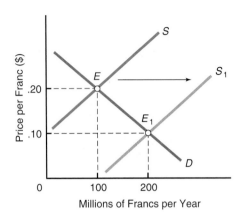

FIGURE 34-6

A Shift in the Supply of French Francs
There has been a shift in the supply curve for French francs. The new equilibrium will occur at E_1, meaning that 10 cents, rather than 20 cents, will now buy one franc. After the exchange rate adjustment, the amount of francs demanded and supplied will increase to 200 million per year.

French wine, it has caused a shift in the demand curve for francs. Alternatively, assume that the supply curve of French francs shifts outward to the right. This may occur for many reasons, the most probable one being a relative rise in the French price level. For example, if the price of all French-made clothes went up 100 percent in francs, American jeans would become relatively cheaper. That would mean that French people would want to buy more American jeans. But remember that when they want to buy more American jeans, they supply more francs to the foreign exchange market. Thus we see in Figure 34-6 that the supply curve of French francs moves from S to S_1. In the absence of restrictions—that is, in a system of flexible exchange rates—the new equilibrium exchange rate will be one franc equals 10 cents, or $1 equals 10 francs. The quantity of francs demanded and supplied will increase from 100 million per year to 200 million per year. We say, then, that in a flexible international exchange rate system, shifts in the demand for and supply of foreign currencies will cause changes in the equilibrium foreign exchange rates. Those rates will remain in effect until supply or demand shifts.

Market Determinants of Exchange Rates

The foreign exchange market is affected by many other changes in market variables in addition to changes in relative price levels, including these:

1. *Changes in real interest rates.* If the United States interest rate, corrected for people's expectations of inflation, abruptly increases relative to the rest of the world, international investors elsewhere will increase their demand for dollar-denominated assets, thereby increasing the demand for dollars in foreign exchange markets. An increased demand for dollars in foreign exchange markets, other things held constant, will cause the dollar to appreciate and other currencies to depreciate.
2. *Changes in productivity.* Whenever one country's productivity increases relative to another's, the former country will become more price competitive in world markets. The demand for its exports will increase, and so, too, will the demand for its currency.
3. *Changes in product preferences.* If Germany's citizens suddenly develop a taste for American-made automobiles, this will increase the derived demand for American dollars in foreign exchange markets.
4. *Perceptions of economic stability.* As already mentioned, if the United States looks economically and politically more stable relative to other countries, more foreigners will want to put their savings into U.S. assets than in their own domestic assets. This will increase the demand for dollars.

CONCEPTS IN BRIEF

- The foreign exchange rate is the rate at which one country's currency can be exchanged for another's.

- The demand for foreign exchange is a derived demand; it is derived from the demand for foreign goods and services (and financial assets). The supply of foreign exchange is derived from foreigners' demands for our goods and services.

- In general, the demand curve of foreign exchange slopes downward and the supply curve of foreign exchange slopes upward. The equilibrium foreign exchange rate occurs at the intersection of the demand and supply curves for a currency.

- A shift in the demand for foreign goods will result in a shift in the demand for foreign exchange. The equilibrium foreign exchange rate will change. A shift in the supply of foreign currency will also cause a change in the equilibrium exchange rate.

THE GOLD STANDARD AND THE INTERNATIONAL MONETARY FUND

The current system of more or less freely floating exchange rates is a recent development. We have had, in the past, periods of a gold standard, fixed exchange rates under the International Monetary Fund, and variants of these two.

The Gold Standard

Gold standard

An international monetary system in which nations fix their exchange rates in terms of gold. All currencies are fixed in terms of all others, and any balance of payments deficits or surpluses can be made up by shipments of gold.

Until the 1930s, many nations were on a **gold standard.** The values of their currencies were tied directly to gold.[3] Nations operating under this gold standard agreed to redeem their currencies for a fixed amount of gold at the request of any holder of that currency. Although gold was not necessarily the means of exchange for world trade, it was the unit to which all currencies under the gold standard were pegged. And because all currencies in the system were linked to gold, exchange rates between those currencies were fixed. Indeed, the gold standard has been offered as the prototype of a fixed exchange rate system. The heyday of the gold standard was from about 1870 to 1914. England had been on such a standard as far back as the 1820s.

There turns out to be a relationship between the balance of payments and changes in domestic money supplies throughout the world. Under a gold standard, the international financial market reached equilibrium through the effect of gold flows on each country's money supply. When a nation suffered a deficit in its balance of payments, more gold would flow out than in. Because the domestic money supply was based on gold, an outflow of gold to foreigners caused an automatic reduction in the domestic money supply. This caused several things to happen. Interest rates rose, thereby attracting foreign capital and improving the balance of payments. At the same time, the reduction in the money supply was equivalent to a restrictive monetary policy, which caused national output and prices to fall. Imports were discouraged and exports were encouraged, thereby again improving the balance of payments.

---

[3]This is a simplification. Most nations were on a *specie metal standard* using gold, silver, copper, and other precious metals as money. Nations operating under this standard agreed to redeem their currencies for a fixed exchange rate.

Two problems that plagued the gold standard were that no nation had control of its domestic monetary policy and that the world's commerce was at the mercy of gold discoveries.

POLICY EXAMPLE
Should We Go Back to the Gold Standard?

In the past several decades, the United States has consistently run a current account deficit. The dollar has become weaker. We have had inflation. We have had recessions. Some economists and politicians argue that we should return to the gold standard. The United States actually operated under two gold standards. From 1879 to 1933, the dollar was defined as 32.22 grains of gold, yielding a gold price of $20.671835 an ounce. During that time period, general prices more than doubled during World War I, there was a major depression in 1920–1921, and the Great Depression occurred. The second gold standard prevailed from 1933 to 1971, when the price of gold was pegged at $35 an ounce. A dollar was defined as 13.714286 grains of gold. During that time period, general prices quadrupled.

Clearly, a gold standard guarantees neither stable prices nor economic stability.

FOR CRITICAL ANALYSIS: Why does no country today operate on a gold standard? •

Bretton Woods and the International Monetary Fund

In 1944, as World War II was ending, representatives from the world's capitalist countries met in Bretton Woods, New Hampshire, to create a new international payment system to replace the gold standard, which had collapsed during the 1930s. The Bretton Woods Agreement Act was signed on July 31, 1945, by President Harry Truman. It created a new permanent institution, the **International Monetary Fund (IMF),** to administer the agreement and to lend to member countries in balance of payments deficit. The arrangements thus provided are now called the old IMF system or the Bretton Woods system.

Each member nation was assigned an IMF contribution quota determined by its international trade volume and national income. Twenty-five percent of the quota was contributed in gold or U.S. dollars and 75 percent in its own currency. At the time, the IMF therefore consisted of a pool of gold, dollars, and other major currencies.

Member governments were then obligated to intervene to maintain the values of their currencies in foreign exchange markets within 1 percent of the declared **par value**—the officially determined value. The United States, which owned most of the world's gold stock, was similarly obligated to maintain gold prices within a 1 percent margin of the official rate of $35 an ounce. Except for a transitional arrangement permitting a one-time adjustment of up to 10 percent in par value, members could alter exchange rates thereafter only with the approval of the IMF. The agreement stated that such approval would be given only if the country's balance of payments was in *fundamental disequilibrium,* a term that has never been officially defined.

Special Drawing Rights. In 1967, the IMF created a new type of international money, *special drawing rights (SDRs).* SDRs are exchanged only between monetary authorities (central banks). Their existence temporarily changed the IMF into a world central bank. The IMF creates SDRs the same way that the Federal Reserve can create dollars. The IMF allocates SDRs to member nations in accordance with their quotas. Currently, the SDR's

International Monetary Fund (IMF)
An institution set up to manage the international monetary system, established in 1945 under the Bretton Woods Agreement Act, which established fixed exchange rates for the world's currencies.

Par value
The legally established value of the monetary unit of one country in terms of that of another.

value is determined by making one SDR equal to a bundle of currencies. In reality, the SDR rises or falls in terms of the dollar.

End of the Old IMF. On August 15, 1971, President Richard Nixon suspended the convertibility of the dollar into gold. On December 18, 1971, we officially devalued the dollar against the currencies of 14 major industrial nations. Finally, on March 16, 1973, the finance ministers of the European Economic Community (now the EU) announced that they would let their currencies float against the dollar, something Japan had already begun doing with its yen. Since 1973, the United States and most other trading countries have had either freely floating exchange rates or managed ("dirty") floating exchange rates.

THE DIRTY FLOAT AND MANAGED EXCHANGE RATES

Dirty float
A system between flexible and fixed exchange rates in which central banks occasionally enter foreign exchange markets to influence rates.

The United States went off the Bretton Woods system in 1973, but it has nonetheless tried to keep certain elements of that system in play. We have occasionally engaged in what is called a **dirty float,** or management of flexible exchange rates. The management of flexible exchange rates has usually come about through international policy cooperation. For example, the Group of Five (G-5) nations—France, Germany, Japan, the United Kingdom, and the United States—and the Group of Seven (G-7) nations—the G-5 nations plus Italy and Canada—have for some time shared information on their policy objectives and procedures. They do this through regular meetings between economic policy secretaries, ministers, and staff members. One of their principal objectives has been to "smooth out" foreign exchange rates. Initially, the G-5 attempted to push the value of the dollar downward to help correct U.S. trade deficits and reduce Japanese foreign trade surpluses. What the five nations agreed to do was supply dollars in foreign exchange markets. This increased supply would reduce the dollar's value.

Is it possible for these groups to "manage" foreign exchange rates? Some economists do not think so. For example, economists Michael Bordo and Anna Schwartz studied the foreign exchange intervention actions coordinated by the Federal Reserve and the U.S. Treasury for the second half of the 1980s. Besides showing that such interventions were sporadic and variable, Bordo and Schwartz came to an even more compelling conclusion: Exchange rate interventions were trivial relative to the total trading of foreign exchange on a daily basis. For example, in April 1989, total foreign exchange trading amounted to $129 billion per day, yet the American central bank purchased only $100 million in deutsche marks and yen during that entire month (and did so on a single day). For all of 1989, Fed purchases of marks and yen were only $17.7 billion, or the equivalent of less than 14 percent of the amount of an average *day's* trading in April of that year. Their conclusion is that neither the American central bank nor the central banks of the other G-7 nations can influence exchange rates in the long run.

CONCEPTS IN BRIEF

- The International Monetary Fund was developed after World War II as an institution to maintain fixed exchange rates in the world. Since 1973, however, fixed exchange rates have disappeared in most major trading countries.

- A dirty float occurs in a flexible exchange rate system whenever central banks intervene to influence exchange rates.

Should We Worry About the Weak Dollar?

Concepts Applied: Flexible exchange rates, current account deficit, depreciation

The dollar became relatively weaker against the yen and deutsche mark in 1985. However, the dollar has held its value when weighted against the currencies of all U.S. trading partners.

Rome's currency was the world's strongest for a period of 400 years, but then it lost its attractiveness in world trade. The United Kingdom saw its currency, the pound sterling, lose its world dominance over a period of 50 years. Now the United States' currency is on top. But need we worry that its days of dominance are numbered?

At first blush, the dollar appears strong. It accounts for over 60 percent of foreign exchange reserves and over 50 percent of global private financial wealth. In addition, almost 70 percent of world trade is invoiced in dollars, as is 75 percent of international bank lending. Not bad for a country that accounts for only 24 percent of world output and 14 percent of world exports.

The Dwindling Value of the Dollar

But the dollar definitely does not seem to buy as much as it used to. Figure 34-7 shows what has happened to dollar exchange rates with respect to the yen and the deutsche mark. The value of the dollar with respect to those two currencies has been falling steadily since 1985. There are several reasons why the yen and the mark have become so strong and the dollar so weak. Both Japan and Germany have had lower rates of inflation than the United States. Also, at least in Germany, investors have earned higher rates of return.

Who Is Hurt by the Falling Dollar?

Besides the outraged American tourist in Germany, France, Switzerland, and Japan, who else is hurt by the weak dollar? The weaker dollar translates into higher prices for imported goods, such as BMWs, Mercedes, Toyotas, NEC computers, and Nintendo videogames. So

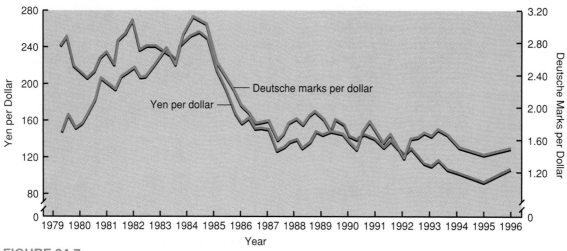

FIGURE 34-7

The Dollar Relative to the Mark and the Yen
Since the mid-1980s, the value of the U.S. dollar in terms of the German (Deutsche) mark and the Japanese yen has tended to decline.
Source: International Monetary Fund.

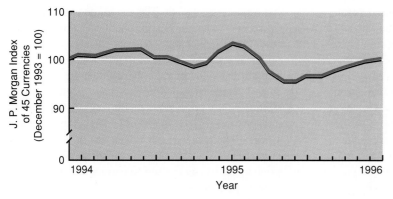

FIGURE 34-8

The Dollar Relative to an Index of 45 Currencies

If we look at the dollar relative to a basket of 45 of the world's currencies, it has held rather firm since the end of 1993.

Sources: J. P. Morgan Company; Federal Reserve Board.

Americans who purchase imported goods from countries whose currencies are stronger relative to the dollar must now pay more than they did before. But there is a flip side to this equation. Foreigners now find our products cheaper, so employees and shareholders in American companies that export find themselves better off.

Is the Dollar Really So Weak?

The dollar is indisputably changing relative to the yen, the deutsche mark, the Swiss franc, the French franc, and a few other currencies. But as you can see in Figure 34-8, the dollar has actually been getting stronger since mid-1995. Weighted against the currencies of *all* of the United States' trading partners, the dollar has been relatively stable since 1988, and in the past few years, it has strengthened considerably against the other North American currencies (those of Canada and Mexico).

The Dollar Is Still in Demand

Almost $400 billion in U.S. currency is held overseas. Much of it is used by Russians, Mexicans, and others because they do not trust their own currencies. To obtain these dollar bills, foreigners have had to give up something of value, such as oil, fur hats, and tomatoes. In return, we were kind enough to give them pieces of paper money that cost us virtually nothing to produce. As long as they hold on to those pieces of paper, we are obtaining an interest-free loan. According to economist Richard Cooper of Harvard University, that saves the United States roughly $15 billion a year in interest.

FOR CRITICAL ANALYSIS

1. Why would a lower rate of inflation in Japan lead to a weaker dollar?
2. Why would foreigners agree to hold dollar bills instead of their own currencies?

CHAPTER SUMMARY

1. The balance of merchandise trade is defined as the value of goods bought and sold in the world market, usually during the period of one year. The balance of payments is a more inclusive concept that includes the value of all transactions in the world market.

2. Americans purchase financial assets in other countries, and foreigners purchase American financial assets, such as stocks or bonds. The buying and selling of foreign financial assets has the same effect on the balance of payments as the buying and selling of goods and services.

3. Our balance of trade and payments can be affected by our relative rate of inflation and by political instability elsewhere compared to the stability that exists in the United States.

4. Market determinants of exchange rates are changes in real interest rates (interest rates corrected for inflation), changes in productivity, changes in product preferences, and perceptions of economic stability.

5. To transact business internationally, it is necessary to convert domestic currencies into other currencies. This is done via the foreign exchange market. If we were trading with France only, French producers would want to be paid in francs because they must pay their workers in francs. American producers would want to be paid in dollars because American workers are paid in dollars.

6. An American's desire for French wine is expressed in terms of a supply of dollars, which is in turn a demand for French francs in the foreign exchange market. The opposite situation arises when the

French wish to buy American jeans. Their demand for jeans creates a demand for American dollars and a supply of French francs. We put the demand and supply schedules together to find the equilibrium foreign exchange rate. The demand schedule for foreign exchange is a derived demand—it is derived from Americans' demand for foreign products.

7. With no government intervention, a market clearing equilibrium foreign exchange rate will emerge. After a shift in demand or supply, the exchange rate will change so that it will again clear the market.

8. If Americans increase their demand for French wine, the demand curve for French wine shifts to the right. The derived demand for francs also shifts to the right. The supply schedule of francs, however, remains stable because the French demand for American jeans has remained constant. The shifted demand schedule intersects the stable supply schedule at a higher price (the foreign exchange rate increases). This is an appreciation of the value of French francs (a depreciation of the value of the dollar against the franc).

9. In a managed exchange rate system (a "dirty float"), central banks occasionally intervene in foreign exchange markets to influence exchange rates.

10. Under a gold standard, movement of gold across countries changes domestic money supplies, causing price levels to change and to correct balance of payments imbalances.

11. In 1945, the International Monetary Fund (IMF) was created to maintain fixed exchange rates throughout the world. This system was abandoned in 1973.

DISCUSSION OF PREVIEW QUESTIONS

1. What is the difference between the balance of trade and the balance of payments?

The balance of trade is defined as the difference between the value of exports and the value of imports. If the value of exports exceeds the value of imports, a trade surplus exists; if the value of exports is less than the value of imports, a trade deficit exists; if export and import values are equal, we refer to this situation as a trade balance. The balance of payments is more general and takes into account the value of *all* international transactions. Thus the balance of payments identifies not only goods and services transactions among nations but also investments (financial and nonfinancial) and gifts (private and public). When the value of all these transactions is such that one nation is sending more to other nations than it is receiving in return, a balance of payments deficit exists. A payments surplus and payments balance are self-explanatory.

2. What is a foreign exchange rate?

We know that nations trade with one another; they buy and sell goods, make and receive financial and nonfinancial investments, and give and receive gifts. However, nations have different currencies. People who sell to, invest in, or receive gifts from the United States ultimately want their own currency so that they can use the money domestically. Similarly, U.S. residents who sell in, invest in, or receive gifts from people in other countries ultimately want U.S. dollars to spend in the United States. Because most people ultimately want to end up with their own currencies, foreign exchange markets have evolved to enable people to sell one currency for other currencies. A foreign exchange rate, then, is the rate at which one country's currency can be exchanged for another's. For example, the exchange rate between the United Kingdom (U.K.) and the United States might dictate that one pound sterling is equivalent to $1.50; alternately stated, the U.S. dollar is worth .667 pound sterling.

3. What is a flexible exchange rate system?

A flexible exchange rate system is an international monetary system in which foreign exchange rates are allowed to fluctuate to reflect changes in the supply of and demand for international currencies. Say that the United States and the U.K. are in payments balance at the exchange rate of one pound sterling to U.S. $1.50. The U.S. demand for sterling is derived from private and government desires to buy British goods, to invest in the U.K., or to send gifts to the British people and is *inversely* related to the number of dollars it takes to buy one pound. Conversely, the supply of sterling is derived from the U.K.'s private and governmental desires to buy U.S. goods and services, to invest in the United States, and to send gifts to U.S. residents. The supply of sterling is *directly* related to the number of dollars one pound is worth. The intersection of the supply and demand curves for sterling determines the market foreign exchange rate of dollars per pound. In a system of flexible exchange rates, shifts in the supply or demand curves will lead to changes in the foreign exchange rates between nations.

4. What is the gold standard?

The gold standard is an international monetary system in which each nation values its currency unit at a specific quantity of gold. Under such a standard, exchange rates are fixed in terms of each other. For example, the U.S. dollar was originally backed by one-twentieth of an ounce of gold, and the British valued their coins (or paper backed by gold) at one-quarter of an ounce of gold; the British monetary unit was therefore worth five times the U.S. monetary unit. The resulting exchange rate was that one pound sterling was worth $5. The gold standard was, in matters of exchange rates, similar to the fixed exchange rate system. However, payment imbalances were automatically corrected by gold flows. For instance, if the United States had a payment deficit with the U.K. (which therefore had a payment surplus with the United States), gold would flow from the United States to the U.K. The result of these gold flows (which, in effect, are equivalent to money movements) would be to raise the price level in the U.K. and lower it in the United States. This would lead to an increase in U.S. exports and a decrease in U.S. imports and a corresponding increase in British imports and decrease in British exports. Thus, in the past, the gold standard brought nations into payment balance by altering price *levels* in each country. The current system of flexible exchange rates corrects payment imbalances leaving price levels unaltered; it changes *one* price—the exchange rate.

PROBLEMS

(Answers to the odd-numbered problems appear at the back of the book.)

34-1. In the graph, what can be said about the shift from D to D_1?

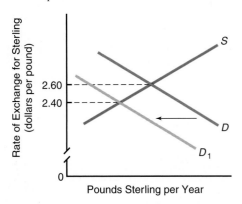

a. It could be caused by Britons demanding fewer U.S. products.
b. It is a result of increased U.S. demand for British goods.
c. It causes an appreciation of the dollar relative to the pound.
d. It causes an appreciation of the pound relative to the dollar.

34-2. If the rate of exchange between the pound and the dollar is $1.45 for one pound, and the United States then experiences severe inflation, we would expect the exchange rate (under a flexible rate system) to shift. What would be the new rate?

a. More than $1.45 for one pound
b. Less than $1.45 for one pound
c. More than one pound for $1.45
d. None of the above

34-3. The dollar, the pound sterling, and the deutsche mark are the currency units of the United States, the United Kingdom, and Germany, respectively. Suppose that these nations decide to go on a gold standard and define the value of their currencies in terms of gold as follows: $35 = 1 ounce of gold; 10 pounds sterling = 1 ounce of gold; and 100 marks = 1 ounce of gold. What would the exchange rate be between the dollar and the pound? Between the dollar and the mark? Between the mark and the pound?

34-4. Examine the following hypothetical data for U.S. international transactions, in billions of dollars.

Exports: goods, 165.8; services, 130.5
Imports: goods, −250.7; services, −99.3
Net unilateral transfers: −20.0

a. What is the balance of trade?
b. What is the balance on goods and services?
c. What is the balance on current account?

34-5. Maintenance of a fixed exchange rate system requires government intervention to keep exchange rates stable. What is the policy implication of this fact? (Hint: Think in terms of the money supply.)

34-6. Suppose that we have the following demand schedule for German beer in the United States per week:

Price per Case	Quantity Demanded (cases)
$40	2
32	4
24	6
16	8
8	10

a. If the price is 30 deutsche marks per case, how many marks are required to purchase each quantity demanded?

b. Now derive the demand schedule for marks per week in the United States to pay for German beer.

c. At a price of 80 cents per mark, how many cases of beer would be imported from Germany per week?

34-7. The accompanying graph shows the supply of and demand for pounds sterling.

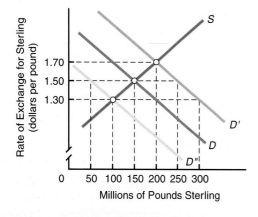

a. Assuming that the demand for sterling is represented by D, what is the dollar price of pounds? What is the equilibrium quantity?

b. Suppose that there is general inflation in the United States. Starting at D, which demand curve could represent this situation? If exchange rates are allowed to float freely, what would be the new dollar price of one pound sterling? What would be the equilibrium quantity?

c. Suppose that the inflation in part (b) occurs and the United States has the dollar price of one pound sterling fixed at $1.50. How would the Federal Reserve be able to accomplish this?

d. Now suppose that instead of inflation, there was general deflation in the United States. Which demand curve could represent this situation? How could the United States maintain a fixed price of $1.50 per pound sterling in this situation?

34-8. Which of the following will cause the yen to appreciate? Explain.

a. U.S. real incomes increase relative to Japanese real incomes.

b. It is expected that in the future the yen will depreciate relative to the dollar.

c. The U.S. inflation rate rises relative to the Japanese inflation rate.

d. The after-tax, risk-adjusted real interest rate in the United States rises relative to that in Japan.

e. U.S. tastes change in favor of Japanese-made goods.

COMPUTER-ASSISTED INSTRUCTION

Suppose that the United States and France have formed a two-country gold standard, and a balance of payments equilibrium exists. What happens if tastes change so that U.S. residents now prefer French goods more than they did previously, other things being constant? This problem shows how balance of payments equilibrium is restored under a gold standard, a specific fixed exchange rate system.

Complete problem and answer appear on disk.

INTERACTING WITH THE INTERNET

Current exchange rates for a number of countries can be found at
http://bin.gnn.com/cgi-bin/gnn/currency
These rates are updated twice a week. More current rates on a just a few countries can be found at
gopher://una.hh.lib.umich.edu/00/ebb/monetary/tenfx.frb
(however, sometimes delays occur with this site).

CHAPTER 35

DEVELOPMENT: ECONOMIC GROWTH AROUND THE WORLD

If you are like many Americans, you do not yet use a home-banking program on your computer in order to make transactions with your local bank. But if you live in Brazil, one of the world's developing countries, you can use a system developed by União de Bancos Brasileiros. How is it possible that such a technological advancement can take place more rapidly in a less developed country than in one of the most developed countries in the world? The answer lies in understanding what causes economic development and why there may be a bright future for the world's developing economies.

PREVIEW QUESTIONS

1. What is a developing country?

2. Must developing countries develop by industrializing?

3. Can developing countries create their own capital stock?

4. Does a lack of protected property rights hinder a developing country's development?

Did You Know That . . . a business best-seller in 1967 called *The American Challenge* predicted that by 1985, the world's economies would be owned and run by a dozen huge American multinationals, producing over 90 percent of the world's manufactured goods? Of course, nothing could be further from the truth today. American companies remain important in the world economy, but they do not dominate. Since that prediction was made, Germany, Japan, South Korea, Hong Kong, Singapore, and Taiwan have grown to become economic powerhouses. Today, there are indeed many "rich" countries, including, of course, the United States. But this nation was not always rich. In fact, it was quite poor 200 years ago. If you go back far enough, every country was poor and undeveloped. Why do some countries develop faster than others? In other words, what causes economic development? Although there are no easy answers to this important question, economists now have enough data to know what conditions favor economic development in the developing world.

PUTTING WORLD POVERTY IN PERSPECTIVE

Most Americans cannot even begin to understand the reality of poverty in the world today. At least one-half, if not two-thirds, of the world's population lives at subsistence level, with just enough to eat for survival. The official poverty level in the United States exceeds the average income in at least half the world. That is not to say that we should ignore problems at home with the poor and homeless simply because they are living better than many people elsewhere in the world. Rather, it is necessary for Americans to keep their perspective on what are considered problems for this country relative to what are considered problems elsewhere.

WHAT IS DEVELOPMENT ECONOMICS?

How did developed countries travel the path out of extreme poverty to relative riches? That is the essential issue of development economics. It is the study of why some countries develop and others do not. Further, it is the study of changes in policies that might help developing countries get richer. It is not good enough simply to say that people in different countries are different and therefore that is why some countries are rich and some countries are poor. Economists do not deny that different cultures create different work ethics, but they are unwilling to accept such a pat and fatalistic answer.

Look at any world map. About four-fifths of the countries you will see on that map are considered relatively poor. The goal of students of development economics is to help the more than 4 billion people today with low living standards join the billion or so who have relatively high living standards.

INDUSTRIALLY ADVANCED ECONOMIES

Any system of defining poor countries and rich countries, developing countries and developed countries, is, of course, arbitrary. Nonetheless, it is instructive to examine some figures on the difference between **industrially advanced countries (IACs)** and so-called developing countries. There are 19 IACs. (Excluded from this classification are countries whose economies are based on a single resource, such as oil, but whose industrial development in other fields is minimal.) The latest data available on the IACs (1995) show an estimated per capita income of $16,341, an annual growth rate of about 2.2 percent, and a population

Industrially advanced countries (IACs)
Canada, Japan, the United States, and the countries of Western Europe, all of which have market economies based on a large skilled labor force and a large technically advanced stock of capital goods.

growth of about .6 percent. At the other end of the scale, the more than 100 developing countries have a per capita income of $980, an annual growth rate of almost 3 percent, and a population growth rate of 2 percent per year, more than three times that of the IACs.

To be sure, we must be careful about accepting such data at face value. There is a tremendous disparity in incomes among the developing countries, and the data are notoriously inaccurate. Nonetheless, it is certain that a tremendous gap exists between average incomes in the IACs and in the developing countries.

Newly Industrialized Economies

Not all developing countries are stuck in abject poverty. The developing countries vary greatly in their ability to experience economic growth, but one group of recently industrialized economies has achieved annual growth rates two and three times that of the United States. These newly industrialized economies are the so-called Four Tigers—Singapore, Hong Kong, Taiwan, and South Korea—all on the Pacific Rim. From 1960 to 1995, per capita income in these economies grew sixfold. One of the reasons the newly industrialized countries have grown so rapidly is that a huge increase in world trade and in international communications has allowed technology to be disseminated much more quickly today than in the past. Indeed, these countries have advanced so quickly that three of the four now have a higher per capita income than Spain, the United Kingdom, and Italy. Yet during the same 35-year period, a number of sub-Saharan African nations experienced a *fall* in real per capita income.

CONCEPTS IN BRIEF

- Any definition of developing countries or industrially advanced countries (IACs) is arbitrary. Nonetheless, we have identified 19 IACs and over 100 developing countries.

- The IACs have per capita incomes that are roughly 17 times the per capita incomes in the developing nations. Population in developing nations is growing more than three times as fast as in the IACs.

- Four newly industrialized nations on the Pacific Rim—Singapore, Taiwan, South Korea, and Hong Kong—have increased their real per capita incomes sixfold since 1960.

ECONOMIC DEVELOPMENT: INDUSTRY VERSUS AGRICULTURE

One of the most widely discussed theories of development concerns the need for balanced growth, with industry and agriculture given equal importance. One characteristic of many developed countries is their high degree of industrialization, although there are clearly exceptions—Hong Kong, for example. In general, nations with relatively high standards of living are more industrialized than countries with low standards of living. The policy prescription then seems obvious: Less developed nations in which a large percentage of the total resources are devoted to agricultural pursuits should attempt to obtain more balanced growth by industrializing.

Although the theory is fairly acceptable at first glance, it leads to some absurd results. We find in many developing countries with steel factories and automobile plants that the people are actually worse off because of this attempted industrialization. Most developing countries currently cannot profitably produce steel or automobiles because they lack the necessary domestic human and physical capital. They can engage in such industrial activities only with heavy government subsidization of the industry itself. Import restrictions abound, preventing the purchase of foreign, mostly cheaper substitutes for the industrial products that the country itself produces. Also, in general, the existence of subsidies leads to a misallocation of resources and a lower economic welfare for the country as a whole.

INTERNATIONAL EXAMPLE
Industrialized Poverty

Amazingly, some of the poorest countries in the world today have some of the highest rates of industrialization. Industry's share of gross output is greater in sub-Saharan Africa than in Denmark, is greater in Zimbabwe, Botswana, and Trinidad and Tobago than in Japan, and is greater in Argentina than in every country in the European Union!

Agriculture represents a relatively low share of gross output in some of the world's poorest countries. For example, agriculture represents a greater share of national output in Denmark than it does in Trinidad and Tobago. The same is true in Spain relative to Botswana and in Portugal relative to Gabon. It is clear that industrialization does not necessarily lead to high standards of living.

FOR CRITICAL ANALYSIS: *If industry represents a large share of gross output in extremely poor countries, what does this tell you about the rate of return on investment in industry in those countries?* ●

The Stages of Development: Agriculture to Industry to Services

If we analyze the development of modern rich nations, we find that they went through three stages. First is the agricultural stage, when most of the population is involved in agriculture. Then comes the manufacturing stage, when much of the population becomes involved in the industrialized sector of the economy. And finally there is a shift toward services. That is exactly what happened in the United States: The so-called tertiary, or service, sector of the economy continues to grow, whereas the manufacturing sector (and its share of employment) is declining in relative importance.

However, it is important to understand the need for early specialization in a nation's comparative advantage. We have repeatedly referred to the doctrine of comparative advantage, and it is even more appropriate for the developing countries of the world. If trading is allowed among nations, a nation is normally best off if it produces what it has a comparative advantage at producing and imports the rest (see Chapter 33). This means that many developing countries should continue to specialize in agricultural production or in labor-intensive manufactured goods.

How Subsidized Agriculture Affects Developing Nations

Modern Western countries have continually subsidized their own agricultural sectors to allow them to compete more easily with the developing countries in this area. If we lived in a world of no subsidization, we would probably see less food being produced in the highly developed Western world (except for the United States, Canada, and Australia) and much more being produced in the developing countries of the rest of the world. They would trade food for manufactured goods. It would seem, then, that one of the most detrimental aspects of our economic policy for the developing countries has been the continued subsidization of the American farmer. The United States, of course, is not alone; virtually the entire European Union does exactly the same thing.

Even with this situation, however, a policy of using higher taxes on imported goods or domestic manufacturing subsidies in order to increase industrialization in the developing countries may do more harm than good. Industrialization is generally beneficial only if it comes about naturally, when the market conditions are such that the countries' entrepreneurs freely decide to build factories instead of increasing farm output because it is profitable to do so.

CONCEPTS IN BRIEF

- A balanced-growth theory predicts that industry and agriculture must grow together in order for a nation to experience growth.
- For many developing countries, balanced growth requires subsidization of manufacturing firms.
- Historically, there are three stages of economic development: the agricultural stage, the manufacturing stage, and the service-sector stage, when a large part of the workforce is employed in providing services.

NATURAL RESOURCES AND ECONOMIC DEVELOPMENT

One theory of development states that for a country to develop, it must have a large natural resource base. The theory continues to assert that much of the world is running out of natural resources, thereby limiting economic growth and development. We must point out that only the narrowest definition of a natural resource could lead to such an opinion. In broader terms, a natural resource is something scarce occurring in nature that we can use for our own purposes. Natural resources therefore include knowledge of the use of something. The natural resources that we could define several hundred years ago did not, for example, include hydroelectric power—no one knew that such a natural resource existed or, indeed, how to make it exist.

In any event, it is difficult to find a strong correlation between the natural resources of a nation and its stage of development. Japan has virtually no crude oil and must import most of the natural resources that it uses as inputs for its industrial production. Brazil has huge amounts of natural resources, including fertile soil and abundant minerals, yet Brazil has a much lower per capita income than Japan. Only when we include the human element of natural resources can we say that natural resources determine economic development.

Natural resources by themselves are not particularly useful for economic development. They must be transformed into something usable for either investment or consumption. This leads us to another aspect of development, the trade-off between investment and consumption. The normal way this subject is analyzed is by dealing with investment simply as capital accumulation.

CAPITAL ACCUMULATION

It is often asserted that a necessary prerequisite for economic development is a large capital stock—machines and other durable goods that can be used to aid in the production of consumption goods and more capital goods in the future. It is true that industrially advanced countries indeed have larger capital stocks per capita than developing countries.

It is also true that the larger the capital stock for any given population, the higher the possible rate of economic growth (assuming that the population makes good use of the capital goods). This is basically one of the foundations for many of the foreign aid programs in which the United States and other countries have engaged. We and other nations have attempted to give developing countries capital so that they, too, might grow. However, the amount of capital that we have actually given to other nations is quite small: a steel mill here, a factory there.

Domestic Capital Formation

How does a developing nation accumulate capital? The answer is that it must save and invest those accumulated savings profitably. Saving, of course, means not consuming. Resources must be released from consumer goods production in order to be used for investment.

Saving and the Poor. It is often stated that people in developing countries cannot save because they are barely subsisting. This is not actually true. Many anthropological studies—of villages in India, for example—have revealed that saving is in fact going on, but it takes forms that we don't recognize in our money economy; for example, saving may involve storing dried onions that can later be traded for other goods. Some researchers speculate that much saving in developing countries takes the form of rearing children who then feel a moral obligation to support their parents during the latter's retirement. In any event, saving does take place even in the most poverty-stricken areas. In general, there is no pronounced relationship between the *percentage* of income saved and the level of income (over the long run).

Basically, then, saving is a method by which individuals can realize an optimal consumption stream throughout their expected lifetimes. The word *optimal* here does not mean adequate or necessary or decent; it means most desirable from the *individual's* point of view (given that individual's resources).

Evidence of Saving in Developing Countries. Savings in developing countries do not necessarily flow into what we might consider productive capital formation projects. We do see the results of literally centuries of saving in the form of religious monuments, such as cathedrals and government buildings. Indeed, one major problem in developing nations is that much of the saving that occurs does not get channeled into productive capital formation. This is also true of much of the foreign aid that has been sent to developing nations. These nations could productively use more factories and a better infrastructure—roads and communications—rather than more government buildings and fancy stadiums built exclusively for merrymaking and sports.

Property Rights and Economic Development

If you were in a country in which bank accounts and businesses were periodically expropriated by the government, how willing would you be to leave your money in a savings account or to invest in a business? Certainly, you would be less willing than if such things never occurred. Periodic expropriation of private property rarely occurs in developed countries. It *has* occurred in numerous developing countries, however. For example, private property was once nationalized in Chile and still is in Cuba. In some cases, former owners are compensated, but rarely for the full value of the property taken over by the state.

Empirically, we have seen that, other things being equal, the more certain private property rights are, the more private capital accumulation there will be. People are more willing to invest their savings in endeavors that will increase their wealth in future years. They have property rights in their wealth that are sanctioned and enforced by the government. In fact, some economic historians have attempted to show that it was the development of well-defined private property rights that allowed Western Europe to increase its growth rate after many centuries of stagnation. The degree of certainty with which one can reap the gains from investing also determines the extent to which businesspeople in *other* countries will invest capital in developing countries. The threat of nationalization in some countries may scare away foreign investment that would allow these nations to become more developed.

In a sentence, economic development depends more on individuals who are able to perceive opportunities and then take advantage of those opportunities than it does on capital or natural resources.[1] Risks will not be taken, though, if the risk takers cannot expect a reward. The political institutions must be such that risk takers are rewarded. That requires well-established property rights, lack of the threat of expropriation of profits, and no fear of government nationalization of businesses.

CONCEPTS IN BRIEF

- Some policymakers believe that a large capital stock is a prerequisite for economic growth and development. They therefore suggest that developing countries need more capital.

- The human element, however, is vital; the labor force must be capable of using any capital that the developing country acquires. This requires training and education.

- Saving is a prerequisite for capital formation.

- Saving goes on even in poor developing countries, although not necessarily in the same form as in rich developed countries.

- Saving and individual capital accumulation will be greater the more certain individuals are about the safety of their wealth.

THE IMPORTANCE OF AN OPEN ECONOMY

The data are conclusive: Open economies experience faster economic development than economies closed to international trade. That is to say, the less government protects the domestic economy by imposing trade barriers, the faster that economy will experience economic development. According to a study by economists Nouriel Roubini and Xavier Sala-i-Martin, when a country goes from being relatively open to relatively closed via government-enacted trade barriers, it will have a 2.5 percentage point decrease in its growth rate.

Open economies accomplish several things. For one, individuals and businesses end up specializing in those endeavors in which they have a comparative advantage. International trade encourages individuals and businesses to discover ways to specialize so that they can become more productive and earn higher incomes. Increased productivity and the subsequent increase in the rate of economic development are the results. Open economies also allow the importation of already developed technology. For instance, no developing country today needs to spend years to figure out how to make computers or how to use them; that has already been done elsewhere.

---

[1]The member nations of OPEC might be considered exceptions to this generalization.

The True Cost of Protectionism

A statistical study of the cost of trade barriers might give the impression that taxes on imported goods simply raise their price to domestic consumers. But there is another cost that is normally hidden. Statisticians call it a *Type II error*—the cost of omission. It is the cost of what would have been had there not been tariff barriers. The best example of a Type II error is the cost of overregulating the pharmaceutical industry. If it causes fewer lifesaving drugs to be introduced, it is a Type II error. When trade is restricted in a developing country, that country's people are deprived of a potential larger range of new goods and production processes. Such new foreign products could spur local support businesses, which in turn would cause other businesses to be created. Developing countries that have restricted the entry of computer products have clearly slowed down the development of their own software industry. Trade barriers sometimes guarantee that new goods and services never appear in protected countries. According to economist Paul Romer of the University of California at Berkeley, because of protectionism, many developing countries do not simply cut back on their consumption of the entire range of goods available to rich countries; rather, they use a smaller quantity of a much smaller range of goods. He calculates that the cumulative forgone benefits from new economic activity blocked by an across-the-board 10 percent tariff in a developing country might be as high as 20 percent of annual national income.

THE IMPORTANCE OF AN EDUCATED POPULATION

Both theoretically and empirically, we know that a more educated workforce aids economic development because it allows individuals to build on the ideas of others. According to economists David Gould and Roy Ruffin, increasing the rate of enrollment in secondary schools by only 2 percentage points, from 8 to 10 percent, raises the average rate of economic growth by half a percent per year. Thus we must conclude that developing countries can advance more rapidly if they invest more heavily in secondary education. Or stated in the negative, economic development cannot be sustained if a nation allows a sizable portion of its population to avoid education. After all, education allows young people who grew up poor to acquire skills that enable them to avoid poverty as adults.

Some of the fastest-growing countries in the world, including the Four Tigers, virtually eliminated illiteracy very early on.

 INTERNATIONAL POLICY EXAMPLE
Should School Tuition Vouchers Be Used in Developing Countries?

Nobel Prize–winning economist Gary Becker has argued in favor of a school voucher system in developing countries. According to his scheme, low-income parents would receive the vouchers, which could then be used at any approved school in their country. The participating schools would also have to provide meals for their students. According to Becker, such vouchers would stimulate competition among private and public schools in developing countries. There is a problem for very poor families, however. They want their children to work to provide income. Becker suggests that such families be given a bonus that offsets the income loss while their children are going to school.

FOR CRITICAL ANALYSIS: Do parents in developed countries have to be compensated for sending their children to school? Explain. ●

LETTING COMPANIES DISAPPEAR: CREATIVE DESTRUCTION

Harvard economist Joseph Schumpeter (1883–1950) championed the concept of *creative destruction*. He pointed out that new technologies and successful new businesses end up destroying old jobs, old companies, and old industries. Change is painful and costly, but it is necessary for economic advancement. Nowhere is this more important than in developing countries, where the principle is often ignored.

Developing countries have had a history of supporting current companies and industries by preventing new technologies and new companies from entering the marketplace. The process of creative destruction has not been allowed to work its magic.

One key element in providing the most favorable condition for economic development is allowing businesses to fail. A corollary to this principle is that governments should not consistently use their taxpayers' money to subsidize or even own businesses. It does little good (and normally lots of harm) for governments in developing countries to own banks, phone companies, electric companies, car companies, or airlines. There are few historical examples of state-owned companies doing other than one thing—draining the public coffers.

Do not get the impression that government-owned and -operated businesses are run by individuals who are somehow less competent than those in the private sector. Rather, the incentive structure for managers in private businesses is different from that for managers in state-owned businesses.

THE RELATIONSHIP BETWEEN POPULATION GROWTH AND ECONOMIC DEVELOPMENT

World population is growing at the rate of 2.8 people each and every second. That turns out to be 242,000 a day, or 88.3 million a year. Today, there are about 5.8 billion people on earth. By the year 2030, according to the United Nations, there will be 8.5 billion. Look at Figure 35-1 on page 784 to see which countries are growing the most.

Just to make sure the message is clear, look at Figure 35-2 on page 784. There you see that virtually all of the growth in population comes from developing nations. Some countries, such as Germany, are expected to lose population over the next several decades.

The Conventional Wisdom

Ever since the Reverend Thomas Robert Malthus wrote his essay *The Principle of Population* in 1798, excessive population growth has been a concern. Modern-day Malthusians are able to generate just as much enthusiasm for the concept that population growth is bad. We are told that rapid population growth threatens economic development and the quality of life. This message was made loud and clear by numerous participants in the United Nations' International Conference on Population and Development held in Cairo, Egypt, in the fall of 1994.

What the Data Show. First of all, Malthus's prediction that population would outstrip food supplies has never held true for the entire world according to economist Nicholas Eberstadt of the Harvard Center for Population Development Studies. Figure 35-3 on page 785 shows how population has grown over the past 35 years. At the same time, the food supply, measured by calories per person, has also increased somewhat steadily.

Also, as you learned in Chapter 32, the price of food, corrected for inflation, has been falling steadily for over a century. That means that the supply of food is expanding faster than the demand caused by increased population.

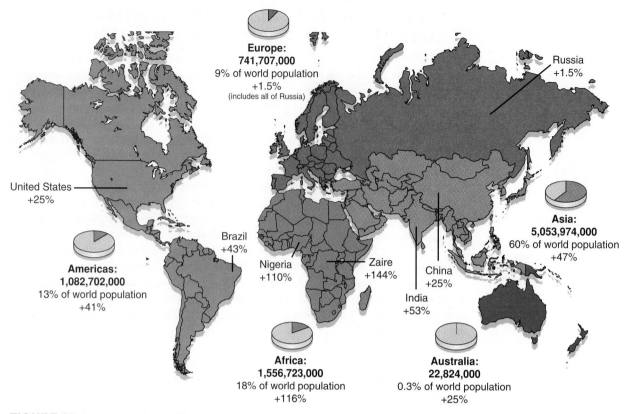

FIGURE 35-1

Expected Growth in World Population by 2030

Asia and Africa are expected to gain the most in population by the year 2030.

Source: United Nations.

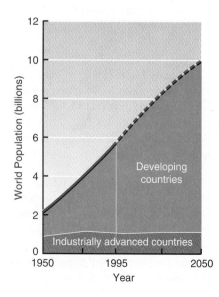

FIGURE 35-2

Population Growth by 2050

Population will increase dramatically in the developing countries. The industrially advanced countries will grow very little in population over the next half century.

Source: Population Reference Bureau.

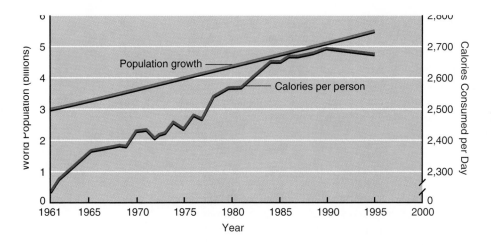

FIGURE 35-3
Population and Food Supplies
Malthus has been proved wrong: Population has not outstripped the world's food supply. In fact, for at least the past half century, calories consumed per person have been increasing at a rate even faster than the increase in population.
Source: U.S. Department of Agriculture.

Population Density and Economic Development. There is no consistent relationship between population density and economic development. Ethiopia has the same number of people per square mile as the United States, but per capita income is only about one-tenth that in the United States. Japan has a higher per capita income than many Western European nations, yet it has more people per square mile than India, one of the poorest nations. Hong Kong is the most densely populated country. Fifty years ago it was one of the poorest, but today its per capita income exceeds that in France and Great Britain. (Hong Kong has almost no natural resources either—it has to import even its drinking water.) As a general proposition, some of the richest countries in the world today are the most densely populated—South Korea, Taiwan, Belgium, the Netherlands, England, Germany, and Japan.

The Relationship Between Population Growth Rates and Economic Development.
Again there seems to be little relationship between economic development and rapid population growth. Consider Malaysia, which grew from a sparsely populated country of villages in the 1890s to a nation of cities in the 1930s. During this period, its population increased from 1.5 million to 6 million, but its standard of living also increased, by about 140 percent. Historically, the largest increases in Western living standards took place during the period when the Western population was growing faster than it is in today's developing countries. Also, in spite of relatively high population growth rates, per capita incomes in many, if not most, developing countries are much higher today than they were four decades ago. Much of the population growth in developing countries has occurred because both adults and children live longer than they used to, not necessarily because families are having more children. There are just fewer deaths caused by malnutrition and contagious diseases than there used to be.

The Relationship Between Average Family Income and Size

One thing that economists know for sure is that over the past century, as nations became richer, the average family size fell. Otherwise stated, the more economic development occurs, the slower the population growth rate. Predictions of birthrates in developing countries have often turned out to be overstated if those countries experience rapid economic growth. This was the case in Hong Kong, Mexico, Taiwan, and Colombia.

786 PART 9 • GLOBAL ECONOMICS

Recent research on population and economic development has revealed that social and economic modernization has been accompanied by what might be called a fertility revolution—the spread of deliberate family size limitation within marriage and a decline in child-bearing. Modernization reduces infant mortality, which in turn reduces the incentive for couples to have many children to make sure that enough will survive to satisfy each couple's demand. Also, modernization lowers the demand for children for a variety of reasons, not the least being that couples in more developed countries do not need to rely on their children to take care of them in old age.

Population and Productivity

Recall the discussion of comparative advantage and specialization in Chapter 33. Specialization turns out to be a function of the size of the market, which is, of course, a function of population. Thus a growing population can help improve the quality of life because it allows individuals to devote their talents to what they are best suited to do—whatever their comparative advantage is. Individuals don't "exhaust" the earth's resources. People create wealth through imagination and innovation. It was not long ago that oil was considered useless. So was sand; today, it is used to make silicone and glass from which computer chips and fiber optics are manufactured.

Three hundred years ago, there were one-tenth the number of humans who now live. Yet the world is incredibly more wealthy than it was three centuries ago. Today, there are four times as many Americans as there were 100 years ago. Yet today we live longer and are about six times richer per capita.

POLICY EXAMPLE
Are the Antinatalists Right?

Paul Ehrlich, the author of several books on the population explosion, argues that the earth can sustain only about 2 billion people. To him and others, the future of the earth looks grim unless the world sustains *negative* population growth—hence the term *antinatalists,* meaning "against births." The nonprofit organization Negative Population Growth (NPG) has produced ads telling us that the optimum U.S. population is about where it was in the 1940s, with 125 to 150 million people. NPG tells us that we should reduce annual immigration to about 200,000 and lower our fertility rate. Pentti Linkola, an amateur biologist in the remote village of Saaksmaki, Finland, wants to go several steps further. He argues that the United States symbolizes the worst ideologies in the world: growth and freedom. He argues that "everything we have developed over the last 100 years should be destroyed." He argues for an end to aid to developing countries, no more asylum for refugees, and other draconian measures to reduce the world's population. His goal is to "save humanity."

FOR CRITICAL ANALYSIS: Would the United States be better off with 100 million fewer Americans? ●

FOREIGN AID

Many nations, including the United States, extend assistance to developing countries. A number of reasons are given to justify this assistance, which can be in the form of grants, low-interest loans, food, military supplies, or technical expertise. Although the humanitarian argument in support of foreign aid is often given, security and economics also enter into the discussion. During the Cold War, the United States gave foreign aid to developing countries in order to support noncommunist regimes or to prevent communist takeovers. The United States also extends foreign aid to help develop foreign markets for the output of U.S. firms. This is particularly true when foreign aid is tied to the purchase of American products. Tied foreign aid requires that the recipient spend all or part of the sum extended as foreign aid on U.S.-produced goods.

The major landmark in the history of foreign aid from the United States was the Marshall Plan. Proposed by Secretary of State George Marshall in an address at Harvard University in June 1948, the plan established the European Recovery Program, which granted over $10 billion ($64 billion in 1996 dollars) in foreign assistance to Europe following World War II. Many observers contend that the Marshall Plan was instrumental in allowing Europe's productive capacity to grow dramatically during the late 1940s and early 1950s.

The United States gives relatively little aid to developing countries on a per capita basis today, and this amount is shrinking in inflation-corrected terms because of the U.S. federal government deficit. Most foreign aid goes to two countries, Israel and Egypt. Japan now gives a greater absolute amount of foreign aid than does the United States.

The Situation in the Developing Countries

The developing countries in the world today cannot be compared to those war-torn European countries at the end of World War II. The modernization of developing countries is a much more complicated task than the restoration of postwar Europe. In many cases, foreign aid to Europe simply helped those countries rebuild an existing and well-functioning capital base. It is one thing merely to replace locomotives and repair tracks in an existing railroad system and quite another to build a railroad system in a country that has none. Perhaps more important is potentially misdirected aid to developing countries. Remember that post–World War II Europe had the human capital of an experienced industrial workforce. Today's developing countries do not, so we cannot expect that foreign aid given to them will have the same result as the aid given to Europe for its restoration after the war. There are many barriers to economic growth in developing countries, including a lack of technical skills and capacities, poorly organized markets, political and social elites unreceptive to change, and non-growth-oriented foreign trade policies.

The Results of Foreign Aid

Since the end of World War II, the developed world has transferred about $2.4 trillion (in today's dollars) to developing countries. The results have been mixed. According to one study by economist Peter Bauer at the London School of Economics, there is little correlation between the level of foreign aid received and changes in living standards. He also found that foreign aid did not necessarily reduce infant mortality rates. His conclusion was that foreign aid simply raised the standard of living of the recipient countries' richest people.

Consider Tanzania. Between 1970 and 1988, this African country received $8.6 billion in aid, four times that country's 1988 gross domestic product. This is the equivalent of someone giving the United States around $20 trillion. During the same period, Sudan was given $9.6 billion, an amount equal to one year's output. Zaire, Togo, Zambia, Mozambique, and Niger each received around $6 billion during the same period. What happened to these billions of dollars? In all of these countries, gross output actually fell. Critics of foreign aid point out that much of the money went into new government centers, showy airports, and grand conference halls. Some of it also went into government officials' Swiss bank accounts. According to economist George Ayittey, Zaire president Mobutu Sese Seko is now worth $10 billion, and Zambia's Kenneth Kaunda is worth $6 billion.

INTERNATIONAL EXAMPLE
The World Bank and the Development of Poor Nations (or Lack Thereof)

The International Bank for Reconstruction and Development, known as the World Bank, was established in 1944. To date it has lent over $300 billion, mostly to poor nations. However, its accomplishments have recently been questioned. For example, since 1951, India has received $55 billion—more foreign aid than any other country on earth—yet over 40 percent of India's population still lives in poverty. In sub-Saharan Africa, massive amounts of money have gone into development planning, yet that region has a lower per capita income than it did before it received aid.

Another criticism of the World Bank is that its lending policies during the 1970s encouraged large-scale, capital-intensive technology, which helped governments in less developed nations to plunder their natural resources. These large-scale projects displaced millions of poor and tribal peoples. In India, World Bank development projects uprooted over 20 million people. Throughout the world, dam projects have altered natural ecologies. Indeed, a mid-1990's internal review of the bank's lending portfolio found that almost 40 percent of recently evaluated projects did not adhere to established environmental and social policies.

The major problem with the World Bank's lending activities is that they help government bureaucracies flourish with funds that could be used to help individuals in the host countries.

FOR CRITICAL ANALYSIS: How does lending to governments in less developed countries hinder market reforms? •

CONCEPTS IN BRIEF

- The openness of an economy can determine it rate, or lack thereof, of economic development. Open economies allow, among other things, the importation of technology from the rest of the world.

- The more educated the workforce, the greater the chance of successful economic development, so enrollment in secondary schools is a key determinant of economic growth.

- While many believe population growth hinders economic development, there is little historic relationship between either population density or growth rates and economic growth rates.

- Critics of foreign aid point out that foreign aid will not increase the rate of economic growth unless a well-functioning capital base and infrastructure are in place.

Can PCs Bridge the Gap Between Less Advanced and More Advanced Economies?

Concepts Applied: International trade, technology, open economies

The PC revolution allows less advanced economies to benefit from new technology at a low investment cost and at a faster rate than in already developed countries.

The PC revolution is showing up in the world's developing countries, sometimes at a faster pace than in the United States. In its wake is a quickly narrowing competitive gap between the more advanced and the less advanced economies. There are several reasons why the PC may be at the heart of improved economies in developing countries.

Low-Price Accessibility

Even in the developed countries, the PC revolution would never have happened without dramatic improvements in microprocessors, memory chips, and software, all occurring while prices continue to drop. Computer technology is now economically viable for most businesses except in the extremely poor countries, according to Eduardo Talero, information technology specialist at the World Bank.

Necessity: The Mother of Invention

Another reason why PC technology has taken off in some countries is simply because of necessity. The advanced home-banking system in Brazil referred to at the beginning of this chapter did depend on cheap technology and software. Also, high inflation rates in Brazil have meant that people who did not deposit their earnings immediately would see the real value of their wealth drop through inflation. Home banking allows for instantaneous transfers of earnings. Necessity is the mother of invention.

The Benefit of Being a Latecomer

Perhaps just as important for developing countries, the fact that they are latecomers has helped them tremendously. Developing countries by definition have had low levels of technology in their business infrastructure. Consequently, they have not invested large amounts in old systems, such as IBM mainframe computers. When the PC revolution came along, they were able to take advantage of it without waiting for their old equipment to wear out. Economic theory predicts that late starters—developing nations—can benefit from new technology at a much faster rate than the already developed countries. And that is what has been happening.

Bringing Down the Trade Barriers

The developing countries that have reduced their trade barriers fastest have seen technology circulate the most freely and have experienced the greatest benefits. Many Latin American countries are leading the way by allowing unfettered imports of computer equipment and software. The PC market in Latin America is growing at a rate of almost 25 percent a year. Sales in Eastern Europe are growing at 15 percent a year. Software sales are growing even faster.

FOR CRITICAL ANALYSIS
1. Why do latecomers adopt technology faster than already established economies?
2. Why is an open economy necessary for technological innovation to spread rapidly?

789

CHAPTER SUMMARY

1. The 19 industrially advanced countries (IACs)—the United States, Japan, Canada, and the countries of Western Europe—have market economies based on a large skilled labor force and a large technically advanced stock of capital goods.

2. One of the major characteristics of developing countries is a high rate of population growth. However, high population growth does not necessarily prevent or retard economic development.

3. Some authorities contend that balanced development of industry and agriculture is necessary for growth in the developing countries. There are, however, exceptions to this rule; Hong Kong is one.

4. Industrialization in many developing countries has involved subsidization of manufacturing. Such subsidization leads to a misallocation of resources and to a lower per capita standard of living for the population even though the country may become more highly industrialized.

5. Capital accumulation is an important determinant of economic development. However, massive transfers of capital to developing countries do not guarantee economic development. Appropriately trained personnel must be available to use the capital given to these countries.

6. Domestic capital formation requires saving—nonconsumption of current income. Even the poorest countries' citizens do some saving. In fact, there is no pronounced relationship between percentage of income saved and level of income.

7. Saving in the developing countries may take on different forms than in more developed countries. For example, having children is a form of saving if those children feel an obligation to support their parents during retirement.

8. The more certain private property rights are, the more private capital accumulation there will be, other things being equal.

DISCUSSION OF PREVIEW QUESTIONS

1. **What is a developing country?**

   Developing countries are arbitrarily defined as those with very low per capita incomes. Relative to developed countries, people in developing countries have lower incomes, life expectancies, literacy rates, and daily caloric intake and higher infant mortality rates.

2. **Must developing countries develop by industrializing?**

   Proponents of the balanced-growth theory point out that the industrially advanced countries (IACs) are highly industrialized and the developing countries are mostly agrarian. They feel that balanced growth requires that the developing countries expand the manufacturing sector; laborers and other resources should be reallocated to promote industrialization. It is often suggested that the developing countries restrict imports of nonagricultural goods to help industrialization. It is alleged that these nations must

   industrialize even if their comparative advantage lies in the production of agricultural goods because they can't compete with the subsidized agricultural sectors of the IACs. Yet it is easy to oversell the pro-industrialization balanced-growth approach. Numerous examples of gross inefficiency can be cited when the developing countries attempted to develop steel and automobile industries. Moreover, when the developing countries restrict the imports of manufactured goods, they lower living standards and promote inefficiency. It would seem that the time to develop the industrial sector would be when it is profitable for businesses to do so.

3. **Can developing countries create their own capital stock?**

   It is often asserted that a large capital stock is necessary for economic development, the developing countries are too poor to save sufficient amounts to develop domestic capital formation, and the IACs should therefore give capital to the developing countries. Experts disagree about the validity of each contention. The question under discussion here deals with the second proposition. A good deal of evidence exists to support the notion that the developing countries do save—although in forms that are not easily observed or cannot be readily converted into capital. Even people with extremely low incomes are forced by economic circumstances to provide for future consumption; they often store dried or cured food. On a nationwide scale, much evidence of capital formation exists: cathedrals, pyramids, great walls, fortresses, government buildings, and so on. Of course, the problem is to get savings into forms that can be used to produce goods or services.

4. Does a lack of protected property rights hinder a developing country's development?
Yes. When individuals fear that their property rights will not be protected, they invest in ways that reflect this risk. Thus people in politically and economically unstable countries prefer to accumulate diamonds, gold, silver, and currency in foreign banks rather than invest in factories, equipment, and savings in domestic bank accounts. Similarly, a nation that expropriates property or nationalizes industry discourages investment by foreign businesses. Many developing countries could be aided to a great extent by attracting foreign investment—but foreign investors will require property right guarantees.

PROBLEMS

(Answers to the odd-numbered problems appear at the back of the book.)

35-1. List five developing countries and five industrially advanced countries.

35-2. What problems are associated with advancements in medicine and health that are made available to developing countries?

35-3. Outline a typical pattern of economic development.

35-4. Suppose that you are shown the following data for two countries, known only as country X and country Z:

Country	GDP	Population
X	$ 81 billion	9 million
Z	135 billion	90 million

a. From this information, which country would you expect to be classified as a developing country? Why?
b. Now suppose that you were also given the following data:

Country	Life Expectancy at Birth (years)	Infant Mortality per 1,000 Live Births	Literacy (%)
X	70	15	60
Z	58	50	70

Are these figures consistent with your answer to part (a)?
c. Should we expect the developing country identified in part (a) to have a much greater population density than the other country?

35-5. Would unrestricted labor immigration end up helping or hurting developing countries? Explain.

35-6. Many countries in Africa have extremely large potential stocks of natural resources. Nonetheless, those natural resources often remain unexploited. Give reasons why this situation continues to exist.

35-7. Sketch a scenario in which population growth causes an increase in income per capita.

COMPUTER-ASSISTED INSTRUCTION

This chapter brings the tutorial full circle; it applies the principles of scientific thinking to questions of economic development, illustrating once again such concepts as observational equivalence, the fallacy of composition, tautologies, and correlation versus causation.

Complete problem and answer appear on disk.

INTERACTING WITH THE INTERNET

Summary macroeconomic data on most countries of the world, including developing ones, can be found in the Penn World Tables at

    http://nber.harvard.edu/pwt56.html

If the release number of the data changes, it might be necessary to search from

    http://nber.harvard.edu

and at

    http://cansim.epas.utoronto.ca:5680/pwt/pwt.html

The latter site allows you to plot the data on-line.

    The World Bank maintains two sites with valuable information on economic development. Perhaps the more important is "Social Indicators of Development," which covers a wide variety of health, demographic, and economic information. It is found at

    http://www.ciesin.org/IC/wbank/sid-home.html

Brief reports on countries that borrow from the World Bank are contained in "Trends in Developing Economies," which is located at

    http://www.ciesin.org/IC/wbank/tde-home.html

ANSWERS TO ODD-NUMBERED PROBLEMS

CHAPTER 1

1-1. A large number of possible factors might affect the probability of death, including age, occupation, diet, and current health. Thus one model would show that the older someone is, the greater is the probability of dying within the next five years; another would show that the riskier the occupation, other things being equal, the greater the probability of dying within five years; and so forth.

1-3. a. We should observe younger drivers to be more frequently involved in traffic accidents than older persons.
   b. Slower monetary expansion should be associated with less inflation.
   c. Professional basketball players receiving smaller salaries should be observed to have done less well in their high school studies.
   d. Employees being promoted rapidly should have lower rates of absenteeism than those being promoted more slowly.

1-5. The decreasing relative attractiveness of mail communication has no doubt decreased students' demand for writing skills. Whether or not the influence has been a significant one is a subject for empirical research. As for the direction of causation, it may well be running both ways. Cheaper nonwritten forms of communication may decrease the demand for writing skills. Lower levels of writing skills probably further increase the demand for audio and video communications media.

1-7. a. Normative, involving a value judgment about what should be
   b. Positive, for it is a statement of what has actually occurred
   c. Positive, for it is a statement of what actually is
   d. Normative, involving a value judgment about what should be

CHAPTER 2

2-1. The law of increasing relative cost does seem to hold because of the principle that some resources may be more suited to one productive use than to another. In moving from butter to guns, the economy will first transfer those resources most easily sacrificed by the butter sector, holding on to the very specialized (to butter) factors until the last. Thus different factor intensities will lead to increasing relative costs.

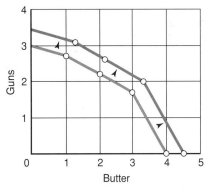

Production Possibilities Curve
for Guns and Butter
(before and after 10 percent growth)

2-3. a. Neither, because each can produce the same total number of jackets per time period (2 jackets per hour)
   b. Neither, because each has the same cost of producing ties ($\frac{2}{3}$ jacket per tie)
   c. No, because with equal costs of production, there are no gains from specialization
   d. Output will be the same as if they did not specialize (16 jackets per day and 24 ties per day)

2-5. a. Only the extra expense of lunch in a restaurant, above what lunch at home would have cost, is part of the cost of going to the game.

b. This is part of the cost of going to the game because you would not have incurred it if you had watched the game on TV at home.

c. This is part of the cost of going to the game because you would not have incurred it if you had watched the game on TV at home.

2-7. For most people, air is probably not an economic good because most of us would not pay simply to have a larger volume of the air we are currently breathing. But for almost everyone, *clean* air is an economic good because most of us would be willing to give something up to have cleaner air.

APPENDIX A

A-1.

y	x
12	4
9	3
6	2
3	1
0	0
-3	-1
-6	-2
-9	-3
-12	-4

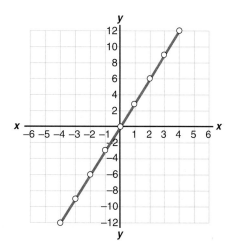

CHAPTER 3

3-1. The equilibrium price is $30. The quantity supplied and demanded is about 10.5 million skateboards per year.

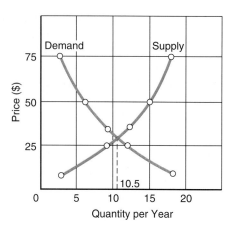

3-3. a. The demand curve for vitamin C will shift outward to the right because the product has taken on a desirable new quality.

b. The demand curve for teachers will shift inward to the left because the substitute good, the interactive educational CD-ROM, is now a lower-cost alternative. (Change in the price of a substitute)

c. The demand curve for beer will shift outward to the right because the price of a complementary good—pretzels—has decreased. Is it any wonder that tavern owners often give pretzels away? (Change in the price of a complement)

3-5. As the graph indicates, demand doesn't change, supply decreases, the equilibrium price of oranges rises, and the equilibrium quantity falls.

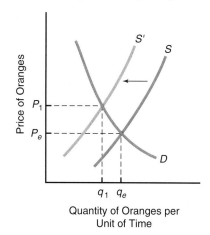

3-7. The speaker has learned well the definition of a surplus but has overlooked one point. The "surpluses" that result from the above-equilibrium minimum prices don't go begging; the excess quantities supplied are in effect purchased by the

Department of Agriculture. In that sense, they are not surpluses at all. When one includes the quantity that is demanded by the Department of Agriculture, along with the quantities being purchased by private purchasers at the support price, the quantity demanded will equal the quantity supplied, and there will be an equilibrium of sorts.

3-9. As the graph illustrates, rain consumers are not willing to pay a positive price to have nature's bounty increased. Thus the equilibrium quantity is 200 centimeters per year (the amount supplied freely by nature), and the equilibrium price is zero (the amount that consumers will pay for an additional unit, given that nature is already producing 200 centimeters per year).

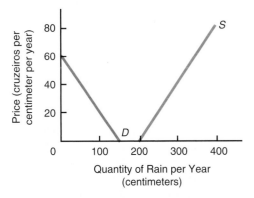

CHAPTER 4

4-1. a. The demand curve will shift to the right (increase).
      b. The supply curve will shift to the right (increase).
      c. Because the price floor, or minimum price, is below the equilibrium price of 50 cents, there will be no effect on price or quantity.
      d. Because the price floor is now greater than the equilibrium price, there will be a surplus at the new price of 75 cents.
      e. Assuming that grapefruits are a substitute for oranges, the demand curve for oranges will shift to the right (increase).
      f. Assuming that oranges are a normal good, the demand curve will shift to the left (decrease).

4-3. The "equilibrium" price is $40 per calculator, and the equilibrium quantity is zero calculators per year. This is so because at a price of $40, the quantity demanded—zero—is equal to the quantity supplied—also zero. None will be produced or bought

because the highest price that any consumer is willing to pay for even a single calculator ($30) is below the lowest price at which any producer is willing to produce even one calculator ($50).

4-5. The equilibrium price is $4 per crate, and the equilibrium quantity is 50 million crates per year. At $2 per crate, the quantity demanded is 90 million crates per year and the quantity supplied is 10. This is called a shortage, or excess quantity demanded. The excess quantity demanded is 80 million crates per year. At $5 per crate, the quantity demanded is 20 million crates per year and the quantity supplied is 80 million crates. This is called a surplus, or excess quantity supplied. The excess quantity supplied is 60 million crates per year.

4-7. As shown in the graph, if the equilibrium price of oranges is 10 cents, a price floor of 15 cents will result in a surplus equal to $Q_s - Q_d$. A price floor of 5 cents per orange will have no effect, however, because it is below the equilibrium price and thus does not prevent suppliers and demanders from doing what they want to do—produce and consume Q_e oranges at 10 cents each.

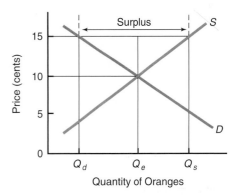

CHAPTER 5

5-1. The marginal tax rate on the first $3,000 of taxable income is 0 percent because no taxes are imposed until $5,000 is earned. The marginal rate on $10,000 is 20 percent, as it is on $100,000 and all other amounts above the $5,000 level, because for each additional dollar earned after $5,000, 20 cents will be taxed away. The average tax rate, which is the tax amount divided by the pretax income, is 0 for $3,000, 10 percent for $10,000, and 19 percent for $100,000. The average tax rate will *approach* a maximum of 20 percent as income increases. It cannot reach *exactly* 20 percent be-cause of the untaxed $5,000 at the beginning. Such is the nature of a *degressive* tax system.

5-3. Mr. Smith pays nothing on his first $1,500 of in-come, 14 percent ($70) on the $500 of earnings be-tween $1,500 and $2,000, and 20 percent ($100) on the $500 that he earns above $2,000. Thus Mr. Smith has a total tax bill of $170 on an income of $2,500; his average tax rate is 6.8 percent, and his marginal tax rate is 20 percent.

5-5. Among the ideas that have been proposed is that a good tax system should meet the requirements of equity, efficiency, and ease of administration. Equi-ty means that each person should pay a "fair share." The efficiency requirement is that the tax system should minimize interferences with economic deci-sions. Ease of administration means that the tax system should not be excessively costly to adminis-ter and that it should be understandable to the tax-payer. Even though the U.S. tax system was not designed through a master plan, these ideas have had their influence on the American system.

5-7. There are both public good and private good as-pects to police protection. When an officer patrols the neighborhood in a police car, criminals are de-terred from burglarizing every home in the neigh-borhood; this is a public good aspect of police pro-tection because the protection afforded one person is simultaneously afforded all of the neighbors. But when an officer spends time arresting the person who broke into Mr. Smith's home, that is time the officer cannot spend arresting the person who broke into Ms. Jones's home; this is the private good aspect of police protection, for when these services are provided Mr. Smith, Ms. Jones is ex-cluded from simultaneously using those services.

5-9. a. If you give and everyone else does also, you account for 1 percent. If you are the only one who gives, you account for 100 percent. If you give nothing, you account for 0 percent, regard-less of what others give.
b. In principle, your contribution matters what-ever the level of participation. But as a practical matter, if participation is near 100 percent, the absence of your contribution may have little practical effect.
c. There is no free ride. If you do not make your contribution, total contributions will be lower, and the quality of the services provided will be lower.

5-11. Strictly speaking, probably all the items except national defense should go into the column labeled "Private Goods," either because residents *could* be excluded from consuming them or because one per-son's consumption reduces the amount available for other individuals. As a practical matter, however, there are several goods on the list (public television, elementary education, and the museum) for which full exclusion generally does not take place and/or consumption by one person reduces the amount that other persons can consume by only a small amount.

CHAPTER 6

6-1. On the supply side, all of the industries responsible for automobile inputs would have to be consid-ered. This would include steel (and coke and coal), glass, tires (and rubber), plastics, railroads (and thus steel again), aluminum (and electricity), and manufacturers of stereos, hubcaps, and air condi-tioners, to name a few. On the demand side, you would have to take into account industries involv-ing complements (such as oil, gasoline, concrete, and asphalt) and substitutes (including bicycles, motorcycles, buses, and walking shoes). More-over, resource allocation decisions regarding labor and the other inputs, complements, and substitutes for these goods must also be made.

6-3. a. Profit equals total revenue minus total cost. Because revenue is fixed (at $172), if the firm wishes to maximize profit, this is equivalent to minimizing costs. To find total costs, simply multiply the price of each input by the amount of the input that must be used for each technique.

Costs of A = ($10)(7) + ($2)(6) + ($15)(2) + ($8)(1) = $120
Costs of B = ($10)(4) + ($2)(7) + ($15)(6) + ($8)(3) = $168
Costs of C = ($10)(1) + ($2)(18) + ($15)(3) + ($8)(2) = $107

Because C has the lowest costs, it yields the highest profits, and thus it will be used.
b. Profit equals $172 − $107 = $65.
c. Each technique's costs rise by the increase in the price of labor multiplied by the amount of labor used by that technique. Because tech-nique A uses the least amount of labor, its costs rise the least, and it thus becomes the lowest-cost technique at $132. (The new cost of B is

$182, and the new cost of C is $143.) Hence technique A will be used, resulting in profits of $172 − $132 = $40.

6-5. a. In the market system, the techniques that yield the highest (positive) profits will be used.
b. Profit equals total revenue minus total cost. Because revenue from 100 units is fixed (at $100), if the firm wishes to maximize profit, this is equivalent to minimizing costs. To find total costs, simply multiply the price of each input by the amount of the input that must be used for each technique.

Costs of A = ($10)(6) + ($8)(5) = $100
Costs of B = ($10)(5) + ($8)(6) = $98
Costs of C = ($10)(4) + ($8)(7) = $96

Because technique C has the lowest costs, it also yields the highest profits ($100 − $96 = $4).
c. Following the same methods yields these costs: A = $98, B = $100, and C = $102. Technique A will be used because it is the most profitable.
d. The profits from using technique A to produce 100 units of X are $100 − $98 = $2.

CHAPTER 19

19-1. For you, the marginal utility of the fifth pound of oranges is equal to the marginal utility of the third ear of corn. Apparently, your sister's tastes differ from yours—for her, the marginal utilities are not equal. For her, corn's marginal utility is too low, while that of oranges is too high—that's why she wants you to get rid of some of the corn (raising its marginal utility). She would have you do this until marginal utilities, for her, were equal. If you follow her suggestions, you will end up with a market basket that maximizes *her* utility subject to the constraint of *your* income. Is it any wonder that shopping from someone else's list is a frustrating task?

19-3. Her marginal utility is 100 at $1, 200 at 50 cents, and 50 at $2. To calculate marginal utility per dollar, divide marginal utility by price per unit.

19-5. Optimum satisfaction is reached when marginal utilities per dollar of both goods are equal. This occurs at 102 units of A and 11 units of B. (Marginal utility per dollar is 1.77.)

19-7. Either your income or the relative price of eggs and bacon must have changed. Without more information, you can't make any judgments about whether you are better or worse off.

19-9. a. 20
b. 10
c. With consumption of the third unit of X

APPENDIX E

E-1. The problem here is that such preferences are inconsistent (*intransitive* is the word that economists use). If this consumer's tastes really are this way, then when confronted with a choice among A, B, and C, she will be horribly confused because A is preferred to B, which is preferred to C, which is preferred to A, which is preferred to B, which is preferred to C, and so on forever. Economists generally assume that preferences are consistent (or *transitive*): If A is preferred to B and B is preferred to C, then A is preferred to C. Regardless of what people may *say* about their preferences, the assumption of transitivity seems to do quite well in predicting what people actually do.

E-3. With an income of $100 and the original prices, you could have consumed *either* 50 pounds of beef *or* 5 units of shelter *or* any linear combination shown by the budget line labeled "Original" on the graph below. With the same income but the new prices, you can now consume 25 pounds of beef or 10 units of shelter or any linear combination shown by the line labeled "New budget." Without information about your preferences, there is no way to tell whether you are better off or worse off. Draw a few indifference curves on the diagram. You will find that if you are a "shelter lover" (your indifference curves are relatively steep), the decline in the relative price of shelter will tend to make you better off. Conversely, if you are a "beef lover" (your indifference curves are relatively flat), the rise in the relative price of beef will make you worse off.

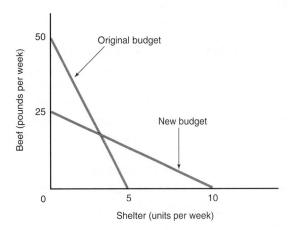

E-5. The first burrito is substituted at a rate of 10 servings of yogurt per burrito; the second burrito is substituted at a rate of 4:1; the third at a rate of 3:1; and the fourth at a rate of 2:1.

E-7. a. This person is simply indifferent between going or staying, an attitude that is perfectly consistent with our assumptions about consumer preferences.

b. This statement denies the law of substitution and so is inconsistent with our assumptions about preferences.

c. If we interpret "if I had my way" to mean "if I had an unlimited budget," this statement simply says that there is nonsatiation for these goods for this consumer—which is perfectly consistent with our assumptions about preferences.

CHAPTER 20

20-1. a.

Quantity Demanded per Week (ounces)	Price per Ounce	Elasticity
1,000	$ 5	$\frac{1}{3}$, or .33
800	10	$\frac{5}{7}$, or .714
600	15	$\frac{7}{5}$, or 1.4
400	20	$\frac{9}{3}$, or 3
200	25	

b. There are several ways to explain why elasticity is greater at higher prices on a linear curve. At higher prices, a given price change will result in a smaller percentage price change. The smaller resulting denominator of the elasticity ratio leads to a larger overall ratio. Similarly, as prices rise, quantities fall, thereby implying greater percentage quantity changes for a given absolute quantity change, and a larger numerator. Alternatively, the sizes of total revenue changes first increase and then decrease as price is lowered throughout a linear demand curve, thus implying declining elasticity.

20-3. a. Using averages in the elasticity equation, the income elasticity of demand for VCRs is .6666 ÷ .2857 = 2.33. It is income-elastic.

b. It is presumably a luxury good.

20-5. The problem is with the denominator, percentage change in P. Because the initial price was zero, any increase in price is of infinite percentage. However, if we take the average elasticity over a segment, there will be no problem. P will become the average of P_1 (= 0) and P_2 (= 10), or $(P_1 + P_2)/2 = 5$.

20-7. a. $E_p = \dfrac{50}{(475 + 525)/2} \div \dfrac{.02}{(.15 + .17)/2} = .8$

b. Demand is price-inelastic.

c. $E_s = \dfrac{75}{(525 + 600)/2} \div \dfrac{.02}{(.15 + .17)/2} = 1.067$

d. Supply is price-elastic (but only slightly so).

20-9. In each case, "before" is before the development of an acceptable substitute for the good in question, and "after" is after the development of that substitute. For example, between 1840 and 1880, the railroad emerged as a good substitute for canal transportation. In general, the better the substitutes for a good, the greater the price elasticity of demand for that good. Thus in each case we would expect the price elasticity of demand to be higher after the emergence of the substitute.

CHAPTER 21

21-1. Taxation of corporate dividend income can be thought of as a tax on the corporate form of organization. Increasing the amount of dividends exempt from taxes thus amounts to reducing taxes on dividends and hence reducing the tax on the corporate form of organization. As a result, more firms would choose to incorporate, and fewer would choose to be proprietorships or partnerships.

21-3. For simplicity, assume that potential lenders care only about the expected value of their lending decisions. If $10,000 is lent to a risk-free borrower at 10 percent interest, the borrower is certain to have ($10,000)(1 + .10) = $11,000 one year from now. If a loan is made to the risky firm, the borrower has a 20 percent chance of ending up with nothing and an 80 percent chance of repayment in full. Hence the amount the borrower expects to end up with is E = (.20)(0) + (.80)($10,000)(1 + R), where R is the rate of interest charged to the risky firm. We seek the value of R that makes E equal to $11,000 because that will make the lender equally well off whether lending to the risk-free borrower or to the risky borrower. Thus we solve $11,000 = 0 + ($8,000)(1 + R) so that at a rate of interest $R = 37.5$ percent, the risky firm will be able to borrow the $10,000.

CHAPTER 22

22-1. The opportunity cost of continuing to possess the van is being ignored. For example, if the van could be sold without much problem for $10,000 and you could earn 10 percent per year by investing that $10,000 in something else, the opportunity cost of keeping the van is $1,000 per year.

22-3. a. $1
    b. 5 cents
    c. $1
    d. 10 cents
    e. It is rising.
    f. When the marginal product of labor is rising, the marginal cost of output falls; when the marginal product of labor is falling, the marginal cost of output rises.

22-5. The long-run average costs represent the points that give the least unit cost of producing any given rate of output. The concept is important when one must decide which scale of operations to adopt. Such a decision usually takes the form of deciding what size "plant" to construct.

22-7. a.

Output	AVC
0	$ 0
5	20
10	18
20	11
40	8

b. The marginal cost is $40 when increasing output from 10 to 20 units and $100 when increasing from 20 to 40.

c.

Output	ATC
0	$ 0
5	60
10	38
20	21
40	13

22-9.

Units of Labor	Total Product	Marginal Product	Average Product
6	120	—	20
7	147	27	21
8	170	23	21.25
9	180	10	20

CHAPTER 23

23-1.

Output (units)	Fixed Cost	AFC	Variable Cost	AVC	Total Cost	ATC	MC
1	$100	$100.00	$ 40	$40	$140	$140.00	$40
2	100	50.00	70	35	170	85.00	30
3	100	33.33	120	40	220	73.33	50
4	100	25.00	180	45	280	70.00	60
5	100	20.00	250	50	350	70.00	70
6	100	16.67	330	55	430	71.67	80

a. The price would have to drop below $35 before the firm would shut down in the short run.

b. $70 is the short-run break-even point for the firm. The output at this price would be 5 units per period.

c. At a price of $76, the firm would produce 5 units and earn a profit of $30 ($6 per unit over 5 units).

23-3. The industry demand curve is negatively sloped; it is relevant insofar as its interaction with the industry supply curve (ΣMC) determines the product price. The demand the individual firm faces, however, is infinitely elastic (horizontal) at the current market price.

23-5. a. $100
  b. $100
  c. $100
  d. $100

23-7. For simplicity, assume that your friend computed her "profit" the way many small businesses do: She ignored the opportunity cost of her time and her money. Instead of operating the car wash, she could have earned $25,000 at the collection agency plus $12,000 ($200,000 $\times$ 6 percent) on her savings. Thus the opportunity cost to her of operating the car wash was $37,000. Subtracting this amount from the $40,000 yields $3,000, which is her actual profit, over and above opportunity costs. You would tell her she really isn't making such great profits.

CHAPTER 24

24-1. a. The rectangle that shows total costs under ATC$_1$ is 0WCQ. Total revenue is shown by 0XBQ.

This monopolist is in an economic profit situation. MC = MR is the output at which profit—the difference between total cost and total revenue—is maximized.
  b. With ATC$_2$, the rectangle showing total costs is 0XBQ. The same rectangle, 0XBQ, gives total revenue. This monopolist is breaking even. MC = MR shows the only quantity that does not cause losses.
  c. Under ATC$_3$, total costs are represented by rectangle 0YAQ, total revenue by 0XBQ. Here the monopolist is operating at an economic loss, which is minimized by producing where MC = MR.

24-3. Four conditions are necessary: (1) market power, (2) ability to separate markets at a reasonable cost, (3) differing price elasticities of demand, and (4) ability to prevent resale.

24-5. If E_p is numerically greater than 1 (elastic), marginal revenue is positive; a decrease in price will result in more total revenues. If E_p is numerically equal to 1 (unit-elastic), marginal revenue is 0; a change in price will not affect total revenues at all. If E_p is numerically less than 1 (inelastic), marginal revenue is negative; a decrease in price will result in less total revenues.

24-7. a.

Price	Quantity Demanded	Total Revenue	Marginal Revenue	Total Cost	Marginal Cost	Profit or Loss
$20	0	$ 0	—	$ 4	—	$−4
16	1	16	$ 16	10	$ 6	6
12	2	24	8	14	4	10
10	3	30	6	20	6	10
7	4	28	−2	28	8	0
4	5	20	−8	40	12	−20
0	6	0	−20	54	14	−54

  b. The firm would operate at a loss if it produced 0, 5, or 6 units.

  c. The firm would break even at a rate of output of 4 units.

d. The firm would maximize its profits by producing either 2 or 3 units. At either of those two outputs, it would be earning a profit of $10.

24-9. a. TR = $10,000, $16,000, $18,000, $16,000, $10,000, $3,000

b. MR = $6,000, $2,000, −$2,000, −$6,000, −$7,000

c. 3,000 units

d. A profit-maximizing firm always sets MR = MC, and at any output level greater than 3,000, MR is negative. Naturally, MC can never be negative, thus ensuring that output levels where MR is negative are impossible for a profit-maximizing firm.

CHAPTER 25

25-1. The marginal revenue of this ad campaign is $1,000. There was an addition of 40 cars per week at $25 per car. To determine whether profits have risen, we would have to know how much additional cost was incurred in the tuning of these cars, as well as the cost of the advertisement itself.

25-3. a. Approximately 64 percent ($525 million ÷ $825 million).

b. The ratio would rise as the industry is more narrowly defined and fall as it is more broadly defined. Because an "industry" is arbitrarily defined, concentration ratios may be misleading.

25-5. The kink arises from the assumptions of the model. It is assumed that if any one firm raises its price, none of the others will follow. Consequently, a maverick firm's price increase will result in a drastic decrease in its total revenue. Conversely, the model assumes that any price decrease will be matched by all rivals. For this reason, the quantity demanded will probably not increase enough to cover increased costs. And profit will probably be less. Under these assumptions, it is in no individual firm's interest to "rock the boat."

25-7. The advertising campaign must increase weekly ticket revenues by at least $1,000 per week or it will be discontinued. This will require an additional 200 movie viewers each week.

25-9. The payoff matrix looks like this:

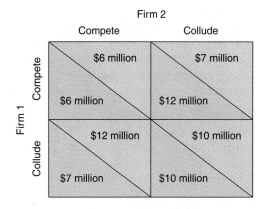

This situation parallels that of the prisoners' dilemma in that it is in the firms' *collective* interest to collude but in their *individual* interests to compete. If the possibility for collusion is a one-time-only arrangement, we have exactly the circumstances of the classic prisoners' dilemma, in which the dominant strategy is to compete, resulting in profits of $6 million for each firm. (This sounds good until you remember that each is *losing* $4 million relative to the joint maximum possible with collusion!) If this is a repeating game and if each firm can observe the behavior of its rival, it may be possible for the firms to overcome their dilemma and reach the joint maximum—for example, by employing the "tit for tat" strategy discussed in the text.

CHAPTER 26

26-1. a. Quantity produced would be Q_b, and price would be P_c.

b. Losses would equal the rectangle P_bBCP_c.

26-3. There will still be political pressure from Congress if you enforce new regulations that dramatically increase the costs and hence the prices of products. Thus you can simply do anything you feel like concerning new rules in the workplace. If you must now consider costs, you might want to estimate the impact each new rule has on the unit cost of each product affected. You would compare the total costs thus incurred because of the new rule with the estimated benefits to the community in terms of higher levels of worker safety and health.

26-5. By definition, a natural monopolist's costs are lower than those of potential entrants. Hence although other firms may be free to enter, they are unlikely to do so. The natural monopolist can thus earn economic profits equal to the difference between its costs and its potential rivals' costs.

26-7. Liquor store owners do not like to compete any more than anyone else does. Nevertheless, simply telling the truth about this distaste is unlikely to garner them much political support in favor of restricting entry into their industry. What the liquor store owners seek is an argument that what is good for them is also good for you, and many people probably find the idea of a liquor store next door distasteful.

CHAPTER 27

27-1.

Quantity of Labor	Total Product per Week	MPP	MRP
1	250	250	$500
2	450	200	400
3	600	150	300
4	700	100	200
5	750	50	100
6	750	0	0

a. Demand schedule for labor:

Weekly Wage	Laborers Demanded per Week
$500	1
400	2
300	3
200	4
100	5

b. $100 each
c. Four

27-3. a. 15 million worker-hours per time period
b. 10 million per time period
c. Buyers can get all the labor they want at W_1; laborers can't sell all they want to sell at W_1.
d. Because a surplus of labor exists, the unemployed will offer to work for less, and industry wage rates will fall toward W_e.

27-5. Suppose that the demand for the output product is highly elastic. Even a relatively small increase in the price of the input factor, which correspondingly raises the price of the output product, will cause a large decrease in the quantity of output demanded and therefore in the employment of the input.

27-7. The MRP of labor is $40 per worker-day ($3,040 less $3,000, divided by a change in labor input of one worker-day). The maximum wage that would still make it worthwhile to hire this additional employee would be $39.99 per day. If the going market wage is above that figure, you will not expand output.

27-9. Imposing limitations such as these implicitly reduces the ability of employers to compete for your services. Thus you can expect to receive a lower wage and to work in a less desirable job.

CHAPTER 28

28-1. a. Marginal revenue product
b. S
c. Q_m
d. W_m

28-3. Some examples would be Coors beer in Golden, Colorado; Bethlehem Steel in Bethlehem, Pennsylvania; Winnebago Corporation in Forest City, Iowa; and many coal-mining companies in towns in West Virginia. As long as your example is one of an employer that is dominant in its local labor market selling in fairly competitive markets, you are correct.

28-5. No, you should not. The MRP when you employ 31 people is $89.50 ($99.50 in revenue from selling the twenty-first unit, less $10 forgone in selling the first 20 units for 50 cents less than originally). The MFC is $91 ($61 to attract the twenty-first employee to your firm, plus the additional $1 per day to each of the original 20 employees). Because MFC exceeds MRP, you should not expand output.

28-7. Because the union acts in the interests of its members and the competitive wage is lower than the highest wage the union can obtain for its members.

28-9. The monopsonist's decisions about how much to purchase influence the price of the good it is buying. As a result, the marginal factor cost curve facing a monopsonist lies above the average factor cost curve (which is the supply curve of the industry producing the good being purchased by the monopsonist).

CHAPTER 29

29-1. The statement is false. Although there may be a substantial portion of rent in the revenues from these museums, we would have to assume that the museums are absolutely costless to keep in their current use in order to make the statement that *all* revenues are economic rent. The most obvious expenses of keeping the museums operating are the costs of maintenance: cleaning, lighting, and other overhead costs. But these may be minor compared to the opportunity cost involved in keeping the museum *as a museum*. The buildings might make ideal government office buildings. They may be on land that would be extremely valuable if sold on the private real estate market. If there are any such alternative uses, the value of these uses must be subtracted from the current revenues in order to arrive at the true level of economic rent. Forgoing these alternative opportunities is as much a cost of operating the museum as the monthly utility bill.

29-3. The statement is false. Because a firm utilizes an input only to the point that the input's MRP is equal to its price, and marginal product is declining, it follows that all the intramarginal (up-to-the-marginal) units are producing more value than they are being paid. This differential is used to compensate for other factor inputs. The residual, if any, would be profits.

29-5. a. 9 percent
      b. The equilibrium interest rate will increase.
      c. 5 percent

29-7. In each case, the asset that qualifies the borrower for a lower interest rate is better collateral (or security) for the lender and thus reduces both the chances of default and the lender's losses in the event that default does occur.

29-9. They would be reduced but not necessarily eliminated (because, for example, economic profits due to entry restrictions might still persist).

CHAPTER 30

30-1. Whites might invest more in human capital; blacks might receive less and lower-quality education and/or training; blacks in the workforce may, on average, be younger; discrimination may exist.

30-3. Productivity and equality.

30-5. Such a program would drastically reduce efficiency. It would eliminate individuals' incentives to maximize the economic value of resources because they would receive no reward for doing so. It would also eliminate their incentive to minimize production costs because there would be no penalty for failing to do so.

30-7. When governments pay for health care, hospitals have reduced incentives to operate efficiently because they are less likely to be penalized for being inefficient. Bureaucrats are less likely to provide the services that patients want at the lowest cost because the rewards from doing so are diminished when the government (rather than the patient) pays for the services. Finally, because the patient is not directly footing the bill, the patient has less incentive to choose wisely (that is, in a manner that equates the true marginal benefits and costs) when choosing health care.

CHAPTER 31

31-1. When the external costs are added to the supply curve (which is itself the sum of marginal costs of the industry), the total (private plus public) marginal costs of production are above the private supply schedule. At quantity Q_1 in the graph on the next page, marginal costs to society are greater than the value attached to the marginal unit. The demand curve is below the social supply curve. To bring marginal cost and marginal benefit back into line, thus promoting an economically efficient allocation of resources, quantity would have to be reduced to Q_2 and price raised to P_2.

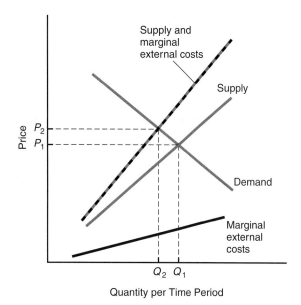

Quantity per Time Period

31-3. a. The price of polluting should be set according to the marginal economic damage imposed by polluters; this means that similar quantities of pollution will cost polluters different prices in different parts of the country; pollution will be more costly in New York City than in a small town in the Midwest.

b. Firms that find it cheaper to treat will do so; firms that find it cheaper to pay to pollute will pollute.

c. Yes, some firms will be forced to shut down due to increased costs; this is efficient, as the true costs to society of their operations were not paid by them and their customers; they were able to remain in business only by imposing costs on third parties.

d. This might be good because now the people who are using the resources will be forced to pay for them instead of imposing costs on others. Those who are *not* using these products were, in effect, subsidizing lower prices to those who were. This new solution seems more fair and is certainly efficient.

31-5. Everyone owns them and nobody owns them. Consequently, there is no incentive for any user to be concerned with the future value of the resource in question. This is perhaps most clearly observable in the behavior of fishing boat owners. The goal of each boat owner is to harvest fish as long as marginal private cost is less than the going price of such fish. The opportunity cost of depleting the stock of fish does not affect the decisions of the proprietor. In light of the nonownership of the fish, any single boat operator would be foolish to behave otherwise.

31-7.

Annual Units of Pollution	a. Marginal Benefits	b. Marginal Costs
0	—	—
1	$ 30	$150
2	40	100
3	80	80
4	120	60
5	160	20

a. The net gain is $(430 - 150) - 80 = 200$.

b. The net gain is $430 - 410 = 20$.

c. The optimal level is between 2 and 3 units, or where marginal benefit equals marginal cost.

31-9. The economically efficient amount of pollution occurs at a level at which the marginal costs of reducing it further would just exceed any benefits from that reduction. If pollution is reduced below this point, we would be better off with more pollution. The government might directly require firms or individuals to generate too little pollution (for example, through inappropriate environmental regulations), or it might establish pollution fees, fines, or taxes that overstate the damages done by the pollution and thus induce firms or individuals to reduce pollution too much.

CHAPTER 32

32-1. The existence of these costs implies the notion of rational ignorance, so that individuals choose not to be informed about certain issues because the cost of being informed is high relative to any benefit forthcoming from the state of the issue. This also contributes to the growth of special-interest groups because individuals have no strong economic incentive to act against them.

32-3. Legislators find themselves in a situation much like a prisoners' dilemma (see Chapter 25): They have a collective incentive to act in the best interests of society as a whole but individual incentives to act in the interests of their own constituents or other narrow special interests. The favors handed out by legislators could, in principle, come in the form of either lower taxes or higher spending. As a practical matter, it is usually easier to disguise higher spending as something socially beneficial for which the recipient is uniquely qualified. Hence spending (and thus the size of the government) tends to increase. (Clearly there is some limit to this process, for the government cannot be larger than the economy as a whole. Nevertheless, the limit does not appear to be in sight.)

32-5. Currently, lobbyists are paid to influence state legislators, the benefits of which may redound to those seeking the political favors for many years, given that often state legislators stay in office for many years. Under a system of term limits, each legislator's time in office is definitely terminated after, for example, 12 years. Thus, using the theory of public choice, we predict that fewer resources will be used to influence each legislator in those states that have term limits. The reason is that the potential payoff will last a shorter time period. More newly elected legislators will have to be influenced under term limits, so fewer resources will go toward influencing each legislator individually, all other things held constant.

32-7. a. 20 percent of 1.9 million is 380,000 farms.
   b. Oligopoly seems highly unlikely in this industry in the foreseeable future—there are simply too many firms.

32-9. One of the trickiest things about handing out subsidies is that everybody wants to receive them but not everyone can receive them (at least not after netting out the taxes used to pay for them). Farmers are uniquely positioned to be the recipients of subsidies because of the natural limiting factor—farmland—that constrains their numbers.

32-11. The demand for farmland would fall, resulting in lower prices for such land and a diversion of some of it to other uses, possibly including residential neighborhoods or national parks. The demand for other farm resources—including the labor of farmers—would also fall, inducing some of these resources to move into alternative occupations as well. The price of food would fall, reducing malnutrition but also possibly increasing obesity. Imports of some crops (such as sugar) would rise sharply, while production of goods that use foodstuffs as inputs would also rise. These (and many other) effects would be greatly dampened today if the change in policy were not to take place until 20 years from now—partly because the present value of distant events is small and partly because Congress would have plenty of opportunities over 20 years to reverse itself.

CHAPTER 33

33-1. a. The opportunity cost to the United States of producing one ounce of caviar is two bushels of wheat. The six hours that were needed to make the caviar could have been used to grow two bushels. The opportunity cost of producing one bushel of wheat is $\frac{1}{2}$ ounce of caviar.
   b. The opportunity cost to Russia of producing one ounce of caviar is $1\frac{1}{2}$ bushels of wheat. The opportunity cost of producing a bushel of wheat in Russia is $\frac{2}{3}$ ounce of caviar.
   c. The United States has a comparative advantage in wheat because it has a lower opportunity cost in terms of caviar. Russia has a comparative advantage in caviar. Less wheat is forgone to produce an ounce of caviar in Russia.

33-3. The assumption given in the question is equivalent to the United States' having an absolute advantage in the production of all goods and services. But the basis of world trade lies in differences in *comparative* advantage. As long as other countries have a lower opportunity cost in producing some goods and services, the United States will benefit from international trade.

33-5. Tariffs yield government revenues; quotas do not.

33-7. a. One million pounds are produced and 2 million pounds are imported.
b. With a 10-cent tariff, 1.5 million pounds would be produced and 1 million pounds would be imported. Government revenues would amount to ($2.5 million − $1.5 million) × $.10 = $100,000.
c. With a 20-cent tariff, domestic growers can receive 70 cents per pound. They will produce 2 million pounds, and no grapes will be imported, in which case government revenues are zero.

33-9. Consider trade between the United States and Canada. The United States purchases timber from Canada, and Canada purchases computers from the United States. Ultimately, the Canadians pay for U.S.-made computers with the timber that they sell here. If the United States imposes a tax on Canadian timber and thus reduces the amount of timber that the Canadians are able to sell to the United States, the necessary result is that the Canadians will be able to buy fewer American computers. American exports of computers will decline as a result of the reduction in American imports of timber.

CHAPTER 34

34-1. The answer is (c). A declining dollar price of the pound implies an increasing pound price of the dollar—appreciation of the dollar. (a) is incorrect because an increase in demand for U.S. products would affect the supply of pounds and the demand for dollars, whereas here we are dealing with the demand for pounds. (b) explains a phenomenon that would have just the opposite result as that shown in the graph: An increased U.S. demand for British goods would lead to an increase in the demand for the pound, not a decrease as shown. (d) is incorrect because the pound depreciates.

34-3. One pound equals $3.50; $1 equals .2857 pound. One mark equals 35 cents; $1 equals 2.857 marks. One mark equals .1 pound; one pound equals 10 marks.

34-5. To maintain the exchange rate, domestic policy variables such as the money supply are also affected. Suppose that the government plans an expansive monetary policy to encourage output growth. A balance of payments deficit leads the government to buy up dollars, which in turn leads to a contraction in the domestic money supply. Therefore, in order to maintain the expansionary monetary policy, the government would have to expand the money supply in larger magnitudes than it would without the balance of payments deficits with a fixed exchange rate system.

34-7. a. The dollar price of pounds is $1.50. The equilibrium quantity is 150 million.
b. Curve D' describes this situation. The new dollar price of pounds would be $1.70, and the equilibrium quantity would be 200 million.
c. At a price of $1.50 per pound, 250 million pounds sterling would be demanded and only 150 million would be supplied, so the Fed would have to supply an extra 100 million to American buyers of British goods or British exporters.
d. Curve D'' describes this situation. 150 million pounds sterling would be supplied at a price of $1.50, but only 50 million pounds would be demanded. Therefore, the Fed would have to buy up 100 million pounds sterling.

CHAPTER 35

35-1. The following countries may be considered developing countries: Burkina Faso, Bangladesh, Afghanistan, India, and China; there are many others. The following are considered IACs: the United States, Canada, Australia, Germany, and France; there are many others.

35-3. Initially, there is an agricultural stage where most of the population is involved in agriculture. Many developing countries are still in this stage. Then comes the manufacturing stage. Industry dominates the economy, and gains from the division of labor lead to rapid increases in output. In the final stage, the service sector becomes prominent in the economy. The United States and other advanced

economy. The United States and other advanced countries are in this stage.

35-5. Economic development depends greatly on individuals who are able to perceive and take advantage of opportunities. Immigrants who possessed attributes such as these started America on the road to greatness. In general, voluntary exchange is mutually beneficial. If the potential immigrants are willing and able to offer their services at prices (wages) that existing residents are willing to pay and to purchase the goods and services offered for sale by existing residents, their arrival is likely to benefit existing residents as well as themselves.

35-7. It is important to remember that all resources are owned by human beings and that in general there is an optimal (wealth-maximizing) mix of land, labor, and capital. So even though population growth (relative to growth in capital or land) would be expected to lower wages, it would also be expected to raise the earnings of capital and land. On balance, if the population growth moved the country closer to the optimal mix of land, labor, and capital, the added income accruing to the owners of land and capital would more than offset the reduced earnings of labor, producing an overall rise in per capita income.

GLOSSARY

Absolute advantage The ability to produce a good or service at an "absolutely" lower cost, usually measured in units of labor or resource input required to produce one unit of the good or service. *Can also be viewed as* the ability to produce more output from given inputs of resources than other producers can.

Accounting identities Statements that certain numerical measurements are equal by accepted definition (for example, "assets equal liabilities plus stockholders' equity").

Accounting profit Total revenues minus total explicit costs.

Action time lag The time required between recognizing an economic problem and putting policy into effect. The action time lag is short for monetary policy but quite long for fiscal policy, which requires congressional approval.

Active (discretionary) policymaking All actions on the part of monetary and fiscal policymakers that are undertaken in response to or in anticipation of some change in the overall economy.

Adverse selection A problem created by asymmetric information prior to a transaction. Individuals who are the most undesirable from the other party's point of view end up being the ones who are most likely to want to engage in a particular financial transaction, such as borrowing. *Can also be viewed as* the circumstance that arises in financial markets when borrowers who are the worst credit risks are the ones most likely to seek loans.

Age-earnings cycle The regular earnings profile of an individual throughout his or her lifetime. The age-earnings cycle usually starts with a low income, builds gradually to a peak at around age 50, and then gradually curves down until it approaches zero at retirement.

Aggregate demand The total of all planned expenditures for the entire economy.

Aggregate demand curve A curve showing planned purchase rates for all goods and services in the economy at various price levels, all other things held constant.

Aggregate demand shock

Any shock that causes the aggregate demand curve to shift inward or outward.

Aggregates Total amounts or quantities; aggregate demand, for example, is total planned expenditures throughout a nation.

Aggregate supply The total of all planned production for the entire economy.

Aggregate supply shock Any shock that causes the aggregate supply curve to shift inward or outward.

Anticipated inflation The inflation rate that we believe will occur; when it does, we are in a situation of fully anticipated inflation.

Antitrust legislation Laws that restrict the formation of monopolies and regulate certain anticompetitive business practices.

Appreciation An increase in the value of a currency in terms of other currencies.

Asset demand Holding money as a store of value instead of other assets such as certificates of deposit, corporate bonds, and stocks.

Assets Amounts owned; all items to which a business or household holds legal claim.

Asymmetric information Information possessed by one side of a transaction but not the other. The side with more information will be at an advantage.

Automatic, or **built-in, stabilizers** Special provisions of the tax law that cause changes in the economy without the action of Congress and the president. Examples are the progressive income tax system and unemployment compensation.

Autonomous consumption

The part of consumption that is independent of (does not depend on) the level of disposable income. Changes in autonomous consumption shift the consumption function.

Average fixed costs Total fixed costs divided by the number of units produced.

Average physical product Total product divided by the variable input.

Average propensity to consume (APC)   Consumption divided by disposable income; for any given level of income, the proportion of total disposable income that is consumed.

Average propensity to save (APS)   Saving divided by disposable income; for any given level of income, the proportion of total disposable income that is saved.

Average tax rate   The total tax payment divided by total income. It is the proportion of total income paid in taxes.

Average total costs   Total costs divided by the number of units produced; sometimes called *average per-unit total costs*.

Average variable costs   Total variable costs divided by the number of units produced.

Balance of payments   A summary record of a country's economic transactions with foreign residents and governments over a year.

Balance of trade   The value of goods and services bought and sold in the world market.

Balance sheet   A statement of the assets and liabilities of any business entity, including financial institutions and the Federal Reserve System. Assets are what is owned; liabilities are what is owed.

Bank runs   Attempts by many of a bank's depositors to convert checkable and time deposits into currency out of fear for the bank's solvency.

Barter   The direct exchange of goods and services for other goods and services without the use of money.

Base year   The year that is chosen as the point of reference for comparison of prices in other years.

Bilateral monopoly   A market structure consisting of a monopolist and a monopsonist.

Black market   A market in which goods are traded at prices above their legal maximum prices or in which illegal goods are sold.

Bond   A legal claim against a firm, usually entitling the owner of the bond to receive a fixed annual coupon payment, plus a lump-sum payment at the bond's maturity date. Bonds are issued in return for funds lent to the firm.

Budget constraint   All of the possible combinations of goods that can be purchased (at fixed prices) with a specific budget.

Bureaucrats   Nonelected government officials who are responsible for the day-to-day operation of government and the observance of its regulations and laws.

Business fluctuations   The ups and downs in overall business activity, as evidenced by changes in national income, employment, and the price level.

Capital consumption allowance   Another name for depreciation, the amount that businesses would have to save in order to take care of the deterioration of machines and other equipment.

Capital gain   The positive difference between the purchase price and the sale price of an asset. If a share of stock is bought for $5 and then sold for $15, the capital gain is $10.

Capital goods   Producer durables; nonconsumable goods that firms use to make other goods.

Capitalism   An economic system in which individuals own productive resources; these individuals can use the resources in whatever manner they choose, subject to common protective legal restrictions.

Capital loss   The negative difference between the purchase price and the sale price of an asset.

Capture hypothesis   A theory of regulatory behavior that predicts that the regulators will eventually be captured by the special interests of the industry being regulated.

Cartel   An association of producers in an industry that agree to set common prices and output quotas to prevent competition.

Central bank   A banker's bank, usually an official institution that also serves as a country's treasury's bank. Central banks normally regulate commercial banks.

Certificate of deposit (CD)   A time deposit with a fixed maturity date offered by banks and other financial institutions.

***Ceteris paribus* [KAY-ter-us PEAR-uh-bus] assumption**   The assumption that nothing changes except the factor or factors being studied.

Checkable deposits   Any deposits in a thrift institution or a commercial bank on which a check may be written.

Closed shop   A business enterprise in which employees must belong to the union before they can be hired and must remain in the union after they are hired.

Collateral   An asset pledged to guarantee the repayment of a loan.

Collective bargaining   Bargaining between the management of a company or of a group of companies and the management of a union or a group of unions for the purpose of setting a mutually agreeable contract on wages, fringe benefits, and working conditions for all employees in all the unions involved.

Collective decision making   How voters, politicians, and other interested parties act and how these actions influence nonmarket decisions.

Common property   Property that is owned by everyone and therefore by no one. Air and water are examples of common property resources.

Communism   In its purest form, an economic system in which the state has disappeared and individuals contribute to the economy according to their productivity and are given income according to their needs.

Comparable-worth doctrine   The belief that women should receive the same wages as men if the levels of skill and responsibility in their jobs are equivalent.

Comparative advantage The ability to produce a good or service at a lower opportunity cost compared to other producers.

Complements Two goods are complements if both are used together for consumption or enjoyment—for example, coffee and cream. The more you buy of one, the more you buy of the other. For complements, a change in the price of one causes an opposite shift in the demand for the other.

Concentration ratio The percentage of all sales contributed by the leading four or leading eight firms in an industry; sometimes called the *industry concentration ratio*.

Constant-cost industry An industry whose total output can be increased without an increase in long-run per-unit costs; an industry whose long-run supply curve is horizontal.

Constant dollars Dollars expressed in terms of real purchasing power using a particular year as the base or standard of comparison, in contrast to current dollars.

Constant returns to scale No change in long-run average costs when output increases.

Consumer optimum A choice of a set of goods and services that maximizes the level of satisfaction for each consumer, subject to limited income.

Consumer Price Index (CPI) A statistical measure of a weighted average of prices of a specified set of goods and services purchased by wage earners in urban areas.

Consumption The use of goods and services for personal satisfaction. *Can also be viewed as* spending on new goods and services out of a household's current income. Whatever is not consumed is saved. Consumption includes such things as buying food and going to a concert.

Consumption function The relationship between amount consumed and disposable income. A consumption function tells us how much people plan to consume at various levels of disposable income.

Consumption goods Goods bought by households to use up, such as food, clothing, and movies.

Contraction A business fluctuation during which the pace of national economic activity is slowing down.

Contractionary gap The gap that exists whenever the equilibrium level of real national income per year is less than the full-employment level as shown by the position of the long-run aggregate supply curve.

Cooperative game A game in which the players explicitly collude to make themselves better off. As applied to firms, it involves companies colluding in order to make higher than competitive rates of return.

Corporation A legal entity that may conduct business in its own name just as an individual does; the owners of a corporation, called shareholders, own shares of the firm's profits and enjoy the protection of limited liability.

Cost-of-living adjustments (COLAs) Clauses in contracts that allow for increases in specified nominal values to take account of changes in the cost of living.

Cost-of-service regulation Regulation based on allowing prices to reflect only the actual cost of production and no monopoly profits.

Cost-push inflation Inflation caused by a continually decreasing short-run aggregate supply curve.

Craft unions Labor unions composed of workers who engage in a particular trade or skill, such as baking, carpentry, or plumbing.

Creative response Behavior on the part of a firm that allows it to comply with the letter of the law but violate the

spirit, significantly lessening the law's effects.

Cross elasticity of demand (E_{xy}) The percentage change in the demand for one good (holding its price constant) divided by the percentage change in the price of a related good.

Crowding-out effect The tendency of expansionary fiscal policy to cause a decrease in planned investment or planned consumption in the private sector; this decrease normally results from the rise in interest rates.

Crude quantity theory of money and prices The belief that changes in the money supply lead to proportional changes in the price level.

Cyclical unemployment Unemployment resulting from business recessions that occur when aggregate (total) demand is insufficient to create full employment.

Decreasing-cost industry An industry in which an increase in output leads to a reduction in long-run per-unit costs, such that the long-run industry supply curve slopes downward.

Deficiency payment A direct subsidy paid to farmers equal to the amount of a crop they produce multiplied by the difference between the target price for that good and its market price.

Deflation The situation in which the average of all prices of goods and services in an economy is falling.

Demand A schedule of how much of a good or service people will purchase at any price during a specified time period, other things being constant.

Demand curve A graphical representation of the demand schedule; a negatively sloped line showing the inverse relationship between the price and the quantity demanded (other things being equal).

Demand-pull inflation Inflation caused by increases in aggregate demand not matched by increases in aggregate supply.

Demerit good A good that has been deemed socially undesirable through the political process. Heroin is an example.

Dependent variable A variable whose value changes according to changes in the value of one or more independent variables.

Depository institutions Financial institutions that accept deposits from savers and lend those deposits out at interest.

Depreciation Reduction in the value of capital goods over a one-year period due to physical wear and tear and also to obsolescence; also called *capital consumption allowance. Can also be viewed as* a decrease in the value of a currency in terms of other currencies.

Depression An extremely severe recession.

Deregulation The elimination or phasing out of regulations on economic activity.

Derived demand Input factor demand derived from demand for the final product being produced.

Diminishing marginal utility The principle that as more of any good or service is consumed, its extra benefit declines. Otherwise stated, increases in total utility from the consumption of a good or service become smaller and smaller as more is consumed during a given time period.

Direct expenditure offsets Actions on the part of the private sector in spending money that offset government fiscal policy actions. Any increase in government spending in an area that competes with the private sector will have some direct expenditure offset.

Direct relationship A relationship between two variables that is positive, meaning that an increase in one variable is associated with an increase in the other and a decrease in one variable is associated with a decrease in the other.

Dirty float A system between flexible and fixed exchange rates in which central banks occasionally enter foreign exchange markets to influence rates.

Discounting The method by which the present value of a future sum or a future stream of sums is obtained.

Discount rate The interest rate that the Federal Reserve charges for reserves that it lends to depository institutions. It is sometimes referred to as the rediscount rate or, in Canada and England, as the bank rate.

Discouraged workers Individuals who have stopped looking for a job because they are convinced that they will not find a suitable one. Typically, they become convinced after unsuccessfully searching for a job.

Diseconomies of scale Increases in long-run average costs that occur as output increases.

Disposable personal income (DPI) Personal income after personal income taxes have been paid.

Dissaving Negative saving; a situation in which spending exceeds income. Dissaving can occur when a household is able to borrow or use up existing owned assets.

Distributional coalitions Associations such as cartels, unions, and cooperatives that are formed to gain special government privileges in order to redistribute wealth by taking small amounts from each of many people and giving large amounts to each of only a few.

Distribution of income The way income is allocated among the population.

Dividends Portion of a corporation's profits paid to its owners (shareholders).

Division of labor The segregation of a resource into different specific tasks; for example, one automobile worker puts on bumpers, another doors, and so on.

Dominant strategies Strategies that always yield the highest benefit. Regardless of what other players do, a dominant strategy will yield the most benefit for the player using it.

Dumping Selling a good or a service abroad at a price below its cost of production or below the price charged in the home market.

Durable consumer goods Consumer goods that have a life span of more than three years.

Economic goods Goods that are scarce.

Economic growth Increases in per capita real GDP measured by its rate of change per year.

Economic profits Total revenues minus total opportunity costs of all inputs used, or the total of all implicit and explicit costs. *Can also be viewed as* the difference between total revenues and the opportunity cost of all factors of production.

Economic rent A payment for the use of any resource over and above its opportunity cost.

Economics The study of how people allocate their limited resources to satisfy their unlimited wants.

Economic system The institutional means through which resources are used to satisfy human wants.

Economies of scale Decreases in long-run average costs resulting from increases in output.

Effect time lag The time that elapses between the onset of policy and the results of that policy.

Efficiency The case in which a given level of inputs is used to produce the maximum output possible. Alternatively, the situation in which a given output is produced at minimum cost.

Efficiency wages Wages set above competitive levels to increase labor productivity and profits by enhancing the efficiency of the firm through lower turnover, ease of attracting higher-quality workers, and better efforts by workers.

Efficiency wage theory   The hypothesis that the productivity of workers depends on the level of the real wage rate.

Effluent fee   A charge to a polluter that gives the right to discharge into the air or water a certain amount of pollution. Also called a *pollution tax*.

Elastic demand   A demand relationship in which a given percentage change in price will result in a larger percentage change in quantity demanded. Total expenditures are invariant to price changes in the unit's elastic portion of the demand curve.

Empirical   Relying on real-world data in evaluating the usefulness of a model.

Endowments   The various resources in an economy, including both physical resources and such human resources as ingenuity and management skills.

Entitlements   Guaranteed benefits under a government program such as Social Security, Medicare, or Medicaid.

Entrepreneurship   The factor of production involving human resources that perform the functions of raising capital, organizing, managing, assembling other factors of production, and making basic business policy decisions. The entrepreneur is a risk taker.

Entry deterrence strategy   Any strategy undertaken by firms in an industry, either individually or together, with the intent or effect of raising the cost of entry into the industry by a new firm.

Equation of exchange   The formula indicating that the number of monetary units times the number of times each unit is spent on final goods and services is identical to the price level times output (or nominal national income).

Equilibrium   The situation when quantity supplied equals quantity demanded at a particular price.

Eurodollar deposits   Deposits denominated in U.S. dollars but held in banks outside the United States, often in overseas branches of U.S. banks.

Excess reserves   The difference between legal reserves and required reserves.

Exclusion principle   The principle that no one can be excluded from the benefits of a public good, even if that person hasn't paid for it.

Expansion   A business fluctuation in which overall business activity is rising at a more rapid rate than previously or at a more rapid rate than the overall historical trend for the nation.

Expansionary gap   The gap that exists whenever the equilibrium level of real national income per year is greater than the full-employment level as shown by the position of the long-run aggregate supply curve.

Expenditure approach   A way of computing national income by adding up the dollar value at current market prices of all final goods and services.

Explicit costs   Costs that business managers must take account of because they must be paid; examples are wages, taxes, and rent.

Externality   A consequence of an economic activity that spills over to affect third parties. Pollution is an externality. *Can also be viewed as* a situation in which a private cost diverges from a social cost; a situation in which the costs of an action are not fully borne by the two parties engaged in exchange or by an individual engaging in a scarce-resource-using activity. (Also applies to benefits.)

Featherbedding   Any practice that forces employers to use more labor than they would otherwise or to use existing labor in an inefficient manner.

The Fed   The Federal Reserve System; the central bank of the United States.

Federal Deposit Insurance Corporation (FDIC)   A government agency that insures the deposits held in member banks; all members of the Fed and other banks that qualify can join.

Federal funds market   A private market (made up mostly of banks) in which banks can borrow reserves from other banks that want to lend them. Federal funds are usually lent for overnight use.

Federal funds rate   The interest rate that depository institutions pay to borrow reserves in the interbank federal funds market.

Fiduciary monetary system   A system in which currency is issued by the government and its value is based uniquely on the public's faith that the currency represents command over goods and services.

Final goods and services   Goods and services that are at their final stage of production and will not be transformed into yet other goods or services. For example, wheat is normally not a final good because usually it is used to make bread, which is a final good.

Financial capital   Money used to purchase capital goods such as buildings and equipment.

Financial intermediaries   Institutions that transfer funds between ultimate lenders (savers) and ultimate borrowers.

Financial intermediation   The process by which financial institutions accept savings from businesses, households, and governments and lend the savings to other businesses, households, and governments.

Firm   A business organization that employs resources to produce goods or services for profit. A firm normally owns and operates at least one plant in order to produce.

Fiscal policy   The discretionary changing of government expenditures and/or taxes in order to achieve national economic goals, such as high employment with price stability.

Fixed costs   Costs that do not vary with output. Fixed costs include such things as rent on a building. These costs are fixed for a certain period of time; in the long run, they are variable.

Fixed investment Purchases by businesses of newly produced producer durables, or capital goods, such as production machinery and office equipment.

Flexible exchange rates Exchange rates that are allowed to fluctuate in the open market in response to changes in supply and demand. Sometimes called *floating exchange rates*.

Flow A quantity measured per unit of time; something that occurs over time, such as the income you make per week or per year or the number of individuals who are fired every month.

Foreign exchange market The market for buying and selling foreign currencies.

Foreign exchange rate The price of one currency in terms of another.

45-degree reference line The line along which planned real expenditures equal real national income per year.

Fractional reserve banking A system in which depository institutions hold reserves that are less than the amount of total deposits.

Free-rider problem A problem that arises when individuals presume that others will pay for public goods so that, individually, they can escape paying for their portion without causing a reduction in production.

Frictional unemployment Unemployment due to the fact that workers must search for appropriate job offers. This takes time, and so they remain temporarily ("frictionally") unemployed.

Full employment As presented by the Council of Economic Advisers, an arbitrary level of unemployment that corresponds to "normal" friction in the labor market. In 1986, the council declared that 6.5 percent unemployment was full employment. Today, it is around 5.5 percent.

Game theory A way of describing the various possible outcomes in any situation involving two or more interacting individuals when those individuals are aware of the interactive nature of their situation and plan accordingly.

The plans made by these individuals are known as *game strategies*.

GDP deflator A price index measuring the changes in prices of all new goods and services produced in the economy.

General Agreement on Tariffs and Trade (GATT) An international agreement established in 1947 to further world trade by reducing barriers and tariffs.

Gold standard An international monetary system in which nations fix their exchange rates in terms of gold. All currencies are fixed in terms of all others, and any balance of payments deficits or surpluses can be made up by shipments of gold.

Goods All things from which individuals derive satisfaction or happiness.

Government, or political, goods Goods (and services) provided by the public sector; they can be either private or public goods.

Gross domestic income (GDI) The sum of all income—wages, interest, rent, and profits—paid to the four factors of production.

Gross domestic product (GDP) The total market value of all final goods and services produced by factors of production located within a nation's borders.

Gross private domestic investment The creation of capital goods, such as factories and machines, that can yield production and hence consumption in the future. Also included in this definition are changes in business inventories and repairs made to machines or buildings.

Gross public debt All federal government debt irrespective of who owns it.

Horizontal merger The joining of firms that are producing or selling a similar product.

Human capital The accumulated training and education of workers.

Hyperinflation Extremely rapid rise of the average of all prices in an economy.

Implicit costs Expenses that managers do not have to pay out of pocket and hence do not normally explicitly calculate, such as the opportunity cost of factors of production that are owned; examples are owner-provided capital and owner-provided labor.

Import quota A physical supply restriction on imports of a particular good, such as sugar. Foreign exporters are unable to sell in the United States more than the quantity specified in the import quota.

Incentive-compatible contract A loan contract under which a significant amount of the borrower's assets are at risk, providing an incentive for the borrower to look after the lender's interests.

Incentives Rewards for engaging in a particular activity.

Incentive structure The motivational rewards and costs that individuals face in any given situation. Each economic system has its own incentive structure. The incentive structure is different under a system of private property than under a system of government-owned property, for example. *Can also be viewed as* the system of rewards and punishments individuals face with respect to their own actions.

Income approach A way of measuring national income by adding up all components of national income, including wages, interest, rent, and profits.

Income-consumption curve The set of optimum consumption points that would occur if income were increased, relative prices remaining constant.

Income elasticity of demand (E_i) The percentage change in demand for any good, holding its price constant, divided by the percentage change in income; the responsiveness of the demand to changes in income, holding the good's relative price constant.

Income in kind Income received in the form of goods and services, such as housing or medical care; to be contrasted with money income, which is simply income in dollars, or general purchasing power, that can be used to buy *any* goods and services.

Income velocity of money The number of times per year a dollar is spent on final goods and services; equal to GDP divided by the money supply.

Increasing-cost industry An industry in which an increase in industry output is accompanied by an increase in long-run per-unit costs, such that the long-run industry supply curve slopes upward.

Independent variable A variable whose value is determined independently of, or outside, the equation under study.

Indifference curve A curve composed of a set of consumption alternatives, each of which yields the same total amount of satisfaction.

Indirect business taxes All business taxes except the tax on corporate profits. Indirect business taxes include sales and business property taxes.

Industrially advanced countries (IACs) Canada, Japan, the United States, and the countries of Western Europe, all of which have market economies based on a large skilled labor force and a large technically advanced stock of capital goods.

Industrial unions Labor unions that consist of workers from a particular industry, such as automobile manufacturing or steel manufacturing.

Industry supply curve The locus of points showing the minimum prices at which given quantities will be forthcoming; also called the *market supply curve.*

Inefficient point Any point below the production possibilities curve at which resources are being used inefficiently.

Inelastic demand A demand relationship in which a given percentage change in price will result in a less than proportionate percentage change in the quantity demanded. Total expenditures and price are directly related in the inelastic region of the demand curve.

Infant industry argument The contention that tariffs should be imposed to protect from import competition an industry that is trying to get started. Presumably, after the industry becomes technologically efficient, the tariff can be lifted.

Inferior goods Goods for which demand falls as income rises.

Inflation The situation in which the average of all prices of goods and services in an economy is rising.

Innovation Transforming an invention into something that is useful to humans.

Inside information Information that is not available to the general public about what is happening in a corporation.

Insider-outsider theory A theory of labor markets in which workers who are already employed have an influence on wage bargaining in such a way that outsiders who are willing to work for lower real wages cannot get a job.

Interest The payment for current rather than future command over resources; the cost of obtaining credit. Also, the return paid to owners of capital.

Interest group Any group that seeks to cause government to change spending in a way that will benefit the group's members or to undertake any other action that will improve their lot. Also called a *special-interest group.*

Interest rate effect One of the reasons that the aggregate demand curve slopes down is because higher price levels indirectly increase the interest rate, which in turn causes businesses and consumers to reduce desired spending due to the higher cost of borrowing.

Intermediate goods Goods used up entirely in the production of final goods.

International Monetary Fund (IMF) An institution set up to manage the international monetary system, established in 1945 under the Bretton Woods Agreement Act, which established fixed exchange rates for the world's currencies.

Inventory investment Changes in the stocks of finished goods and goods in process, as well as changes in the raw materials that businesses keep on hand. Whenever inventories are decreasing, inventory investment is negative; whenever they are increasing, inventory investment is positive.

Inverse relationship A relationship between two variables that is negative, meaning that an increase in one variable is associated with a decrease in the other and a decrease in one variable is associated with an increase in the other.

Investment Any use of today's resources to expand tomorrow's production or consumption. *Can also be viewed as* the spending by businesses on things such as machines and buildings, which can be used to produce goods and services in the future. The investment part of total income is the portion that will be used in the process of producing goods in the future.

Job leaver An individual in the labor force who quits voluntarily.

Job loser An individual in the labor force who was employed and whose employment was involuntarily terminated or who was laid off.

Jurisdictional dispute A dispute involving two or more unions over which should have control of a particular jurisdiction, such as a particular craft or skill or a particular firm or industry.

Keynesian short-run aggregate supply curve The horizontal portion of the aggregate supply curve in which there is unemployment and unused capacity in the economy.

Labor Productive contributions of humans who work, involving both mental and physical activities.

Labor force Individuals aged 16 years or older who either have jobs or are looking and available for jobs; the number of employed plus the number of unemployed.

Labor force participation rate
The percentage of noninstitutionalized working-age individuals who are employed or seeking employment.

Labor market signaling The process by which a potential worker's acquisition of credentials, such as a degree, is used by the employer to predict future productivity.

Labor productivity Total real domestic output (real GDP) divided by the number of workers (output per worker).

Labor unions Worker organizations that seek to secure economic improvements for their members; they also seek to improve the safety, health, and other benefits (such as job security) of their members.

Laissez-faire French for "leave [it] alone"; applied to an economic system in which the government minimizes its interference with economy.

Land The natural resources that are available from nature. Land as a resource includes location, original fertility and mineral deposits, topography, climate, water, and vegetation.

Law of demand The observation that there is a negative, or inverse, relationship between the price of any good or service and the quantity demanded, holding other factors constant.

Law of diminishing (marginal) returns The observation that after some point, successive equal-sized increases in a variable factor of production, such as labor, added to fixed factors of production, will result in smaller increases in output.

Law of increasing relative cost The observation that the opportunity cost of additional units of a good generally increases as society attempts to produce more of that good. This accounts for the bowed-out shape of the production possibilities curve.

Law of supply The observation that the higher the price of a good, the more of that good sellers will make

available over a specified time period, other things being equal.

Least-cost combination The level of input use that produces a given level of output at minimum cost.

Legal reserves Reserves that depository institutions are allowed by law to claim as reserves—for example, deposits held at Federal Reserve district banks and vault cash.

Lemons problem The situation in which consumers, who do not know details about the quality of a product, are willing to pay no more than the price of a low-quality product, even if a higher-quality product at a higher price exists.

Liabilities Amounts owed; the legal claims against a business or household by nonowners.

Limited liability A legal concept whereby the responsibility, or liability, of the owners of a corporation is limited to the value of the shares in the firm that they own.

Limit-pricing model A model that hypothesizes that a group of colluding sellers will set the highest common price that they believe they can charge without new firms seeking to enter that industry in search of relatively high profits.

Liquidity The degree to which an asset can be acquired or disposed of without much danger of any intervening loss in *nominal* value and with small transaction costs. Money is the most liquid asset.

Liquidity approach A method of measuring the money supply by looking at money as a temporary store of value.

Logrolling The practice of exchanging political favors by elected representatives. Typically, one elected official agrees to vote for the policy of another official in exchange for the vote of the latter in favor of the former's desired policy.

Long run The time period in which all factors of production can be varied.

Long-run aggregate supply curve A vertical line representing real output of goods and services based on full information and after full adjustment has occurred. *Can also be viewed as* representing the real output of the economy under conditions of full employment—the full-employment level of real GDP.

Long-run average cost curve The locus of points representing the minimum unit cost of producing any given rate of output, given current technology and resource prices.

Long-run industry supply curve A market supply curve showing the relationship between price and quantities forthcoming after firms have been allowed the time to enter into or exit from an industry, depending on whether there have been positive or negative economic profits.

Lorenz curve A geometric representation of the distribution of income. A Lorenz curve that is perfectly straight represents perfect income equality. The more bowed a Lorenz curve, the more unequally income is distributed.

Lump-sum tax A tax that does not depend on income or the circumstances of the taxpayer. An example is a $1,000 tax that every family must pay, irrespective of its economic situation.

M1 The money supply, taken as the total value of currency plus checkable deposits plus traveler's checks not issued by banks.

M2 M1 plus (1) savings and small-denomination time deposits at all depository institutions, (2) overnight repurchase agreements at commercial banks, (3) overnight Eurodollars held by U.S. residents other than banks at Caribbean branches of member banks, (4) balances in retail money market mutual funds, and (5) money market deposit accounts (MMDAs).

Macroeconomics The study of the behavior of the economy as a whole, including such economywide phenomena as changes in unemployment, the general price level, and national income.

Majority rule A collective decision-making system in which group decisions are made on the basis of 50.1 percent of the vote. In other words, whatever more than half of the electorate votes for, the entire electorate has to accept.

Marginal cost pricing A system of pricing in which the price charged is equal to the opportunity cost to society of producing one more unit of the good or service in question. The opportunity cost is the marginal cost to society.

Marginal costs The change in total costs due to a one-unit change in production rate.

Marginal factor cost (MFC) The cost of using an additional unit of an input. For example, if a firm can hire all the workers it wants at the going wage rate, the marginal factor cost of labor is the wage rate.

Marginal physical product The physical output that is due to the addition of one more unit of a variable factor of production; the change in total product occurring when a variable input is increased and all other inputs are held constant; also called *marginal productivity* or *marginal return.*

Marginal physical product (MPP) of labor The change in output resulting from the addition of one more worker. The MPP of the worker equals the change in total output accounted for by hiring the worker, holding all other factors of production constant.

Marginal propensity to consume (MPC) The ratio of the change in consumption to the change in disposable income. A marginal propensity to consume of .8 tells us that an additional $100 in take-home pay will lead to an additional $80 consumed.

Marginal propensity to save (MPS) The ratio of the change in saving to the change in disposable income. A marginal propensity to save of .2 indicates that out of an additional $100 in take-home pay, $20 will be saved. Whatever is not saved is consumed. The marginal propensity to save plus the marginal propensity

to consume must always equal 1, by definition.

Marginal revenue The change in total revenues resulting from a change in output (and sale) of one unit of the product in question.

Marginal revenue product (MRP) The marginal physical product (MPP) times marginal revenue. The MRP gives the additional revenue obtained from a one-unit change in labor input.

Marginal tax rate The change in the tax payment divided by the change in income, or the percentage of additional dollars that must be paid in taxes. The marginal tax rate is applied to the highest tax bracket of taxable income reached.

Marginal utility The change in total utility due to a one-unit change in the quantity of a good or service consumed.

Market All of the arrangements that individuals have for exchanging with one another. Thus we can speak of the labor market, the automobile market, and the credit market.

Market clearing, or equilibrium, price The price that clears the market, at which quantity demanded equals quantity supplied; the price where the demand curve intersects the supply curve.

Market demand The demand of all consumers in the marketplace for a particular good or service. The summing at each price of the quantity demanded by each individual.

Market failure A situation in which an unrestrained market economy leads to too few or too many resources going to a specific economic activity.

Market share test The percentage of a market that a particular firm controls, used as the primary measure of monopoly power.

Medical savings accounts (MSAs) A tax-exempt health care account to which individuals would pay into on a regular basis and from which medical care expenses could be paid.

Medium of exchange Any asset that sellers will accept as payment.

Merit good A good that has been deemed socially desirable through the political process. Museums are an example.

Microeconomics The study of decision making undertaken by individuals (or households) and by firms.

Minimum efficient scale (MES) The lowest rate of output per unit time at which long-run average costs for a particular firm are at a minimum.

Minimum wage A wage floor, legislated by government, setting the lowest hourly rate that firms may legally pay workers.

Mixed economy An economic system in which decisions about how resources should be used are made partly by the private sector and partly by the government, or the public sector.

Models, or theories Simplified representations of the real world used as the basis for predictions or explanations.

Monetarists Macroeconomists who believe that inflation is always caused by excessive monetary growth and that changes in the money supply directly affect aggregate demand both directly and indirectly.

Monetary rule A monetary policy that incorporates a rule specifying the annual rate of growth of some monetary aggregate.

Money Any medium that is universally accepted in an economy both by sellers of goods and services as payment for those goods and services and by creditors as payment for debts.

Money illusion Reacting to changes in money prices rather than relative prices. If a worker whose wages double when the price level also doubles thinks he or she is better off, the worker is suffering from money illusion.

Money market deposit accounts (MMDAs) Accounts issued by banks yielding a market rate of interest with a minimum balance requirement and a limit on transactions. They have no minimum maturity.

Money market mutual funds Funds of investment companies that obtain funds from the public that are held in common and used to acquire short-maturity credit instruments, such as certificates of deposit and securities sold by the U.S. government.

Money multiplier The reciprocal of the required reserve ratio, assuming no leakages into currency and no excess reserves. It is equal to 1 divided by the required reserve ratio.

Money multiplier process The process by which an injection of new money into the banking system leads to a multiple expansion in the total money supply.

Money price The price that we observe today, expressed in today's dollars. Also called the *absolute, nominal,* or *current price.*

Money supply The amount of money in circulation.

Monopolist A single supplier that comprises its entire industry for a good or service for which there is no close substitute.

Monopolistic competition A market situation in which a large number of firms produce similar but not identical products. Entry into the industry is relatively easy.

Monopolization The possession of monopoly power in the relevant market and the willful acquisition or maintenance of that power, as distinguished from growth or development as a consequence of a superior product, business acumen, or historical accident.

Monopoly A firm that has great control over the price of a good. In the extreme case, a monopoly is the only seller of a good or service.

Monopsonist A single buyer.

Monopsonistic exploitation Exploitation due to monopsony power. It leads to a price for the variable input that is less than its marginal revenue product. Monopsonistic exploitation is the difference between marginal revenue product and the wage rate.

Moral hazard A situation in which, after a transaction has taken place, one of the parties to the transaction has an incentive to engage in behavior that will be undesirable from the other party's point of view. *Can also be viewed as* a problem that occurs because of asymmetric information *after* a transaction occurs. In financial markets, a person to whom money has been lent may indulge in more risky behavior, thereby increasing the probability of default on the debt.

Multiplier The ratio of the change in the equilibrium level of real national income to the change in autonomous expenditures; the number by which a change in autonomous investment or autonomous consumption, for example, is multiplied to get the change in the equilibrium level of real national income.

National income accounting A measurement system used to estimate national income and its components; one approach to measuring an economy's aggregate performance.

National income (NI) The total of all factor payments to resource owners. It can be obtained by subtracting indirect business taxes from NDP.

Natural monopoly A monopoly that arises from the peculiar production characteristics in an industry. It usually arises when there are large economies of scale relative to the industry's demand such that one firm can produce at a lower average cost than can be achieved by multiple firms.

Natural rate of unemployment The rate of unemployment that is estimated to prevail in long-run macroeconomic equilibrium, when all workers and employers have fully adjusted to any changes in the economy.

Near monies Assets that are almost money. They have a high degree of liquidity; they can be easily converted into money without loss in value. Time deposits and short-term U.S. government securities are examples.

Negative-sum game A game in which all players are worse off at the end of the game.

Net domestic product (NDP) GDP minus depreciation.

Net investment Gross private domestic investment minus an estimate of the wear and tear on the existing capital stock. Net investment therefore measures the change in capital stock over a one-year period.

Net public debt Gross public debt minus all government interagency borrowing.

Net worth The difference between assets and liabilities.

New classical model A modern version of the classical model in which wages and prices are flexible, there is pure competition in all markets, and the rational expectations hypothesis is assumed to be working.

New entrant An individual who has never held a full-time job lasting two weeks or longer but is now in the labor force.

New growth theory A relatively modern theory of economic growth that examines the factors that determine why technology, research, innovation, and the like are undertaken and how they interact.

New Keynesian economics Economic models based on the idea that demand creates its own supply as a result of various possible government fiscal and monetary coordination failures.

Nominal rate of interest The market rate of interest expressed in today's dollars.

Nominal values The values of variables such as GDP and investment expressed in current dollars, also called *money values;* measurement in terms of the actual market prices at which goods are sold.

Nonaccelerating inflation rate of unemployment (NAIRU) The rate of unemployment below which the rate of inflation tends to rise and above which the rate of inflation tends to fall.

Noncooperative game A game in which the players neither negotiate nor collude in any way. As applied to firms in an industry, this is the common situation in which there are relatively few firms and each has some ability to change price.

Nondurable consumer goods Consumer goods that are used up within three years.

Nonincome expense items The total of indirect business taxes and depreciation.

Nonprice rationing devices All methods used to ration scarce goods that are price controlled. Whenever the price system is not allowed to work, nonprice rationing devices will evolve to ration the affected goods and services.

Normal goods Goods for which demand rises as income rises. Most goods are considered normal.

Normal rate of return The amount that must be paid to an investor to induce investment in a business; also known as the *opportunity cost of capital*.

Normative economics Analysis involving value judgments about economic policies; relates to whether things are good or bad. A statement of *what ought to be*.

Number line A line that can be divided into segments of equal length, each associated with a number.

Oligopoly A market situation in which there are very few sellers. Each seller knows that the other sellers will react to its changes in prices and quantities.

Open economy effect One of the reasons that the aggregate demand curve slopes downward is because higher price levels result in foreigners' desiring to buy fewer American-made goods while Americans now desire more foreign-made goods, thereby reducing net exports, which is equivalent to a reduction in the amount of real goods and services purchased in the United States.

Open market operations The purchase and sale of existing U.S. government securities (such as bonds) in the open private market by the Federal Reserve System.

Opportunistic behavior Actions that ignore the possible long-run benefits of cooperation and focus solely on short-run gains.

Opportunity cost The highest-valued, next-best alternative that must be sacrificed to attain something or to satisfy a want.

Opportunity cost of capital The normal rate of return, or the available return on the next-best alternative investment. Economists consider this a cost of production, and it is included in our cost examples.

Optimal quantity of pollution The level of pollution for which the marginal benefit of one additional unit of clean air just equals the marginal cost of that additional unit of clean air.

Origin The intersection of the *y* axis and the *x* axis in a graph.

Partnership A business owned by two or more co-owners, or partners, who share the responsibilities and the profits of the firm and are individually liable for all of the debts of the partnership.

Par value The legally established value of the monetary unit of one country in terms of that of another.

Passive (nondiscretionary) policymaking Policymaking that is carried out in response to a rule. It is therefore not in response to an actual or potential change in overall economic activity.

Patent A government protection that gives an inventor the exclusive right to make, use, or sell an invention for a limited period of time (currently, 17 years).

Payoff matrix A matrix of outcomes, or consequences, of the strategies available to the players in a game.

Perfect competition A market structure in which the decisions of individual buyers and sellers have no effect on market price.

Perfectly competitive firm A firm that is such a small part of the total industry that it cannot affect the price of the product it sells.

Perfectly elastic demand A demand that has the characteristic that even the slightest increase in price will lead to zero quantity demanded.

Perfectly elastic supply A supply characterized by a reduction in quantity supplied to zero when there is the slightest decrease in price.

Perfectly inelastic demand A demand that exhibits zero responsiveness to price changes; no matter what the price is, the quantity demanded remains the same.

Perfectly inelastic supply A supply for which quantity supplied remains constant, no matter what happens to price.

Personal income (PI) The amount of income that households actually receive before they pay personal income taxes.

Phillips curve A curve showing the relationship between unemployment and changes in wages or prices. It was long thought to reflect a trade-off between unemployment and inflation.

Physical capital All manufactured resources, including buildings, equipment, machines, and improvements to land that is used for production.

Planning curve The long-run average cost curve.

Planning horizon The long run, during which all inputs are variable.

Plant size The physical size of the factories that a firm owns and operates to produce its output. Plant size can be defined by square footage, maximum physical capacity, and other physical measures.

Policy irrelevance proposition The new classical and rational expectations conclusion that policy actions have no real effects in the short run if the policy actions are anticipated and none in the long run even if the policy actions are unanticipated.

Positive economics Analysis that is strictly limited to making either purely descriptive statements or scientific predictions; for example, "If A, then B." A statement of *what is*.

Positive-sum game A game in which players as a group are better off at the end of the game.

Precautionary demand Holding money to meet unplanned expenditures and emergencies.

Present value The value of a future amount expressed in today's dollars; the most that someone would pay today to receive a certain sum at some point in the future.

Price ceiling A legal maximum price that may be charged for a particular good or service.

Price-consumption curve The set of consumer optimum combinations of two goods that the consumer would choose as the price of one good changes, while money income and the price of the other good remain constant.

Price controls Government-mandated minimum or maximum prices that may be charged for goods and services.

Price differentiation Establishing different prices for similar products to reflect differences in marginal cost in providing those commodities to different groups of buyers.

Price discrimination Selling a given product at more than one price, with the price difference being unrelated to differences in cost.

Price elasticity of demand (E_p) The responsiveness of the quantity demanded of a commodity to changes in its price; defined as the percentage change in quantity demanded divided by the percentage change in price.

Price elasticity of supply (E_s) The responsiveness of the quantity supplied of a commodity to a change in its price; the percentage change in quantity supplied divided by the percentage change in price.

Price floor A legal minimum price below which a good or service may not be sold. Legal minimum wages are an example.

Price index The cost of today's market basket of goods expressed as a percentage of the cost of the same market basket during a base year.

Price leadership A practice in many oligopolistic industries in which the largest firm publishes its price list ahead of its competitors, who then match those announced prices. Also called *parallel pricing*.

Price searcher A firm that must determine the price-output combination that maximizes profit because it faces a downward-sloping demand curve.

Price system An economic system in which relative prices are constantly changing to reflect changes in supply and demand for different commodities. The prices of those commodities are signals to everyone within the system as to what is relatively scarce and what is relatively abundant.

Price taker A competitive firm that must take the price of its product as given because the firm cannot influence its price.

Price war A pricing campaign designed to drive competing firms out of a market by repeatedly cutting prices.

Primary market A financial market in which newly issued securities are bought and sold.

Principal-agent problem The conflict of interest that occurs when agents—managers of firms—pursue

their own objectives to the detriment of the goals of the firms' principals, or owners.

Principle of rival consumption The recognition that individuals are rivals in consuming private goods because one person's consumption reduces the amount available for others to consume.

Principle of substitution The principle that consumers and producers shift away from goods and resources that become relatively higher priced in favor of goods and resources that are now relatively lower priced.

Prisoners' dilemma A famous strategic game in which two prisoners have a choice between confessing and not confessing to a crime. If neither confesses, they serve a minimum sentence. If both confess, they serve a maximum sentence. If one confesses and the other doesn't, the one who confesses goes free. The dominant strategy is always to confess.

Private costs Costs borne solely by the individuals who incur them. Also called *internal costs*.

Private goods Goods that can be consumed by only one individual at a time. Private goods are subject to the principle of rival consumption.

Private property rights Exclusive rights of ownership that allow the use, transfer, and exchange of property.

Privatization The sale or transfer of state-owned property and businesses to the private sector, in part or in whole. Also refers to *contracting out*— letting private business take over government-provided services such as trash collection.

Producer durables, or capital goods Durable goods having an expected service life of more than three years that are used by businesses to produce other goods and services.

Producer Price Index (PPI) A statistical measure of a weighted average of prices of commodities that firms purchase from other firms.

Product differentiation The distinguishing of products by brand name, color, and other minor attributes. Product differentiation occurs in other than perfectly competitive markets in which products are, in theory, homogeneous, such as wheat or corn.

Production Any activity that results in the conversion of resources into products that can be used in consumption.

Production function The relationship between inputs and output. A production function is a technological, not an economic, relationship.

Production possibilities curve (PPC) A curve representing all possible combinations of total output that could be produced assuming (1) a fixed amount of productive resources of a given quality and (2) the efficient use of those resources.

Profit-maximizing rate of production The rate of production that maximizes total profits, or the difference between total revenues and total costs; also, the rate of production at which marginal revenue equals marginal cost.

Progressive taxation A tax system in which as income increases, a higher percentage of the additional income is taxed. The marginal tax rate exceeds the average tax rate as income rises.

Property rights The rights of an owner to use and to exchange property.

Proportional rule A decision-making system in which actions are based on the proportion of the "votes" cast and are in proportion to them. In a market system, if 10 percent of the "dollar votes" are cast for blue cars, 10 percent of the output will be blue cars.

Proportional taxation A tax system in which regardless of an individual's income, the tax bill comprises exactly the same proportion. Also called a *flat-rate tax*.

Proprietorship A business owned by one individual who makes the business decisions, receives all the profits, and is legally responsible for all the debts of the firm.

Public debt The total value of all outstanding federal government securities.

Public goods Goods to which the principle of rival consumption does not apply; they can be jointly consumed by many individuals simultaneously at no additional cost and with no reduction in quality or quantity.

Purchasing power The value of money for buying goods and services. If your money income stays the same but the price of one good that you are buying goes up, your effective purchasing power falls, and vice versa.

Purchasing power parity Adjustment in exchange rate conversions that takes into account differences in the true cost of living across countries.

Quota system A government-imposed restriction on the quantity of a specific good that another country is allowed to sell in the United States. In other words, quotas are restrictions on imports. These restrictions are usually applied to one or several specific countries.

Random walk theory The theory there are no predictable trends in security prices that can be used to "get rich quick."

Rate of discount The rate of interest used to discount future sums back to present value.

Rate-of-return regulation Regulation that seeks to keep the rate of return in the industry at a competitive level by not allowing excessive prices to be charged.

Rational expectations hypothesis A theory stating that people combine the effects of past policy changes on important economic variables with their own judgment about the future effects of current and future policy changes.

Rationality assumption The assumption that people do not intentionally make decisions that would leave them worse off.

Reaction function The manner in which one oligopolist reacts to a change in price, output, or quality made by another oligopolist in the industry.

Real-balance effect The change in the real value of money balances when the price level changes, all other things held constant. Also called the *wealth effect.*

Real business cycle theory An extension and modification of the theories of the new classical economists of the 1970s and 1980s, in which money is neutral and only real, supply-side factors matter in influencing labor employment and real output.

Real-income effect The change in people's purchasing power that occurs when, other things being constant, the price of one good that they purchase changes. When that price goes up, real income, or purchasing power, falls, and when that price goes down, real income increases.

Real rate of interest The nominal rate of interest minus the anticipated rate of inflation.

Real values Measurement of economic values after adjustments have been made for changes in the average of prices between years.

Recession A period of time during which the rate of growth of business activity is consistently less than its long-term trend or is negative.

Recognition time lag The time required to gather information about the current state of the economy.

Recycling The reuse of raw materials derived from manufactured products.

Reentrant An individual who used to work full time but left the labor force and has now reentered it looking for a job.

Regressive taxation A tax system in which as more dollars are earned, the percentage of tax paid on them falls. The marginal tax rate is less than the average tax rate as income rises.

Reinvestment   Profits (or depreciation reserves) used to purchase new capital equipment.

Relative price   The price of a commodity expressed in terms of another commodity.

Rent control   The placement of price ceilings on rents in particular cities.

Rent seeking   The use of resources in an attempt to get government to bestow a benefit on an interest group.

Repricing, or menu, cost of inflation   The cost associated with recalculating prices and printing new price lists when there is inflation.

Repurchase agreement (REPO, or RP)   An agreement made by a bank to sell Treasury or federal agency securities to its customers, coupled with an agreement to repurchase them at a price that includes accumulated interest.

Required reserve ratio   The percentage of total deposits that the Fed requires depository institutions to hold in the form of vault cash or deposits with the Fed.

Required reserves   The value of reserves that a depository institution must hold in the form of vault cash or deposits with the Fed.

Reserves   In the U.S. Federal Reserve System, deposits held by Federal Reserve district banks for depository institutions, plus depository institutions' vault cash.

Resource allocation   The assignment of resources to specific uses by determining what will be produced, how it will be produced, and for whom it will be produced.

Resources   Things used to produce other things to satisfy people's wants.

Retained earnings   Earnings that a corporation saves, or retains, for investment in other productive activities;

earnings that are not distributed to stockholders.

Ricardian equivalence theorem   The proposition that an increase in the government budget deficit has no effect on aggregate demand.

Right-to-work laws   Laws that make it illegal to require union membership as a condition of continuing employment in a particular firm.

Saving   The act of not consuming all of one's current income. Whatever is not consumed out of spendable income is, by definition, saved. *Saving* is an action measured over time (a flow), whereas *savings* are a stock, an accumulation resulting from the act of saving in the past.

Savings deposits   Interest-earning funds that can be withdrawn at any time without payment of a penalty.

Say's law   A dictum of economist J. B. Say that supply creates its own demand; producing goods and services generates the means and the willingness to purchase other goods and services.

Scarcity   A situation in which the ingredients for producing the things that people desire are insufficient to satisfy all wants.

Seasonal unemployment   Unemployment resulting from the seasonal pattern of work in specific industries. It is usually due to seasonal fluctuations in demand or to changing weather conditions, rendering work difficult, if not impossible, as in the agriculture, construction, and tourist industries.

Secondary boycott   A boycott of companies or products sold by companies that are dealing with a company being struck.

Secondary market   A financial market in which previously issued securities are bought and sold.

Separation of ownership and control   The situation that exists in corporations in which the owners (shareholders) are not the people who control the operation of the corpora-

tion (managers). The goals of these two groups are often different.

Services   Mental or physical labor or help purchased by consumers. Examples are the assistance of doctors, lawyers, dentists, repair personnel, housecleaners, educators, retailers, and wholesalers; things purchased or used by consumers that do not have physical characteristics.

Share of stock   A legal claim to a share of a corporation's future profits; if it is *common stock,* it incorporates certain voting rights regarding major policy decisions of the corporation; if it is *preferred stock,* its owners are accorded preferential treatment in the payment of dividends.

Share-the-gains, share-the-pains theory   A theory of regulatory behavior in which the regulators must take account of the demands of three groups: legislators, who established and who oversee the regulatory agency; members of the regulated industry; and consumers of the regulated industry's products or services.

Shortage   A situation in which quantity demanded is greater than quantity supplied at a price below the market clearing price.

Short run   The time period when at least one input, such as plant size, cannot be changed.

Short-run aggregate supply curve   The relationship between aggregate supply and the price level in the short run, all other things held constant; the curve is normally positively sloped.

Short-run break-even price   The price at which a firm's total revenues equal its total costs. At the break-even price, the firm is just making a normal rate of return on its capital investment. (It is covering its explicit and implicit costs.)

Short-run shutdown price   The price that just covers average variable costs. It occurs just below the intersection of the marginal cost curve and the average variable cost curve.

Signals Compact ways of conveying to economic decision makers information needed to make decisions. A true signal not only conveys information but also provides the incentive to react appropriately. Economic profits and economic losses are such signals.

Slope The change in the y value divided by the corresponding change in the x value of a curve; the "incline" of the curve.

Small-menu cost theory A hypothesis that it is costly for firms to change prices in response to demand changes because of the cost of renegotiating contracts, printing price lists, and so on.

Social costs The full costs borne by society whenever a resource use occurs. Social costs can be measured by adding private, or internal, costs to external costs.

Socialism An economic system in which the state owns the major share of productive resources except labor. Socialism also usually involves the redistribution of income.

Special drawing rights (SDRs) Reserve assets created by the International Monetary Fund that countries can use to settle international payments.

Specialization The division of productive activities among persons and regions so that no one individual or one area is totally self-sufficient. An individual may specialize, for example, in law or medicine. A nation may specialize in the production of coffee, computers, or cameras.

Standard of deferred payment A property of an asset that makes it desirable for use as a means of settling debts maturing in the future; an essential property of money.

Stock The quantity of something, measured at a given point in time—for example, an inventory of goods or a bank account. Stocks are defined independently of time, although they are assessed at a point in time.

Store of value The ability to hold value over time; a necessary property of money.

Strategic dependence A situation in which one firm's actions with respect to price, quality, advertising, and related changes may be strategically countered by the reactions of one or more other firms in the industry. Such dependence can exist only when there are a limited number of major firms in an industry.

Strategy Any rule that is used to make a choice, such as "Always pick heads"; any potential choice that can be made by players in a game.

Strikebreakers Temporary or permanent workers hired by a company to replace union members who are striking.

Structural unemployment Unemployment resulting from fundamental changes in the structure of the economy. It occurs, for example, when the demand for a product falls drastically so that workers specializing in the production of that product find themselves out of work.

Subsidy A negative tax; a payment to a producer from the government, usually in the form of a cash grant.

Substitutes Two goods are substitutes when either one can be used for consumption to satisfy a similar want—for example, coffee and tea. The more you buy of one, the less you buy of the other. For substitutes, the change in the price of one causes a shift in demand for the other in the same direction as the price change.

Substitution effect The tendency of people to substitute cheaper commodities for more expensive commodities.

Supply A schedule showing the relationship between price and quantity supplied for a specified period of time, other things being equal.

Supply curve The graphical representation of the supply schedule; a line (curve) showing the supply schedule, which generally slopes upward (has a positive slope), other things being equal.

Supply-side economics The notion that creating incentives for individuals and firms to increase productivity will cause the aggregate supply curve to shift outward.

Surplus A situation in which quantity supplied is greater than quantity demanded at a price above the market clearing price.

Sympathy strike A strike by a union in sympathy with another union's strike or cause.

Target price A price set by the government for specific agricultural products. If the market clearing price is below the target price, a *deficiency payment*, equal to the difference between the market price and the target price, is given to farmers for each unit of the good they produce.

Tariffs Taxes on imported goods.

Tax bracket A specified interval of income to which a specific and unique marginal tax rate is applied.

Tax incidence The distribution of tax burdens among various groups in society.

Technology Society's pool of applied knowledge concerning how goods and services can be produced.

Terms of exchange The terms under which trading takes place. Usually the terms of exchange are equal to the price at which a good is traded.

Theory of contestable markets A hypothesis concerning pricing behavior that holds that even though there are only a few firms in an industry, they are forced to price their products more or less competitively because of the ease of entry by outsiders. The key aspect of a contestable market is relatively costless entry into and exit from the industry.

Theory of public choice The study of collective decision making.

Third parties Parties who are not directly involved in a given activity or transaction. For example, in the relationship between caregivers and patients, fees may be paid by third parties (insurance companies, government).

Thrift institutions Financial institutions that receive most of their funds from the savings of the public; they include mutual savings banks, savings and loan associations, and credit unions

Time deposit A deposit in a financial institution that requires notice of intent to withdraw or must be left for an agreed period. Withdrawal of funds prior to the end of the agreed period may result in a penalty.

Tit-for-tat strategic behavior In game theory, cooperation that continues so long as the other players continue to cooperate.

Total costs The sum of total fixed costs and total variable costs.

Total income The yearly amount earned by the nation's resources (factors of production). Total income therefore includes wages, rent, interest payments, and profits that are received, respectively, by workers, landowners, capital owners, and entrepreneurs.

Total revenues The price per unit times the total quantity sold.

Transaction costs All of the costs associated with exchanging, including the informational costs of finding out price and quality, service record, and durability of a product, plus the cost of contracting and enforcing that contract.

Transactions accounts Checking account balances in commercial banks and other types of financial institutions, such as credit unions and mutual savings banks; any accounts in financial institutions on which you can easily write checks without many restrictions.

Transactions approach A method of measuring the money supply by looking at money as a medium of exchange.

Transactions demand Holding money as a medium of exchange to make payments. The level varies directly with nominal national income.

Transfer payments Money payments made by governments to individuals for which in return no services or goods are concurrently rendered. Examples are welfare, Social Security, and unemployment insurance benefits.

Transfers in kind Payments that are in the form of actual goods and services, such as food stamps, low-cost public housing, and medical care, and for which in return no goods or services are rendered concurrently.

Traveler's checks Financial instruments purchased from a bank or a non-banking organization and signed during purchase that can be used as cash upon a second signature by the purchaser.

Unanticipated inflation Inflation at a rate that comes as a surprise, either higher or lower than the rate anticipated.

Unemployment The total number of adults (aged 16 years or older) who are willing and able to work and who are actively looking for work but have not found a job.

Union shop A business enterprise that allows the hiring of nonunion members, conditional on their joining the union by some specified date after employment begins.

Unit elasticity of demand A demand relationship in which the quantity demanded changes exactly in proportion to the change in price. Total expenditures are invariant to price changes in the unit-elastic portion of the demand curve.

Unit of accounting A measure by which prices are expressed; the common denominator of the price system; a central property of money.

Unlimited liability A legal concept whereby the personal assets of the owner of a firm can be seized to pay off the firm's debts.

Util A representative unit by which utility is measured.

Utility The want-satisfying power of a good or service.

Utility analysis The analysis of consumer decision making based on utility maximization.

Value added The dollar value of an industry's sales minus the value of intermediate goods (for example, raw materials and parts) used in production.

Variable costs Costs that vary with the rate of production. They include wages paid to workers and purchases of materials.

Vertical merger The joining of a firm with another to which it sells an output or from which it buys an input.

Voluntary exchange An act of trading, done on a voluntary basis, in which both parties to the trade are subjectively better off after the exchange.

Voluntary import expansion (VIE) An official agreement with another country in which it agrees to import more from the United States.

Voluntary restraint agreement (VRA) An official agreement with another country that "voluntarily" restricts the quantity of its exports to the Unted States.

Wait unemployment Unemployment that is caused by wage rigidities resulting from minimum wages, unions, and other factors.

Wants What people would buy if their incomes were unlimited.

Wealth The stock of assets owned by a person, household, firm, or nation. For a household, wealth can consist of a house, cars, personal belongings, bank accounts, and cash.

World Trade Organization (WTO) The successor organization to GATT, it handles all trade disputes among its 117 member nations.

x **axis** The horizontal axis in a graph.

y **axis** The vertical axis in a graph.

Zero-sum game A game in which any gains within the group are exactly offset by equal losses by the end of the game.

INDEX

China
  economic growth, 132
  transition to capitalism, 117,
    128–132
Chirac, Jacques, 21
Chlorofluorocarbons, 74
Choices
  between consumer/capital goods,
    28–29
  faced by society, 23–27
  and scarcity, 20–21
Chrysler Corporation, 565–566
Cigarettes, 87–88, 455–456, 575
Cigars, 53
CIO. *See* Congress of Industrial
    Organizations
Civil Aeronautics Board, 591
Clayton Act (1914), 594–595
Clinton, Bill, 690
Closed shops, 630
Coal, 510, 703
Coalitions, 716, 726
Coase, Ronald, 702
Coase theorem, 702
Coffee, 442
Colbert, Jean-Baptiste, 103
Cold War, 787
Collateral, 473
Collective bargaining, 629,
    632–633
Collective decision making,
    712–714
College financial aid, 104
College students, 54, 68–69
Collusion, 574–575, 644
Columbus, Christopher, 86
Command socialism, 125, 128
Commerce Department, U.S., 126,
    474, 742, 744
Common agricultural policy,
    723–724
Common property, 700–703, 707
Common stock, 465
Communications technology, 4
Communism, 119–120, 125–126,
    129
Compact discs (CDs), 47, 51, 606,
    617
Comparable-worth doctrine, 676

Comparative advantage, 30–32,
    735–736, 748
Competition, 528, 748. *See also*
    Monopolistic competition;
    Perfect competition
  defined, 509
  international, 740
  in product market, 606
  promotion of, 99
  and public choice, 713
Competitive price determination,
    521
Competitive pricing, 525–527
Complements, 53–54
CompuServe, 75
Computers, 4, 522–523
  in developing countries, 780,
    789
  and education, 54
  laptops, 744–745
  microprocessors, 535
  on-line services, 15–16, 75
  software applications, 509, 598
  substitution of software for labor,
    622
  and unemployment, 780
Concentration ratio, 566–567
Congress, U.S., 714–715
  control over unions, 630–631
  logrolling, 717–718
  rent seeking, 725
  tariffs, 745–746
Congressional Budget Office, 689
Congress of Industrial Organiza-
    tions (CIO), 630
Conscription (military draft), 21
Constant-cost industries, 523–524
Constant returns to scale,
    499–501
Construction, and rent control, 82
Consumer capitalism, 121
Consumer expectations, as demand
    determinant, 55
Consumer goods, 27–29
Consumer optimum, 434–435
  affected by price changes,
    421–423
  defined, 419–420
  in mathematical terms, 421

Consumer Price Index (CPI), 680
Consumer Product Safety
    Commission (CPSC), 588
Consumers
  ability/willingness to pay market
    prices, 119
  demand for loanable funds, 655
Consumption, 27–29
Consumption choices, optimization
    of, 419–421
Consumption-income curve,
    435–436
Consumption possibilities curve,
    433
Consumption-price curve, 436
Consumption taxes, 111–112
Contestable market theory,
    592–593
Contingent valuation, 425
Contracting, 122, 701–702
Contributive standard, 677
Convention on International Trade
    and Endangered Species, 701
Cooperative games, 568
Coordinate axes, 40
Copyrights, 537–538
Corporate income taxes, 106–107
Corporations
  advantages/disadvantages,
    464–465
  defined, 464
  governance of, 471–473
  government, 713
  methods of financing, 465–467
Corsica, brush fires in, 8
Cost minimization, 621–622
Cost-of-service regulation, 587
Costs, 13, 503–504
  average, 492–494
  average total, 492–494
  dispersion of, 716–718
  entry, 576
  explicit, 482
  external, 96, 695–696
  fixed, 490, 492–494
  health care, 684
  implicit, 482–483
  input, 60
  internal, 695–696